*Secondary School
Literacy Instruction*

THE CONTENT AREAS

Ninth Edition

Betty D. Roe
Tennessee Technological University, Cookeville

Barbara D. Stoodt-Hill
John Tyler Community College and Old Dominion University

Paul C. Burns
Late of University of Tennessee at Knoxville

Houghton Mifflin Company
Boston   New York

To my husband, Mike Roe, with appreciation and thanks for all his help
on this project
   —B.D.R.

and

To my family, with appreciation for their assistance with this project
   —B.D.S.-H.

Publisher: Patricia A. Coryell
Executive Editor: Mary Finch
Senior Development Editor: Lisa Mafrici
Editorial Assistant: Dayna Pell
Senior Project Editor: Kimberly Gavrilles
Senior Art and Design Coordinator: Jill Haber
Senior Photo Editor: Jennifer Meyer Dare
Composition Buyer: Chuck Dutton
Associate Manufacturing Buyer: Brian Pieragostini
Senior Marketing Manager: Elinor Gregory
Marketing Associate: Evelyn Yang

Cover image: © Bruce Rogovin/Getty Images

Printed in the U.S.A.

Library of Congress Control Number: 2006920291

Instructor's examination copy
ISBN-10: 0-618-73301-9
ISBN-13: 978-0-618-73301-9
For orders, use student text ISBNs
ISBN-10: 0-618-64282-X
ISBN-13: 978-0-618-64282-3

23456789-DOC-10 09 08 07 06

Brief Contents

Contents

Online Study Center

HM Video Case
Middle School Reading
Instruction: Integrating
Technology 42

Online Study Center

HM Video Case
Integrating Technology
into the Middle School
Curriculum 51

Online Study Center

HM Video Case
Metacognition: Helping
Students Become
Strategic Learners   183

Online Study Center

HM Video Case
Student Self-Esteem:
Peer Editing Process   228

Online Study Center
HM Video Case
Performance Assessment:
Student Presentations
in a High School English
Class 279

Online Study Center
HM Video Case
Reading in the Content
Areas: An Interdisciplinary
Unit on the 1920s 302

Online Study Center

HM Video Case
Formative Assessment:
High School History
Class 406

Online Study Center

HM Video Case
Grading: Strategies and
Approaches 423

Preface

Secondary school teachers use textbooks, trade books, and electronic reference sources extensively as vehicles to convey content area information to their students. Content area teachers often discover, however, that their students are not maximizing their learning potential and do not read at levels necessary for understanding the types of material the teachers would like to use. These students also often do not use appropriate reading and study strategies or writing-to-learn strategies. In view of the current push nationwide to establish literacy standards for secondary school students, this situation is particularly frustrating to teachers who do not know how to help their students learn literacy strategies to support learning of content area material. Teachers and administrators may feel unprepared to find solutions for students' literacy problems, especially as more and more English language learners and students who have special needs are being included in regular classrooms.

This book offers all content area teachers detailed and practical explanations of reading, writing, and study strategies that students need to allow them to acquire and use new information that is available in electronic and traditional print media. Techniques for assessing student performance and for teaching needed strategies in a broad range of disciplines are included. Teachers using these techniques help their students become more efficient, effective readers of their content materials and facilitate their students' learning of the subject matter content.

Audience and Purpose

Secondary School Literary Instruction: The Content Areas, Ninth Edition, has been written primarily for preservice teachers preparing for secondary school certification in teacher education programs and for experienced secondary school teachers who want to help their students read content assignments with more understanding. Neither group is likely to have substantial background knowledge in literacy instruction. This book has thus been written at an introductory level, with the needs and concerns of these teachers in mind. The text also contains information that is useful for reading specialists who work cooperatively with content teachers in helping secondary students with reading difficulties and for secondary school administrators who must know about the reading needs of secondary school students if they are to set school policies appropriately.

This book provides a strategy-based approach to content reading. Much secondary content area material is written at a high difficulty level, and students are required to read extensively. Teachers who know how to teach the reading and study skills strategies appropriate to their content area enhance their students' success in the classroom.

Revisions in This Edition

The ninth edition of *Secondary School Literacy Instruction: The Content Areas* has been thoroughly updated and revised. Information on content literacy for diverse students, which was isolated in a separate chapter in the eighth edition, has been integrated into the other chapters where it is pertinent, in order to make the material more accessible. Some of this material has been called out in the appropriate chapters to highlight applications for struggling readers and English language learners. Several new "Meeting the Challenge" features show how teachers in secondary schools have applied the ideas presented in this book. These vignettes can make the information in the chapters easier to understand because they are placed in the context of real situations.

Also new to the ninth edition are marginal notes containing linkage to relevant **Houghton Mifflin Video Cases.** Available on the Online Study Center (http://college .hmco.com/pic/roeSSLI9e), these 4-6 minute videos bring topics in the text to life by presenting actual classroom scenarios.

Chapter 1, "Content Area Literacy in a Changing World," has an updated section on digital literacy, as well as new material on fluency, gender issues, writing instruction, the impact of legislation such as No Child Left Behind, struggling readers, and English language learners. A new "Meeting the Challenge" addresses English language learners.

Chapter 2, "Integrating Technology in Content Area Literacy Instruction," is extensively updated. Media literacy, including critical viewing of television programs, videotaping and production of videos, use of web logs (blogs), writing of "fanfiction" to be e-mailed or posted to the Web, use of cell phones and digital cameras, and use of collaboration software (including some multiuser video games), is given extensive treatment. A new "Meeting the Challenge" on the use of web logs is included. There are new sections on evaluation of websites, media use to help English language learners and struggling readers, and media to assist physically challenged students. Suggestions for new websites to use for instruction are included.

Chapter 3, "A Conceptual Approach to Developing Meaningful Vocabulary," defines the meaning of *knowing words* and the relationship of words and comprehension. Word knowledge is a major problem for struggling readers. Direct vocabulary instruction that introduces multiple contexts is important for all students. Multiple opportunities to experience word meanings in a variety of contexts enrich students' word knowledge. A new "Meeting the Challenge" illustrates vocabulary instruction for secondary students.

Chapter 4, "The Process of Constructing Meaning in Texts," introduces the changes in content comprehension due to the rapidly changing demands of information and communication technologies. This chapter highlights the importance of fluency in comprehension. Students will study the ways that the contexts of readers, texts, and reading situations impinge on comprehension. A new "Meeting the Challenge" illustrates the relationship between context and comprehension.

Chapter 5, "Strategies for Constructing Meaning in Text," emphasizes the significance of active reading in comprehension development. The strategies and skills that good readers use to comprehend are introduced. Among the goals of strategy application are retaining important information, understanding topics deeply, and actively using knowledge application. A new "Meeting the Challenge" illustrates a "webquest" that uses technology to develop understanding. Chapter 6, "Location and Organization of Information," and Chapter 7, "Reading-Study Strategies for Textbook Use," present useful strategies for all content areas. Both chapters have been updated and streamlined, and both have new sections on study skills for English language learners and struggling readers. Chapter 7 includes discussions of interactive whiteboards and of using cartoons to enhance study in content areas.

Four chapters that focus more specifically on instruction in content area classes follow. Chapter 8, "Writing in the Content Areas," has new material on written conversations, writing multigenre reports and books, using good published nonfiction materials as models for nonfiction writing, mentoring projects, editing, and choosing topics for writing. There is a new "Meeting the Challenge" on writing zines and a new example of a multigenre report that includes a traditional research report. New sections on writing instruction for English language learners and struggling readers are also included.

Chapter 9, "Literature-Based and Thematic Approaches to Content Area Teaching," has new material on the use of text-picture books and graphic novels, read-alouds, and readers' theater. A new "Meeting the Challenge" shows development of a unit on the Holocaust. Sections on use of literature with English language learners and struggling readers have also been added.

Chapter 10, "Reading in the Content Areas: I," has been updated to address the curriculum goals and expectations of current content. This chapter focuses on strategies to help students interpret and use the knowledge they acquire.

Chapter 11, "Reading in the Content Areas: II," focuses on understanding the complex and layered combinations of the messages that students will encounter. The strategies will help students transform information through writing, speaking, and visual representation.

Chapter 12, "Classroom Literacy Assessment," has been streamlined and updated. Additional information about high-stakes tests has been added. More information on self-evaluation, resilience, and evaluation of written retellings of nonfiction material has been incorporated. Sections on considerations in evaluation of English language learners and struggling readers are included.

Features of the Text

This text presents a balance of theory and applications related to secondary school literacy. It provides unique emphasis on the content areas, with practical strategies and illustrations of content materials from all secondary school subject areas. In all chapters, extensive use is made of actual secondary school material to explicitly bring theory into practice. A major strength of this book is the guidance it provides teachers in helping students improve their reading performance through the application of reading and study skills. To help the reader gain a more complete understanding of content, each text chapter contains the following features:

Overview. This section provides a brief description of the most important concepts and themes of each chapter. Readers can use the overview to create a mental set for reading the chapter.

Purpose-Setting Questions. Purpose-setting questions focus readers' attention on the important aspects of chapter content.

Meeting the Challenge Vignettes. These vignettes illustrate how teachers have used the ideas discussed in the chapter to meet their teaching challenges. The vignettes put the concepts from the chapter into realistic contexts for readers and help answer the question that content teachers often ask: How will I use this information on reading in my future classroom teaching?

New **Focus on English Language Learners and Focus on Struggling Readers.** These features highlight the important applications for students with special needs in separate, easy-to-locate sections in each chapter.

New **Houghton Mifflin Video Cases.** Video Cases that correlate to chapter content have been highlighted in the margins for quick reference. The Online Study Center icon with case title in the margin denotes where students can go to the website to watch the corresponding teaching strategies in practice.

Margin Questions. These questions focus attention on important terminology and concepts in the material.

Content Area Marginal Icons. These icons easily alert content area teachers to material specific to their content areas.

Summary. The summary pulls together the main ideas of the chapter. Readers can use the summary to review their knowledge and to reinforce chapter content.

Discussion Questions. Instructors can use these higher-level essay questions as homework assignments or as the basis of class discussion.

Enrichment Activities. Application activities that go beyond chapter content provide students with opportunities to practice what they have learned in each chapter. These range from ideas for research papers to creating lesson plans and using strategies.

Glossary. The glossary helps readers unfamiliar with specialized literacy terminology understand key terms.

Teaching and Learning Supplements

The *Instructor's Resource Manual*, available on the Online Teaching Center, offers learning objectives, suggested teaching and learning strategies, and instructional materials for each chapter. Appropriate performance-based assessment activities are also included. Model syllabi that could be used for a course in secondary school reading instruction and a study skills learning activity packet are provided in this manual, along with a transition guide that outlines the changes from the eighth edition to the ninth edition.

Test items are available on the *HM Testing CD*. Sets of examination items provided for chapters include multiple-choice, true-false, and essay questions.

Online Teaching and Study Centers (http://college.hmco.com/pic/roeSSLI9e) is available to enhance instruction. The Online Study Center provides links to related standards, lesson plans, and professional organizations. It also includes links to website resources from McDougal Littell, a Houghton Mifflin company that publishes secondary school content area textbooks, as well as HM Video Cases, glossary terms, and definitions. For instructors, the Online Teaching Center offers the *Instructor's Resource Manual* online to provide flexibility for using the various instructor resource and assessment materials, Web links, PowerPoint slides, HM Video Cases, and more.

Acknowledgments

We are indebted to many people for their assistance in the preparation of our manuscript. Although we would like to acknowledge the many teachers and students whose inspiration was instrumental in the development of this book, it is impossible to name them all. Particular appreciation is due Barbara Vaughn, Larry Lynn, Katherine M. Dooley, Lance Jasitt, Rory Lewelyn, Annette Littrell, Cathy McCurdy, and Jill Ramsey. Grateful recognition is also given to our editors, Lisa Mafrici and Dayna Pell, and the following reviewers whose constructive advice and criticism helped greatly in the writing and revision of the manuscript:

Charlotte Boger, *Fayetteville State University*
Roberta L. Sejnost, *Loyola University*
Heather K. Sheridan-Thomas, *Binghamton University*

In addition, appreciation is expressed for those who have granted permission to use sample materials or citations from their works.

Betty D. Roe, *Professor Emerita, Tennessee Technological University, Cookeville*
Barbara Stoodt-Hill, *John Tyler Community College and Old Dominion University*

Part 1

Contexts of Literacy Instruction in a Technological Age

Chapter 1

Content Area Literacy in a Changing World

OVERVIEW

This chapter opens by addressing literacy demands on secondary school students and by looking at literacy instruction needs in content areas. Then it provides an overview of the nature of reading and the strategy and skill areas involved, the personnel responsible for secondary school literacy instruction, and the five aspects of a secondary school literacy program. Faulty assumptions about literacy instruction are examined next. Finally, we discuss current concerns about literacy performance and the resulting development of standards, taking into consideration the diversity of students found within content area classrooms.

PURPOSE-SETTING QUESTIONS

As you read this chapter, try to answer these questions:

1. What occurs during the reading process?
2. What literacy demands do secondary school students face?
3. What school personnel are responsible for literacy instruction?
4. What are some faulty assumptions about developing literacy in secondary schools?
5. What are some concerns about the literacy performance of secondary school students?
6. How have new standards for literacy learning affected secondary school instruction?
7. What is the range of students in content area classrooms?

MEETING THE CHALLENGE

"My students aren't doing their reading assignments for my class. I don't know whether they *can't* or just *won't* read the material. Either way, my lessons haven't been going smoothly," a new secondary school teacher complained to a colleague.

"First, you need to find out if they *can* read the material," the colleague replied. "Do you know how to construct a cloze test or a group reading inventory?"

"No. Are they hard to do?" the new teacher responded.

"Cloze tests are easier to construct. However, you may feel that you get more specific information from the inventory," the colleague answered.

"Will you show me how to make these assessments?" asked the new teacher. "And will you help me interpret the results?"

"I'll lend you a book that describes them," the colleague said. "I got it for a college methods course. I'm sorry that I don't have more time to help, but you might ask the special reading teacher or the reading consultant for some assistance, too."

"I didn't think of that," the new teacher admitted. "Thanks for your advice."

After studying the book's description of the two assessment measures, the teacher chose to prepare and administer a cloze test to the students. The results surprised her. Only a small number of the students appeared to be capable of reading the text independently. The majority could read it with teacher assistance, but some could not read it with understanding, even with teacher assistance.

"Thank goodness for the independent-level group," she thought, "but what can I do to help the others?"

She returned to her colleague with her new question. He replied, "Check out that book some more. It suggests strategies that help prepare students for reading, guide them through reading, and direct them in analysis after reading. It describes study methods and ideas for study guides and other instructional activities for those students who can learn from the text with help. It suggests alternative materials and strategies for the other, less capable readers, but I still think you should talk to the reading specialists about this as well."

The teacher examined more sections of the recommended book and gained ideas from it. Then she talked to the reading staff in her school. She now had a better idea of what she needed to do, and she had more specific questions to ask them.

"Where can I locate lower-level reading material for the students who can't read this text?" she asked.

Reading specialists can help classroom teachers learn how to help their students read content materials with understanding.
© Bob Daemmrich Photography

"Enlist the help of the media specialist," she was told. "Also make some transcripts of class discussions that can be duplicated and used as reading material for these students."

"Oh, yes. I remember that idea," she said. "The book called it 'use of language experience materials.' What would you suggest that I do to prepare the ones who can read the text with help for successful reading?"

"For *all* your students, try developing the new vocabulary through semantic webs or semantic feature analysis. Provide purposes for their reading that involve higher-level thinking. Perhaps use anticipation guides," she was told.

"The book explains all those activities," she said with relief. "I guess I had better get busy."

"If you need help when you get into the process, call me," the reading consultant said. "I'll be glad to lend a hand with specifics."

"It's sure good to have some direction for this," the teacher sighed. "Who would have thought I'd be so concerned about *reading*? I'm a *science* teacher."

Although the scenario in the "Meeting the Challenge" vignette is not based on the experience of a single teacher, the situation it depicts is a common one. Teachers who have not had courses in secondary reading methods often find themselves in this situation. It would be good if they could all find colleagues with the right books and advice to offer!

This text is designed to help teachers know what to do about their students' literacy problems and whom to ask for assistance when they need it. All the techniques and activities mentioned in the scenario and many others are explained in detail in later chapters. "Meeting the Challenge" sections in the remainder of this book are based on the experiences of individual teachers in various school settings, as are the new features that focus on struggling readers and English language learners.

Literacy Demands on Secondary School Students

How will the levels of literacy that your secondary school students have affect their content area learning?

The term **literacy** refers to the ability to comprehend and produce written language and the willingness to do so in order to operate effectively in a particular social context. Venezky (1995, p. 142) says that it "differs from simple reading and writing in its assumption of an understanding of the appropriate use of these abilities within a print-based society. Literacy, therefore, requires active, autonomous engagement with print."

Secondary school students have to read content textbooks and supplementary materials (including trade books, magazines, and newspapers) in school and for homework outside of school. This may include reading electronically transmitted text from a computer monitor. Some of the material is likely to be highly technical in nature. Students also need to write in-class and homework papers and to write responses to test questions, study questions, and assigned readings. However, they have even more varied literacy needs in their activities outside school.

Even if students ignore purely recreational reading, they need to read signs found in their environment, recipes, menus, manuals for operating equipment, instructions for assembling items, job applications, television schedules, transportation schedules, road maps, labels on food or medicine, newspapers, public notices, advertisements, bank statements, bills, and many other functional materials. Failure to read some of these materials with adequate understanding can result in their committing traffic violations, becoming lost, having unpleasant reactions to food or medicine, being ejected from unauthorized areas, missing desirable programs, failing to make connections with needed transportation, losing employment opportunities, and other undesirable outcomes.

Secondary students also need to write letters to family and friends, instructions to people who are doing things for them (such as feeding their pets), notes to themselves about tasks to be completed, phone messages for other members of their households, responses to a multitude of forms, and many other items. Mistakes in these activities can have negative results. For example, an inaccurately written phone message may cause someone to fail to pick up a young child at school on time. Our culture places a high value on literacy, and we are inundated with reading and writing demands in order to carry out everyday tasks.

The job market also affects students' literacy needs. Research shows that the number of low-literacy jobs has decreased, and even jobs considered to be low in literacy demands may require the ability to read materials such as manuals for operating equipment. The literacy demands of schools and the workplace are different (Mace, 1992; Gerber and Finn, 1998). "The nature of reading in the workplace generally involves locating information for immediate use and inferring information for problem solving" (Gerber and Finn, 1998, p. 33). Workers need to be able to understand graphic aids, categorize information, and skim and scan to locate information. These skills are often not emphasized in secondary school instruction (Gerber and Finn, 1998). The reading and writing of a variety of types of documents—memos, manuals, catalogs, letters, reports, graphs, charts, and instructions—are necessary literacy skills for the workplace. Mikulecky (1996, p. 155) says that "the ability to set purposes, self-question, summarize information, monitor comprehension, and make useful notes distinguishes superior job performers from merely adequate job performers." Workers have to put together information from a variety of sources to solve problems and to perform job requirements.

Good literacy skills are especially important to students who plan to attend college. Educators have realized for years that reading at grade level is not good enough for these students because students entering college are expected to be able to read at higher than twelfth-grade level, as determined by traditional reading tests.

Today's high school students do engage in many literacy practices: "they e-mail, Instant Message, surf the Web, read video game magazines . . . , participate in online chat rooms, and read bulleted information on teacher handouts" (Alvermann, Huddleston, and Hagood, 2004, p. 532). They also construct their own web pages and blogs (web logs). They don't do a great deal of reading from their textbooks, however, and they may balk at completing traditional writing assignments. On the High School Survey of Student Engagement, conducted by Indiana University, "55% of the respondents reported spending three hours or less per week on homework, readings, rehearsals, or other school assignments" ("Survey Gauges Engagement Among High School Students," 2004, p. 4). However, they did spend more time than that on personal reading online. The survey also revealed that 30 percent of the respondents had not written a paper longer than five pages so far during that school year, but nearly 40 percent had written seven or more papers of less than three pages during that time period.

Smith and Wilhelm's research (2004) shows that boys may reject literacy activities in school because they lack competence in them, and they generally pursue activities in which they are competent. They may, however, engage in literacy activities at home in areas in which they feel competent, for example, working with hypermedia and Web design. Some complained about the difficult language of school texts, especially those laden with description, and reading in unfamiliar genres. Several indicated that teachers should do more to support their learning of strategies needed to interpret these materials. Alvermann, Huddleston, and Hagood (2004) believe that teachers should instruct students in a way that encourages them to make connections between personal literacies, such as reading comics or watching World Wrestling Federation matches, with school literacies, such as textbook reading.

Legislation Related to Secondary School Literacy

Currently, federal legislation has entered the picture for all of our students. *No Child Left Behind* legislation makes continuous reading instruction and learning of vocabulary and comprehension strategies a current concern, as secondary literacy educators have always believed them to be. The legislation also promotes assessment-based, individually appropriate reading instruction and many opportunities to use a wide variety of texts, also practices that literacy educators support. Its recommendations fail to address many of the issues in adolescent literacy, however. Secondary teachers need to acquire strategies to build bridges between adolescents and the community, as well as between adolescents and the school, involving parents as partners in the adolescents' education, and designing interventions for struggling adolescent readers (Conley and Hinchman, 2004).

Literacy Lens—The Content Areas

In everyday situations, all people, secondary students included, must identify and seek the information they need. Therefore, in a secondary classroom, it is appropriate for instruction to center on issues and problems that are relevant to the students in everyday life. Such instruction addresses finding and understanding information, comparing and evaluating sources of information, and going beyond the printed material by interpreting, generalizing, synthesizing, and applying the information.

Providing a variety of reading and writing experiences using varied materials can help students develop the background they need to read real-world material and the skill to express themselves in clear and functional ways. Reading short textbook assignments to answer factual check-up questions and writing single-word or single-phrase answers to questions or circling correct responses are not sufficient.

Reading Instruction in the Content Area Curriculum

WHAT IS READING?

How would you define reading?

Reading is described in different ways by different people. Despite continuing disagreement about the precise nature of the reading process, there are points of general agreement among reading authorities. One such point is that comprehension of written material is the purpose of reading instruction. In fact, we consider *reading comprehension* and *reading* to be synonymous because when understanding breaks down, reading actually has not occurred.

During the reading process, there is an interplay between the reader's preexisting knowledge and the written content. Competent reading is an active process in which the reader calls on experience, language, and schemata (theoretical constructs of knowledge related to experiences) to anticipate and understand the author's written language. Therefore, readers both bring meaning to print and take meaning from print. It is, as Rosenblatt (1989) and Goodman (in Aaron et al., 1990) would say, transactive.

The nature of the reading process alters as students mature. In the early stages of reading, word identification requires a reader's concentration. Eventually, however, readers are able to use their reading ability (ability to interpret written language) for pleasure, appreciation, knowledge acquisition, and functional purposes. Thus, reading competence has many faces. Competent readers locate materials and ideas that enable them to fulfill particular purposes, which may be to follow directions, to complete job applications, or to appreciate Shakespeare's plays. In addition, competent readers adjust their reading style as they move from narrative to expository content. Finally, they read with various types of understanding—literal, interpretive, critical, and creative.

The terms *literal, interpretive (inferential), critical,* and *creative* refer to the types of thinking that are commonly associated with reading comprehension. *Literal understanding* refers to the reader's recognizing or remembering ideas and information that are explicitly stated in printed material. *Interpretive comprehension* occurs when the reader synthesizes ideas and information from printed material with knowledge, experience, and imagination to form hypotheses. Interpretive comprehension requires that the reader use ideas and information that are not stated on the printed page; that is, the reader must "read between the lines," use deductive reasoning, and make assumptions based on the facts given. *Critical comprehension (evaluation)* requires that the reader make judgments about the content of a reading selection by comparing it with external criteria. The reader may have developed these criteria through experience, through reference to resource materials, or through access to information provided by authorities on the subject. *Creative understanding* (*reading beyond the lines*) has to do with the reader's emotional responses to printed material (appreciation) and his or her ability to produce new ideas based on the reading experience. Creative understanding is built on literal, inferential, and critical understanding. A reader's intellectual understanding provides a foundation for his or her emotional reaction. For example, a reader may respond to an author's style or may identify with a certain character, a story incident, or the author's use of symbolism.

Good readers exercise comprehension monitoring (metacognitive) strategies as they read. They constantly ask if the material they are reading makes sense, and if not, what they should do to remedy their lack of understanding.

Reading Orally

Because there are times when students must read orally to convey information to others, oral reading fluency is important. **Fluency** involves reading with expression, appropriate phrasing, and accuracy. Rasinski and Hoffman (2003) report that the National Assessment of Educational Progress showed that oral reading fluency was positively related to overall reading achievement.

Good ways to work on fluency with secondary-level students are Readers Theatre (discussed in Chapter 9) and the method of repeated readings (discussed in Chapter 4). Current research and theory support instruction in oral reading fluency for older students who are not fluent readers (Rasinski and Hoffman, 2003).

Word Identification

Do students need to be able to use all of the different word identification skills and strategies? Why or why not?

Word identification skills and strategies include sight-word recognition, contextual analysis, structural analysis, phonic analysis, and use of the dictionary's respellings to determine pronunciation. The goal of word identification instruction is to develop students' independence in identifying words.

Sight words are words students have memorized and are able to identify immediately. Secondary students usually have a good store of sight words that help them read content materials with understanding. Each time a content teacher introduces a new technical or specialized term that is important to understanding the content area, the teacher hopes to turn the new word into a sight word for the students; the study of the subject would be inefficient if many of the important words had to be analyzed carefully before recognition occurred. The content teacher can help impress new words on the students' memories and thus turn them into sight words by writing them on the chalkboard, pronouncing them, and discussing them with the students. Knowledge of sight words also enables students to use contextual analysis.

Contextual analysis is the use of the context in which an unknown word occurs (the surrounding words and sentences) to identify the word. Contextual analysis skills are powerful tools for secondary students to use in reading content area materials, and content area teachers will benefit from helping students become aware of the usefulness of context in word identification. Contextual analysis not only plays a role in word identification, but also is an important tool for determining word meaning.

Structural analysis entails the use of word parts, such as affixes, root words, syllables, and smaller words that are joined to form compound words, to help in the identification of unfamiliar words. Structural analysis is extremely helpful in analysis of content area words because in many cases certain prefixes, suffixes, and root words appear repeatedly in the related technical terms of a discipline. Learning to recognize these word parts can be very helpful in decoding the vocabulary of the discipline.

Phonic analysis involves breaking words into basic sound elements and blending these sounds together to produce spoken words. Phonic analysis is not taught by the content area teacher but lies in the province of the special reading teacher.

Use of the dictionary's respellings to determine pronunciation is an important skill for students to master. Many students need lessons in using the dictionary's pronunciation key to help them decode the respellings.

Comprehension

Why is reading comprehension a central concern of the content area teacher?

Reading comprehension is an interactive process of meaning construction. The reader's background knowledge structures (schemata), the information in the text, and the context in which the reading takes place all interact to produce comprehension. Schemata related to the reading material must be activated if students are to comprehend material as fully as possible.

Word identification skills and strategies help students pronounce words, but they must understand word meanings before reading comprehension can occur. Many of the words that content readers encounter represent labels for key concepts in the content areas. A reader learns word meanings through experience, word association, discussion, concept development, contextual analysis, structural analysis, and use of a dictionary and a thesaurus. Content teachers can help students comprehend content materials by teaching them the meanings of key vocabulary terms. Structural analysis plays an important part in the determination of word meaning in content area classes. Morphemes, the smallest meaningful units of a language, include prefixes, suffixes, and root words. Each content area has common word parts such as these that are frequently found in instructional materials for the class. Analogy exercises, semantic feature analysis, word sorts, and word webs (or semantic webs or arrays) are all good vocabulary development activities. These activities are explained in detail in Chapter 3.

To read with comprehension, readers must also be able to perceive the internal organization of reading materials, understand the various writing patterns used to structure content materials, and understand the material at the appropriate cognitive levels.

A reader's perception of the internal organization of a selection is based on the ability to identify main ideas and supporting details as well as on familiarity with various organizational writing patterns. Expository writing patterns may include cause-effect, comparison-contrast, sequence of events, or one or more of a variety of other organizations. For narrative materials, knowledge of story grammar (or story structure) is important. Readers understand content better when they are able to follow the particular writing pattern and organization used. Content area teachers need to be familiar with the types of writing patterns encountered frequently in their particular disciplines so that they can help students to understand these patterns.

When reading, students must comprehend material literally, interpretively, critically, and creatively, as each type of comprehension is appropriate. Modeling, discussion, a problem-solving approach to reading, comprehension monitoring, visualization strategies, judicious use of questioning techniques, use of writing to learn, use of study guides, and directed reading lessons serve as vehicles for developing these types of understanding. Chapters 4 and 5 address comprehension instruction.

Content reading requires flexible use of reading rate. The concept of rate can be examined best as it relates to comprehension. Rate is governed by purpose for reading, type of comprehension desired, familiarity with content, and type of content. Content area teachers need to help students learn to vary their reading rates to fit particular instructional materials and different purposes for reading. Chapter 7 discusses reading rate.

Study Skills

How can poor study skills affect content area learning?

In secondary school, students are expected to become more independent in applying their reading skills and strategies in work-study situations. **Study skills** include the application of reading skills and strategies to the learning of written content area material. There are three basic types of study skills: those that involve locating information through reading; those that are concerned with understanding and remembering content; and those that are concerned with the organization of information once it has been located and read. Content area teachers need to help students learn to use these study skills efficiently so that they can study the content assignments more effectively. Teaching study skills in the situations in which they are expected to be used is more effective than teaching them in isolation. Examples of location and study skills can be found in Chapters 6 and 7, and applications of these skills to particular content areas are discussed in Chapters 10 and 11.

PERSONNEL RESPONSIBLE FOR SECONDARY SCHOOL LITERACY INSTRUCTION

The secondary school literacy program is the responsibility of a number of individuals. Those responsible for various portions of the program include content area teachers, special reading teachers, reading consultants, principals and other administrators, and librarians or media center specialists.

Content Area Teachers

How does the content area teacher's responsibility for his or her students' reading skills differ from that of the special reading teacher?

The content area teacher's responsibility is to help students *read* their textbooks and supplementary materials more effectively in order to *learn* the content more effectively. **Content area teachers** need to know what reading skills are necessary for successful reading of the materials in their particular disciplines, and they need to be capable of assisting students in applying these skills as they complete their content area assignments. In most cases, such as in teaching technical vocabulary, reading instruction and content instruction are identical. Content teachers may often find that mini-lessons in a particular reading strategy will pay large dividends in the students' understanding of an assignment.

Content area teachers do not have the *primary* responsibility for teaching reading strategies. The responsibility for helping students with significantly impaired reading abilities belongs to a special reading teacher. However, content teachers do have to adjust assignments for these students. It may be necessary to provide alternate materials and teaching methods for these students if their content learning is to be successful.

Content area teachers need to know the reading skills that secondary students require in order to read content materials in their disciplines effectively; assessment measures that can help them identify students who cannot read the standard assignments, students who can read the assignments only with much assistance, and those who can read the assignments with ease; ways to help students learn specific skills and strategies needed for their content areas; study aids and procedures that can help students achieve success in content area reading; and effective ways to differentiate assignments for students reading at different levels of proficiency. They also need to be able to identify specific learning problems that should be referred to a specialist for help, and they need to be willing to cooperate with other school personnel, such as the special reading teacher, to help students reach their full potential in content reading.

Even though some content area teachers are initially hesitant about reading strategy instruction, they often change their attitudes when they learn useful strategies. Poindexter (1994) found that four strategies—the jigsaw method, anticipation/reaction guides, What I Know (essentially K-W-L), and self-questioning—helped students in her content area reading class to see that they could teach reading strategies successfully and thereby enhance comprehension of their content area material. The jigsaw method is a form of cooperative learning. (See Chapter 5 for an explanation of the other three strategies.)

Hesitancy about assisting students to improve their writing proficiency in related content areas may also exist for teachers who have not been taught appropriate strategies. There are many strategies that can be helpful to teachers in the area of writing as well. The process writing approach works well with any type of writing to be learned. Content journals, RAFT assignments, research reports, laboratory reports, photo essays, and Internet writing projects are just a few of the many ways that content area teachers can use writing to accomplish content objectives while helping students become more effective communicators. Chapters 8 and 9 provide information about these and other approaches that teachers may use. A wonderful writing teacher and researcher, Donald Graves (2004) believes, as we do, that teachers are more important to student learning than are teaching methods. However, having a working knowledge of effective methods makes a good teacher even better.

Special Reading Teacher

What kinds of interactions do the special reading teacher and the content area teacher need to have?

The special reading teacher generally works directly with students on reading skills. Although the specific responsibilities of reading specialists may vary from locale to locale, these educators also often administer and interpret reading assessments; plan and teach reading classes; and work with the reading consultant, content area teachers, and paraprofessionals who have responsibilities in the reading program.

Jaeger (1996) makes the case that reading specialists should spend more time working with school personnel, rather than working directly with children for all, or the large majority, of their time. She believes that they would have more impact working with curriculum development, instructional problem solving, assessment, and parent liaison activities, essentially serving as a reading consultant at the building level.

Henwood (1999/2000) collaborated with content teachers in her high school in paired, partnership relationships to promote student learning and stimulate professional development. Sometimes, in response to a teacher request, she modeled a teaching strategy. At other times she demonstrated learning strategies or observed the teacher's instruction and student response and provided feedback. She helped teachers learn how to provide individualized instruction and deal with large classes, as well as how to choose and implement appropriate strategies. She also acted as a liaison among the various teachers and departments.

After a review of research on the role of the reading specialist, Quatroche, Bean, and Hamilton (2001, p. 292) stated that "although reading specialists have many responsibilities, a major role seems to be the assessment and instruction of students with difficulties. . . . The new configurations for meeting the needs of at-risk students . . . require reading specialists who are able to collaborate and communicate effectively" with classroom teachers, special education teachers, administrators, and parents.

Reading Consultant

What are the main differences between the job of the reading consultant and that of the special reading teacher?

The reading consultant works with administrators and other school personnel to develop and coordinate schoolwide reading programs. The reading consultant may work from the central office with more than one school. This person is freed from classroom teaching and instruction of special reading classes.

Again, although the specific responsibilities of reading consultants may vary somewhat from place to place, these educators often assist in planning comprehensive reading programs; keep school personnel informed about the philosophy, procedures, and materials for the programs; evaluate reading programs and materials; provide in-service training; and provide resources for other personnel.

Principal or Administrator

A most significant prerequisite for a good secondary literacy program is administrative direction. The administrator alone possesses the prestige and authority to carry through a sound literacy program. He or she needs to understand the literacy program's philosophy.

The administrator should know about literacy and students, provide a good teaching/learning environment, work with teachers in creating an appropriate organizational plan for instruction, see that appropriate instructional and assessment tools are available, make sure that all components of a secondary school literacy program are included in the school's plan, communicate with parents about literacy concerns, and hire capable personnel.

Librarian or Media Center Specialist

The librarian or media center specialist provides assistance to the special reading teacher and the content area teacher alike by locating books and other printed materials on different subjects and at different reading levels, by making available audiovisual aids that can be used for motivation and background building, and by providing students with instruction in location strategies related to the library or media center, such as doing online computer searches for information or searching electronic or printed reference books. The librarian may set up special displays of printed materials or may create specialized bibliographies or lists of Internet addresses on specific subjects at the request of the teachers, and he or she also may provide students with direct assistance in finding and using appropriate materials. Recreational reading may be fostered by the librarian's book talks or attractive book displays on topics with high levels of interest to students.

Teamwork

All of the personnel responsible for the literacy program need to work together as a team. The content area teacher is definitely a part of the team concerned with the development of secondary school students' literacy skills. This teacher is concerned with proficiency in literacy largely because it can either enhance or adversely affect the learning of content.

Content area teachers may ask for the reading consultant's assistance in identifying approaches that will best meet the special reading needs of their students. They may send students who are reading far below the level of the instructional materials assigned for the grade to the special reading teacher for assessment and remedial instruction, or the special reading teacher may come into the content classrooms to provide assistance. Content teachers should work closely with the special reading teacher in planning reading assignments for students who are receiving remedial assistance; they should consult with the special reading teacher about what instructional materials will meet the reading needs of their students; and they may ask the special reading teacher to teach lessons in some aspects of reading. They may also cooperate with special tutors for some students with special needs.

Content area teachers should expect to work hand in hand with the librarian or media center specialist when assembling materials for teaching units and when teaching library skills. Content magazines, print and electronic reference materials, and recreational reading materials should be a part of the library's yearly budget allocation, and it should be the content teachers who recommend appropriate materials.

Other content area teachers may team with the English teachers for projects that require writing skills that their students have not mastered. The English teachers can teach the writing skills and evaluate the resultant writing products, and the other teachers can evaluate the level of learning achieved in the specific content area subject matter.

The principal sets the tone of the school's literacy program. The content area teacher should be able to approach the principal for funding for instructional materials that are needed to meet the diverse reading and writing needs of the students in content classes and for help with organizational arrangements, such as special grouping practices that will enhance the content area literacy program.

ASPECTS OF A SECONDARY SCHOOL LITERACY PROGRAM

In an excellent secondary school literacy program all school personnel cooperate to advance effective reading and writing skills, and all students are offered literacy instruction according to their needs. Such instruction may be offered in special reading classes, special writing labs, or English classes, but it is also a priority in all content area classes. Barry (1994) points out that some schools are moving away from special reading classes. The specialist may come into content classrooms and offer assistance there instead. Reading strategies and skills are taught as they are needed, facilitating meaningful application of the instruction. Additionally, many schools do not have writing labs for students who are having difficulties with written assignments in various content areas. In an excellent secondary school literacy program, all components of literacy instruction are included:

Why is developmental reading instruction needed in secondary school?

1. *Developmental reading* is taught to students who are progressing satisfactorily in acquiring reading proficiency. The developmental component of the program is for average and above-average readers. A special reading teacher, who directs the program, helps students to develop further comprehension skills and strategies, vocabulary knowledge, rate of reading, and study skills.

How does reading in content area materials pose special problems for students?

2. *Content area reading* is taught. In the content area component of the program, the students are helped to comprehend specific subject matter. Reading skills and strategies required for effective reading of the content area material are considered. Within each content area—English, mathematics, social studies, science, and so forth—reading materials with which students can experience reading success must be used. Such materials may include multilevel texts, materials from library sources with levels of reading difficulty that correspond with the students' abilities, interactive computer programs, videos, and audiotapes. The main focus of this book is on content area literacy.

Why should content teachers be concerned with recreational reading?

3. *Recreational reading* is encouraged. The recreational reading component is an important, although frequently neglected, aspect of the comprehensive literacy program since the ultimate goal of reading instruction is to develop good life-long reading habits. Although English teachers and reading specialists have particularly strong reasons for motivating students to read for pleasure, everyone involved with students should actively encourage recreational reading.

Content area teachers should encourage recreational reading for three major reasons:

PHYSICAL EDUCATION

SOCIAL STUDIES

AGRICULTURE

ENGLISH/ LANGUAGE ARTS

- The content area teacher may have a special rapport with some students who do not like to read and with whom no other secondary teacher has established this special relationship.
- A certain content area may be the only one that holds a student's interest at a particular time. For example, a physical education teacher might be able to motivate a particular boy or girl to read extracurricular books on sports.
- Particular subject matter becomes more "real" as a reader experiences events through imaginative literature. For example, the topic of the American Revolution, which might take up only one chapter in a social studies textbook, will be more meaningful to a student who reads Esther Forbes's *Johnny Tremain* and becomes involved in Johnny's experiences of that period's political intrigue and his preparation for war. *Across Five Aprils* by Irene Hunt gives students broadened perspectives on the Civil War. Good nonfiction selections can also add interest to the study of history. Teachers may want to recommend *Eyes on the Prize: America's Civil Rights Years, 1954–1965* by Juan Williams. Teachers of agriculture can use literature to sustain student interest; for example, Henry Billings's *All Down the Valley* is an interesting story of the Tennessee Valley Authority. Teachers of composition may find Lois Duncan's *Chapters: My Growth as a Writer* useful. Extra effort by each content area teacher to find interesting supplementary reading material may lead to enduring reading habits and tastes in the students.

4. *Writing instruction* is provided to facilitate completion of meaningful and purposeful content area assignments that involve writing. Some content teachers may team with English teachers to accomplish both literacy and content area goals.

5. *Instruction for struggling readers* is important for students who are experiencing difficulties. Students who are performing at one year below their grade levels or less are usually served by the regular classroom teacher through in-class adjustments to assignments and materials. Students who are further behind usually need to work on basic word recognition and comprehension strategies and skills. Good comprehenders, in general, tend to use more strategies and be more flexible in their use than do poor comprehenders (Kletzien, 1991), so developing strategies and the ability to use them is very important to these students. As their fluency improves, the students can learn how to apply general study skills. This part of the program is directed primarily by the special reading teacher, often in a separate class.

San Diego's Morse High School has offered a multidimensional reading course to those ninth- and tenth-graders who are reading at the seventh-grade level or below. The course includes vocabulary building through dictation of natural language and through reading. Students are encouraged to read both in school and at home, and teachers read aloud to them and "think aloud" about their reading strategies. Students induce phonetic and structural principles as they examine banks of words they have collected. Teachers also provide explicit reading comprehension instruction. A research study of this program showed that it was extremely successful (Showers et al., 1998).

SOME FAULTY ASSUMPTIONS ABOUT TEACHING READING

Several faulty assumptions about the teaching of reading should be recognized.

1. *Teaching reading is a concern only in the elementary school.* In many school systems, formal reading instruction ends at the sixth grade. The idea that a child who has completed the sixth grade should have mastered the complex process of reading fails to take into account that learning to read is a continuing process. People learn to read over a long period of time, attempting more advanced reading materials as they master easier ones. Even after encountering all the reading skills through classroom instruction, readers continue to refine their use of them, just as athletes first learn the techniques of a sport and then practice and refine their abilities over time.

2. *Teaching reading in the content areas is separate and distinct from teaching subject matter.* Teaching reading and study skills is an integral part of teaching any content area, and content teachers' efforts to do so are important to the success of any secondary school literacy program. A teacher is obligated to teach students how to use the printed materials that he or she assigns. When a teacher employs printed materials to teach a content area, that teacher is using reading as a teaching aid—and should use it for maximum effectiveness. Teaching reading in subject matter areas is a complementary learning process, inseparable from the particular subject matter.

3. *Reading needs in the secondary school can be met through remedial work alone.* Some schools fail to make an essential distinction between *developmental reading*, which is designed to meet the needs of all students, and *corrective reading* and *remedial reading*, which provide specific assistance to struggling readers. Not only should developmental (as well as remedial) classes be made available, but also within each class the content teacher can promote developmental reading by helping students learn the concepts and vocabulary of that content area, and teachers can enhance their students' reading comprehension by assisting them in interpreting and evaluating the text material. Corrective reading assistance can also be given within each class, as needed.

   Teachers can help students develop better reading study skills and other specialized skills associated with their particular content areas. For example, reading written directions with understanding is a necessary skill in every secondary classroom. Students must also be able to read to discover main ideas, details, and inferences. Even more important than absorbing the vast amount of printed material that they encounter every day is secondary school students' development of critical reading ability. Before they leave secondary school, students should know how to sort out fact from opinion, truth from half-truth, information from emotion.

Schema = Background Information

4. *A reading specialist or an English teacher should be responsible for the teaching of reading.* Reading specialists have distinct responsibilities in secondary literacy programs, but the results of their efforts are negligible without the help of classroom teachers. Responsibility for teaching reading cannot be delegated solely to English teachers. Reading as a tool for learning is no more important in English class than it is in most other classes, and English teachers do not necessarily have any better preparation for teaching reading skills and strategies than do other teachers, although they generally have been prepared to teach writing skills and strategies. All content teachers (English, science, health, social studies, mathematics, computer science, human environmental science, business education, technology, agriculture, physical education, music, art, and others) have a responsibility to teach the language and organization of their particular content areas, and to do so they must help students read that content.

**ENGLISH/
LANGUAGE
ARTS**

5. *The teaching of reading and the teaching of literature are one and the same.* Reading skills are important to the study of literature, as they are to the study of every content area. It should be understood, however, that teaching literature should not consist merely of having students read stories and then giving them vocabulary drills and exercises to find details and main ideas. It is dangerous to assume that a student will improve content reading skills by practicing with only literature selections, for reading in other content areas involves primarily expository, rather than narrative, selections and requires integration of information gained from graphic aids, such as pictures, maps, graphs, charts, and diagrams, with the written text.

SOME FAULTY ASSUMPTIONS ABOUT TEACHING WRITING

1. *Students learn what they need to know about **how** to write in elementary school.* After that they just use writing as a basic tool in other subjects. People who believe this fail to recognize the developmental nature of writing competency. Teachers know that older students need assistance to learn more advanced and complex reading skills for necessary reading activities in secondary school after mastering basic word recognition and comprehension skills. After mastering the basics of sentence structure and writing conventions, these students also need help to learn more advanced writing techniques in order to meet ever more demanding writing tasks as they work in different content area studies.

2. *Writing skills are only important to secondary school students in English class.* Although writing receives attention in English classes, as direct instruction in writing and writing for the purpose of analysis of literature, writing is important in every class. Not only that, but clarity of expression is important. Scientists must be able to write coherent and precise reports on experiments and observations

of phenomena, and science students need to be able to perform such tasks, as well. Almost all classes require written projects or reports to demonstrate learning both from class and from outside research. Learning cannot be adequately demonstrated if the writing is inexact, unfocused, or unclear. Failure to observe writing conventions and standard spellings and failure to use clear sentence constructions may completely mask the learning that has taken place. If the report or project represents a typical real-world task, it has not been successful if it would not be acceptable in a real-world situation, such as a business meeting.

Literacy Performance and Standards

There is widespread concern in the United States about the literacy skills of secondary students. This concern has manifested itself in much testing.

LITERACY PERFORMANCE

The wide range in literacy achievement among secondary school students presents their teachers with a difficult problem. For example, in a group classified as seventh-graders, there may be boys and girls whose literacy skills equal those of many tenth- or eleventh-graders. Some twelfth-graders may have a fifth- or sixth-grade reading ability, whereas others may read at the level of college seniors. The same differences are found in the area of writing. In addition to having students with a wide range of reading and writing abilities, secondary schools often have large numbers of struggling readers. Thus, teachers in secondary schools should know that a student's grade placement may not reflect his or her literacy levels. Teaching literacy skills and strategies in the secondary schools includes strengthening the performance of students who are reading and writing well for their grade placements *and* giving more basic assistance to students who are reading and writing at levels significantly below their grade placements.

The National Assessment of Educational Progress (NAEP) is a study to determine competence in a number of learning areas, including reading and writing. NAEP assessments involve nationally representative samples of students in the fourth, eighth, and twelfth grades. Overall assessment results are analyzed by placement on a single proficiency scale, showing the kinds of tasks the students can perform at different achievement levels (Donahue et al., 1999).

Since 1992, the NAEP has reported results in terms of three achievement levels. Those students scoring at the *basic* level showed "partial mastery of the knowledge and skills fundamental for proficient work at each grade" (Mullis, Campbell, and Farstrup, 1993, p. 12). Those scoring at the *proficient* level exhibited "solid academic performance and demonstrated competence over challenging subject matter" (Mullis, Campbell, and Farstrup, 1993, p. 12). Students who scored at the *advanced* level displayed even higher levels of performance, including the ability to integrate prior knowledge with text information at the eighth-grade level and the ability to integrate text and document directions to accurately complete a task at the twelfth-grade level (Mullis, Campbell, and Farstrup, 1993).

In the 2002 NAEP, average reading scores for eighth-graders were higher than they were in 1992, but the average scores for twelfth-graders were lower than they were in 1992. In addition, the percentages of eighth-graders who performed at or above the basic level and at the proficient level were higher than they were in 1992, although there was not a significant change from what they were in 1998. At the twelfth-grade level there were declines in performance at or above the basic level and at the proficient level ("Good News, Bad News," 2003; "Reading," 2002).

In 2002, eighth-graders made gains in writing over the 1998 results, but the changes for twelfth-graders were not statistically significant. In this assessment the students were asked to do narrative, informative, and persuasive writing in a variety of forms and for different audiences. The stimuli for the writing varied from pictures and cartoons to letters and poems (*The Nation's Report Card*, 2002).

Some educators have questioned the use of NAEP results. For example, Jerome Harste asserted that "standardized tests that reduce literacy to a single scale are, put bluntly, invalid, and invalid, generic tests of literacy have zero instructional usefulness" (Farstrup, 1989/1990, p. 12).

Some educators are concerned that the standards may have been set too high; some wonder if the "NAEP achievement levels are valid measures of what students should know" ("Analyzing the NAEP Data," 1993/1994, p. 1); and some have questioned the adequacy of the test questions and complained about the overlapping definitions of the achievement levels ("NAEP Achievement Standards Draw Criticism," 1993/1994). Further analysis and clarification of the validity of the findings will emerge with further study. For now, teachers should be cautious in interpreting information from these test results.

Such test results continue to spur demands for the development of standards related to classroom knowledge or performance. Many states have developed standards for literacy of students at specific grade levels, specifying minimum competencies that students must acquire. Students may have to pass a minimum competency test in order to receive a high school diploma. Such actions have caused Tierney (1998, p. 387) to lament, "In some ways the quest for educational improvement via standards and in turn proficiency testing places a premium on uniformity rather than diversity and favors prepackaged learning over emerging possibilities."

Professional organizations have also sought to develop standards to improve instruction in various areas of the curriculum, such as language, mathematics, science, and social studies. The National Council of Teachers of English and the International Reading Association cooperatively developed a set of standards for the English language arts for kindergarten through twelfth grade. (See Figure 1.1.) Faust and Kieffer (1998) feel that *Standards for the English Language Arts* (1996) can be used as a guide for discussion about learning and evaluation, but this document resists "widespread calls for a national core curriculum requiring definitive, grade-level performance standards" (Faust and Kieffer, 1998, p. 541), the basis for minimum competency testing approaches. Instead, it specifies a range of areas in the

FIGURE 1.1

Standards for the English Language Arts (Sponsored by NCTE and IRA)

Source: *Standards for the English Language Arts*, by International Reading Association and the National Council of Teachers of English. Copyright 1996 by the International Reading Association and the National Council of Teachers of English. Reprinted with permission.

The vision guiding these standards is that all students must have the opportunities and resources to develop the language skills they need to pursue life's goals and to participate fully as informed, productive members of society. These standards assume that literacy growth begins before children enter school as they experience and experiment with literacy activities—reading and writing, and associating spoken words with their graphic representations. Recognizing this fact, these standards encourage the development of curriculum and instruction that make productive use of the emerging literacy abilities that children bring to school. Furthermore, the standards provide ample room for the innovation and creativity essential to teaching and learning. They are not prescriptions for particular curriculum or instruction.

Although we present these standards as a list, we want to emphasize that they are not distinct and separable; they are, in fact, interrelated and should be considered as a whole.

1. Students read a wide range of print and nonprint texts to build an understanding of texts, of themselves, and of the cultures of the United States and the world; to acquire new information; to respond to the needs and demands of society and the workplace; and for personal fulfillment. Among these texts are fiction and nonfiction, classic and contemporary works.

2. Students read a wide range of literature from many periods in many genres to build an understanding of the many dimensions (e.g., philosophical, ethical, aesthetic) of human experience.

3. Students apply a wide range of strategies to comprehend, interpret, evaluate, and appreciate texts. They draw on their prior experience, their interactions with other readers and writers, their knowledge of word meaning and of other texts, and their understanding of textual features (e.g., sound-letter correspondence, sentence structure, context, graphics).

4. Students adjust their use of spoken, written, and visual language (e.g., conventions, style, vocabulary) to communicate effectively with a variety of audiences and for different purposes.

5. Students employ a wide range of strategies as they write and use different writing process elements appropriately to communicate with different audiences for a variety of purposes.

6. Students apply knowledge of language structure, language conventions (e.g., spelling and punctuation), media techniques, figurative language, and genre to create, critique, and discuss print and nonprint texts.

7. Students conduct research on issues and interests by generating ideas and questions, and by posing problems. They gather, evaluate, and synthesize data from a variety of sources (e.g., print and nonprint texts, artifacts, people) to communicate their discoveries in ways that suit their purpose and audience.

8. Students use a variety of technological and information resources (e.g., libraries, databases, computer networks, video) to gather and synthesize information and to create and communicate knowledge.

9. Students develop an understanding of and respect for diversity in language use, patterns, and dialects across cultures, ethnic groups, geographic regions, and social roles.

10. Students whose first language is not English make use of their first language to develop competency in the English language arts and to develop understanding of content across the curriculum.

11. Students participate as knowledgeable, reflective, creative, and critical members of a variety of literacy communities.

12. Students use spoken, written, and visual language to accomplish their own purposes (e.g., for learning, enjoyment, persuasion, and the exchange of information).

English language arts in which students must be proficient, rather than providing performance standards that specify levels of achievement (Smagorinsky, 1999).

Because use of technology in education has become so widespread, in 1998 the International Society for Technology in Education (ISTE) produced the *National Educational Technology Standards for Students (NETS)* and in 2000 produced *National Educational Technology Standards for Students: Connecting Curriculum and Technology,* for which "teams of writers created English language arts learning activities, essentially thematic units, across the grade levels, as well as multidisciplinary resource units for pre-K–2 to 9–12 grade levels" (Valmont, 2003, p. 79).

Students are often expected to meet not only standards set forth by learned societies in various curricular disciplines, but also standards developed by individual states in all or some of those areas. Virginia, for example, has standards in the areas of English, mathematics, science, history and social science, and computer technology. The standards-based tests are given in grades three, five, and eight in English, mathematics, science, and history and in grades five and eight in computer technology (Thayer, 2000). "There are 11 tests administered after students complete certain high school courses in the four core areas" (Thayer, 2000, p. 70). Beginning in 2004, in order to graduate from high school, students in Virginia must pass a certain number of the high school tests.

Competency tests have been developed at the state level in some states and at the local level in others. Instructional objectives commonly included on these tests are identifying main ideas and details, finding sequence and cause-and-effect patterns, making inferences, following written directions, using an index and table of contents, using a dictionary, extracting information from graphic aids, and interpreting and completing common forms. Some secondary schools use a commercially available standardized survey reading test (such as the Gates-MacGinitie Reading Test: Survey); other schools use commercially available standardized reading tests that measure survival reading skills or basic skills. In some cases, students who fail the tests must take remedial classes; in others, no remedial program is required.

Noble (1999, p. G1) states, "Virginia's reform rests on a commonsense concept: Set high, clear, and measurable academic standards for each grade on a statewide basis, then test in grades 3, 5, 8 and high school to measure student progress in meeting those standards. Help the children who are falling behind, and tie school accreditation to student achievement to measure accountability." Passing the tests depends upon mastering a body of skills and knowledge. Noble does point out that the standards "represent a floor, not a ceiling, of knowledge" (p. G1). Students who can exceed these standards should be helped to do so. The Virginia high school tests are not one-shot tests. They can be retaken until they are passed, and after a failure in a subject test, students will get remedial help before trying again.

Schmoker and Marzano (1999, p. 19) point out that "the official documents generated by 49 states and the professional subject-area organizations have had unintended consequences." Indeed, some of them identify so much content that it would take far too much teaching time to cover the material. Schmoker and Marzano believe that "U.S. schools would benefit from decreasing the amount of content they try to cover," but covering the chosen content well. Clear standards that are aligned with appropriate assessments can lead to higher student achievement, but murky standards that are not easily assessed may be counterproductive.

Some educators feel that minimum competency tests are unfair to some subgroups of our population. Some teachers feel that standardized curricula, brought about because of minimum competency testing requirements, impair their ability to match learning objectives to particular student needs. They worry about covering all the skills with all the students, even though some students have not mastered the skills already presented. Such concerns often result in inappropriate instructional pacing, which, according to research, accounts for poor reading performance on the part of students of low socioeconomic levels (Rosenholtz, 1987).

Ellman (1988) feels that the tests used are not valid for testing verbal skills. He points out such problems with all standardized tests that focus on speed, remarking that some students work more slowly than others and are adversely affected by the timing of the tests. He also believes that the test producers overlook individual differences in students' development of skills and knowledge, assuming that they all should have mastered the same material or skills by the same date. He states that the tests discourage holistic teaching approaches because isolated factors are easier to test and that generally such tests do not attempt to test for creativity and higher-order thinking skills.

Making important decisions based on a single test score is not wise. Multiple sources of assessment data, such as teacher observation, student work samples, and tests, collected over a period of time, are essential to informed decision making.

RANGE OF STUDENTS IN CONTENT AREA CLASSROOMS

Teachers are faced with a wide range of students in their classrooms. The cultural and linguistic diversity of the population of the United States has greatly increased in recent years, and the country's racial and ethnic makeup is more diverse than census data indicate. There are at least 276 ethnic groups in the United States (Garcia, 2002; Gollnick and Chinn, 2002). Federal laws have mandated inclusion of many students with disabilities in regular content area classrooms, and many students from low socioeconomic backgrounds have had limited experiences and opportunities, putting them at risk for failure.

Language and Cultural Diversity

In recent years, **English language learners (ELLs)** who have limited English proficiency have been rapidly increasing in numbers in U.S. classrooms. Secondary school teachers must be prepared to teach these students from these different cultural, linguistic, and educational backgrounds who have been included in regular classrooms. However, many of these teachers have not been prepared to do so effectively. To accomplish this difficult task, they must determine which language demands in their subject areas offer the most challenges to ELLs. Just exposing the students to English is not enough to help them reach grade-level proficiency. Secondary school textbooks and classroom activities and presentations contain complex language and present many abstract concepts for students to comprehend. Therefore, help with grammatical, morphological, and phonological aspects of English and with the language of classroom discourse is important to students' mastery of the content presented. Providing both oral and written directions for assignments may be beneficial for ELLs who have culturally different learning approaches from those of the dominant classroom culture (Gibbons, 2002; Harper and de Jong, 2004). Individual tutoring may also help these students, as is described in the following "Meeting the Challenge."

MEETING THE CHALLENGE

During his tutoring experiences with high school Hispanic English language learners (ELLs), Lance Jasitt has strived to provide literacy instruction that has been fully understandable to his tutees. New vocabulary and fresh concepts and content can be assimilated and applied with a confidence that ultimately results in independent learning when comprehension is the focus of instruction. Therefore, Lance has focused on providing comprehensible, but challenging, input for English language comprehension.

Particularly in the content areas of science and social studies, Lance finds that bilingual resources for supporting comprehensible input for Spanish-speaking ELLs are extremely scarce. Other factors that limit the acquisition of content area knowledge and access to supplemental resources for many local Hispanic ELLs are family economic restrictions, the limited formal education of their parents, and lack of familiarity and experience with the educational system.

Maria is a ninth-grade ELL from Mexico who enrolled in the local high school during the middle of the 2003–2004 academic year. Although she could read Spanish, her ability to comprehend English text was limited. One weekend she brought home a health sciences research assignment that involved drafting a one-page paper on the topic of cerebral palsy. She had no significant background knowledge about either the topic or the research process. Compounding her academic dilemma, she did not have access to resources necessary to meet the project requisites and her family did not own a personal computer.

Lance determined that in order to write a paper on cerebral palsy, Maria would have to enhance her schema on that topic. To do so she would require comprehensible input. Together they traveled to the Tennessee Technological University library and found Spanish language references (i.e., online *Wikipedia* encyclopedia and *Infotrac ¡Informe!* database of Spanish periodical articles) to build background for Maria. After she read briefly about her topic in Spanish, she was able to synthesize some basic English reference articles and write a short paper. She could read and understand her report and retell key facts orally.

Because she had access to comprehensible input in her primary language and a knowledgeable guide, Maria was able to complete her report and acquire important content knowledge, in addition to locating new research tools and resources for future homework and projects. Tutoring such as Maria received was integrated with her content area assignments.

Students who speak languages other than English often come from diverse cultural backgrounds. Those whose cultural backgrounds differ from that of the dominant culture encounter information outside their background knowledge but that the general population is assumed to know. They may need to build new schemata to understand concepts that authors expect to be a part of their background knowledge. For example, students may lack knowledge about famous U.S. leaders that is assumed in textbooks. Another area that is commonly problematic for readers is use of figurative expressions in American English. Because of these types of problems, students may comprehend better when they read materials about their own cultures. Teachers and media specialists can work together to identify literature, videos, and Internet resources for these students.

Students whose families speak little or no English often have no help with schoolwork at home. Moreover, their families may need the assistance of an interpreter to understand the educational system and the schooling process. Teachers should make a special effort to include families in the planning process and to keep them informed of their children's progress (Fitzgerald, 1993). They may also make use of individual tutoring to help ELLs accomplish academic assignments, as in the case of the following "Meeting the Challenge" vignette.

MEETING THE CHALLENGE

Lance Jasitt has served as a literacy tutor of children of Mexican and Guatemalan immigrants to Tennessee for nearly two years. His tutees have included two sisters who are in the eighth grade and tenth grade, respectively.

The sisters arrived in the school district with fluency in Spanish but only limited conversational ability in English. In spite of their lack of proficiency and confidence in the English language, they were mainstreamed with the general student population for all of their core classes and electives, which included biology, earth sciences, mathematics, language arts, world geography, social studies, lifetime wellness, and computer productivity. In addition, both were enrolled in daily English as a Second Language (ESL) classes at their respective schools.

As his weekly tutoring sessions progressed through the sisters' first year of school, Lance found that their literacy interests were not primarily inclined toward acquiring formal language and usage conventions. Instead, these bright girls desired assistance in social conversational skills, such as translation of the idioms that are used in everyday speech, and in completing daily homework and special projects for which their specific content-related vocabulary (particularly in the sciences) and understanding of standard project constructs were inadequate.

When the older sister, Maria, brought home project guidelines for a three-dimensional diorama that was to illustrate a particular Tennessee ecosystem (e.g., woodland, marsh, river), guided assistance included conducting focused research using the student's textbook and periodical resources supplied by the tutor; identifying fauna and flora unique to the chosen habitat; labeling illustrations; composing and revising a supporting one-page written summary of the ecosystem; and practicing oral presentation of the informational essay, with particular concentration on proper pronunciation. The actual construction of a diorama was a first-time event for the student. It involved pasting images in the foreground of a shoebox after drawing and coloring a background that reflected both the shoreline and submarine environs of her freshwater community of river-dwelling plants and animals. Once she was helped to understand the concepts of *three-dimensional* and *diorama*, she was able to complete the project successfully. She and her tutor were pleased with her work. Because she had access to comprehensible input in her primary language and a knowledgeable guide, Maria was able to complete her report and acquire important content knowledge, in addition to locating new research tools and resources for future homework and projects.

A caring environment fosters literacy learning for all students, especially at-risk students. One way that teachers can exhibit a caring attitude is to work at understanding and responding with sensitivity to their students' cultures (Sanacore, 2004).

Students with Educational Challenges

Increasing numbers of challenged learners, who were once taught in special education classes, are now enrolled in regular classrooms through **inclusion** programs. This component of diversity arises largely from the special needs of individuals who have mental, physical, sensory, communication, and learning challenges or who are emotionally or behaviorally challenged (Kirk, Gallagher, and Anastasiow, 2003).

Exceptional students differ from average students in a variety of ways. "These differences must occur to such an extent that the child requires a modification of school practices, or special educational services, to develop to maximum capacity" (Kirk, Gallagher, and Anastasiow, 2003, p. 2). Some have multiple handicapping conditions.

What is the purpose of the IDEA?

Students with disabilities have often received a portion of their education in public school classrooms since the Education for All Handicapped Children Act (EHA) was passed. Congress reaffirmed the federal commitment to students with disabilities in 1983 with the passage of legislation that extended this act to focus on secondary education, parent training, and preschool children. The 1990 amendments to this law (PL101–476) changed the name of the EHA to the **Individuals with Disabilities Education Act (IDEA)**. The legislation was updated again as the Individuals with Disabilities Education Act of 1997. This legislation ensures the right to a free and appropriate public education to all students from age five to twenty-one who have disabilities.

Why is participation in regular classrooms increasing for special education students?

In recent decades, advocates for students with learning problems have actively pursued increased integration of students with disabilities into the regular classroom. The Regular Education Initiative (REI) calls for **full inclusion** of disabled students in the regular classroom, thus increasing the likelihood that many students with disabilities will receive all or a significant portion of their instruction in the regular classroom. In such programs, the special education teacher collaborates with the classroom teacher about the student's goals, achievement, and appropriate instruction. Then the classroom teacher integrates the student with special needs entirely into the regular classroom (Mastropieri and Scruggs, 2000).

What is the purpose of an IEP?

Each student identified as handicapped must have an **individualized education plan (IEP)**, which includes a description of the student's problem, the program's long-term goals and its short-term objectives, the special education services needed for the student, and the criteria for assessing the effectiveness of the services. Classroom teachers serve on the committees that develop IEPs for students who are eligible for special education services, but not every content teacher will be on the IEP committee. Content teachers who do not serve on the IEP committee for a student can learn about the student's IEP requirements through collaboration with special education personnel.

At-Risk Students

Students enter school expecting to learn to read and write, but failing over and over again may cause them to give up. **Socioeconomic status** is the single best predictor

What reasons can you suggest to explain the relationship between socio-economic status and school achievement?

of students' reading achievement. Through no fault of their own, many students of low socioeconomic status are at risk of failing to learn and of failing to complete high school. Other risk factors commonly associated with school dropouts include low achievement, retention in grade, behavior problems, poor attendance, and attendance at schools with large numbers of poor students (Slavin, 1989; Polloway, Patton, and Serna, 2001). They may be from any racial, ethnic, and linguistic background (Mastropieri and Scruggs, 2000).

SUMMARY

Secondary school students today face a wide array of literacy demands. Secondary school teachers must decide how to help these students handle the literacy demands they face in their content area classes. A variety of reading skills is necessary for effective content area learning. The content area teacher is responsible for helping students apply these skills, and necessary writing skills, in content area assignments. Other educators—special reading teachers, reading consultants, administrators, and librarians or media center specialists—are responsible for other aspects of the secondary school literacy program.

Secondary school literacy programs include five components: developmental reading instruction, content area reading instruction, recreational reading, writing instruction, and instruction for struggling readers. Content area teachers are responsible for content area reading and writing and for encouraging recreational reading, but they should also cooperate with other literacy professionals who deal with the other components.

There are a number of misconceptions about the teaching of reading at the secondary school level. These faulty assumptions include the notions that (1) teaching reading is a concern only in the elementary school; (2) teaching reading in the content areas is separate and distinct from teaching subject matter; (3) reading needs can be met through remedial work alone; (4) a reading specialist or an English teacher should be totally responsible for the teaching of reading; and (5) the teaching of reading and the teaching of literature are one and the same.

There are two basic misconceptions about the teaching of writing at the secondary school level: that students learn all that they need to know about *how* to write in the elementary school, and that writing skills are only important to secondary students in English class.

Currently there is much concern about secondary school students' reading and writing performance, and various groups are developing standards for judging this performance. Teachers face this concern about performance while encountering a wide range of students in their classrooms. Many of these students exhibit language diversity and disabilities of various types and come from backgrounds that leave them at risk for failure in literacy tasks.

DISCUSSION QUESTIONS

1.   Which of the faulty assumptions about teaching reading listed in the chapter seem most evident in your school situation?

2.   Do you see evidence of the two faulty assumptions about writing instruction in your school situation? What can you do to refute these beliefs?

3.   Do you believe that it is possible to increase learning in the content areas by providing appropriate help to students in their study of printed materials? Give as many examples as possible to support your position.

4.   What factors account for many secondary school graduates' inability to read well enough to cope with basic reading requirements? Give reasons for your answer.

5.   What factors account for the wide range of reading and writing ability of secondary school students? Defend your answer.

6.   What particular problems do English language learners face in content area classrooms?

ENRICHMENT ACTIVITIES

1.   What do you think are the most important things about reading that a content area teacher should know? Interview a content area teacher about this question. Compare the teacher's response with your own views.

2.   Keep a log of your literacy activities for a week. What do your findings suggest about reading and writing to meet the daily needs of young adults?

*3.   Interview four students, one of each of the following types: (a) accelerated reader, (b) average reader, (c) struggling reader, and (d) English language learner. Try to learn each student's perspective on the effect of his or her reading ability regarding school achievement, self-image, and life goals. Share your findings with the class.

*4.   Visit a secondary classroom. Try to identify the range of reading and writing abilities. Compare your impressions with those of the teacher.

*These activities are designed for in-service teachers, student teachers, and practicum students.

Chapter 2

Integrating Technology in Content Area Literacy Instruction

OVERVIEW

Many students today are immersed in technology daily. They encounter it in store checkout lanes, as well as in popular video games. They communicate by e-mail and listen to music stored in digital form. They play computer games incessantly. They use videocassettes, CDs, or DVDs from which to learn new skills, rather than using instructional books. They watch the news on television instead of reading it in a daily newspaper. They communicate with cell phones that also serve as digital cameras, rather than by writing traditional letters. Many of these phones even allow access to e-mail and text messaging. Students have MP3 players that can store thousands of songs that may be downloaded from the Internet, rather than using older tape and CD players. In short, many students are familiar with technology outside of school and are comfortable with it as a tool and information source.

However, other students have only superficial contact with technology outside of school. They may not have computers in their homes or may not have the desire, guidance, or money to purchase instructional videos, CDs, or DVDs. These students need exposure to technology use in school because technology will be an integral part of their lives when they enter the work force. They need to expand their grasp of literacy to include informed use of technology and interpretation and production of multiple forms of representation—receiving and transmitting information with multiple symbol systems, such as visual symbols and images, color, shapes, and so on (Kist, 2002; Smolin and Lawless, 2003). As Love (2004/2005, p. 304) points out, "Meaning is being made in ways that are becoming more multimodal because the way language is used is continually being reshaped by new forms of communication media."

Classrooms of today often reflect a technological environment as well, but many classrooms have limited computer access for the number of students being served. In some cases the schools are not as thoroughly equipped as are many of the students' homes. Cost, of course, is a factor in poorly equipped schools. Another problem is that some educators did not grow up in a technological environment and did not have training that covered some of the newer technologies. As a result, available equipment often lies unused in classrooms, laboratories, or media centers, a situation that is not acceptable in current educational settings.

Educators must learn how to harness technology for the benefit of their instructional programs. Any type of technology in a classroom should be used to advance the learning of the students and/or facilitate the job of the teacher. No technological application should be used just because it is available. Each decision to use technology should be made because that particular technological application will be more effective for the task at hand than would other approaches.

Nevertheless, today's world demands that students acquire a degree of media literacy. Literacy learning naturally accommodates the use of technology. Teachers find that everything from overhead projectors, television, and audiotapes to computers, videotapes, CDs, DVDs, and multimedia has an application to the literacy curriculum.

PURPOSE-SETTING QUESTIONS

As you read this chapter, try to answer these questions:

1. What is media literacy, and why is it currently of concern?
2. How can media use help English language learners (ELLs)?
3. How can media use help struggling readers?
4. What are some valid applications of overhead projectors, televisions, and audiotapes in literacy learning?
5. How can word-processing and desktop-publishing programs benefit literacy instruction?
6. What kinds of software can be helpful in writing instruction?
7. How do database programs and spreadsheet programs differ?
8. What are some valuable aspects of using the Internet for literacy learning?
9. What are the types of computer-assisted instruction, and what purpose does each type serve?
10. What are some applications of videotapes, CDs, and DVDs in literacy instruction?
11. What multimedia applications might be used in literacy instruction?

Media Literacy

Media literacy is the ability to comprehend and produce material for media other than print, including the ability to interpret and develop electronic messages that include images, sounds, movements, and animations (Valmont, 2003). According to Scharrer (2003), it involves critical analysis of what students watch, see, and read and the effects the material may have on the viewers and readers, so that students can become critical viewers. Other media literacy concerns include critical thinking about how the messages from different media are created and learning how to produce media messages. Some educators are particularly concerned about negative effects of media violence, propaganda, and sexual content on viewers (Scharrer, 2003).

Students come to media literacy, as to all literacy experiences, with varying backgrounds of experiences. Many have done extensive viewing, but much of it has been uncritical absorption of the material with which they have been presented. Scharrer (2003) believes that sustained instruction in media literacy has a chance to reduce the negative effects of media on adolescents. Knowing how advertising uses propaganda, being aware of how fake but realistic-looking violence is used for sensationalism, and distinguishing how different types of people are portrayed, often in stereotyped ways, are all part of becoming critical viewers, as well as critical readers. Chapter 5 discusses critical thinking and reading in more detail.

Many of today's secondary school students have developed some media literacy through playing electronic games. With these games they have also learned some critical literacy skills as a by-product. They have to make decisions, and they learn about consequences when they take risks. They learn to evaluate the trade-offs they must make between risk and possible benefits. Prensky (2001), cited in Norton-Meier (2005), discovered that the average college graduate today has spent more than 10,000 hours playing video games. Unfortunately, this compares to less than 5,000 hours spent reading. They do acquire critical reading skills to some extent through playing video games, and they also learn to perform multiple tasks at the same time and to respond rapidly when confronted with new information. They interpret words, pictures, sounds, and actions as part of their play. The games also sometimes offer new worthwhile experiences (although many do not) and content that can be applied to life experiences. The line between learning and playing becomes blurred during a game. When playing, the gamers interact and create within the game environment, which may be more engaging to them than reading books, and even students who are believed to have short attention spans often persevere with the games for extended periods (Norton-Meier, 2005; Gee, 2003).

Some of the technology that students must master in order to attain media and technological literacy include digital imaging technologies, such as Microsoft PowerPoint's slide show feature; research on the Internet to locate information for classes; web page construction; and use of electronic communication, such as e-mail. Acquiring these skills will prepare students to construct meaning with and obtain meaning from a variety of texts (Smolin and Lawless, 2003).

Focus on English Language Learners

Media Use to Help English Language Learners (ELLs)

English language learner (ELL) programs need well-designed bilingual instruction to afford students full English literacy (Grant and Wong, 2003). Technology and electronic literacy transform learning for ELLs (Seal, 2003; Matthews, 2000). For example, research shows the importance of extensive reading in second-language instruction (Jacobs and Gallo, 2002), and Black (2005) points out advantages to ELLs of participation in an online "fanfiction" community. ("Fanfiction" is discussed in the section on electronic communications later in this chapter.) The Internet, computer software, and electronic books offer extensive opportunities for second language learning.

Text-to-speech (TTS) software helps ELLs learn to read and comprehend, according to research (Balajthy, 2005). The goal of TTS is presenting electronic book (e-book) files with electronic voice synthesis software to provide oral reading of electronic text files. Students using this software see the visual text and hear the auditory version of the text at the same time. Currently marketed TTS word processors include such programs as OutLoud (Don Johnston) and IntelliTalk3 (IntelliTools). Balajthy (2005) identifies the following related software: ReadPlease 2003 and HelpRead are available as free downloads from the Internet, and they provide simple text-to-speech. The CAST eReader and TextHelp are not free, nor are Kurzweil 3000 and WordSmith; however, they offer more options in their software.

Websites such as the following offer digitized materials that can be used with TTS software. This is not an exhaustive list since additional materials are developed constantly:

The World Fact Book by the U.S. Central Intelligence Agency
(http://www.odci.gov/cia/publications/factbook/index.html) is one source.
The Electronic Text Center at the University of Virginia
(http://etext.lib.virginia.edu/collections/languages) includes an extensive collection of materials by African American, Native American, and women writers.
The Internet Public Library includes TeenSpace for adolescents
(http://www.ipl.org/div/teen/aplus/toc.htm), a site that offers a step-by-step approach to research and writing.

Text-to-speech materials provide instructional support for programs such as the neurological impress method (Heckelman, 1969) and echo reading (Anderson, 1981). Each of these programs involves reading a print text aloud in unison with a teacher or classmate. Text-to-speech materials and taped books can serve the same function as a teacher or classmate up to a point. However, teachers must also provide instructional support to develop student understanding.

ELL students can build background for understanding content assignments by consulting sites such as that of the Library of Congress (includes recorded information), Smithsonian Institution (includes recorded information), and the World Wide Web Virtual Library (includes many subjects and cultures), among others. Teachers can find lists of Internet sites that will assist themselves and their students at http://www.eduref.org/Resources/Specific_Populations/Minority. This site lists addresses such as the Center for the Study of Books in Spanish for Children and Adolescents. Teaching ideas, activities, and units are found on the site http://www.thegateway.org/browse/makes. Teachers will find dictionaries and translations available on many websites.

Focus on Struggling Readers

Media Use to Help Struggling Readers

The Internet provides a variety of sites that will help struggling readers acquire word meanings that will enhance their comprehension. Some of these sites are discussed in Chapter 3. Teachers can use search engines to find online dictionaries and thesauruses. For example, the site http://www.bibliomania.com contains an up-to-date list of useful sites.

Struggling readers will benefit from many of the same resources as ELLs will. They too need extensive practice reading; however, they are not transferring knowledge of reading and language from their native languages. Struggling readers also need the support provided by electronic books, the Internet, and computer programs (Matthews, 2000; Anderson-Inman and Horney, 1999). Electronic books (e-books), talking books, and books on compact disc (CD-ROM) are valuable sources of reading material. These books include the actual text, as well as supplementary information selected to provide assistance and increase comprehension. This information may include graphics, video, and sound. English language learners may learn synonyms for words and find explanations of new words in their primary languages (Johnson, 2001).

Some readers struggle because of physical challenges. Visually challenged learners may benefit from text-to-speech software, such as the programs previously cited as helpful for ELLs.

Struggling readers need reading practice that contributes to their developing accurate, fluent, high-comprehension-level reading ability (Allington, 2001). However, struggling readers need to read books that are "just right" (Allington, 2001). "Just right" books are those written at a level where they can read successfully. Teachers can use informal reading inventories to identify the students' correct reading levels (see Chapter 12). After identifying the appropriate reading level, teachers can consult sites such as http://www.Leveledbooks.com and the Barahona Center (http://www.csusm.edu/csb/) at California State University, San Marcos, which provides information about recommended books in Spanish (Johnson, 2001). Project LITT: Literacy Instruction through Technology, which was based at San Diego State University and funded through the U.S. Department of Education, focused on the use of technology to improve the reading skills of students with learning disabilities (Johnson, 2001). Information about Project LITT can be found at http://edtechfm.sdsu.edu/SPEDProjectLITT/LITTinfo.html. The following are just a sampling of the riches on the Internet that are available to teachers: Children's Storybooks Online (http://www.magickeys.com/books/links.html) lists e-books for older children and young adults; the University of Pennsylvania's On-Line Books (http://onlinebooks.library.upenn.edu/)page is a searchable digital library; and the Free Library of Classics (http://www.utm.edu/vlibrary/docust2.shtml) includes over two hundred free e-texts.

Building on Past Experiences with Technology

Bruce (2001) pointed out that it is important to understand the antecedents of current technologies and to be able to evaluate current technologies in light of knowledge gained from past technologies. Sometimes older technologies are more appropriate and efficient to use for a particular purpose than are newer technologies. Teachers should consider the needs of the lessons and carefully choose technology to assist each lesson.

OVERHEAD PROJECTORS

For many years now, teachers have generally had access to overhead projectors, televisions, and audiotape recorders/players as enhancements to their instruction.

**ENGLISH/
LANGUAGE
ARTS**

The use of transparencies displayed on overhead projectors has for many years benefited those who needed to display complex diagrams and illustrations. Many artistically challenged teachers have bought sets of well-prepared transparencies to help them illustrate their classroom explanations of various topics. Transparencies can be made out of material that teachers have typed or illustrated themselves at a more leisurely pace than is possible when trying to produce materials in class. Many computer programs, such as Microsoft PowerPoint and mPower (Multimedia Design), allow teachers to design transparencies with a variety of fonts, colors, and appropriate graphics. Teachers can also obtain many inexpensive or free graphics from the Internet and CDs of clip art.

Overhead transparencies may be used to advance literacy learning in a number of ways. When describing the stages in developing a written product, for example, the teacher can use a series of transparencies with overlays that show each succeeding step as he or she describes it. Transparencies can allow the teacher to record ideas for writing that result from a brainstorming session held prior to writing. Students can then organize the recorded ideas, and volunteers can put their organizational arrangements on transparencies for sharing. Transparencies can allow teachers to display students' work for class analysis of accuracy, clarity, and organization of ideas. Student permission for use of the work should be obtained in advance, or the teacher could use work from classes other than the one in question, with identifying labels deleted, in order to highlight problems that are common to the current class.

Transparencies can be used before reading about any topic to record semantic maps or webs of prior knowledge about the topic or entries for a K-W-L chart. After reading, they can be used to elaborate the chart and fill in the last stage of the K-W-L chart. (See Chapter 3 for an example of a semantic map or web and Chapter 5 for a discussion of K-W-L charts.)

TELEVISIONS

Televisions also have many uses. Public broadcasting programs may fit in with the curricula of teachers in many different disciplines. Videotaping programs to show them later for educational purposes is often a possibility, when pertinent programs are not broadcast during class hours. However, teachers must be careful to adhere to copyright laws.

Many schools currently have cable television connections, and some cable operators offer schools special programming and teachers' guides. The most popular cable TV service in schools is Cable in the Classroom, a noncommercial service designed for school audiences.

SOCIAL
STUDIES   SCIENCE AND
HEALTH

Sometimes television programs contain historical or scientific information that can fit into unit study. Students who watch television to obtain this information will need to use their note-taking skills to record what they learn to add to the information gathered from other sources. Newscasts or news specials may highlight a class topic—an ongoing military action somewhere in the world, a current election campaign, or a new archaeological discovery, for example. Critical analysis of the information presented could take the form of reports that compare the information obtained from this source with information gathered from primary sources, such as military personnel, participants in the campaign, or archaeologists, and current print media, such as newspapers or newsmagazines.

ENGLISH/
LANGUAGE
ARTS

Sometimes movies that are based on books that are being studied in the class are available. In this case, students may also take notes, in order to compare and contrast the story in the book and the story as presented in the movie. Movies based on literature selections that the students have not read may be viewed and critiqued, and students may be encouraged to read these selections for extra credit or for personal enjoyment and to report back to the class on the experience.

Because, as Prensky (2001) discovered, the average college graduate has spent 20,000 hours watching television, teachers would be wise to help them view critically. Such instruction can help them with recreational viewing as well as informational viewing. Many of the negative messages that teachers hope students will learn to recognize and evaluate are seen during recreational viewing.

Some educators use media literacy as a bridge to print literacy. Like print presentations, television and video presentations are developed with particular audiences in mind, and they can be divided into a number of recognizable genres. Secondary school students readily identify the audiences for which television programs and movies have been developed, and they recognize such genres as soap operas, mysteries, sitcoms, and documentaries. This knowledge can be a stepping stone in teaching about how to determine the audiences for whom the authors are writing, authors' purposes, techniques used to accomplish purposes or focus on particular audiences, and common characteristics of a particular genre. Electronic and print media have many commonalities and connections that should be explored in the classroom (Williams, 2003).

AUDIOTAPES

ENGLISH/ LANGUAGE ARTS

SCIENCE AND HEALTH

Audiotapes can be used to provide prerecorded information on a topic, but they are probably most useful when they are used to record group discussions or class lectures for later review and note taking, interviews with primary sources for use in writing reports, or findings from experiments being done in science class. Students can use them to record themselves practicing oral reports that they must give in class, so that they can play the tapes back and critique their performances. Much material that lends itself to audiotaping now is being videotaped instead.

ENGLISH/ LANGUAGE ARTS

Having students listen to a challenging book on tape before reading it as a part of a class activity can lead to better comprehension of the material when it is covered in class. Struggling readers may benefit from listening to an unabridged book on tape while following along in the book to help them increase their sight vocabularies and comprehend the material better as they hear it read with proper phrasing and inflections. Tapes of content area text materials, recorded by the teacher or by a gifted reader, could be used in the same way. If a student reader makes tapes for this purpose, the teacher must check the tapes before using them for instruction.

Audiotapes of oral presentations may make good material to place in portfolios for assessment purposes. Written explanations about how the presentation was developed and what the student learned from the experience can add to the usefulness of such tapes.

Working with Newer Technologies

Whereas the technological applications in the previous sections still have many valid classroom uses, many teachers now often employ computer applications, videotapes, CDs, and DVDs. Teachers must learn to use these tools at the appropriate times to enhance literacy learning.

COMPUTERS

Computers are the key to future success in most walks of life. Not only are computers found in businesses for communications, record keeping, and accounting, they also are found in the cash registers of retail stores and restaurants, in household appliances, and in children's toys and games, and they are used in homes for e-mail, game playing, and music sources. They have many potential functions in literacy education.

Appropriate use of computers involves **digital literacy**, a subset of media literacy. According to Paul Gilster, author of *Digital Literacy* (1997), "[d]igital literacy is the ability to understand information and—more important—to evaluate and integrate information in multiple formats that the computer can deliver" (Pool, 1997, p. 6). Valmont (2003, p. 92) points out that it "includes the active interpretation of non-verbal symbolic systems that authors include in electronic messages" and "the construction of sounds, images, graphics, photos, videos, animations, and movements to add nonverbal components to electronic messages."

There are many other new terms that must be understood in order to read about computer applications with ease. Bruce (1999/2000, p. 354) suggests that the Webopedia website (www.pcWebopedia.com) provides a good online glossary of computer terms.

Word-Processing and Desktop-Publishing Programs

What are some advantages of having students use word-processing programs to write creative works or research reports?

The writing of student papers, both creative efforts and research reports, is an obvious application of computers to literacy education. The ease of revision and editing that **word-processing programs** provide makes students more likely to reconsider content, organization, wording, and mechanical aspects of their papers and to make changes after a draft has been completed. Spelling checkers and grammar checkers alert students to spellings and syntactic constructions that they may need to change. They then have to make their own decisions about the correctness of their material and the best ways to change it. These programs do not merely serve as crutches; they stimulate thought about the writing and initiate decision making. This revision and editing process often results in better-written products and offers a learning experience as students see the benefits of trying different organizations and approaches. Word-processing programs often include a dictionary and a thesaurus. The dictionary can be used to decide if the chosen word has the correct meaning for the context. The thesaurus can be used to choose a synonym when a word has been overused in a selection or to pick a word with just the right connotations. More on word processing is found in Chapter 8.

What are some applications of desktop-publishing programs that could be useful in your content area?

Desktop-publishing programs allow for integration of text and graphics. Generally, users can flow text around graphics, choose from a variety of styles and sizes of type, format text into columns, and set up special formats (such as greeting cards, business cards, and banners). Creating posters, flyers, and class newsletters and magazines are the most common uses of desktop publishing for literacy and content development.

At one time, there was a clear-cut delineation between word-processing software and desktop-publishing software. Today's deluxe word-processing programs, such as Microsoft Word, contain many features that once were available only from desktop-publishing programs, including the ability to combine text and graphics, use different fonts, and set up text in columns. Therefore, creative writing, class reports, newsletters, and magazines may all be produced with the same software. Microsoft Word and many other word-processing programs also offer a function that converts word-processed documents to hypertext markup language (HTML), the format needed to post material on the World Wide Web (WWW).

Writing Development Software

ENGLISH/ LANGUAGE ARTS

Some electronic outliners are now available to help students organize the content of a paper by enabling them to put ideas in outline format. When an outline has been created, the student can easily add or delete items, as the program reconfigures the material to fit the new content (Geisert and Futrell, 2000). Concept maps, or semantic maps, are often developed as a result of brainstorming as a prewriting activity. Inspiration®, an outlining and diagramming program, is useful for creating semantic maps. A projection device or large monitor can be used with the computer to allow the class to see the development of the map. Symbols can be dragged around the screen to organize them. New symbols can be inserted as labels for categories that are formed as the material is organized. More ideas or categories can be added, graphics can indicate the importance or order of ideas on the map, and specific instructions can be added to the map. Such mapping allows students to record information from multiple sources on a single map to aid in synthesizing information. It is also possible to link items on the map, clarifying the relationships among the terms. Inspiration can have multiple layers of smaller maps that are hidden until the user accesses them, keeping the screen from becoming crowded and confusing.

Writer's Studio (Computer Curriculum Corporation) offers process-writing instruction appropriate for students in grades seven and eight. This program incorporates the writing process (prewriting, drafting, revising, proofreading, and publishing) and includes graphic organizers (cluster maps, story maps, sequencers, and checklists).

Microsoft Word and similar word-processing programs are useful during the drafting stage. The online version of the *American Heritage Dictionary* and Microsoft Word and other word-processing programs are also useful during the revising, editing, and publishing stages.

Conference and Collaboration Software

What are some examples of conference and collaboration software?

Special software is also available that allows students to hold conferences electronically about their reading and writing in any area. The Daedalus Integrated Writing Environment (Daedalus Group) and Norton Textra Connect (W.W. Norton & Company) allow students to hold networked real-time conferences about reading and writing that they do for class and examine drafts of peers' papers. Norton Textra Connect facilitates the creation of collaborative documents. Chat programs can be used to connect students in geographically diverse locations for real-time written conversations. Computer-mediated discussions of reading among students allow students to participate as often as they like, take as much time as they need to compose responses, and respond directly to each other (Anderson-Inman, Knox-Quinn, and Tromba, 1996; Jody and Saccardi, 1996).

One type of collaboration software is the multiplayer video game. Since 2000, many video games are Internet-based multiplayer games, often known as MMORPGs (massively multiplayer online role-playing games). As players become immersed in these online games, they seek and form relationships, both cooperative and antagonistic, with others sitting at keyboards all over the world. Entire social communities (often taking the form of "guilds" of players) are created, and they have many of the same characteristics as social organizations and relationships formed face to face. It is common for players to begin to view others as extensions of the avatars or icons that the others have chosen to represent themselves. These MMORPGs require a type of social and cultural literacy within a technological medium.

Databases and Spreadsheets

What are some applications of database programs in your content area?

A database is an organized collection of data. **Database programs** make possible a search of the database by the computer. The information in a database is filed so that it can be retrieved by category. Many commercial, governmental, and educational databases are available for students to use in their research, and students can form their own databases of information that they collect when doing personal research. Students in U.S. history classes might develop databases of facts related to various states; students in biology classes, databases of the characteristics of certain species; students in English classes, databases of characteristics of particular literature selections; and so on. Creating databases helps students decide what data are relevant to particular topics, and they learn to analyze and synthesize large amounts of information. Many libraries catalog their holdings in a computer database that students can search by author, title, or subject. More on databases is found in Chapter 6.

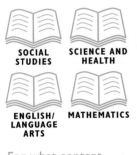

SOCIAL STUDIES   **SCIENCE AND HEALTH**

ENGLISH/ LANGUAGE ARTS   **MATHEMATICS**

For what content areas are spreadsheets most useful?

Spreadsheets also organize data into a pattern, using a grid of rows and columns. They are ordinarily used to store and manipulate numerical data. Spreadsheet programs often make it possible for data to be presented in chart and graph form. The reading and production of meaningful charts and graphs are important parts of literacy in today's society. Science, economics, and business math teachers may choose to have students use and interpret spreadsheets.

The Internet

What types of resources are available on the Internet that classroom teachers can use?

The **Internet** is a network of computer networks that links more than 600 million computers throughout the world (Nua Internet Surveys, 2002). Communication is the most common use of the Internet. Information in the form of text, sound, video, and graphics can be obtained from the Internet. Different "server" computers supply different material, including software, graphs, maps, movies, still pictures, sound, and databases. The World Wide Web is a portion of the Internet that makes use of hypertext links to allow users to click a mouse on special words or symbols that will automatically connect them to related Web locations.

Hypertext refers to nonsequential text. Hypertext links allow computer users to access documents in an order chosen by the user. Highlighted words and symbols serve as links to other texts, which can be accessed by clicking on the highlighted elements. **Hypermedia** refers to nonsequentially linked text, graphics, motions, and sounds. This nonsequential linkage makes accessing information for research quicker and easier than it would be if each individual location had to be separately addressed. It also presents a problem in terms of navigating among different texts, even for some students who do quite well in following the linear text in books. Students must learn to select links in a reasonable order to create their individual paths through information (Ryder and Graves, 1996/1997; Bruce, 1998; Laspina, 2001; Schmar-Dobler, 2003). Many students are quite comfortable using the Internet. They can search for information to use in research papers and other class assignments. Some students, however, will need to be taught appropriate search strategies.

The text found on Internet sites is primarily expository. Students need to have skills and strategies for reading expository text in order to get the most from such sites.

Much information is available on the Internet about any topic that is studied in school. One problem, however, is that not all of the information is accurate. If students are to use the Internet as a research source, they have to learn to check the credentials of the authors of information found on the Net, to double-check information with print or other sources when possible, and to look for documentation of information presented. Anonymous information, accompanied by no documentation, must be approached skeptically. Some sites are known to be reputable, such as the Smithsonian site (http://www.si.edu), the Library of Congress site (http://www .loc.gov), and the National Geographic site (http://www.nationalgeographic.com), and can be used with confidence as sources. In some instances, the teacher may wish to supply the students with a list of sites to use in their research. The teacher may wish to bookmark acceptable sites on the classroom computers and ask the students to use these sites for their research. This action eliminates some of the higher-order thinking needed to evaluate sites, but it can be a major time saver in a classroom in which time or computer availability is limited, and it can help to lessen the danger of students' accessing unacceptable sites (Forbes, 2004). Many schools have installed filter software, such as SurfControl (http://www1.surfcontrol.com/) and Cyber Patrol (http://www.cyberpatrol.com) to restrict access to undesirable sites.

Uniform Resource Locators (URLs) are Internet addresses. URLs for sites in the previous paragraph are shown in parentheses. One of the problems with specifying sites on the Web to students or in a book such as this one is that, because the World Wide Web is changing so rapidly, a site may be relocated or may be removed. Unlike books, whose contents never change from one reading to another, the text on the Internet changes constantly. A site that a student visits today may not be there tomorrow, or it may contain additional or different information tomorrow.

Finding information on the Internet is facilitated by a browser, such as Lynx (a text-based browser) or Mozilla Firefox, Netscape, or Microsoft Internet Explorer (all graphical browsers). In addition, there are many search engines, such as Google, AltaVista, and WebCrawler, and metasearch engines (such as Dogpile, at http://www .dogpile.com) that will provide the user with the results from several search engines with a single request. These tools allow users to conduct key word searches. (See Chapter 6 for more about locating information on the Internet.) A group or individual doing a research project might complete the first two sections of a K-W-L

**ENGLISH/
LANGUAGE
ARTS**

about the topic and use the "W" (Want to Know) column to generate key words to guide an Internet search. The results of the search would go in the "L" (Learned) column.

Scavenger hunting for specific information on school topics on the Internet is fun and educational. Rekrut (1999) helped her tenth-graders become familiar with searching the Internet by designing a scavenger hunt/trivia game about King Arthur and allowing the students to work in cooperative groups to locate the information in books, in the vertical file, or on the Internet. Some students used bookmarked websites that were already identified, but some went in unexpected directions and accessed unrelated or inappropriate sites. Filtering software could have helped alleviate this problem.

**ENGLISH/
LANGUAGE
ARTS**

**SOCIAL
STUDIES**

The teacher can also download files to be used for class. Sharon Bailey, a high school teacher in New Mexico who teaches English and history, downloads such materials as science fiction and bestsellers, novels from Project Gutenberg, book reviews, authors' biographies, and interviews. For example, she "retrieved the archive for *Zlata's Diary*. Zlata became known to many as the Anne Frank of war-torn Sarajevo. There was a chat on the Scholastic Network, . . . where she discussed her book, her experiences in Sarajevo, and her fears for her family, friends, and country" (Serim and Koch, 1996, p. 40). (The Scholastic Network is available at http://www.scholastic.com.) This material, of course, was pertinent to both an English class (novel study) and a history class (study of war, violence, and racism).

**ENGLISH/
LANGUAGE
ARTS**

In Kathleen Litkey's seventh-grade English class, students researched the life and writings of Mark Twain, with some guidance from the teacher. They located information on the Internet, copied it to a word-processing file, and answered the questions the teacher had posed. Then they impersonated Mark Twain, answering the teacher's interview questions as they thought he would have. The language skills used in the project included searching the Internet, writing descriptive paragraphs, punctuating quotations, and using proper attribution in the final product (Serim and Koch, 1996).

**SCIENCE AND
HEALTH**

**ENGLISH/
LANGUAGE
ARTS**

Ken Hartman, a high school chemistry teacher, had his students use the Internet to research the topic of solid waste. Groups worked to collect data on six aspects of the issue. They published their findings for use by others (Serim and Koch, 1996).

A teacher of a secondary English class might want to search the Web for an appropriate site where students can publish work and get critiques. These sites must be carefully chosen.

Online Study Center

HM Video Case
Middle School Reading
Instruction: Integrating
Technology

Online discussion groups can be implemented with students in English classes in a number of ways. They can e-mail their fellow students about classwork or read classmates' papers and write comments. English language learners can benefit from online discussion groups because they are motivational and interactive in nature. Students practice their writing skills, share experiences, and learn from others (Cote Parra, 2000). Love (2002) cautions that teachers' success with online discussions depends on the clarity with which they define the purposes of the discussions and communicate these purposes to their students.

**SOCIAL
STUDIES**   **MATHEMATICS**

A social studies, mathematics, or English class (or a multidisciplinary class) might want to use an Internet project like Good News Bears (http://www.ncsa.uiuc.edu/edu/RSE/RSEyellow/gnb.html), a stock market game that allows students to use

**ENGLISH/
LANGUAGE
ARTS**

**SCIENCE AND
HEALTH**

online stock market data and try to develop the best portfolio in competition with others. This site is designed for middle school students (Leu and Leu, 1999).

Using the Internet allows the development of virtual learning communities that reach beyond cultural, geographic, generational, and institutional boundaries. The "Meeting the Challenge" box below describes one such community.

Vanderbilt University has a Virtual School that instructs teachers in using the Internet in daily classes. Vanderbilt's Virtual Watershed Institute is focused on teaching students about conducting and analyzing field research and sharing their results. Debbie Carroll, an intermediate school teacher in Williamson County, Tennessee, used Virtual Watershed activities in her class to prepare her students for a field trip to a creek, "where they calculated water flow, measured dissolved oxygen and pH levels and identified leaves and trees" ("Local Educators," 1999, p. 3C). Using the

MEETING THE CHALLENGE

Larry Lynn, a teacher at Homestead Elementary School in Cumberland County, Tennessee, enrolled three of his classes in the International Telecomputing Consortium's World Class project. World Class is an online forum for the discussion of real problems by students, teachers, and field experts. Citizen's Energy, an energy company, brought in experts from across the country to answer questions posed by students during the project. Larry's classes were in contact with students worldwide, including students from China, Brazil, Ethiopia, Germany, and the United States. During the project, the students learned about alternative energy sources.

Larry had this to say about the project:

Each week during the project we would receive e-mail with a lot of information for us to read and respond to. I would print the e-mail, and my classes would read the mail and discuss it in their groups. When they had arrived at a consensus about the answers to any questions that were asked, I would let them e-mail their answers to World Class so that the other participants could view them. We did the same thing with their responses. We would also pose questions to experts in the field of discussion and receive their answers by e-mail.

During the time that we were involved in World Class, we were able to send e-mail directly to some of the participating schools. My students really enjoyed this part because they could learn firsthand about the cultures and circumstances in which others live.

I encouraged my students to be open-minded about what they were reading and learning. They realized that everyone does not have the same things they do. Also, they enjoyed analyzing the grammar of the students from other countries. It was good practice without a textbook! Sometimes my students would have to try to understand what the other students were trying to say. Most of the participating teachers did not correct their students' grammar when they were sending their e-mail. I explained to my students that English was not the native language of these students, and my students treated their foreign peers with respect.

It was a very interesting project for my students and for me. You have to be willing to give some of your class time to something other than what's in the book to do this kind of activity, but I believe it is worth the time and trouble.

SCIENCE AND HEALTH

What kinds of information might a student or a class put on a homepage?

Internet, Carroll's students compared their data with the data collected by other Tennessee schools. This project helped students see the importance of protecting rivers and streams ("Local Educators," 1999).

NASA sponsors Online Interactive Projects (http://quest.arc.nasa.gov/) that involve students in authentic scientific explorations through television broadcasts, videotapes, online interaction, and workbooks (Grabe and Grabe, 2000).

Many classrooms or individual students now have their own **homepages** on the Web. Although a discussion of homepage development is beyond the scope of this section, students can learn to use HTML to code the material for their own homepages. They may be able to use a special function of their word-processing program to convert their word-processed text to HTML, or they can use a special program, such as PY Software's Actual Drawing, Microsoft's FrontPage, or Macromedia's Dreamweaver, that is designed to aid in web page publishing. Knowledge of HTML is not essential to the development of web pages. Text, graphics, photographs, and even animations may be included. Classes may develop web pages to display class newspapers, students' creative writing or written reports, students' artwork, and so on. The importance of careful composition, proofreading, and editing becomes evident when writing is to be displayed to the world on the Internet. Web pages produced by students should be examined for accurate information, correct grammar and mechanics, interesting presentation, readable and attractive page layout, useful links, and appropriate graphics.

Sefton-Green (2001, p. 728) points out the need to teach students to work in new media. She notes that "[t]he skill will not spontaneously erupt from young people." Time spent showing students how to use new media will pay dividends in the works that they are capable of producing as a result of content area learning. There is a high level of uncertainty in many Web-based activities, encouraging collaborative learning and problem solving, with the teacher and student both working to solve problems (Kapitzke et al., 2000/2001). Kapitzke and others (2000/2001, p. 341) discovered that the young people they worked with "felt comfortable with computer-mediated learning because it enabled them to make mistakes privately . . . [and] the computer is a patient instructor that provides space and time for student experimentation, reflection, and reassessment."

One Web-based activity that is currently popular with secondary school students is the **web log** (**blog**). Littrell (2005, p. 7) defines *blog* in the following manner: "Web log; web-based journal. A blog takes the form of an online diary but allows the user to personalize the appearance, add hyperlinks to other websites, add multimedia components such as audio or video, and invite comments from readers." Blogs usually contain personal comments, reflections, and links to other sites on the Web (Winer, 2002). Because the blogs are maintained over a period of time and most are updated frequently, their authors are involved in ongoing writing—a goal of secondary literacy programs (Richardson, 2004). Blogs give adolescents an audience for their ideas and accomplishments and a place to collaborate with others, and they can give teachers a place to post assignments and other material (Curry and Ford, 2005; Littrell, 2005). Free hosting services, such as are found at http://www.blogger.com, and ease of use and maintenance make blogging attractive to both secondary school students and adults. The following "Meeting the Challenge" vignette tells of a way that blogging may be useful in an English classroom.

ENGLISH/ LANGUAGE ARTS

MEETING THE CHALLENGE

To examine the possible uses of blogs for writing, Annette Littrell involved ten eighth-grade girls in using both blogs and traditional literature response journals. The students were initially interviewed to determine their existing uses of technology and journaling.

Over the course of eight weeks, they read two books by Joan Bauer, while alternating their methods of literature response in two-week intervals between blogging and traditional journaling. Both the frequency with which the students made journal entries and the average length of the entries were monitored.

At the end of the eight weeks, the students were interviewed again and asked to elaborate on their journaling experiences. During these interviews, 90 percent of the students reported that they preferred using a blog over the traditional journal. When asked why she would choose a blog, one participant said, ". . . hello, this is 2004."

In reviewing the project, Annette found that the students wrote an average of 50 percent more often when using their blogs and wrote 30 percent longer entries than they did when using the traditional journal. Although adolescent girls are generally viewed as more resistant to the adoption of technology than are boys, the use of blogs appeared to motivate them to write. All of the participants categorized using the blog as "easy," while 70 percent also found it "fun." Students who participated in the study reported that they enjoyed customizing the appearance of the blog and that they enjoyed having a place to write that was free from criticism. Thirty percent of the participants mentioned the positive feelings they received from publishing their work for an audience.

Electronic Communications

Electronic mail (e-mail), subscriptions to electronic mailing lists (called listservers), posting to electronic bulletin boards (newsgroups), and electronic videoconferencing are all ways of communicating by way of the Internet, although not all electronic mail nor all electronic videoconferencing is sent or conducted over the Internet.

What are some ideas for using video-conferencing in your content area?

Few classrooms have the cameras and software necessary for **videoconferencing** at present, but the future may offer more opportunities for students to hold conferences over the Internet with someone who can be seen on a computer's monitor and heard through its speakers. Videoconferencing allows students to interview authors, scientists, historians, mathematicians, business people, and others who can shed light on a current area of study. The students can compile interview questions; conduct the interview, taking notes; and write up a report of the findings, which they then might integrate into a larger project's report. In Dade County, Florida, advanced computer students use videoconferencing to converse with students in other countries ("Wired Education," 1996). Maring's Cyber Mentoring projects at Washington State University have involved the use of videoconferencing. In these projects, Washington State University preservice education students interact with K–12 students (Maring, 2002).

E-mail has many potential benefits for the classroom. Students can e-mail students in schools in other parts of the world to discuss such things as current study topics, current events, differences in their schools and environments, and the literature they are studying. Students may also e-mail experts in various fields to get answers to questions for class studies. In one Kentucky project, for example, students in different Kentucky schools read the same books and use e-mail to communicate with each other about their reading, and in another project students interact with published authors, sharing personal information and their works-in-progress. Authors provide feedback to individual students. Students also can discuss authors' works with the authors through online conferences (Bell et al., 1995; Paeth et al., 1995). Secondary school students can e-mail college students in methods courses to discuss matters related to the content of their curricula. A number of e-mail connections have been set up between college students and public school students to discuss books that both are reading (Moore, 1991; Bromley, 1993; Roe and Smith, 1996; Roe and Smith, 1997; Sullivan, 1998). The "Meeting the Challenge" section on page 47 describes the project that Roe and Smith developed and implemented at Tennessee Technological University.

Some secondary school students e-mail "fanfiction" pieces to friends and acquaintances whom they have met electronically. Fanfiction is developed by using media texts, such as cartoons (particularly Japanese *anime* cartoons) and video games, as the starting point for writing creative stories. Chandler-Olcott and Mahar (2003) found that the Japanese cartoons were written in many genres, including fantasy, romance, and science fiction. Some students post their fanfiction on websites for like-minded adolescents to read. The fanfiction that is produced is often multimodal; that is, it integrates visual, linguistic, and audio designs in one text. Additionally, Chandler-Olcott and Mahar (2003, pp. 562–563) say that "fanfictions make intertextuality visible because they rely on readers' ability to see relationships between the fan-writer's stories and the original media sources." They result in hybrid texts that integrate different discourses and genres, a process that definitely involves creativity. The fact that many students choose this activity as a recreational one emphasizes the fact that students will work on writing skills with the right motivation. Teachers should consider how they can tap into the abilities that are displayed by writers of fanfiction for use in school-related pursuits.

Stivers (1996) paired college students in junior-year methods courses with children with special learning needs for e-mail exchanges. Some letters were general conversation, and some were lessons in which the college students modeled a skill, explained it, and then led the middle school students to use it in their writing. The middle school students responded well to the attention the college students paid to them, and even the college students showed evidence of increased self-esteem because of the young students' positive responses to the correspondence.

Doherty and Mayer (2003) participated in a project in which Aboriginal and Torres Strait islanders in Queensland, Australia, were given the opportunity to use a

ENGLISH/
LANGUAGE
ARTS

ENGLISH/
LANGUAGE
ARTS

computer laboratory to exchange e-mail with members of the teaching team. They found that strong interpersonal relationships that enhance students' commitment to learning were built through the e-mail exchanges.

Electronic mailing lists send out messages to a group of readers interested in the same topic. Readers "subscribe" to a particular list and thereafter every member in the list receives all communications sent to the list until they choose to "unsubscribe" to stop the flow of mail. Although the subscriber may be interested in the topic, the volume of mail generated by some mailing lists is often too difficult to handle. It must be read and deleted on a regular basis, generally daily. Mailing lists of interest may be subscribed to for only the period of time when a topic is being studied.

How may electronic mailing lists be used for assignments?

MEETING THE CHALLENGE

E-mail exchanges about literature can promote analysis of the literature selections.
© Susie Fitzhugh

An entire section of Betty Roe's undergraduate reading methods students, plus graduate students in reading and language arts methods courses who chose this activity as a class project, were paired with the seventh-graders in Barbara Vaughn's and Melinda Beaty's homerooms. Both the university students and the seventh-graders read the book *Bridge to Terabithia* on a predetermined schedule and exchanged e-mail messages about the reading on a weekly basis. They discussed literary elements of the book and connections that they could see between the book and their lives. Both groups also viewed a video based on the book; then, in an e-mail exchange, the partners compared and contrasted the book and the video. The seventh-graders produced an mPower multimedia presentation based on the book to show the university students. At the end of the project, the partners met on the university campus and discussed the experience.

The seventh-grade students, the university students, the two seventh-grade teachers, and the university professor all felt the project was beneficial and enjoyable. One seventh-grader wrote to Betty Roe, "Dear Dr. Roe, I liked reading the book. I thought it was a good learning experience. I liked the feeling that I'm not the only one who sometimes doesn't understand something that I read. She helped me understand it. It was like she was my sister. I talked to her all the time. Your friend, Angie Adkins." The two seventh-grade teachers wrote, "Reading the book *Bridge to Terabithia* and e-mailing their thoughts concerning the book improved our seventh-graders' reading, writing, and communicative skills. Our students were very enthusiastic about the project and

continued

continued

really enjoyed the trip to TTU to meet their e-mail partners. We have found our students continuing to communicate with their partners even though, technically, the project is concluded for this semester. We also noticed a marked improvement in some students' self-expression. Over time, the letters became longer and more focused on the book's contents. This positive association with older students, responsible for the same work, enhanced our seventh-graders' self-esteem. Some students felt that they were 'almost doing college work.' " University student Stacy Webb said, "I think it gives students a sense of responsibility and promotes the idea of discussing and enjoying what they read. It was also helpful for me in the sense that I was able to practice responding and interacting with the kind of students I will be teaching one day." Noel Roberts, another university student, said, "I read *Bridge to Terabithia* through the eyes of a child." The university students appeared to enjoy the e-mail interactions. The mPower presentation developed by the seventh-graders was extremely well done, and the university students were impressed.

The project was so successful that it was continued for years, with many professors, public school teachers and students, and university students involved. The students read and discussed a variety of books, some assigned and some self-selected.

Teachers may wish to do a scan of the mail from the mailing list and delete any messages containing inappropriate language. Then they may ask students to examine the remaining messages and to delete irrelevant ones and print and annotate any that appear to contain inaccurate material, as well as ones that appear to have truly useful material. The class should check out both types for accuracy. This evaluation is a good critical reading activity.

The International E-mail Classroom Connections (IECC), http://www.iecc.org, is an electronic mailing list for K–12 teachers seeking international and cross-cultural partner classrooms for e-mail exchanges. IECC-PROJECTS is an electronic mailing list that provides an avenue for teachers to publicize or ask for assistance with classroom projects that involve international or cross-cultural e-mail.

What are newsgroups?

Electronic bulletin boards, or **newsgroups**, conferences, or forums, have messages "posted" to a network location. Interested readers can read these messages electronically if they know the address of the newsgroup. Messages may be posted and read by people from all over the world (Grabe and Grabe, 2004). One good way to locate newsgroups is to go to http://groups.google.com, which has links to many newsgroups that could be of interest. Like mailing lists, newsgroups also may contain inappropriate material. They should be used with caution.

Electronic Reference Works

Dictionaries, thesauruses, encyclopedias, atlases, and specialized reference books are available on disk, CD, and DVD for use with computers. Many reference works can also be found on the Internet. More on electronic reference works is found in Chapter 6.

Computer-Assisted Instruction (CAI)

What types of computer-assisted instructional programs exist, and what is the value of each type?

Computer-assisted instructional programs are generally of four types: drill-and-practice, which offer practice on skills that teachers have already taught; tutorial, which offer actual instruction; simulations, which set up situations that simulate reality and give students the opportunity to use decision-making and problem-solving skills; and educational games, which take a variety of formats to give students experiences related to educational goals. All of these types of programs may be used to enhance the instructional program, but some programs are not pedagogically sound, so they must be evaluated carefully before they are used with students. CAI programs need to be focused on legitimate educational objectives; appropriate for the maturity levels of the students; user friendly; and manageable, timewise, in the classroom.

Many drill-and-practice, tutorial, and game programs focus on such skills as vocabulary development, parts of speech, punctuation, and spelling. A frequently used computerized reading program is the Accelerated Reader (Renaissance). This is a reading practice and assessment program that involves no actual reading instruction. Students read books and take computer-generated tests to earn points and incentives (Biggers, 2001). Simulation programs for any content area are good to encourage critical reading and thinking and problem solving, areas in which students have not shown proficiency on the National Assessment of Educational Progress. Although it is beyond the scope of this text to identify software for each application, a few examples follow.

SOCIAL STUDIES

Making History: The Calm and the Storm (Muzzy Lane) is appropriate for history classes. The Calm and the Storm is the first program in a series called Making History. In this simulation video-game program, the players "act as world leaders, make momentous decisions, and discover the consequences" (Brumfield, 2005, p. 28). The series is designed to help students learn history by taking on leadership roles in different nations during World War II. The students compete against other "national leaders" and the program's scoring considers the players' performance against actual historical events. They make major decisions related to the economy, the military, and foreign and domestic issues. They may even perform better than the real leaders did historically. The game involves analysis of situations, synthesis of information, recognition of cause and effect, detection of bias, and negotiation—all necessary language skills (Brumfield, 2005).

SCIENCE AND HEALTH   **ENGLISH/ LANGUAGE ARTS**

MATHEMATICS

Other useful simulations include Operation Frog (Scholastic) for science, which simulates a dissection, and the Math Shop Series (Scholastic) for math, which has the students solve problems in everyday situations related to customer services provided for stores. Any one of a wide variety of interactive fiction story programs can be used as recreational reading in an English class.

VIDEOTAPES

Videotapes on many topics can be used to enhance learning in those areas. They can be used to illustrate text materials for less proficient readers or for students with limited experiential backgrounds; for example, they may be used to help bring a literary selection to life for students or to make a process (such as pasteurization) that

**ENGLISH/
LANGUAGE
ARTS**

is discussed in their text more comprehensible. Showing videos can provide students with much support for comprehending texts, while at the same time being motivational and enjoyable (Hibbing and Rankin-Erickson, 2003). Prerecorded tapes on a multitude of topics are available for purchase, for rental from video stores, or from libraries. Students can view these tapes, take notes, and use the information for classroom discussion, reports, and projects. Videotapes based on literature selections are often available for use in English classrooms, and many are now also available on CDs or DVDs. Students can compare and contrast the video presentations with the books. When the students described in the preceding "Meeting the Challenge" section did this comparison, they decided that the book was much more effective than the video. Several studies have indicated that viewing a related video before reading a book has a positive effect on comprehension of the text (Lapp, Flood, and Fisher, 1999). Videos are available on most topics of study.

In these days of relatively inexpensive media production resources, such as camcorders and editing equipment, some teachers have involved students in making videos (Sefton-Green, 2001). The process of producing videos not only helps students learn to communicate in another medium, but also helps them to see how the producers of these videotapes have put together sound, action, and images to communicate ideas to them.

**PHYSICAL
EDUCATION**

Videotaping sports skill practice (tennis strokes, golf swings, and so on) can provide students with the opportunity to critique their own and their classmates' performances, helping to meet Standard 1 of the National Association of Sport and Physical Education's *National Standards for Physical Education*. After some of these activities, students can record fitness information from such technology as heart and blood pressure monitors, further using technology to meet Standard 4 (Mohnsen, 1997).

Students can also make their own videotapes of class presentations or field trip activities. They can prepare special video presentations for which they write scripts and practice polished presentations, such as simulated newscasts.

CDs AND DVDs

What are the advantages of using CDs and DVDs?

CDs and **DVDs** (digital videodiscs or digital versatile discs) are large-capacity storage media. Entire reference books or novels may be stored on them. They provide high-quality images and sound. Some are interactive, in that words can be selected to be pronounced, defined, or pictured, and nonlinear sequences of presentation can be followed. Information on a CD or DVD may be selected through keystrokes or mouse clicks. Both CDs and DVDs offer instant random access. DVD players are capable of playing CDs, although DVDs cannot be played on CD players. Both of these media have good instructional applications (Grabe and Grabe, 2004; Stabenau, 1999; Glencoe/McGraw Hill, 2000).

MULTIMEDIA APPLICATIONS

What is meant by multimedia?

Multimedia refers to the mixing of different media. A multimedia presentation may include text, photographs, line drawings, video clips, sounds, and animated figures.

The sounds and images may be drawn from videotapes, videodiscs, audiotapes, and clip art available on discs. Images may be scanned in from printed documents. Multimedia computer systems allow teachers to combine text, graphics, animation, music, voice, and full-motion video that are controlled by a computer. These systems have interactive capabilities. Multimedia encyclopedias are common in schools today, and they allow students to read text, see video clips, hear audio clips, or see still pictures related to the subject being accessed.

Students can develop their own multimedia presentations with special software, as the students in the preceding "Meeting the Challenge" section did with mPower (Multimedia Design). Such a presentation takes much organization, composition, and critical reading and thinking. It is truly a good literacy activity.

**ENGLISH/
LANGUAGE
ARTS**

The use of multimedia in a unit on *Huckleberry Finn* by Mark Twain is suggested by Willis, Stephens, and Matthew (1996). One resource for the unit could be the electronic version of *Huckleberry Finn* by Bookworm, which uses graphics, audio recordings, and movies to bring the text alive. In such a unit students may plan a debate about whether the book should be banned or not. Groups of students could research their arguments and write persuasive essays using a writing program that allows two or more students to work on a single document from different computers. Then the students could use these essays as the basis for a debate. Students might search for information about Mark Twain, the time period in which the novel is set, and public reactions to the novel when it was published. This could be partially done on the Internet. Some students might want to write poems or short stories based on their findings. These could be written with a word-processing program. A class presentation might be developed using Microsoft PowerPoint. The project's culminating activity could be a newsletter produced with a desktop-publishing program.

Copeland and Goering (2003) taught the Faustian theme of selling one's soul to the devil for personal gain through use of music, film, and literature. This theme has been the nucleus of books such as Goethe's *Faust*, Nolan's *Born Blue*, and Gantos's *Hole in My Life*. It has also been the theme in music such as Liszt's *Faust Symphony*, Gounod's opera *Faust*, and the Charlie Daniels Band's "The Devil Went Down to Georgia." Movies such as *O Brother, Where Art Thou?* contain the theme, as do *Damn Yankees*, *The Devil and Daniel Webster*, and *Bedazzled*. Several blues musicians, including Robert Johnson, were said to have sold their souls to the devil for outstanding musical talent.

In the unit that Copeland and Goering (2003) taught, the students brainstormed, used a process writing approach, wrote based on a model, did research and produced visual aids about a blues artist's life with partners, and viewed and analyzed films. Their culminating activity was a project in which they used "the devil's pact legend to bring a contemporary ethical, social, or political issue into sharp (and often entertaining) focus" (p. 441). They could choose to create a hypertext and graphics presentation, write blues song lyrics, videotape a movie, or write a short story. This project helped the students connect popular culture with classical and literary content.

According to Watts Pailliotet and others (2000, p. 209), "[l]iteracy learning acquired through one medium or context complements learning in others," since all

FIGURE 2.1

Guiding Questions
for Critical Media
Literacy

What type of medium is this? Is it effective for communicating this material? Does it take advantage of the capabilities of the technology?

Is the material up-to-date? Does it contain misperceptions based on datedness?

Does it contain stereotypes of people or groups? What people are represented?

What images, sound, and motions are used? Are they effective?

Who developed this medium? Are they qualified to communicate accurately about the subject? Do they have obvious biases about the topic or project a particular values orientation?

Is there documentation of the information presented? How is the documentation handled?

Who is the target audience? How can you tell? Is it appropriate for this audience? Will the audience understand the vocabulary and images used?

Does this presentation make personal connections and evoke particular feelings in the user?

Is the material accessible to people with physical or mental challenges?

texts have commonalities in such elements as structures and genres. Teachers can help students to locate and interpret common textual elements, as well as to challenge the authority of the texts through critical analysis. Textual information, verbal and audio input, and visual images are all used, along with background experiences, to construct meaning through viewing audio-visual media, just as printed words, sentences, and longer selections are examined in light of background experiences to construct meaning from print. Students can use media logs to record the time they spend with various media and to answer guiding questions about the content of each medium (Watts Pailliotet et al., 2000). See Figure 2.1 for guiding questions to ask about media in order to critically analyze their appropriateness.

Evaluating Literacy Applications

Teachers have the job of evaluating literacy applications of technology. They should decide if each application addresses content that is needed, motivates the students to learn the content, clarifies the material for the students, and lends itself to use in the classroom. They also need to ask if the application is easy to implement, instructionally sound, cost-effective, and more effective than other ways to accomplish the task (Roe, Smith, and Burns, 2005). Evaluation of computer software involves asking other questions as well. Roe, Smith, and Burns (2005, p. 426) present a set of questions to ask when evaluating computer software. Some are specific to computer-assisted instructional software, but most are applicable to any software that is to be used in the school. These questions are found in Figure 2.2. Websites also must be evaluated. Questions to ask to evaluate websites are found in Figure 2.3.

FIGURE 2.2

Evaluating Computer Software

Source: Betty D. Roe, Sandy H. Smith, and Paul C. Burns. *Teaching Reading in Today's Elementary Schools* (Boston: Houghton Mifflin, 2005). Used with permission.

When evaluating computer software, ask the following questions:

1. Is the program compatible with the available hardware and operating system?

2. Does the program meet a curricular need better than another approach would?

3. Is the program well documented?

   a. Are the objectives of the program clearly presented?
   b. Are steps for initiating and running the program clearly stated?
   c. Are hardware requirements for the program clearly specified, and is this hardware available?
   d. Are time requirements for program use described, and are they reasonable for classroom use? (If a program can be saved at any time and re-entered at the same place, some of the problems with time are alleviated.)

4. Is the program user-friendly?

5. Is there a management system that keeps up with a student's performance on the program, if that would be appropriate?

6. Are the screens well designed and readable?

7. Is the program essentially crash-proof?

8. Is feedback about performance offered to the students? Is the feedback appropriate for them?

9. Do the students have control over the

   a. speed of the program presentation?
   b. level of difficulty of the program?
   c. degree of prompting offered by the program (including seeing instructions for use)?
   d. sequence of presentation of material?

10. Is the program highly interactive, requiring more of the student than just page-turning?

11. Is sound used appropriately, if at all? Can the sound be turned off without destroying the effectiveness of the program?

12. Is color used effectively, if at all?

13. Is the program adaptable for a variety of levels of students? Are your students within this range?

14. Is the material free of stereotypes and bias?

15. Is there a way that the teacher can modify the program for a particular class, set of data, or student? Is this procedure protected against student tampering?

16. Is information presented in the program accurate and presented clearly and in grammatically correct form?

When you are evaluating websites, you must consider the reliability of the sources of the material, accuracy of the content, clarity of the material presented, and purposes of the sites. Ask yourself the following questions when judging a website:

1. Can you determine who has developed the site? (If not, you may not want to place undue confidence in its contents.) If so, is the developer a reliable source for the information you are seeking? (A noted authority on the topic or an agency of the government would be considered reliable. Someone you have not heard of before may need to be investigated.)

2. Is there enough information given on the site developer that qualifications can be checked? (If not, be cautious.)

3. Are sources provided for information displayed on the site, so the user can cross-check information? (If they are, this is a definite plus.)

4. Does any of the information conflict with reliable sources that you have consulted? (If some of the information is in question, all of it is suspect.)

5. Is the layout of the site busy and confusing, making information difficult to evaluate? (Disorganization, particularly, is a bad sign.)

6. Is site navigation easy? (Sloppy navigational methods sometimes indicate a lack of attention to detail.)

7. Is the presented material grammatically correct, and is it free from errors in spelling and mechanics? (If it is not, the clarity is badly affected.)

8. Is the site free of advertising? (If not, look for possible bias of information presented, based on the advertising present.)

9. If currency of information is important, can you tell when the page was developed and last updated? (If not, be careful in accepting the information. If currency is not a factor—for example, for a Civil War site on which the material is not likely to become dated—this will not be a major concern.)

Advantages of Technology in the Classroom

McGrath (1998) found that technology use resulted in increased student motivation, increased cooperation and collaboration among students, more in-depth conversations between teachers and students and among students, more equity between students and teachers, more student persistence in solving problems, improved communication skills, and more opportunities for interdisciplinary activities. She also indicated that use of computers allowed for more effective work with diverse students. Many other educators have echoed these sentiments, and activities cited in this chapter support these ideas as well.

Students also are becoming familiar with technologies that are increasingly important to them in the world of work and even in home activities. Students who use technology in the classroom enter life activities better prepared to face the challenges they present.

Integrating Technology into the Curriculum

BUSINESS EDUCATION **ENGLISH/ LANGUAGE ARTS**

SOCIAL STUDIES **SCIENCE AND HEALTH**

Teachers at Woodham High School in Pensacola, Florida, developed a planned approach to "emphasizing using technology as a learning tool to increase student achievement in the areas of academics, behavior, and attitude" (Kaczynski and White, 1999, p. 1). Their students work on projects that blend learning objectives from the students' academic and business technology courses. The freshman-level KEGS (Keyboarding, English, Geography, Science) Program lets students learn word-processing skills and produce written documents for their English, geography, and earth science classes. During this year the students complete projects, such as a research paper about a country they are studying.

The sophomore-level BECAH (Biology, English, Concepts, Application, History) Program includes the learning of word-processing, spreadsheet, and database applications and applying these skills in biology, English, and world history classes. One of the activities is the production of a Roman newsletter.

The junior-level ITECH (Integration of Technology, English, Chemistry, History) Program has students integrating the use of CD-ROMs, presentation software, the Internet, word processing, spreadsheets, and databases in English, chemistry, and American history courses. One project is a book of student autobiographies.

The senior-level ET (Emerging Technologies) Program gives students a chance to do desktop publishing, multimedia presentations, and Web design. It also involves research using multimedia and telecommunications. Students have developed newsletters, brochures, and a school web page. The teachers believe that these programs have been successful because of computer lab availability, block scheduling that assigns students to common teachers, and a team-teaching approach to instructional projects in all but the senior year (Kaczynski and White, 1999; Slover and Payne, 1999). Figure 2.4 shows one project from the BECAH Program.

FIGURE 2.4

"Know Your Body Parts!" Assignment

Source: Michelle Kaczynski and Jill White. "Integrating Language Arts, Social Studies, and Science Through Technology." Handout at International Reading Association Convention, May 1999. Used with permission.

Woodham High School BECAH Program

Biology, English, Computer Applications, and History

W. J. Woodham High School • 150 East Burgess Road • Pensacola, FL 32503
Telephone (904) 478-4020

KNOW YOUR BODY PARTS!!!

Situation/Scenario: You are a first year biology teacher at Woodham High School. Your next unit to teach is human anatomy.

Solution/Problem Statement: Select and teach one of the ten human systems to your students. Not only must the students demonstrate mastery of this system, but also your teaching ability is being evaluated by an administrator. The evaluation by your administrator will determine if you will return as a second year teacher.

Resources:

People: All BECAH students

Information of Knowledge: Knowledge of the system and effective teaching techniques

Tools/Equipment: Furnished by students and brought from home

Materials: Supplied by students

Capital: Students decide on cost of model, materials needed, etc.

Energy: Human and other as required

Time: March 26–27 until May 20–21

	Task
	Prepare a written lesson plan covering all stated objectives for your system (see your science supervisor for objectives). Must be keyed in computer lab. (Biology)
	Oral presentation of systems to your students, including handouts, drawings, etc. (Biology)
	Complete a lab or demonstration about your system. (Biology)
	Design and construct a working model of your system. (Biology)
	Design a test about your system to be taken by your students. (Biology/computer)
	Design a database in Lotus Approach identifying all aspects of your system. (Computer)
	Create a vocabulary list (with terms and definitions) pertaining to your system. Must be keyed in computer class. (English/computer)
	Create an original poem (at least 8–12 lines) about your system. Must be keyed in computer class. (English/computer)
	Research the medical/surgical advances associated with your system. (Include diseases, treatments, or other interesting factoids.) (History)
	Attend open house to view displayed models of systems. (Reception following!!!) (Computer)
	Turn in completed ILA to science supervisor. Supervisor's signature _____

Perspective on Technology Use for Literacy Learning Tomorrow

The incredible pace of emergence of new technology makes it clear that educational technology is here to stay. Schools can't keep up with the cutting-edge applications, but they will continually be advancing to higher levels of applications. It is impossible to know what new technologies will evolve into educational tools. Virtual reality applications are already making some advances, and much effort is being expended to offer greater access to telecommunications. Web-based courses (instruction via the World Wide Web) are likely to spread in the future.

Teachers may wish to learn more about technological applications but may not know where to turn. Today there are many resources for teachers to help them learn about and have successful experiences with today's literacy learner. The technology section of most large bookstores and the magazine racks in a variety of stores provide many publications that will explain emerging technologies at various levels of sophistication. Professional organizations, such as the International Reading Association (IRA) (http://www.reading.org) and the National Council of Teachers of English (NCTE) (http://www.ncte.org), which offer increasing numbers of sessions on technology at their conferences and conventions each year, are good resources. The locations of these conferences and conventions vary from year to year, so one may be within easy reach in the near future. The Technology, Reading and Learning Difficulties Conference focuses on technology and literacy; the National Educational Computing Conference, managed by the International Society for Technology in Education (ISTE), is more general; and ED-MEDIA: World Conference on Educational Media and Hypermedia, an Association for the Advancement of Computing Education (AACE) conference, covers multimedia.

IRA and NCTE also include articles about integrating technology into the classroom in their journals: *The Reading Teacher* (focus on elementary and middle school) and the *Journal of Adolescent & Adult Literacy* (focus on middle school through adult)—both are IRA journals; and *Language Arts* (focus on elementary and middle school) and *English Journal* (focus on middle school through senior high)—both are NCTE journals. ISTE has many helpful publications, including *Learning & Leading with Technology, Journal of Research on Technology in Education*, and *Journal of Computing in Teacher Education*. AACE has several journals also, including *Journal of Interactive Learning Research, Information Technology in Childhood Education Annual*, and *Journal of Educational Multimedia and Hypermedia*.

The World Wide Web is a treasure trove of resources, but, unfortunately, the locations of the treasures are anything but stable, since Web addresses change constantly. Figure 2.5 shows a few sites that you may wish to check. A search engine, such as AltaVista or Google, will help you find many more.

FIGURE 2.5

Selected Websites

(Remember that Web addresses change frequently.)

Amazon Online Bookstore—http://www.amazon.com
The Complete Works of William Shakespeare—http://www-tech.mit.edu/
    Shakespeare/works.html
Children's Literature Web Guide—http://www.acs.ucalgary.ca/~dkbrown
Educational Web Design—http://www.oswego.org/staff/cchamber/webdesign/
    edwebdesign.htm
Eisenhower National Clearinghouse for Mathematics and Science Education—
    http://www.enc.org
Houghton Mifflin's Education Place—http://www.eduplace.com
International Reading Association—http://www.reading.org
Library of Congress—http://lcweb.loc.gov
NASA's Website— http://www.nasa.gov/home/index.html?skipIntro=1
National Council of Teachers of English—http://www.ncte.org
National Science Foundation—http://www.nsf.gov
Northwest Regional Educational Laboratory—http://www.nwrel.org
Reading Online—http://www.readingonline.org
Regional Educational Laboratory Network—http://www.relnetwork.org
Smithsonian—http://www.si.edu
U.S. Geological Survey—http://www.usgs.gov/education
WebMuseum, Paris— http://www.ibiblio.org/louvre
Welcome to the White House—http://www.whitehouse.gov

SUMMARY

Teachers in today's schools have a wide variety of technological applications available for use in their content area instruction. These applications include older technologies, such as overhead projectors, televisions, and audiotape recorders, as well as newer technologies, such as computers, videotape recorders, CD drives, and DVD drives. Many multimedia applications are possible, often through computer technology.

Teachers must be able to evaluate the technological applications available to them because they are of varying quality. Some are appropriate for particular curricular uses, and some have little instructional value. Careful evaluation of the applications facilitates their wise integration into the curriculum.

There are many advantages to using technology for content area literacy, both in classroom instruction and in preparing students for the world of work. These advantages are evident in working with a wide variety of students, including struggling readers and English language learners.

The use of technology in schools is increasing rapidly, with new applications becoming more widely available and more affordable. Teachers must strive to keep up-to-date in order to optimize their instruction.

DISCUSSION QUESTIONS

1. What are valid applications for overhead projectors, televisions, and audiotapes in literacy learning?
2. How can word-processing, desktop-publishing, writing development, and conference and collaboration software be used in writing instruction?
3. What are some applications of databases and spreadsheets in literacy learning?
4. What literacy skills are involved in using the Internet for research?
5. What are some cautions about using the Internet for gathering information?
6. What are the benefits of e-mail for literacy learning?
7. What type of computer-assisted instructional programs involves the highest levels of literacy activities? Why do you think so?
8. How can videotapes be used to enhance literacy learning?
9. For what purposes would multimedia presentations be useful in a literacy classroom?
10. What are some uses of technology that are effective for English language learners?
11. What are some uses of technology that are effective for struggling readers?

ENRICHMENT ACTIVITIES

1. Develop a set of transparencies to teach vocabulary from a content area chapter.
2. Videotape or audiotape presentations made by your students and play them back to allow students to critically analyze their own presentations.
*3. Develop and teach a procedure for conducting an Internet search for information on a research topic.
*4. Set up an e-mail exchange between your students and the students in another school about a topic of study.
5. Develop a multimedia presentation to teach students a reading strategy.

*These activities are designed for in-service teachers, student teachers, and practicum students.

Part 2

Strategies for Learning: Constructing Meaning and Studying

Chapter 3

A Conceptual Approach to Developing Meaningful Vocabulary

OVERVIEW

Content reading instruction revolves around increasing students' comprehension of content materials. The larger readers' vocabularies are, the easier it is for them to make sense of text (NIH, 2000). Therefore, reading comprehension depends on word knowledge, as do writing and content learning (Snow, Burns, and Griffin, 1998; Brynildssen, 2000). Word knowledge enables students to connect concepts and meaning with printed words (Bromley, 2002). Limited vocabulary creates significant reading difficulties for struggling readers. English language learners (ELLs) may have mastered the vocabulary and concepts in their primary language, but they have to transfer them to English.

The importance of developing word meanings becomes more clear when we realize that the estimated number of words students encounter in their reading at school exceeds one hundred thousand (Ruddell and Shearer, 2002). Content concepts make up the majority of words found in printed materials for secondary students. This chapter focuses on direct instruction for cultivating students' vocabulary growth and increasing their command of words and context, thus enhancing comprehension of content textbooks. Computer technology and the Internet offer students motivating avenues for vocabulary growth.

PURPOSE-SETTING QUESTIONS

As you read this chapter, try to answer these questions:

1. How are experiences, concepts, and words interrelated?
2. Why is direct instruction an important aspect of teaching challenged readers?
3. Why do students need multiple encounters with vocabulary?
4. Why does vocabulary play an important role in content reading?

Word Knowledge

How are words
related to concepts?

Knowledge of words determines how we understand texts, define ourselves for others, and define the way we see the world (Stahl, 1999). Words, our labels for concepts, shape meaning in oral and written language. Word knowledge and the ability to apply it are significantly related to reading comprehension, intelligence, thinking abilities, and academic achievement (Baker, 1995; Smith, 1998; Nagy and Scott, 2000). Students who know the important words in a reading assignment are better able to learn new concepts and ideas from content textbooks. Direct vocabulary instruction results in greater vocabulary growth (Curtis and Longo, 2001; Biemiller, 2003). The key instructional ideas in this chapter are concerned with active student engagement in learning words, beginning with direct teaching of targeted vocabulary, using word context, engaging in conceptual learning, and providing repeated exposures to words from multiple sources (Rhoder and Huerster, 2002).

CONCEPTUAL KNOWLEDGE

What are concepts?

Concepts are the categories into which our experiences are organized and our webs of ideas created through categorization. Items in a category share similar characteristics. In the process of conceptualizing, we group objects, experiences, or information into categories based on common features. For example, the concept of measurement includes *meter, ounce, gram,* and *inch.* However, a word can refer to a number of different referents. For example, the word *butterfly* can represent a monarch butterfly or the opera *Madame Butterfly.* In this instance, the context helps readers know whether the author is writing about an insect or an opera.

How is schema
theory related to
concepts?

Conceptual knowledge is a component of schema theory. According to this theory, knowledge is composed of organized, structured experiences, concepts, and information. These networks of knowledge in memory structure our thoughts. Therefore, they influence learning, as well as thinking. Sharing similar schemata, concepts, and vocabulary enables people to communicate without explaining every idea, event, or object. New schemata build on preceding ones; this cumulative pattern makes each experience essential to those that follow. When communication falters, it is probably because one person lacks the schemata basic to the discussion. This problem occurs in textbooks when a textbook author or a teacher incorrectly assumes that students have acquired certain concepts.

WHAT DOES IT MEAN TO KNOW A WORD?

Knowing a word is having a core meaning for that word and recognizing how the meaning changes in different contexts (Stahl, 1999). Readers need more than definitions for words, and more than the knowledge derived from context. Both context and definitions can be misleading for students. Misleading context is illustrated in the following student's response on a vocabulary quiz. The student gave the word *dumb* as a synonym for *genius.* When asked about his answer, he said, "My mom says 'what a genius,' when I do something dumb." Students need to understand the ways words function in various contexts, as well as acquiring synonym and antonym knowledge. Experience with words enriches students' range of meaning, so their knowledge grows from superficial to in-depth knowledge.

In content reading, concepts related to the subject usually have specific meanings that are essential to comprehension. An example of specific content meaning is apparent in science with the word *matter*. In science, *matter* has a unique meaning that differentiates it from how *matter* is used in the question, "What is the matter, Tyler?"

Another example is the word *credit*. Students understand *credit* when referring to a credit card or the credits needed for high school graduation. However, a credit report may be an unknown concept for them. An economics student will acquire an understanding of *credit* through a formal definition such as "the provision of money, goods, or services at the present in exchange for the promise of future payment" (Lowe, Malouf, and Jacobson, 1997). Additional uses, such as *credit bureau, credit disclosure form, credit rating, credit references, credit union*, and *creditor*, may be encountered in the student's consumer economics class. In history class, this student may read, "Abraham Lincoln is often credited with freeing the slaves," thus encountering the word *credit* in yet another context. In-depth word knowledge is usually reserved for those words that an individual uses frequently in reading, listening, speaking, and writing.

When students develop special interests or prepare to enter a vocation or profession, they generally develop some in-depth word knowledge. For example, a student who is interested in sailing will have a vocabulary that includes *jib, main sail*, and so forth. An individual who is planning a nursing career develops a vocabulary including words such as temperature, chart, IV (intravenous), ICU (Intensive Care Unit), and so forth.

What is the range of word knowledge?

How Do Students Learn Words and Concepts?

What is a receptive vocabulary?

Listening and reading develop students' **receptive vocabularies**, the words they recognize when they hear them or see them. Speaking and writing develop students' expressive vocabularies, the words they know well enough to use in speaking and writing. Receptive vocabularies are usually substantially larger than **expressive vocabularies**, because learners have to know a word rather well before using it. While students may recognize many words in their listening and/or reading vocabularies, their knowledge may be partial, lacking the richness of the in-depth word knowledge that they require for effective content learning. Appropriate teaching and learning strategies are essential to developing the word knowledge that students need to succeed. The hallmarks of successful vocabulary instruction are the following:

Sensitize students to important words and unknown words.
Provide direct instruction.
Present words in multiple contexts.
Offer multiple opportunities to develop and expand meanings.
Assess progress.

SENSITIZE STUDENTS TO IMPORTANT WORDS AND UNKNOWN WORDS

Alerting students to key words helps their vocabulary grow and improves their comprehension. These words include key vocabulary for chapters or sections of their content textbooks. For example, when introducing mathematics content, teachers can call students' attention to words such as *commutative, metric, symmetrical, pentagon,* and *hexagon.* Students need a system to use when they encounter words that are not in their own vocabularies. They can learn how to use context and/or a glossary to aid their understanding of vocabulary. One mode of focusing on important words is to use direct instruction.

PROVIDE DIRECT INSTRUCTION

Direct instruction is systematic, explicit, teacher-led instruction. Direct instruction in content area vocabulary is focused on targeted vocabulary related to content area concepts (Szymborski, 1995; Smith, 1998; Curtis and Longo, 2001). To facilitate direct instruction, teachers identify key vocabulary that will prepare students to comprehend and acquire important content concepts. After introducing key words and their meanings, teachers activate prior knowledge, thus connecting the new with the known (Johnson and Rasmussen, 1998). Research emphasizes that for learning to occur, new information must be integrated with what the learner already knows (Christen and Murphy, 1991). Readers use the words they know to learn new words. Effective instruction focuses on identifying targeted words and teaching those words before the student reads content materials.

Teachers encourage students to build associations and contexts that elaborate their word knowledge (Curtis and Longo, 2001). Although direct instruction is a useful strategy for developing vocabulary, Stahl (1999) states that three hundred to five hundred words are all that can be reasonably taught in a year. However, according to White, Graves, and Slater (1989) students learn three to four thousand words a year. This information indicates that context plays an important role in incidental learning of vocabulary.

PRESENT WORDS IN MULTIPLE CONTEXTS

Context narrows a word's field of reference and helps specify its meaning. It also builds connections between known and new information. Context is most useful when students are fluent readers who automatically recognize most of the words in a sentence, because they can use the surrounding words to determine the meanings of unknown words. Context can help students understand content text; however, context alone may not provide enough clues to word meaning. In content reading, students may read long selections that lack neat contextual explanations. For this reason, content teachers should teach important words in a text prior to assigning the text to students. The following figure shows a content text teacher's edition that illustrates this concept.

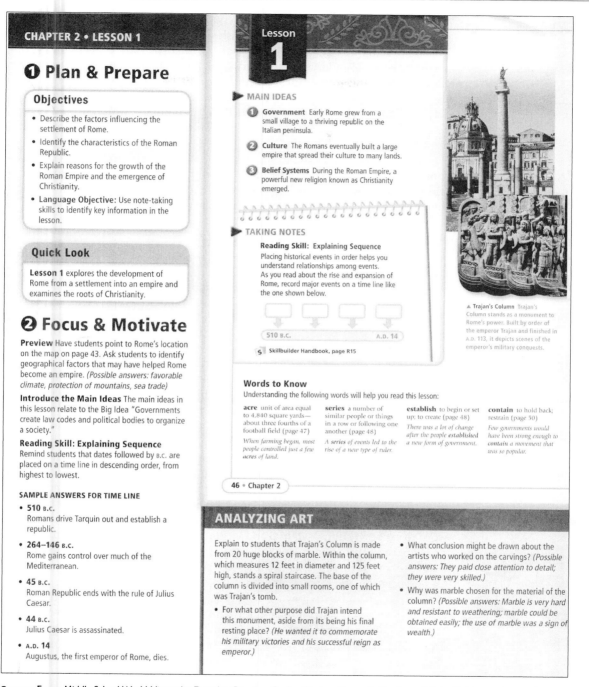

❶ Plan & Prepare

Objectives

- Describe the factors influencing the settlement of Rome.
- Identify the characteristics of the Roman Republic.
- Explain reasons for the growth of the Roman Empire and the emergence of Christianity.
- **Language Objective:** Use note-taking skills to identify key information in the lesson.

Quick Look

Lesson 1 explores the development of Rome from a settlement into an empire and examines the roots of Christianity.

❷ Focus & Motivate

Preview Have students point to Rome's location on the map on page 43. Ask students to identify geographical factors that may have helped Rome become an empire. *(Possible answers: favorable climate, protection of mountains, sea trade)*

Introduce the Main Ideas The main ideas in this lesson relate to the Big Idea "Governments create law codes and political bodies to organize a society."

Reading Skill: Explaining Sequence Remind students that dates followed by B.C. are placed on a time line in descending order, from highest to lowest.

SAMPLE ANSWERS FOR TIME LINE

- **510 B.C.**
  Romans drive Tarquin out and establish a republic.

- **264–146 B.C.**
  Rome gains control over much of the Mediterranean.

- **45 B.C.**
  Roman Republic ends with the rule of Julius Caesar.

- **44 B.C.**
  Julius Caesar is assassinated.

- **A.D. 14**
  Augustus, the first emperor of Rome, dies.

Lesson 1

▶ MAIN IDEAS

① **Government** Early Rome grew from a small village to a thriving republic on the Italian peninsula.

② **Culture** The Romans eventually built a large empire that spread their culture to many lands.

③ **Belief Systems** During the Roman Empire, a powerful new religion known as Christianity emerged.

▶ TAKING NOTES

Reading Skill: Explaining Sequence
Placing historical events in order helps you understand relationships among events. As you read about the rise and expansion of Rome, record major events on a time line like the one shown below.

510 B.C.   A.D. 14

Ⓢ **Skillbuilder Handbook, page R15**

▲ **Trajan's Column** Trajan's Column stands as a monument to Rome's power. Built by order of the emperor Trajan and finished in A.D. 113, it depicts scenes of the emperor's military conquests.

Words to Know

Understanding the following words will help you read this lesson:

acre unit of area equal to 4,840 square yards—about three fourths of a football field (page 47)
When farming began, most people controlled just a few acres of land.

series a number of similar people or things in a row or following one another (page 48)
A series of events led to the rise of a new type of ruler.

establish to begin or set up; to create (page 48)
There was a lot of change after the people established a new form of government.

contain to hold back; restrain (page 50)
Few governments would have been strong enough to contain a movement that was so popular.

46 • Chapter 2

ANALYZING ART

Explain to students that Trajan's Column is made from 20 huge blocks of marble. Within the column, which measures 12 feet in diameter and 125 feet high, stands a spiral staircase. The base of the column is divided into small rooms, one of which was Trajan's tomb.

- For what other purpose did Trajan intend this monument, aside from its being his final resting place? *(He wanted it to commemorate his military victories and his successful reign as emperor.)*

- What conclusion might be drawn about the artists who worked on the carvings? *(Possible answers: They paid close attention to detail; they were very skilled.)*

- Why was marble chosen for the material of the column? *(Possible answers: Marble is very hard and resistant to weathering; marble could be obtained easily; the use of marble was a sign of wealth.)*

Learning words from context is incidental learning. Context reveals one of several possible meanings because many English words have multiple meanings (Gergen, 1999). Students who read widely in material that includes challenging words will improve their vocabularies (Kuhn and Stahl, 2000). Increasing the amount that students read significantly improves their vocabularies. Unfortunately, the reverse is also true; students who do not read widely fail to acquire vocabulary, creating a self-defeating cycle. However, direct instruction can build the word knowledge that will permit these students to read more and subsequently acquire more vocabulary through context, as well.

In readings written expressly for students, such as textbooks, context clues may be contrived, neatly providing information about an unfamiliar word. However, some selections will not contain clear contextual explanations. After all, authors write to transmit ideas rather than to define vocabulary.

OFFER MULTIPLE OPPORTUNITIES TO DEVELOP AND EXPAND MEANINGS

Multiple exposures to words give readers opportunities to move from an initial level of knowing to greater familiarity with the words and concepts. This familiarity enables learners to use the words to acquire additional words and concepts. The activities and strategies introduced throughout this chapter provide opportunities for multiple exposures to words and exploring words in multiple contexts. For instance, elaboration is a means of developing and expanding word meanings.

Elaboration involves associations between words and meanings. Students who have many associations acquire richer vocabularies. Word knowledge is most effectively elaborated through meaningful, concrete experiences.

The initial level of elaboration is association, wherein the reader associates the term with other words that are often synonyms, which indicates that he or she has some sense of the word's meaning. The second level is comprehension; at this level, the reader recognizes the word and understands its meaning when encountering it in a reading context. Generative processing is the most sophisticated level of word understanding, one that reflects a deep level of cognitive processing. At this level, the reader is fluent enough to produce the target word in a novel context and can use the word to express thoughts in oral and written language. Association, comprehension, and generative processing involve active processing and transfer of knowledge. The latter section of this chapter includes a variety of association activities such as history association and science association.

Comprehension activities for vocabulary expansion that are illustrated in this chapter include classification activities for science, **open and closed word sorts** for secretarial office procedures, and an open-ended sort for biology. Graphic organizers build comprehension, as does the Super Word Web. Generative processing includes activities that cause students to generate words for writing and speaking.

ASSESS STUDENTS' PROGRESS IN DEVELOPING VOCABULARY

Consistent assessment of students' progress in learning the vocabulary that is presented in direct instruction lessons enables both teacher and students to recognize their progress. Assessments are often multiple-choice tests in which the students identify the synonym or phrase that best defines a word. Other simple assessments involve giving students lists of words and instructing them to respond with synonyms or antonyms for the target words, having them complete crossword puzzles containing the vocabulary terms, and having teams of students compete in a vocabulary-based quiz show. Each student should maintain a record of his or her vocabulary scores and the words missed.

Focus on English Language Learners

Vocabulary for English Language Learners (ELLs)

In a sense, English vocabulary may be easier to acquire for secondary ELLs who have previously learned to read in their first language than for those who have not done so. These ELLs are usually in a position to transfer their existing vocabulary knowledge to English. The linguistic resources that these students bring into the classroom provide a foundation for learning English (Lu, 1998). Their initial English lessons can focus on existing concepts and vocabulary (Myers, 1995). ELLs must be able to recognize opportunities for language transfer from their first language to English and be motivated to make the transfer (Ngeow, 1998).

Developing a working English vocabulary is especially important for ELLs because it permits them to learn in English-speaking content classrooms. ELLs have special needs in learning English vocabulary; they need language to use for various contexts, audiences, and purposes. Many of the activities suggested later in this chapter are useful for teaching ELLs. Activities such as "Possible Sentences" and illustrated vocabulary cards are especially useful for ELLs because they help students explore English context. The following list identifies important emphases the teacher must provide for these students:

1. Understand correct word meaning.

2. Use correct pronunciation.

3. Use correct spelling.

4. Use words correctly in context.

5. Use common English phrases correctly.

Focus on Struggling Readers

Vocabulary for Struggling Readers

Many struggling readers populate the content classes in middle and secondary schools. These students are not unable to read; they simply do not read well enough to understand and apply content texts and related materials. Many of these students read well below their grade placement. In fact, it is not uncommon to find such students reading at third or fourth grade level. Struggling readers have weak vocabularies, and the gap between the vocabulary they need for success and the vocabulary they actually have widens as they go through school (Stahl, 1999).

Curtis and Longo (2001) and Stoodt-Hill (2005) found that direct instruction is essential since these students do not acquire vocabulary incidentally, because they lack the foundational vocabulary to permit this. Teachers of struggling readers need to devote an adequate amount of instructional time to the task. This amount of time is greater than that needed in average classes. Struggling readers need at least ten to fifteen encounters with each word's meaning (Curtis and Longo, 2001).

Research indicates that the most successful vocabulary programs for struggling readers are based on direct teaching of word meanings. Moreover, research shows that struggling readers need many opportunities to generate contexts for the words they are learning (Stoodt-Hill, 2005; Curtis and Longo, 2001). Understanding the various contexts in which a word makes sense is difficult for struggling readers (Stoodt-Hill, 2005). Activities such as generating contexts for the words they are studying are important for learning. (In the following sections, there are a variety of activities such as "Possible Sentences" and word cards that will help students enrich their understanding of vocabulary.) Struggling readers should have regular vocabulary quizzes to assess their progress. The following guidelines for teaching struggling readers emerged from research (Stahl, 1999; Curtis and Longo, 2001; Stoodt-Hill, 2005):

Students need

Direct instruction.
Daily instruction.
Vocabulary presented with definitions.
To make connections to what is already known.
Repeated encounters with the same words in various contexts.
To develop their own contexts for the vocabulary they are studying.
Strategies for developing a deeper knowledge of vocabulary, such as word maps, association activities, in-depth word study, sorts, classifications, and mnemonic instruction.

MEETING THE CHALLENGE

Tinsley Washington teaches developmental reading to students in grades nine, ten, eleven, and twelve in a county school system that serves a culturally diverse student population of suburban, city, and rural students. The school system recognized the students' significant vocabulary problems and adopted instructional materials that introduce ten words per week. Definitions and context are the focus of lessons. Multiple-choice tests are included for assessment. The description below illustrates the challenges Tinsley encounters in teaching vocabulary.

Tinsley introduced a lesson that included these words: *delete, menace, impartial, morale, integrity, naïve, legitimate, overt, lenient, undermine.* On a pretest, all of the students received a grade of zero. Then she introduced the words in the context provided by the text.

After organizing the students in groups of three, she instructed them to write sentences using the target words in an appropriate context. The students loudly objected. Their argument was that they had never heard any of these words and they had no use for them because they would never use them in their daily writing or conversation. She explained the importance of vocabulary knowledge in learning and in employment. The students remained unconvinced.

She decided that a new plan was essential. After considerable thought, she collected newspapers, magazines, speeches (from the Internet), and pages from content textbooks that the students would be required to read. Her next assignment required each student to read two selections from the collection and circle all of the unknown words. Through this assignment the students began to recognize that they needed to learn words in order to succeed. She started with the words they identified as unknown and expanded their word bank by having them examine more written materials and listen to television news, as well as to science and history television programs. After the students grew accustomed to recognizing unknown words and learning them, she was able to integrate words from the class text. The students continued to have problems with appropriate context because they did not understand the multiple meanings of many English words. However, they became more motivated as they saw the value of words in their lives. These students illustrate the difficulties that struggling secondary students face as they attempt to gain more education. In later sections, we introduce teaching and learning strategies to help students like these to succeed.

Teachers cannot teach all of the words that students will need to know for successful content area learning, but direct instruction can be a springboard for independent vocabulary growth. The words learned through direct instruction create a foundation for acquiring additional words. Moreover, students can use the strategies learned in direct instruction for amassing a larger bank of word knowledge.

To build background and vocabulary for content area reading, students need to see multiple relationships (Hodapp and Hodapp, 1996). Conceptual activities, mind maps, and activities for multiple intelligences contribute to the building of multiple relationships through instruction.

BUILD BACKGROUND

Vicarious experiences can support vocabulary development, but learning is more complete when it is attached to concrete experience. A student who encounters the term *intersect* in a mathematics text will understand it better because of his or her familiarity with street intersections. However, students cannot have direct experience with every concept they encounter in reading. Thus, teachers must help students build both direct and indirect experience through field trips, exhibits, dramatizations, videos, television, resource persons, and pictures. They can help students relate their own experiences to the passages they read. Computerized encyclopedias such as the interactive multimedia *Encarta* enable students to hear different languages, the sounds of musical instruments, and so forth, which enrich conceptual understanding. Moreover, the networking of concepts in multimedia materials enhances conceptual development. Of course, there are many multimedia programs that enhance learning in diverse areas of study. For example, the Microsoft program Dangerous Creatures explores the endangered world of wildlife, while a program called Golf gives students ways of refining their golf game.

SCIENCE AND **PHYSICAL**
HEALTH **EDUCATION**

DISCUSSION

How does discussion clarify word meaning?

Discussion helps students associate word pronunciation and meaning, as well as relate existing experiences and word knowledge to new vocabulary. For example, vocabulary instruction can proceed by asking students to think of and share ideas, synonyms, definitions, and associated words related to specified vocabulary terms. These words and ideas can be grouped in a chart, a computerized matrix, or a mind map.

Another strategy to help students see a word in a broader context is to have them answer questions like these: (1) What is it? (2) What is it like? (3) What are some examples? (Schwartz and Raphael, 1985). These questions help students see relationships between familiar and less familiar terms and bring the meaning of an unknown term into focus.

The many instructional ideas we discuss in the following sections represent procedures and methods that teachers should build into their content area instruction. As with all vocabulary instruction, the overall goal is students' autonomy in word work. As teachers model and demonstrate the various word strategies and ways of figuring out word meanings and associations, the underlying goal is to help students internalize these strategies for eventual independent use in their reading.

MIND MAPPING

Mind mapping is a way of pouring ideas onto paper. Through mapping, teachers and learners can enhance their thinking skills (Margulies, 1991). It is visual note taking and a way of showing connections among ideas. Mind mappers use a central image, key words, colors, codes, and symbols to put ideas on paper; all of these components make ideas more concrete and the connections more vivid. Moreover, mind maps are flexible and adaptable to many situations, such as learning words, showing comprehension, making plans, and studying for tests. The following steps make a good starting point for mind mapping. They are adapted from *Mapping Inner Space* by Nancy Margulies (1991).

1. Select a word, concept, or topic, and draw a small picture or symbol that represents the subject. Place the image in the center of the paper.

2. Let your mind freely associate with the topic. Use colors as you draw.

3. Use key words in the map, but only one word per line. Next, branch out and add other words associated with the first word. Then generate more words until you have branched out in many directions. Select the words that communicate the most information.

4. Develop symbols or pictures to use instead of words.

The mind map in Figure 3.1 illustrates science vocabulary.

FIGURE 3.1

Mind Map for Science Vocabulary

SCIENCE AND
HEALTH

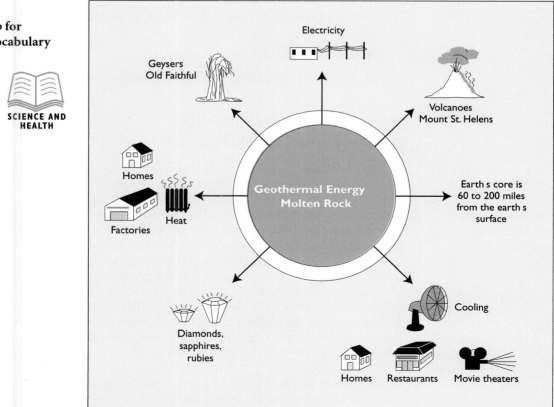

Conceptual Relationships

How is conceptual
learning different
from learning facts?

**SCIENCE AND
HEALTH**

Conceptual learning is based on understanding relationships among ideas rather than on learning lists of independent facts. Students can be overwhelmed by the constant learning required when responding to each separate incident, object, or idea as unique. For example, developing a science concept of "organ" would include linking it to familiar ideas, as in "organs of the body such as liver and kidney," which is more effective than learning "The kidney is defined as . . . . The liver is . . . ." Recognizing the connections enhances understanding and memory.

Conceptual relationships are shown on **semantic maps** or webs, that don't have the illustrations that are found in mind maps, but rely completely on printed words that are connected with lines. These maps are important in content area study because they develop concepts. According to Simpson (1987), conceptual understanding evolves from four mental operations, which are emphasized in the reinforcement activities of this chapter. Reinforcement activities to build vocabulary should incorporate these mental operations:

1. Recognizing and generating critical attributes—both examples and nonexamples—of a concept

2. Seeing relationships between the concept to be learned and what is already known

3. Applying the concept to a variety of contexts

4. Generating new contexts for the learned concept

CONCEPTUAL REINFORCEMENT INSTRUCTIONAL ACTIVITIES

How do learners use
attribute relations?

What is the purpose
of semantic feature
analysis?

MATHEMATICS

Attribute relations provide an organizational network focusing on concept characteristics. Students use their existing concepts to learn new concepts and conceptual relationships. For example, students know about horses, which helps them to understand a connected concept, *unicorns*. Related concepts can be compared using **semantic feature analysis**. Semantic feature analysis works best with related words, such as those connected to a specific concept or within a content area. The attributes of the familiar words in a feature analysis give students a basis for comparison with the new words. For example, in the following semantic feature analysis (Example 3.1), students could begin with geometric figures. Then the teacher might develop the grid of vocabulary words and features, or attributes, related to them and let the students complete the grid by putting Xs in appropriate cells—the ones in which the rows for specific terms intersect with columns that represent features related to those terms—or the students and teacher could develop the grid together as the terms are discussed.

Conceptual relationships can be organized in various ways, such as class relations and examples and nonexamples. *Class relations* are hierarchical networks.

EXAMPLE 3.1 **Semantic Feature Analysis for Geometric Figures**

MATHEMATICS

	3 sides	All sides of equal length	2 sides of equal length	Contains a 90-degree angle
Isosceles triangle	×		×	
Scalene triangle	×			
Equilateral triangle	×	×		
Right triangle	×			×

How can conceptual relationships be organized?

SCIENCE AND HEALTH

Words are related to one another by superordinate and subordinate concepts. For example, chromosomes are a part of the hereditary material in cells, and genes are found within chromosomes. *Examples* demonstrate a concept, whereas *nonexamples* demonstrate what the concept is not; both facilitate learning. For example, both dominant genes and recessive genes are examples of genes. Chromosomes are nonexamples of genes.

The **Frayer Model** (Frayer, Frederick, and Klausmeier, 1969) helps students develop a more complete understanding of the facets of a newly acquired concept. This model calls for inclusion of both examples and nonexamples to extend learning. In developing a concept of democratic government, for example, students can identify governments that are not democratic as well as ones that are democratic and can explain why a particular government is an example or nonexample. Schwartz and Raphael (1985) developed a word map based on categories devised by Frayer and others (1969); Example 3.2 illustrates a variation of this activity. Example 3.3 illustrates another activity based on the Frayer Model.

KINDS OF CONTEXT CLUES

There are both syntactic context clues, derived from the grammatical function of the unfamiliar word in the sentence, and semantic context clues, derived from the meaning of the other words in the sentence. Sometimes context clues define or explain an unfamiliar word. Sometimes they provide a comparison or contrast of the unknown word with a word that is known or a synonym or antonym of the unfamiliar word. **Figurative language** provides context clues by making abstract and uncommon ideas more concrete. Types of figurative language include the following:

ENGLISH/ LANGUAGE ARTS

1. *Personification.* Human or personal qualities are given to inanimate things or ideas. Katherine Paterson used personification in *Bridge to Terabithia:* "Through his top ear came the sound of the Timmonses' old Buick—'Wants oil,' his dad would say" (Paterson, 1987, p. 7).

EXAMPLE 3.2
 Word Map

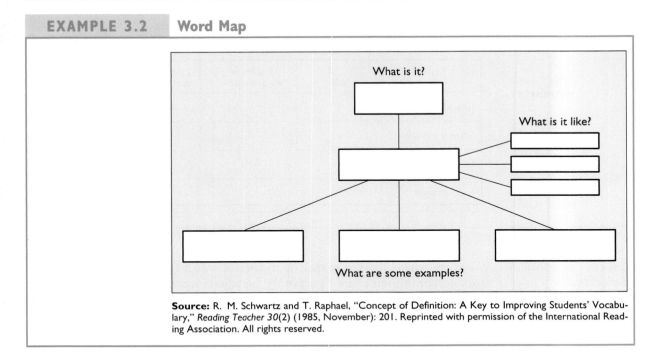

Source: R. M. Schwartz and T. Raphael, "Concept of Definition: A Key to Improving Students' Vocabulary," *Reading Teacher 30*(2) (1985, November): 201. Reprinted with permission of the International Reading Association. All rights reserved.

EXAMPLE 3.3
 Frayer Model

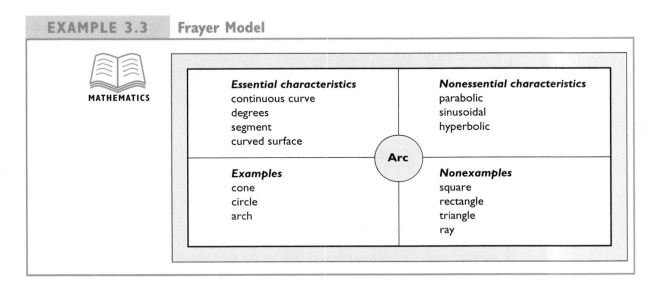

ENGLISH/
LANGUAGE
ARTS

2. *Simile.* A direct comparison is made between things. The words *like, as . . . as,* and *so . . . as* are frequently used in making the comparisons in similes. An example of a sentence containing a simile is "The thunder reverberated like an entire corps of bass drums."

MUSIC   ENGLISH/
            LANGUAGE
            ARTS

3. *Metaphor.* This figure of speech helps writers and speakers create clearer pictures through comparisons. These comparisons, however, do not use clue words such as *like* or *as.* Bruce Brooks used the following metaphor to describe music in *Midnight Hour Encores*: "Just give me the equivalent of antiseptic kitchens in which crew-cut husbands eat lime Jell-O with banana slices and miniature marshmallows suspended in it, served by perky housewives who got the recipe from a television commercial earlier in the day. 'I get it. The Fifties'" (Brooks, 1986, p. 68).

ENGLISH/
LANGUAGE
ARTS

4. *Hyperbole.* This is an exaggeration used for effect. Katherine Paterson used hyperbole to describe a girl in *Bridge to Terabithia*: "And the littlest one cried if you looked at her cross-eyed" (Paterson, 1987, p. 2).

5. *Euphemism.* Euphemism is used to express disagreeable or unpleasant facts indirectly. Death is often described as "passing away," "going to one's reward," or "going to the final rest."

ENGLISH/
LANGUAGE
ARTS

6. *Allusion.* Allusions are references to information believed to be common knowledge. Allusions are based on the assumption that the reader knows the characters or events, and this knowledge causes the reader to make associations that clarify a point. Mary E. Ryan used the following allusion in *The Trouble with Perfect*: "Brian started making ravenous gurgling sounds and lurching around the kitchen like the Hunchback of Wheaton" (Ryan, 1995, p. 9).

CONTEXT CLUE STRATEGIES

Blachowicz and Zabroske (1990) found that students did not automatically use **context** to comprehend text. They found that students have to learn to look for and use **context clues**. Stahl (1999) found that learning the different types of context clues and related exercises did not increase students' vocabulary growth. However, a teacher who used a think-aloud that involved revealing his thinking as he read a selection and called students' attention to context clues and how to implement them was successful with the approach. Example 3.4 illustrates a type of think-aloud for business education terms.

Teachers facilitate students' learning by encouraging them to read backward and forward to locate clues and to generate hypotheses about word meaning; then students can test alternative possibilities to see if their predicted meaning makes sense. To refine word meaning, readers can use context clues in combination with the dictionary or glossary. For example, the word *rendezvous* appears in this passage: "Bourgoyne took four weeks to reach the Hudson. Still confident, he looked forward to the rendezvous" (Garcia et al., 2001, p. 197). The glossary provides this definition:

**SOCIAL
STUDIES**

"rendezvous (RAHN day voo) n. a meeting" (Garcia et al., 2001, p. R56). The reader who combines these two sources of information learns that Bourgoyne was planning to meet someone or something. However, the authors of this text also helped the reader by explaining *rendezvous* in the text. The reader continued through the sentence: "Still confident, he looked forward to the rendezvous, or meeting, with St. Leger and Howe in Albany."

Another strategy for developing students' understanding of context clues is "Possible Sentences." "Possible Sentences" give students opportunities to experience a variety of contexts for the vocabulary they are studying. Stahl and Kapinus (1991) found that "Possible Sentences" significantly improved students' recall of word meanings and their comprehension of text containing those words. In this strategy the teacher supplies target words from a selection and the students try to make sentences that are true or "possible," using two or more of the target words. Then students read the textbook to verify the accuracy of the sentences they constructed and modify the sentences, if necessary. In a variation of this strategy, the instructor chooses target words and constructs sentences with these words. The sentence context should be "Possible" in some instances and "Impossible" in others. Students can suggest ways to change "Impossible" ones to make them "Possible." When working with struggling readers, this is a practice activity for students to use after they have studied the words and read content including those words. The following sentences illustrate this activity:

1. After lengthy consideration, Melissa made an (impetuous) decision.

2. My mother was (maudlin) after my father's death.

3. Kay was (euphoric) after her dog died.

EXAMPLE 3.4   **Business Concepts**

**BUSINESS
EDUCATION**

How does the author help you understand total quality management (TQM)?

Why is it important to ensure quality control?

Deming began by studying how companies ensure that the products they produce are not defective. He came up with a mathematically based approach to quality control that became known as total quality management. **Total quality management** (TQM) is a system of management based on involving all employees in a constant process of improving quality and productivity by improving how they work. This approach, which has been widely adopted by American businesses, focuses on totally satisfying both customers and employees.

Source: Leslie W. Rue and Lloyd L. Byars, *Business Management* (New York: Glencoe McGraw-Hill, 2001), p. 45. Reprinted by permission of Glencoe McGraw-Hill.

CHOOSING WORDS

How are general
vocabulary, specialized
vocabulary, and
technical vocabulary
different from one
another?

Teachers should examine content reading materials to identify potentially difficult words before giving reading assignments. In time, their experience will enable them to recognize words that give students problems year after year. Teachers should also decide which vocabulary-development technique is most likely to help students learn the identified words. Some words are best learned through context clues, whereas others must become sight words, and others are learned best with morphemic analysis (i.e., based on word roots and affixes). Example 3.5 shows a page from a content textbook with troublesome words underlined by the teacher.

In general, learners need three categories of words. The first is general vocabulary, consisting of common words that have generally accepted meanings. These words appear in both content reading materials and general reading materials. Words such

EXAMPLE 3.5   Identifying Troublesome Words

The Physical Evidence

Shigemura uses <u>physics</u> and math to reconstruct an accident, charting the precise path the vehicles must have taken before the crash to end up as they did. For example, he uses the formula $S = \sqrt{30df}$ to <u>calculate</u> a car's minimum speed S in miles per hour at the moment the car begins to <u>skid</u>. In the formula, d = the length in feet of the skid mark left by the car and f = the <u>coefficient</u> of <u>friction</u>. The coefficient of friction is a measure of the slipperiness or stickiness of the road. Shigemura finds d with a tape measure, and determines f with a special device. The <u>matrix</u> at the right shows speeds calculated for several different combinations of d and f.

MATHEMATICS

Calculated Speed S			
		d	
	76	**98**	**123**
0.40	30.19	34.29	38.41
f **0.80**	42.70	48.49	54.33
1.20	52.30	59.39	66.54

$\sqrt{30 \cdot 123 \cdot 0.40} = 38.41$

If d = 123 and f = 0.40, the car was traveling about 38 mi/h when it began to skid.

Source: Miriam A. Leiva and Richard G. Brown, *Algebra I Explorations and Applications* (Boston: McDougal Littell, 1997), p. 238. Photograph courtesy of Nathan S. Shigemura, Illinois State Police.

SOCIAL STUDIES

SCIENCE AND HEALTH

as *neutral* and *mobilize* are in this group. The second category, specialized vocabulary, consists of words having both general and specialized meanings. The word *mouth* is in this group. In general use, *mouth* refers to a facial feature. The word *mouth* also has a specialized meaning in social studies content, as in "mouth of a river." The last category is technical vocabulary, consisting of words representing specific concepts that are applicable to specific content subjects. *Photosynthesis* is an example of a technical word used in scientific content. The vocabulary in all of these categories appears not only in textbooks, but also in literature and reading materials that students encounter in daily life. Therefore, teachers can use real-life reading materials to enhance vocabulary development.

Students are likely to encounter many unknown, or partially known, words as they read literature and textbooks. Teachers generally find it impossible to teach all of the unknown words that students will encounter. If an assignment has twenty-five or thirty unfamiliar words and a teacher devotes one minute to each word, twenty-five to thirty minutes have been spent in vocabulary development, which cuts into other instructional time. Since time and energy constraints make it impossible to devote this amount of time to vocabulary instruction on a regular basis, teachers need to focus on words that are essential to comprehension of the major points in the selection.

Research indicates that teaching key words, or those words essential to understanding concepts developed in a text, prior to reading a selection enhances understanding (Beck, Perfetti, and McKeown, 1982; Kameenui, Carnine, and Freschi, 1982). Students need to learn words they are likely to encounter in subsequent reading in the subject area (high-utility words). Key words are combined to form main ideas and important supporting details. In content area reading, key words are often technical terms whose referents are central to understanding the concepts of the content area. Teachers should examine textbook reading assignments carefully to determine whether the author has assumed that students know words that are actually unknown. After identifying these words, teachers can provide direct instruction focusing on them.

ENGLISH/ LANGUAGE ARTS

Literary material presents a somewhat different vocabulary problem than does exposition because literature includes more symbolic, abstract meanings. Chase and Duffelmeyer (1990) explain that literary text requires a higher level of student involvement than exposition. They want students to realize that knowing a single word can help them accomplish such things as visualizing a character, comprehending a character's motivation, perceiving a theme, and understanding an author's point of view. To achieve this, they created a strategy, VOCAB-LIT, to teach the significant words, like *ingratiating* as used to describe Brother Leon in *The Chocolate War* (Cormier, 1974). This type of word is one that, when fully understood, would reveal an important aspect of the novel. The students complete study sheets that require them to reflect on their personal levels of word knowledge, write the sentence in which the word appears, make connections with content, look the word up in a reference, and discuss what they have learned about the word. After the students learn this strategy, they are each assigned a day for presenting a word to the group. This program has been quite successful.

Having students create a file of vocabulary that they are studying gives them a tool for learning words. The students can develop word cards similar to their study sheets. They should write the word's meaning, three contexts for the word, two or three synonyms, and a sentence using the word. Students can study these cards for quizzes and for exercises similar to "Possible Sentences." Word cards are especially useful for struggling readers and English language learners. They can carry the cards with them to study and to refer to when they are writing.

INSTRUCTIONAL ACTIVITIES

Once specific words have been chosen for a selection, teachers have many options for actually teaching them to students. For instance, a teacher could ask students to write about an experience to illustrate a concept, to write a nonexample for the concept, and, finally, to compose word meanings. Example 3.4, for instance, shows some questions that will help students think about conceptual relationships in exploring business concepts.

A number of the activities presented here could have been discussed under the "Conceptual Reinforcement Instructional Activities" section because they develop concepts and relationships among concepts. We have chosen to highlight them here instead, however, because they are particularly well suited to the instruction of specific targeted words and terms.

Association activities can help students relate concepts to the words that represent them. We can learn unknown words by connecting them with known words that have similar meanings. Students can learn vocabulary for a field trip by viewing a video, listening to a speaker, or reading a text. Students preparing to visit a local courthouse may encounter such terms as *attorney, litigation, defendant,* and *prosecutor.* Teachers can introduce appropriate words on the board, pronounce them, and discuss their meanings, thus giving students opportunities to associate the visual forms of the words with the pronunciations and the meanings. In addition to discussion (see p. 72), association activities include matching exercises, in-depth word study, crossword puzzles, analogies, sorts, and graphic organizers, which can be used for prereading activities or for review. Example 3.6 is an association activity based on a world history text, Example 3.7 is based on a science chapter entitled "States of Matter," and Example 3.8 is based on a chapter on disease in a biology textbook.

SOCIAL STUDIES   SCIENCE AND HEALTH

EXAMPLE 3.6   **History Association Activity**

SOCIAL STUDIES

Directions: Draw a line to connect the words in Column A with the words and phrases that have almost the same meaning in Column B.

A	B
laissez-faire	based on usefulness
capitalism	opposition to government interference in commerce
utilitarianism	perfect living place
socialism	privately owned or corporately owned means of production
utopia	government in control of production and distribution of goods

---

EXAMPLE 3.7   Science Association Activity

SCIENCE AND HEALTH

Directions: Write *S* on the line beside a set of terms if they have the same meaning. Write *D* on the line if the terms have different meanings.

_____ tensile strength—can be pulled apart easily
_____ matter—gas
_____ malleability—lumpiness
_____ ductility—can be drawn into wires

EXAMPLE 3.8   Science Association Activity

SCIENCE AND HEALTH

Directions: Write each term from the list below on the line beside its meaning.

_____ the science of disease
_____ departure from a state of health
_____ biologically inherited disease
_____ signs of illness

pathology	hereditary disease
disease	symptoms
immunity	infectious disease

Describe an in-depth word study.

In-depth word study increases knowledge of word meanings through association. Students using this strategy study all aspects of a word, along with words that are related to it. The content teacher may identify specific words for such study or may ask students to identify words they feel they need to study in greater depth. Students can use their textbooks, a dictionary, and a thesaurus to obtain the necessary information. This activity is illustrated in Example 3.9, which is an in-depth word study of the word *economy*, selected from a social studies text.

How do analogies develop students' vocabulary?

MATHEMATICS

Analogies show a relationship or similarity between two words or ideas. Analogy activities are conceptual and associational, comparing two similar relationships. On one side of the analogy, the two objects or concepts are related in a particular way; on the other side, the objects are related in the same way. For example, in the analogy *triangle : three :: square : four*, the relationship is "geometric figure is to number of sides." An analogy has equal or balanced sides, like those in a mathematical equation.

Content teachers can demonstrate to students how analogies work and how to construct them. After learning how to form analogies, students can create their own.

EXAMPLE 3.9   In-Depth Word Study

SOCIAL STUDIES

Economy: The management of the resources of a country, community, or business: the American economy.

Related Words and Meanings

Economy: (a second meaning) The careful or thrifty use or management of resources; freedom from waste; thrift.
Economics: The science of the production, distribution, and consumption of wealth.

Word Forms
economic, economical, economically, economics, economize, economization, economizer

Opposing Concepts	Related Concepts
liberal	frugal
generous	thrifty
wasteful	save
careless	accumulate
bounteous	amass

This kind of study is especially helpful for college-bound students, who will discover that analogies are popular items on college entrance examinations. Secondary school students are often unfamiliar with the format of analogies; therefore, teachers should explain that the colon (:) represents the words *is to,* and the double colon (::) represents the word *as.* The teacher can provide examples of analogies for the entire class to work through in preparation for analogy practice activities. When working through an analogy example, students should identify the relationship, complete the analogy, and explain their reasoning. Example 3.10 shows an analogy example prepared for a science textbook chapter.

Classification activities help students learn words and concepts by connecting new words with known concepts. When classifying, the student arranges items or information into a given set of categories. There are three steps: (1) identify the categories and their meaning, (2) read the items, and (3) group the items by similarities and association (Johnson and Rasmussen, 1998). To prepare for this activity, the teacher identifies focus words to introduce and writes familiar synonyms or associated words on cards. After being introduced, the new words become category headings, and the students classify the cards according to their relationships to the new words. A classification activity is illustrated in Example 3.11.

EXAMPLE 3.10   Science Analogy Exercise

SCIENCE AND HEALTH

Directions: Select the answer that completes each analogy. Identify the relationship expressed in the analogy, and be prepared to explain your answer.

1. water : dehydration :: vitamins : (mumps, deficiency diseases, jaundice, appendicitis)
2. taste buds : tongue :: villi : (mouth, stomach, small intestine, colon)
3. pepsin : protein :: ptyalin : (oils, fats, starch, sucrose)
4. liver : small intestine :: salivary glands : (mouth, stomach, small intestine, colon)
5. mouth : large intestine :: duodenum : (esophagus, jejunum, ileum, cecum)
6. protein : organic compound :: magnesium : (peptide, vitamin, mineral, salt)
7. pancreas : pancreatic fluid :: stomach : (water, saliva, gastric juices, intestinal fluid)
8. saliva : ptyalin :: pancreatic fluid : (trypsin, amylase, lipase, peptones)

EXAMPLE 3.11   Classification Activity for Science

SCIENCE AND HEALTH

Directions: Read the target words, and classify the words in the word bank into the correct classifications. Then write a short paragraph that includes these words on the back of this paper.

Target words:
Geothermal energy   Fossil fuel

Word bank:
(Written on cards for students to sort.)

coal	oil	renewable	nonrenewable	clean
earth's heat	lava	hot springs	toxins	emissions
foreign fuel dependence	clean air			

Sorts are a classification activity. The items in sorts are categorized according to common characteristics. Sorts may be closed-ended or open-ended. In closed-ended sorts, the common properties of the category are stated, and the students sort words into the categories. In open-ended sorts, no category is stated, and students have to identify the relationships among the concepts, group them together, and define the connection. Example 3.12 illustrates a closed-ended sort, and Example 3.13 illustrates an open-ended sort.

EXAMPLE 3.12 **Closed-Ended Sort for Human Environmental Science (Human Ecology)**

HES/HUMAN ECOLOGY

Directions: Sort the list of words into the following categories: protein, carbohydrates, calcium.

fish	nuts	bread	apples
spaghetti	cheese	kale	broccoli
eggs	sugar	peaches	milk
potatoes	cereal		

EXAMPLE 3.13 **Open-Ended Sort for Secretarial Office Procedures**

BUSINESS EDUCATION

Directions: Classify the following list of words into groups, and identify the common characteristic of each group.

sales invoice	multicopy
purchase order	purchase invoice
bills	horizontal spaces
sales order	binding space
credit memorandum	credit approval

Visual Organizers

Visual organizers can develop depth and breadth of word knowledge and are very useful as prereading activities with large or small groups (Johnson and Rasmussen, 1998). The new vocabulary is introduced and defined in advance. Figure 3.2 shows a Super Word Web (SWW).

Graphic organizers or structured overviews can illustrate hierarchical and/or linear relationships among the key concepts in a content textbook, chapter, or unit. Graphic organizer use is based on Ausubel's (1978) theory that an orderly arrangement of concepts helps students learn them. A graphic organizer gives students a structure for incorporating new concepts with existing concepts, thus helping them anticipate the words and concepts in a content selection.

Hierarchical graphic organizers are used when the relationships portrayed fit into a subordinate-superordinate array. The social studies content in Example 3.14 fits

Which strategy gives students a structure for incorporating new concepts with existing concepts?

FIGURE 3.2

Super Word Web

Source: Andrew Johnson and Jay Rasmussen, "Classifying and Super Word Web: Two Strategies to Improve Productive Vocabulary," *Journal of Adolescent and Adult Literacy* 42(3) (1998, November): 204–207. Reprinted with permission of Andrew Johnson and the International Reading Association. All rights reserved.

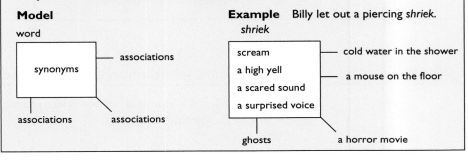

SWW is a technique designed to increase vocabulary development by expanding the breadth as well as the depth of students' word knowledge. This technique can be used in any subject area and implemented as either a pre-reading exercise, an advanced organizer, or a separate vocabulary lesson. While SWWs can be constructed individually, they are generally more effective when two or more students work together and share their ideas.

Procedures

Step 1: See the word in context.
Step 2: List three or four synonyms or defining phrases.
Step 3: List or draw three or four associations.

into a hierarchical array. Barron (1969) recommended the following steps for developing structured overviews:

1. Identify the words (concepts) that are important for students to understand.

2. Arrange the words (concepts) into a structure that illustrates the interrelationships among them.

3. Add to the structure words (concepts) that the students understand in order to show the relationship between the specific learning task at hand and the discipline.

4. Analyze the overview. Are the major relationships shown clearly? Can the overview be simplified and still communicate the important relationships?

The relationships in a structured overview are usually arranged in the following manner:

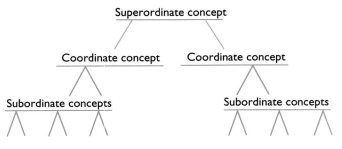

EXAMPLE 3.14   Graphic Organizer for Social Studies

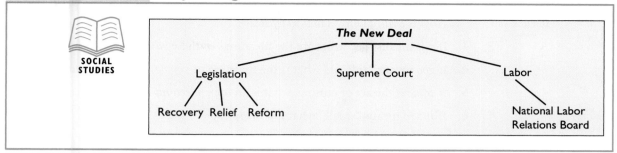

SOCIAL STUDIES

The New Deal

Legislation   Supreme Court   Labor

Recovery   Relief   Reform   National Labor Relations Board

Additional Strategies for Students' Vocabulary Learning

The following additional strategies focus on giving students autonomy in acquiring word meanings. They include morphological analysis, using reference books, expanding definitions, and using computer programs and the Internet.

MORPHOLOGICAL ANALYSIS

What is morphological analysis?

Morphological analysis enables students to identify words rapidly and accurately (Ruddiman, 1993). Morphological analysis is based on identification of a root that carries the base meaning of the word. Affixes, primarily prefixes and suffixes, change the base meaning. *Graph* is a root that means "write," as in *autograph*. Prefixes are word parts added to the front of roots, and suffixes are word parts added to the end of roots. Many of the roots used in content area writing originated in Greek or Latin. Morphological analysis is especially valuable when used in combination with context clues, which help students determine the correct meaning of an affix. Many affixes have multiple meanings, so all meanings that occur frequently should be taught. For example, the suffix *ways* in the word *sideways* can mean "course," "direction," or "manner." When a multiple-meaning affix occurs, students can use context clues to determine which meaning is appropriate. Students can practice using morphological analysis through building new words by combining prefixes and suffixes with various root words. For instance, the word *construct* can be changed in a variety of ways, some of which are illustrated here:

construct	constructing	reconstruct
construction	constructed	reconstruction

To develop morphological analysis, teachers can pose questions that will stimulate students to examine the structural aspects of words. Sample questions that might be used to develop vocabulary in a science class follow:

SCIENCE AND HEALTH

1. If *thermo* means "heat," what is a *thermostat*? a *thermometer*?

2. If *hydro* means "water," what do these words mean: *dehydrate*? *hydrophobia*? How is *hydroplane* related to *hydrant*?

3. If *tele* means "far," what are the meanings of these words: *telescope*? *television*?

4. If *zoo* means "animal," what is the meaning of *zoology*? Who is a *zoologist*?

5. If *tome* is the act of cutting, what is an *appendectomy*?

6. If *micro* means "small," what is a *microscope*?

7. Why would you call *dynamite* and *dynamo* first cousins?

Students can create a web of words (a type of graphic organizer) structured upon a root. Webs may be developed by groups of students or by students working alone. Example 3.15 illustrates a web for the root *migr*, and Example 3.16 illustrates a word web for mathematics.

EXAMPLE 3.15   **Web Graphic Organizer**

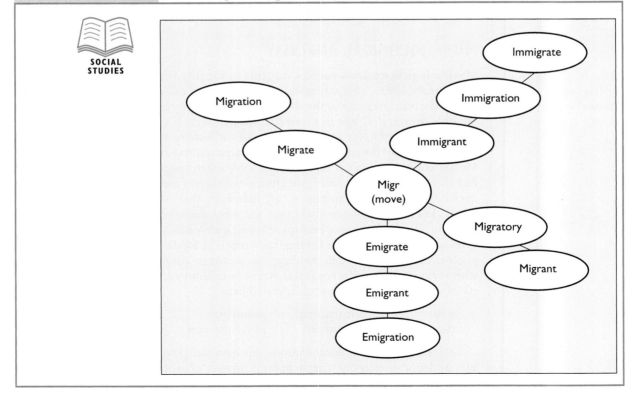

EXAMPLE 3.16   **Word Web for Mathematics**

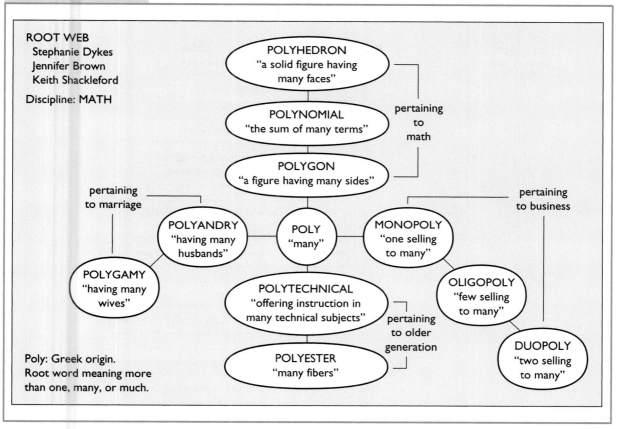

ROOT WEB
Stephanie Dykes
Jennifer Brown
Keith Shackleford

Discipline: MATH

POLYHEDRON
"a solid figure having many faces"

POLYNOMIAL
"the sum of many terms"

POLYGON
"a figure having many sides"

pertaining to math

pertaining to marriage

POLYANDRY
"having many husbands"

POLY
"many"

MONOPOLY
"one selling to many"

pertaining to business

POLYGAMY
"having many wives"

POLYTECHNICAL
"offering instruction in many technical subjects"

OLIGOPOLY
"few selling to many"

pertaining to older generation

Poly: Greek origin.
Root word meaning more than one, many, or much.

POLYESTER
"many fibers"

DUOPOLY
"two selling to many"

Learners find it easier to assimilate new information and to use prior knowledge when they have more connections and interconnections (Rosenshine, 1997). Having a well-connected network of words and rich relationships among concepts makes information meaningful to students and gives them structures for enlarging their word knowledge. Example 3.17 illustrates one approach to "Finding Connections" applied to earth science vocabulary.

USING REFERENCE BOOKS

Reference books, such as dictionaries, thesauruses, and encyclopedias, either printed or computer-based, are useful for developing word meanings. Students can use these reference books in conjunction with prior knowledge, context, and morphological

EXAMPLE 3.17   **Finding Connections: Earth Science Vocabulary**

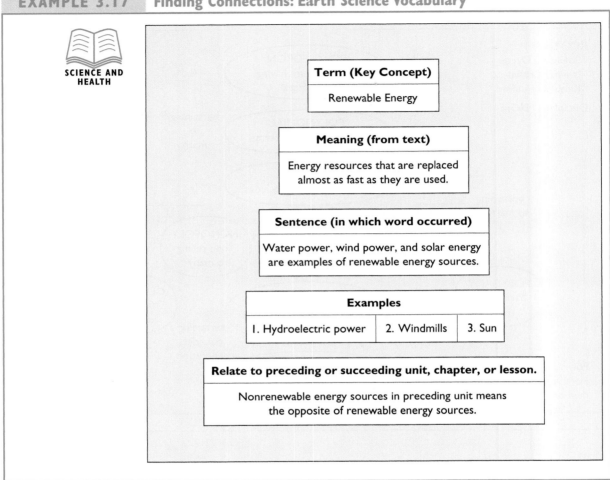

SCIENCE AND HEALTH

Term (Key Concept)
Renewable Energy

Meaning (from text)
Energy resources that are replaced almost as fast as they are used.

Sentence (in which word occurred)
Water power, wind power, and solar energy are examples of renewable energy sources.

Examples		
1. Hydroelectric power	2. Windmills	3. Sun

Relate to preceding or succeeding unit, chapter, or lesson.
Nonrenewable energy sources in preceding unit means the opposite of renewable energy sources.

analysis to build understanding. The following guidelines are useful when teaching the use of references in content classrooms:

1. Help students select the appropriate dictionary definition by using the context in which the word appears. The multiple meanings in dictionary entries are problematic for some students, but with practice, most students can learn how to use content context to identify the appropriate meaning.

2. Identify only a few key concepts for dictionary study. It is perfectly legitimate for teachers to tell students the meanings of unknown words. Secondary students generally are more willing to use the dictionary when they need it if the teacher has not forced them to use it constantly.

EXPANDING DEFINITIONS

Readers have to integrate new words and concepts with existing knowledge in order to apply them in subsequent learning (Nagy and Scott, 2000). Definitions alone provide only superficial word knowledge. Looking up words in a dictionary or memorizing definitions does not reliably increase reading comprehension (Nagy and Scott, 2000). Teachers who have tried this method alone will attest to its failure.

A strictly definitional approach to teaching word meanings fails for a variety of reasons. First, many definitions are not very clear or precise, as illustrated in the following examples:

Sedimentary: Of, containing, resembling, or derived from sediment.
Hogweed: Any of various coarse, weedy plants.

These definitions are accurate, but they would not help a person who did not already know the word meanings. Most of the words in a definition should be familiar to students if they are to understand the definition. In addition, using a form of the defined word in its definition further obscures the meaning, and this occurs in both of the preceding examples.

A second reason that strictly definitional approaches fail is that students may have difficulty choosing the correct definition for a particular context from the several definitions that are given in a dictionary or glossary. Third, many definitions do not give enough information to help students understand words for concepts with which they are unfamiliar. Fourth, definitions do not help learners use a new word. Research shows that students have difficulty writing meaningful sentences utilizing new words when given only definitions of those words (Miller and Gildea, 1987).

Definitions that students themselves generate help them relate new words to prior experiences. Thus, activities like the ones shown in Examples 3. 18 and 3.19 are useful in developing students' understanding.

EXAMPLE 3.18   **Expanding Definitions**

1. Use the word in a sentence that shows its meaning.
   Magnanimous—A magnanimous person would give you the shirt off his back.
2. Give a synonym for the word.
   Magnanimous—generous
3. Give an antonym for the word.
   Magnanimous—selfish
4. State a classification for the word.
   Magnanimity can be classified as a quality of mind and soul.
5. Provide an example of the word. Either draw an illustration or locate a picture to illustrate it.
6. Compare the word with another word.
   Magnanimity is like generosity, but it implies more noble unselfishness.

EXAMPLE 3.19	Content Concept Development for Business Management					

	Concept word and definition	Classification	Example	Synonym	Antonym	Benefits
BUSINESS EDUCATION	*Networking:* talking to people who may offer you job leads, contacts, or other information	Career strategy	Talking with the school guidance counselor or business acquaintances	*connecting*	*disassociating*	Career planning Job leads Informed planning

MNEMONIC STRATEGIES

Mnemonics is a memory-enhancing instructional strategy that involves teaching students to relate new information to existing knowledge. Research with mnemonic strategies verifies the value of these approaches (Mastropieri and Scruggs, 2000; Stoodt-Hill, 2005).

In the classroom, teachers can use these steps to create mnemonics for vocabulary words:

Identify the word (e.g., "ostentatious").
Define the word (e.g., "showy, elaborate").
Write the word on a file card.
Think of a key word (Students discuss key words, but each chooses one that will trigger his or her memory.) Write this on the card.
Draw a picture on the card to help memory (Students may use stick figures, cartoon-like pictures, or magazine pictures).

Example 3.20 shows mnemonic vocabulary cards prepared by students.

COMPUTER PROGRAMS AND THE INTERNET

Computer programs that can help students to develop extensive word understanding are available. Such programs can be motivational learning tools for students, and students can use them independently. The most common types of computer software for vocabulary instruction are cloze passage programs; structural analysis programs; homonym, synonym, and antonym programs; computer dictionaries; and computer thesauruses. The specific software selected depends both on the type of computer available and on the instructional objectives. Software and computers are constantly being changed and upgraded; therefore, it is difficult to recommend specific materials. We do recommend that teachers read this chapter carefully to establish criteria for the vocabulary software they wish to use and that they evaluate available materials based on their own requirements. They will also find it helpful to read the article "Computer-Assisted Vocabulary Instruction" (Wheatley, Muller, and Miller, 1993). Many computer companies and salespeople will provide demonstration copies of software to potential customers for examination before purchase. It is wise to take advantage of this opportunity.

EXAMPLE 3.20   Mnemonic Vocabulary Cards Prepared by Students

The Internet offers a variety of excellent vocabulary sites. One such site is found at http://www.vocabulary.com. This is a dynamic site, so the activities it provides will vary from time to time. An example from this site is shown in the following "Meeting the Challenge" that tells about Emily, who is an eighth-grade student in a Virginia middle school.

MEETING THE CHALLENGE

Emily was a student with average grades who was eager to improve them, so she asked her guidance counselor for assistance. The counselor arranged for testing, which revealed that Emily's vocabulary and fluency were limited. These limitations were influencing her achievement in social studies, science, and English. Unfortunately, the reading teacher reported a full schedule of students whose needs were greater. However, the reading teacher suggested that she go to the computer lab for assistance in accessing http://www.vocabulary.com.

Emily was skeptical about using the computer, but she agreed to give it a try. With the instructor's assistance in the computer lab, she logged on to http://www.vocabulary.com.

Level II, the middle school level, seemed to be the right one for Emily. She started with fill-in-the-blank items based on the roots *ject, lect, leg, lig, pend, pent*. The meanings of these roots and the context provided in the puzzle were very helpful. After completing the blanks, she submitted the exercise to the site administrator; she received a page that showed her answers and the correct answers and a page of correct definitions with examples of the words used in sentences. Then she moved to a match-the-definition exercise with the same words, including *objective, pendant, diligently, perpendicular, intelligentsia, illegible, conjecture, legacy, pendulum, adjacent, projection*, and *appendage*. Synonym-and-antonym word encounters with the

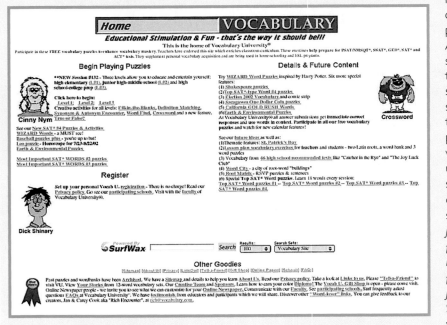

Reprinted with permission of Vocabulary University.

same set of words came up next, followed by a crossword puzzle based on these words. After completing these four meaningful exercises with a single set of words, Emily developed some confidence that significantly increased the following day, when she encountered two of these words in textbook assignments.

As Emily progressed, her content teachers became interested and encouraged other students to use the computer to expand their vocabularies. The teachers also discovered vocabulary activities for novels they were teaching as well as topical vocabularies that fit into their teaching plans.

SUMMARY

Students who have large stores of word meanings comprehend content materials better than students who have limited vocabularies. Since many of the words used in content materials are labels for concepts, concept development is also an important goal of content area instruction. Knowing a word means understanding the concept it represents and the ability to use it in various contexts. Because content materials frequently contain a high proportion of unknown words, it is impossible for teachers to teach students every word they do not know. Therefore, teachers should focus on key vocabulary as well as on developing students' independent word-learning skills. Research shows that direct teaching of vocabulary increases students' word knowledge. Struggling readers and English language learners are especially responsive to direct instruction.

DISCUSSION QUESTIONS

1. Why is experience central to vocabulary instruction?
2. What does it mean to know a word?
3. What are the weaknesses of a definitional approach to developing vocabulary?
4. Explain the meaning of *concepts* in your own words.
5. What are the strengths and weaknesses of context clues in deriving word meanings?
6. Why do you think practice is so important in developing students' ability to derive meaning from context?
7. What basic principles should teachers know in order to develop vocabulary with struggling readers?
8. Compare vocabulary instruction for English language learners with instruction for struggling readers.
9. Why is learning English vocabulary and concepts usually easier for students who have a well-developed first language?

ENRICHMENT ACTIVITIES

1. Prepare a categorization activity, as illustrated in Examples 3.11 through 3.13, for a chapter from a content area textbook or nonfiction trade book of your choice.
*2. Prepare seven activities to develop vocabulary for a particular trade book or textbook.
3. Select a chapter in a content area book, and identify the vocabulary you would teach to a class. Plan ways to teach the chosen terms. Following is a list of content areas and the key concepts that might be found in a chapter in each area.

MUSIC   **SCIENCE AND HEALTH**

FOREIGN LANGUAGES   **ART**

SOCIAL STUDIES

Music: choreographer, prologue, prompter, score, overture, prelude, libretto, aria

Health: bacteria, virus, protozoan, metazoan, fungus, carbuncle, psoriasis, shingles, scabies, eczema

Foreign language: masculine, feminine, gender, predicate, cognate, singular

Art: introspective, mural, appreciation, technique, expression, property, exhibition, contemporary, interpret

Psychology: learning curve, plateau, hierarchy, massed practice, feedback, frame, negative transfer, retention, overlearning

Government: delinquent, incorrigibility, omnibus, exigency, indeterminate, adjudicated, arbitrariness, interrogation, formulation, juvenile

4. Develop a procedure for in-depth study of a word.

*5. Make a graphic organizer for a selection in a content area textbook or a nonfiction trade book.

6. Prepare an analogy exercise sheet (similar to the one in Example 3.10) for a chapter or unit in a content area text.

*7. Visit www.vocabulary.com and complete some of the exercises available.

*8. Plan a lesson for struggling readers using a text chapter from a content area text.

*9. Plan a lesson for English language learners (ELLs) using a text chapter from a content area text.

---

*These activities are designed for in-service teachers, student teachers, and practicum students.

Chapter 4

The Process of Constructing Meaning in Texts

OVERVIEW

Transactions among the reader, the text, and the situational context result in comprehension, an understanding of what the student has read. Change is a defining element of life today. Comprehension needs have changed to meet the demands of the information and communication technologies that are continuously emerging in our world (Leu, 2002). Existing comprehension strategies can be adjusted and applied to meet the demands of multiple literacies, as well as emerging technologies (Schmar-Dobler, 2003).

Readers today face the challenge of comprehending multiple types of content in varying contexts for complex purposes. They may read text on a computer screen and communicate about it with another student across the United States or around the world. High-stakes tests that are a part of the standards-based movement are another source of escalating literacy demands. Successful comprehenders are active readers who read fluently. They use strategies to actively monitor their own cognitive processes (applying metacognitive ability). In this chapter, the first of two chapters that address the process of acquiring meaning and constructing knowledge, the goals are to develop your understanding of the comprehension process and to present strategies that students can implement as they read from various media. Chapter 5 focuses on comprehension strategies employed before, during, and after reading.

PURPOSE-SETTING QUESTIONS

As you read this chapter, try to answer these questions:

1. How are multiple literacies related to content reading?
2. What do successful readers do when they read?
3. Why are good comprehenders active readers?
4. Why is fluency an important aspect of reading comprehension?

Multiple Literacies and Reading Comprehension

Why are multiple
literacies important
today?

Literacy cannot be considered a single generic skill or ability. The scope of literacy has greatly broadened to include **multiple literacies**, such as understanding information on CDs, on World Wide Web browsers, on the Internet, in e-mail, in video-conferences, and in games (Leu, 2002). "New literacies build on, but do not replace, previous literacies" (Leu, 2002, p. 3). Secondary students today need conceptually rich engagements with a broad array of materials to develop comprehension in these varied and rapidly changing materials. However, the rapidly changing nature of the new media makes *learning how to learn* a significant aspect of addressing multiple literacies. Moreover, readers have to read critically, since anyone can publish material on the World Wide Web (Leu, 2002). The importance of fluency to comprehension has escalated because students have to comprehend more text from more sources for multiple purposes.

The challenge of multiple literacies is illustrated by the literacy activities of an adolescent girl during one day:

- She went on the Internet to find coupons for purchases she wished to make.
- While online she consulted a weather site to determine whether she could go sailing.
- She read the e-mail messages delivered to the in-box of her Internet e-mail account and responded to them.
- She used an Internet search engine to locate material for a science paper and then discussed the science paper with a classmate via instant messaging.
- She read class assignments in content textbooks and reference books.
- She read CD labels and selected a CD to play.
- She used the public library computer to search for books, located the books, and checked them out.
- She called friends and invited them over to watch a movie on a DVD and read an article in a fashion magazine while she waited for them to arrive.
- She read a mystery novel before bedtime.

READING COMPREHENSION

What is reading
comprehension?

Reading comprehension has been defined in many ways, each of which contributes to our understanding of the process. However, for our purposes we use a common definition for teachers. Comprehension is a process in which active readers construct meaning by interacting with text through the combination of prior knowledge and previous experience, information in the text, and the stance the reader takes in relationship to the text (Pardo, 2004). Although it is insufficient by itself, the text provides the knowledge, language, and framework for understanding. Meaning is expressed differently in fiction, nonfiction, and poetry; therefore, text form (genre) has an impact on comprehension.

What is a reading transaction?

The word *transaction* indicates that readers interact with the text content, using their vocabulary, experiences, world knowledge, skills, motivation, and strategies to construct meaning. Readers use schemata, mental organizations of personal experiences and world knowledge that provide a basis for interpretation, comprehension, and expectations of text. Schema theory is discussed in later sections of this chapter.

Reading comprehension includes the reader's characteristics (reader context), the text being read (text context), and the total situation (e.g., audience, purpose, importance to the reader), all of which affect the process. All of these areas are discussed in this chapter.

What is fluency?

The emphasis on reading **fluency** is increasing because we have come to realize that fluent readers comprehend at high levels (Griffith and Rasinski, 2004; Kuhn, 2004/2005). "Reading fluency is the ability to read accurately, quickly, effortlessly, and with appropriate expression and meaning" (Griffith and Rasinski, 2004, p. 24). Readers who have to decode words in a text cannot concentrate on understanding. On the other hand, readers who automatically read words can concentrate fully on the text meaning; thus, they are able to comprehend the text at higher levels than their less fluent counterparts (Wren et al., 2000). This explains why vocabulary and comprehension are so closely related (see Chapter 3).

Active Readers

Active readers are engaged. They are motivated and thoughtful (Guthrie, 2000). Active readers seek to understand; they enjoy reading and learning. When content makes sense, readers actively engage in the reading process because they have some ownership of the activity (Langer and Applebee, 1987). When readers understand this relationship, and the relevance of reading to their lives, they will invest greater energy and increase comprehension (Guthrie, 2000).

Readers who actively engage with text increase their level of comprehension. Active reading focuses attention on the text and eliminates students' tendencies to allow their thinking to wander from the text. Self-Questioning and Question/Answer Relationships are useful strategies to encourage active reading.

THE CONTEXT FOR ACTIVE READERS

The reader's context is composed of his or her attitudes, interests, purposes, predictions, prior knowledge, and skills. Reading comprehension is situated in the reader's world, including his or her world knowledge, as well as his or her social and cultural world. The contexts of comprehension include all of the activity that occurs around the reading transaction (Jetton and Alexander, 2001).

Teachers are a part of the classroom environment. Teachers create contexts for active reading when they supply knowledge goals (purposes); real-world connections for text; and choices about what, when, and how to read. Teachers can teach comprehension strategies. Students are invited into reading in a classroom where teachers value reading and provide books at various levels on a broad array of subjects. When students are asked to discuss a text, generate questions from the text, or identify the big idea, these activities form a context for them to interact with the text. The same reading assignment at another time or place might result in a different meaning (Pardo, 2004).

In summary, the three contexts of reading comprehension are the reader's context, the context of the text, and situational context. Active readers also apply metacognitive skills to assess their own comprehension. These thinking skills enable students to reflect on whether they have comprehended the text. The next "Meeting the Challenge" addresses concerns with the context of the text.

MEETING THE CHALLENGE

Group work can help with comprehension instruction.
© Susie Fitzhugh

Sam Yung, a first-year teacher, faced early problems with his world history class. The opening unit in the text was on Rome. He discovered that the students read their assignments, but they could not sort out important details from unimportant ones and they could not recognize main ideas. This caused them to answer main idea questions with trivial details. He reviewed his objectives for this section of the textbook and identified three concepts or main topics that he planned to develop with the students. These main topics structured the chapter: Roman government, Roman culture, and Roman beliefs (religions). After reviewing his objectives, Sam thought about ways that he could help the students identify the main ideas and the details that supported each main idea. He recognized that he needed to work with the students in a way that would stimulate their thinking. First, he did a think-aloud with a paragraph from the text that modeled his thinking as he identified the main idea and supporting details. This model helped his students understand ways they could think when identifying main ideas and supporting details. Then he explained the three major concepts developed in the chapter and related the paragraph to the concept of Roman government.

After his initial preparation, Sam divided the class into three groups. He assigned each group one of the concepts he planned to develop. Then he explained that the group members were to read the assignment and identify the important details related to their topic. The students wrote each detail on an index card and the group discussed each detail and its relationship to the concept. The members of each group were expected to agree regarding the important details that were related to their topic. When they completed reading and categorizing text information, group members served as experts on their topic and answered questions posed by the other groups. Finally, each group prepared a map of their main ideas and supporting details that they shared with the other groups. This process helped the students understand the relationship between main ideas and supporting details.

After completing the chapter, Sam decided to use this strategy with the next chapter to further the students' understanding of main ideas and supporting details and to give them additional practice in discerning these ideas and details.

SELF-QUESTIONING

What is an example of self-questioning?

Self-questioning is a means of encouraging active reading, and students can learn to control their own thought processes by employing this technique. Self-questioning can be initiated with questions such as "What is the main idea in this paragraph (selection)?" and "Is there anything I don't understand in this paragraph (selection)?" Teachers can demonstrate the different types of questions (literal, inferential, evaluative, and creative) and then have students work individually or in pairs to generate questions related to their readings. (See Chapter 5 for additional discussion of questions or more information about question types.)

An exercise like that in Example 4.1 is useful in guiding students to generate questions after they are given instruction on question types.

EXAMPLE 4.1   **Guide for Generating Questions**

Directions: Read the assigned selection, then write a question about the selection at each level indicated, and answer the remaining questions.
1. Literal question:
2. Inferential question:
3. Evaluative question:
4. Creative question:
5. What is the main idea of the selection?
6. What things in this selection do you not understand?

QUESTION/ANSWER RELATIONSHIPS (QARs)

Question/answer relationships (QARs) provide another strategy that can be used to increase comprehension and active reading. This strategy focuses on the processes for generating answers to questions and on the relationships between questions and answers. Students are encouraged to think of sources for answers to questions. The following ideas are included to help teachers guide students when using this strategy:

1. First, the student looks in the text for the words used in the question and tries to identify these words in a sentence that answers the question. If he or she does this, the answer is "Right There," because the question is directly answered in the text.

2. Next, the student tries "Think and Search," which involves using information from one or more sentences or paragraphs to answer the question.

3. If the question does not have an answer in the text, it is considered "On My Own" and is answered from the reader's knowledge.

4. Still other questions, referred to as "Author and Me," are inferential questions that the reader answers by combining his or her knowledge with the information in the text.

When teaching students to use QARs, teachers should begin with short texts and work up to longer ones. Students should have immediate feedback on their responses. The goal is to have them become independent in applying the four relationships: Right There; Think and Search; On My Own; Author and Me. Example 4.2 illustrates the QAR strategy applied to mathematics.

EXAMPLE 4.2

QAR for Math (Developed by Stephanie Dykes, Jennifer Brown, and Keith Shackleford)

MATHEMATICS

1. *Right There:* State the multiplicative identity.

   answer: For any number a, $a \cdot 1 = 1 \cdot a = a$.

2. *Think and Search:* Name the property illustrated by the following statement: If $8 + 1 = 9$, then $9 = 8 + 1$.

   answer: symmetric

   *This is a Think and Search because the book gives a problem similar to it.

3. *Author and Me:* Lincoln's Gettysburg address began "Four score and seven years ago, . . ." Write an expression to represent four score and seven. How many years is that?

   answer: $4(20) + 7 = 87$ years

   *This is Author and Me because it involves the material in the section, but incorporates the learner's own experience. (score = 20)

4. *On My Own:* If 4 quarters = $1.00 and $1.00 = 10 dimes, then 4 quarters = 10 dimes. Is this true? On your own, think of a money combination similar to the one above using any amount of money.

   answer: may vary

   *This is On My Own because this problem could be done without even reading the textbook, yet it is related to the section.

Based on material from: Foster, Gell, Gordon, et al. *Algebra 1: Applications and Connections* (Lake Forest, Illinois: Glencoe, 1992), pp. 22–25.

Linguistic and Cognitive Components of Comprehension

What linguistic factors function in comprehension?

Language and cognitive competence are foundations for understanding content texts. **Literacy** involves the reader's language and thought that he or she engages in to make sense of and communicate ideas in a variety of situations. The student's underlying cognitive and linguistic skills are precursors of his or her ability to comprehend. A student comprehends most successfully when he or she reads meaningful materials that connect with his or her schemata, while studying for relevant purposes that link text with listening, speaking, and writing. Literacy above all involves communication. An understanding of both semantics and syntax is essential to comprehension (McKenna, Robinson, and Miller, 1990). **Semantics** refers to word meaning. **Syntax** is concerned with the word order in sentences and paragraphs. Both semantics and syntax are important when a reader uses context clues to aid comprehension.

A content text comprises the author's explanations, descriptions, and information. Authors use vocabulary and syntax to express the meaning they wish to convey. Textbook language is more formal than readers' conversational language. Moreover, the vocabulary in content texts is more technical, which imposes additional comprehension difficulties for some students. When the language of the text is different from the students' language, students have more difficulty understanding it.

Schema theory explains cognitive functions that undergird both comprehension and content reading instruction. Figure 4.1 shows some of the major aspects of readers' cognitive processing in comprehension.

What cognitive and metacognitive abilities function in comprehension?

Metacognition (metacomprehension) is thinking about one's own thinking and controlling one's own learning (Pressley, 2002). Researchers generally agree that metacognition involves knowledge and self-regulation, as well as motivation. According to research, reading metacognition includes knowledge of (1) the self as a learner; (2) the demands of the reading task; and (3) the relationships among text, prior knowledge, reading strategies, and reading comprehension. When students are conscious of their own thinking and comprehension, they try different strategies to fix their comprehension. They are responsible for their own comprehension. Acquiring metacognitive skills helps students to become independent readers.

Cognitive strategies that are most useful in the metacognitive process include activating prior knowledge, establishing a purpose for reading, identifying important ideas, reading critically, and using reflection and self-questioning to evaluate understanding. The following scenario illustrates the metacognitive process.

MATHEMATICS

Chris Thompson, a secondary school math student, was assigned a unit about sampling that served as preparation for statistical analysis. He established prereading purpose questions to guide his reading. After reading the text, he reviewed these questions. This helped him realize that he understood the overall process of sampling, but could not define the terms *variance*, *population*, and *population parameter*. He recognized that he needed to reread specific portions of the text to locate and study the important terms.

FIGURE 4.1

**Major Aspects of
Thinking in
Comprehension**

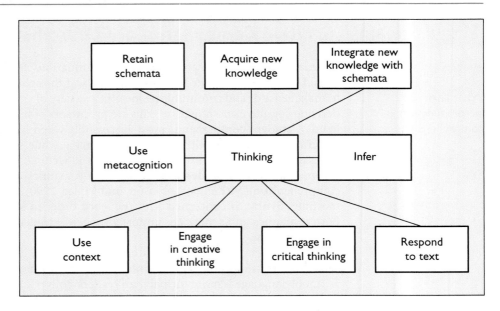

COGNITIVE FLEXIBILITY AND
THE SITUATIONAL CONTEXT

What learning
situations require
cognitive flexibility?

**SCIENCE AND
HEALTH**

Cognitive flexibility is concerned with more complex learning situations that go beyond what can be described by a simple application of schema theory (Jetton and Alexander, 2001; Bean, 2001). For example, an earth science instructor developed a schema for renewable energy with his class studying energy sources. He then decided to extend students' learning by exploring the multiple perspectives of the various groups that could be concerned with renewable energy sources and the impact of these sources on their lives, earning power, environment, and so forth. The students drew from a variety of schemata as they explored the issues that could arise from developing renewable energy sources. Example 4.3 illustrates the various multiple perspectives the students explored. This example illustrates the fact that a single schema could not account for the multiple interrelationships examined. Cognitive flexibility is related to the **situational context**.

THE SITUATIONAL CONTEXT

Readers have a situational context for reading. Consider the differences in perspective among a physician, a pharmacist, and a patient reading a text. Readers have to adjust their points of view to fit the purpose, to apply cognitive flexibility, and to activate schemata appropriate to the literary experience. Situational context involves the *stance*, the *purposes*, that readers have for reading, writing, and learning. It gives form to the literacy experience as well as the mode for expressing a response (reaction).

EXAMPLE 4.3   Multiple Perspectives

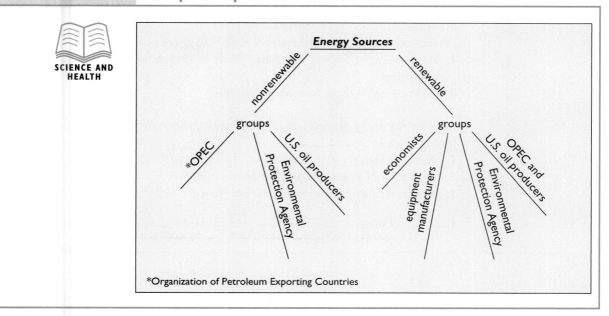

SCIENCE AND
HEALTH

*Organization of Petroleum Exporting Countries

Authentic purposes help students recognize that content is meaningful and connected to their lives. When giving students a reading assignment or an inquiry task that involves reading and writing, teachers guide and focus readers' attention through identifying a **stance**, which is a point of view or perspective that integrates the text and the situational context. Reader stance influences the reader's response and comprehension. The two major stances are aesthetic and efferent (Rosenblatt, 1985). Aesthetic reading is that which leads to a pleasurable, interesting experience for its own sake. Efferent reading focuses on the meanings and ideas in the text.

Readers may interpret a text one way when reading for general understanding, but their interpretation changes when they apply ideas in real life because the context has changed. A reader's interpretation often changes after discussing a story with another student who has a different slant on a character or story incident. Research indicates that students' understanding changes over time, with readers relating ideas to a larger context and focusing on bigger ideas rather than the details that initially captured their interests (Stoodt and Amspaugh, 1994). Considering various points of view and connections among ideas helps students organize main ideas and clarify their importance relative to details (Jetton and Alexander, 2001). Example 4.4 illustrates a point-of-view guide for U.S. history.

The situational context is also concerned with the group in which the instruction occurs, which may be a large group, a small group, an individual, or a pull-out group meeting outside of the classroom. Reading purposes and assignments often determine the nature of the group.

EXAMPLE 4.4   Point-of-View Guide for U.S. History

SOCIAL STUDIES

Topic: War Breaks Out in Europe

Look at the murder of Archduke Ferdinand from these points of view:

1. As an average citizen of the United States in 1914, how would you feel about this event?
2. As President Wilson, how would you feel?

Examine the entry of the United States into World War I from these perspectives (points of view):

1. A recent immigrant from Hungary
2. The family of a person who died on the *Lusitania*
3. The child of a man who was gassed in France

Source: Guide based on four sections from *Creating America: A History of the United States* by J. Garcia, D. Ogle, C. F. Risinger, J. Stevos, and W. Jordan (Boston: McDougal Littell, 2001).

SOCIAL STUDIES

A situational context may address real-life or simulated circumstances that focus students' comprehension (Tierney, 1990). The contexts build students' motivation, curiosity, and insight, and students need literacy skills to acquire information or skills to solve problems that have meaning for them. A simulated situational context for social studies could provide a student with the context of an individual who was elected to the House of Representatives. As a woman and parent of three children, she has a particular perspective. She needs to understand government, law, and the economic impact of various proposals as she debates issues.

The role of situation-based comprehension and its relationship to real-life learning will be further discussed in Chapter 5.

Schema Theory

Schemata are mental networks of knowledge, information, and experiences stored in long-term memory. Learning occurs when we integrate new ideas with the ideas stored in long-term memory. "This can occur through adding new information to preexisting schemata (assimilation), or discarding prior knowledge and replacing it with something different (accommodation)" (Lloyd, 1998, p. 185). As learning occurs, the categories within a schema are modified, and new categories are built to form additional schemata within a more general schema.

The most efficient reading occurs when the schemata established in a reader's mind match the organization of the reading material. When stored knowledge relates to new information, readers can use both their schemata and the incoming information to predict language, organization, and ideas and to form hypotheses about the text. Then they read to confirm, discount, and revise their theories. Readers' schemata enable them to read actively and comprehend. These expectations about text increase comprehension and fall into two categories: those based on content schemata and those based on textual schemata.

SCHEMATA TYPES AND RELATIONSHIPS

Content schemata are based on world knowledge. We have only to contrast a sports-loving student's comprehension of the sports section of the newspaper with his or her understanding of a chapter of social studies to understand the significant role schemata play in comprehension. This student uses schemata developed from years of experience for a context, or frame of reference, just as a child development student who has had baby-sitting experiences with younger brothers and sisters has a context for understanding a child development text.

How are content schemata different from textual schemata?

Textual schemata are the basis for multiple literacies. Readers' knowledge of and experience with different forms of written discourse prepare them to read a variety of content. Prior knowledge of the structural characteristics of written language enables readers to anticipate, follow, and organize it. Prior knowledge also enables students to find information within a text and to sort important ideas from unimportant ideas (Pressley, 2000). For example, a reader expects a textbook to have a particular form, and that form differs greatly from that of a novel. Readers expect the essential information in textbooks to be organized with headings, subheadings, theses, and main ideas, whereas fiction reveals its plot, characters, theme, and so forth throughout the story. Structural knowledge like this creates links to future literacy experiences.

What is the technical term for links built from one text to another?

Intertextuality is concerned with the links between the ideas gleaned from one text and those discovered in another text or texts. Gradually, readers build a complex series of connections among the texts they have read (Carrney, 1990). Research reveals that, as readers generate links between ideas, events, and people, they use links within a given passage as well as links between different passages. They also use textual resources such as videos, class lectures, conversations, and books (Hartman, 1992). Comprehension is facilitated when text materials provide intertextual links. Moreover, intertextual links help students develop schemata.

BUILDING SCHEMATA

What are some schemata-building activities?

Teachers can help students build schemata in a variety of ways, using activities such as discussion; drama; storytelling; oral reading of all types of literature; viewing television shows, videos, and Internet sites; examining models; and using computer software. Preteaching vocabulary, as discussed in Chapter 3, increases background experience and conceptual development. Multimedia presentations of related knowledge build secondary students' interests, knowledge, textual schemata, multicultural schemata, and so on. For instance, in an eleventh-grade American literature course,

**ENGLISH/
LANGUAGE
ARTS**

teachers used folklore and family sayings such as those found in Benjamin Franklin's *Autobiography* and *Poor Richard's Almanac* to develop students' schemata for the U.S. colonial period. Then these students sought personal family materials, such as letters, diaries, and photographs, to build a sense of history (Renner and Carter, 1992).

ACTIVATING SCHEMATA

What is the function
of reading guides?

When students activate appropriate schemata, they can anticipate the author's ideas and information and make inferences about content (filling in missing ideas and information) because an author cannot concretely explain all of his or her ideas. Teachers can help students activate schemata by posing questions or developing vocabulary, which also encourages students' active, engaged reading.

What is a preview
guide?

Many of the strategies and activities in this chapter are designed for activating students' schemata. For example, **reading guides**, especially **preview guides**, can help students relate what they are about to read to their own experiential backgrounds. In its simplest form, the preview guide may be a request to, for example, "list everything you already know about word processing." Another style of preview guide provides students with a list of statements to review and respond to before reading; after completing the assignment, students return to the guide to verify whether or not their statements are substantiated by the reading (resulting in a *reaction guide*). Students may also be asked to revise statements that were proved wrong by the text and to put question marks beside items that were not addressed in the reading. All three types of items are appropriate for class discussion; teachers can ask students to respond to items before reading and have them check their answers after reading. The highly structured preview guides are often called *anticipation guides*. One such guide is shown in Example 4.5. Another type of reading guide is presented in Example 4.6.

Reader-Response Theory

According to **reader-response theory**, a literary work is actualized only through a transaction between a reader and a text. Readers' responses related to a reading assignment or selection can range from total absorption to complete lack of interest. Response theory is based on a continuum that ranges from aesthetic response at one end and efferent response at the opposite end (Rosenblatt, 1978).

Aesthetic response is characterized by readers' personal feelings about a story or text. This response may be expressed through art, music, drama, or composition. At the other end of the continuum, **efferent responses** focus on knowledge, information, and facts. Content teachers are usually most interested in the efferent response; however, they should encourage and respect both students' aesthetic and efferent responses.

Lloyd (1998) points out that a reaction log like the one shown in Example 4.7 provides a means of expressing both aesthetic and efferent responses. The comparison/contrast guide shown in Example 4.8 illustrates efferent response.

EXAMPLE 4.5   Preview Guide

Directions: Before you read the chapter, respond to the following statements by placing a check mark beside those statements that you think will be supported by the material in the chapter. After you finish reading the chapter, check the accuracy of your responses.

1. Reference sources made available by computer technology include the Internet, CDs, and DVDs.
2. CDs are useful only for games.
3. A CD or DVD can hold large amounts of information.
4. A CD or DVD can store text material and sound, but it cannot store video information containing motion.
5. To use a CD or DVD, your computer must be connected to the Internet.
6. Material found on the Internet has been carefully checked by authorities and is certified to be true.
7. Using a search engine is a good way to search for material on the Internet.
8. Computers connected to the Internet that hold information available to Internet users are called "servers."
9. Since Internet addresses are all permanent, if you find an Internet address in a textbook, you can be sure it will connect you to a server that has the material described in the textbook.
10. Since the information available through the Internet is stored on only a few computers, it is likely that all the information you need for a report will be on one server.

EXAMPLE 4.6   Social Science Guide

SOCIAL
STUDIES

Topic: Terrorism
Purpose Question: How does terrorism relate to me?

A What I already knew	B What I now know	C What I don't know
Terrorism is extending to many countries.	Terrorists are secretive; even those closest to them do not know what they are doing.	How much danger are we in?
Great Britain is the latest country to suffer from terrorism.		Where in the U.S. are terrorists most likely to strike?
The ways that our lives have changed since 9/11.	They use various bombs and tricks to kill and injure people.	What can I do?

Answer to Purpose Question: I have to be vigilant, because terrorists are a danger worldwide.

EXAMPLE 4.7   Reaction Log for Human Environmental Science

HES/HUMAN ECOLOGY

I learned	My response
How to find quality childcare.	I did not realize that babysitters had to be so knowledgable.
The personal characteristics that a caregiver needs.	I liked babysitters who read to me.
The skills a caregiver needs.	I think a caregiver should be able to prepare food and feed a child.
The knowledge a caregiver needs.	I read in the newspaper that you should not put a baby on its stomach because of SIDS.

THE TEXTUAL CONTEXT OF READING COMPREHENSION

The quality of a text is important in the comprehension of both fiction and nonfiction. Both **text organization** and **text coherence** contribute to comprehension, for example, whether or not readers develop logical understandings of historical periods and historical topics. Two major flaws are common in the content and presentation of texts. First, textbook authors often assume that students have a greater variety and depth of prior knowledge than is actually the case, providing an excellent argument for teachers to develop schemata in preparation for reading.

Second, the presentation in texts can lack **coherence**. Logical organization of the material can help students follow the ideas presented. Beck and others (1991) found that texts tended to present many facts with little explanation. This situation makes it difficult for readers to adjust their thinking to the organization of the selection and to follow the author's line of thought. Well-developed paragraphs are easier to understand, because each of them focuses on a single major topic, and a logical sequence of sentences is used in the structure. The sentences have coherence; they are related to the paragraph topic and to one another. In contrast, a poorly organized paragraph does not establish a focus, and the sentences frequently are not related to one another and are not presented in a logical order.

The following are examples of a well-developed paragraph and a poorly developed paragraph.

How can authors create coherence?

Why are well-organized paragraphs easier to comprehend?

Paragraph A: Flowers bloom throughout the world. They grow on high mountains at the edges of the snow. Other flowers grow in the shallow parts of oceans. Even hot, dry deserts have bright blossoms. The only places where flowers do not grow are on the ice-covered areas of the Arctic and Antarctic and in the open seas.

Paragraph B: Flowers are the reproductive parts of flowering plants. Flowers bloom throughout the world. They grow on high mountains and in the oceans. Many flowers have a smell that attracts birds and insects. Flowers bloom in the hot, dry desert during the rainy season. The only places flowers do not grow are the Arctic, the Antarctic, and the open seas.

SCIENCE AND HEALTH

If you identified Paragraph A as the well-developed paragraph, which is easier to understand, you are correct. Notice that this paragraph sticks to the subject—the fact that flowers grow throughout the world. The ideas are presented in a logical order, and the sentences have coherence. No loosely related ideas are introduced to divert the reader's attention. On the other hand, Paragraph B lacks a clear focus.

Critics of textbook writing also suggest that good writing with active verbs, vivid anecdotes, lively quotations, and other literary devices contributes to readers' interest and recall (Wade and Adams, 1990; Wade et al., 1993). Moreover, the quality of readers' recall of main ideas and interesting details increases when the text includes a greater number of interesting, memorable details.

Considerate Text

What makes a text considerate or inconsiderate?

Effective readers use a variety of strategies and processes to construct text meaning. They understand the components and patterns of text structure, such as paragraphs. The initial sections of this chapter addressed the current emphasis on the reader's active role in comprehension. However, to read actively and responsibly, students also must understand the nature of *considerate* and *inconsiderate* text, so that they can compensate for text limitations.

Five characteristics account for the ease or difficulty students are likely to encounter when reading a text:

1. Organization and structure

2. Whether the text addresses one concept at a time or tries to explain several at once

3. The clarity and coherence of the explanations

4. Whether the text is appropriate for the students' reading levels and the purpose

5. Whether the information is accurate and consistent (Armbruster and Anderson, 1981)

Organizational Patterns

Students who recognize the various patterns of text structure perform better on recall, summarization, and other comprehension tasks than readers who do not. Text structures are organizational frameworks that students can learn to identify, giving the students a predictable means to interpret explanatory discourse. The common **organizational patterns** found in content textbooks and nonfiction and informational writing are illustrated in the following paragraphs.

What are five common organizational patterns found in textbooks?

1. *Sequential or chronological order.* Paragraphs in sequential or chronological order present information in the order of its occurrence to clarify the ideas presented, as illustrated in the following example. Readers can use time or sequential order patterns to organize and remember this information. These words may signal this text organization: *after, before, begin, beyond, during, finally, first, next, now, second, then, third, until,* and *when.*

SCIENCE AND
HEALTH

The gravel settles first, followed by the sand, and then the clay. Heavier particles settle first because they require the greatest water velocity to be moved. In step 3, the gravel does not move, but the clay becomes suspended (Spaulding and Namowitz, 2005).

2. *Comparison/contrast.* Authors use comparison/contrast to clarify certain points. Questions like the following may help readers to understand this structure: What is the author's main idea? What similarities and/or differences does he or she use to illustrate the point? Student-constructed tables that list similarities and differences also enhance understanding. Some words that may signal the use of this pattern are *although, but, yet, nevertheless, meanwhile, however, on the other hand, otherwise, compared to, despite,* and *similarly.* The following paragraph illustrates the comparison/contrast pattern:

SOCIAL
STUDIES

Past— As you have learned, the large deposits of gold throughout Africa brought great wealth and power to kingdoms in the west and south. Back then miners used picks and other light tools to dig gold from the land.
Present—Gold remains a key resource of Africa; in fact Africa is a world leader in gold production. Modern miners in Africa and elsewhere use powerful drills to dig out gold thousands of feet underground (Carnine, Cortes, Curtis, and Robinson, 2006).

3. *Cause and effect.* Authors use this pattern to explain relationships among facts and ideas. Readers need to identify stated and implied causes and their related effects. The following words may signal the use of cause and effect: forms of the verb *cause,* as well as *because, since, so that, thus, therefore, if, consequently,* and *as a result.* An example of a cause-and-effect paragraph follows:

SOCIAL
STUDIES

The area that experienced the Dust Bowl disaster had been largely grassland on which ranchers raised livestock during World War I. After that millions of acres were converted to wheat growing. Overcultivation and incorrect land use in the 1920's left the region vulnerable not only to the years of drought conditions, but to strong winds that easily carried away the top soil (Arreola, Deal, Peterson, and Sanders, 2003).

4. *Definition or explanation.* This pattern explains a concept or defines terms that are essential to understanding in many content areas. An example of a definition or explanation pattern follows:

MATHEMATICS

A box and whisper plot is a data display that divides data values into four parts. Ordered data are divided into a lower and an upper half by the median. The median of the lower half is the lower quartile. The median of the upper half is the upper quartile. The lower extreme is the least data value. The upper extreme is the greatest data value (Larson, Bosewell, Kanold, and Stiff, 2005).

5. *Enumeration or simple listing pattern.* Paragraphs in this pattern list items of information (such as facts or ideas), either in order of importance or simply in logical order. Clues to this pattern are the words *one, two, first, second, third, to begin, next, finally, most important, when, also, too,* and *then.* An example of the enumeration or simple listing pattern follows:

SCIENCE AND
HEALTH

Because earthquakes produce different types of wave motions, there are different types of seismographs. Some record side-to-side motions. Others record up-and-down motions. Another records side-to-side motions in a north-south direction and a third records side-to-side motions in an east-west direction (Spaulding and Namowitz, 2005).

This paragraph also has an embedded cause and effect. Many paragraphs exhibit more that one organizational pattern.

Instructional Activities for Teaching Organizational Patterns

Instruction should involve a communication approach and include speaking, listening, reading, and writing. The instruction should make use of the actual texts and materials that students have to read. Strategies for teaching text structure include use of preview guides, graphic organizers (also called *visual organizers*), and questions. Pattern guides are based on the organizational pattern of the text. If a text is organized according to a cause-and-effect pattern, for example, the guide would highlight causes and effects. Some possible focuses for pattern guides other than cause and effect are sequence, comparison/contrast, and categorization. Pattern guides activate a reader's schemata for the particular organizational patterns frequently found in various subject areas. Example 4.8 is a filled-out comparison/contrast guide for a selection from a world history text.

EXAMPLE 4.8   Comparison/Contrast Guide

SOCIAL STUDIES

Directions: Read the selection about the revolutions in food production and then fill in the chart below to help you compare the characteristics of the green revolution and the biorevolution.

Green revolution	Biorevolution
Increased crop yields	Gene alteration
High-yield grain	Plants resistant to pests and disease
Doubled wheat production	Increased retention of flavor and freshness of tomatoes
Four rice crops a year required irrigation	Raised issues about negative consequences
Required chemicals for growth	

Revolutions in Food Production

One response to the problem of rapid population growth has been to boost food production. Two important examples of this effort are the **green revolution** and the **biorevolution**.

The Green Revolution   In the 1950s, agricultural scientists began to look for ways to increase crop yields. Their success, known as the green revolution, has helped to boost food production greatly.

Scientists focused their efforts on producing high-yield varieties of grain. Their first great success occurred in Mexico in the 1950s. An American-led team developed high-yield wheat plants. Thanks to these new plants, Mexican farmers doubled their wheat production. In the 1960s, another American-backed team helped to develop a hybrid rice plant in the Philippines. It allowed rice farmers to harvest up to four rice crops every year. Soon, Asian governments were funding their own scientists to develop other hybrid plants to meet the needs of people in their nations.

Unfortunately, the techniques of the green revolution often call for much irrigation, or watering, of crops. Because many African nations have limited water supplies, they have not been able to make full use of the new seeds. This severely limits the usefulness of these methods in much of Africa, where there is little water.

In addition, the new hybrid varieties of plants require chemicals, such as fertilizers, herbicides, and pesticides, to help them grow. This requirement has caused a number of problems. First, the chemicals are expensive. Peasants usually cannot afford them. Second, the use of such chemicals often clashes with age-old methods of farming. Third, these chemicals pose a threat to the environment.

The Biorevolution In addition to the methods of the green revolution, genetic research has played a growing role in agricultural science in recent years. In this approach, scientists alter plant genes to produce new plants that are more productive and more resistant to pests and disease.

This biorevolution, or gene revolution, has led to some important developments. For example, one American company has developed a genetically altered tomato that ripens more slowly than other tomatoes. This means that the altered tomatoes keep much of their flavor and freshness longer. Similar work is being tried with other kinds of produce.

But the biorevolution has raised some troubling issues. Critics fear that altering genes may accidentally create new disease-causing organisms. Another fear is that plants produced by altering genes may become diseased more easily. As with the green revolution, science offers great opportunities in the search for more food, but results may also have negative consequences.

Graphic, or visual, organizers and structured overviews are graphic arrangements of terms that apply to the important concepts in a reading selection. (See Figure 4.2.) They represent different kinds of thinking processes and text organizations that can be applied to listening, reading, and writing. These strategies also develop readiness for reading and writing. They help students to visualize what they are thinking

FIGURE 4.2

Graphic Organizers for Thinkers

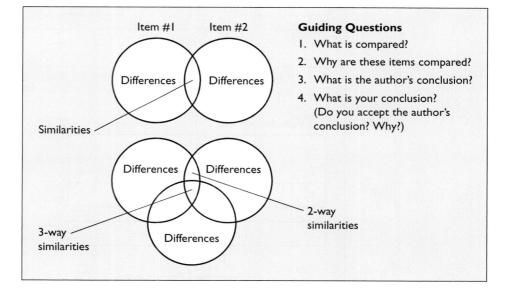

Items Compared	#1	#2
1st attribute		
2nd attribute		
3rd attribute		
4th attribute		

Guiding Questions

1. What is compared?
2. Why are these items compared?
3. What is the author's conclusion?
4. What is your conclusion? (Do you accept the author's conclusion? Why?)

Item #1   Item #2

Differences   Differences

Similarities

Differences   Differences

2-way similarities

3-way similarities

Differences

Guiding Questions

1. What is compared?
2. Why are these items compared?
3. What is the author's conclusion?
4. What is your conclusion? (Do you accept the author's conclusion? Why?)

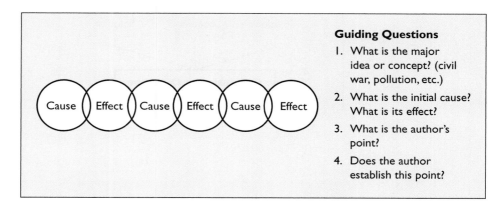

Cause Effect Cause Effect Cause Effect

Guiding Questions

1. What is the major idea or concept? (civil war, pollution, etc.)
2. What is the initial cause? What is its effect?
3. What is the author's point?
4. Does the author establish this point?

FIGURE 4.2

continued

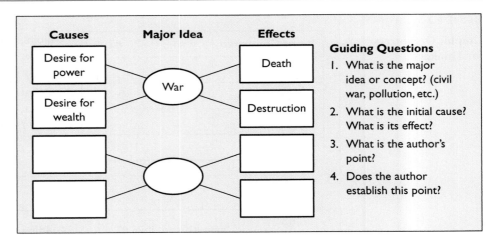

Causes   **Major Idea**   **Effects**

Desire for power

War

Desire for wealth

Death

Destruction

Guiding Questions

1. What is the major idea or concept? (civil war, pollution, etc.)
2. What is the initial cause? What is its effect?
3. What is the author's point?
4. Does the author establish this point?

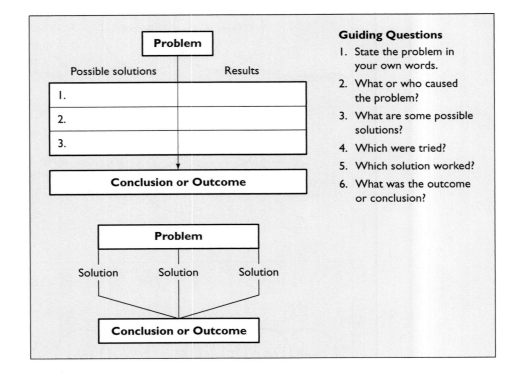

Problem

Possible solutions   Results

1.
2.
3.

Conclusion or Outcome

Problem

Solution   Solution   Solution

Conclusion or Outcome

Guiding Questions

1. State the problem in your own words.
2. What or who caused the problem?
3. What are some possible solutions?
4. Which were tried?
5. Which solution worked?
6. What was the outcome or conclusion?

and/or trying to understand. (See Chapter 3 for more on graphic organizers.) The following questions are guides for teachers to ask themselves when developing graphic organizers:

1. As I look at this content, what central facts, ideas, arguments, processes, or procedures do students need to comprehend? (This is related to purpose and/or objectives.)

2. What pattern or organization best holds the material together and makes it meaningful?

3. What kind of visual organizer will show students how to think their way through the content?

4. What problems or challenges can I pose that will force students to work through the steps of a thinking process?

Teachers can use these questions as they prepare graphic organizers for students to complete. The graphic organizers and questions in Figure 4.2 can be applied to most content area materials, and they are effective for main ideas and details, which are major tools for structuring information and knowledge.

Students can use computer graphics to create their own illustrations to show their thinking or the text organization. Our experiences indicate that students can be very creative when formulating their own graphic organizers. Student-created graphics are usually prepared as a follow-up or summary of reading content.

Teachers can model the development of overviews on overhead transparencies as the students watch each step and discuss it. Teachers can develop overviews on sentence strips by using bulletin boards and having the students organize the sentence strips. Then students can work in small groups, and finally individually, to develop overviews for their reading assignments. Example 4.9 shows a sample structured overview in the area of atomic structure.

EXAMPLE 4.9   Structured Overview

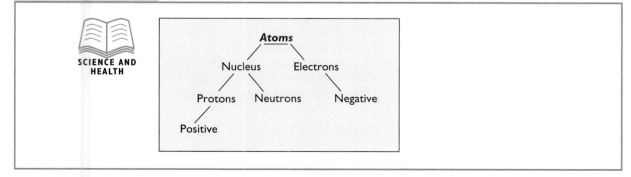

FIGURE 4.3

**Steps for Finding the
Topic, Main Idea, and
Details**

A. Identify the topic by asking who or what the paragraph is about. Ask yourself, What general word or phrase identifies the subject? Remember that the topic is based on a broad idea such as sports, flowers, wars, cells (science), or communication.

B. Identify the supporting details. Search for details that seem important and the idea they point to. For example, details about sports might include facts about baseball, football, and basketball.

C. Identify the main idea the author is communicating about the topic. The author's main idea about sports could be that these sports all involve teamwork and competition.

Main Ideas and Details

Why are main ideas and details so important in content reading?

How are details related to main ideas?

The writing in most content area materials is structured around topics, main ideas, and details; therefore, teaching students to identify topics and main ideas of paragraphs and entire selections is a high priority in reading programs. Topics are frequently presented as titles, words, or phrases that label the subjects.

The main idea of a paragraph is the significant idea or central idea that the author develops about the topic and supports with details throughout the paragraph. Details are the smaller pieces of information or ideas that are used to support this idea. See Figure 4.3 for the steps for finding the topic, main idea, and details in a paragraph.

Main ideas are interrelated with organizational patterns because they can be expressed in patterns such as cause and effect, comparison/contrast, sequential order, enumeration, and explanation. For example, a paragraph in a cause-and-effect pattern has a main idea and supporting details that are expressed through this pattern. The main idea of such a paragraph could be "causes and effects of erosion." The details are the specific causes and effects. Similarly, in a paragraph written with a comparison/contrast pattern, the details might be the contrasting points and the main idea the overall comparison (Palincsar and Brown, 1986).

Teachers need to go beyond simply presenting instructional strategies and must *show* students how to identify main ideas and details. Instructions requiring students to generate the main idea of a selection or paragraph lead them to recall and understand content better than simply identifying the main idea from multiple-choice items. Therefore, students should practice writing the main idea in their own words. Students who learn to summarize main ideas improve their ability to answer questions and to identify important information. They also need to identify and write both stated and unstated (implied) main ideas. Some authors include details that are interesting but that do not elaborate the main idea.

Main Idea and Detail Activities

Activities such as the following give students help with and practice in identifying and stating main ideas and supporting details:

1. Have students use categorization activities to separate important from unimportant details. For instance, students can write down the details they have identified in a paragraph and categorize them as either important or unimportant to the communication of the main idea. Having students state reasons that they classified details into either of these categories permits the teacher to clear up any misconceptions about the points the author stressed.

Important Details	Unimportant Details

2. Model the procedure of finding main ideas for students before asking them to locate main ideas themselves. See the examples of modeling that are included in this chapter.

3. Have students ask themselves these questions: What is this sentence or paragraph about? What do most of the key words seem to point to? What words occur most frequently? What do these frequently occurring words relate to? What idea is related to most of the supporting details? What sentence would best summarize the frequently occurring ideas? Is the main idea stated or implied? Where is the main idea located in the paragraph (at the beginning, in the middle, or at the end)?

4. Teach students to look for words and phrases that often indicate the main idea, for instance, *first, last, the most important factor, the significant fact.*

5. Prepare blank diagrams on which students can place main ideas and supporting ideas. Following is an example of a generic diagram.

Main Idea
Detail #1
Detail #2
Detail #3
Detail #4

6. Have students create their own diagrams for main ideas and supporting details.

7. Encourage students to write, in their own words, concise statements of main ideas.

Selection Organization

Selections are longer units of discourse composed of series of paragraphs. In content reading, we are concerned largely with expository discourse. The organizational patterns presented earlier in this chapter (sequential, comparison/contrast, cause and effect, definition or explanation, and enumeration or simple listing pattern) are found in many selections, and they are frequently combined in structuring discourse. When these patterns are identified in longer selections, they can be interpreted in the same ways as in paragraphs. However, these common patterns become parts of a macrostructure in longer discourse.

Well-written expository content—such as a content textbook chapter—begins with an *introductory section*, which previews the subject. This introduction can be compared to an inverted triangle, because it starts with a broad, general idea of the topic and narrows the topic to a more specific point. This section may be developed in a variety of ways, such as comparison and cause and effect.

The second part of a selection is the *body*, which develops the ideas that have been stated in the introduction. Each of the paragraphs that make up the body usually has a main idea and details that relate to the topic presented in the introductory section. These paragraphs may be developed through any organizational pattern the author chooses.

The chapter or selection usually concludes with a *summary paragraph* that pulls together the ideas presented in the body. A triangle can be used to illustrate this section, which begins with a specific idea and broadens and becomes more general as it develops. The pattern of the summary is the reverse of that of the introductory section. Content teachers can illustrate organizational patterns with the table of contents, which is discussed in Chapter 6. Textbook headings, which are helpful in understanding, remembering, and locating information, are widely used in content textbooks and nonfiction trade books.

Story Grammars.   In the preceding sections we examined the common structures found in expository and descriptive text. Now we consider the structural elements of narrative texts. Structure is in some ways a container for communicating a story. In stories, there are plots, characters, problems or conflicts, and themes that revolve around characters' goals and actions. Story structure, or story grammar (*grammar* means "structural relationships"), is a mental representation of the parts of a typical story and the relationships among those parts.

Students can identify the important elements in stories and relate these elements to one another by mapping them. Our discussion is based on the six major story elements posited by Mandler and Johnson (1977). These elements are setting, beginning, reaction, attempt, outcome, and ending. The *setting* introduces the main character and the time and place. A precipitating or initiating event occurs in the *beginning*, and the main character's response to the precipitating event is identified as the *reaction*. *Attempt* is concerned with the main character's efforts to attain his or her goal. The success or failure of the attempt is identified in the *outcome*. The *ending*, the last component of story structure, is the long-range consequence of the action, the final response of a character, or an emphatic statement. A story may be composed of one story grammar, or it may include a series of story grammars. In an episodic story, each episode has a story grammar. Example 4.10 shows the

What is a synonym for story structure?

EXAMPLE 4.10   Story Grammar

**ENGLISH/
LANGUAGE
ARTS**

When My Name Was Keoko by Linda Sue Park

Setting	Korea during the Japanese occupation 1940–1945. Sun-hee and Tae-yul, a brother and sister, alternate as narrators of the story.
Beginning	The Japanese had imposed many restrictions on the Koreans. Then they announced that all Koreans must take Japanese names.
Reaction	Sun-hee and Tae-yul and their family find this very threatening to their identity. Members of the family react in different ways to protect their identities.
Attempt	Sun-hee keeps a journal where she can be herself rather than Keoko (her Japanese name). Tae-yul resents his father's compliance with the Japanese to choose a Japanese name.
Outcome	An uncle who publishes an underground newspaper is arrested and forced to become a Kamikaze pilot. Tae-yul becomes a pilot for the Japanese.
Ending	Sun-hee preserves her Korean self through her journal. Tae-yul understands his father at the end of the novel.

---

story grammar for the young adult novel *When My Name Was Keoko* by Linda Sue Park.

Readers use their knowledge of fiction and nonfiction text structure to guide their expectations, understanding, recall, and production of text. When reading, listening, and writing, students use a structural outline of the major story and text components in their minds to make predictions and hypotheses about stories and information. These expectations focus students' attention on story events, help them understand the unfolding of time and sequence, and cue recall of text. When writing their own essays or analyses, students use knowledge of text structures to shape their discourse.

Focus on Struggling Readers

Helping Struggling Readers Comprehend

Giving struggling students reading materials they can comprehend is fundamental to developing comprehension. Secondary classrooms include students who read anywhere from one to five (and possibly more) grades below or above their placement. The students reading below grade level may need alternate materials that are easier to read than texts that the rest of the class is reading. Teachers often need to locate interesting readable supplementary materials. They can use readability formulas to measure the difficulty of text. Most of these formulas measure vocabulary and sentence difficulty. These formulas are discussed in Chapter 12.

Vocabulary is a significant problem for struggling readers (see Chapter 3). Research shows that struggling readers often get off track because they do not automatically recognize words. Spear-Swerling (2004) found that the reading comprehension of struggling readers is usually weak due to deficient word knowledge and below average oral language comprehension. Furthermore, poor readers lack knowledge or application of reading comprehension strategies. Struggling readers often have experiences and schemata that differ from textbook content, a situation that limits their ability to connect with the texts. Figure 4.4 shows comprehension interventions for struggling readers that are supported by research (Ash, 2002; Samuels, 2004; Spear-Swerling, 2004).

Finding topics, main ideas, and supporting details is a difficult task for struggling readers. They have to learn to sort important details from unimportant ones. This will lead them into writing summaries and paraphrasing. Paraphrasing requires the student to state important ideas in his or her own words. Teach strategies through explicit instruction and scaffold reading (see Chapter 5). Struggling readers tend to avoid reading because they are not successful at it; unfortunately,

FIGURE 4.4

Comprehension Interventions for Struggling Readers

Comprehension Intervention	
	Focus on main ideas; use prereading experiences.
Motivate/build interest	Activate/build schemata.
Vocabulary	Preteach vocabulary.
	Relate to concepts.
Purposes for reading	Provide questions to answer when reading.
Oral and shared reading	Students read with taped textbook/coach.
Guided reading	Small group or partner (coach) reading.
Self-selected reading	Literature circles (see Chapter 9, "Literature Response Groups (Literature Circles)").

they do not improve because they are not motivated to read. Internet activities and computerized programs motivate students and increase both vocabulary and comprehension. Reading coaches also motivate struggling secondary readers. Bacon (2005) describes a program she designed to prepare her at- and above-grade readers to act as coaches for the struggling students in her classes. She found that the student coaches provided the intense, specific, and frequent instruction that struggling readers need; the program fostered a learning community. The reading coaches modeled comprehension strategies for the struggling readers in a cooperative learning environment. Teachers have found that coaches make a remarkable difference in the learning of struggling students. The comprehension strategies shown in this chapter and the other chapters of this book can be demonstrated, and teachers can use think-alouds to demonstrate the kind of thinking that occurs when reading silently.

Focus on English Language Learners

Helping English Language Learners (ELLs) Comprehend

Above all else, English language learners need assistance to read; they need to understand, learn from, and feel successful in reading (Graves and Fitzgerald, 2003). They bring world knowledge and schemata developed in their home language to aid them in comprehending English text. However, there are individual differences among ELLs because they bring different world knowledge and experience to learning language (Hernandez, 2003). Another difference depends on the native language of the learner; for example, English and Dutch are linguistically closer than English and German and the Romance languages (Myers, 1995).

There is a rich connection between language and cognition (Wood et al., 1995). Therefore, learning English vocabulary and English grammatical structure are foundations of the reading fluency needed for reading comprehension. Students tend to use English vocabulary in the syntactic patterns of their first language. Teachers can help ELLs through comparing their first and second languages, showing them the structures that are the same. This enables students to use English words to make complete and accurate sentences.

Instructional materials should be meaningful and interesting to ELLs. ELLs may need schemata development and prereading preparation for the texts they are expected to read. They need meaningful opportunities to interact with classmates and will benefit from a peer coach or a peer tutor (Coppola, 2003). Hernandez (2003) suggests a strategic worksheet that ELLs could complete alone or with a partner. Figure 4.5 is adapted from an example in Hernandez (2003).

FIGURE 4.5

A Guide for Developing the Reading Comprehension of ELLs and Partners

---

Directions: Write answers to the questions.

1. Before reading, look at the following:

   Title and subtitles   Highlighted vocabulary   Illustrations, including graphs and charts

   What is the topic?

   _____

   _____

   Predict the main idea.

   _____

   _____

2. Read the first paragraph and the last paragraph and write what you have learned.

   _____

   _____

3. Ask yourself questions about the topic; if there are subheads they can become questions. Write your questions here.

   _____

   _____

4. Begin reading and stop at the end of each section to summarize in a sentence or two. Write the sentences here.

   _____

   _____

5. Identify the important vocabulary. _____

   _____

6. Did you find the text easy to read or hard to read? _____

   Why? _____

7. Tell your partner what you learned, and whether your prediction was accurate.

SUMMARY

Students must acquire multiple literacies to comprehend the many text forms they will encounter both in and out of school. Comprehension is a strategic process during which readers simultaneously extract and construct meaning through interaction with written language. Readers' comprehension depends on their ability to manage themselves as readers, the text, and the situation or activity. Students use their skills, fluency, stance, social and cultural background, and interest in authentic assignments to read content texts. In addition, vocabulary knowledge, experiences, abilities, motivation, and strategies enable readers to construct meaning.

Readers' language and cognitive competence create students' foundation for acquiring the skills and strategies that they need to understand content texts of various types such as textbooks, novels, magazines, and Internet materials (Bean, 2001). The texts students read provide the knowledge, language, and framework for understanding. Teachers create aspects of the reading situation because they establish time, place, participants, the assignment, and the purposes, as well as guide stance or perspective.

Teaching students comprehension strategies gives them the tools for enhancing their content comprehension. Strategies for vocabulary were introduced in Chapter 3. In this chapter, reaction logs, comparison/contrast logs, identifying various text organizations, and using graphic organizers are introduced to help students improve their comprehension of content texts. Struggling readers and English language learners need comprehension instruction and strategies to develop understanding of content materials.

DISCUSSION QUESTIONS

1. How could reading comprehension occur without prior knowledge?
2. What are textual schemata? How do they function in reading comprehension?
3. Compare the characteristics of active readers with those of passive readers.
4. How are reading comprehension and content reading related?
5. Why are main ideas significant in content area comprehension?
6. How is intertextuality related to reading comprehension?
7. How do you think an active reader would employ metacognition?
8. What do content teachers need to know about teaching English language learners?
9. What do content teachers need to know about teaching struggling readers?

ENRICHMENT ACTIVITIES

1. Read an article in the local newspaper, and write down all the thinking processes that you use to understand what you are reading.
2. Read a current bestseller, and write a brief paragraph that presents the theme (main idea) of the book. Have a classmate who has read the same book analyze your comprehension.
3. Find examples of paragraphs in content area textbooks that follow organizational patterns illustrated in this chapter. Bring these examples to class to share and discuss.
*4. Use the key word idea to analyze several paragraphs in a content textbook.
*5. Choose one of the metacognitive activities presented in this chapter, and plan ways to adapt it to your content area.
*6. Observe a class that includes English language learners and identify the adjustments that the teacher makes to enhance learning.
7. Identify a content text that you might use in teaching and plan the adjustment necessary for struggling readers. (This could include locating adapted reading materials and/or Internet sites.)

*These activities are designed for in-service teachers, student teachers, and practicum students.

Chapter 5

Strategies for Constructing Meaning in Texts

OVERVIEW

Students who are fortunate enough to have large vocabularies, good listening comprehension, and well-developed stores of world knowledge are prepared to read with comprehension (Rand Corporation, 2002). Understanding, according to Perkins (1995, p. 13), enables students "to explain, muster evidence, find examples, generalize, apply concepts, analogize, represent in a new way, and so on." Current research demonstrates that directly teaching comprehension strategies improves students' understanding of texts (Duke and Pearson, 2002). To develop comprehension, teachers need to ensure that students accomplish three tasks: retain important information; understand topics deeply; and actively use the knowledge they gain (Graves, 1999). Instruction and practice help students learn to implement strategies for understanding (Alfassi, 1998). This chapter focuses on teaching the strategies that readers can use to build understanding.

PURPOSE-SETTING QUESTIONS

As you read this chapter, try to answer these questions:

1. Describe a teacher of strategic reading.
2. How can readers identify appropriate comprehension strategies?
3. What are the stages of learning to use comprehension strategies?
4. What do good readers do?

Good Readers

A picture of the strategies that successful readers use has emerged from research (Block and Pressley, 2001; Barry, 2002; Applebee and Langer, 2002; Duke and Pearson, 2002; Beck, 2005). This image enables teachers to plan instruction and select strategies that will help their students become good readers. Students who understand text use these strategies:

Good readers preview the text to identify unknown vocabulary, headings, and subheadings and the structure of the text.
Good readers make predictions about the information or story they are reading.
Good readers ask themselves questions.
Good readers draw inferences from the text.
Good readers monitor their own comprehension and clarify misunderstandings.
Good readers synthesize new information and ideas to create new thinking.

What are cognitive strategies?

Cognitive strategies are systematic plans that students consciously use to monitor and improve reading comprehension. These strategies allow students to gain control of the comprehension process (Barry, 2002). **Strategic readers** actively interact with the text and the context (reading task and purpose); they connect information in the text with preexisting knowledge. They have a repertoire of strategies and know how to use these strategies to comprehend. Strategic readers stop to reflect on what they have read. These and other strategies are developed throughout this book.

What is the teacher's role in developing strategic readers?

Strategy instruction involves the explicit teaching of strategies that enable students to acquire relevant knowledge from text. Explicit strategy instruction includes modeling, scaffolding, and coaching with direct explanations of why strategies are valuable, as well as how and when to use them. The teacher's role in teaching strategies begins with engaging students in the learning process. Engagement is a key factor in reading comprehension because engaged readers are motivated and they seek to understand (Guthrie, 2000; Pflaum and Bishop, 2004).

Scaffolding is a strategy for supporting learning experiences. The most useful form of scaffolding for secondary students is organizing students' engagement with text through prereading activities, during reading activities, and post reading activities. Prereading activities include relating students' experiences to the text, activating background knowledge, developing prereading questions, and prediction of text content or story plot. During reading activities include guided reading and summarizing. Post reading activities include discussion, answering questions, responding to text, and writing summaries. The preceding activities are suggestions, but they are not exhaustive. Application of scaffolding activities is discussed later in this chapter.

Teachers create contexts for engagement when they develop knowledge goals, real-world connections, and meaningful choices about reading (Guthrie, 2000). Teachers choose interesting texts that are vivid, important, and relevant to students (Pflaum and Bishop, 2004). Teachers learn what students bring to their reading and create bridges or scaffolds between prior knowledge and new information (Jacobs, 2001).

FIGURE 5.1

Teaching Process for Comprehension Strategies*

1. **Teacher engages students**—The teacher motivates students, activates their interests and prior knowledge. The teacher gives the strategy a label and explains its value for reading comprehension.

2. **Teacher models strategy**—The teacher shows students how to use the strategy. The teacher may use a think-aloud to demonstrate. A think-aloud is a process that teachers use to illustrate ways of thinking about reading content. The teacher reads from a text aloud, stopping periodically to tell his thoughts about the content he has read. Following the demonstration, the students should practice "thinking" aloud. The teacher may demonstrate this process several times and then use sticky notes to mark the places he has stopped. Then students can use sticky notes to mark the places they stopped.

3. **Teacher monitors guided student practice**—Students practice the strategy until they can apply it in their own reading.

4. **Teacher steps back**—Students independently apply the strategy to comprehend.

Strategic instruction enables students to assume responsibility for independent comprehension gradually. Figures 5.1 and 5.2 illustrate these concepts. Figure 5.1 summarizes the steps that content teachers can use when teaching comprehension strategies.

COGNITIVE PROCESSING

What activities stimulate cognitive processing?

The comprehension process is one of thinking about content. Thinking about content calls on both general knowledge and specialized knowledge, as well as thinking strategies (Perkins, 1995). **Cognitive processing** leads to schema development, which facilitates storage of knowledge in memory. Teachers can stimulate students' cognitive processing through a variety of activities such as **rehearsal** (practicing use of information), review, comparing and contrasting, and drawing connections (Rosenshine, 1997). Strategies that stimulate cognitive processing are summarized in Figure 5.2.

THINKING AND QUESTIONING

Teachers should raise questions about real-world problems, projects, and tasks that relate to students and focus their thinking. Follow-up discussion strategies, such as asking for elaboration, influence the degree and quality of classroom discussion. Thinking is more likely to flourish when ideas are valued and varying points of view are encouraged. In a thoughtful environment, students' answers and ideas are accepted, clarified, and expanded, often by the teacher's asking, "Why do you think that?"

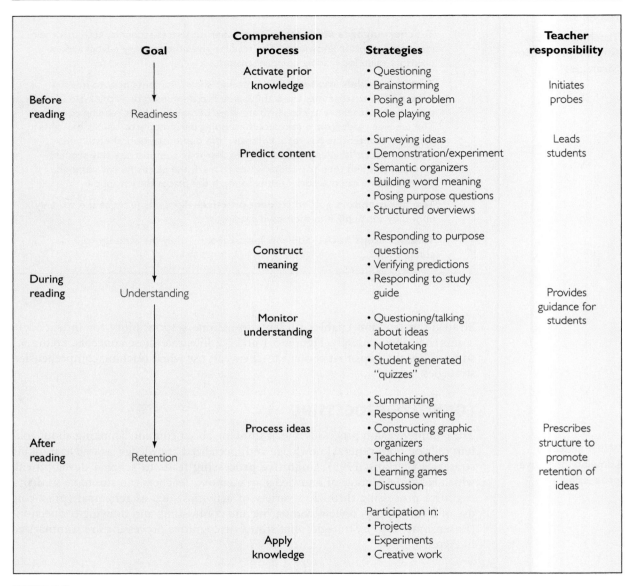

FIGURE 5.2

Mediated Instruction of Text: A Framework of Teaching Options for Content Area Instruction

Source: Figure 1 from "A Framework of Teaching Options for Content Area Instruction: Mediated Instruction of Text," by Judith C. Neal and Margaret A. Langer, *Journal of Reading 36*(3) (1992, November): 227–230. Reprinted with permission of Judith C. Neal and the International Reading Association. All rights reserved.

MEETING THE CHALLENGE

SOCIAL STUDIES

After the principal of Woodridge High School censored material in the school newspaper, Jeff Colson's eleventh-grade social studies students began to complain that he had violated their freedom of speech. Jeff asked the students to identify the ways that the principal had violated specific rights encoded in the Bill of Rights. After discussion, the students discovered they could not cite violations because they didn't know anything about the Bill of Rights. Jeff decided to develop a *webquest* to explore the topic. Webquests are inquiry-oriented projects in which the information that students read and study comes from the Internet. Students may e-mail questions to Internet sites and they may use videoconferencing. In this webquest students were to work in small groups and individually. Their evaluation would be based on writing and debating.

The students were to study the Bill of Rights and relate that document to the principal's decision concerning the school newspaper. After phase one of the webquest, Jeff planned to have the students research challenges to the Bill of Rights and compare those challenges to their school situation. In the final phase of the webquest, the students were to study the Fourteenth Amendment to the Constitution and relate it to the Bill of Rights. All of the students started in groups of three to locate copies of the Bill of Rights from the Library of Congress Internet site. After they did that, Jeff identified related Internet sites: ACLU Briefing Papers—The Bill of Rights (http://archive.aclu.org), and the Bill of Rights Institute (http://www.billofrightsinstitute.org).

The students then organized into small groups to study the Bill of Rights word by word. After this thorough study, the students discussed their various interpretations of the document in relation to the incident in their school. Then the students wrote position papers in which they explained what they believed and cited portions of the Bill of Rights and related documents to support their positions. They asked the principal to write a position paper regarding the school paper incident. The first part of the study concluded with a debate to which they invited the principal. They challenged his position and wrote a rebuttal. They were pleased that he agreed to listen to them and to discuss their grievances, and they looked forward to his response to their rebuttal. The students were highly motivated by this experience and very interested in studying the challenges to the Bill of Rights.

EFFECTIVE QUESTIONING

Questioning can effectively guide and extend comprehension. In addition, asking and answering questions reveals our thoughts and feelings, to ourselves as well as to others. Strategies such as providing relevant questions before students read the selection help them focus on major ideas and concepts. Asking questions that require interpretation and critical thinking stimulates higher levels of cognitive processing. In contrast, focusing on literal questions that require specific correct answers limits thinking, because students can memorize the required answers. Stimulating questions are those that have several appropriate responses; such questions give students opportunities to experience success when expressing their own ideas. Good questions require multiple-word answers that foster cognitive growth. When students offer one-word answers, a teacher might say, "Can you tell me any more about . . .?" or "Why do you think that?" or "Can you give me examples of this?" To increase comprehension, teach students to ask themselves and others clarification questions such as these: "Is this what you mean: _____?" "Can you give me a nonexample of _____?" "Would you say more about _____?" "What is the main point?"

What could happen when you allow "wait time" after asking a question?

Giving students ample time to reflect on their answers improves the quality of answers. Allowing three to five seconds of "**wait time**" after asking a question gives students time to process the question and formulate a response. The wait time for questions that focus on stimulating students' higher levels of thinking and those that encourage independent thinking should be longer than the time given for literal-level questions. Thoughtful answers require more processing time. Teachers should expect individual differences in the amount of wait time that students need to formulate thoughtful answers. Some students process quickly and others process slowly, but the answers from both types of students can be of equal quality.

Providing appropriate wait time for students is a challenge for teachers who are concerned about silence in the classroom. Some teachers may feel compelled to ask follow-up questions to encourage students' answers, when waiting would improve the quality of answers.

Questions can be posed before, during, and after reading. Questions asked before reading activate schemata and focus attention on important ideas and concepts; at this point, students can generate questions about a topic or concept. During reading, students can ask questions about how well they are comprehending. After reading, teachers can ask questions such as "Did you find the answers to your questions?" "What are they?" "Which questions are still unanswered?" "What did you learn that we didn't ask questions about?" "What did the writer do to make readers feel or think a certain way?" "How did the writer use language to convey a particular idea?" "What evidence to support a particular idea did the writer give?" Students who read a passage and answer questions about it generally learn more than students who only read the passage. Teaching unsuccessful readers to raise questions as they read helps them acquire the ability to comprehend complex verbal material. It appears that students who ask themselves questions engage in self-monitoring of their understanding, which leads them to independent comprehension. Teachers who are preparing questions for a discussion should review the following points:

1. What are the important ideas in this selection?

2. What ideas and concepts do I want the students to remember from this selection?

3. What questions will lead students to understand these ideas and concepts?

4. What thinking abilities have the students in this group already developed?

5. What thinking abilities do the students in this group need to develop?

Student Questions

What is divergent
thinking?

Cognitive processing enables students to internalize new information and to perform higher-level thinking operations (Rosenshine, Meister, and Chapman, 1996).
Self-questioning is a powerful strategy for stimulating content learning. Question
generation prompts learners to seek answers that they want to know (Jacobs, 2001;
Duke and Pearson, 2002). Self-questioning stimulates **divergent thinking** and encourages independent learning. Divergent thinking is "thinking outside the box." It
is thinking that follows different paths and moves beyond the original material. Research shows that students need direct strategy instruction to become successful
generators of higher-level questions (Duke and Pearson, 2002; Rosenshine, Meister,
and Chapman, 1996). The strategy instruction approach introduced in Figure 5.1
can be applied to self-questioning.

Types of Thinking and Reading

LITERAL THINKING AND READING

What is the focus of
literal thinking?

Literal thinking is concerned with directly stated facts and ideas that answer the
question "What did the author say?" Readers often quote the text to answer literal
questions. The major forms of literal thinking are recognizing and recalling stated
main ideas; recognizing and recalling stated details; recognizing and recalling stated
sequences; following stated directions; and recognizing stated causes and effects.

ENGLISH/
LANGUAGE
ARTS

SOCIAL
STUDIES

SCIENCE AND
HEALTH

The following are examples of literal-level questions based on *The Land*, by Mildred
D. Taylor, which is the fictionalized biography of the author's great-grandparents,
and *Shipwreck at the Bottom of the World*, by Jennifer Armstrong. Taylor's great-
grandfather was the son of a slave owner and a slave. Taylor's book won the Coretta
Scott King Award in 2002. *Shipwreck at the Bottom of the World* is an informational
account of Sir Ernest Shackleton's expedition to the Antarctic. The members of this
expedition were stranded in the Antarctic with no way to contact the outside world,
but they all survived.

Students learn best when teachers model the process of answering questions. For
example, the teacher could model answering the first question for *Shipwreck at the
Bottom of the World* by sharing his or her thoughts in a think-aloud. The teacher
might begin with "I wonder why the author asked readers to imagine the most hostile place on earth and then proceeded to tell what was not the most hostile place?"
The author's use of contrast in the introduction dramatized the hostility of the
South Pole. This discussion alerts students to the author's writing style and her manner of presenting information.

Teachers can provide students with opportunities to demonstrate their own thinking strategies. Questions that lead students to relate the text to their prior knowledge,
to support their answers from the text or prior knowledge, or to apply knowledge
are especially useful for encouraging them to model thinking processes. In listening to the students present their thinking, the teacher should focus on the cognitive
process, as well as the answer. After students have some experience with thinking
strategies, they can work in pairs, modeling thinking for each other.

| EXAMPLE 5.1 | Literal-Level Questions Based on *The Land* and *Shipwreck at the Bottom of the World* |

The Land
1. How does Paul describe his father?
2. Who tells this story?
3. What information provided the author with the foundation for this story?
4. How did Paul feel that he was different from other slaves?

Shipwreck at the Bottom of the World
1. What is the most hostile place on earth (according to this author)?
2. Why is the South Pole more hostile than the North Pole?
3. How does the author describe Ernest Shackleton?
4. What kind of men made up the crew of the *Endurance*?
5. What kind of stores were taken on the *Endurance*?
6. What activities kept the men busy?

INFERENTIAL THINKING AND READING

How does literal thinking contrast with inferential thinking?

Inferential thinking is concerned with deeper meanings that are difficult to define because they involve several types of reasoning. This is further complicated by the fact that inferential questions often have more than one "correct" answer. To make inferences, readers must relate facts, generalizations, definitions, and values. Inferential questions emphasize finding relationships among elements of the written text. Essentially, making inferences involves using one's schemata to fill in information that the author assumes the reader knows. Building on readers' background knowledge is essential, due to space and time limitations. For example, in the sentence "Nancy pulled on her mittens and her parka before opening the door," the reader draws upon personal experience to infer that Nancy is going outdoors into cold weather. Students should always be prepared to support and explain their answers. Two activities that can help students develop their ability to make inferences are comparing and contrasting historical figures and identifying generalizations in their content textbooks.

In making inferences about reading content, readers examine the author's words, reading between the lines for implications that are not explicitly stated. To do this, readers combine information from their own experiences with text information. The main types of inferences include *location* inferences, in which the reader infers the place; *agent* inferences, which require the reader to infer the person acting; *time* inferences, which are concerned with the time designation (e.g., when the action occurs); *action* inferences, which have to do with the action occurring in the text; *instrument* inferences, which are concerned with tools or devices involved in the text;

object inferences, which require readers to infer objects the author has implied; *cause-and-effect* inferences, which have to do with implied causes and/or effects; *category* inferences, which require the reader to infer a category to which objects mentioned in the text belong; *problem-solution* inferences, which have to do with problems and solutions implied by the author; and *feeling-attitude* inferences, which are concerned with the feelings and attitudes implied by the author.

To demonstrate the inferential reasoning process, teachers can employ the think-aloud strategy by expressing their reflections aloud. For instance, in the final inferential question for *The Land*, the teacher might say, "Paul has a number of conflicts in this story. He has conflicts within himself, conflicts with his mother and father, conflicts with his brothers, and conflicts with his friend. These conflicts cause him to leave home and search for a way to buy his own land." The teacher could also discuss the cause of each of these conflicts. For example, Paul is in conflict with his father because his father has given Paul many opportunities that only white people had at that time in history, but he expects Paul to act like a slave rather than to stand up to white men even when they are wrong.

To answer the final question based on *Shipwreck at the Bottom of the World*, the reader could say that Ernest Shackleton experienced many conflicts. He was in conflict with the weather because the weather destroyed his ship, *Endurance*. This disaster led to conflicts related to food and shelter for the crew. He encountered many conflicts with the members of his crew as they struggled to survive.

ENGLISH/
LANGUAGE
ARTS

SOCIAL
STUDIES

ENGLISH/
LANGUAGE
ARTS

SCIENCE AND
HEALTH

EXAMPLE 5.2

**Inferential Questions Based on *The Land*
and *Shipwreck at the Bottom of the World***

The Land
1. What is the difference between a friend and an ally?
2. Why did Paul call himself a "man of color" when another person called him a "colored boy"?
3. Why is this book biographical fiction?
4. What makes it fiction?
5. Why is the setting of this story so important?
6. What are the conflicts in this story?

Shipwreck at the Bottom of the World
1. Why did the sun never set?
2. Why were the men prone to disagreements and fights?
3. Why do you think Reginald James declared that he never wanted to see another scrap of ice for the rest of his life?
4. Why is the setting critical to this book?
5. What are the conflicts in this book?

CRITICAL THINKING AND READING

How are literal thinking and inferential thinking related to critical thinking?

Many educators believe that **critical thinking** is central to the curriculum because schools strive to educate minds rather than to train memories. The importance of critical thinking is well established because everyone needs to consider critically the information they receive about the world around them (Perkins, 1995). Critical readers recognize that they receive a limited amount of information when they read (or listen). Moreover, the information is usually presented from a particular point of view, filtered through the writer's perceptions. These varying perceptions lead to discrepancies in different accounts of the same incident. To think critically, readers must begin with an understanding of what the author is saying, so literal and interpretive thinking are necessary to critical thinking skills.

What do critical readers do?

Critical readers question what they read, suspend judgment until all facts are presented, evaluate, and decide. Critical thinking is evaluative thinking that focuses on what to believe or to do. To make such judgments, the reader compares text with external criteria derived from experience, research, teachers, and experts in the field; therefore, background knowledge is essential to critical reading. Critical readers recognize the author's purpose and point of view or context, and they distinguish fact from opinion. They test the author's assertions against their own observations, information, and logic. The major facets of critical reading are summarized below:

The reader is open-minded and suspends judgment until adequate data are available, thus avoiding jumping to conclusions.

The reader constantly questions the content.

The reader has a problem-solving attitude.

The reader is knowledgeable regarding the topic.

The reader discerns the author's purpose.

The reader evaluates the author's qualifications.

The reader evaluates the validity of the material.

The reader evaluates the use of propaganda.

The reader evaluates the author's logic.

The reader evaluates the author's use of language.

Critical reading involves three major types of abilities: semantics, logic, and evaluating authenticity (Lewis, 1991). *Semantics* abilities include understanding the denotative and connotative uses of words, the use of vague and precise words, and the use of words in a persuasive manner. *Logic* skills include understanding the reliability of the author's argument and statements; recognizing the use of propaganda; distinguishing fact from opinion; and recognizing the various forms of persuasive writing. *Authenticity* skills include determining if adequate information is included, comparing this information with other relevant information, examining the author's qualifications, and using authoritative research sources. Critical reading in the content areas consists of explicit applications of the principles of critical thinking, which are discussed further in Chapters 10 and 11. Suggestions for teaching critical reading procedures are given in later sections of this chapter.

Critical reading questions based on *The Land* and *Shipwreck at the Bottom of the World* are shown in Example 5.3.

EXAMPLE 5.3

Critical Reading Questions Based on *The Land* and *Shipwreck at the Bottom of the World*

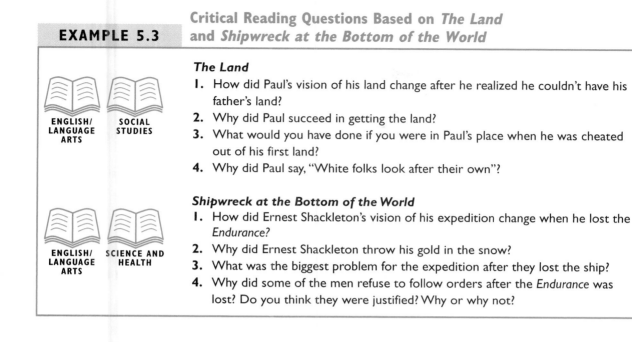

ENGLISH/ LANGUAGE ARTS

SOCIAL STUDIES

ENGLISH/ LANGUAGE ARTS

SCIENCE AND HEALTH

The Land

1. How did Paul's vision of his land change after he realized he couldn't have his father's land?
2. Why did Paul succeed in getting the land?
3. What would you have done if you were in Paul's place when he was cheated out of his first land?
4. Why did Paul say, "White folks look after their own"?

Shipwreck at the Bottom of the World

1. How did Ernest Shackleton's vision of his expedition change when he lost the *Endurance*?
2. Why did Ernest Shackleton throw his gold in the snow?
3. What was the biggest problem for the expedition after they lost the ship?
4. Why did some of the men refuse to follow orders after the *Endurance* was lost? Do you think they were justified? Why or why not?

ENGLISH/ LANGUAGE ARTS

When modeling critical thinking, the teacher could say, "To answer the last question for *The Land* you might think about the number of times that Paul experienced treatment that he considered mistreatment at the hands of his mother, father, and brothers because they insisted that he behave in ways that would not endanger him."

The final question based on *Shipwreck at the Bottom of the World* is concerned with naval law. The teacher might say, "Some of the crew refused to follow orders because naval law stipulated that the Ship's Articles were canceled when the ship sank. But the ship broke up; it did not sink. Once the crew was on shore, Shackleton was the master, and disobedience was legally punishable. It seems to me that the crew members who refused to obey were foolhardy, because they had to work together to survive."

Semantic Learning Activities

1. Since "loaded" words play on readers' emotions, students will benefit from practice in identifying them. Words like *un-American* and *extremist* call forth a negative reaction, whereas words such as *freedom*, *peace*, and *human rights* stimulate positive feelings. Students can practice identifying "loaded" words in newspapers, magazines, and textbooks.

2. Critical readers discover that words used in vague, general ways interfere with content clarity (e.g., the expressions "Everyone is doing it" and "They say"). Students should locate examples of vague word usage in their reading material.

Logic Learning Activities

SOCIAL
STUDIES

1. Have students create syllogisms that state an author's premises and conclusions, similar to this one based on a social studies text chapter:

   Premises. People with undesirable characteristics were rejected. Some "new" immigrants had undesirable characteristics.

   Conclusion. Those "new" immigrants were rejected.

2. Have students verify statements found in local newspaper stories through research.

ENGLISH/
LANGUAGE
ARTS

3. Have students examine sentences to identify words that signal the author's opinion, such as these qualifying words: *think, probably, maybe, appear, seem,* and *believe.* The following sentences are examples:
   a. I believe this is the best cake I have ever eaten.
   b. Jane will probably come home for vacation.

4. Making a graphic representation (chart) of the facts and opinions presented by an author will help the reader examine ideas critically. Example 5.4 is a chart based on information taken from a social studies textbook.

ENGLISH/   SOCIAL
LANGUAGE   STUDIES
ARTS

5. Recognizing propaganda is one of the abilities required for critical reading. Discussions of propaganda techniques and methods for analyzing propaganda could be held in class. Make sure that students realize that these propaganda techniques are usually used in combination.
   a. *Bad names.* Disagreeable words are used to arouse distaste for a person or a thing.
   b. *Glad names.* Pleasant words are used to create good feelings about a person or a thing.
   c. *Plain folks.* This kind of propaganda avoids sophistication. Political candidates use this technique when they kiss babies and play with dogs.
   d. *Transfer.* This type of propaganda attempts to transfer to a person or thing the reader's respect for the flag, the cross, or some other valued symbol.
   e. *Testimonial.* This technique is like transfer except that a famous or well-informed person gives a testimonial for a product or a person. Positive feelings for the famous person are supposed to be transferred to the product.
   f. *Bandwagon.* This is an attempt to convince readers that they should accept an idea or purchase an item because "everyone is doing it."
   g. *Card stacking.* This technique utilizes accurate information but omits some data so that only one side of a story is told.

6. After learning to identify propaganda techniques, the reader should analyze the propaganda using the following questions:
   a. What technique is used?
   b. Who composed the propaganda?
   c. Why was the propaganda written?
   d. To what reader interests, emotions, and prejudices does the propaganda appeal?
   e. Will I allow myself to be influenced by this propaganda?

EXAMPLE 5.4   Fact and Opinion Chart

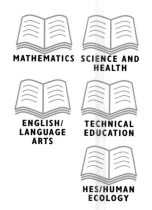

SOCIAL STUDIES

Facts	Opinions
"Old" immigrants were from British Isles, Germany, Scandinavia.	"Old" immigrants were acceptable.
"New" immigrants were from Slavic countries, Italy, Greece.	"New" immigrants were unacceptable, ignorant, greedy, diseased, criminal, insane, wild-eyed, bad-smelling.

Critical Thinking Activities

1. Writers should support their conclusions in the text; however, readers often need additional data to evaluate the validity of content. Ask students to consult other sources of information to evaluate the validity of the content of an article, book, or chapter.

2. Ask students to evaluate the author's qualifications for writing on the topic at hand. Questions like these will guide them:
   a. Would a lawyer probably be qualified to write a book on writing contracts?
   b. Would a football player probably be qualified to write a book on foreign policy?
   c. Would a chef probably be a qualified author for a book on menu planning?
   d. Would a physician probably be qualified to write a book on music theory?

CREATIVE THINKING AND READING

What is the most important aspect of creative thinking?

Creative thinkers find new ways of viewing ideas, incidents, or characters that stimulate original or novel thinking or production of new materials. They strive for originality and ideas that are fundamental, far-reaching, and powerful (Perkins, 1995). Creative thinkers are able to view their experiences from different perspectives. Good **creative thinking** always involves a measure of critical thinking, or it would be nonsensical (Perkins, 1995). Creative thinkers generate possibilities, then critically sift through and rework them. They need to be knowledgeable about a subject to think more creatively about it.

Creative thinkers and readers may come up with several ways of solving a math problem or of performing an experiment in science class. They may turn a situation from a literature selection into a puppet show, a skit, or a painting. They may make a unique table in wood shop or develop a design in human environmental science that surpasses those suggested in the book. To do these things, creative thinkers translate existing knowledge into new forms. Creativity is stifled when all school activities must be carried out according to the precise specifications of the teacher and when deviations from prescribed forms are always discouraged.

Creative thinking is based on knowledge about the subject and opportunities to solve problems and to respond to authentic situations. Creative thinking and reading activities related to *The Land* and *Shipwreck at the Bottom of the World* are illustrated below.

MATHEMATICS   **SCIENCE AND HEALTH**

ENGLISH/ LANGUAGE ARTS   **TECHNICAL EDUCATION**

HES/HUMAN ECOLOGY

Creative Thinking and Reading Activities

**ENGLISH/
LANGUAGE
ARTS**

**SOCIAL
STUDIES**

**ENGLISH/
LANGUAGE
ARTS**

1. In the book *The Land*, Paul expresses strong feelings about the land where he grew up and the land that he wanted to buy. Find these descriptions and reread them, examining his thoughts. Then write a description of land that you like, expressing your feelings about it.

2. Discuss the ways that Paul's feelings might have changed after a white man helped him.

3. What do you think it would feel like to be caught between the colored world and the white world?

4. Read the author's notes at the end of this book. Then discuss the ways that Paul and his wife influenced the author.

5. The author of *Shipwreck at the Bottom of the World* vividly describes the sounds of the ship, *Endurance*, as it was caught in the ice. How did the description make you feel? What music sounds like the ship sounds? How do you think these sounds made the crew feel?

6. The author of *Shipwreck at the Bottom of the World* describes one of the pictures of the *Endurance* as looking like a negative. Why did he describe it in this way? Can you create a picture that has this same effect? How?

7. The author of this book is an especially vivid writer of nonfiction. Analyze her use of language and suggest the ways that she uses language to create strong feelings.

Figure 5.3 summarizes types of questions and strategies to increase quality thinking.

Authentic Reading Tasks

Reading comprehension instruction should link classroom literacy activities with real-world, authentic reading and writing experiences (Brophy, 1992). These experiences help students connect the use of print with the home or the wider culture (Kucer, 1991).

Thematic units are one approach to developing authentic literacy tasks that integrate the language arts and other curricular areas. The integrated curriculum can be authentic and can provide learning experiences more closely attuned to the way children and adults learn (Lipson et al., 1993). **Integrated units** promote higher-order thinking, concept development, and transfer of knowledge.

Integrated units make teaching and learning meaningful by interrelating content and process. **Themes** give instruction a focus, create coherence across content and process, and enable students to understand what and why they are learning. Integrated units of study help students transform knowledge into the schemata and tools for learning that will be helpful throughout their lives. Themes also provide a framework for students to discover the connections among literature selections. To capitalize on the merits of integrated, thematic units, teachers need to serve as

What processes are promoted in integrated units?

Give an example of a theme that would help students discover connections among literature selections.

FIGURE 5.3

Questioning for Quality Thinking

Source: J. McTighe and F. Lyman Jr., "Cueing Thinking in the Classroom: The Promise of Theory-Embedded Tools," *Educational Leadership 54*(7) (1988, April): 18–24 (Figure p. 21).

Front	Back
QUESTIONING FOR QUALITY THINKING	**STRATEGIES TO EXTEND STUDENT THINKING**

Front

QUESTIONING FOR QUALITY THINKING

Knowledge — Identification and recall of information
　Who, what, when, where, how _____ ?
　Describe _____ .

Comprehension — Organization and selection of facts and ideas
　Retell _____ in your own words.
　What is the main idea of _____ ?

Application — Use of facts, rules, principles
　How is _____ an example of _____ ?
　How is _____ related to _____ ?
　Why is _____ significant?

Analysis — Separation of whole into component parts
　What are the parts or features of _____ ?
　Classify _____ according to _____ .
　Outline/diagram/web _____ .
　How does ___ compare/contrast with ___ ?
　What evidence can you list for _____ ?

Synthesis — Combination of ideas to form a new whole
　What would you predict/infer from ___ ?
　What ideas can you add to _____ ?
　How would you create/design a new ___ ?
　What might happen if you combined ___ with _____ ?
　What solutions would you suggest for ___ ?

Evaluation — Development of opinions, judgments, or decisions
　Do you agree _____ ?
　What do you think about _____ ?
　What is the most important _____ ?
　Prioritize _____ .
　How would you decide about _____ ?
　What criteria would you use to assess ___ ?

Back

STRATEGIES TO EXTEND STUDENT THINKING

- **Remember "wait time I and II"**
  Provide at least three seconds of thinking time after a question and after a response
- **Utilize "think-pair-share"**
  Allow individual thinking time, discussion with a partner, and then open up the class discussion
- **Ask "follow-ups"**
  Why? Do you agree? Can you elaborate? Tell me more. Can you give an example?
- **Withhold judgment**
  Respond to student answers in a non-evaluative fashion
- **Ask for summary (to promote active listening)**
  "Could you please summarize John's point?"
- **Survey the class**
  "How many people agree with the author's point of view?" ("thumbs up, thumbs down")
- **Allow for student calling**
  "Richard, will you please call on someone else to respond?"
- **Play devil's advocate**
  Require students to defend their reasoning against different points of view
- **Ask students to "unpack their thinking"**
  "Describe how you arrived at your answer." ("think aloud")
- **Call on students randomly**
  Not just those with raised hands
- **Student questioning**
  Let the students develop their own questions
- **Cue student responses**
  "There is not a single correct answer for this question. I want you to consider alternatives."

mediators of comprehension strategies and skills as they guide students who are discovering the connections that are the heart of integrated instruction. The role of themes, topics, and real literature in developing literacy is discussed throughout this book, and Chapter 9 focuses on literature in content classrooms. In the following "Meeting the Challenge" vignette, the integrated unit approach to using literature in the classroom is demonstrated.

MEETING THE CHALLENGE

News stories may serve as the basis for thematic units.
© Susie Fitzhugh

Kyle Richards overheard his eighth-grade students discussing a news story about skiers who had survived five days without food or shelter following an avalanche. Then another student told the group about people who survived long periods of time in collapsed buildings after an earthquake. These discussions gave him an idea for a thematic unit on survival in various environments. On the basis of the students' discussion, he thought they would recognize the authenticity of this unit. Furthermore, he could integrate it with the science and social studies curriculum. An abridged version of the unit he taught follows.

Major Concepts of the Unit

1. Many survivors do not have special skills; instead, they are people who refuse to give up.
2. Many survivors are ordinary people who are thrust into extraordinary circumstances that force them to find ways to solve their problems and keep on living.
3. Survivors often have to meet basic needs, such as finding food, water, shelter, and protection. People who lack basic knowledge about their environment have greater difficulties in solving their problems.
4. The sources of food, water, shelter, and protection differ with the nature of the environment. For example, a person stranded on a tropical island would face different problems from those faced by one caught in a blizzard.
5. Survivors' lives are changed by the problems they faced and overcame.

Unit Initiation

Kyle asked the students to brainstorm the concept of survival as it related to newspaper articles about hurricanes, earthquakes, and floods, as well as stories about

ENGLISH/
LANGUAGE
ARTS

individuals who had survived other environmental traumas. Then he had the students map survival situations and create individual definitions of the term *survival*. The map they created is illustrated in Figure 5.4.

Following the brainstorming and semantic mapping of survival, the class studied the book *Hatchet* by Gary Paulsen. They also read newspaper and magazine articles related to survival.

FIGURE 5.4

Survival Map Created by Students

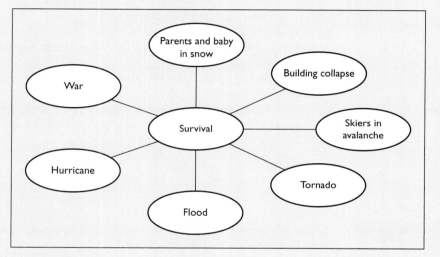

Before Reading

1. The students identified the problems and dangers they would face if they were alone in a Canadian wilderness without assistance or equipment. They discussed the topic, and the teacher recorded their ideas on a transparency. When they finished brainstorming, they fit their ideas into categories of food, shelter, clothing, protection from animals, and so forth. They summarized these ideas in their journals and on a class chart.

2. Students were told they could choose just one piece of equipment to take into the wilderness with them. Then they wrote a paragraph or more about what they chose and why they chose that particular piece of equipment. Many students cited points from newspaper and magazine articles that helped them choose their equipment.

During Reading

SCIENCE AND
HEALTH

SOCIAL
STUDIES

1. The students identified the various ways the main character in *Hatchet*, Brian, solved his problems, and they compared his strategies with those discussed in newspaper and magazine articles.

2. The protagonist in *Hatchet* was struggling with several problems throughout the book, so the teacher asked students to identify the words associated with these

continued

continued

**SCIENCE AND
HEALTH**

concepts: *divorce, fire, mistakes,* and *the secret.* They listed these words in their journal for class discussion.

3. The students identified scientific and geographic knowledge that would have helped Brian survive.

Following Reading

The students discussed the following questions:

1. "Why did Brian call the fire a 'hungry friend,' and 'close and sweet'?"
2. "What was the most valuable thing Brian invented or had in this story? Why did you choose this?"
3. "What did Brian mean when he called himself a city boy in this story? Was he complimenting himself?"
4. "Why did Brian want to tell somebody about his success in building a fire?"
5. "What did Brian learn from his experience? How did he learn this?"
6. "Who taught Brian?"

**ENGLISH/
LANGUAGE
ARTS**

Students also did the following:

1. They identified additional figurative language that made the writing especially effective. They compared the writing style of the newspaper and magazine stories with that of the novel.
2. They contrasted Brian's character traits at the beginning and at the end of the story and made charts to show the contrasts.
3. They identified and discussed the theme of the book.
4. They identified the three types of conflict in the book and explained each one.
5. They discussed how this experience changed Brian's life.

Extensions

The students chose projects from the following list that could be related to the novel or a newspaper or magazine article.

1. Research flora and fauna that might exist in the Canadian wilderness that Brian could have used for food.
2. Identify other kinds of shelters that he could have constructed or found in this setting.
3. Research the concept of light refraction, which played such an important role in this book.
4. Research fire, and find different ways to build fires.
5. Find a map of a similar area. Then create a map of Brian's camp and the lake.
6. Identify ways of measuring time when one lacks the usual means.

**SCIENCE AND
HEALTH**

Language Arts Extensions

1. Write a script in which Brian is interviewed on a television program. The students may role-play this activity.
2. Write about Brian's first meal after returning home.

**ENGLISH/
LANGUAGE
ARTS**

3. Compare survival situations depicted in various stories and articles. Discuss the elements to be survived, the means of survival, and the aftermaths of the situations.
4. Compare characters, character development, and character traits in various books.
5. Compare the plot lines in several books.
6. Prepare a television show or play that illustrates the survival theme.

Related Books

Slake's Limbo by Felice Holman
Julie of the Wolves by Jean George
The Goats by Brock Cole
Dogsong by Gary Paulsen
My Side of the Mountain by Jean George
Tracker by Gary Paulsen
No Pretty Pictures by Anita Lobel
Away Is a Strange Place to Be by H. M. Hoover
What's Going to Happen to Me? When Parents Separate and Divorce by Eda Le Shan
Animal Ecology by Mark Lambert and John Williams
Shelters from Tepee to Igloo by Harvey Weiss
Plants That Heal by Millicent Selsam

Strategies to Increase Comprehension

Throughout this text, strategies and activities are introduced to improve students' comprehension. These strategies focus on literacy and constructing meaning. Initially, most of the strategies involve direct teacher instruction and guidance, but the universal goal is for students to use the strategies independently. Ultimately students should internalize and implement appropriate strategies.

Some of the following suggestions should be implemented before reading, some during reading, and others after reading; some strategies are used throughout the reading process.

SCAFFOLDS FOR COMPREHENSION

Scaffolds are temporary structures that enable a student to successfully complete a task he or she could not complete without the assistance of the scaffold. Scaffolding connects students to the text and the comprehension task. Scaffolds are instructional frameworks that support students as they develop content literacy (Stephens and Brown, 2005). Scaffolds focus on the task and how to complete it, but the ultimate goal is to help students become independent learners. In reality, all of the strategies in this book are scaffolds because they support the teacher who is giving students the support they need to comprehend.

Scaffolding strategies can be adapted to any content area and they can be structured through various organizational formats. Teachers can work with the entire class, especially when working toward common goals. A small group of students may work with specific goals and tasks. These groups should be flexible and changeable, depending on the purposes and tasks. Some students work well with partners who are working to achieve the same goals. In some instances, individual students work well when assigned specific responsibilities (Stephens and Brown, 2005). Moreover, the varied groups enable the teacher to develop a clear picture of individual students' progress.

Think alouds, which were discussed earlier, are strategies that teachers and students use for scaffolding. Additional strategies are found throughout this text and the following scaffolding strategies are examples:

Directed reading-thinking activity (DRTA)
Discussion
Know–Want to Know–Learned (K-W-L)
Problem-solving approach
Reciprocal teaching
Writing strategies
Visualization strategies

DIRECTED READING-THINKING ACTIVITY (DRTA)

How does a directed reading lesson compare with a directed reading-thinking activity?

Stauffer (1969) developed the **directed reading-thinking activity (DRTA)** to encourage students' thinking. In a DRTA, students develop their own purposes for reading when the teacher asks them to predict what the material will be about from the title clues and the graphic aids in the text. Predictions may be listed on the board and modified or deleted as the students request. Students may change their ideas about the predictions, and they can explain their predictions during class discussion.

The teacher divides the reading material into portions that provide good prediction points. Students read to a specified point, stop, assess their previous predictions, either confirm or reject the predictions, and make new predictions if they have rejected the old ones. Students discuss the confirmation or rejection of predictions and support their decisions by referring to information gathered from the text. This process is continued until the entire selection has been read. Students' early predictions are likely to be diverse because the reading clues are sparse at that point, but the predictions become more convergent as the reading continues.

The four steps in a content area directed reading-thinking activity are as follows (Haggard, 1986):

1. Activate prior knowledge.

2. Predict the content of the next text portion.

3. Read the selection.

4. Confirm, reject, revise, or elaborate previous predictions.

Example 5.5 illustrates the application of DRTA to an earth science lesson on modern methods of mapmaking.

EXAMPLE 5.5   Earth Science DRTA

SCIENCE AND
HEALTH

STEP 1 Activate prior knowledge.

Teacher: What kind of surveying was used for the first topographic maps?

Student A: A ground survey.

Teacher: Why do you think it is called a ground survey?

Student B: I think it's because the surveyor stood on the ground.

STEP 2 Predict.

Teacher: What topics do you predict will be covered in the section on remote sensing?

Student C: I guess they'll discuss ways of surveying that are not used in ground surveying.

Teacher: What methods do you predict will be discussed?

Student D: I think they'll probably talk about magnetic methods because magnetic declination was in the last section.

Teacher: That is a thoughtful prediction.

Student E: I predict that the methods will be something like radar because the book says "remote sensing" and radar senses things far away.

Student F: Well, it seems to me that remote sensing for maps would have to have pictures or photographs of some kind.

STEP 3 Read.

Teacher: Now read this section to learn whether your predictions are accurate.

STEP 4 Confirm, reject, revise, or elaborate predictions.

In Step 4 the students discussed and concluded the following:

a. They confirmed that remote sensing involved both photography and radar.

b. They rejected magnetic imaging as a factor in this discussion.

c. They revised their predictions to include imaging radar, side-looking radar, and photogrammetry.

d. They elaborated their predictions to include a series of satellites called *Landsat*.

DISCUSSION

What are the major
values of discussion in
content classrooms?

Creating a social environment in the classroom promotes dialogue and discussion, as well as developing a learning community (Brophy, 1992; Wollman-Bonilla, 1994). **Discussion** is a powerful tool for developing higher-order thinking because participants interact as they present multiple points of view and listen to counterarguments. Students who participate in discussions learn to listen to and validate other students' perspectives. Meanings shared in discussion groups are more than a collection of individual ideas; they are part of new sets of meanings developed as members talk and listen to one another.

In a well-planned discussion, students interact with one another as well as with the teacher, and they are encouraged to make comments and to ask questions that are longer than two- or three-word phrases. Such discussions offer students opportunities to enrich and refine knowledge gained from the text.

KNOW–WANT TO KNOW–LEARNED (K-W-L)

What additional
columns could you
add to K-W-L?

The Know–Want to Know–Learned (**K-W-L**) strategy encourages students to activate prior knowledge and stimulates cognition and metacognition (Ogle, 1986; Carr and Ogle, 1987). Initially, the students brainstorm what they already know about the reading topic. Then they write the brainstormed information in the K (Know) column of a chart like the one shown in Example 5.6. As the students work, the teacher should encourage them to categorize the information and list their categories at the bottom of the column. The students generate questions about the text, which are listed in the W (Want to Know) column. Additional questions may be generated as the students proceed. Finally, information learned from the text is entered in the L (Learned) column. The students map the material and use the map to write a summary.

EXAMPLE 5.6   K-W-L for Eleventh-Grade Government—"Civil Liberties": The First Amendment Freedoms

SOCIAL STUDIES

K Know	W Want to Know	L Learned
Freedom of speech	Does the First Amendment mean we	
Personal freedom	can do *anything* we want to? Are we	
Freedom to write	free to do things that will hurt us?	
Language		
Civil liberties		

PROBLEM-SOLVING APPROACH

What kinds of thinking are stimulated in a problem-solving approach?

A **problem-solving approach** to reading encourages students to spend time understanding a problem before attacking it (McTighe and Lyman, 1988). In this approach, the teacher introduces various methods of problem solving and poses problem situations for students to analyze. Then students identify a problem and state it in their own words, after which they brainstorm possible solutions. Critical thinking is the next stage because students have to examine the possibilities generated and eliminate the unworkable ones. Students can compare this problem with others that they know about or discuss it with another person to clarify thinking. In addition, students may gather relevant information and find out how other people have solved similar problems. A problem can be broken into parts or restated to expand students' understanding. Finally, writing out a problem often helps students solve it. Completing a guide similar to the one in Example 5.7 is helpful for students who need practice with problem solving.

EXAMPLE 5.7   **Problem-Solving Paradigm Based on *Hatchet* by Gary Paulsen**

Problem: Brian needed food to survive.

Possible solutions	Evaluate possible solutions	Support for evaluations
Eat what birds eat	+	He could eat some things birds eat, but some he couldn't.
Fish	+	Needs fishing line
Catch animals	+	Needs traps or other equipment

Solution: He used all three solutions to obtain food.

Evaluate Solution
The solution worked well, but some of the food the birds ate made Brian sick. He was able to fish and catch animals after he made equipment and found additional equipment in the airplane.

The following are examples of problems that could be used in problem-solving reading activities:

SOCIAL STUDIES

SCIENCE AND HEALTH

TECHNICAL EDUCATION

HES/HUMAN ECOLOGY

1. *Social studies:* During a World War II unit give the students contradicting quotations concerning Franklin Delano Roosevelt. Then ask them to research to determine which point of view they espouse.

2. *Science:* Assign students to read news articles related to the tsunami that occurred in South Asia at the end of 2004 and to research the kinds of problems that victims of a tsunami may face.

3. *Technology education:* During a unit on finishing various types of materials, such as wood, concrete, plastic, and compressed wood, have the students explore the finishes that are most appropriate, most economical, and most durable.

4. *Human environmental science:* Students should use the new food pyramid as a basis for planning the nutritional needs of individuals with various diseases, such as diabetes, or allergies.

Controversial issues provide material for the problem-solving approach to content area reading. In such an approach, teachers may select issues related to assigned reading or from newspapers, newsmagazines, and television programs. Controversial issues that may be used follow:

BUSINESS EDUCATION

SCIENCE AND HEALTH   **SOCIAL STUDIES**

1. The president's economic changes at the beginning of a new term of office (economics class)

2. The moral and/or scientific issues in genetic engineering (science class)

3. The role of computers in education and in other facets of life (social studies class)

RECIPROCAL TEACHING

What are the strategies involved in reciprocal teaching?

Reciprocal teaching features "guided practice" in applying simple, concrete strategies to text comprehension (Palincsar and Brown, 1986; Rosenshine and Meister, 1994; Alfassi, 1998). This very successful instructional procedure consists of these four strategies:

1. Summarize the paragraph or assignment in a sentence.

2. Ask one or two higher-level questions.

3. Clarify any difficult parts.

4. Predict what the next paragraph or section will discuss.

The teacher models the process and then gradually turns it over to the students while providing feedback and encouragement. This activity may be done with pairs or triads (three students, or one adult and two students).

WRITING STRATEGIES

Educators have recognized for some time that writing improves comprehension. Writing forces students to shape and form their responses to the text—to bring these thoughts to conscious awareness. Refer to Chapter 8 for additional information about writing and its relation to reading comprehension and retention.

VISUALIZATION STRATEGIES

What is visualization?

Visualization is the process of forming mental images that depict reading content, such as story settings, characters, story action, geographic areas, famous historical figures, scientific experiments, and steps in mathematics problems. Visualization activities like these will benefit students:

SOCIAL STUDIES

1. *Social studies:* Develop a "You Are There" activity. The students could act out the process of approval for judges appointed to the Supreme Court. This will involve a certain amount of research to understand the process. They could discuss the emotions engendered by the occasion. At another time, students might visualize a battle in a war they are studying, discussing the placement of various battle lines, and giving descriptions of weapons and uniforms. They could also use models to develop an understanding of the action.

2. When working with problem-solving activities in any subject, students can be asked to visualize alternative solutions that will help them work through the various ways of solving a problem.

Enhancing Comprehension Before, During, and After Reading

The unit plan in the "Meeting the Challenge" vignette in this chapter integrates strategies for all three phases of reading, as do the following study guide, the directed reading lesson, and the graphic organizer in Figure 5.5. These plans are used most appropriately after students have acquired strategies for the three phases of reading comprehension.

STUDY GUIDES

What value do study guides have?

One of the most valuable strategies for increasing students' comprehension is the **study guide**. A study guide is a set of statements and/or questions designed to direct students' attention to the key ideas in a passage and sometimes to suggest the skills to apply for successful comprehension (Harris and Hodges, 1981). A study guide creates a point of contact between the student and the written material, showing readers *how to comprehend* content.

The instructor's goals and the students' needs determine the composition of a study guide. It may cover a chapter, a larger unit, or merely part of a long chapter. If

A What I know definitely	B What I think I know	C D Read/Verify	E Questions about the reading	F Where to find answers
1 _____ _____ _____ 2 _____ _____ _____ 3 _____ _____ _____ 4 _____ _____ _____	1 _____ _____ _____ 2 _____ _____ _____ 3 _____ _____ _____ 4 _____ _____ _____	(Discussion may take place here) R + Item is accurate. E – Item is not accurate. A ? Not enough information D is given.	1 _____ _____ _____ 2 _____ _____ _____ 3 _____ _____ _____ 4 _____ _____ _____	1 _____ _____ _____ 2 _____ _____ _____ 3 _____ _____ _____ 4 _____ _____ _____

1. List information that is definitely known about the topic.
2. List information that is tentatively known about the topic.
3. Read the material.
4. After reading, verify the accuracy of the information given in Columns A and B by marking the items with a plus (+), minus (–), or a question mark (?).
5. Decide which questions still remain or which questions have arisen after the reading.
6. Identify which sources can be consulted to find the information.

Note: This organizer may be modified to suit instructional purposes. Lines were drawn to help the reader maintain continuity among items in different columns.

FIGURE 5.5

Graphic Organizer SSTG (Six-Step Topical Guide)

Source: Margaret Egan, "Reflections on Effective Use of Graphic Organizers," *Journal of Adolescent & Adult Literacy* 42(8) (1999, May): 641–645. Reprinted with permission of Margaret Egan and the International Reading Association. All rights reserved.

students are given a study guide to read before they study an assignment, they can respond to the questions and activities as they read the material. Study guides may take a variety of forms. Examples of these forms are found throughout this text.

A single study guide may set purposes for reading, provide aids for interpretation of the material, or do both. Study guides are particularly valuable when the teacher uses grouping in the content class. Each small group of students can sit together, work through their study guide individually, and then discuss their answers with one another, reconciling any differences in their answers. Handling material this way causes the students to think about the material they are reading; critical thinking is necessary as students try to reach a consensus about their answers.

Example 5.8 shows a science selection related to oceanography; a study guide follows.

EXAMPLE 5.8   Science Selection and Study Guide

SCIENCE AND HEALTH

Oceanography

Throughout history, poets and sailors alike have been awed by the size of the world's oceans. When viewed from space, Earth appears mostly blue, because oceans cover more than 70 percent of its surface. For this reason, Earth is sometimes called the water planet. The immense volume of water on Earth is hard to imagine; the average depth of the oceans is more than four times the average elevation of the continents.

As vast and interesting as they are, the oceans remain largely a mystery. Aided by new technology, scientists are continually discovering and learning about interactions between the oceans and Earth's other environments.

The Beginnings of Oceanography

Oceanography is the scientific study of the ocean using chemistry, biology, physics, geology, and other sciences. In the mid-1800s, a U.S. Navy officer named Matthew F. Maury conducted one of the first modern ocean studies. Maury used the logbooks of U.S. Navy captains to compile charts of ocean currents and winds. In 1855, he published his findings in the book *The Physical Geography of the Sea*.

The first large-scale ocean research project came in 1872, when scientists aboard the British ship H.M.S. *Challenger* used their onboard laboratory equipment to measure ocean depths, take water samples, record temperatures, and study currents. Oceanographers today still use data gathered during this expedition.

World War II brought about the next great advance in oceanography. The military's development of submarines and surface ships led to more accurate ocean charts and new instruments, such as sonar and magnetic recorders. These devices became the basic tools of modern ocean research.

Analysis
Why is oceanography an important science?

Study Guide
Overview Question: Since extensive research has been used to explore the oceans, why do they continue to be mysterious?
1. Identify the various scientists involved in oceanography.
2. How does the author illustrate the depth of oceans?
3. Describe the oceanographic research conducted in 1872.
4. Why are scientists studying the interactions between oceans and earth's other environments?
5. How does oceanographic research relate to your life?

Source: From *Earth Science* by Nancy E. Spaulding and Samuel N. Namowitz. Copyright © 2003 by McDougal Littell Inc., a division of Houghton Mifflin Company. All rights reserved. Reprinted by permission of McDougal Littell Inc., a division of Houghton Mifflin Company.

The teacher's instructional intent in the study guide in Example 5.8 is apparent in the overview question, which is designed to focus on the understandings that students are expected to acquire from the selection; moreover, this question focuses the reading while requiring critical or creative reading abilities. The balance of the guide provides a series of questions that relate to the ideas in the text.

This study guide could be used for all students who can read the textbook, with or without teacher assistance; however, if a teacher wanted to reduce the guide's length, some questions could be assigned to all students, and other questions could be divided between those who need assistance from the teacher and those who do not. The teacher may work closely with the instructional-level group members as they discuss their assigned questions and may monitor the independent-level group less intensively. The group that cannot handle the text material should be given another reading assignment in order to learn the content. This group should have its own study guide, geared to its assignment. The whole-class discussion that follows the small-group sessions with the guides will help all the students clarify their concepts and see relationships among the ideas.

A three-level study guide directs students toward comprehension at the literal level (directly stated ideas), the interpretive level (implied ideas), and the applied level (using information to solve problems). See Chapter 9, Example 9.1, for an example of a guide designed for the short story "Man Without a Country" by Edward Everett Hale.

DIRECTED READING LESSONS

What are the steps in a directed reading lesson?

A **directed reading lesson** (DRL) is a method for guiding students' comprehension of a reading selection. Directed reading approaches vary from source to source, but the following components are present in all the plans: motivation and building background, skill-development activities, guided reading, and follow-up activities. The following directed reading lesson is based on a selection from Shirley Haley-James et al., *Houghton Mifflin English*, Boston: Houghton Mifflin, 1986, p. 417.

Directed Reading Lesson

Motivation and Building Background

ENGLISH/
LANGUAGE
ARTS

1. Ask the students if they know what a *villain* is. After discussing the word's current meaning, tell them that it originally meant "a person from a villa" and that its meaning has changed for the worse.

2. Ask the students if they know what *nice* means. After discussing the word's current meaning, tell them that it once meant "ignorant" and that its meaning has changed for the better.

3. Ask the students if they know any words that have come from place names or names of people. Let them name as many as possible. Be ready to provide some examples for them, such as *pasteurization*.

Skill-Development Activities

4. Remind students that words presented in boldface print are important words for which to know meanings.

5. Review types of context clues that are often found in textbooks. Give special attention to definition clues, since there is a definition clue for the word *etymology* in the assignment.

6. Review the meaning of *-logy* (the study of). Have students name and define words ending in *-logy* (*biology, geology,* and so forth).

7. Review the meaning of the word part *un-* (not). Have students name and define words with this part (*unhappy, unwanted*).

8. Review the meaning of the word part *-able* (able to be). Have students name and define words with this part (*workable, marketable*).

Guided Reading

9. Silent reading—Have students read the selection silently for the following purposes:
   a. Determine the meaning of the word *etymology.*
   b. Find two words whose names have come from the names of places.
   c. Determine the meaning of *unpredictable.*
   d. Find a word that had a negative meaning change over the years.
   e. Find a word that had a positive meaning change over the years.

10. Discussion and oral reading—Choose some students to read aloud and discuss the parts related to the silent reading purposes, especially if the students find the purpose questions difficult to answer.

Follow-up Activities

11. Have the students do the two practice activities at the bottom of the selection and discuss their results in class.

12. Have the students list five words that they find that have interesting etymologies. Have a class discussion of the words.

Focus on Struggling Readers

Comprehension I

Students who must struggle with decoding text will find it difficult to comprehend; therefore, teachers may need to assign alternative text material on the topic. Students need to know 95–99 percent of the words and the concepts they represent in order to comprehend. The majority of struggling readers do not know the words or the concepts they represent. Therefore, struggling readers need to focus on concepts related to the topic in order to comprehend. Many struggling readers lack the necessary schemata to permit them to connect with the text and predict the ideas they will be reading. Many struggling readers lack concepts and world knowledge that more accomplished readers take for granted. Therefore, teachers may have to introduce background information that would prepare students to read.

Struggling readers should be guided to realize how the assigned material relates to them and to identify the value of assigned reading. Scaffolding strategies are especially important to support their comprehension efforts. These strategies will help them read with understanding and organize the information so that students increase their ability to remember what they have read. The strategies in Chapters 3, 4, and 5 will help struggling readers comprehend.

Struggling readers should have a clear understanding of the reading assignment and the teacher's purposes for their reading. After they grow more competent, they should be encouraged to state their own purposes. Moreover, they should write the questions they are seeking to answer prior to reading; after reading, they should write the answers to their questions. Struggling readers should be encouraged to look back at the text to find answers or the information they need to infer answers; otherwise, they will guess rather than using a logical thought process.

Struggling readers will benefit from working with partners or coaches. They tend to achieve more success working in small groups. Multimedia materials are motivating for struggling readers. Furthermore, these materials require the same comprehension strategies as do books. A comparison of these media is shown in Figure 5.6.

"Repeated Readings" are valuable for both struggling readers and ELLs. The purpose of this strategy is to increase students' automatic recognition of words, which increases their fluency and their comprehension. This technique is developed in several ways. Initially, students can read aloud with the teacher, who reads a little faster than the students, so they are echoing the teacher. Students also do three-minute readings, and, reading the same text, they try to read more words each time they read it. They may read for different purposes each time (e.g., to identify the characters, to determine the setting), to provide some reason for reading again. Additional practice is developed through giving students tape recordings of books so they can continue practicing.

Strategy	Book	Internet
Activate schemata	Reader relates prior experience to the reading content and purpose.	Needs these strategies.
Ask questions	Reader asks questions.	Student does the same.
Identify main ideas and thesis	Reader uses these strategies.	Reader uses the same strategies.
Use literal, inferential skills	Reader uses these thinking skills.	Student uses these skills and critical thinking.
Synthesizes information and ideas	Reader synthesizes.	Student synthesizes.
Monitor understanding and correct as needed	Reader skims and scans to correct.	Student does the same.
Navigate	Readers uses typographical information and index, table of contents, headings, and glossary.	Student uses different navigational skills including identification of related sites to search.

This figure was adapted from Schmar-Dobler (2003).

FIGURE 5.6

Focus on English Language Learners

Learning How to Comprehend Written English

English language learners (ELLs) can acquire basic vocabulary and concepts, but teachers cannot assume that ELLs have the comprehension skills necessary to succeed in content classes. ELLs need to be taught comprehension strategies through explicit modeling and scaffolding (Harper and de Jong, 2004). Therefore, the strategies introduced in this chapter are important to ELLs' comprehension.

Moreover, teachers who have ELLs in class should be aware that English is a word-order language; other languages are based on word case, and many Asian languages originated as pictographic languages. These factors are related to the syntactic differences that ELLs experience in functioning with English.

ELLs will experience cultural and historical differences in text because they are unacquainted with concepts that are common to fluent readers of English. Therefore, teachers need to prepare students to read, particularly in the content areas of history, English, and literature. On the other hand, many math and science concepts transcend culture. While teaching a Korean student, Barbara discovered there are some Korean concepts that cannot be translated into English, and English concepts that cannot be translated directly into Korean. Even students whose first language is English, such as some students originally from India, will exhibit conceptual differences in their language. When assessing their oral language and written language, teachers must ask them to explain their ideas. The comprehension of ELLs is enhanced by multimedia materials and bilingual books. This is illustrated in Figure 5.6. Bilingual books are becoming more widely available and teachers will find them useful for both ELLs and the other students in their classes because they can learn words in the ELLs' language (Ernst-Slavit and Mulhern, 2003). Teachers can obtain information about bilingual books from these sources: American Library Association; *English Journal; Journal of Adolescent and Adult Literacy;* University of Wisconsin, Cooperative Children's Book Center.

SUMMARY

Comprehension is an active, constructive process based on interactions among a reader, a text, and the reading situation or purpose. Readers implement strategies before, during, and after reading text. Effective readers use strategies that are appropriate to the material and the task. Their strategies are plans for using skills to comprehend. Struggling readers and English language learners need to learn the strategies introduced in this chapter in order to become competent comprehenders. Figure 5.7 summarizes comprehension strategies.

FIGURE 5.7

Comprehension Strategies

1. Develop a positive attitude toward reading
2. Identify important ideas
3. Identify the organizational pattern of the text
4. Identify the sequence of events
5. Monitor understanding
6. Paraphrase
7. Predict
8. Question
9. Relate new knowledge to prior knowledge
10. Reread
11. Search for relationships
12. Summarize

DISCUSSION QUESTIONS

1. Why do you think critical reading is so important for today's students?
2. What strategies and activities can a teacher use before having students start a reading assignment to aid their comprehension?
3. How is discussion related to reading comprehension?
4. What is the purpose of a think-aloud exercise?
5. How do strategies function in reading comprehension?

6. What attributes characterize fluent readers?
7. How are struggling readers like their classmates?
8. How do ELLs differ from their classmates?

ENRICHMENT ACTIVITIES

1. Visit a secondary school classroom to watch questioning procedures. Identify the type of questioning used most often. Also note how much time the students are allowed for formulating answers.
2. Select a chapter in a content textbook, and make a plan to help secondary school students comprehend the chapter, using strategies suggested in this chapter.
*3. Adapt one of the strategies suggested in this chapter to your content area.
*4. Examine the exercises suggested in this chapter, and identify those that will be most useful in your content area.
*5. Prepare a strategy lesson for an English language learner.
6. Visit a classroom that includes struggling readers and observe the teaching adaptations used.

---

*These activities are designed for in-service teachers, student teachers, and practicum students.

Chapter 6

Location and Organization
of Information

OVERVIEW

In this chapter we discuss location skills related to use of the library or media center, books, computer databases, and the Internet. We also give attention to the organizational skills of outlining, summarizing, and note taking. These skills are important to students' success with assignments such as written reports, research papers, and class presentations in all content area classes.

PURPOSE-SETTING QUESTIONS

As you read this chapter, try to answer these questions:

1. What location skills do secondary school students need in order to use the library or media center effectively?
2. What location skills do students need in order to use books effectively for content area classes?
3. What skills do students need in order to use computer databases effectively?
4. What skills do students need in order to use the Internet effectively to locate information?
5. What organizational skills are helpful to students who are reading material that they will use later in some manner?
6. What special help with location and organization skills do struggling readers and English language learners need?

Location Skills

To take part in many study activities (primarily content area reading and writing assignments), students must be able to locate specific reading materials. Teaching students to use location aids in libraries or media centers and in books and to use computer databases and the Internet will enable them to find the materials they need.

LIBRARIES OR MEDIA CENTERS

A study done by Ross Todd and Carol Kuhlthau showed that learning, in general, and information literacy, in particular, are facilitated by an effective school library with a credentialed librarian. Students indicated that the library helped them learn to find and use information, work out questions for topics they are researching, and learn more about their topics ("New Study Supports Value of School Libraries," 2004).

"In schools, libraries are places where text, technology, and literacy converge in concentrated form" (Kapitzke, 2001, p. 451). Teachers and librarians/media specialists should work cooperatively to help students develop the skills needed for effective use of the library or media center. (For easy reference, the library or media center will hereafter be referred to as the library and the librarian/media specialist as the librarian, but the expanded role of this facility and these personnel in dealing with multimedia should not be overlooked.) Lambeth (1998, p. 79) says, "Ultimately a library media center will offer teachers and students the service of connecting the school to the world of information in the form of online access as well as other information sources such as LaserDisc, CD-ROM, DVD, videotape and cable TV." All these functions are important to content area instruction.

The librarian can help by showing students the locations of books, periodicals, card catalogs, computer terminals, and reference materials in the library; by explaining the procedures for checking out books and returning them; and by clarifying the rules relating to behavior in the library. The librarian can also demonstrate the use of the card catalog (either manual or electronic) and the *Readers' Guide* and can explain the arrangement of books in the library. (Dewey decimal classification is the arrangement most commonly used in school libraries in the United States for classifying nonfiction books, although some libraries classify books by Library of Congress numbers.) Posters displayed in the library can remind students of checkout procedures, library rules, and arrangement of books, as well as ways to use card catalogs (computerized or manual) and the meanings of terms involved in computer searches.

The librarian can be extremely helpful to teachers. He or she may

1. help teachers locate both printed and other materials related to current units of study;

2. help teachers plan a unit on use of reference materials in the library;

3. help teachers discover reading interests of individuals and specific groups of students;

4. alert teachers to professional reading materials in their content areas;

5. give presentations to students on the availability and location of materials for particular content areas; and

6. put materials on particular content topics on reserve for a class.

LOCATING INFORMATION IN BOOKS

Secondary teachers tend not to teach textbook use to their students, perhaps thinking that it has been covered previously. Since elementary teachers do not always provide such instruction, possibly because they use trade books rather than textbooks in their classes, secondary school content teachers need to consider adding this component to their classes (Alvermann and Moore, 1991; Dreher, 1992).

In a study of the ability of eleventh-grade students to search texts for information, Dreher and Guthrie discovered that many students could locate the appropriate text pages. However, although the students' responses showed that they knew highlighted terms were important in locating information, they did not seem to be able to evaluate the appropriateness of particular terms to the question posed (Dreher, 1992). This indicates a need to pay attention to metacognitive (self-monitoring) skills in classroom instruction.

In a study of college students, Dreher and Brown reported similar findings, with many students locating the correct page, but not evaluating the answers chosen. Some were not able to decide on an appropriate search term and therefore were unsuccessful in their search. Help in deciding on key words when searching for information is important (Dreher, 1992). The need to determine appropriate search terms is also critical in the use of computer databases and the Internet. Teachers should help students locate appropriate key words because some research indicates that teachers and students do not necessarily perceive the same words as being key words in a particular passage (Mealey et al., 1992; Schumm, 1993).

Dreher (1992) suggests that students' search skills can be improved with more use of textbooks for varied purposes. Students who are searching texts for information need to have a plan of action; decide on text sections to examine for the information (table of contents, index, etc.); extract the needed information from the text section or sections chosen (deciding if the information makes sense in terms of the search task); integrate that information with prior knowledge; and repeat the procedure until all the needed information has been found.

Most informational books include special features that students can use to locate needed material. Content area teachers will find that explaining the functions of prefaces, tables of contents, indexes, appendixes, glossaries, footnotes, and bibliographies is well worth the effort in increasing students' efficiency as they use books. Some things that teachers may wish to teach about text features are discussed next.

Preface

When a content area teacher presents a new textbook to secondary school students, he or she should ask the students to read the preface and/or introduction to decide why the book was written and to discover the manner in which the material is presented.

Table of Contents

The table of contents of a textbook should also be examined on the day the textbook is distributed. Students can be reminded that the table of contents indicates the topics that the book includes and the pages on which those topics begin. The teacher can ask questions, such as the following, during the text introduction:

1. What topics are covered in this book?

2. What is the first topic that is discussed?

3. On what page does the discussion about _____ begin? (This question can be repeated several times with different topics inserted in the blank.)

Index

Students need to understand that an index is an alphabetical list of the important items and proper names mentioned in a book, with the pages where each item or name appears. Students generally need practice in using index headings and subheadings to locate information in their books.

A preliminary lesson on what an index is and how to use it to locate information can be presented. Afterward, the teacher can use the students' own textbooks to teach index use. The lesson idea shown in Example 6.1 can be modified for use with an actual index in a content area textbook.

Appendix

Students can be shown that the appendixes in textbooks and other books contain helpful information, such as documents, maps, and tables.

Glossary

Glossaries are often found in content area textbooks. Students need to know that glossaries are similar to dictionaries but include only words presented in the books in which they are found or terms related to a specific subject and include only the definitions of multiple-meaning words that are specific to the subject. Glossaries of technical terms can greatly help students in understanding a book's content. The skills needed for proper use of a glossary are the same as those needed for using a dictionary.

Footnotes and Bibliography

Footnotes and bibliographies are extremely valuable aids for students doing assigned research activities. Footnotes usually tell the source of information in the text

EXAMPLE 6.1   Sample Index and Questions

MATHEMATICS

Sample Index
Absolute value, 145, 174–175
Addition
    of decimals, 101
    of fractions, 80–83
    of natural numbers, 15–16, 46–48
    of rational numbers, 146–148
    of real numbers, 170
Angles, 203
    measurement of, 206–207
    right, 204
Axiom, 241
Base
    meaning of, 5
    change of, 6–7

Index Questions
1. On what page would you look to find out how to add decimals? Under what main topic and subheading did you have to look to discover this page number?
2. On what pages will you find *base* mentioned?
3. What pages contain information about absolute value?
4. On what pages would you look to find out about measurement of angles? What main heading did you look under to discover this? What subheading did you look under?
5. Where would you look to find information about adding real numbers? Would you expect to find any information about real numbers on page 146? Why or why not?
6. Is there information about addition of natural numbers on pages 46–48? Is information on this topic found on any other pages?
7. Find the meaning for *base*, and read it aloud. Did you look in the index to find the page number? If not, could you have found it more quickly by looking in the index?

and can guide a student to the original source if further clarification is needed. Sometimes the footnotes directly supply clarifying information. Bibliographies may refer students to other sources of information about the subjects discussed in a book. The chapter bibliographies in textbooks are generally lists of references that the authors consulted when preparing the chapters and references that contain additional information about the subjects.

SPECIAL REFERENCE BOOKS

Secondary school students are often called on to find information in reference books such as encyclopedias, dictionaries, almanacs, and atlases. Unfortunately, many students reach junior high or high school without knowing how to use such books effectively.

Prerequisites for effective use of reference books include the following:

1. Knowledge of alphabetical order and the fact that information in encyclopedias, dictionaries, and some atlases is arranged in alphabetical order (Most secondary school students have mastered the principles of alphabetical order, but a few need help, especially with alphabetization beyond the first letters of words.)

2. Ability to use guide words (i.e., knowing the location of guide words on a page and understanding that they represent the first and last entry words on a dictionary or encyclopedia page)

3. Ability to use cross-references (related primarily to use of encyclopedias)

4. Ability to use pronunciation keys (related primarily to use of dictionaries)

5. Ability to choose from several possible word meanings the one that most closely fits the context in which the word was found (related to use of dictionaries)

6. Ability to read maps—interpreting the scale and legends and locating directions on maps (related to use of atlases)

7. Ability to determine which volume of a set will contain the information being sought (related primarily to use of encyclopedias)

8. Ability to determine key words under which related information can be found

Because encyclopedias, almanacs, and atlases are often difficult to read, teachers should use caution in assigning students work in these reference books. Students will not benefit from attempting to do research in books written on a level they find frustrating. When the material is too difficult, students tend to copy the material word for word instead of extracting the important ideas.

Many reference works are available online, including dictionaries, encyclopedias, and collections of maps. Students need to learn to use these sources as well. Search techniques using key words (discussed in Chapter 2 and later in this chapter) are important when using online references. Online references often contain helpful aids to understanding, such as links to pictures, word pronunciations, and definitions.

Encyclopedias

Some secondary school students need help with the use of encyclopedias. They may need to practice locating varied subjects in the encyclopedia. Teachers should lead the students to decide on the key words that will help them find the specified information by first explaining and modeling the procedure. For example, for "Education

SOCIAL
STUDIES

in Sweden" they should look first under "Sweden" and then find the section on education. Example 6.2 can be used to assess students' ability to locate information in encyclopedias.

A surprising number of junior high school students and a few high school students do not realize that the name of a person in an encyclopedia is alphabetized by the last name, not the first. A student who had to write a report on James Otis came to Betty Roe and announced that James Otis was not in the encyclopedia. Puzzled, Betty asked the student to show her how he had proceeded in looking for the name. He went to the "J" volume of the encyclopedia and began to look for "James." He seemed surprised when he was told that proper names are listed alphabetically by last name and then followed by the first name. The last two items in Example 6.2 can be used to check on or work with students' understanding of this concept.

A number of encyclopedias are available on CD or DVD for use with computers. (See the section "Using Computer Databases" later in this chapter for more detail about electronic encyclopedias.) These references have many hypertext and hypermedia links (see Chapter 2) that help to illuminate the material for students.

Dictionaries

Students frequently lack familiarity with dictionary content and use. A few have some trouble with alphabetical order. A much larger number have trouble with guide words and use of the pronunciation key, and many do not realize the variety of information, such as parts of speech, principal parts of verbs, degrees of adjectives, etymologies, and illustrations, found in a dictionary entry. Spending some time familiarizing students with dictionary use can pay dividends in their future learning.

EXAMPLE 6.2   Activity for Using an Encyclopedia

Directions: Look up each of the following topics in the encyclopedia. On the line beside each topic, write the letter of the volume in which you found the topic and the page number on which the topic is discussed.

I. Solar system   _____

2. U.S. Constitution   _____

3. Oleander   _____

4. Education in Sweden   _____

5. Computer use in library systems   _____

6. Martin Luther King Jr.   _____

7. John Paul Jones   _____

A particular need for secondary school students is determining which definition of a word fits the context in which it was found. Students have the tendency to try to force the first definition they find to fit all situations.

FOREIGN LANGUAGES

With more and more English language learners (ELLs) in U.S. schools, use of bilingual dictionaries gains importance. Such dictionaries can be useful both to ELLs in dealing with use of words in class and to English speakers in communication with classmates who are ELLs. They also are useful for students enrolled in foreign language classes.

MOTIVATIONAL ACTIVITIES

Since location skills are presented to students repeatedly during their school careers, they may seem boring, even though they may not be thoroughly learned. The introduction of games, audiovisual presentations, and other motivational activities may enhance interest in the instruction. For example, paper-and-pencil scavenger hunts in the library, like the one described in the following "Meeting the Challenge" vignette, may be fun for students. Teachers can use library scavenger hunts to help students learn to use many types of library resources, including CD-based indexes and the online search catalog. Online scavenger hunts could be similar to the pencil-and-paper one described, with items such as the following:

SCIENCE AND HEALTH   **ENGLISH/ LANGUAGE ARTS**

1. Locate a picture of the moon, taken from space, on the NASA website. Print the picture.

2. Locate a site that has student writing posted. Print a sample page. Write down the URL for the site.

USING COMPUTER DATABASES

What value do computer databases have for students?

The location skills that students need in today's schools include the ability to retrieve information stored in **computer databases**, either ones that the students have compiled themselves or others that are available in the school.

A database is an organized collection of information. Conceptually, a database is like a filing cabinet (or several cabinets), with separate file folders for each article in the database. The information may be categorized by subject or by another categorization scheme and is indexed for easy access. Typically, the computer system supporting a database allows the user to construct complicated search requirements, for example, "Find all articles on distortion in optics used for telescopes published after 1980 in Sweden." Databases can be user created (student created) or preexisting, large or small, general or specific.

SCIENCE AND HEALTH

Increasingly, finding information is becoming a computer-oriented task involving databases. More and more occupations rely on the use of such databases, making the need for information-retrieval skills and an understanding of database maintenance important for today's students. The use of these sources requires knowledge of how to construct search questions for the particular database system, of the organizational scheme of the subject matter, and of search techniques in general. The user

MEETING THE CHALLENGE

Ms. MacMurray wants to check on the reference skills of the inner-city eighth-graders in her English class. She confers with Mrs. Freedle, the librarian, after school the day before she has a library period. Together they pull out a variety of reference books that the students need to know how to use. Then Ms. MacMurray writes a series of

questions that can be answered using each of twenty different reference books of many types, including atlases, encyclopedias, dictionaries, and almanacs. (For example: 1. What is a book by Herman Melville? [Write down its name, call number, and location.] 2. What is a catamaran, according to the *American Heritage Dictionary*? 3. Write the phonetic respelling for the word *catamaran*. 4. What volume and page of the *World Book Encyclopedia* contains a discussion of catamarans? 5. What states border Colorado? 6. Who is Madame Curie?) After the questions have been constructed, Ms. MacMurray and Mrs. Freedle return the reference books to their accustomed places.

Back in her own room, Ms. MacMurray takes the list of students in the English class and arranges the students in pairs. Then she duplicates her list of questions so that each pair of students will have a copy. Choosing from among several prizes that she has solicited from local businesses, she decides which prize to give the team with the most correct answers within the time limit. (If there is a tie, the first team to finish with the highest number of correct answers wins.)

Reference skills can be checked by letting teams search for answers to a series of research questions in the library or media center.
© Michael Zide

**ENGLISH/
LANGUAGE
ARTS**

The next day, Ms. MacMurray assigns the students to their teams, gives a list of questions to each team, and escorts the students to the library. Teammates confer to choose a strategy and then begin their searches. As they intently work to win the contest, Ms. MacMurray quietly notes the good and poor strategies of library use they exhibit—guidance for future lessons in her class. She later uses explanations and activities such as ones described in this chapter to work on the understanding and use of indexes, tables of contents, glossaries, computer databases, the card catalog, the basic library arrangement, alphabetical order, guide words, and dictionary respellings, if these prove to be problem areas.

must be able to phrase complex questions that limit the retrieval process to pertinent information without omitting any desired information.

A database can be organized in a wide variety of ways. A limited database might contain the names, symbols, and basic properties of chemical compounds used in the manufacture of paper, or the names, dates of inauguration, and birthplaces of the presidents of the United States. A large database is *Who's Who in America*. The contents are the same as those in the printed volume, but its structure as a database allows searching by such things as birthplace (e.g., what famous people are from Claysville, Idaho), profession, or college of matriculation.

Schools now have access to both local and remote databases. A local database resides on the computer system of the user, whereas a remote database resides on a computer system other than the user's. The most prevalent means of remote access is through the Internet.

A local database in a classroom might range from a small quantity of information collected as part of a class project to a complete encyclopedia. Several encyclopedias are available in computer-readable form, on CDs or DVDs. Examples are *The New Grolier Multimedia Encyclopedia* (Grolier Electronic Publishing), *Microsoft Encarta Multimedia Encyclopedia* (Microsoft), and *Compton's Interactive Encyclopedia* (Compton's NewMedia). The *Encarta* is written for ages 9 to 15, but it is applicable for all ages. *Compton's Interactive* is recommended for fifth-graders to adults, and *New Grolier Multimedia* is recommended for high school level to adult. Therefore, there is an electronic encyclopedia to fit the needs of any level of learner in the secondary school. A number of dictionaries are also available on CD.

MUSIC

SCIENCE AND HEALTH

An entire multivolume encyclopedia can be contained on a single disk. Multimedia encyclopedias contain more than text; they include pictures, maps, animated diagrams, voice recordings, music recordings, and sound effects (such as sounds that animals make). Users might read about Bach, view his picture, and hear a recording of one of his musical compositions. They might also read about grizzly bears, see a video of one, and hear its sound.

Creating small databases in the classroom can give students valuable experience in categorizing and organizing material. For this type of work on the computer, the teacher needs access to a database utility program, such as FileMaker Pro or Appleworks (for both Macintosh and Windows operating systems). After the information for the database has been collected and entered into the computer, the database system can be used for critical analyses, such as comparing similarities and differences (e.g., "What problems do urban areas have in common? How are these problems different from those in rural areas?"), analyzing relationships, examining trends, and testing and refining hypotheses.

One important application of databases for students is the computerized card catalog in many libraries. Such databases replace the traditional card catalogs, providing the traditional indexing plus complex search capabilities. Many libraries also provide access to the ERIC (Educational Resources Information Center) index of educational material, as well as to the card catalogs of other libraries and even Internet sites that contain electronic books and magazines and homepages that have links to a wide variety of types of information, which may include multimedia as well as text.

USING THE INTERNET

What kinds of
information can be
found by searching
Internet sites?

**ENGLISH/
LANGUAGE
ARTS**

**SOCIAL
STUDIES**

The Internet offers a multitude of online resources, including "encyclopedias, dictionaries, and collections of quotes; libraries of poetry, short stories, images, and music; critical studies and research articles on every conceivable topic; information about authors and historical figures; government and public policy data; current events; and much, much more" (Bruce, 1999/2000, p. 348)—a bounty that can lead to problems, such as easy plagiarism, exposure to commercialism or pornography, and waste of instructional time. Teachers must understand both the benefits and the hazards of Internet use. Both primary and secondary sources of information can be found on the Internet. Primary sources include diaries, government documents, photographs, videotapes, and other types of original materials. Secondary sources include summaries and analyses of information from other sources. The information available on the Internet is not controlled for accuracy, however, so students must do more than simply locate material on the appropriate topic; they must also evaluate the information they locate.

Searching for information on the World Wide Web can be made easier with the use of search engines. Search engines check terms that a user enters into the computer against key words found on web pages that have been indexed by the search service. Frequently used search engines are AltaVista, Excite, Dogpile, Google, and Ask Jeeves. Because different search engines use different search techniques, they often provide different results based on the same search terms, and some are better at finding particular types of information than others. A site that can help students evaluate which search engine fits their needs is http://www.noodletools.com. Teachers can also find reviews of search engines and search tips for each engine at http://daphne.palomar.edu/TGSEARCH/.

Simple searches on search engines require students to decide on relevant key words for the search. Often a search on a key word will return far more "hits" (matches that indicate potentially useful sites) than the user could realistically check. When this happens, many engines allow users to do advanced searches with quotation marks around phrases to indicate that the entire phrase must be found, Boolean searches (that use Boolean logic), or other refined searches. These techniques are specific to the search engine being used, and teachers and students would do well to familiarize themselves with the search engines they use most often. Search engines frequently have Help options that connect to detailed explanations of how to use advanced search techniques.

Organizational Skills

**ENGLISH/
LANGUAGE
ARTS**

When participating in study activities such as writing reports, secondary school students need to organize the ideas they encounter in their reading. Three helpful organizational skills are outlining, summarizing, and note taking. All require recognition and recording, in an organized form, of important ideas from the materials read. The act of organizing information helps students comprehend and retain it better. According to Friend (2001/2002, p. 321), "[I]n order to organize new information, students must draw on prior knowledge and pay attention to the nature of relationships among ideas. As they organize information by constructing a summary, an outline, or a graphic organizer, students generate links among new ideas they are studying."

Pearson and Santa (1995) found that students recalled terms in categorized lists more readily than those in random order, and they demonstrated this to the students by having class members try to learn lists of terms in each condition. Students then saw the value of organizing material in order to learn it.

OUTLINING

What different ways can be used to outline material that is read for class?

Teachers should help their students to understand that **outlining** is recording information from reading material in a way that makes clear the relationships between the main ideas and the supporting details. Before students can learn to construct an outline properly, they must know how to identify main ideas and supporting details in reading selections. Information about how to assist students in locating main ideas and recognizing related details is found in Chapter 4.

Readiness for formal outlining tasks may be developed by having students work with *arrays*, which are freeform outlines. When constructing arrays, students are required to arrange key words and phrases in ways that show the relationships set forth by the author. They can use words, lines, and arrows to do this. It is important to use a simple, familiar story or an uncomplicated expository selection for this activity, so that the students can focus on the logical arrangement of the terms rather than worrying about the details of the story or selection. Example 6.3 shows a story array for the familiar story "Johnny Appleseed."

Teachers can guide students to learn how to make arrays by supplying the words and phrases and then letting the students work in groups to complete the arrays. First the students read the selection; then they arrange the words and phrases appropriately, using lines and arrows to indicate relationships. The teacher questions students about the positioning and direction of arrows, asking for reasons for the choices made. In addition, the teacher is available to answer students' questions. Eventually, the students are expected to choose key words and concepts themselves and to arrange them without the teacher's help.

Two other types of outlines that students may find useful are the *sentence outline* and the *topic outline*. In a sentence outline, each point is stated in the form of a complete sentence; in a topic outline, the points are written in the form of key words and phrases. The sentence outline is generally easier to master because the topic outline involves an extra task—condensing main ideas, already expressed in sentence form, into key words and phrases.

The first step in making an outline is extracting the main ideas from the material and listing them beside Roman numerals in the order in which they occur. The next step is locating the details that support each of the main ideas and listing them beside capital letters below the main idea that they support. These details are indented to indicate subordination to the main idea. Details that are subordinate to these details are indented still more and preceded by Arabic numerals. The next level of

ENGLISH/ LANGUAGE ARTS

EXAMPLE 6.3   **Story Array**

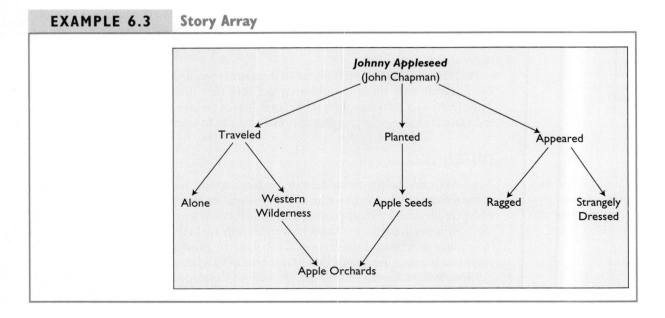

subordination is indicated by lowercase letters. Although other levels of subordination are possible, secondary school students will rarely need such fine divisions.

An important idea about outlining that a teacher may wish to stress is that the degree of importance of ideas in an outline is shown by the numbers and letters used, as well as by the indentation of entries. Points that have equal importance are designated by the same number or letter style and the same degree of indentation.

Teachers can help students see how a textbook chapter would be outlined by showing them how the headings within the chapter can indicate different levels of subordination. For example, in some textbooks the title for the outline would be the title of the chapter. Roman numeral headings would be centered, or major, headings in the chapter, capital letter headings would be side headings, and Arabic numeral headings would be italic or paragraph headings.

Another approach to helping students to learn to outline their reading assignments is for the teacher to supply the students with partially completed outlines of the material and then have them complete the outlines. The teacher can vary the difficulty of the activity by gradually leaving out more and more details until the students create the entire outline alone.

Many current word-processing programs have outlining functions that students may use. These functions can facilitate the students' outlining activities.

Outlining can be helpful in any subject area. A standard form of outlining, used throughout the school, will decrease confusion among the students.

SUMMARIZING

What should be
included in a good
summary?

Good summaries of reading assignments can be extremely valuable to students when they are studying for tests. To write a good **summary**, a student must restate what the author has said in a more concise form. Summary writers should preserve the main ideas and essential supporting details of selections in their summaries but should not include illustrative material and statements that merely elaborate on the main ideas. The ability to locate main ideas is therefore a prerequisite for learning how to write good summaries. (Development of this skill is discussed in Chapter 4.)

The topic sentence of a paragraph is a good summary of the paragraph, if it is well written. Practice in finding topic sentences of paragraphs, therefore, is also practice in the skill of summarizing paragraphs.

Summaries of longer selections may be constructed by combining the main ideas of the component paragraphs into summary statements. Certain types of paragraphs can generally be disregarded when making summaries. Introductory and illustrative paragraphs do not add new ideas and therefore are not helpful in constructing a concise overview of the material. Students who write summaries of their reading assignments may wish to compare their summaries with the author's concluding or summary paragraphs to make sure that they have not omitted essential details.

When writing summaries, students should try not only to limit the number of sentences they use but also to limit the number of words within sentences. For example:

Original sentence. A match, carelessly discarded by an unsuspecting tourist, can cause the destruction by fire of many acres of trees that will take years of work to replace.

Changed sentence. Carelessly discarded matches can result in extensive destruction of forested areas by fire.

Teachers should show students that they must delete trivial and redundant material to create good summaries. They should use superordinate terms to replace lists of similar items or actions (e.g., "animals" for "pigs, dogs, and cats"). A superordinate action can be used to replace steps in an action (e.g., "made spaghetti sauce" for "took tomato sauce, sliced mushrooms, chopped onion, oregano, and salt, . . . and placed on the stove to cook on low heat"). As mentioned above, each paragraph can be represented by an implied main idea sentence or by a directly stated topic sentence. Paragraphs can then be examined to see which ones are most needed. Only necessary paragraphs should be kept, and some that are kept can be combined (Brown and Day, 1983; Brown, Day, and Jones, 1983; Hare and Borchardt, 1984; Recht, 1984).

Practice in summarizing is most effective if it is based on material in current textbooks or other reading material for classes. The teacher may give students a textbook section to read, along with three or four summaries of the material. Then students can choose the best summary from those presented and explain why it is best. This is good preparation for independent student writing of summaries.

To write good summaries, students must identify the important material to include as well as the unnecessary material and then reorganize the material for clarity. Since ideas have to be understood, evaluated, and condensed, they are transformed in summarizing in a way that is not typical of simple recall (Friend, 2000/2001). Therefore, retention is more likely to result when students summarize assignments.

Précis writing is a special form of summarizing that is discussed in detail in Chapter 8. Teachers can use it with English language learners (ELLs) to develop abstracting and synthesizing skills and to develop vocabulary through use of synonyms. ELLs can begin by writing a précis in a group setting and continue by writing individual ones.

NOTE TAKING

Taking notes on material read for classes can be a helpful memory aid. Well-constructed notes can save students time and effort. To take good notes, students must think about the material they are reading and organize it in a meaningful way; as a result, they will be more likely to remember it. It is also true that the simple act of writing ideas helps fix them in students' memories.

Students should be encouraged to use the form of note taking that helps them the most. Some may use semantic webs, outlines, or mind mapping when taking notes on an assignment in a textbook. Others may write a summary of the textbook materials. Some may use graphics that show description, time/order, cause-and-effect, problem-solution, comparison/contrast, and definition-examples patterns visually through the form in which the notes are taken. For example, the description pattern could have notes taken in a sunburst shape, with the concept being described in the center of the circle and the descriptive details on the rays; and the time/order pattern could have a stair-step numbered listing of events in order. Teachers should teach each pattern and the structure for notes taken in that pattern.

What are the characteristics of the Cornell Note-Taking System?

Pauk (2001) suggests use of the **Cornell Note-Taking System**, which he developed. With this system, the student draws a vertical line two and a half inches from the left-hand side of each page to create a cue column and a horizontal line two inches from the bottom of the page to create a summary area. Students take notes on the material in the area to the right of the cue column and above the summary area. When the students review the notes, they write questions answered in the notes in the cue column to clarify the information in their minds and to strengthen their memory for the material. In the summary area of the page, they sum up that page of notes in one or two sentences. This summarization helps them look at the main ideas covered instead of a collection of details. Example 6.4 shows the Cornell System in use.

What advantages can you see in using an I-Chart for note taking?

Note taking for a research report can also be done in the form of I-Charts (inquiry charts) (Hoffman, 1992; Randall, 1996). An **I-Chart** is composed of a grid that has questions about the subject at the tops of columns and references consulted along the left-hand margin, providing the headings for the rows. There is also a place for other interesting facts that the students know and a summary of the findings. Hoffman (1992) wrote out the references in the right-hand column, but Randall

EXAMPLE 6.4   Cornell Note-Taking System

Psych. 105 – Prof. Martin – Sept. 14 (Mon.)

MEMORY

Memory tricky – Can recall instantly many trivial things of child-hood, yet forget things recently worked hard to learn & retain.

How do psycholo-gists account for remembering?

Memory Trace
— Fact that we retain information means that some change was made in the brain.
— Change called "memory trace."
— "Trace" probably a molecular arrangement similar to molecular changes in a magnetic recording tape.

What's a "memory trace"?

What are the three memory systems?

Three memory systems: sensory, short term, long term.
— Sensory (lasts one second)
   Ex. Words or numbers sent to brain by sight (visual image) start to disintegrate within a few tenths of a second & gone in one full second, unless quickly transferred to S-T memory by verbal repetition.
— Short-term memory [STM] (lasts 30 seconds)
   • Experiments show: a syllable of 3 letters remembered 50% of the time after 3 seconds.
     Totally forgotten end of 30 seconds.
   • S-T memory — limited capacity — holds average of 7 items.
   • More than 7 items — jettisons some to make room.
   • To hold items in STM, must rehearse — must hear sound of words internally or externally.
— Long-term memory [LTM] (lasts a lifetime or short time).
   • Transfer fact or idea by
     (1) Associating w/information already in LTM.
     (2) Organizing information into meaningful units.
     (3) Understanding by comparing & making relationships.
     (4) Frameworking – fit pieces in like in a jigsaw puzzle.
     (5) Reorganizing – combining new & old into a new unit.
     (6) Rehearsing – aloud to keep memory trace strong.

How long does sensory memory retain information?

How is information transferred to STM?

What are the reten-tion times of STM?

What's the capacity of the STM?

How to hold information in STM?

What are the reten-tion times of LTM?

What are the six ways to transfer information from STM to LTM?

Three kinds of memory systems are sensory, which retains information for about 1 second; short-term, which retains for a maximum of 30 seconds; and long-term, which varies from a lifetime of retention to a relatively short time.
   The six ways (activities) to transfer information to the long-term memory are associating, organizing, understanding, frameworking, reorganizing, and rehearsing.

(1996) let the students number the references and make a bibliography, and she used a separate I-Chart for each question, rather than having multiple questions on a page. Students were encouraged to paraphrase the answers to questions on their charts. Sometimes students had trouble keeping their answers focused, as you can see in Example 6.5, in which plants are mentioned in answer to a question about animals, but the charts do help students to be more organized in their note taking. Example 6.5 shows a modification of Hoffman's I-Chart (1992) used by Randall (1996).

Before students take notes for a research paper, they must identify the questions that the paper should answer. The questions can be listed under categories important to the topic, and students can go to appropriate reference sources to find out about the categories. For example, "What types of printers exist?" and "What are some advantages of a laser printer?" could be categorized under the topic "Printers." All notes taken on the topic "Printers" could be labeled with this term, to facilitate organization of notes. Other categories might be "Monitors," "CPUs," and "Keyboards," for example.

Notes for a research paper can be especially effective when made on index cards that can later be sorted into topics to be covered in the paper. If note cards are used, each one should include the source of information so that the paper is well documented. Some guidelines for note taking that may be helpful to students follow:

1. Key words and phrases should be used in notes.

2. Enough of the context must be included to make the notes understandable after a period of time has elapsed. Consider using telegraphic sentences, that is, sentences that leave out unnecessary words.

3. The bibliographical reference should be included with each note card or page.

4. Direct quotations should be copied exactly and should be used sparingly.

5. Notes should differentiate clearly between direct quotations and reworded material.

6. Notes should be as brief as possible.

7. Use of abbreviations can make note taking less time-consuming. Examples: w/ for "with" or = for "equals." Only abbreviations that are easy for the writer to remember should be used.

Teachers may be able to help their students learn to take good notes by "thinking through" a textbook assignment with them orally in class, emphasizing the points that should be included in a good set of notes by writing them on an overhead transparency. This provides them with a model of the process of note taking. Students then can be encouraged to take notes on another assignment and compare them with a set of notes the teacher has constructed on the same material.

EXAMPLE 6.5   Modified I-Chart

SCIENCE AND
HEALTH

Name: Melanie	Topic: Rainforest Destruction

Subtopic: What animals live in the Rainforest?

What I already know: There are alot of birds an other animals big and small.
Some of the animals living in rainforests are going extinct.

Bibliography #: 1	Colorful birds, chattering monkeys, butterflies
2	Monkeys, squirrels, birds, jaguar, giant armadillo, plants: giant water lilies, stiltroots, strangler, and buttresses, an aerial roots, palm. Anaconda, geometrid moth, poison arrow frog, Matamata turtle, Kinkajou
3	Keel-billed toucan, rare butterflies, howler monkeys, the 3-toed sloth, tamandua (related to the anteater), jaguar, the ruby-topaz humming bird, genus Denodraba, a bird-eating spider, leaf cutter ants, and the red brocket deer.

Interesting related facts: 6% of the earth's land surface is covered by Rainforests which are a home to over half the planets species. 1/3 of earth's species are beleived to live in this rainforest, only a fraction of them have been given scientific names.

Key words: Biodeversity

New questions to research: What types of tree species live in the rainforest?

Source: Sally N. Randall, "Information Charts: A Strategy for Organizing Student Research," *Journal of Adolescent and Adult Literacy 39*(7) (1996, April): 538. Reprinted with permission of Sally N. Randall and the International Reading Association. All rights reserved.

Focus on Struggling Readers

Location and Organization Skills for Struggling Readers

Location and organization skills are especially important for struggling readers. They often do not know where to find information because they have never used reference books or the Internet for research purposes. Once they are acquainted with sources of information, they have to learn how to locate the information within the source to complete assignments. Once they find the needed information, struggling readers tend to write a word-for-word copy of the material or they may write details rather than main ideas; therefore, they must learn to sort important ideas from unimportant ideas. Outlining, summarizing, and note-taking skills will help them experience success in the content areas. Direct instruction and application practice can help them develop these skills.

Focus on English Language Learners

Location and Organization Skills for ELLs

Secondary English language learners can develop location and organization skills after they have a working knowledge of English. They have a special need to learn about English reference works, but if they are fluent readers in their native language, they will be able to understand how to use those works. Bilingual dictionaries are especially helpful to these learners. Electronic references that provide bilingual options can also help ELLs. English language learners may need instruction on taking notes and writing summaries. Outlining may not present a challenge because it addresses the existing text. Recorded class instructions and lectures are useful in helping English language learners develop organizational skills.

SUMMARY

Students in content area classes must be able to locate information in the library or media center; in textbooks, other informational books, and reference books; in computer databases; and on the Internet in order to do effective research for class presentations and written reports. To use the library, they often must know how to use the card catalog, computer terminals, and the library's system for book arrangement. To use books successfully, they need to know the parts of a book and the functions of each part. To use reference books, they need to know about alphabetical order, guide words, cross-references, pronunciation keys, map legends, map scales, and other location and interpretation aids. To use computer databases, they must know how to construct search questions for specific systems. Use of the Internet to locate information requires the understanding of key words and search engines.

Also important to students who are writing reports are the skills of outlining, summarizing, and note taking. All these skills require the ability to recognize main ideas and supporting details. Outlining requires showing relationships among the main ideas and supporting details, whereas summarizing requires stating the important information in a more concise way. Notes may be taken in outline or summary form, in the form of graphic organizers, in split-page format, on I-Charts, or in another form that the student finds useful to organize the information. Notes are frequently taken on note cards when they will be used for a research paper. Struggling readers and ELLs may need extra support in learning location and organization skills.

DISCUSSION QUESTIONS

1. How can the librarian and the content area teacher cooperate to teach library skills that students need for research activities?
2. What parts of a book must students be able to use effectively if they are to locate needed information efficiently?
3. What types of reference books need special attention from you, if your students are to do effective research for your class?
4. What are necessary skills for locating information on the Internet?
5. How can outlining help students to understand the material in the textbook for your content class?
6. What helpful guidelines for note taking can you share with students?
7. Which technique for teaching note taking mentioned in this chapter seems to hold the most promise for your classes? What others do you know of that you could use instead?
8. What computer skills might students need to make use of today's libraries and media centers?
9. What location and organization skills are most likely to be problems for struggling readers and English language learners?

ENRICHMENT ACTIVITIES

1.   Plan a lesson on use of the index of a secondary-level textbook of your choice. Teach the lesson to a group of your classmates. *Teach the lesson in a secondary school classroom, if possible.

2.   Take a content area textbook at the secondary level and plan procedures to familiarize students with the parts of the book and with the reading aids the book offers.

3.   Plan a lesson on how to use the Internet to locate information. *Teach the lesson in a secondary school classroom, if possible.

4.   Visit a secondary school library, and listen to the librarian explain the reference materials and library procedures to the students. Evaluate the presentation, and decide how you might make changes if you were responsible for it.

*5.   Make a bulletin board display that would be helpful to use when teaching either outlining or note taking. Display it either in your college classroom or in a secondary school classroom.

*These activities are designed for in-service teachers, student teachers, and practicum students.

Chapter 7

Reading-Study Strategies
for Textbook Use

OVERVIEW

In this chapter we consider the development of strategies that enhance both comprehension and retention of information in printed material. We describe study methods such as SQ3R, ROWAC, SQRC, and SQRQCQ and discuss their usefulness in helping students manage content area reading assignments. Teaching procedures such as PSRT are also included.

Ways to help students learn to read to follow directions are suggested. How to help students learn from the graphic aids (maps, graphs, tables, diagrams, and pictures) in their content area reading materials is discussed, as well as how to help them learn to adjust their reading rates to fit their purposes and the materials to be read. The final topics are fluency, retention, and test taking.

PURPOSE-SETTING QUESTIONS

As you read this chapter, try to answer these questions:

1. What are some study methods designed for use with content area reading selections, and how do they help?
2. What are some teaching procedures for helping students learn study skills and helping them read with more comprehension, and why are they effective?
3. How can a teacher help students of varying abilities learn to follow written directions accurately?
4. What types of graphic aids are found in textbooks, and what must students know about each one to read it effectively?
5. What are some factors to consider in instruction related to reading rate?
6. Why is flexibility of rate important to secondary school students?
7. What activities can help students retain what they read?
8. How can teachers help students read test questions with understanding?
9. What can teachers do to help struggling readers and English language learners develop needed reading-study skills?

Preparation for Study

Time spent discussing effective study preparation is well spent because it allows students to be more productive when they study. Following are some tips for teachers to pass along.

1. Take time to record assignments in a special notebook and mark your calendar with the deadlines for the assignments.

2. Under each long-term assignment, list component tasks (e.g., brainstorming, library research, organization, rough draft, final paper). Give yourself a deadline for completing each component task so that you will finish the entire assignment on time. Enter dates on your calendar.

3. At the beginning of every week, make a separate page for each day of that week. On the page for each day, list the tasks to be worked on that day, including both the parts of long-term assignments and assignments your teachers give during the week.

4. Each day work on the most important tasks first at the times of day when you are most alert and energetic. If tasks are equally important, work on the harder tasks during your most productive times. On days when not much daily work is assigned, look at your list of long-term activities, and try to get ahead on them.

5. Study in a place with as few distractions as possible and at the time of day when you are most alert.

6. Gather all your materials before you sit down to study. You will usually need pencils, pens, paper, textbooks, and reference books (especially a dictionary), although you may need more specialized materials for some assignments. Check the requirements for your assignments ahead of time, and assemble all the items you will need.

7. If you are a visual learner (you learn best through seeing), use reading and graphic aids for studying. If you are an auditory learner (you learn best through hearing), talk about the material and possibly listen to tapes of lectures. You may even want to read the material aloud to yourself. If you are a kinesthetic learner (you learn best through movement), take notes on the material or find a way to use the ideas in a practical manner. In other words, take advantage of your strengths when you study.

8. Choose a study procedure that your teacher has presented that best fits your personal needs, although you may want to modify it to fit the way you think and learn.

Importance of a Study Method

What are metacognitive skills, and why are they important?

Secondary school students can often read narrative material effectively, but they have difficulty with expository text. They also frequently do not study effectively because they *do not know how*. They have never learned how to focus on the important material, identify the organization of material, make use of graphic aids, vary reading rates and study procedures to fit the material, or connect new learning to things they already know. They often approach all content reading material with the same attention and speed used for pleasure reading of narrative material.

Many students fail to make use of **metacognitive skills**—that is, they do not monitor their comprehension of the material they read as they are reading it. The topic of metacognition was introduced in Chapter 4. To summarize, metacognition means knowing what is known already, knowing when comprehension of new material has been accomplished, knowing how the understanding was attained, and knowing what to do if comprehension has not been accomplished. Students frequently look at or pronounce the words in a selection and feel that they have read it, without checking to see if they have located important ideas and have understood the content and how it fits in with information that they already know. They fail to ask, "Do I understand this point?" and "Does this make sense?" Even if they ask these questions, when the answers are negative, they may not remedy the situation by choosing and applying appropriate strategies, such as rereading, checking word meanings in a glossary or dictionary, looking for relationships among ideas, and identifying the organizational pattern of the text in order to clear up problems with meaning (Babbs and Moe, 1983). All these activities are part of effective studying. Instruction in how to ask appropriate questions can be beneficial (Ciardiello, 1998).

Teachers must show students the importance of activating prior knowledge about a topic, relating new information to the prior knowledge, and deciding whether the new information makes sense in light of previous knowledge. They must also make students aware of the strategies they can use to help them figure out meanings that are not immediately apparent. Teacher modeling of self-questioning about meaning and deciding on strategies to use when meaning is unclear is a good approach for increasing metacognitive activities among students.

Having purposes for their reading activities can increase the likelihood that students will apply metacognitive skills. If they have purposes for reading, they can check to see if those purposes were met. If they have no purposes, they may not know what to look for or what questions to ask about the material.

Study methods have been developed that help students approach content area reading in ways that make comprehension and retention of the material more likely. These methods help students to establish purposes for reading the material and to monitor their reading to determine if they have understood the concepts. They often cause the student to look at the material more than once for different purposes, thereby making retention of the ideas more likely.

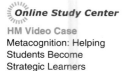

Online Study Center

HM Video Case
Metacognition: Helping
Students Become
Strategic Learners

MATHEMATICS

Students need to become aware of the advantages of using a study method. They need to be told how to apply each method and how to decide when to apply it. For example, SQRQCQ is appropriate for use with reading word problems in mathematics, but not appropriate for reading a history text.

Students who do not know a study method to use when reading content area assignments may resort to pronouncing all the words in the selections as they read without actually thinking about the content. They may then rely on rote memorization to get them through tests on the material and, therefore, may never find meaning in the content they are studying because such memorization does not require understanding.

TEACHING PROCEDURES

Teachers find certain teaching procedures particularly helpful in enhancing students' study skills. The PSRT strategy and some recitation techniques can be useful approaches.

What does PSRT stand for?

Simons (1989) suggests use of the **PSRT** strategy. The steps in this strategy are *Prepare, Structure, Read,* and *Think.* The *Prepare* step includes finding out what the students already know about the concepts in the material and, if necessary, supplementing this background information. Brainstorming about the key concepts should take place during this step. The *Structure* step involves helping students understand the text's organization through use of a graphic overview that is partially completed on the board with them. During the *Read* step, the students read the text independently for a purpose and individually complete the overview presented in the previous step. During the *Think* step, a discussion of the text is held, the overview on the board is completed as a class activity, and the students summarize the text and answer higher-order, teacher-developed questions about it. This procedure is effective because of its high levels of teacher-student interactions. It also takes into account the importance of background knowledge and text organization to reading comprehension.

Classroom recitation techniques can be used to encourage good study practices. Recitation involves saying aloud the information to be remembered. It may serve as a motivational factor for studying material because students feel the need to prepare when they may be required to make presentations in class. It also can strengthen memory for the material, as a student must think about the information, say it, and hear the result. Some forms of recitation include paraphrasing previous contributions to the content discussion, telling something that was learned from the day's lesson, discussing answers to questions presented by teachers or students, and responding simultaneously with the rest of the class to true-false or multiple-choice questions. The total-class response activities allow students to respond without feeling the pressure of being singled out. Students may hold up a "true" or "false" symbol at the same time that others do. The teacher can question the students to discover the thinking behind both correct and incorrect responses when not all students respond correctly.

EXAMPLE 7.1   PSRT Lesson

SOCIAL
STUDIES

The students are being asked to read the selection called "Revolutions in Food Production" from *Modern World History,* which is reproduced in Chapter 4 on pages 113–114. The teaching session might proceed like the following one:

Prepare

Teacher:	What do you think a section called "Revolutions in Food Production" will be about?
Student:	Changes in the way food is produced.
Teacher:	What do you already know about food production from our previous reading and your other experiences?
Student A:	Hunter-gatherer societies depended on food that was in nature, but agricultural societies planted, tended, and harvested crops.
Student B:	The weather affected crop production. You know, droughts and floods and storms ruined crops.
Student C:	Pests sometimes spoiled crops.
Student D:	Early on, people just produced crops for their own families; then they started having some people produce for others who worked at other jobs. Now there are huge companies who raise and process food for lots of people.
Student E:	The soil can wear out.
Student F:	Bigger populations make it hard to produce enough food for everybody.
Student G:	This was made worse in some places by wars.
Teacher:	What might be considered a revolution in food production?
Student A:	Better ways to protect crops from weather.
Student B:	Better ways to kill pests.
Student C:	Ways to get bigger crops from the same amount of land.

Structure

The teacher puts the following organizer on the board and helps the students see that it can be completed from their reading passage.

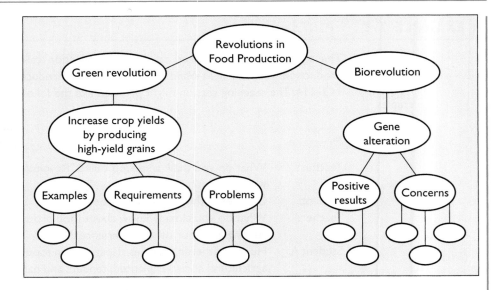

Read

Students read the text to answer the question "What are the results of revolutions in food production?" and to fill in the rest of the graphic organizer on their own papers.

Think

The students and teacher discuss the selection and complete the overview on the board together. Then the students summarize the text. One summary might be "The green revolution has been successful in increasing crop yields by producing high-yield grains, but not all nations can meet the requirements for this technique, and there are potential problems, especially related to use of chemicals. The biorevolution has successfully altered tomato genes, resulting in longer-lasting flavor and freshness, but there are concerns about negative effects related to plant diseases."

Finally the teacher may ask such questions as the following:

1. What countries would have major problems taking advantage of the green revolution?
2. Should chemicals be used for agriculture? Why, or why not?
3. Why do some people fear eating gene-altered vegetables?
4. Is this fear reasonable?

Teacher modeling of the steps in study skills procedures before students are asked to perform the steps can be a very useful technique. The teacher can move through a procedure, verbalizing the steps being used and letting the students see how each step is accomplished.

Then teachers should provide students with opportunities to practice the methods before asking them to use the methods independently. The teacher should guide students through the use of each study method during a class period, using an actual reading assignment. At the teacher's direction, the students should perform each step in the chosen method. For example, with the use of SQ3R, all students should be asked to survey the material together, reading the chapter title, the introduction to the chapter, the headings, and the chapter summary. At this time they should also be asked to inspect graphic aids within the chapter. Each of the other steps, in turn, should be carried out by all students simultaneously. This technique can be applied to any of the study methods described in this chapter.

SPECIFIC STUDY METHODS

Many methods of approaching study reading have been developed. Probably the best known and most widely used, especially for social studies and science selections, is the SQ3R method, developed by Robinson (1961). ROWAC, developed by Roe, and SQRC, recommended by Sakta (1998/1999), are also methods that are good to use with expository texts. SQRQCQ is a study method appropriate for use with word problems in mathematics. Each of these methods is considered in turn. No teacher would want to use all these methods but should choose the ones that best fit his or her classes' needs.

Study Methods for Expository Texts

SQ3R. When the five steps of the **SQ3R** method are applied to a content area reading selection, a variety of reading activities must be employed (Robinson, 1961). The five steps of SQ3R encourage metacognitive strategies: previewing the text, establishing purposes for reading, monitoring comprehension, summarizing, and reviewing. The steps are as follows.

1. *Survey.* During the survey step, the readers read the chapter title, the introductory paragraph(s), the headings, and the summary paragraph(s). At this time the readers should also inspect any graphic aids, such as maps, graphs, tables, diagrams, and pictures. This survey provides readers with an overview of the material contained in the reading assignment and a framework into which they can organize the facts contained in the selection as they read, enhancing the potential for comprehension. Readers who have this knowledge about what they are going to be reading and this grasp of the structure of the text are likely to have better comprehension of the material. This step gives the readers enough information to generate individual purposes for reading the text.

     Manz (2002) suggests a memory device for carrying out a preview (such as the survey step requires) of a text assignment: THIEVES. As mentioned in the

With what types of printed materials should SQ3R be used?

previous paragraph, teachers encourage students to read or examine the *Title*, the *Headings, Every* paragraph's first sentence, *Visuals* and vocabulary, *End*-of-chapter questions, and the *Summary*.

2. *Question.* During this step, readers formulate questions that they expect to find answered in the selection. The author may have provided purpose questions at the beginning of the chapter or follow-up questions at the end. If so, the students may utilize these questions as purpose questions for the reading. If not, the readers can turn the section headings into questions and read to answer self-constructed questions.

3. *Read.* This is the step in which the students read to answer the purpose questions formulated in the previous step. Notes may be taken during this careful reading.

4. *Recite.* In this step, the students try to answer the purpose questions formulated during the second step without referring to the book or to their notes. This step helps to "set" the information in memory, facilitating later recall. This rehearsal process aids the transfer of information from short-term to long-term memory (Jacobowitz, 1988). This activity gets the students involved and provides feedback on learning (Pauk, 2001).

5. *Review.* At this point the students review the material by rereading portions of the book or by rereading notes taken during the careful reading, to verify the answers given during the previous step. This activity aids the students' retention of the material; immediate reinforcement of ideas helps them overcome the tendency to forget material shortly after reading it.

The SQ3R method, like other study techniques, seems to be learned best when taught in the context of content materials and during, rather than before, content classes.

What are the differences in SQ3R and ROWAC?

ROWAC. Another general study method related to the SQ3R approach, but one that utilizes the reading/writing connection and emphasizes the importance of organization more than SQ3R does, has been devised by Betty Roe. The **ROWAC** steps are explained next.

1. *Read.* Read each heading and subheading in the assigned material. (This introduces the student to the nature of the content to be covered and helps to activate his or her background knowledge about the material.)

2. *Organize.* Organize the headings and subheadings in some way (e.g., outline or semantic web). (This gives the student a framework into which to insert the details gained from a careful reading.)

3. *Write.* Write a few paragraphs about what you predict the material will contain, based on the organizer. (This causes the student to engage with the topics to be covered in an active manner, examining connections and sequences and making inferences. This active engagement with the topics should provide motivation and purpose for the reading of the assignment.)

4. *Actively read.* Actively read the material. (This means that the student should constantly be checking the written predictions for accuracy, questioning the reasons for variations between what was expected and what is presented, and filing information in the categories provided by the advance organizer.)

5. *Correct predictions.* Correct your original predictions by revising the paragraphs that you wrote originally. You don't have to rewrite material. Mark out words, phrases, and sentences; use carats to insert ideas; and make marginal notes. The important thing is that the final version, although not neat, is an accurate reflection of the content of the chapter. (This helps the student to integrate the new material into the organizational structure more solidly.)

How does the SQRC strategy work?

SQRC. Sakta (1998/1999) recommends the use of the **SQRC** strategy. SQRC stands for *State, Question, Read,* and *Conclude.* Before reading takes place, the teacher prepares the students for reading by introducing the topic, developing vocabulary knowledge, and building or activating background knowledge. Students then *state* their position on the topic in writing. They turn their statements into *questions,* which give each student a purpose for reading. As they *read,* they look for support for their positions. Finally, when the reading is finished, they write a *conclusion* that supports or refutes the position statement they made before reading. A debate between two groups, taking different positions, follows. Students decide which position has the most support.

A Study Method for Mathematics

Why is SQRQCQ valuable for reading mathematics materials?

MATHEMATICS

SQRQCQ. Since mathematics materials present special problems for readers, the **SQRQCQ** study method was developed for use with statement or word problems in mathematics (Fay, 1965). The steps are as follows:

1. *Survey.* The student reads the problem rapidly to obtain an idea of its general nature.

2. *Question.* In this step, the student determines the specific nature of the problem, that is, "What is being asked in this problem?"

3. *Read.* The student reads the problem carefully, paying attention to specific details and relationships.

4. *Question.* At this point, the student must make a decision about the mathematical operations to be carried out and, in some cases, the order in which these operations are to be performed.

5. *Compute.* The student does the computations decided on in the previous step.

6. *Question.* The student checks the entire process and decides whether or not the answer seems to be correct. He or she asks if the answer is reasonable and if the computations have been performed accurately.

Like SQ3R, this method encourages use of metacognitive skills. Students preview the problem in the survey step, set purposes in the first two question steps, and monitor their success with the problem in the final question step.

Reading to Follow Directions

Another skill that secondary school students need for effective study is the ability to read to follow directions. Students are constantly expected to follow written directions both in the classroom and in everyday life. Teachers write assignments on the board and distribute duplicated materials with directions written on them. Textbooks in different content areas contain printed directions that students are expected to follow. There are also many aspects of everyday activities that require us to follow directions: reading traffic signs, recipes, assembly and installation instructions, forms to be completed, voting instructions, and registration procedures, to name a few. A traffic sign gives a single direction that is vital for a person to follow in order to avoid bodily injury, misdirection, fines, or other penalties. The other activities mentioned involve multiple steps to be followed. Failure to complete the steps properly may result in penalties such as inedible food, nonworking appliances, and receipt of incorrect merchandise.

Many people fail at a task either because they do not know how to follow written directions or because they ignore the directions and try to perform the task without understanding its sequential steps. Almost everyone is familiar with the saying, "When all else fails, read the directions." This tendency to take printed directions lightly may have been fostered in the classroom. Teachers hand out printed directions and then explain them orally. Teachers also often tell students each step to perform as they progress through the task, rather than asking them to read the directions and ask about which parts are unclear. These actions promote a general disregard for reading directions.

Following directions requires two basic comprehension skills: the ability to locate details and the ability to detect sequence. Because each step in a set of directions must be followed exactly and in the appropriate sequence, reading to follow directions is a slow and deliberate task. Rereading is often necessary. The following procedure may prove helpful:

1. Read the directions from beginning to end to get an overview of the task to be performed.

2. Study any accompanying pictorial aids that may help in understanding one or more of the steps or in picturing the desired end result.

3. Reread the directions carefully, visualizing each step to be performed. Read with an open mind, disregarding any preconceived ideas about the procedure involved.

4. Take note of such key words as *first, second, next, last,* and *finally.* Let these words help you picture the order of the activities to be performed.

5. Read each step again, just before you actually perform it.

6. Carry out the steps in the proper order.

Students will learn to follow directions more easily if the presentation of activities is scaled in difficulty from easy to hard. Teachers can start with directions that have few steps and progress to longer sets of directions as the students' proficiency increases.

Some activities for developing skills in following directions are suggested below.

ART

1. Give students a paragraph containing key direction words (*first, next, then, last, finally,* etc.), and ask them to underline the words that help to show the order of events.

2. Prepare duplicated directions for Japanese paper-folding activities. Provide the students with paper, and ask them to follow the directions.

3. Make it a practice to refer students to written directions instead of telling them orally how to do everything. Ask students to read the directions silently and then tell you in their own words what they should do.

4. Teach the meanings of words commonly encountered in written directions, such as *array, estimate, example, horizontal, phrase,* and *vertical.*

5. Have students follow directions to make something from a kit.

6. Use activities similar to the one in Example 7.2 to make a point about the importance of following directions.

Any exercises designed to improve students' ability to understand details and detect sequence will also help them improve their skills in following directions. Activities in which students must integrate information from graphic aids, such as charts or diagrams, with printed information in the text will also be helpful.

Graphic Aids

How do graphic aids help students to understand content material?

The ability to interpret **graphic aids** requires visual literacy, the ability both to interpret and create nonverbal messages (Valmont, 2003). Textbooks contain numerous graphic aids—maps, graphs, tables, charts, diagrams, and pictures—that students often disregard because they have had no training in their use. These aids can help students understand the textbook material better if teachers help them learn to extract the information from each type of graphic aid, but the students need to be explicitly directed to use them to find *specific* information. Simply having a reliable approach to each of the types of graphic aids may be all many secondary students need to benefit from the aids in their textbooks.

Graphic aids serve different purposes in different textbooks. At times, they include information not discussed in the text, although it is related to the text discussion. Sometimes they contain information stated in the text, but they present it in a more visual form. At other times, they may contain a mixture of information from

EXAMPLE 7.2   **Activity on Following Directions**

Questionnaire: Read this entire questionnaire before you begin to fill in the answers. Work as quickly as you can. You have three minutes to finish this activity.

Name _____

Address _____

_____

Phone number _____ Age _____

What is your father's name and occupation? _____

What is your mother's name and occupation? _____

Do you plan to go to college? _____ If so, where? _____

What career are you most interested in? _____

How many years of study past high school will you need for this career? _____

Who is the person that you admire most? _____

What is this person's occupation? _____

After you have completed reading this questionnaire, turn the paper over and write your name on the back. Then give the paper to your teacher. You should have written nothing on this side of the page.

the text and information not from the text, making connections apparent. Whatever their content, graphic displays have been found to improve students' comprehension. This may be true because graphic aids often allow readers to scan large collections of information to see meaningful patterns and to help them visualize certain kinds of information (Gillespie, 1993).

MAPS

Maps are found in many content area materials, although they are most common in social studies textbooks. Since maps are generally included in textbooks to help

SOCIAL STUDIES

clarify the narrative material, students need to be able to read them to understand fully the material being presented.

Some students may have been taught map-reading techniques in elementary school, but many have not had any structured preparation for reading maps. Therefore, secondary school students may vary greatly in their abilities to handle assignments containing maps. A survey of map-reading skills should be administered early in the school year by teachers who expect map reading to be a frequent activity throughout the year. A sample map and some useful questions for surveying map-reading skills are shown in Example 7.3.

After administering a survey of map-reading skills and evaluating the results, the teacher should systematically teach any of the following skills that the students have not yet mastered:

1. Locating and comprehending the map title

2. Determining directions

3. Interpreting a map's legend

4. Applying a map's scale

5. Understanding the concepts of latitude and longitude

6. Understanding common map terms

7. Making inferences concerning the material represented on a map

The first step in map reading should be examining the title of the map to determine the area being represented and the type of information being given about the area. Map titles are not always located at the tops of the maps, as students often expect them to be. Therefore, students may overlook the title of a map unless they have been told to scan the map to find it.

Next, students should locate the directional indicator on the map and orient themselves to the map's layout. They should be aware that north is not always at the top of the map, although most maps are constructed in this manner.

Interpretation of the legend or key is the next step in map reading. The map legend contains an explanation of each of the symbols used. If students do not understand these symbols, the map will be incomprehensible to them.

To determine distances on a map, students must apply the map's scale. Because it would be highly impractical, if not impossible, to draw a map the actual size of the area represented (for example, the United States), maps show areas greatly reduced in size. The relationship of a given distance on a map to the same distance on the earth is shown by the map's scale.

An understanding of latitude and longitude will be helpful in reading some maps. Understanding the system of parallels and meridians enables a reader to locate places on a map by using coordinates of degrees of latitude and longitude. Parallels of latitude are lines on a globe that are parallel to the equator. Meridians of longitude are lines that encircle the globe in a north-south direction, meeting at the poles.

Students need to understand many common map terms to comprehend maps fully. Among these are *latitude* and *longitude*, of course, as well as *equator, hemisphere, peninsula, continent, isthmus, gulf, bay,* and many others.

EXAMPLE 7.3   Map of the United States and Latin America

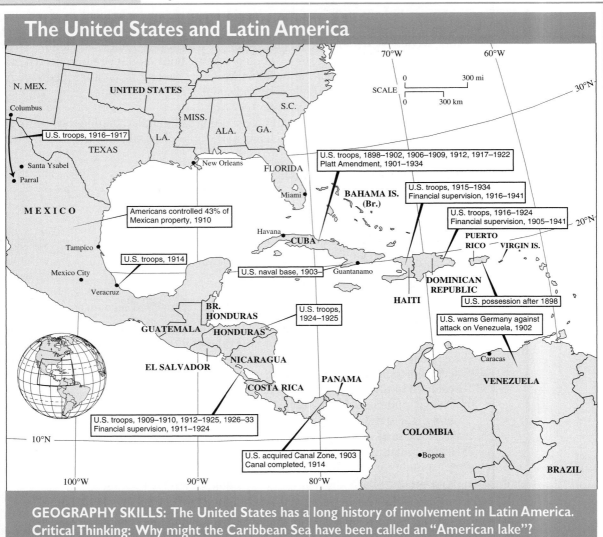

The United States and Latin America

N. MEX.
Columbus
U.S. troops, 1916–1917
UNITED STATES
TEXAS
Santa Ysabel
Parral
MEXICO
Tampico
Mexico City
Veracruz
Americans controlled 43% of Mexican property, 1910
U.S. troops, 1914

MISS.   ALA.   GA.   S.C.
LA.
New Orleans   FLORIDA
Miami

70°W   60°W
0   300 mi
SCALE
0   300 km
30°N

U.S. troops, 1898–1902, 1906–1909, 1912, 1917–1922 Platt Amendment, 1901–1934

BAHAMA IS. (Br.)

Havana
CUBA
U.S. naval base, 1903–   Guantanamo

U.S. troops, 1915–1934 Financial supervision, 1916–1941

U.S. troops, 1916–1924 Financial supervision, 1905–1941
20°N

PUERTO RICO   VIRGIN IS.

DOMINICAN REPUBLIC

HAITI

U.S. possession after 1898

U.S. warns Germany against attack on Venezuela, 1902

BR. HONDURAS
GUATEMALA   HONDURAS
EL SALVADOR   NICARAGUA
COSTA RICA   PANAMA
U.S. troops, 1924–1925

Caracas
VENEZUELA

U.S. troops, 1909–1910, 1912–1925, 1926–33 Financial supervision, 1911–1924

10°N

COLOMBIA
●Bogota

U.S. acquired Canal Zone, 1903 Canal completed, 1914

100°W   90°W   80°W

BRAZIL

GEOGRAPHY SKILLS: The United States has a long history of involvement in Latin America. **Critical Thinking:** Why might the Caribbean Sea have been called an "American lake"?

Questions

SOCIAL STUDIES

1. What area does this map cover?
2. What information about the area is provided?
3. What is the distance from Havana to Miami in miles? In kilometers?
4. What information does the inset map provide?

5. Which Latin American country has had the most recent U.S. involvement, according to this map?
6. Where is a U.S. naval base located on the map? Why would that location be strategically important?
7. Using degrees of latitude and longitude, what is the location of Puerto Rico?
8. In what country is Caracas located?
9. What is a canal? What canal is shown on this map?

Teachers should encourage students to perform more than simple location activities with maps. They should ask students to make inferences about the material represented on maps. For example, for a map showing the physical features of an area (such as mountains, rivers, lakes, deserts, and swamps), the students might be asked to decide what types of transportation would be most appropriate in that area. This kind of activity is extremely important at the secondary school level.

It may be helpful to students to relate a map of an area they are studying to a map of a larger area that contains the smaller one. For example, a map of Tennessee can be related to a map of the United States. In this way, the position of Tennessee within the United States becomes apparent.

Some educators use interactive whiteboards to teach map-reading skills ("Ideas for Teaching with Interactive Whiteboards," 2005). Whiteboards, which are essentially digital dry-erase boards and can serve to replace overhead projectors, allow teachers to "project text, data, images, video, and sound from a computer onto a 66-inch screen using whatever programs teachers have running on their computers, including PowerPoint, Excel, AutoCAD, or a standard web browser" (Levin-Epstein, Murray, and Pierce, 2005, p. 22).

Further suggestions for working with map-reading skills follow.

PHYSICAL EDUCATION

MATHEMATICS

1. Before presenting a chapter in a textbook that requires much map reading, ask students to construct a map of an area of interest to the class. (In a health or physical education class, this might be a map of recreation facilities in the town.) Help students draw the map to scale. (A mathematics teacher may be enlisted to help with this aspect.) Ask students to include a title, a directional indicator, and a legend. This exercise will give students the opportunity for direct experience with important tasks in map reading and will help prepare them to read the maps in their content textbooks with more understanding.

2. When students encounter a map in a content area textbook, encourage them to use the legend by asking questions such as the following:

   Where is there a campground on this map?
   Where do you find a symbol for a state capital?
   Are there any national parks in this area? If so, where are they located?

3. Help students with map terminology by first identifying map features with examples and then asking them to point out on a wall map features such as a *gulf* and a *peninsula* when these features are pertinent to the content presentation.

MEETING THE CHALLENGE

The seventh-graders in Mr. Kyle's urban classroom have been having trouble learning to read maps. Mr. Kyle has come up with a creative approach to this problem. He takes heavy-grade poster board on which he has drawn an outline map of an area and cuts it up with a knife-blade saw. He gives the puzzle pieces that he has created in this manner to his students. First, the students have to put the pieces of the map back together. Then they have to fill in the details of the area on the map (e.g., cities, rivers, land-marks, etc.). To accomplish this task, they must supply a legend with the appropriate symbols, directional indicators, and map scales, as well as place names. When they finish, they use puzzle glue to hold their production together. It can be displayed for other groups, and class members can refer to it as they study the area. The students take pride in their accomplishment.

Map-reading instruction is important for students in social studies classes.
© Dennis McDonald/Photo Edit

SOCIAL STUDIES

4. Have students map the locations of the events in a novel or the events in a history chapter or nonfiction trade book that does not provide a detailed map. Make sure they include a title, legend, directional indicator, and scale.

GRAPHS

SOCIAL STUDIES   SCIENCE AND HEALTH

Graphs often appear in social studies, science, and mathematics books, and sometimes in books for other content areas. Graphs are used to make comparisons among quantitative data.

Types of Graphs

MATHEMATICS

There are four basic types of graphs.

1. *Picture graphs (or pictographs).* Picture graphs use pictures to compare quantities. They aid in visualization of data and are often thought to be the easiest type of graph to read. Readers must realize, however, that only approximate amounts can be indicated by pictographs, making estimation of amounts necessary when interpreting them.

2. *Circle or pie graphs.* Proportional parts of a whole can be shown most easily through use of circle or pie graphs. These graphs show the percentage of the whole represented by each individual part.

3. *Bar graphs.* Bar graphs are useful for comparing the quantities of several items or the quantities of a particular item at different times. These graphs may be either horizontal or vertical.

4. *Line graphs.* Line graphs can depict changes in amounts over a period of time or under different circumstances. They have vertical and horizontal axes. Each point that is plotted on a line graph has a value on both axes.

Representative samples of each of these types of graphs and accompanying sample questions are shown in Examples 7.4, 7.5, 7.6, and 7.7.

EXAMPLE 7.4   Sample Picture Graph and Questions

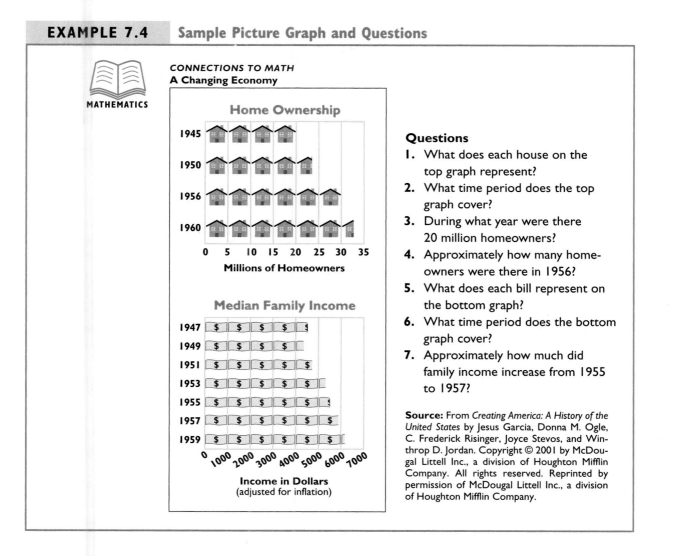

MATHEMATICS

CONNECTIONS TO MATH
A Changing Economy

Home Ownership

Millions of Homeowners

Median Family Income

Income in Dollars
(adjusted for inflation)

Questions

1. What does each house on the top graph represent?
2. What time period does the top graph cover?
3. During what year were there 20 million homeowners?
4. Approximately how many homeowners were there in 1956?
5. What does each bill represent on the bottom graph?
6. What time period does the bottom graph cover?
7. Approximately how much did family income increase from 1955 to 1957?

Source: From *Creating America: A History of the United States* by Jesus Garcia, Donna M. Ogle, C. Frederick Risinger, Joyce Stevos, and Winthrop D. Jordan. Copyright © 2001 by McDougal Littell Inc., a division of Houghton Mifflin Company. All rights reserved. Reprinted by permission of McDougal Littell Inc., a division of Houghton Mifflin Company.

EXAMPLE 7.5 Sample History Text with Circle Graphs and Questions

SOCIAL
STUDIES

CONNECTING WITH THE

PRESENT ▷ A CHANGING AMERICA

If you could take a snapshot of America in 1920 and 1990 you would have two very different pictures. In 1920 the nation was at the end of a huge immigration wave. Most of those immigrants were European. Immigration was sharply reduced until the 1960s. Then waves of immigrants came from Mexico, South America, the Caribbean, and Asia.

As you can see from the charts, the 1920 Census did not even include a figure for Hispanics (people from Spanish-speaking countries). In 1990 Hispanics were the fastest-growing minority group. The charts also show that whites make up a smaller majority of Americans than they used to.

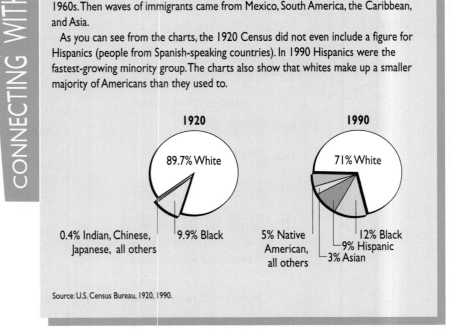

1920

89.7% White

0.4% Indian, Chinese, Japanese, all others   9.9% Black

1990

71% White

5% Native American, all others   12% Black
9% Hispanic
3% Asian

Source: U.S. Census Bureau, 1920, 1990.

Source: *America's Past and Promise*, by Lorna Mason, Jesus Garcia, Frances Powell, and C. Frederick Risinger. Copyright © 1995 by Houghton Mifflin Company. All rights reserved.

[Note to readers: See how information from the text and from the graphic aid must be integrated for full understanding of the material.]

Questions

1. How did the percentage of whites in the United States change from 1920 to 1990?

2. How did the nonwhite population of the United States change from 1920 to 1990?

3. What are some possible reasons for the changes that occurred between 1920 and 1990?

EXAMPLE 7.6   Sample Bar Graph and Questions

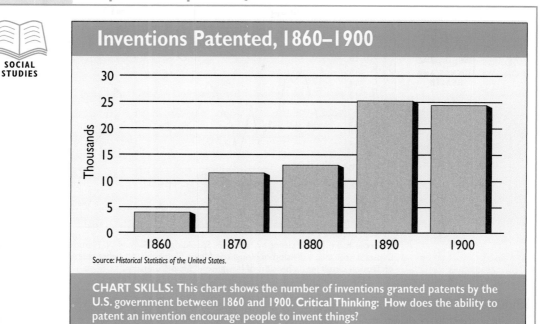

SOCIAL
STUDIES

Inventions Patented, 1860–1900

Source: *Historical Statistics of the United States.*

CHART SKILLS: This chart shows the number of inventions granted patents by the U.S. government between 1860 and 1900. **Critical Thinking:** How does the ability to patent an invention encourage people to invent things?

Source: *America's Past and Promise,* by Lorna Mason, Jesus Garcia, Frances Powell, and C. Frederick Risinger. Copyright © 1995 by Houghton Mifflin Company. All rights reserved.

Questions

1. What is the topic of the bar graph?
2. How many inventions were patented in 1860?
3. In what year shown were the most inventions patented?
4. What is the general trend in the numbers of inventions patented? What might be some reasons for this trend?

Graph-Reading Skills

Students should be taught to check the title of a graph to discover what comparison is being made or what information is being supplied. They must also learn to interpret the legend of a picture graph and to derive needed information from a graph accurately.

Teachers can help students discover the following information about the graphs in their textbooks:

1. The purpose of the graph (Usually indicated by the title, the purpose becomes more evident when the accompanying narrative is studied.)

EXAMPLE 7.7 Sample Line Graph and Questions

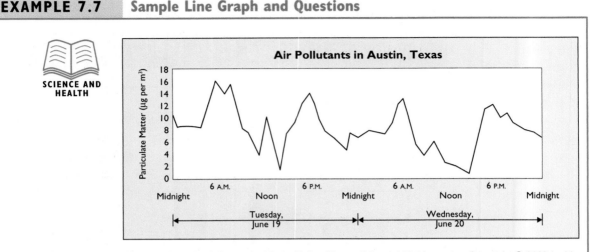

SCIENCE AND
HEALTH

Source: From *Earth Science* by Nancy E. Spaulding and Samuel N. Namowitz. Copyright © 2003 by Mc-Dougal Littell Inc., a division of Houghton Mifflin Company. All rights reserved. Reprinted by permission of McDougal Littell Inc., a division of Houghton Mifflin Company.

Questions

1. How does the concentration of pollutants at 6 a.m. Tuesday compare with the concentration of pollutants at 6 a.m. Wednesday?

2. Air pollution can worsen the health of people with lung disease. According to the graph, when is the best time for such a person to run errands?

3. At what time does the concentration of pollutants peak on both days?

4. What could be the cause of the peaks in the amounts of pollution on the two days?

5. Falling rain tends to clean pollutants from the air. What evidence is there that no rain fell Tuesday morning before 6 a.m.?

6. Assume these trends continue into Thursday, June 21. Predict the time on that day when the amount of pollutants is most likely to be greatest.

2. The scale of measure on bar and line graphs

3. The legend of picture graphs

4. The items being compared

5. The location of specific pieces of information within a graph (e.g., the intersection of the point of interest on the vertical axis with the point of interest on the horizontal axis)

6. The trends indicated by a graph (For example, does an amount increase or decrease over a period of time?)

7. The application of graphic information to actual life situations (A graph showing the temperatures for each month in Sydney, Australia, could be used for planning what clothes to take on a trip to Sydney at a particular time of the year.)

Fry (1981, pp. 388–389) points out that "graphical literacy—the ability to both comprehend and draw graphs—is an important communication tool that needs more emphasis in the school curriculum." He urges teachers to include graphing in their assignments, perhaps taking a section of the content textbook or an outside reading and asking students to make as many graphs as they can to illustrate ideas in the material. One of the best ways to help students learn to read graphs is to have them construct their own after the teacher has modeled how to do this. They can graph such things as fund-raising activities, number of students participating in extracurricular activities, time spent on different activities, outside readings done by various students, or quiz scores over a period of time. The teacher can construct graphs such as the ones in Examples 7.4 through 7.7 and ask students to answer questions about them. Questions can also be asked about particular graphs in the students' textbooks or related trade books.

TABLES

Tables, which are found in reading materials for all subject areas, contain information arranged in vertical columns and horizontal rows. One problem that students have with reading tables is extracting the needed facts from a large mass of information presented.

Like the titles of maps and graphs, the titles of tables contain information about their content. Also, because tables are arranged in columns and rows, the headings for the columns and rows also provide information. Specific information is obtained by locating the intersection of an appropriate column with an appropriate row. Example 7.8 shows a sample table. The questions that follow the table are presented as models for the types of questions that teachers might ask about the tables in their students' content textbooks.

CHARTS AND DIAGRAMS

Charts and diagrams appear in textbooks for many different content areas. They are designed to help students picture the events, processes, structures, relationships, or sequences described by the text. At times they may be used as summaries of text material. Example 7.9 is a chart from a history book that summarizes text material and shows a process.

Students must be made aware of the abstract nature of diagrams and of the fact that they often distort or oversimplify information. Interpretation of the symbols found in diagrams and understanding of the perspectives used in diagrams are not automatic; teachers must provide practice in such activities.

Numerous types of charts and diagrams are used in the various content areas. Examples include tree diagrams (English), flow charts (mathematics), and process charts (science). Careful instruction in reading such charts and diagrams must be provided for interpretation of content material. Example 7.10 shows a diagram from a science textbook.

EXAMPLE 7.8   Sample Table and Questions

SCIENCE AND HEALTH

Common Air Pollutants

Air Pollutant	Major Sources	Effects
Carbon monoxide (CO)	Automobile exhaust	Reduces delivery of oxygen to body tissues; impairs vision and reflexes
Nitrogen dioxide (NO2)	Burning of fossil fuels in power plants and automobiles	Irritates lungs and lowers resistance to respiratory infections; contributes to acid rain and smog
Sulfur dioxide (SO2)	Burning of fossil fuels in power plants, oil refineries, paper mills, volcanoes	Irritates respiratory system; contributes to acid rain
Particulate matter (dust, smoke, soot, ash)	Factories, power plants, oil refineries, paper mills, volcanoes	Contributes to respiratory problems; linked to some cancers
Lead (Pb)	Smelters, battery plants	Damages nervous and digestive systems
Ozone (O3)	Reactions of nitrogen oxides and hydrocarbons in the presence of sunlight	Reduces lung function and causes inflammation

Source: From *Earth Science* by Nancy E. Spaulding and Samuel N. Namowitz. Copyright © 2003 by Mc-Dougal Littell Inc., a division of Houghton Mifflin Company. All rights reserved. Reprinted by permission of McDougal Littell Inc., a division of Houghton Mifflin Company.

Questions

1. What type of information is located in this table?
2. What are the column headings?
3. What does nitrogen dioxide cause?
4. What is a major source of carbon monoxide?
5. What pollutant damages nervous and digestive systems?

The teacher can point out that distortions are frequently found in textbook drawings. Students can be helped to see that the diagrams in Example 7.10 are views of the human body's bone structure, which is not visible because it is covered by flesh and skin. The teacher can also identify the front and rear views and discuss the differences between them. Diagrams such as this might also appear in health textbooks. Students may be asked to label unlabeled diagrams similar to this one as a check on retention of the concepts and terminology presented in the text.

A semantic map, one type of graphic organizer, is a diagram of the relationships among concepts in a text. Having students draw semantic maps of content material can help them comprehend it better. (See Chapter 3 for details on semantic mapping.) Fisher (2001) suggests the use of Graphic Organizer Notebooks, collections of blank organizers and webs, designed by the teacher to fit particular text material. Students are asked to fill in these graphic organizers after they have read the content material.

Diagramming the word problems presented in mathematics textbooks can help students visualize the problems and subsequently solve them (Rakes, Rakes, and Smith, 1995). Such approaches to math problem solving are fairly common in ele-

MATHEMATICS

EXAMPLE 7.9   History Chart

SOCIAL STUDIES

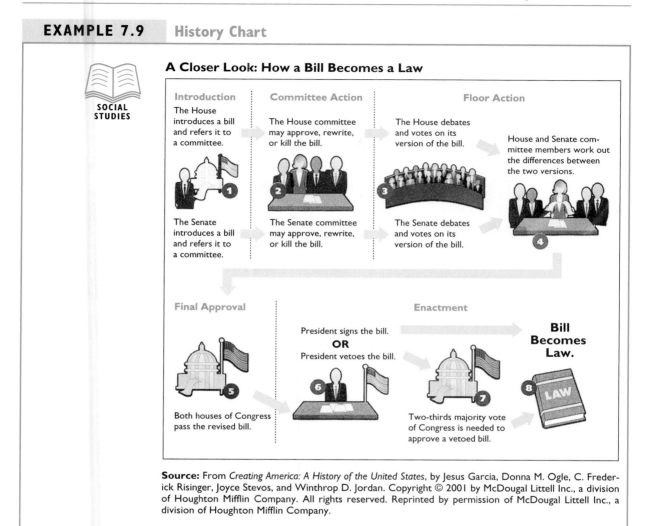

A Closer Look: How a Bill Becomes a Law

Introduction

The House introduces a bill and refers it to a committee.

The Senate introduces a bill and refers it to a committee.

Committee Action

The House committee may approve, rewrite, or kill the bill.

The Senate committee may approve, rewrite, or kill the bill.

Floor Action

The House debates and votes on its version of the bill.

The Senate debates and votes on its version of the bill.

House and Senate committee members work out the differences between the two versions.

Final Approval

Both houses of Congress pass the revised bill.

Enactment

President signs the bill.
OR
President vetoes the bill.

Two-thirds majority vote of Congress is needed to approve a vetoed bill.

Bill Becomes Law.

LAW

Source: From *Creating America: A History of the United States*, by Jesus Garcia, Donna M. Ogle, C. Frederick Risinger, Joyce Stevos, and Winthrop D. Jordan. Copyright © 2001 by McDougal Littell Inc., a division of Houghton Mifflin Company. All rights reserved. Reprinted by permission of McDougal Littell Inc., a division of Houghton Mifflin Company.

mentary schools, but they often are dropped at the secondary level, even though they are still valid.

PICTURES AND CARTOONS

Content area textbooks contain pictures that are designed to illustrate the material described and to interest students. The illustrations may be photographs offering a realistic representation of concepts, people, and places, or they may be line drawings that are somewhat more abstract in nature.

EXAMPLE 7.10   Science Diagram

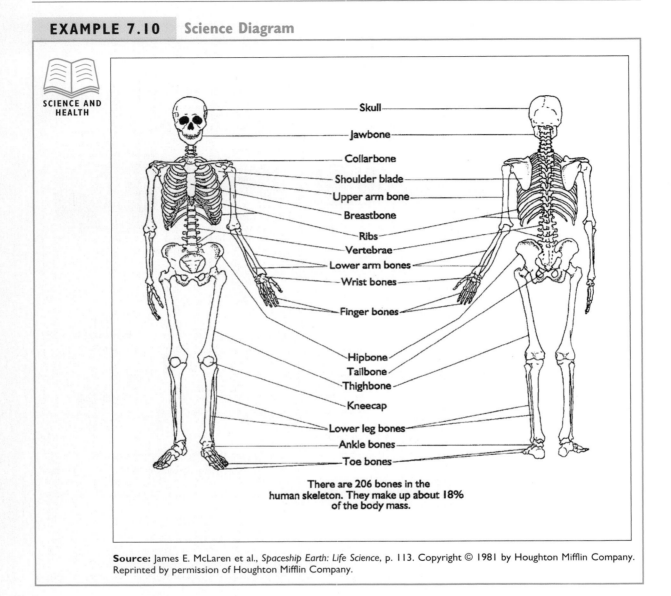

SCIENCE AND
HEALTH

Skull
Jawbone
Collarbone
Shoulder blade
Upper arm bone
Breastbone
Ribs
Vertebrae
Lower arm bones
Wrist bones
Finger bones
Hipbone
Tailbone
Thighbone
Kneecap
Lower leg bones
Ankle bones
Toe bones

There are 206 bones in the
human skeleton. They make up about 18%
of the body mass.

Source: James E. McLaren et al., *Spaceship Earth: Life Science*, p. 113. Copyright © 1981 by Houghton Mifflin Company. Reprinted by permission of Houghton Mifflin Company.

Students frequently see pictures merely as space fillers, reducing the amount of reading they will have to do on a page. Therefore, they may pay little attention to pictures, although the pictures are often excellent sources of information.

Since pictures are representations of experiences, they may be utilized as vicarious means of adding to a student's store of knowledge. Teachers should help students extract information from textbook illustrations by encouraging them to study

**SCIENCE AND
HEALTH**

the pictures before and after reading the text, looking for the purpose of each picture and its specific details. Studying pictures may help students understand and retain the information illustrated.

   Example 7.11 depicts marine animals and the different ocean levels in which they live. The picture helps students visualize these animals.

EXAMPLE 7.11   **Science Textbook Illustration**

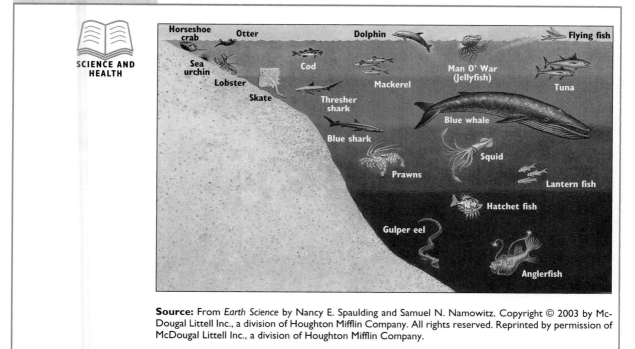

Source: From *Earth Science* by Nancy E. Spaulding and Samuel N. Namowitz. Copyright © 2003 by Mc-Dougal Littell Inc., a division of Houghton Mifflin Company. All rights reserved. Reprinted by permission of McDougal Littell Inc., a division of Houghton Mifflin Company.

   Cartoons are special types of pictures that contain special symbols. They often distort the things they represent in order to make a point. Students should be encouraged to read cartoons critically. Example 7.12 shows a cartoon that might appear in a literature textbook. This cartoon makes the point that allusions to literature are often used in cartoons.

   The *Six Chix* comic strip in Example 7.13 might be used in an explanation of metamorphosis.

   Example 7.14 can be used as an exercise in examining how a cartoon delivers a message. Teachers can help the students connect the environmental issue involved with the situation depicted in the cartoon. In the cartoon, oil spills in the ocean are referred to indirectly by equating the smell of oil, rather than fresh salt air, with the ocean.

EXAMPLE 7.12 Literature-Related Cartoon

© R. Daniel Proctor/Knoxville News-Sentinel. Reprinted with permission.

EXAMPLE 7.13 Biology-Related Comic Strip

Copyright © SIX CHIX – MARGARET SHULOCK. Reprinted with permission of King Features Syndicate.

EXAMPLE 7.14   Science Textbook Cartoon

Source: Joseph H. Jackson and Edward D. Evans, *Spaceship Earth: Earth Science*, p. 511. Copyright © 1980 by Houghton Mifflin Company. Reprinted by permission of Houghton Mifflin Company.

Students can illustrate sections of content text with their own pictures or cartoons as they read. This action causes them to process the material more deeply and results in increased comprehension. Students should understand that their artistic ability is not the point and is not being evaluated. Evidence of insight into the content is the focus of the evaluation.

Adjusting Rate to Fit Purpose and Materials

What is meant by flexibility of rate?

Students will use study time most efficiently if they are taught to vary their reading rates to fit their purposes and the materials they are reading. The ability to make these adjustments, which is important for good comprehension, is called **flexibility of rate**. Good readers adjust their rates, thinking, and approaches automatically and are not aware that they make several changes when reading a single page.

Flexible readers can distinguish between important and unimportant ideas, and they read important ideas carefully, giving less attention to the less important ideas. Information about familiar topics is read more quickly than information about new topics because familiarity with a topic allows the reader to anticipate ideas, vocabulary, and phrasing. A selection that has a light vocabulary burden, more concrete concepts, and an easily managed style of writing can be read more rapidly than

SCIENCE AND HEALTH

MATHEMATICS

material with a heavy vocabulary load, many abstract concepts, and a difficult writing style. Light fiction that is read strictly for enjoyment can and should be absorbed much faster than the directions for a science experiment; newspapers and magazines can be read more rapidly than textbooks; theoretical scientific content and statistics must be read more slowly than much social studies content.

Students often think that everything should be read at the same rate. Thus, some of them read light novels as slowly and deliberately as they read mathematics problems. These students will probably never enjoy reading for recreation because they work so hard at reading and it takes them so long. Other students move rapidly through everything they read. In doing so, they usually fail to grasp essential details in content area assignments, although they "finish" reading all of the assigned material. Rate of reading should never be considered apart from comprehension. Therefore, the optimum rate for reading any material is the fastest rate at which an acceptable level of comprehension is obtained. Teachers who wish to concentrate on improving their students' reading rates should include comprehension checks with all rate exercises.

Work on increasing reading rate should not be emphasized until basic word recognition and comprehension skills are thoroughly under control. Improvement in these skills often results in increased rate without any special attention to it. For best results, flexibility of rate should be developed with the content materials that students are expected to read.

FACTORS AFFECTING RATE

Many factors influence the rate at which a person can read a particular selection. Some are related to the material, but some are related to the reader. Factors related to the material include size and style of type, format of the pages, use of illustrations, organization, writing style of the author, and abstractness or complexity of ideas in the material. Factors related to the reader include the reader's background of experiences, reading ability, attitudes and interests, and reason for reading the specific material. Obviously, these factors differ with each selection. Therefore, different rates are appropriate for different materials.

Poor reading habits may greatly decrease reading rate. Poor habits include excessive vocalizing (forming each word as it is read); sounding out all words, those familiar and those unfamiliar; excessive regressing (going back and rereading previously read material); and pointing at each word with the index finger. Concentrated attention to the elimination of these problems can yield good results. Often, secondary school students simply need to be made aware of the habits that are slowing them down and need to be given some suggestions for practice in overcoming them.

TECHNIQUES FOR INCREASING RATE AND FLEXIBILITY

Many methods have been devised to help students increase or adjust their rates of reading. The approaches most classroom teachers use are having timed readings, teaching skimming and scanning techniques, and providing flexibility exercises.

Timed Readings

SCIENCE AND MATHEMATICS HEALTH

To help students increase their rates of reading in material that does not require intensive study reading, teachers may use timed readings. Like other study skills, techniques for improving rate may be learned best in situations in which they are actually used. In choosing appropriate selections for rate instruction, the content teacher should avoid material that includes many small details (e.g., a science experiment or a mathematics statement problem). Materials that present general background and recreational reading in the content area are more useful for this activity (e.g., the story of a scientific discovery or the biography of a mathematician).

Timed readings should always be accompanied by comprehension checks. An extremely high rate score is of no use if the student fails to comprehend the material. Teachers should encourage rate increases only if comprehension does not suffer. Some students need help in basic reading skills before they can participate profitably in these rate-building activities.

Graphs can be kept of the results of timed rate exercises over a period of weeks or months. Seeing visible progress can motivate students to continue to work on improving their rates. Comprehension charts should also be kept so rate increases can be viewed in the proper perspective.

Skimming and Scanning Techniques

When might you need to skim text? How is scanning of text accomplished?

Skimming and **scanning** are special types of rapid reading. Skimming refers to reading to obtain a general idea or overview of the material, and scanning means reading to find a specific bit of information. Skimming is faster than rapid reading of most of the words in the material because, when readers skim material, they read selectively. Scanning is faster than skimming because only one piece of information is being sought. When scanning, readers run their eyes rapidly down the page, concentrating on the particular information they seek. Workplace reading often requires skimming and scanning of material (Gerber and Finn, 1998).

Skimming techniques are used in the survey step of the SQ3R method discussed earlier in this chapter. Teachers can help develop skimming skills as they work to teach this study method.

When teaching students to skim, the teacher should tell them to read all of the first two paragraphs of a chapter or selection to get an overview and then begin to leave out material as they read, reading only key sentences and phrases to get the main ideas. The teacher should point out that, if the final paragraph summarizes the material, students may want to read it more carefully.

Students should try to read as fast as possible when they skim. Students should use skimming when they do not have much time and need to cover the material as fast as possible.

Some skimming activities include the following:

1. Give the students a short time to skim an assigned chapter and write down the main ideas covered.

2. Ask students to skim newspaper articles and match them to headlines written on the board. Have a competition to see who can finish first with no errors.

3. Give students the title of a research topic and have them skim an article to decide whether it is pertinent to the topic.

Scanning activities are easy to design. Some examples follow:

SOCIAL STUDIES

1. Have students scan a history chapter to find the date of a particular event.

2. Have students scan a textbook to find information about a particular person.

Students need to scan for key words related to the specific facts they seek. An exercise in generating key words that are related to a specific topic may be beneficial.

Flexibility Exercises

Since not all materials should be read at the same rate, students need assistance in determining appropriate rates for different materials. The table in Example 7.15 shows three reading rates of a good reader, each of which is appropriate for a particular type of reading material.

One type of flexibility exercise is to ask a series of questions such as the following ones and then discuss students' reasons for their answers:

MATHEMATICS

1. What rate would be best for reading a statement problem in your mathematics textbook?

2. Which could you read most quickly and still achieve your purpose—a television schedule, a newspaper article, or a science textbook?

3. Is just skimming an appropriate way to read directions for a science experiment?

SCIENCE AND HEALTH

4. What reading technique would you use to look up a word in the dictionary?

EXAMPLE 7.15 **Rate Chart**

Kind of Reading	Rate	Comprehension
Slow: *Study reading* speed is used when material is difficult or when high comprehension is desired.	200 to 300 w.p.m.	80–90%
Average: An *average reading* speed is used for everyday reading of magazines, newspapers, and easier textbooks.	250 to 500 w.p.m.	70%
Fast: *Skimming* is used when the highest rate is desired. Comprehension is intentionally lower.	800+ w.p.m.	50%

Source: Reprinted by permission of Edward Fry.

Fluency

People sometimes equate fluency with rate, but fluency "consists not only of rate, accuracy, and automaticity, but also of phrasing, smoothness, and expressiveness" (Worthy and Broaddus, 2001/2002, p. 334). Fluent reading is important to comprehension. Students beyond the primary grades who are not fluent readers face problems in dealing with classroom reading demands as material becomes more difficult and assignments become longer and require more processing.

ENGLISH/ LANGUAGE ARTS

The method of repeated reading has proven successful in helping students develop fluency. With this method, "students practice rereading a familiar text with teacher guidance and feedback . . . until they reach an appropriate level of accuracy and speed" (Worthy and Broaddus, 2001/2002, p. 336). Worthy and Broaddus use reading performances in Readers' Theater to provide purposeful repeated readings for students. Readers' Theater is reading aloud from scripts in a dramatic, expressive manner. This technique is started by model read-alouds performed by the teacher. Students may follow along in the text. Sometimes they may read chorally with the teacher. Guided practice may take the form of reading in groups with teacher feedback. Independent practice should follow before the Readers' Theater is performed for others (Worthy and Broaddus, 2000/2001).

ENGLISH/ LANGUAGE ARTS

Daily self-selected silent reading in comfortable materials is also important in developing fluency. Thematic units (see Chapter 9) often allow some choice of reading materials. They offer opportunities for students to read materials at their own reading levels and still participate actively in a unit of study. Teachers need to be familiar with the wide variety of trade books available to supplement their units of study. Any genre, from picture books to realistic fiction to science fiction to nonfiction, may be of use.

Rasinski (2000) points out that slow, disfluent reading needs to be taken seriously. It can turn any reading activity into a frustrating struggle for a student. When that happens, little learning will occur.

Retention

Secondary school students are expected to retain much of the material from their content area textbooks. Use of study methods to enhance **retention** has already been discussed extensively in this chapter. Teachers can help students apply these techniques and others that will facilitate retention of material. Concentrating on material as it is read is important to retention. Some suggestions that the teacher may offer include these:

1. Always read study material with a purpose. If the teacher does not supply you with a purpose, set a purpose of your own. Having a purpose for reading will help you extract meaning from a passage, and you will retain material that is meaningful to you longer.

2. Try to grasp the author's organization of the material. This will help you to categorize concepts to be learned under main headings, which are easier to retain than small details and which facilitate recall of the related details. To accomplish this task, outline the material.

3. Try to picture the ideas that the author is attempting to describe. Visualization of the information being presented will help you remember it longer.

4. As you read, take notes on important points in the material. Writing information down can help you to fix it in your memory. (See Chapter 6 for note-taking guidelines.)

5. After you have read the material, summarize it in your own words. If you can do this, you will have recalled the main points, and rewording the material will demonstrate your understanding.

6. When you have read the material, discuss the assignment with a classmate or a group of classmates. Talking about the material facilitates remembering it.

7. Apply the concepts that you read about, if possible. Physical or mental interaction with the material will help you retain it.

8. Read assignments critically. If you question the material as you read, you will be more likely to remember it.

9. If you wish to retain the material over a long period of time, use spaced practice (a number of short practice sessions extended over a period of time) rather than massed practice (one long practice session). Massed practice facilitates immediate recall, but for long-term retention, distributed practice produces the best results.

10. If you plan to recite the material to yourself or to another student in order to increase your retention, do so as soon as possible after reading the material. Always check your accuracy and correct any errors immediately, so that you will not retain inaccurate material.

11. Overlearning facilitates long-term retention. To overlearn something, you must continue to practice it for a period of time after you have initially mastered it.

12. Mnemonic devices can help you retain certain types of information. (For example, remember that there is "a rat" in the middle of "separate.")

13. A variety of types of writing can improve retention. Langer (1986) reported the effects of different types of writing tasks on learning from reading in the content areas. Writing answers to study questions fostered recall of isolated bits of information. Essay writing produced more long-term and reasoned learning of a smaller amount of material. Note taking fell somewhere in the middle, causing students to deal with larger chunks of meaning than did study questions, but not involving reorganization of material, as did essay writing.

14. Relate the material you are reading to things you already know. Making such connections can aid in the acquisition of new concepts and in the retention of material read.

15. Monitor your reading to determine if you understand the material. If not, reread it or take other steps to ensure understanding.

16. Avoid studying in a distracting setting.

17. Study more difficult and less interesting material when you are most alert.

18. Anticipate what is coming next as you read a passage, and read to see if your prediction was accurate.

Teachers can also facilitate student retention of material by offering students ample opportunities to review information and to practice skills learned and by offering positive reinforcement for correct responses given during the practice and review periods. Class discussion of material to be learned tends to aid retention. Emphasis on classifying the ideas found in the reading material under appropriate categories can also help.

Test Taking

Secondary school students sometimes fail to do well on tests, not because they do not know the material, but because they have difficulty reading and comprehending the test. Teachers can help students by suggesting ways to read different types of tests effectively.

Essay tests often contain the terms *compare, contrast, diagram, trace the development, describe, discuss,* and others. Teachers can explain how they expect students to answer questions containing each of these terms and any other terms they plan to use. This will help prevent students from losing points on the test because they "described" instead of "contrasted." Teachers can point out that, if students are asked to compare two things or ideas, both similarities and differences should be mentioned. If students are asked to contrast two things or ideas, differences are the important factors. If students are asked to describe something, they are expected to paint a word picture of it. If they are asked to diagram something, an actual drawing is required. Sample answers to a variety of different test questions utilizing the special vocabulary may be useful in helping students understand what the teacher expects. An example follows:

Question. Contrast extemporaneous speeches and prepared speeches.

Answer. Extemporaneous speeches are given with little advance thought. Prepared speeches are usually preceded by much thought and research. Prepared speeches often contain quotations and paraphrases of the thoughts of many other people about the subject. Extemporaneous speeches can contain such material only if the speaker has previously become very well informed in the particular area involved. Assuming that the speaker has little background in the area, an extemporaneous speech would be likely to have less depth than a prepared speech since it would involve only the speaker's immediate impressions. Prepared speeches tend to be better organized than extemporaneous speeches because the speaker has more time to collect thoughts and arrange them in the best possible sequence.

What are the steps in the PORPE technique?

PORPE is a technique developed by Simpson (1986) to help students study for essay examinations. The steps in PORPE are as follows:

1. *Predict.* Construct potential essay questions, based on your reading of the material. Use words such as *explain*, *criticize*, *compare*, and *contrast*. Focus on important ideas.

2. *Organize.* Organize the information necessary to answer the questions.

3. *Rehearse.* Memorize material through recitation and self-testing. Space practice over several days for long-term memory.

4. *Practice.* Write out in detail the answers to the questions that you formulated.

5. *Evaluate.* Judge the accuracy and completeness of your answers.

Simpson suggests teaching this procedure through teacher modeling and a series of group and individual activities. Many students may need help in the self-questioning portion of PORPE or in self-questioning for ordinary study. Teachers should familiarize students with different types of questions and should show them how to generate these questions, perhaps through think-aloud procedures. Research has shown that secondary students can be taught to generate their own questions about texts and that doing so helps low-ability students more than average- or high-ability students (Andre and Anderson, 1978/1979; Gillespie, 1990).

The teacher may suggest ways for students to study for tests. Some techniques are to read class notes, apply some of the retention-enhancement techniques suggested previously, rewrite notes more concisely, and compose possible test questions and practice answering them.

It is important for the students to know exactly what the test will cover and what type of test will be given, for this information will affect the study procedures used. The teacher should provide this information, but the students should ask about it if the teacher is vague about the content or fails to mention the type of test.

Students need to realize the importance of working carefully when they are taking tests and of following directions exactly. They should examine the test before they begin, to determine if they have questions about what they are to do, the point values of the questions, or the manner of responding to the questions. They should answer the ones they know well first and then allocate the remainder of their time to the harder questions (Strichart and Mangrum, 1993). They should be aware of the time available to complete the test and should avoid spending too much time on items they are not likely to be able to answer. Before they turn in their papers, they should always check to make sure that they have not inadvertently left one or more answers blank. In general, it is wise to answer all questions with a best guess, but this suggestion is invalidated if the teacher imposes a penalty for guessing.

The student must read objective tests carefully. Generally, every word in an item must be considered. Teachers should emphasize the importance of considering the effect of words such as *always*, *never*, and *not*, as well as others of this general nature. Students need to understand that all the parts of a true-false question must be true if the answer is to be true. They must also be taught to read all possible responses for a multiple-choice question before choosing an answer.

Teachers can also help students improve their performance on tests by offering the following useful hints:

1. When studying for essay tests:
   a. Remember that your answers should include main ideas accompanied by supporting details.
   b. Expect questions that cover the topics most emphasized in the course, since only a few questions can be asked within the limited time.
   c. Expect questions that are broad in scope.
   d. Read your class notes and rewrite them more concisely.
   e. Consider the important topics covered, and try to guess some of the questions that the teacher may ask. Prepare good answers for these questions, and try to learn them thoroughly. You will probably be able to use the points you rehearse in your answers on the actual test, even if the questions you formulated are not exactly the same as the ones the teacher asks.

2. When studying for objective tests:
   a. Become familiar with important details.
   b. Consider the types of questions that have been asked on previous tests, and study for those types. If dates have been asked for in the past, learn the dates in the current material.
   c. If listing questions are a possibility, especially sequential listings, try preparing mnemonic devices to help you in recalling the lists.

3. Learning important definitions can be helpful for any kind of test and can be useful in answering many essay questions.

4. Apply the suggestions listed in the earlier section, "Retention."

When teachers construct tests, they should take care to avoid making the test harder to read than the original material. Otherwise, students could know the material required but be unable to comprehend the questions because the readability level of the test was so high. Students might then receive low test scores because of the teacher's inappropriate test preparation rather than because of their own lack of knowledge of the concepts involved.

The preceding discussion focuses primarily on how to take teacher-made tests, because they are the most frequently given tests during the year. Less frequently students are faced with taking standardized tests, although many of these tests are high-stakes governmentally mandated tests, increasing their importance to teachers and students. These tests are given under strictly controlled conditions. Because of the desire for objective assessment, they tend to be objective in nature, and the previously given tips for taking objective tests apply. The strict timing on these tests and the very specific directions for marking answer sheets cause many students problems. Practice with similar answer sheets under timed conditions could familiarize students with the procedures and decrease anxiety about taking the tests.

Focus on Struggling Readers

Study Skills and Struggling Readers

Struggling readers are frequently disorganized, a state that is detrimental to their school progress. For example, a struggling reader named Ethan stumbles into the classroom after class has begun. He bumps into a desk and drops all of his books, along with a variety of crumpled papers. When the teacher asks for his homework, he says that he started it, but he thinks it is at home because he didn't remember that it was due.

Study skills instruction can give struggling readers the essential organizational skills that will enable them to learn from text. First, struggling readers need assistance in learning how to attend to teachers and how to sustain their attention. In addition, they need help in understanding the vocabulary in a spoken presentation or written selection, in recognizing important points, in following a sequence of ideas, and in understanding verbal and nonverbal cues. Teachers can help students by modeling good listening practices and providing them with practice in the listening skills necessary to accomplish these learning tasks as a basis for developing study skills.

Struggling readers often need assistance in organizing and completing assignments. Teachers can help struggling readers by giving them all of their assignments in written form, which may include detailed, step-by-step instructions. For example, students need to know exactly what the assignment is, when it is due, and the sequence of steps involved in completing it. Study methods are very helpful to struggling readers as they learn how to learn from textbooks and how to complete assignments. SQ3R is a good beginning study method because it can be applied effectively to expository texts. However, struggling readers need direct instruction in using this study method and they need teacher-directed practice with SQ3R until they can apply it automatically. Ten teacher-directed practices are usually necessary for them to achieve fluent application of this method.

Focus on English Language Learners

Study Skills and ELLs

English language learners will also benefit from learning study skill strategies because they are learning content from textbooks written in their second language. The teaching strategies described in this chapter are useful for ELLs. However, they should be fluent comprehenders of English in order to learn a study method and apply it to their textbooks. A beginning point for ELLs is to study SQ3R and then to add additional methods as they are needed.

SUMMARY

Reading-study skills are skills that enhance comprehension and retention of information contained in printed material. They help students manage their reading in content area classes.

Study methods such as SQ3R, ROWAC, and SQRC are applicable to a number of different subject areas, including social studies and science. SQRQCQ is effective for use with statement or word problems in mathematics. Instructional procedures such as the PSRT strategy and some recitation techniques can be used to enhance the development of study skills.

The ability to follow written directions is vitally important to secondary school students. Teachers should plan activities to help students develop this important skill.

Content area textbooks are filled with graphic visual aids such as maps, graphs, tables, diagrams, and pictures. Teachers should give students guidance in interpreting these helpful text features.

Other areas to which teachers should give attention are adjustment of reading rate to fit the purpose for which the reading is being done and the material to be read, developing fluency, retention of material read, and test-taking skills.

DISCUSSION QUESTIONS

1. Which of the study methods listed in this chapter is best for use in your content area? Why?

2. What is a useful procedure for teaching students to read directions with understanding?

3. What graphic aids occur most commonly in your content area? What can you do to help students interpret them effectively?

4. What is the best setting in which to offer students instruction concerning flexibility of rate? Why is this so?

5. What are some techniques for helping students increase reading rate with acceptable comprehension?

6. How can you help your students retain as much of the material that they read in their content textbooks as possible?

7. Should you give attention to helping your students develop test-taking skills? Why, or why not?

8. What can you do to help struggling readers develop needed reading-study strategies?

9. What can you do to help English language learners develop needed reading-study strategies?

ENRICHMENT ACTIVITIES

*1. Teach one of the study methods described in this chapter to a class of secondary school students. Work through it with them step by step.

2. Collect materials that include directions that secondary-level students often need to read. Discuss with your classmates how you could help the students learn to read the materials more effectively.

3. Collect a variety of types of maps. Decide which features of each map will need the most explanation for students.

4. Collect a variety of types of graphs. Make them into a display that could be used in a unit on reading graphs.

5. Develop a procedure to help secondary school students learn to be flexible in their rates of reading. Use materials of widely varying types.

*6. Examine several of your old tests. Decide what reading difficulties they may present for your students. Isolate special words for which meanings may have to be taught.

*These activities are designed for in-service teachers, student teachers, and practicum students.

Part 3

Applying Literacy Instruction in the Content Areas

Chapter 8

Writing in the Content Areas

OVERVIEW

In this chapter we consider the relationships among reading, writing, and thinking in content area classes; the process approach to writing instruction; and types of writing-to-learn strategies that content area teachers may employ. The goal is to help content area teachers learn to use writing to advantage in their classes.

The process approach to writing emphasizes prewriting, drafting, revision, editing, and publication procedures. It requires the student to be concerned with the message and the audience from the beginning, whereas a focus on the product often gives inordinate attention to the mechanics of writing without emphasizing the development of the message. Publication procedures include sharing the products in written or oral form with classmates, the larger audience of the community, or perhaps a global audience on the Internet. Writing-to-learn strategies in content areas include use of the language experience approach, content journals, dialogue journals, RAFT assignments, research reports (including multigenre reports), laboratory reports, photo essays, pen pals, and Internet writing projects. The process approach to writing is useful with many types of content area writing, especially research reports and RAFT assignments, as well as creative writing endeavors. It can be implemented on computers, and the Internet offers writing labs for students.

PURPOSE-SETTING QUESTIONS

As you read this chapter, try to answer these questions:

1. What is the relationship between reading and writing activities in content area classes?
2. What are some types of writing that are useful in the content areas?
3. What are the steps in the process approach to writing instruction?
4. What are some ways to evaluate writing?
5. What writing instructional practices work best with struggling readers and writers?
6. What writing instructional practices work best with English language learners?

The Relationships Among Reading, Writing, and Thinking

THE NATURE OF WRITING

Each incidence of writing occurs "at a particular moment in the writer's biography, in particular circumstances, and under particular external and internal pressures. In short, the writer is always transacting with a personal, social, and cultural environment" (Rosenblatt, 1989, p. 163). Writers are also transacting with the texts that they are producing, using the reservoirs of past linguistic experiences at their disposal. Freewriting (discussed later in this chapter) is a way of tapping the individual's linguistic reservoir without concern about organization or form of expression.

A writer necessarily reads what he or she has written as it is being produced. When this happens, the writer is checking to see if the writing is projecting a meaning that meets the purpose for the writing. The writer weighs words against an internal standard to see if they are right. The writer also may attempt to read the material as potential audiences will read it to see if the meaning they will construct is congruent with his or her purpose (Rosenblatt, 1989).

VALUES OF WRITING IN THE CONTENT AREAS

Study in the content areas is designed to promote the learning of facts, principles, and procedures related to the disciplines involved. Such learning involves both literal and higher-level thinking skills and retention of material studied.

Writing is a tool for thinking, and it helps develop thinking skills. Its "linear and structured form imposes its own sense of order on our attempts to think about relationships. And, as 'frozen speech,' it makes metalinguistic reflection more easily accomplished" (Glatthorn, 1989, p. 284). Writing can help readers explore what they know. Through writing, students come to terms with their own thoughts, solve problems, and discover new ideas; in other words, writing helps them clarify their thinking. As Britton and others (1975, p. 28) explain, "*An essential part of the writing process is explaining the matter to oneself. . . .* There are plenty of things we are sure we know but cannot articulate" because we are still working toward understanding the situation or concept. Sometimes we surprise ourselves when we realize after we've said or written something that we have finally clarified a previously partially formed idea. Elbow (1978) agrees that writing enhances thinking, and he also believes that it leads to an ongoing process of self-knowledge.

Frequent use of writing activities of various types can help students develop fluency, an aspect of writing that can be achieved only with practice. The advantages of writing as a tool for thinking are more available to fluent writers than to those who are not fluent.

SOCIAL
STUDIES

Sanacore (1998, p. 393) suggests that students in a secondary school social studies class might "work as individuals or in small teams to chronicle their perceptions of major historical events, to complete a short biography of a poignant character who added a personal dimension to the time period, to produce a challenging comparison and contrast essay, to write a miniresearch paper, or to do another creative project," letting students see that "learning is both personal and social." Other content areas also lend themselves to such activities, all valuable ways of studying content. Research findings should be made available to the rest of the class, providing an authentic audience for the writing (Rekrut, 1997).

THE RELATIONSHIP BETWEEN READING AND WRITING IN CONTENT AREA CLASSES

What are the links between reading and writing?

Secondary school students need both reading and writing skills for learning. Teachers of content area classes *have* generally perceived reading as a means of learning, but few have viewed writing in this way. Consequently, many content area classes exhibit a noticeable lack of writing activities. This situation is unfortunate, since both reading and writing are valuable learning techniques for students in these classes.

Reading and writing have the obvious link of being written language skills. They are both concerned with communication: readers consider the biases and expertise of the author, and writers consider the natures and backgrounds of their audiences. Both make use of written words that represent thoughts, and oral language vocabulary development is a key ingredient in successful reading and writing activities.

Another link between reading and writing is that the construction of meaning in reading is related to the organization of written material. Raphael and others (1986) have found that teaching students about expository text structure has a positive effect on both report writing and content area reading. (See Chapter 4 for more on teaching expository text structure.) Learning to write using a particular organizational pattern has the potential to help students understand material that others write in that pattern.

Reading and writing are complementary skills. Written material is necessary for reading to take place, but written material is useless until it is read. A focus on one of these skills naturally involves the other. Fisher and Frey (2003) found that the best writing they got from struggling readers and writers occurred after discussions of readings. Connecting reading and writing in meaningful ways was highly beneficial.

We have previously stated that reading is a thinking process. Elaboration on this idea can be found in Chapter 5. This relationship to thinking is another link between reading and writing.

TECHNIQUES OF COMBINING READING AND WRITING EFFECTIVELY

ENGLISH/
LANGUAGE
ARTS

Despite the connections between reading and writing, use of random writing activities in a content course may not help students in reading. Ferris and Snyder (1986) found that use of a process approach to writing instruction (discussed extensively later in this chapter) increased writing skills, but not reading skills, for students in eleven-grade English classes. Therefore, use of random writing assignments in an effort to improve reading performance is not advisable. Assignments must focus on the relationships between the two disciplines. For example, after students read a selection from a text, teachers can discuss its organization in relation to the organization of some of the students' own compositions. Teachers may also have students write paraphrases of difficult texts to help them understand these texts better and to make the students more aware of the depth of their understanding.

Konopak and others (1987) did find, however, that a writing treatment resulted in students' production of higher-level ideas gained from their reading and synthesis of information from various class activities. The writing treatment included making jot lists to activate prior knowledge, brainstorming and classification of ideas, preliminary writing based on the classifications, reading, and further writing.

> What are some ways students can use writing to activate prior knowledge before reading?

Writing before starting the reading assignment can help students retrieve background knowledge that they need in order to comprehend ideas in the written material. Activation of such knowledge can be beneficial to reading achievement. Writing responses to prereading questions can be particularly helpful. Writing can be based on organizational devices, such as feature matrixes, webs, outlines, or timelines, that help students understand relationships among various areas of content knowledge. The students and teacher may cooperatively develop a class organizer containing aspects of a topic, or students may develop individual organizers based upon personal knowledge and research. A teacher may introduce the idea of writing with this approach by directing the development of an organizer from a text chapter, and then may lead the group through the writing of a paragraph based on a portion of the organizer (i.e., an item on a feature matrix, a strand of a web, a main division of an outline). Subsequently, the teacher may let individuals or small groups write on other parts of the organizer, supplementing information from the textbook with information gained from reading in other research materials. Eventually students can completely develop their own organizers and write entire compositions from them.

SCIENCE AND HEALTH

Example 8.1 shows an organizer both in its early stages of development during the prereading period and in completed form. This organizer was developed for information included in a chapter in a physics text. Notice how the organizer shows the relationships described in the chapter. Types of electricity, aspects of electricity, units of measurement of electricity, and theory related to electricity are all discussed in the chapter. Each of these topics also has subtopics discussed under it. These subtopics are connected by lines in the organizer. Because the subtopics of the major topics, aspects of electricity and units of measurement of electricity, are related, the organizer also shows these subtopics connected with lines; for example, resistance is one aspect of electricity and resistance is measured in ohms.

EXAMPLE 8.1   Incomplete and Completed Organizer

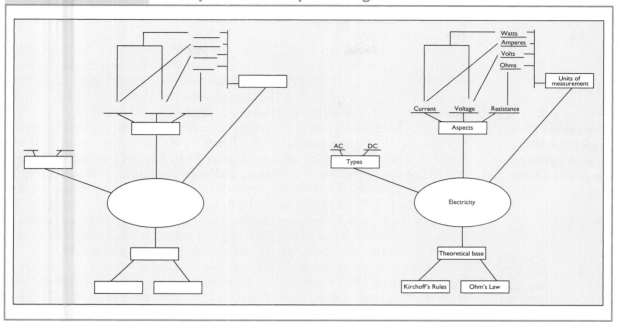

The Process Approach to Writing in the Content Areas

If teachers are to implement writing across the curriculum, they need to know how to guide students through the writing process, regardless of the type of content. In content classes, writing has often been treated as a two-step process: (1) the writing assignment is given, and (2) the students write a paper and turn it in to the teacher. This is an inadequate and inaccurate picture of what writing in content classes should be. Students are not helped to develop their writing products, but they are graded on their effectiveness, which could have been improved considerably by developmental instruction. Fisher and Frey (2003, p. 404) point out that "often instructional minutes are wasted when students are given independent writing prompts for which they are unprepared."

Research has indicated that a process approach to writing instruction is a good way to support writing development in students (Patthey-Chavez, Matsumura, and Valdes, 2004). When a process approach to writing is used, the development of the written material is guided through various stages, with students receiving feedback from the teacher and from peers at each stage. Students are encouraged to think about their topics, the organization for their writing, and a variety of possible audiences. The papers may be shared with peers, younger students, parents, or the community at large in letters to the editor of the local paper or postings on web pages.

Realizing that other people will see their material, students tend to produce papers that are more coherent and have more complete explanations than they do when they assume that the teacher, who knows all about the topic anyway, is the only audience for the paper.

The writing process can be divided into steps in several different ways, but all the systems of division have multiple stages. The system we will discuss divides the process into five basic steps that are *overlapping* and *recursive*: prewriting, writing a draft, revising, editing, and publishing and sharing (Roe and Ross, 2006). Each of these steps is discussed in detail in the following sections.

Students need instruction in the various aspects of the writing process if they are to achieve at the highest possible levels (Power, 1996). Literature can be used as a model of quality writing for students. Harvey (2002) points out that using well-crafted nonfiction books and newspaper and magazine articles as models for nonfiction writing results in richer, more compelling nonfiction writing. Possible choices are books by Russell Freedman or articles from *National Geographic*. Nonfiction selections serve as models for using headings, boldface and italic print, and captions for photographs and illustrations. Modeling and guided practice with such materials and features are essential to development of skill in writing nonfiction.

From these nonfiction models teachers can also point out such techniques as writing beginnings that excite interest, organizing material in logical sequence to aid understanding, and offering concrete details to support main ideas. Broaddus and Ivey (2002) point out the dependence of writers on distinct terms and details. Collecting fascinating information from a variety of sources lends richness to nonfiction writing. Some nonfiction materials have unusual formats, such as letters or diary entries, that can provide opportunities for creative choices in writing. Much nonfiction material today describes practical real-life applications of content concepts through literary devices that involve the same techniques that are used in fiction selections. Other possibilities for lessons on expository writing include choosing topics, techniques for revision, paraphrase writing, feature matrix development, and webbing.

Obviously, process writing is easily linked to English classes, but the procedure is equally valuable in other content area classes. Mini-lessons in classes such as science and social studies, for example, would be likely to focus more on choosing and delimiting topics for inquiry, on using a feature matrix for organizing related material, or on webbing ideas than on paraphrase writing or sentence combining. They would emphasize the use of writing to express knowledge, show connections between ideas, and gain new insights into the material through organization of information from multiple sources.

Effective writing lessons include teacher modeling, guided practice, and feedback. High-quality feedback is particularly important (Patthey-Chavez, Matsumura, and Valdes, 2004). Writing and conferences should take place after the mini-lessons. This procedure allows students to apply what they learn from the mini-lessons in authentic writing experiences. Conferences are valuable opportunities for students in any content area to get feedback on the effectiveness and accuracy of their written communication. The writing teacher must be a coach and mentor. Students need

How can use of mini-lessons in writing enhance teaching in the various content areas?

**ENGLISH/
LANGUAGE
ARTS**

**SCIENCE AND
HEALTH**

**SOCIAL
STUDIES**

the teacher's help in learning to *shape* their writing—to structure it so that it says what they want it to say (Power, 1996). Romano (1996) reminds teachers that writers develop their authentic voices by crafting what they write to accomplish the language rhythms and effects that they seek. Encouraging students to attend to the strategic arrangement of words and ideas and to the choice of words that convey unmistakable meaning is an important function for teachers.

Teachers should be careful to emphasize the recursive nature of the stages in the writing process. These stages are components among which students move—often in a nonlinear fashion (e.g., returning to prereading activities in the midst of writing a draft)—with different writers approaching the process in different ways (Latta, 1991).

PREWRITING

What activities take place during the prewriting stage?

Prewriting is often neglected in content classes. This stage is used for:

- Selection and delimitation of the topic
- Determination of the audience for the writing
- Decisions about the general approach for the writing
- Activation of the students' prior knowledge of the subject
- Discussion of ideas with classmates
- Organization of ideas

The topic for the writing is sometimes selected by the teacher in a content class, but the other activities can be assumed by the students. In composition classes, and sometimes in other areas, even topic selection is included in the prewriting activities. For example, high school teacher Jessie Singer let her seniors choose something that they were passionate about. They first listed passions, then wrote turning-point essays telling when in their lives their passion was sparked. These activities guided the topic selection (Singer and Hubbard, 2002/2003). Van Horn (2001) had seventh-graders write about objects of personal significance to them. She felt that using objects that were physically present, as well as significant, helped the students be successful with the assignment.

Secondary students often do not adequately *limit the scope of topics* they choose. Therefore, they face researching a seemingly insurmountable amount of material on a broad topic. When they discover the scope of the task ahead of them, their response is often to inquire, "How long does the paper have to be? How many sources do we need to consult?" when they should ask themselves, "What is needed to cover this topic adequately?" A social studies student may decide to write about a topic as broad as "The Revolutionary War" when he or she should be considering something much more specific, such as a single battle, a particular general, or a single theme related to the war. The teacher's modeling of topic delimitation can help students to perform this task effectively.

Students need to *practice writing for audiences other than the teacher*. The audience can be their classmates, with peers listening to and/or reading each other's drafts during the development of the drafts. Students also often have access to each

SOCIAL STUDIES

Online Study Center

HM Video Case
Developing Student
Self-Esteem: Peer Editing
Process

other's revised writings in the form of classroom "books" composed of the collected writings of several students or of a single student, bulletin board displays, or oral sharing sessions. During peer conferences, students can learn to ask each other questions that request clarification or expansion of the information given. The peers, therefore, let each other know when the needs of the audience are not being taken into consideration. Students may find that having an audience response form to guide them in giving feedback to their classmates about the effectiveness of a piece of writing can be helpful (Aubry, 1995).

Teachers may also want to plan lessons that focus on other audiences or *take other approaches*. Letters to the editor of the local newspaper on timely subjects such as water pollution, unfairness of restrictions on youth gatherings, a local health hazard, or the drug problem in the schools give students the larger community as an audience. Students may also be asked to write simplified explanations of concepts they are studying for students in lower grades who need the information to enrich their study units, or composition students may write short stories designed for younger readers and share them with classroom teachers of lower grades. Students may write directions for carrying out procedures for their classmates to follow in class or explanations of steps in scientific experiments that other students may be curious about or want to duplicate.

Deciding on an approach to the writing may include choosing a format, such as a letter, a short story, a poem, a memorandum, or an essay. It also can include choosing the manner of presenting expository information, such as comparison/contrast, chronological order, problem/solution, cause-and-effect, or some other organizational pattern.

The student's *prior knowledge about the topic can be activated* through activities such as class discussion, brainstorming, webbing, freewriting, and making comparison charts or feature matrixes. Students *listen to the contributions of others* in class activities and remember related items to contribute. Interaction among students at this stage is extremely desirable.

Ideas may be organized through a web or map, a feature matrix, a timeline, or an outline. Students should be taught all of these techniques and be allowed to choose the one that appears to fit the task best for each assignment.

SCIENCE AND
HEALTH

SOCIAL
STUDIES

ENGLISH/
LANGUAGE
ARTS

WRITING A DRAFT

What takes place during the stage of writing a draft?

The stage of **writing a draft** is designed to allow the writer to put his or her ideas on paper without worrying about mechanics or neatness. Ideally, the writing time should be in an uninterrupted block so that intervening activities do not break the student's train of thought. As Noskin (2000, p. 36) points out, "When students draft, they are not continuously writing. Instead, the act is interrupted with pauses where students revisit their purpose, change their focus, brainstorm additionally, or talk through a trouble spot." This is evidence that the writing process is recursive.

Some sharing of ideas with classmates may take place during this period in the form of spontaneous conversation among students seated close together. This should be allowed if it is not disruptive to the other students. This conversation is essentially a continued rehearsal of students' writing ideas and, as such, represents a return to the prewriting stage—more evidence of the recursive nature of the writing process. Peer responses may help to shape the writing in some cases, and the interaction may make a sense of audience easier to attain. Certainly if the paper is to be a collaborative effort, the collaborators need to converse as the draft progresses.

Although Britton and others (1975) have characterized the production stage of the writing process as a lonely one, they do perceive the value of talking about the project. They feel that the relationship of talking to writing is a central one, that good talk encourages good writing, and that talk permits writers to express tentative conclusions and opinions. They say, "It is probable that of all the things teachers are now doing to make their pupils' approach to writing more stimulating, and the writing itself a more integral part of the manifold activities of the classroom, it is the encouragement of different kinds of talk that is the commonest and most productive factor" (Britton et al., 1975, p. 29).

Teachers may need to help students overcome their reluctance to take risks related to spelling and punctuation and their reluctance to produce messy first drafts by bringing in examples of their own first drafts, which are double-spaced to allow for changes, with words, phrases, and sentences struck out and others inserted between lines or in margins and with some incorrectly spelled words circled to be looked up later. Students often have the impression that the draft has to be perfect from the beginning. Thus, to avoid imperfection, they substitute less exact words for ones they cannot spell without using the dictionary and substitute shorter, less complex sentences for ones they cannot punctuate without additional thought and time.

In the midst of drafting a paper, peer and teacher conferences about the writing may take place. Quick, informal teacher conferences may occur as the teacher circulates among the students to see how work is progressing. The teacher may ask students how their writing is going and, when problems are revealed, ask pertinent questions to help the writers think through the problem areas effectively. For example, if a student says, "I'm not sure what order to use to tell about these events," the teacher might say, "What order did the author of your history book use to tell about the events that came just before those events?" The student may answer, "Time order," and the teacher may ask, "Is that an appropriate order for you to use here, or do you have a reason to want to use another order? What would be the value of chronological order or some other order to your presentation?" These conferences are brief but help productive writing to continue. The teacher does not tell the student what to do with the writing but leads him or her to think in channels appropriate for the task.

In some areas, conferences between secondary student writers and university methods students are taking place online. Prospective teachers learn about the characteristics of the students that they will be teaching as they help them craft their writing through e-mail conversations (Robbins and Fischer, 1996). More about such e-mail partnerships, including writing and other aspects, is found in Chapter 2 of this book. Betty Roe has carried out such a project in her methods courses.

Students may request peer conferences for the purpose of asking for help with some part of the writing that is giving them trouble. They may read their writing to one or more peers and say something to this effect: "I'm having trouble with this ending. What can I do to improve it?"

The peers should first respond to the piece by indicating their understanding of what it says; then they should offer positive comments on good points. Finally, they should give suggestions that they may have for improvement or ask questions such as, "Would it help if you left out the last paragraph? How would it sound if you referred to the beginning statement here?" When a student has an entire first draft finished, he or she may wish to read it to a peer or several peers for further response. At this point in development, the student should read the work to his or her peers rather than having them read it. This procedure keeps the mechanical problems of the draft from interfering with a content analysis by the other students. Peers need to offer specific revision suggestions, or their comments will not be as helpful as they should be. They should tell the writer what they believe is good about the piece and why they think so, what parts need clarification, and what specific ways they believe the piece can be improved. Teachers may need to give some instruction in generating more specific, helpful comments, perhaps by telling the students why certain responses to a piece would or would not be effective.

REVISING

Why is revision unnecessary for some types of student writing?

How do revision and editing differ?

For pieces that others will read, **revision** is a necessary step, although it is not necessary for everything students write. Revision should not be expected, for example, in journals or class notes unless the student does it spontaneously.

The first step in the revision process is for the student to read his or her own piece carefully, considering the criteria for writing that have been established in the class. Students should realize that revision is not just **editing** for spelling, grammar, and punctuation. It involves reorganizing the material, clarifying ideas, and adding and deleting information as needed. Although revision is listed here as the third step in the writing process, it is important to realize that revision is recursive and can occur at any point in the writing process. For example, revision may happen during planning, as ideas are clarified in the writer's mind, or while writers review material that they have written.

A list of criteria to use in judging students' written work may be cooperatively developed by the teacher and students, or the teacher may provide it. A set of criteria that a group might develop is as follows:

1. *Beginning.* Does it arouse the reader's interest from the start? It should get the reader "hooked" right away.

2. *Middle.* Is the information or action presented in a logical order? Is the organizational pattern evident to the reader? The organizational pattern should fit your information.

3. *Ending.* Does the ending tie up the piece satisfactorily? It should not leave the reader "hanging."

4. *Sentence structure.* Have you used complete sentences? Do your sentences make sense? Sentence fragments should be avoided, except in special cases, such as dialogue.

5. *Vocabulary.* Have you used words that say exactly what you want to say? Consider the precise meanings of the words that you used, and make sure they fit the context.

6. *Point of view.* Did you maintain a single point of view in the story? Make sure that you have not shifted from third person to second person or first person, for example.

7. *Focus.* Does your piece stay on the main topic? Delete portions that stray from the main point.

8. *Audience.* Is your story appropriate for the intended audience? Read the piece with your audience in mind, and make sure that you have taken their backgrounds into consideration.

A revision guide, such as the one in Example 8.2, could be used by a peer who is participating in a peer conference activity with the writer. It can prompt the peer to provide specific suggestions for revision.

Students can make their paper and pencil revisions by using carets and writing additional material between lines, marking out or erasing unwanted material, using circles and arrows to move material around, or even cutting and pasting. Their markings need to be clear, but the paper does not necessarily need to look neat.

If the piece has been written on a computer with a word-processing program, the revision activity is much easier, and the final copy will be cleaner. A few clicks of the mouse will delete material, insert material, and move material around. Papers revised in this manner never need to look messy.

EXAMPLE 8.2   Revision Guide

1. As you listen to your classmate read the material, write notes about positive points, such as precise and vivid word usage, good ideas, coherent organization, good transitions, attention-getting beginnings, and satisfying endings.
2. Write down any questions you have when the writer has finished.
3. Identify for the writer any section that was confusing, and suggest what would make it clearer. You may suggest that the writer add more information in specific places or clarify parts, start the piece with an attention-getting statement, change the order of the ideas presented, add signal words or transitions, or add personal reflections on the material or conclusions the writer has drawn based on the information collected. Be sure to point out factual errors or explanations that are incomplete.

EDITING

Editing involves polishing the writing for consumption by others. It includes checking for grammar, punctuation, and spelling. A computer's spell checker can highlight suspicious words for the student to check, and grammar checkers are available to check for incomplete sentences, incorrect punctuation, redundancies, wordiness, and other problems. These tools just alert students to potential problems and force them to look closely at their writing; they do not make changes for the students. The students must take responsibility for making judgments about the flagged material. Many flagged parts may be perfectly acceptable, whereas some errors will not be flagged. Computers cannot consider meaning in their analyses, and therefore they are understandably inaccurate at times when a human editor would understand the situation. If students write their pieces on the computer, they should run the grammar and spell check programs to help them detect errors, but this should be in addition to proofreading in the usual manner.

Have students ask themselves the following questions as an editing guide:

1. Have I used punctuation marks correctly?

2. Have I capitalized appropriately?

Students can be taught strategies to help them use spell checkers more effectively. They can alter words that are identified as misspelled, but for which alternative spellings are not suggested, until the checker is able to offer alternatives. Different spellings for sounds must be tried in order to accomplish this. Students can also check dictionary definitions of alternatives that are offered to be sure which one fits their context. (The word processor may have a dictionary included, or there may be an electronic dictionary on the computer as a separate program.) If the checker or dictionary supports sound, the students can ask for pronunciation of the alternatives through speech synthesis. They may be able to tell from its pronunciation if an option is the one they want (Anderson-Inman and Knox-Quinn, 1996).

INTERNET ASSISTANCE IN REVISION AND EDITING

ENGLISH/ LANGUAGE ARTS

Help with revision and editing can also be found on the Internet. Online writing labs (OWLs) offer such services as writing aids, online tutoring, grammar and style guides, reference works, and links to writing and research aids. OWLs may offer interaction with other writers and critiques of writing samples as well (Zucca, 1996). The Dakota State University OWL is located at http://www.departments.dsu.edu/owl. The University of Illinois at Urbana-Champaign's Writers Workshop (http://www.english.uiuc.edu/cws/wworkshop) has on its website a writing techniques handbook, an online grammar handbook, and links to style manuals. Additionally, students may find the Good Grammar, Good Style™ pages (http://www.protrainco.com/grammar.htm) useful.

After students have read and revised their papers to the best of their abilities, they may submit their work for peer editing. They may have regular partners for peer editing or they may choose different peer editors at different times. Peer editors read and mark their classmates' papers with the class writing criteria in mind, write positive comments about the material, and make suggestions for changes or ask for clarification about parts of the writing. The author may confer with the peer editor before deciding which changes may be necessary and which ones are not desirable. This process should be modeled by the teacher before the students are expected to use it. Both the writers and the editors can learn from this process. Teacher analysis and feedback on the finished product will enhance the learning.

PUBLISHING

In what ways may student writing be "published"?

HES/HUMAN ECOLOGY   ENGLISH/ LANGUAGE ARTS

TECHNICAL EDUCATION   SCIENCE AND HEALTH

The pieces that students carefully revise for sharing with others, as just described, are "**published**" in one of a number of ways. They may simply be shared orally by the student author, or they may be posted on bulletin boards, bound into a "book" to be placed in the classroom library or school library, or published in a school magazine or newspaper. Many types of writings may be "published" in various classes. Members of a shop class could develop directions for assembly of various items. Students in a health or human environmental science class could produce meal plans for family members with special dietary needs, such as low-cholesterol diets or low-calorie diets. Literature students could turn a short story into a play for presentation in class or to a wider audience, and science students could write descriptions of science fair exhibits or class experiments.

MEETING THE CHALLENGE

ENGLISH/ LANGUAGE ARTS

Bott (2002) and several other teachers in her school have their students develop *zines* to publish personal writing for English classes. Zines are "independently created and published magaZINES" (Bott, 2002, p. 27). The teachers developed their own personal zines first to familiarize themselves with the process. Then they decided on guidelines for the zines that their students would develop. The idea was to have students produce poems, stories, memoirs, lists, puzzles, reviews, graphics, drawings, cartoons, word plays, advice columns, or collections of writings on themes. They all had to have a cover with an appropriate title, an introduction to the zine, a table of contents, and at least nine personally created pages of each student's writing. Students were allowed to use pseudonyms if they wanted to protect their identities, since the zines would be "published" at the school and copies would be placed in the library. One day a week for seven weeks the students worked on their zines on computers. Some zines were autobiographical; and some were about students' interest areas, such as music. The zines were graded on mechanics, originality, creativity, and completeness of thought and execution. Some students participated in public readings of their work, and the students read one another's zines.

**ENGLISH/
LANGUAGE
ARTS**

Publishing on school, class, or personal web pages has also become common. This type of publishing gives students a worldwide audience. Civello (1999) had her students each choose a character from *Jane Eyre* and design a web page for that character as if the character had designed the page. Students included information that demonstrated their close study of the novel. Students who are developing web pages will find the HTML Writer's Guild helpful (http://www.hwg.org/resources/) (Iannone, 1998).

Students see the reason for careful crafting of their writing when others are going to read it for information or entertainment. They get much satisfaction from seeing others reading their work, and they appreciate the opportunities to read the work of their peers. A new avenue of writing for an audience that is currently gaining popularity with adolescents is blogging (Curry and Ford, 2002; Littrell, 2005). On *eSchool News Online*'s "Ed-Tech Insider" (http://www.eschoolnews.com/eti/index.php), Anne Davis, a longtime classroom teacher and current instructional technology specialist at Georgia State University, points out that there are a number of ways that blogs can be used in school. She says, "I would like to see them used with students in ways that help make them better writers and thinkers" ("Best of the Blogs," 2005, p. 8). She cautions that this will not be accomplished without teachers being involved with the students by talking about what is posted to their blogs ("Best of the Blogs," 2005). Chapter 2 has a detailed discussion of blogging.

Types of Writing-to-Learn Activities in the Content Areas

Many types of writing are used in content area classes to enhance learning. The types discussed here are some of the more common ones with which teachers have reported positive results. Knowledge of the steps in the process approach to writing can help teachers to implement some of these writing-to-learn strategies more effectively.

Writing assignments need to have the purpose of communicating with a specific, real audience. For example, students can write letters to authors of books they have read or to newspaper editors.

LANGUAGE EXPERIENCE WRITINGS

How can language experience materials be used in a content area classroom?

Language experience writings are materials written in the students' own words. In the elementary school, language experience stories are usually developed by a group of students who have had a common experience. In the secondary school, **language experience materials** may be written by a group of students who have read about a common topic and wish to summarize their findings. The teacher can record all significant contributions on the board as they are offered. At the conclusion of the discussion, the teacher and students together can organize the contributions in a logical order (e.g., chronological or cause-and-effect). The teacher can then duplicate the group-composed material and distribute it to the class members. This approach works well with struggling readers and writers and English language learners (Fisher and Frey, 2003; Furr, 2003).

Students who can handle the textbook with ease may file the experience material to use for review for tests. A group that is unable to handle the textbook presentation may use the material more extensively. For example, the teacher may meet with this group and guide the members through the reading of the material by using purpose questions. The students are likely to succeed in reading this material because they have seen the content written on the board and because it is in the words of fellow students. Having heard a discussion of the content, the students will find it easier to apply context clues as they read. Any technical vocabulary or multiple-meaning words can be located and discussed thoroughly. These words may be written in a special notebook with accompanying pronunciations and definitions and a reference to the experience material in which they occurred. A booklet made up of experience material can serve as a reference source for these words when they are encountered again and can be used in studying for tests. English language learners (ELLs) and other at-risk students may especially benefit from such special word notebooks.

SCIENCE AND HEALTH

Experience materials may also be developed by individuals and groups who wish to record the results of scientific experiments or the periodic observation of some natural phenomena. These materials may be shared with the rest of the class in oral or written form. Such activities are extremely valuable for students who are not able to gain much information from a textbook that is too difficult for them.

MATHEMATICS

Wood (1992) found the language experience approach to be effective for use with content instruction in math classes. Wood suggested having mathematics problems assigned to small groups of students, with each student solving the problems and writing the processes involved in the solutions. Then the students would share their solutions with the rest of the group. This type of language experience activity could be extended by having the group as a whole revise a written solution to make it clearer, more accurate, or less wordy, if necessary.

SOCIAL STUDIES   **SCIENCE AND HEALTH**

Many others have found the language experience approach to work well in social studies and science classes. This approach motivates struggling readers and English language learners, builds their self-esteem, provides them with concepts that allow participation in content classes, builds reading vocabulary (including technical vocabulary), and activates and organizes the students' prior knowledge in the content areas.

CONTENT JOURNALS

What are some of the benefits of using content journals?

Content journals, or learning logs, allow students to keep a written record of content area learning activities that is personal and informal. They help students to clarify their thoughts and feelings about topics under study. Students usually choose what to write in these journals, although teachers may suggest general areas of consideration and types of things they may wish to record, if appropriate. For example, the teacher may ask that the students record any questions that occur to them as they read a content chapter or listen to a class lecture and discussion, new ideas that they have gained, confusion about a topic or procedure, feelings about the subject area, predictions about the assigned reading, explanations of a recently taught concept, or some other general category—such as the answers to some broad content-related questions—at specific times. When the teacher makes a request or notes a specific thing to be recorded, journal entries may be shared by volunteers. The teacher should give prior warning that sharing will be encouraged. At other times the students may choose among the many possibilities that arise in the classroom for their daily entries.

Commander and Smith (1996) have used learning logs to promote students' metacognitive awareness. They asked questions about students' learning behaviors to which the students responded in log entries, helping them achieve insight about their learning and begin to assume responsibility for it.

SCIENCE AND HEALTH

Bachman-Williams (2001) uses daily journal writing at the beginning of her science classes to promote thinking. She writes prompts on the board or a transparency. Some prompts are content oriented, but others ask for personal knowledge, reflection, or pattern poetry related to the class.

The student who is doing the writing is the primary audience for the content journal, although the teacher may periodically collect the journals and read them. However, content journals are not graded in the ordinary sense; spelling and grammatical errors are not marked, for example.

When teachers take up journals, they may occasionally make encouraging comments to students in response to their entries. These comments should focus on the message that the student was trying to convey and ignore problems with punctuation, spelling, and grammar. Teachers should not red-pencil journals, no matter how tempting it may be. This frees students from the fear of writing something that they are not perfectly sure about and results in more comprehensive, creative, and revealing journal entries.

Teacher comments should always be written in correctly spelled and punctuated standard English, which will serve as a model to the student for future writing. If a word has been repeatedly misspelled by the student, the teacher may write a comment in the journal that uses the word spelled correctly, without referring to spelling. The example can be more potent than the admonition would have been.

Freewriting

What is freewriting, and what purposes does it serve?

Some teachers have students use content journals for true **freewriting**—that is, writing that has no teacher restrictions on content. Students simply write in a sustained manner for a specified period of time. This freewriting is intended to make thinking conscious and visible (Collins, 1990). Students write without stopping to correct mistakes or ponder the content. This writing may be in response to something that students have read. In content classes the teacher often specifies that the journal entries focus on a specific topic, even though the writing will not be graded. Freewriting is good for encouraging interpretation and evaluation of the material read. It may result in the discovery of alternative interpretations of the text as students strive to continue to write without pauses for correction or reflection (Andrasick, 1990). Language teachers may obtain more direct benefit from true freewriting than other content teachers do because part of their curriculum centers on self-

ENGLISH/
LANGUAGE
ARTS

SCIENCE AND
HEALTH

ART

SCIENCE AND
HEALTH

expression. Elbow (1978, p. 67) believes, "If you are really interested in good quality writing, then you must make it your immediate goal that people write copiously, not well. Only when people begin to use writing on other occasions than when it is required—only when they have written for diverse purposes over a period of years—will they eventually come to produce good writing." Writing consistently in journals on a daily basis is valuable to the development of ease in writing.

Teachers usually designate times in class for students to write in their journals. At the beginning of a class, students may write summaries of what they learned on the previous day, or at the end of class they may write summaries of what they learned that day. They may write predictions about the lesson that they are about to begin, list everything that they think they already know about the topic, or do both. They may explain how they will apply the day's lesson in everyday life. They may record the progress of a laboratory experiment or observational study.

Franks (2001) collaborated with an art teacher and a science teacher to bring writing across the curriculum to her classroom. She had students make daily weather observations, focusing first on cloud types. As part of the observation, the students were asked to sketch the cloud formations. Then they responded daily to one of five writing prompts concerning their observations, questions that came to mind, reflections about personal memories, associations of things observed with other things or with moods, or forecasting. Franks (2001, p. 323) found that "prior to sketching the cloud types, only a handful of students could pull them out of their heads on a recall quiz that asked them to define the types through drawing and writing. But after sketching and writing, 90% could do it."

Some teachers set aside the same time period each day for journal writing, and students are asked to write for the entire five or ten minutes about the class or observations related to the class, such as their difficulty in finding time at home to study for it. Andrasick (1990, p. 69) believes that "anything less than ten minutes is not productive."

MATHEMATICS

Gordon and MacInnis (1993) provided prompts to guide students' journal writing about decimals but allowed the students to write open-ended entries about any mathematics topic that concerned them. The prompts were much like essay questions (e.g., asking how decimals are similar to and different from fractions), but the open-ended responses were simply a type of freewriting. Gordon and MacInnis made these journals into dialogue journals (discussed later in this chapter) as well, responding to all of the entries by the following week. They "found that the journals provided a window on students' thinking processes. . . . Information gleaned from the journal entries allowed guidance and instruction on a more individualized level" (Gordon and MacInnis, 1993, p. 42). The journals also encouraged students to reflect upon their mathematical understandings.

Teachers can use the journals to discover gaps in understanding and any confusion that the students have about the topics. They may also gain insight into students' lives that helps explain class performance. For example, if a student writes in his or her journal, "I don't know what the chapter for last night was about. I worked late at my after-school job, and I was too tired to study," the teacher has an idea of the reasons behind this student's failure to answer questions in class.

Reading Response Journals

ENGLISH/
LANGUAGE
ARTS

What types of entries are included in reading response journals?

Reading response journals are a type of learning log for literature classes. With these journals, typically the students read or listen to a chapter of a book and then write about it for about five minutes immediately afterward. They comment about the characters, setting, plot, author's writing style and devices, and their personal reactions. The teacher writes while the students are writing and shares his or her entries frequently as a model for the students. Students also may volunteer to share their material. The sharing can be followed by discussion. The teacher can read the journals and comment on entries, clarifying points of confusion for the students and giving positive reinforcement to those who show that they have gained insight into the story.

In a reading response journal, teachers can ask students to select characters from their books and write journal entries for the characters at points in the progress of the stories when there is much descriptive action.

Kletzien and Hushion (1992) used graphic thinking symbols, such as an arrow to indicate a prediction or a scale to indicate a judgment or an evaluation, to mark examples of particular response types in the students' journals. Recalling information, giving ideas and examples, indicating causes and effects, indicating similarities and differences, making inferences, making personal identifications, using analogies, using metacognitive strategies, and analyzing authors' techniques were among the types of responses recognized and marked by the teachers. This approach resulted in responses that went beyond summaries, ones that were more varied and thoughtful.

Some teachers use reading response journals more like learning logs and have students write before, during, and after reading. Prereading writing prompts are given to arouse curiosity about the topic, activate prior knowledge and experiences that are related, encourage personal connections with the material, and generate hypotheses about the characters and action. During reading, writing prompts may ask students to react to such features of the text as character and setting, respond personally to events or people, draw conclusions and make further predictions, or adjust previous predictions. Postreading writing prompts may lead students to apply themes to current situations; to consider the contributions of particular literary elements to the effect of the whole piece; to show changes that took place in people, places, and things over the course of the story; or to compare the work to similar works or works by the same author (Pritchard, 1993).

Andrasick (1990) discusses a type of journal in which students write quotations, paraphrases, or summaries of the ideas in the book on the left-hand pages of a notebook. The students use the corresponding right-hand pages to respond to the entries on the left-hand side. They may both ask questions and make comments about the material. The important thing is that they reflect on the content. Andrasick says the students are having a dialogue with the author of the text about the material. Example 8.3 shows an excerpt from such a journal (Alfred, 1991).

EXAMPLE 8.3   Student's Journal Entries

Dialogue Journal
Chapter Three

Andrasick, K. D. (1990). *Opening Texts: Using Writing to Teach Literature.* Portsmouth, NH: Heinemann.

What the Text Says	What I Say
p. 40 ". . . shouldn't be concerned so much with particular data as with student's ability to use data."	I'm not sure if I agree . . . The way kids are tested, e.g., ACT, other standardized tests, they must know factual data. If we can change this, then I *might* agree.
p. 40 "Many students deny the value of their experiences with texts, dismissing them prematurely."	This really bothers me. Sure, some teachers listen to students' ideas, but that's it. They say, "That's nice," and then continue with their lecture. How else can kids be expected to react?
p. 41 "When we focus on text content by asking students to respond . . . to a series of short answer questions, we deflect attention from larger textual elements and may actually interfere with students' abilities to approach thematic issues."	No way! When I read a novel, for example, I always look for specific elements that may tie into a theme. Answering . . . questions [is] a good way to increase knowledge about themes that are prevalent throughout a work.
p. 41 "Learning to discriminate between the solidity of the visible surface structure and the fluctuating, invisible text world the pages potentially contain requires practice" (Andrasick, pp. 40–41).	What a yucky sentence! Engfish! Engfish! Engfish!

Source: Suellen Alfred, "Dialogue Journal," *Tennessee Reading Teacher* 19 (Fall 1991): 14.

Character Journals

In what content areas would character journals be most useful?

Character journals are diaries in which students assume the role of one of the main characters in a book. In them, each student makes first-person journal entries for a chosen character on episodes throughout the book. These entries help the students attain insight into the characters and their actions. This process also helps students examine their own beliefs, actions, and values.

**ENGLISH/
LANGUAGE
ARTS**

Social Justice Notebooks

What kind of entries would be included in a social justice notebook?

SOCIAL STUDIES

Proctor and Kantor (1996) use **social justice notebooks** as a writing-to-learn experience. The students use their writing in these notebooks to examine controversial human rights issues. Students read and discuss news articles or editorials on the issue. Then a question about the issue is posed, and the students respond to it in writing. They are encouraged to recognize different points of view on the issue, then to take a personal stand.

The students share their writing orally, with classmates commenting and asking questions. This discussion is followed by more research on the issue, more class discussion, and rewriting. In some cases the writing leads to student-initiated action, such as letters to the editor of the local newspaper. Critical reading, enhanced by writing, results in important content learning.

Responses to Thought Questions

How can teachers prepare students to answer essay questions?

Thought questions resemble the essay questions that teachers use on tests. Writing responses to essay questions is probably the most traditional writing task that teachers expect of students. Teachers often assign study questions to classes for homework as study aids. Unfortunately, they may not prepare students to respond effectively to such questions, as was pointed out in Chapter 7. If the students do not know the meanings of the terms used in the questions, they will not understand what is being asked of them. Teachers should use the procedures suggested in Chapter 7 for helping students learn to answer essay questions before asking them to respond in their journals. Teachers should define terms (such as *compare*, *contrast*, and *discuss*), model answers that fit questions with each of the important terms, and provide students with practice questions for writing and discussion in class. Since the journal activity is ungraded, this practice in answering such questions is not threatening to the students, and they can be free to experiment with the technique without fear of failure.

Langer (1986) found that use of study questions did not increase students' topic knowledge as much as use of written essays or note taking on the topic. The study questions seemed to cause the students to focus on specific ideas chosen by the teacher and, therefore, "may best be used to invoke quick recall of isolated items of information" (p. 406). Teachers who use study questions as a part of journal writing should be aware that they may cause the students to focus on details of the content rather than on the overall picture.

Simpson (1986) uses the PORPE (Predict, Organize, Rehearsal, Practice, Evaluate) procedure to alleviate her students' apprehension about essay examinations. This procedure, described in detail in Chapter 7, should result in better performance in answering study questions in journals or otherwise, as well as better performance on essay tests by many students, because of the intense involvement with text that it requires.

Creative Applications

SOCIAL
STUDIES

ENGLISH/
LANGUAGE
ARTS

BUSINESS
EDUCATION

ENGLISH/
LANGUAGE
ARTS

SCIENCE AND
HEALTH

ENGLISH/
LANGUAGE
ARTS

TECHNICAL
EDUCATION

SOCIAL
STUDIES

Some teachers have students use their journals for a variety of creative applications of writing in the subject area. The students may be asked to write stories about a historical period that they are studying in social studies class, making sure that they construct characters, settings, dialogues, and plots that fit the time that has been chosen. They may also write fictional interviews with historical characters or characters from novels, news stories about historical events, or letters to historical figures or from one historical figure to another. Swiderek (1998, p. 407) models each type of writing and gives examples before asking her seventh-grade students to do it. Some types that her students use are "student résumés, cartoon strips, business letters to raise money for student programs, newspaper articles, advertisements, books for younger siblings, and poetry." We recommend that teachers use such modeling to enhance students' written products.

Cruz (2001) uses sent and unsent letters about the things the class is studying. For example, students might write letters to friends explaining the topic under study. Partners in the class may listen to the letters and give feedback about the clarity of the explanations. Then she may have the students write about the topic in a different genre, perhaps an analysis paper or a research report. This process helps them make the transition from informal to formal writing. Sometimes the students may role-play the part of someone else—a homeless person, an underpaid police officer, or a city official—and write a letter on a current area of study from that person's perspective.

In Pennsylvania, teachers are participating in an oral history project that incorporates state language arts, science and technology, and social studies standards as students learn a research technique. The students choose a person as a subject for the project. When elderly subjects are chosen, the project often turns into a gripping history lesson, covering political and social movements and/or historical periods. Many subjects lead into a study of careers, as well. Students in some classes may be allowed to choose community members or even classmates. They interview their subjects and research the subjects' history and interests. They generally present their results to others through a "'triptych'—a presentation board folded into three parts that holds the memoir, photos, and artifacts collected during the interview and research processes" (Dickson et al., 2002, p. 2). "In this Oral History Project, a triptych is a three-paneled backboard display which portrays a person's life experiences. It can consist of a picture/portrait of the person, artifacts important to the person which help to tell his/her story, a news article about the person, based on the interview and artifacts, a memoir that has been written or told by the person about a meaningful experience in his/her life, and anything else that helps convey the personality and life experiences that make up that person's story" (Dickson et al., 2002, p. 3). Teachers model each component for the students before the students are expected to implement it. Rubrics are used to evaluate each step of the project and the final result. An example of a rubric is shown in Example 8.4. An Oral History Project Grades K–16 CD (Oral History Project Consortium, 2000) was developed through an "Educate America" Act grant obtained by the Oral History Project Consortium. The CD helps

EXAMPLE 8.4   Rubric for Writing Assessment

Pennsylvania Writing Assessment Domain Scoring Guide

	Focus	Content	Organization	Style	Conventions
	The single controlling point made with an awareness of task (mode) about a specific topic.	The presence of ideas developed through facts, examples, anecdotes, details, opinions, statistics, reasons and/or explanations.	The order developed and sustained within and across paragraphs using transitional devices including introduction and conclusion.	The choice, use and arrangement of words and sentence structures that create tone and voice.	The use of grammar, mechanics, spelling, usage and sentence formation.
4	Sharp, distinct controlling point made about a single topic with evident awareness of task (mode)	Substantial, specific and/or illustrative content demonstrating strong development and sophisticated ideas	Sophisticated arrangement of content with evident and/or subtle transitions	Precise, illustrative use of a variety of words and sentence structures to create consistent writer's voice and tone appropriate to audience	Evident control of grammar, mechanics, spelling, usage and sentence formation
3	Apparent point made about a single topic with sufficient awareness of task (mode)	Sufficiently developed content with adequate elaboration or explanation	Functional arrangement of content that sustains a logical order with some evidence of transitions	Generic use of a variety of words and sentence structures that may or may not create writer's voice and tone appropriate to audience	Sufficient control of grammar, mechanics, spelling, usage and sentence formation
2	No apparent point but evidence of a specific topic	Limited content with inadequate elaboration or explanation	Confused or inconsistent arrangement of content with or without attempts at transition	Limited word choice and control of sentence structures that inhibit voice and tone	Limited control of grammar, mechanics, spelling, usage and sentence formation
1	Minimal evidence of a specific topic	Superficial and/or minimal content	Minimal control of content arrangement	Minimal variety in word choice and minimal control of sentence structures	Minimal control of grammar, mechanics, spelling, usage and sentence formation

	Non-scorable		Off-prompt
0	• Is illegible; i.e., includes so many indecipherable words that no sense can be made of the response • Is incoherent; i.e., words are legible but syntax is so garbled that response makes no sense • Is insufficient; i.e., does not include enough to assess domains adequately • Is a blank paper		• Is readable but did not respond to prompt

Source: Pennsylvania Department of Education.

teachers implement the project and provides information and opportunities to develop lessons and assessments for the project (Dickson et al., 2002).

Dean and Grierson (2005), taking a cue from Murray (1968), have students write multigenre books to "provide different lenses on a topic" (p. 456). The use of multiple genres allows students to produce richer and more insightful texts. Students also learn to use the structures of different genres in their writing. Dean and Grierson have students first study the texts of multigenre books to analyze their structure as a model for their own writing. Lessons that involve modeling of the required tasks and guided practice are taught, culminating in the writing of such books by the students. *The Magic School Bus* series by Joanna Cole is a series of examples of multigenre writing. Avi's *Nothing But the Truth* is another example. Pictures, diagrams, lists, brief reports, memos, diary entries, letters, transcripts, newspaper articles, telegrams, timelines, and poems are some of the possible genres in multigenre books.

SCIENCE AND HEALTH   **SOCIAL STUDIES**

The information presented in this way can make an informational book more interesting and informative to readers.

When students study the use of pictures and varying text patterns and their contributions to the model books, they are encouraged to activate their prior knowledge; skim, scan, and underline as they read; and analyze new vocabulary terms. The students can construct Venn diagrams to show how the same and different ideas are presented in different genres. The actual writing may be done in groups or individually. Students are guided in generating ideas for the writing, researching the topics, writing drafts, revising drafts, and preparing bibliographies.

SOCIAL STUDIES

Grierson, Anson, and Baird (2002) had sixth-grade students use multigenre writing to explore and honor the past. The students used multigenre writing to create original works based on their own heritages, after researching personal ancestors and developing artifacts to create a paper about their lives. The use of varied genres helped them bring facts to life. Jane Yolen's *The Devil's Arithmetic* was used as a stimulus to write about the past in order for it to be remembered.

MATHEMATICS SCIENCE AND HEALTH

TECHNICAL EDUCATION

Students in math classes may write their own statement problems. In a class on electronics, students can write imaginative accounts of things such as what life would be like without electron flow. Students in an industrial technology class can write sets of instructions for performing a specific type of task that classmates will be asked to follow. In science class, students can write scripts for weather forecasts (Hightshue et al., 1988; Jenkinson, 1988b). Sanacore (1998) believes that students need to explore a variety of forms of discourse in order to discover their strengths and interests. To come up with other ideas for assignments, teachers may wish to refer to the list of discourse forms for content writing presented by Tchudi and Yates (1983, p. 12), shown in Example 8.5.

As Hall (2001) points out, some genres of content area writing are writing to display learning and some are writing to learn. Examples of writing-to-display-learning genres are essays, book reports, research papers, laboratory reports, essay exams, and formal letters. Examples of writing-to-learn genres are journals, laboratory notebooks, notes taken on assigned readings, and freewriting.

Paraphrasing and Summarizing

What are paraphrasing and summarizing?

Paraphrasing and **summarizing** material learned in content area classes and from content area textbooks provide material for content journals. A surprising number of secondary school students do not know how to paraphrase the text material in their content subjects. In fact, when asked to paraphrase, many do not realize that they are simply expected to put the material into their own words. This process can just be rewording, or new forms may be used to represent the meaning of the text; for example, material from expository text may be described in tabular or graphic form. Dictionaries and thesauruses are helpful tools for paraphrasing. Paraphrase writing can result in improved listening, speaking, reading, and writing vocabularies and increased comprehension and recall (Shugarman and Hurst, 1986). Therefore, paraphrase writing in content journals can be a fruitful activity.

How can you help students learn to paraphrase?

To teach paraphrasing, teachers should define the concept, demonstrate it for the students first with short paraphrases, offer the students guided practice in providing

| EXAMPLE 8.5 | Discourse Forms for Content Writing |

Journals and diaries
  (real or imaginary)
Biographical sketches
Anecdotes and stories:
    from experience as told
    by others
Thumbnail sketches:
    of famous people
    of places
    of content ideas
    of historical events
Guess who/what
    descriptions
Letters:
    personal reactions
    observations
    public/informational
    persuasive:
        to the editor
        to public officials
      to imaginary people
      from imaginary places
Requests
Applications
Memos
Résumés and summaries
Poems
Plays
Stories
Fantasy
Adventure
Science fiction
Historical stories
Dialogues and conversations
Children's books
Telegrams
Editorials

Commentaries
Responses and rebuttals
Newspaper "fillers"
Fact books or fact sheets
School newspaper stories
Stories or essays for local
    papers
Proposals
Case studies:
    school problems
    local issues
    national concerns
    historical problems
    scientific issues
Songs and ballads
Demonstrations
Poster displays
Reviews:
    books (including
        textbooks)
    films
    outside reading
    television programs
    documentaries
Historical "you are there"
    scenes
Science notes:
    observations
    science notebook
    reading reports
    lab reports
Math:
    story problems
    solutions to problems
    record books
    notes and
        observations

Responses to literature
Utopian proposals
Practical proposals
Interviews:
    actual
    imaginary
Directions:
    how-to
    school or neighborhood
        guide
    survival manual
Dictionaries and lexicons
Technical reports
Future options, notes on:
    careers, employment
    school and training
    military/public service
Written debates
Taking a stand:
    school issues
    family problems
    state or national issues
    moral questions
Books and booklets
Informational monographs
Radio scripts
TV scenarios and scripts
Dramatic scripts
Notes for improvised drama
Cartoons and cartoon
    strips
Slide show scripts
Puzzles and word searches
Prophecy and predictions
Photos and captions
Collage, montage, mobile,
    sculpture

Source: Stephen N. Tchudi and Joanne Yates, *Teaching Writing in the Content Areas: Senior High School*, © 1983 National Education Association. Reprinted with permission.

short paraphrases, and then provide planned independent practice. Instruction in paraphrases of longer passages can follow.

Practice in paraphrasing can be enjoyable. The teacher can present students with statements such as "A fowl in the palm is of the same value as a pair in the shrub." Students can be asked to paraphrase this sentence to produce a familiar saying. Students are permitted to refer to dictionaries and thesauruses for the activity. Later, the students may be asked to locate familiar expressions, paraphrase them, and present the paraphrases to the class for decoding. Eventually, the students can be asked to locate key sentences in the textbook assignment for the day and write paraphrases in clear language. Judging the clarity and accuracy of the paraphrases can be done in small groups, with all group members presenting their own paraphrases and participating in the evaluation of those of other students. Both paraphrasers and evaluators have to examine the text material closely in order to complete this activity. Students in math classes can paraphrase statement problems; those in social studies classes can paraphrase news articles, campaign literature, and advertisements; those in shop class can paraphrase instructions for a project; and so on for any subject area.

A form of summarizing is précis writing. Précis are abstracts of materials that retain the point of view of the original materials. D'Angelo (1983) credited skill in précis writing with improving both writing and research skills, and Bromley and McKeveny (1986) suggested that the use of précis writing enhances comprehension and recall of content material.

MATHEMATICS **SOCIAL STUDIES**

TECHNICAL EDUCATION

What are the steps in writing a précis?

Students need to understand the purposes for précis writing, including vocabulary improvement and enhanced comprehension and retention. The teacher should demonstrate the process to the students, showing them how to analyze the original material, select main ideas for inclusion in the précis, reject nonessential material, and paraphrase the ideas through the use of synonyms and the restructuring of sentences. Encouraging the use of the thesaurus is a good technique. Taking such a close look at the content makes learning and remembering the material much more likely than if the material were processed less actively. Models of acceptable précis should be provided for students to help them understand the task and to help them evaluate and revise their own products. Students can study their précis to help them review for tests.

Group composition of a précis is a good beginning step. This can be done by having the students dictate as the teacher or one of the students records the précis. This is an application of the language experience technique described earlier in this chapter.

Students definitely need direct instruction in summary writing, which is not offered by many teachers. More information on summarizing is found in Chapter 6.

DIALOGUE JOURNALS

What is the distinctive feature of dialogue journals?

Although dialogue journals *could* be content journals, they need not be. The distinctive feature of **dialogue journals** is that they set up a two-way written conversation between the teacher and each student. Their primary purpose is to open lines of communication. Students write about anything they choose, including both in-class and out-of-class experiences and concerns. They may offer their opinions, state grievances, provide information, make predictions, ask questions, answer questions, apologize, make promises, offer thanks, make evaluations, or give directions, among other possibilities. The written statements, questions, or observations are not evaluated by the teachers; the teachers respond to them as personal communications.

Each day, time is made available for the students to write in their journals. The teachers read all the entries (generally after school) and respond to them. The responses may include recognition of what the students are saying, clarification of things about which the students are confused, answers to students' questions, questions for students to answer related to the writing or to some common interest, and sharing of personal thoughts and feelings. Grammatical and spelling errors in journal entries are never marked. The next day the students read the teachers' responses and continue the written dialogue with another entry. Bromley (1993) suggests that, if classes are large and create too heavy a reading load, the teacher read only a specified number of journals each day. Teachers who follow this suggestion should rotate the reading of the journals, so that students have equal numbers of teacher responses. Since grading is not a part of the reading, most teachers will be able to manage reading each student's journal at least every other day.

WRITTEN CONVERSATIONS

SOCIAL STUDIES

Similar to dialogue journals, but involving communication between two students, written conversations have been used by Karen Shelton to integrate reading, writing, and social studies in middle school language arts classes. Her students work in pairs and hold a conversation through writing, much as they do when they pass notes in class. They pass the same booklet or paper back and forth, writing comments and responses each time. She had students hold written conversations about Japanese internment camps. Partners wrote notes to one another about their reactions to a book on this topic at several key points in the action.

Students respond positively to this approach when they can choose their own partners. Connecting fun with learning tends to engender active involvement in the lessons. Written conversations were personally meaningful for many students in Shelton's classes. They acknowledged the ideas of their partners and indicated that they gained new perspectives on the material by doing so (Bintz and Shelton, 2004).

ENGLISH/ LANGUAGE ARTS

Bloem (2004) paired university students with fifth-graders to correspond through dialogue journals. The journals were small notebooks created by the fifth-graders. At the beginning of the project, university students read polished stories written by their partners, and then wrote their initial letters to their partners in the notebooks provided. Each of the partners wrote seven letters during the exchange, and the fifth-graders also sent two polished drafts to their partners for reading and comments. The university students became both audiences and mentors for their younger partners. This project was an opportunity for reflection and productive discussions that benefited both partners.

RAFT ASSIGNMENTS

"RAFT simply stands for (R) role, (A) audience, (F) format, and (T) topic, the key ingredients for making writing assignments" (Santa, Havens, and Harrison, 1989, p. 148). **RAFT assignments** are explicit as to each of these factors: the student is told

How can RAFT
assignments be
beneficial to content
area learning?

who the writer is, who the audience is, what form the writing will take, and the topic for the writing. Student roles may vary widely; they can be scientists, blood cells, trees, animals, or other animate or inanimate objects. The audiences can be classmates, younger children, or the general public. Formats can include letters, editorials, memoranda, and poems. A sample assignment might be as follows: You are the brother of a boy who is considering experimenting with cocaine (role). Through a letter (format) to your brother (audience), try to persuade him not to do this, backing up your arguments with facts about this drug (topic).

RESEARCH REPORTS

Research reports involve organizing and outlining numerous facts. Writers must also synthesize information from various sources. Research papers can promote critical thinking about topics under study. They also offer practical applications of various study skills, such as library use, reference book use, note taking, outlining, and summarizing. Nevertheless, research papers should not be assigned without careful assessment of students' prerequisite skills, so that appropriate instruction can be offered if necessary skills are not in evidence (Rekrut, 1997). These skills should be taught as needed and connections made between the skills and the current task of answering the research questions that have been raised. Students may be allowed to choose note-taking, footnoting, and bibliographic forms; or the teacher may specify forms that are required.

When content area teachers assign reports to be written for their classes, they sometimes allow students to choose their own topics. In other instances, a teacher may ask each student to write on a predetermined topic. Some educators feel that students should have a great deal of control over what they write. Britton and others (1975, p. 23) say, "however controlled the situation, the writer is *selecting* from what he knows and thinks . . . and embodying that knowledge and thought in words which he produces, no matter how much he draws on the language of a book or of the teacher's notes." Therefore, from the perspective of Britton and others, having the teacher assign topics and guide students in writing procedures does not negate the ownership of the writing.

Davis and Hunter (1990) suggest having gifted students research the accuracy of historical novels as a project that can result in research papers that solve real problems. Anachronisms and other inaccuracies can be located by consulting reference books about the period. The students thus can have a choice of the novel to write about and a choice of focus for the paper, but they also have a well-defined task.

**SOCIAL
STUDIES** **ENGLISH/
LANGUAGE
ARTS**

The process that follows can be used to help students prepare good reports. The first step listed obviously is not applicable if the teacher chooses the topic.

> **Step 1.** Select a topic. The topic selected must be pertinent to the content area material being studied. It should be chosen because of its interest value for both the reporter and the rest of the class, if the reports are going to be shared. Ordinarily, students tend to choose topics that are much too broad for adequate coverage. The teacher needs to help students narrow their topics so that the task of preparing the report is more manageable.

Step 2. Collect information on the topic. Students should use the location skills discussed in Chapter 6 to collect information from a variety of sources. The organizational skill of note taking, covered in Chapter 6, is also essential for use at this point.

Step 3. Organize the material. Outlining or webbing the information collected is the main activity in this step. Material from the different sources used must be fused together. The sequence and relationship of main ideas and details are important considerations in forming the outline or web.

Step 4. Write a first draft. Utilizing the outline or web just formulated and the notes compiled, the students write an initial draft of the report.

Step 5. Read the first draft for revision and editing. The students read the first draft and check for organization, sentence and paragraph sense, cohesiveness of the information, appropriate usage, correct spelling, and proper punctuation. They also confirm that all material is properly documented. At this point, peer editing may be utilized. With this approach, a peer editor carefully reads the report of his or her classmate, answering questions provided by the teacher. Some sample questions are as follows: "Does the report have a title that accurately reflects its contents? Does the report have a good beginning that sparks interest in the topic? Is the sequence in which the information is presented logical? If not, what do you think is wrong with it? Is enough information included? In your opinion, what questions remain to be answered by the report? Does the report have errors in mechanics (e.g., spelling, capitalization, punctuation)? If so, mark them for the author. Does the report have a conclusion that sums up the material adequately? Do you have any questions or suggestions for the author?" After answering these questions, the peer editor returns the report and comments to the author, who revises it for submission to the teacher, carefully considering the editor's comments. Often two students work together, each acting as peer editor for the other.

Step 6. Revise the report. The students make needed changes in the initial draft and rewrite the report in a form acceptable for submission to the teacher. Revision is easier if the report has been written using word-processing software on a computer.

The teacher can do much to help prepare students to perform effectively on an assigned written report. A procedure that a teacher might follow is described next.

1. Name a broad topic related to the course of study. Ask students for suggestions as to how the topic could be narrowed to make it more manageable. Consider a number of acceptable topics that might be derived from the original topic.

2. Choose one of the acceptable narrowed topics. Take the students to the library and have them locate sources of information on the topic. Ask each of them to take notes from at least one source and to record bibliographical information. Remind them to make use of skimming and scanning techniques as they search for information. (See Chapter 7 for information on skimming and scanning.) Encourage use of computer databases and electronic encyclopedias, if they are available. (See Chapter 6 for a discussion of these resources.)

3. Return to the classroom. As a class, synthesize the notes into a single outline. (Use a dry-erase board, computer projection device, or overhead projector.)

4. Write the report from the outline as a whole-class or small-group activity, with the teacher working as the scribe or assigning a student to be the scribe. The scribe may be writing manually or on a computer.

5. Have the students read the draft for content, organization, and mechanics.

6. Make needed changes in organization, spelling, and expression on the basis of the proofreading.

The teacher who follows this procedure has essentially walked the students through the steps of report writing before asking them to attempt it on their own. Thereafter, the students will know what to expect when they are assigned individual reports to write. Help with the skills of note taking, outlining, summarizing information, and locating information should be a prerequisite for assignment of a written report if students have not previously mastered these skills. Help should also be given with composing footnotes and bibliographic entries.

In addition to preparing students for report writing, the content area teacher should contact the school's librarian before assigning a research report. The librarian can help students locate relevant resources.

Rekrut (1997) recommends having students work in teams on research reports, following steps similar to those just enumerated. Working with partners or small groups may be less threatening to many students than working alone would be, and greater learning appears to result from team reports than from individually produced reports. Teachers must monitor the teams' work regularly and should also encourage self-monitoring of progress by team members.

Expository Writing Program

Raphael and others (1988) developed the Expository Writing Program (EWP) to help students learn how to write well-organized reports with data collected from a number of sources. The EWP is designed around "think sheets" that stimulate strategy use for planning the report, gathering data, drafting, editing, and revising. The EWP Prewriting Think Sheet focuses on planning concerns, such as considering the topic, things the students already know about the topic, and the audience for the paper. The Organizing Think Sheet focuses students' attention on different sets of questions that fit different text structures, such as comparison/contrast, problem/solution, and explanation. Students use the sheet that is appropriate for their chosen organizational pattern. A lined sheet of colored paper forms the think sheet for writing the first draft. Edit and Peer Editor Think Sheets provide the framework for first self-editing and then peer editing. These sheets focus on the content and organization of the paper and on planning the next step of the writing. A Revision Think Sheet encourages the students to integrate the feedback from others into a revision plan. Two types of think sheets are shown in Example 8.6. Raphael and Englert (1990) have developed a variety of examples of different types of think sheets. They also have encouraged modeling of the writing process through "thinking aloud."

EXAMPLE 8.6   Sample Think Sheets

Think Sheet for Editing a Comparison/Contrast Paper

Author's name _____   Editor's name _____

Read to check information. (Authors: Read your paper aloud to your editor.)

What is the paper mainly about?

What do you like best? Put a ***** next to the part you liked best and tell why you like it here:

What parts are not clear? Put a **?** next to the unclear parts, and tell what made the part unclear to you:

Is the paper interesting? Tell why or why not here:

Question yourself to check organization.

Did the author:

Tell what two things are compared and contrasted?	Yes	Sort of	No
Tell things they are being compared and contrasted on?	Yes	Sort of	No
Tell how they are alike?	Yes	Sort of	No
Tell how they are different?	Yes	Sort of	No
Use keywords clearly?	Yes	Sort of	No

Plan revision.

What two parts do you think should be changed or revised? (For anything marked "Sort of" or "No," should the author add to, take out, reorder?)

1. _____
   _____
   _____
   _____

2. _____
   _____
   _____
   _____

What could help make the paper more interesting?

Talk.

Talk to the author of the paper. Talk about your comments on this editing think sheet. Share ideas for revising the paper.

Think Sheet for Planning

Author's name _____   Date _____

Topic: _____

Who: Who am I writing for?
Why: Why am I writing this?
What: What do I already know about my topic? (Brainstorm)

1. _____
2. _____
3. _____

How: How do I group my ideas?

Source: Taffy E. Raphael, Carol Sue Englert, and Becky W. Kirschner, "Acquisition of Expository Writing Skills," in Jana M. Mason (ed.), *Reading and Writing Connections.* Copyright © 1989 by Allyn and Bacon. Reprinted with permission of Jana Mason.

MEETING THE CHALLENGE

Teaching students to do research papers can be approached in a number of ways. The following is the procedure that a first-year teacher in a rural high school, Katherine Dooley, used.

1. Kathy held a class-long brainstorming session to answer two questions: "What are you an expert at?" and "What do you want to know more about?" For the purposes of this assignment, she specified that they were *expert* at anything they had ever done themselves. She gave the following topics as examples: expert at being a son/daughter, eater, talker, and tooth brusher. She also gave examples of what she would want to know more about. Her students had many interesting habits, hobbies, and ideas.

2. Kathy read their lists, circling interesting topics and writing her own brainstorming in the margins.

3. Then she took her class to the library, returned their papers, and held individual writing conferences to discuss ideas. Some surprising ideas surfaced. An "expert gum chewer" chose to write about gum and began what he called his "quest" for

continued

information. During the process, the student learned how to use a variety of types of technology, sharpened his problem-solving skills, and actually enjoyed the experience. He came to Kathy daily and said things like "Yuck! Did you know gum contains...?" or "Wow! Look at this, Ms. Dooley." An "expert reader of children's books" listed sexism as something she would like to know more about. Kathy had circled both of the ideas, and during the conference they decided that she could write about the portrayal of women in ten Caldecott-winning books from several decades. For this topic the vast majority of the information came, not from copying directly from another source, but from the student's own evaluation. The student's connection to the topic led her to show Kathy illustrations that particularly angered her. Her feeling about the research topic was evident from her paper.

If the piece has been written on a computer with a word-processing program, the revision activity is much easier.
© Muntz/Taxi Collection/ Getty Images

With this method, Kathy received interesting, unusual papers with what one of Kathy's college professors called "spunk." "When I allowed them to choose topics that were meaningful to them, they actually enjoyed learning about their topics," she said.

Kathy Dooley met the challenge of getting the students to write research papers by giving them some personal choice that led to motivation. Teachers in areas other than English could offer structured choices. For example, a science teacher might ask, "Which of these scientific breakthroughs or procedures has the most impact on *your* life? About which one do you have the most background knowledge? In which one do you have the most interest?" With the answers to these questions as a starter, each student could be led to choose a topic that would provide some personal motivation.

Beyersdorfer and Schauer (1992) describe a special type of research report—the personality profile. They teach about the personality profile in a two-week project. First they have students read about interesting people and decide about things that influenced their lives. Next, students select subjects to profile. Then they learn interviewing and note-taking techniques, write scripts for their interviews, and carry out the interviews. Next they make decisions based on the data collected, write the profiles, and present the profiles orally to their classmates.

Some educators offer other variations to enhance students' motivation to write. Moulton (1999) recommends using Romano's (1995; 2000) multigenre approach to writing research papers, having students include many research tools (for example, the Internet) in the data collection and then vary the form of presentation of information. Instead of having students meld their findings into a traditional paper format, the teacher has them write several pieces based on their research, presenting their information through different genres. "For instance rather than stating that someone was born in a particular year and place, the student might create a birth certificate, the flyleaf of a Bible, a birth announcement, a hospital invoice, or a letter to or from the new parents" (Moulton, 1999, p. 529). Events might be related through personal letters, journal entries, or newspaper articles. Such a presentation requires students to interpret the material from another person's point of view, and it requires them to understand multiple genres. A formal bibliography is included with such research writing, but internal citations are not. Students may use endnotes to explain why they chose particular genres and to cite the sources for their information. Many of Moulton's students used computer technology to prepare realistic-looking documents—a natural integration of technology and writing.

Allen (2001) has suggested an approach to multigenre research papers for middle school students. She also based her approach on Romano's writing. Romano wrote in the Foreword to Allen's book, "*Multigenre* simply means 'composed of many kinds of writing.' Multigenre papers are many-voiced and rhetorically diverse" (p. vii). Allen describes multigenre papers in this way: "each piece in the paper utilizes a different genre, reveals one facet of the topic, and makes its own point. Conventional devices do not connect the pieces in a multigenre paper, nor are the pieces always in chronological order. The paper is instead a collage of writing and artistic expression with an overarching theme that engulfs and informs the reader" (p. 2). Allen's students often used the Internet, videos, personal interviews, other primary sources, and field trips, as well as books from the library, for some references. As the students prepared their papers, Allen provided instruction related to research skills, writing in a variety of genres, and planning and organizational skills. The students cooperatively developed a rubric to evaluate the presentations based on their papers. A sample multigenre report is shown in Example 8.7.

EXAMPLE 8.7   Multigenre Report

Haiku
Water gently flows
Freshly cleaned and purified
Free from pollutants

Example 1

Poem
I was lost in a flood of trash
My beauty not seen
Animals steered clear
Because my water was green

Example 2

WANTED
Water Quality Specialist
Temporary position for an experienced scientist

Benefits:
Office located in town square
Flexible hours
Vacation package

Salary is negotiable

Minimum of Doctor's Degree
in Biology or related field

Interview required
Applications available at Cookeville City Hall
or call 555-9562

Equal Opportunity Employer

Example 3

Example 4

Don't Drink That Water Research Report
By Meagan Jasitt

Problem

If a community's public water supply is contaminated, what is the most effective way to purify water from local sources (streams, lakes, rivers, or wells) to make it potable?

Hypotheses

1. I believe that by using materials that are available in the home, people can make natural sources of water drinkable.
2. I think that of the different methods, distillation will be the most effective way to purify water.

Materials

Coliscan Easygel (20 ml) in sterile bottle
Aquachek 5-in-1 Water Quality Test Strips for Chlorine, Hardness, Alkalinity, and pH
Aquachek 5-in-1 Water Quality Test Strips for Nitrate and Nitrite
Iodine solution (2%)
Clorox Ultra bleach (6.00% sodium hypochlorite)
Sterile, pretreated Petri dishes with lids
Sterile collection bottles
3 ml sterile droppers
Plastic cups
1-gallon plastic collection bottle

Pots for boiling and collecting water
Glass cover
Coffee filters and large funnel
Sand
Ice
Timer
Digital camera
Safety glasses
Disposable gloves

Procedure

1. Collect water samples from a local stream
2. Test these water samples for nitrite level, nitrate level, pH, hardness, alkalinity, chloride level, and free chlorine using chemical test strips.
   a. Tap water
   b. Untreated stream water
   c. 500 ml stream water treated with 2 drops of 6.00% sodium hypochlorite (Clorox Ultra)
   d. 500 ml stream water treated with 3 drops of 2% Iodine
   e. Untreated stream water filtered through a coffee filter
   f. Untreated stream water filtered through sand and a coffee filter
   g. Untreated stream water boiled for 20 minutes in an aluminum pot
   h. Untreated stream water vapor that was condensed

3. Steps for bacteria testing
   a. Place 5 ml of each water sample (2.a-2.h) into a bottle of Coliscan Easygel
   b. Pour solution into sterile Petri dish
   c. Cover and turn each dish over after 45 minutes
   d. Count colonies formed after 48 hours
   e. Determine kinds of bacteria found in Petri dishes and bacteria count

Results

In drinking water, any bacteria can cause illness, especially fecal coliform bacteria. If the fecal coliform bacteria are plentiful, it can cause typhoid fever, hepatitis, dysentery, and ear infections. By using Coliscan Easygel, both fecal and non-fecal bacteria can be identified by the colors of their colonies after letting samples set for at least 30 hours.

My water samples came from a local stream that contained mostly non-fecal bacteria. Chemically treating this water with small amounts of sodium hypochlorite and iodine killed the bacteria. Treating the water with these household chemicals was easy and effective, though there may be some health problems for some people. Boiling is effective in killing bacteria, but the container may help to contaminate the water. Distillation is a slow process that requires boiling and condensation, but pure water is the result.

Conclusions

1. By using household materials, people can make natural sources of water potable.
2. Distilled water was the purest water produced in this experiment, but making it consumed much time and energy.
3. Water treated with iodine most closely resembled tap water, but iodine can be hazardous to some people.

References

Curtis, R. (1998). Outdoor action guide to water purification. Retrieved February 23, 2005, from http://www.princeton.edu/~oa/manual/water.shtml.

Jarrett, D. (2005, March 10). Monterey water system water quality report 2004. *Cookeville Herald-Citizen*, p. 8.

LaMotte Company. (2004). *ColiQuant EZ* (Code 3-0034). Chestertown, MD: LaMotte Company. Pacific Crest Trail Association. (n.d.). Water sources and purification. Retrieved February 23, 2005, from http://www.pcta.org/planning/before_trip/health/water.asp.

Thompson, G., & Turk, J. (1992). *Earth and its environment*. Fort Worth, TX: Saunders College Publishing.

University of Missouri Extension. (2005). *Bacteria in drinking water* (WQ102). Retrieved March 7, 2005, from http://muextension.missouri.edu/xplor/envqual/wq0102.htm.

Photo Essay

Multigenre Science Project

Meagan Jasitt
Cookeville High School
Cookeville, TN
March 2005

Hypotheses

1. I believe that by using materials that are available in the home, people can make natural sources of water drinkable.
2. I think that of the different methods, distillation will be the most effective way to purify water.

Materials

Local stream

Collecting water sample

Treating sample with 2% iodine

Treating sample with
2% iodine

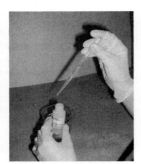

Adding 5ml sample to
Coliscan Easygel

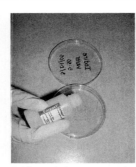

Adding solution to treated
Petri dish

Chemical analysis with test
strips

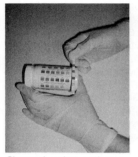

Chemical analysis with test
strips

Water samples after
48-hour treatment

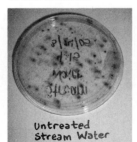

Counting colonies
of bacteria

Counting colonies
of bacteria

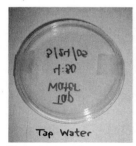

Tap water sample

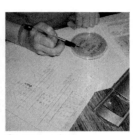

Untreated stream water
bacteria colonies

Coffee filter method

Sand filter method

Stream water sample
treated with 6% sodium
hypochlorite

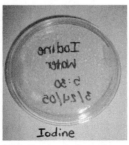

2% iodine treated sample

Distilled water sample

Boiled water sample

Conclusions

1. By using household materials, people can make natural sources of water potable.
2. Distilled water was the purest water produced in this experiment, but making it consumed much time and energy.
3. Water treated with iodine most closely resembled tap water, but iodine can be hazardous to some people.

Example 5

Homeland Security Chief Discusses Emergency Water Supply Awareness
By Meagan Jasitt
Associated Press Reporter

COOKEVILLE (TN) - In case of a disaster, when tap water is not available, citizens should have some of the following supplies available to purify local water sources: iodine, bleach, and an assortment of cooking pots for distillation.

The Secretary of Homeland Security stated that adding 2-3 drops of iodine or Clorox to a quart of water and letting it sit for 30 minutes can purify contaminated water. However, there may be some risks to pregnant women and people with thyroid disease. The Secretary also said that distillation and boiling are probably the most effective methods but not always the most convenient. For more information you can go to http://www.fema.gov/rrr/waterf.shtm

Example 6

(Letter to the editor of the Cookeville Herald-Citizen)

Editor:

"Hello, I was sent by the city to test your water." This is the greeting that many residents of my Cookeville neighborhood have been receiving when they open their front doors.

Unfortunately, after hearing from the "city employee" that their water is contaminated, some citizens have been convinced or conned into buying hundreds of dollars worth of water filtering equipment.

I'm concerned and ask your assistance to help us determine if the water in our community is potable and safe to use. Do these "employees" work for the city or are they part of a new scam that is spreading across Cookeville?

M. Jasitt
Concerned Citizen

Example 7

(Chief of Police response to the letter to the editor)

Editor:

This letter is a response to the letter by the Concerned Citizen about a possible water testing scam. My office has received quite a few calls about fraudulent water testing, and we are currently investigating the problem.

The Director of the Cookeville Water Department told me that the water supplied by Cookeville meets all of the health requirements of the state of Tennessee. City workers are not going to homes and asking to conduct water tests. If you are concerned about the cleanliness of your water, you may call the Water Department and discuss the problem.

If anyone has any information about possible crimes, please phone the police headquarters. Report anyone who comes to check the water quality at homes in your neighborhood.

J. Smith
Cookeville Chief of Police

End Notes

Examples 1 and 2, *Haiku* and *Poem*— These poems were created after reviewing examples of short poems. *Haiku* is a haiku. *Poem* is a quatrain (abcb). Both are about water quality, which was the topic of my science fair project.

Example 3, *Wanted: Water Quality Specialist*— After thinking about the qualifications for someone who could be hired by the city to test water, I wrote this advertisement. I used actual newspaper employment advertisements as examples.

Example 4, *Don't Drink That Water*—This is my actual research project for tenth-grade Honors Chemistry at Cookeville High School. Most of the work on the project was done during my two weeks of spring break in March 2005. I started my research in February and followed the scientific method. I tested my hypothesis, collected data, and developed conclusions. My project won third place at the Cookeville High School Science Fair and was an honorable mention at the Upper Cumberland Regional Science Fair at Tennessee Tech University.

Example 5, *Homeland Security Newspaper Article*—While looking for information about water purification, I read about preparing for emergencies on the Department of Homeland Security and Federal Emergency Management Agency websites. This letter is important because I think that people should be prepared for any catastrophes that may occur.

Examples 6 and 7, *Letters to the Editor*—Letters to the editor and responses are good ways for people to get action and to have their questions answered. Having public officials publish responses is also good because many citizens can be informed with just one short letter. The *Cookeville Herald-Citizen* newspaper publishes a lot of letters to the editor and I used some of them as examples.

Source: Reprinted by permission of Meagan and Lance Jasitt.

LABORATORY REPORTS

Secondary science classes often have laboratory components for which laboratory reports must be written. A student lab guide, such as the one in Example 8.8, may be used to guide students through experiments.

The writing of a laboratory report can be modeled by doing an experiment and writing a cooperative laboratory report on the board or on a transparency. The

---

EXAMPLE 8.8   Student Lab Guide

SCIENCE AND
HEALTH

Purpose of This Lab: Why are you doing this lab?

Problem: What problem are you investigating?

Hypothesis: What do you think the outcome of this lab will be? Think about what you already know about the topic, and make an educated guess about the outcome.

Materials: List all materials that you will need to conduct this laboratory.

Procedure: List in step-by-step fashion the procedure you are going to use to collect the data.

Data or Results: Draw, record, or chart all detailed observations noted from the procedure above.

Analysis or Conclusion: Reread your problem statement. Did your results resolve the problem? Explain why. If the results did not help clarify the problem, explain why.

Class Conclusion: Final conclusion after class discussion. Modify your own conclusion, if necessary.

Source: Santa/Havens/Harrison, "Teaching Secondary Science Through Reading, Writing, Studying, and Problem Solving," in *Content Area Reading and Learning: Instructional Strategies,* Lapp/Flood/Farnan eds., © 1989, p. 150. Reprinted by permission of Prentice Hall, Inc., Englewood Cliffs, New Jersey.

teacher can lead the students through each step in the process; then the students can use their lab guides to write reports independently.

PHOTO ESSAYS

ART

Sinatra and others (1990) found that the use of photo essays and various types of semantic maps was effective for building background knowledge of culturally diverse students and for helping them to organize their thoughts into writing. The students worked in pairs initially to develop photo essays with meaningful conceptual frameworks and then reconstructed the photos on storyboards, using semantic mapping formats. The images in the photos helped to bridge the language differences of the student population and to provide a common base for communication.

**ENGLISH/
LANGUAGE
ARTS**

The procedure was to plan topics or themes, take photos to illustrate the topics, organize the pictures on a storyboard, and then write a composition on the topic with the storyboard in view. Students brainstormed ideas for photos before actually taking the pictures. When the pictures had been processed, the student pairs worked together on the arrangement on the storyboards. The assignments elicited sequential, thematic, and classification writing styles. Example 8.9 shows these three patterns for organizing essays. An example of a photo essay is included as a part of Example 8.7.

PEN PALS

**ENGLISH/
LANGUAGE
ARTS**

Writing to pen pals is a way to provide students with authentic reading and writing experiences because it involves real communication activities (Damico, 1996). A number of teachers have discovered the advantages of e-mail pen pals for motivating students to do meaningful reading and writing. E-mail applications were addressed in Chapter 2. Garcia-Vazquez and Vazquez (1994) paired Latino/a high school students with Latino/a university students with great success. The high school students carefully drafted their messages to their pen pals and often edited them several times before mailing them. McDermott and Setoguchi (1999) have had college methods students converse with seventh-graders about literature in pen-pal letters in a program much like the one Betty Roe conducted through e-mail. (See Chapter 2 for details.)

INTERNET WRITING PROJECTS

**ENGLISH/
LANGUAGE
ARTS**

Internet writing projects can be motivational for secondary school students. If a teacher wants to get students involved in a writing project on the Internet, Education Place (http://www.eduplace.com/projects) includes a section called Project Center that lists such projects—or the teacher can submit his or her own project. This site has links to other sites related to writing and computer technology, as does the Wisconsin Department of Public Instruction's Education Resource List (http://www.dpi.state.wi.us/dpi/dltcl/imt/ed_res.html) (Iannone, 1998).

EXAMPLE 8.9   Three Patterns of Storyboard Organization for Photo Essay and Written Composition

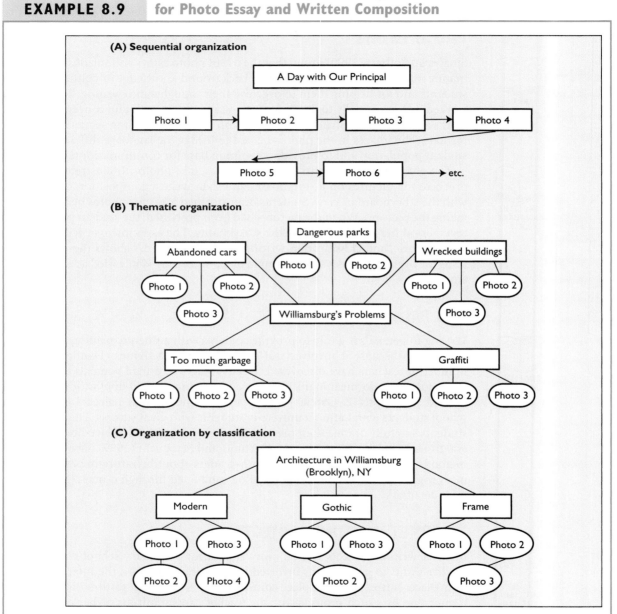

(A) Sequential organization

(B) Thematic organization

(C) Organization by classification

MENTORING PROJECTS

**ENGLISH/
LANGUAGE
ARTS**

To help middle school students improve their writing skills through writing work-shops and to help university students learn about writers' workshops, university students were paired with sixth- or seventh-grade students (Smith-D'Arezzo and Kennedy, 2004). Both groups were taught about the six traits of writing from the Northwest Regional Educational Laboratory (2003): ideas, organization, voice, word choice, sentence fluency, and conventions. The partners critiqued each other's writing, using a rubric based on the six traits. The students in both groups completed three writing projects. There were two or three face-to-face conferences about writing for the partners. In the last meeting, the students gave partners their scores on the pieces and explained how they derived the scores.

Evaluation of Writing

Not all writing that students are asked to do in content area classrooms is formally evaluated. Writing in journals, for example, is done for its learning value and is not formally evaluated for a grade. Language experience writing is usually evaluated by the students who develop it as it is produced. Generally it is not graded by the teacher but is used as a learning aid in the classroom.

If the process approach to writing is used, there is much ongoing evaluation as a written piece is developed. Students elicit feedback about their writing from their peers, they proofread their own work with revision checklists in mind, and they receive feedback from their teachers during student-teacher conferences. In addition to the evaluative efforts that have gone on as materials are written, there are times when teachers must formally evaluate a final draft of a written assignment. These grading procedures may be holistic or analytic in nature.

When *holistic grading* is used, the teacher evaluates the written material as a whole. The paper is read for general impression and overall effect. It may be compared with pieces that have already been graded or scored for the inclusion of features important to the particular type of writing involved (*INC Sights*, 1989). Scoring guides, called *rubrics*, can be developed, which list the characteristics of high-quality, medium-quality, lower-quality, and lowest-quality papers for a particular assignment with a specified purpose and audience. This approach is referred to as *primary trait scoring* (Graser, 1983). Kirby and Liner (1988, p. 221) point out that holistic grading "focuses on the piece of writing as a whole and on those features most important to the success of the piece. . . . The rating is quick because the rater does not take time to circle errors or make marginal notations." Kirby and Liner suggest that teachers may use a list of criteria related to the impact of the writing, the inventiveness of the approach, and the individual flavor of the writing as a guide for their holistic grading. They refer to this type of grading as impression marking.

Analytic scales not only focus readers' attention on the features that are needed for the writing to be effective but also attach point values to each feature. The reader sums the scores for each feature in determining the overall grade. The Diederich

Scale is an example of an analytic scale. It leads the scorer to assign a score of 1 (poor), 2 (weak), 3 (average), 4 (good), or 5 (excellent) to quality and development of ideas *and* organization, relevance, and movement (both of which are weighted heavier than the other considerations); style, flavor, and individuality and wording and phrasing (both of which are given intermediate weights); and grammar and sentence structure, punctuation, spelling, and manuscript form and legibility (all of which receive the lowest weights). Content and organization represent 50 percent of the grade; aspects of style, 30 percent; and mechanics, 20 percent. Scales such as this keep raters focused on the carefully defined criteria and keep them from being unduly influenced by surface features rather than considering all the factors contributing to the effectiveness of a piece of writing (Kirby and Liner, 1988). If students are asked to keep folders of written work over the course of a semester or year, their progress can be noted by comparing the earlier pieces with the latest ones. Students may gain more satisfaction from this type of final evaluation than from many other methods because they can see the differences in the writing and often can see that early teacher comments led to improvements in later products.

A sample rubric is found in Example 8.4. More on assessment, especially portfolio assessment, can be found in Chapter 12.

Focus on Struggling Readers

Writing Instruction for Struggling Readers and Writers

Furr (2003) uses a modified writing workshop with Title I students who read three to four years below their current grade level. He has found that these students need much support as they work toward becoming independent writers. They need procedures to help them decide such things as how to begin and what to do next. They also are more comfortable beginning with expository prose on topics that have been covered in school because they have more control of the vocabulary and syntax they need to use when they have had guided reading experiences with the subject matter. In sustained silent reading time, nonfiction texts with little reading difficulty are popular with these students. The short, accessible text in these books is a major reason they are preferred.

Before beginning writing workshop, Furr has his students participate in guided reading of a variety of nonfiction texts. These books are discussed, important vocabulary is clarified, and the words are used in meaningful written sentences. The information in these texts is supplemented by teacher read-alouds and an abundance of books on the same topics for independent reading by the students.

The first expository piece is developed through shared writing, similar to the language experience approach. The class cooperatively begins a web on the chosen topic after the teacher explains and models the webbing process. Students brainstorm for categories and sometimes return to the text to confirm details. Students then complete the web individually. The teacher next explains the need for and the development of a hook and a general statement about the topic for the report, as a way to begin. This process is modeled and some brainstorming by the students follows.

The class composes part of the draft of the body of the report together. Each box on the web is used as the focus of a paragraph. The students are encouraged to move from the general to the more specific. Furr circulates and holds conferences with the students as they finish the report independently. Students are allowed to consult one another as they write, as well. They finish by editing their material for mechanics, using four categories to check: capitals, agreement, punctuation, and spelling. They are encouraged to read through their report four times, focusing on a different element each time. Finished reports are illustrated and displayed.

Fisher and Frey (2003) use a gradual release model for writing instruction with ninth-grade struggling readers. This means that control of the writing gradually shifts from the teacher to the student. This model began with a language experience approach in which the teacher acted as a scribe and wrote the students' thoughts about a topic on a dry-erase board. The topic chosen was often based on a shared reading experience. As the teacher wrote, various aspects of the writing were discussed— mechanics, spelling, grammatical constructions, or vocabulary. The students had interesting and deep thoughts to share in the writing, even though their independent writing was a struggle. The language experience approach was followed by interactive writing in which the students did the actual writing of the class's ideas. Fisher implemented this by having different students write single words from the chosen sentence. The class repeated the sentence each time a student wrote a word, until the students had written the entire sentence in their combined effort at the board. The teacher sometimes focused on elements of mechanics and spelling as the writing progressed.

Fisher also used published writing to provide patterns that the students could emulate in their own individual writing. The patterns offered a scaffold for these students. For example, in Shelley Moore Thomas's book *Somewhere Today: A Book of Peace*, each page starts with "Somewhere today" in the first sentence. After discussion of newspaper articles and lectures on a topic, students wrote their own sentences beginning with "Somewhere today," typed them on the classroom computer, and illustrated them. They were bound into a class book.

Harvey (2002) suggests using more short nonfiction to teach reading and writing skills to struggling readers and writers. The length is less intimidating to these students; there are usually eye-catching illustrations; they can be reread easily and quickly; and they are short enough for read-alouds of complete, well-crafted pieces that provide writing models.

Generative sentences beginning with single words were turned into topic sentences for paragraphs by Fisher and Frey (2003) in their procedure. The topic sentences were developed under supervision in class, and the paragraphs were assigned to be completed as homework—homework that had a high probability of being completed because it was off to a good beginning. Freewriting that had as its focus the production of as many words on a given topic as quickly as possible was used to provide the students with written material that they could take through the revision process. This procedure culminated in independent writing to prompts based on reading that had been done in class. The entire procedure resulted in improved reading and writing skills for the students in the class.

In other settings, less-motivated and "difficult" students were actively engaged by multigenre writing (Grierson, Anson, and Baird, 2002). They often turned in assignments early and indicated that they really cared about their writing projects.

Focus on English Language Learners

Writing Instruction for ELLs

Fisher and Frey's (2003) gradual release model for writing instruction (see "Focus on Struggling Readers" above) also worked extremely well with the English language learners in the class. One good example was Mubarak, who was from Somalia. He was able to write fewer than five words a minute when the rapid freewrites were started, but in four months he was averaging 40 words a minute. The language experience approach that was used in the gradual release model has also been suggested by many educators as a good procedure for English language learners (Fisher and Frey, 2003).

Dolly (1990) suggests the use of dialogue journals with ELLs. She points out that such journals ensure that this reading material will be somewhat adjusted to the students' individual reading abilities because teachers can modify their writing to fit the language proficiency of the students.

SUMMARY

Writing is valuable in content area classes because it is a tool for thinking and for attaining self-knowledge and because it enhances retention of the material studied. As these benefits are gained, fluency in writing is also promoted.

Reading and writing are closely related skills. Both are written language skills, are concerned with communication, involve construction of meaning, and make use of vocabulary. Still, use of random writing activities in a content course may not help students in reading. To foster reading progress, writing assignments must focus on the relationships between reading and writing. Writing before reading can help students activate their background knowledge about a topic, enhancing reading comprehension. Reading is a thinking process, and reading comprehension requires thinking at various cognitive levels, as does writing production.

A process approach to writing tends to produce superior writing products and a better understanding of the writing process than an approach in which the teacher assigns a paper and the students write it and turn it in without process guidance. The writing process can be broken down into five overlapping and recursive steps: prewriting, writing a draft, revising, editing, and publishing. Many types of writing-to-learn activities have been used in content classes. They include language experience writings, content journals, dialogue journals, RAFT assignments, research reports, laboratory reports, photo essays, pen pals, Internet writing projects, and multigenre projects.

Not all writing done in class needs to be evaluated. Journal writing is a prime example of this. Writing that is developed through a process approach is subject to ongoing evaluation as the writing progresses. Sometimes teachers need to evaluate a final draft of a piece of writing for grading purposes. When this is the case, they may use either holistic or analytic grading procedures.

A modified writing workshop preceded by guided reading and teacher read-alouds of nonfiction texts is effective with struggling readers and writers. A gradual release model for writing instruction is also helpful with these students and with English language learners. Use of short nonfiction is beneficial in this process. Multigenre writing is motivational for students who are not generally eager to write. English language learners benefit from the use of dialogue journals and the language experience approach.

DISCUSSION QUESTIONS

1. In what ways is writing valuable in content area instruction?
2. What are some types of activities in which writing can positively influence reading achievement?
3. Which types of writing-to-learn activities would be most helpful in your content area? Why?
4. Why is the prewriting stage so important to the writing program?
5. What are some advantages to publishing and sharing students' writing?
6. What method of evaluation of final drafts seems most appropriate to you? Why?
7. What are the values of Internet writing projects?
8. What procedures are most helpful to struggling readers and writers and to English language learners?

ENRICHMENT ACTIVITIES

*1. Observe one period of a content area class. List the types of writing that the students are asked to do and the length of time spent on each writing activity.
*2. Try using one of the prereading writing activities suggested by Oberlin and Shugarman (1988) with a content reading assignment that you give. Share your feelings about its effectiveness with your classmates in written or oral form.
*3. Try using content journals, or learning logs, in your classroom for a three-week period. Report your reaction to this technique to your classmates.
4. List creative applications of writing to your subject area.
5. With a partner from this class, role-play the use of dialogue journals for a specific type of class (e.g., a tenth-grade biology class). One of you write as the teacher and one as the student. Be prepared to discuss with the class your reactions to the technique.
*6. Guide a group of secondary school students through the process of writing a group report.
7. Write a multigenre report on a topic in your subject area to use as an example for your students.
8. Develop a photo essay on a topic in your subject area to use as an example for your students.
9. Prepare a lesson plan for using the process approach with a writing assignment. Role-play the teaching of this lesson to your classmates. *If possible, teach the lesson to a class of secondary school students.
10. List Internet sites that are good resources for secondary school writing instruction.

*These activities are designed for in-service teachers, student teachers, and practicum students.

Chapter 9

Literature-Based and Thematic Approaches to Content Area Teaching

OVERVIEW

Literature has many values in the secondary curriculum, not only in English classes, where it has an undisputed place as an important subject area, but also in other content areas, where it can illuminate events and issues that are treated only briefly in textbooks. It is also valuable because it offers material on various subjects at different difficulty levels. Literature is often incorporated into thematic units in a variety of content areas. Thematic units also include resources other than literature and require much planning on the part of the teacher.

Students need instruction on reading strategies needed to approach literature and related to literary elements. Teachers can use a number of activities to encourage deeper responses to literature.

PURPOSE-SETTING QUESTIONS

As you read this chapter, try to answer these questions:

1. How can literature enhance instruction in the secondary school?
2. How can teachers approach use of literature in content area instruction?
3. What activities can be used to encourage student response to literature?
4. What four basic types of activities are part of a teaching unit?
5. How can use of literature and thematic units benefit struggling readers and English language learners?

Values and Uses of Literature in the Secondary School Curriculum

Secondary school instruction is often highly textbook oriented, but textbooks by their nature cannot cover the material as well as it needs to be covered. The need to cover too many topics in a single textbook often leads to superficial coverage of each topic, often reducing it to dry facts that have little interest for students. Trade books can help to remedy this situation. Since a single trade book covers a limited amount of material—a single process, a short time period, or a single individual, for example—it has the room to elaborate on the material and to use detail that brings the situations to life for the readers.

Another problem with textbooks is that, generally, all of the textbooks in a class are on a single reading level. Many students do not have the reading skill to access the information in these texts. Teachers may use alternate textbooks for some of their students, but if such materials are unavailable, teachers can use trade books. Of course, any book intended for use to develop content concepts *must* be examined for accuracy before it is used. Donovan and Smolkin (2002, p. 508) point out that "many books suggested for science instruction deliver incorrect information."

Trade books with various difficulty levels are available for almost any topic in the school curriculum. Some publishers supply information about readability and interest levels of many of the trade books they produce, and teachers can apply readability measures to other books of interest. However, since many factors outside the text itself influence readability, teacher judgment may work as well as a formula in deciding what to use for particular students.

PICTURE BOOKS

What are the benefits of using picture books in secondary content area classes?

Motivation to read is a problem with many students, and trade books often offer more motivation than do textbooks. Danielson (1992) and Johnson-Weber (1989) have found that picture books serve as motivators for reading with junior high students. They also can be used to develop critical thinking skills, to make a connection between reading and writing, and to develop vocabulary, even for high school students. They add spice to content classes. Some picture books that are good for young children, such as *Jumanji* by Chris Van Allsburg (good for inferential reasoning), can be used with secondary students, but there are also some picture books that have themes especially appropriate for older readers, such as *My Hiroshima* by Jinko Morimoto and *Hiroshima No Pika* by Toshi Maruki, both of which make good accompaniments to a study of World War II. These books allow students to apply critical reading skills and serve as stimuli for discussion and writing.

SOCIAL STUDIES

ENGLISH/ LANGUAGE ARTS

Books like Graeme Base's *Animalia* and *The Eleventh Hour* could be used for vocabulary and concept development and for critical thinking, respectively. English teachers might find *A Cache of Jewels*, *Merry-Go-Round*, *Many Luscious Lollipops*, and *Kites Sail High*, all by Ruth Heller, useful when discussing parts of speech, a traditionally low-interest topic for older students. Richard Lederer's *Anguished English* and *More Anguished English* are also good materials for alerting students to such problems as dangling modifiers and words that are not quite appropriate for the context (Nilsen and Nilsen, 1999).

Picture books work well in middle school classrooms partly because the texts are brief, the artwork is appealing, and the language is accessible. They are good to use as parts of thematic units or as prompts for creative writing activities (Miller, 1998). Wordless picture books "have been shown to be valuable for developing reading, writing, and oral language with virtually all students who have the proper guidance and encouragement" (Cassady, 1998, p. 432).

Guided reading of combined text-picture books works well with middle and high school students. Examples of such books that teachers may choose to help students gain more from their reading include Jacqueline Briggs Martin's *Snowflake Bentley* and Peter Sis's *Starry Messenger*. "Picture walks" through the illustrations in such books provide good prereading activities. Students can examine the pictures for themes and details and tie them into prior knowledge through discussion. Instruction related to comprehension of the printed text can follow (Dean and Grierson, 2005).

A relative of picture books is now on the scene in many schools. Many teachers and librarians have come to recognize the value of comics and graphic novels in enticing adolescents to read and for some instructional purposes, as well. Graphic novels are comics in book format. Adaptations of literary classics are available and may be useful to English teachers in teaching literary terms and techniques, although many English teachers feel that use of such adaptations is inappropriate because the students do not get the full impact of the original works. Some graphic novels relate to content classes such as history, art, science, and math, and some relate primarily to English classes. D. Aviva Rothschild's *Graphic Novels: A Bibliographic Guide to Book-Length Novels* reviews over 400 graphic novels (Schwarz, 2002). For example, *Batman* has been used by some in a study of mythology, and Spiegelman's *Maus* has been used in history instruction about the Holocaust. In one special after-school program, conducted at Columbia University, students have been given the opportunity to write and publish their own comics on a variety of issues. Some schools in Maryland are using the comic *Dignifying Science* to study the lives of women scientists (Toppo, 2005).

YOUNG ADULT LITERATURE

Young adult literature selections can be used to introduce students to the various literary genres before more difficult traditional classics are tackled. Joan Lowery Nixon's excellent young adult mysteries can be used to help secondary students become familiar with the mystery genre, for example. Her writing can introduce the students to "the form of the narrative, chapters, rising action, climax, and resolution," as well as "foreshadowing, flashbacks, and point of view" (Pavonetti, 1996, p. 454). She presents a variety of characterizations, from flat to well-rounded ones, typical of the variety that students will encounter later. She thereby allows them to build the needed schemata for the genre (Pavonetti, 1996).

When teaching T. S. Eliot's "The Love Song of J. Alfred Prufrock," Soles (1999) has his English students write "makeover" suggestions to the title character to help

SCIENCE AND HEALTH **SOCIAL STUDIES**

SOCIAL STUDIES **ART**

SCIENCE AND HEALTH **MATHEMATICS**

ENGLISH/ LANGUAGE ARTS

ENGLISH/ LANGUAGE ARTS

ENGLISH/ LANGUAGE ARTS

ENGLISH/
LANGUAGE
ARTS

him acquire self-confidence. The assignment engages the students personally and helps them understand the character and the theme of the poem.

By pairing adolescent novels with adult novels that have related themes, styles, or other literary traits, teachers help students make a step up to more sophisticated reading and learn how to recognize connections between the works. Pairing themes is a good beginning technique. Gallagher (1995) suggests several such pairings, including the teaching of Harper Lee's *To Kill a Mockingbird* along with Nathaniel Hawthorne's *The House of the Seven Gables* for the theme of the power of love and the study of historical settings, and the teaching of S. E. Hinton's *The Outsiders* along with Herman Melville's *Billy Budd* for the theme of loneliness and isolation and the study of character development. Joan Lowery Nixon's *The Name of the Game Was Murder* can be paired with Agatha Christie's *And Then There Were None* (Pavonetti, 1996) to explore the mystery genre. John Steinbeck's *The Grapes of Wrath* can be paired with Karen Hesse's *Out of the Dust* to identify similarities of themes and motifs (Knickerbocker and Rycik, 2002). Han Nolan's *If I Should Die Before I Wake* could be paired with Elie Wiesel's *Night* to help students examine similar struggles of protagonists who face the horrible experiences associated with the Holocaust, and the graphic novel *Maus: A Survivor's Tale* addresses such an experience, as well (Schwarz, 2002).

ENGLISH/
LANGUAGE
ARTS

Young adult literature can also be used to address literacy concerns directly. Jerry Spinelli's *Maniac Magee*, Elizabeth Speare's *Sign of the Beaver*, and Cynthia Voigt's *Dicey's Song* all deal with characters who read well and ones who are struggling to learn to read. Additionally, Brozo and Schmelzer (1997) believe that exposing boys to literature with positive male role models can lead to increased motivation to read and can enhance literacy growth.

Literature can serve other functions, as well. For example, Andrews (1998) feels that literature can increase students' sensitivity to diversity. Landrum (1998/1999; 2001) has compiled annotated bibliographies of novels that feature characters with disabilities and has provided criteria for evaluating novels that feature characters with disabilities. Patricia Hermes's *I Hate Being Gifted* allows students to see problems faced by gifted students.

ENGLISH/   MATHEMATICS
LANGUAGE
ARTS

Schon (1999) has collected lists of young adult books about Latinos/as. Daisey and Jose-Kampfner (2002) encourage the use of biographical storytelling about successful Latinos by language arts and mathematics teachers. Latino students "respond positively to knowledge that is presented in a humanized or story format" (Daisey and Jose-Kampfner, 2002, p. 581). An example of such a biography is that of Cleopatria Martinez, who grew up in a housing project, but earned a Ph.D. in mathematics (Daisey and Jose-Kampfner, 2002). Teachers need to act as cultural mediators when students are reading and discussing multicultural books, or "there is the potential for a pooling of misinformation" (Lehr and Thompson, 2000, p. 484), but Naidoo (1995, p. 16) points out that "[f]or those of us brought up mono-culturally, literature which springs from outside our own boundaries can be a life-line."

Literature must be chosen carefully to meet the needs and abilities of the students. The Newbery Award books are excellent sources of young adult novels that may meet curricular needs. One study showed that the majority of Newbery Award books have secondary readability levels (Leal and Chamberlain-Solecki, 1998), so the frequent use of these books in upper elementary grades does not mean that they are necessarily going to be "easy reading" for secondary students. Teachers should be aware of the varying difficulty levels of the books being used and should offer scaffolding as needed.

Even students who are effective in reading and interpreting literature need to read some relatively easy material with content that is relevant to their daily lives. This reading helps maintain motivation to read (Knickerbocker and Rycik, 2002).

READ-ALOUDS

For what types of materials may teachers best use read-alouds?

Read-alouds by the teacher from literature that would cause reading difficulty for some students can enhance content area studies and can entice students to read other sources. Middle school teachers find value in reading to their students daily (Sharer, Peters, and Lehman, 1995; Albright and Ariail, 2005). Read-alouds can broaden students' horizons, encourage listening skills, model expressive reading, engender pleasure in reading, spark writing and discussion, and invite listeners to read. The National Commission on Reading (Anderson, Hiebert, Scott, and Wilkinson, 1985) encouraged reading aloud to students throughout the grades, including secondary school. Read-alouds may be used to introduce topics, to make situations in texts that students read for themselves more comprehensible, and to show how content area material applies to real life. Read-alouds also serve to introduce students to more types (or genres) of books than they might otherwise encounter. These read-alouds have been found to provide motivation for middle school students and catalysts for their learning.

SOCIAL STUDIES

MATHEMATICS

SCIENCE AND HEALTH

Many award-winning books are related to content area studies, and they make excellent read-aloud choices. Possible choices include picture books that delve into complex issues and newspaper and magazine articles that are related to class content (Albright and Ariail, 2005). High school history students could enjoy an excerpt from Richard Lederer's *Anguished English* (1987, p. 101) that includes these statements: "Ancient Egypt was inhabited by mummies, and they all wrote in hydrolics. They lived in the Sarah Dessert and traveled by Camelot." This book was compiled from parts of essays that students in the United States wrote. *The Phantom Tollbooth* by Norton Juster has a good explanation of infinity that middle school math students may want to use; E. Annie Proulx's *Postcards* has a description of a ground blizzard that could be used in a science class; and Annie Dillard's *Pilgrim at Tinker Creek* has a description of a giant water bug devouring a frog. Christopher Lampton's *Endangered Species* contains a number of sections that make good science read-alouds (Richardson and Breen, 1996).

Teachers must prepare for read-alouds and make their purpose obvious to the students. Material to be read aloud must be previewed to ensure appropriate content and fluent presentation. Teachers can model their thinking processes while reading through think-alouds. They should hold class discussions before, during, and after read-alouds (Albright and Ariail, 2005). Selecting related books for students to read independently can be a good technique (Fisher, Flood, Lapp, and Frey, 2004). Reading aloud to students models fluent reading, exposes students to material that they cannot read themselves, helps increase understanding of content text concepts and reinforce content knowledge, and engages students. Reading aloud from a variety of

What are the advantages of using audiobooks in a secondary school classroom?

types of books helps students make decisions about choices for personal reading (Ivey, 2003).

An extension of the idea of read-alouds is the use of **audiobooks**. Listening to audiobooks can add the dimension of hearing authentic accents, phrasing, and emphasis for characters in stories. Dialects become more manageable than they are on the printed page. Correct pronunciations of proper names are heard. Good timing, emphasis, pause, and stress make humor more understandable for some readers. Poetry can be presented with a model of expert phrasing, accent, rhythm, and pronunciation that can enhance comprehension (Baskin and Harris, 1995). Students, especially those who cannot read at the level necessary to perform adequately in a secondary class, can read along with unabridged, single narrator audiobooks. This can help students sense text subtleties. Such selections as William Golding's *Lord of the Flies* (Listening Library; Greenwich, CT, 1977) and Madeleine L'Engle's *A Wrinkle in Time* (Listening Library; Greenwich, CT, 1993) are available on tapes read by the authors, with accompanying commentary. Abridgments should be used with caution (Baskin and Harris, 1995).

The temptation to ease the reading burden on students by using videos in place of the books from which they were made should be resisted in many cases. Video versions of books often have simplified vocabulary, dialogue, plots, settings, themes, and characterizations. They may sometimes be used, however, to prompt an interest in reading the books. For example, teachers may have students read a book that will soon be released as a video. They may ask students to write and perhaps perform their own screenplays based on these books or to create multimedia presentations based on the literature. After the students see the videos, they can compare the videos with the books or write traditional reviews (Baines, 1996). They could also compare the videos with the screenplays that they wrote.

ENGLISH/
LANGUAGE
ARTS

Literature Instruction

ENGLISH/
LANGUAGE
ARTS

Literature instruction is designed to turn students into lifelong readers who enjoy good literature. Incorporating interesting literary selections into secondary classes helps teachers achieve this goal. These selections may be presented in a literature anthology or as trade books. Students need some direct instruction in literary analysis and guided experiences with reading required literature selections, especially classics that may have unfamiliar settings and characters. Learning about authors also can help students analyze their writing. Good choices may be Walter Dean Myers's *Bad Boy*, Gary Paulsen's *Guts*, and Bruce Brooks's *What Hearts* (Knickerbocker and Rycik, 2002; Ernst-Slavit, Moore, and Maloney, 2002; and Louie, 2005).

MINI-LESSONS

Teachers may teach mini-lessons on literary topics or reading strategies before the students begin reading, if a reading workshop approach is used in which students read, write in response journals, meet in literature circles to discuss their reading, and develop projects from the reading to share with their classmates (Noll, 1994;

McGee and Tompkins, 1995). Modeling a strategy through a think-aloud is a good technique to use for a mini-lesson. When teaching a difficult piece, such as *Romeo and Juliet*, for example, the teacher may use a think-aloud based on the beginning of the work to demonstrate paraphrasing, using background knowledge, predicting, visualizing, and using metacognitive strategies when readers do not understand (Adams, 1995). (Think-alouds are discussed in detail in Chapter 5. Paraphrasing is discussed in Chapter 8, and the other strategies mentioned are covered in Chapters 4 and 5.)

USE OF READING GUIDES

If the selections are related to students' schemata, they will be easier to comprehend. Reading guides, such as anticipation guides and three-level study guides, can help many students comprehend literature selections better. Study guides are described in more detail in Chapter 5.

A three-level guide can be especially useful with literature selections. The guide in Example 9.1 is designed for use with the short story "The Man Without a Country" by Edward Everett Hale.

The main value of reading guides is the discussion that follows their completion. Students should share their answers and their reasons for the answers.

ELECTRONIC DISCUSSIONS

English teachers have found that use of a networked computer lab equipped with collaboration software allows students to discuss literary works by keying in responses to their classmates' comments, using a simple word-processing program. This technique often encourages shy students to respond more. The discussions can be controlled through the choice of questions presented to the students. The discussions work best with only one question per conference. There can be several conferences in a fifty-minute class, covering different questions.

Internet discussion groups that are password protected, to allow only students from designated classes to participate, can also promote writing. Additionally, there are Internet sites where writers can post their work to be critiqued.

E-mail discussions of literature can be shared by placing all students and the teacher on a class mailing list. "Reply to all" responses allow all class members to see the comments made by each individual.

WHOLE-CLASS NOVEL STUDY

What is a social constructivist perspective of learning?

Unrau and Ruddell (1995) present a Text and Classroom Context model "designed with a **social constructivist perspective** of learning in which the teacher fosters a learning environment that engages students in a meaning negotiation process" (p. 21). Meanings evolve from interactions among the reader, the text, the classroom community, the teacher, and the context. Readers must confirm that the constructed interpretations of the text are grounded in the text, reasonably supportable by reference to the content of the text. As Rosenblatt (1983, p. 133) has said, "The process of understanding a work implies a recreation of it, an attempt to grasp completely all

EXAMPLE 9.1   **Three-Level Study Guide**

Directions: Check the statement or statements under each level that answer the question.

Literal—What Did the Author Say About Philip Nolan?

_____ **1.** Philip Nolan said, "I wish I may never hear of the United States again!"

_____ **2.** Philip Nolan never actually met Aaron Burr.

_____ **3.** The court decided that Nolan should never hear the name of the United States again.

_____ **4.** Nolan was placed on board a ship and never allowed to return to the United States.

_____ **5.** Nolan was often permitted to go on shore.

_____ **6.** Nolan did not intentionally make it difficult for the people who were supposed to keep him from knowing about his country.

Interpretive—What Did the Author Mean by His Story?

_____ **1.** Nolan never seriously regretted having denied his country.

_____ **2.** Nolan spoke against his country without realizing how much it had meant to him.

_____ **3.** Nolan never really missed hearing about his country.

Applied—How Can the Meaning Be Applied to Our Lives?

_____ **1.** People should consider the consequences of their actions before they act.

_____ **2.** People can live comfortably away from home.

_____ **3.** Punishment is not always physical; it may be mental.

the sensations and concepts through which the author seeks to convey the qualities of his sense of life. Each of us must make a new synthesis of these elements with his own nature, but it is essential that he assimilate those elements of experience which the author has actually presented."

When applying this model to class study of a novel, the students can first read the novel and then write about it in their learning logs. They can write summaries or interpretations in the logs. Then they can discuss the novel in groups of three. Each member of the group is given a responsibility—recorder, reporter, or prompter (who keeps the group on task). Interpretations voiced during discussion are not seen as final but are revised as the dialogue continues. The text is fixed, but its meanings for readers change over time. Whole-class discussions can follow small-group meetings or can be guided by use of a directed reading-thinking activity (DRTA) or other strategies that encourage individual responses and group sharing (Unrau and Ruddell, 1995). (See Chapter 5 for a discussion of the DRTA.)

LITERATURE RESPONSE GROUPS (LITERATURE CIRCLES)

What are the benefits of literature response groups?

In **literature response groups**, or literature circles, several students who have chosen to read the same novel read a specific number of chapters each week and meet in a group each week to discuss the reading. Students choose novels from several for which the teacher has multiple copies (preferably six to eight copies). Students can indicate their top three choices, and the teacher can form groups to read the top choices, taking preferences into account. Each time the groups complete their novels, new groups may be formed for different selections. Students who did not get their first choices for the first books read should be given preference in getting their first choices for the next books.

As students read, they can make notes on "sticky notes" and place them on the appropriate pages. These notes can be used as a basis for the small-group discussion and for a written response to the reading that the teacher may require them to do either before or after the discussion. These responses can be read aloud as a review to begin the next week's discussion.

Alternatively, students may write responses in reading response journals. They may include changes in a character, things they questioned, things they felt about the characters or the plot, and/or things that they can relate to personal experiences or other books they have read. The teacher can respond to these journals periodically, and the entries can be shared aloud in class and discussed.

The teacher may meet with the groups, or they may meet independently. The teacher should only intervene in the discussion when the students have strayed from the topic or missed important points (Simpson, 1994/1995).

SUSTAINED SILENT READING (SSR)

What are the benefits of sustained silent reading in a content area class?

Readers become more fluent in reading by actually reading. In a **sustained silent reading** (SSR) program, students are given a block of time to read self-selected materials for pleasure. Secondary students may be given from fifteen to thirty minutes to read without interruption and without the threat of testing or reporting that inhibits some readers. The teacher also reads self-selected material during this time. Nobody is allowed to interrupt the reading of the others. Simpson (1994/1995) points out that students can be allowed to discuss the books read during SSR, but we feel that discussion should not be required. Offering students time in class for self-selected reading shows that teachers value it.

READERS' THEATER

Readers' Theater is the expressive interpretation of a story through oral reading by a cast of readers who use a script developed from the story. Different students read characters' dialogue and narration. As a response to a literature selection that is read, small groups or individual students can be asked to prepare Readers' Theater scripts to be performed for the class. If an individual develops the script, he or she can assign classmates to the different parts. If a small group develops the script, the members may perform the reading themselves.

Students who take the parts practice reading their parts until they are reading fluently with good expression. Then they perform the Readers' Theater for the class. The performance consists of sitting or standing before the class and reading the script, as a cast would read a play.

Quinn, Barone, Kearns, Stackhouse, and Zimmerman (2003) found that developing and performing Readers' Theater scripts was motivational for reluctant readers. They expanded the activity to have the students role-play the scripts, and they found that the students were more successful when they acted out the story than when they simply read it.

DIRECTED READING LESSONS

A directed reading lesson such as that in Example 9.2 is another way for teachers to help students read and understand books. Directed reading lessons are discussed in detail in Chapter 5.

EXAMPLE 9.2   Directed Reading Lesson: Literature

Motivation and Building Background
1. Ask the students these questions: Do you know any good ghost stories? Have you ever sat around with a group of friends telling ghost stories? How did you feel later, particularly if you had to go some place alone? You probably felt the way Ichabod Crane felt in this story after he listened to some ghost stories and rode home alone over country roads.
2. Tell the students that the story they are going to read is a ghost story. The characters in this story include a pedagogue; a hero; a ripe, melting, and rosy-cheeked maiden; and a contented farmer. After they read the story, they should try to name each of the characters listed.

Skill Development Activities
3. Have the students match a number of words from the story with their definitions.

Words	Definitions
continual reverie	German soldiers
Hessian troopers	singing of psalms
spectre	constant daydream
psalmody	ghost

Guided Reading
4. Silent—Have the students read the story silently. Tell them to think about these purpose questions as they read: What factors created an atmosphere for the ghost to appear? What happened to Ichabod?

5. Discussion—After the students have read the selection, use these questions for further discussion:
   a. How would you characterize the residents of Sleepy Hollow?
   b. Is the setting important in this story? Why?
   c. Do you think Katrina was really interested in Ichabod? Why?
   d. How are Brom Bones and Ichabod Crane alike? How are they different?
   e. What was the point of view of this story?
   f. Do you agree with the old man about the purpose of this story? What do you think the purpose was?

Follow-Up Activities
6. Have students write a paragraph telling what they would have done if they were Ichabod.
7. Ask students to read another story written by Washington Irving and compare it with "The Legend of Sleepy Hollow."
8. Have students draw a picture of the way they visualize Ichabod.

Activities to Encourage Students' Response to Literature

ENGLISH/
LANGUAGE
ARTS

Whether literature is used as the focus of study in an English class or literature selections are used as tools for study in other content areas, students need to be led to respond to the content of the selections.

WRITTEN RESPONSES

Written responses are valuable tools. Reading response journals, character journals, dialogue journals, learning logs, freewriting in response to reading, paraphrasing and summarizing, and creative responses (e.g., writing letters to story characters or news stories about characters) are all written responses that have been covered in detail in Chapter 8 or in this chapter. Knickerbocker and Rycik (2002) endorse journal writing as a response technique. Lehr and Thompson (2000) suggest the use of assigned journal writing activities (for example, letters supposedly written by a character in the book to someone, explaining the character's problems or feelings). They say that assigned writing "can stimulate children's thinking about characters' problems and themes explored by authors that children might not otherwise consider. Free response will not always get the same results" (p. 488). Assigned writing could be a good way to help students see things from the perspective of others who are different from them in culture, race, age, gender, or some other aspect. Other written responses could include writing letters to the author for clarification of information, comparing and contrasting the work with other works, making timelines for the stories, or mapping the story's literary elements (setting, characters, plot, etc.).

Ollmann (1996) tried seven different reading response formats and found the hexagonal essays, in which the students responded to the literature from the perspectives of the levels of Bloom's Taxonomy, to result in more higher-level thinking. She believed that this was true because it required the students to "summarize the plot, make a personal association with text, analyze the theme, analyze literary techniques, compare and contrast with other literature, and evaluate the work as a whole" (Ollmann, 1996, p. 579).

ORAL RESPONSES

The most valuable oral responses to literature are the small-group and whole-class discussions that have been mentioned repeatedly as important learning tools in the

MEETING THE CHALLENGE

ENGLISH/ LANGUAGE ARTS

As a way to motivate students to read *Macbeth* and build their background for reading it, Cindy McCloud made use of a Readers' Theater activity. Before class, she gave a Readers' Theater script of the witches' scene in Macbeth to a selected group of students, who would take the parts of the witches and Macbeth. These students were asked to practice and polish the reading of their parts. The other students in the class were not told about this activity ahead of time.

When class started, Ms. McCloud told the class to close their eyes. Then she said, "Imagine a fantastical cave filled with fog. In the entrance of the cave you see lights flickering. These lights grow dim and get brighter, then dimmer, then brighter. This piques your curiosity: you must know what these strange lights are. You walk further into the cave and spot three of the strangest looking women you have ever seen. Of course, their very appearance gives you a terrible scare, and you hide behind a rock and peer over it just enough to see what they are doing. These three cloaked, bearded figures are conjuring up a powerful spell."

As the rest of the class continued to imagine the scene, Ms. McCloud cued the designated students to take the parts they had been assigned and begin to read the scene in character. The other students

Visualizing the setting of a story can help build student interest in reading the story.
© Michael Zide

were allowed to open their eyes as the selected students read the scene, acting out the part in which the witches conjure up their potion with appropriate gestures.

This interest-grabbing introduction to the play prepared the students for the subsequent reading. Students who previously had no interest in the play now saw that it had possibilities and were willing to give it a chance.

classroom. Group members share insights that individuals might not achieve alone (Knickerbocker and Rycik, 2002). Another type of oral response is the conversion of the material into a Readers' Theater presentation, with students dividing the material into speaking parts along content or character lines and reading the material orally with good oral expression.

Perhaps the most difficult oral response option is dramatization of the material. This dramatization can range from a spontaneous reenactment of an event or scene, without written script, costumes, properties, scenery, or audience beyond the class members, to a carefully planned presentation, with a student-developed script, memorized lines, costumes, properties, scenery, and an outside audience. Drama can evoke an aesthetic response to the literature. In addition, interpretation of literature is expanded through drama because it takes the students into the events to experience them vicariously. This immersion in the experience helps the students to see the points of view of the people involved in the events (Fennessey, 1995). For example, Leslie Kahn encouraged students to use drama to help them reflect on prejudice expressed in *We Remember the Holocaust* by David Adler (Short, Kauffman, and Kahn, 2000).

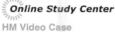

Online Study Center

HM Video Case
Performance Assessment: Student Presentations in a High School English Class

SOCIAL STUDIES

How can you incorporate activities that use multiple intelligences in your content area lessons?

RESPONSES BASED ON MULTIPLE INTELLIGENCES

Glasgow (1996) suggests a series of activities that can be used as responses to adolescent literature that are appropriate for use of Gardner's **multiple intelligences**. Example 9.3 contains a list of these activities. (Note: Whereas Gardner's most recent publications include discussion of nine intelligences, most educators are still focusing primarily on the seven shown here.)

EXAMPLE 9.3   Activities for Adolescent Literature Based on Gardner's Multiple Intelligences

Intelligence	Activities
Musical/rhythmic	Create a radio or TV advertisement for an honor book.
	Compose a rap based on a theme of a historical novel.
	Compose a musical background for the reading of a poem, myth, or folktale.
	Compose the main character's favorite song.
	Compose a poem or song describing the main character of an honor book.
Visual/spatial	Make a collage of the main images in a science fiction book.
	Make a map of the setting for a dystopian or utopian novel.
	Create a model or diorama for the setting of an honor book.
	Market a novel by creating a magazine advertisement.
	Paint the setting or main character of the novel or poem.
	Make a story or character web of a novel.
	Videotape the context for realistic fiction.

Intelligence	Activities
Body/kinesthetic	Compose a dance expressing a theme of an honor book.
	Impersonate a main character from a problem novel.
	Mime a character from a fantasy novel.
	Act out a challenge facing a character in a quest.
	Make puppets and perform a dialogue between two or more characters in a problem-solving situation.
	Create a living sculpture portraying a theme of a book, play, or poem.
Interpersonal	Interview a character or an author of an honor book.
	Prepare dramatic dialogue of two characters in a sports novel.
	Write script and perform Readers Theatre for a fantasy novel.
	Write a collaborative paper discussing the themes and implications of an honor book.
	Keep a dialogue journal with a friend for a problem novel.
	Do choral reading of a dialogue or poem.
Intrapersonal	Keep a reading or process log for an honor book.
	Do reader response activities such as associative recollections; character probes; most important words, passages, and aspects (Milner and Milner, 1993).
	Keep a metacognitive journal of your own reading process.
Logical/ mathematical	Review a book by discussing different categories such as economics, politics, education, lifestyle, and/or religion.
	Create a timeline for a historical fiction book.
	Create a chart pairing a poem with a book, myth, or folktale.
	Map the story structure.
	Create a literature web.
	Write a critical analysis paper.
Verbal/linguistic	Compare and contrast two variants of a folktale.
	Prepare a book review.
	Do a profile of an author.
	Keep a reader response journal.
	Write a formal paper.
	Create a poetry anthology.
	Explicate a poem.

Source: Jacqueline N. Glasgow, "Motivating the Tech Prep Reader Through Learning Styles and Adolescent Literature," *Journal of Adolescent & Adult Literacy* 39(5) (1996, February): 364. Reprinted with permission of Jacqueline N. Glasgow and the International Reading Association. All rights reserved.

Developing Thematic Teaching Units

A **thematic teaching unit** is a series of interrelated lessons or class activities organized around a theme, a literary form, or a skill. Such a unit allows holistic study of the topic. Barton and Smith (2000, p. 59) believe that "teachers should strive to re-create the kinds of situations in which people learn outside of school. . . . Units are most meaningful when they include such authentic activities." Because unit activities are varied in terms of the amount of reading skill and the levels of thinking required to complete them, they offer excellent opportunities to adjust reading assignments to fit all students. Different students may complete different activities, such as reading, listening to, and/or viewing different resource materials, and share the results of these varied activities with their classmates.

Use of teaching units takes a great deal of teacher planning. The teacher must develop objectives for a unit that are in keeping with the overall goals of the class, must decide on skills to be developed, and must plan activities designed to help meet these objectives and to help develop these skills. The students may be involved in deciding on objectives and activities, within the framework of the curriculum requirements. Parents may also become involved in unit activities if teachers send home memos about the themes that the class is studying and suggestions on how the parents can help the learning process by purchasing books related to the themes for their children or by sharing personal knowledge about the topic with their children or with the entire class.

The web shown in Figure 9.1 depicts the parts of a unit graphically. A unit generally involves four basic types of activities:

1. Introduction of the unit

2. Development of the unit

3. Organization of findings

4. Culmination activities

INTRODUCTION OF THE UNIT

The students are introduced to the unit's theme or central idea, the literary form to be explored, or the skills to be developed. Through class discussion and/or pretests, the teacher determines the extent to which the students' backgrounds of experience in the area can contribute to the unit activities. The teacher helps students develop questions that they need to answer about the unit theme. During this discussion, the teacher assists the students in relating the area of study to their own personal experiences or needs. Doing brainstorming or using semantic webs of concepts or terms related to the unit theme may be effective in activating the students' background knowledge and in facilitating the discussion. The teacher may supply motivation for participating in the unit activities by playing tapes, DVDs, or CDs related to the subject.

What is a thematic teaching unit?

What are the steps in creating a thematic unit?

FIGURE 9.1

Unit Development Web

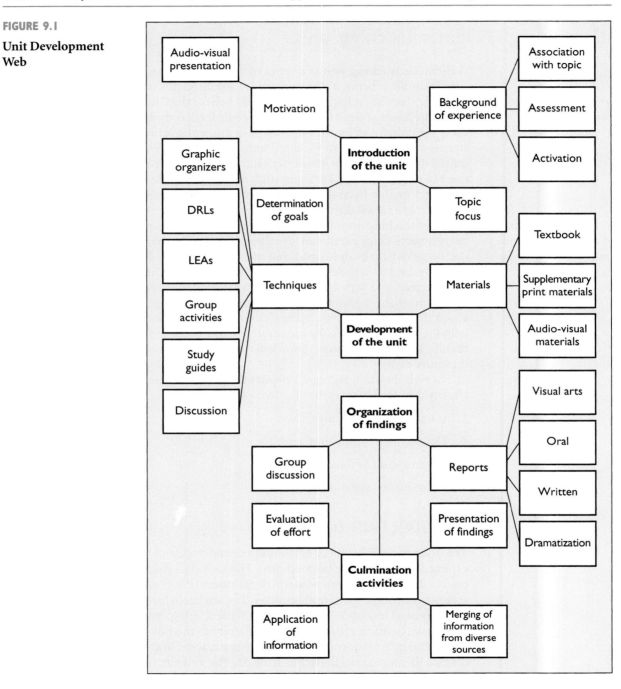

DEVELOPMENT OF THE UNIT

The teacher begins teaching the unit by presenting core instructional material to the whole class. This material will probably consist of the textbook material and supplementary material that the teacher has carefully chosen for those students who cannot benefit from reading the text because of its difficulty level. The teacher may develop directed reading lessons (DRLs) for both the textbook material and the supplementary material.

During the first step of some of the directed reading lessons, the teacher may use structured overviews to develop needed background for reading. Next, using techniques presented in Chapters 3, 4, 5, 6, and 7, he or she may teach needed vocabulary, comprehension, and study strategies and skills that are vital to the understanding of the particular passages involved. As a part of the directed reading lesson, the teacher may guide the actual student reading of the material by means of a study guide. All the students can combine what they have learned through class discussion and language experience activities. The follow-up activities will be included among the independent assignments for different research groups or interest groups formed by the teacher or by student choice after the core material has been read.

After the core instructional presentation, the teacher may either assign areas of concern to the students or allow them to choose areas in which they have a particular interest. Self-selection may have the advantage of providing internal motivation for the unit study.

Students then form several small groups (research groups that may or may not also be interest groups) that attempt to answer specific questions, clarify specific areas of concern, or analyze particular literary works. These research groups may be formed to capitalize on the special abilities of various class members. The teacher may meet with each group to discuss the possible reference sources that are available: textbooks, library books (fiction and nonfiction), encyclopedias, other reference books, magazines, newspapers, original documents, the Internet, CDs, DVDs, videos, and a variety of other audio-visual aids.

Whenever possible, the teacher should choose books that reflect a multicultural environment, and there should be access to large-print books, Braille materials, or audiotapes that cover the class material if there are visually impaired students in the class. Multicultural resources provide the students with a realistic picture of the world at large, even if the cultural diversity within the particular school is narrow, and they allow students whose cultural backgrounds vary from the mainstream culture to feel more comfortable and see how their culture fits into the overall picture. Godina (1996) urges integration of both selections from the traditional canon and multicultural selections into the instructional program. Materials for students with physical disabilities allow these children to participate in unit activities without undue stress and difficulty.

The teacher must be alert to the variety of reading abilities within the group and must make available books and reference aids on a number of different levels. Students then can choose books for their thematic study that are appropriate to their own reading abilities. A review of study skills, such as using the library, using reference books, outlining, taking notes, skimming, and scanning, may be helpful for some members of each research group. (See Chapters 6 and 7 for a discussion of these skills.) In addition, nonprint resources, such as audiotapes, videotapes, CDs, and DVDs may be used for some less able readers.

Each member of each research group is responsible for collecting data. Differentiated assignments within the groups may be developed by the teacher or by group leaders guided by the teacher.

ORGANIZATION OF FINDINGS

The research groups meet after ample time has been allowed for individual members to collect data. Each group then reviews the information collected from the various sources, discusses and attempts to resolve differences of opinion, and forms the findings into a coherent report. The discussion allows the students to share the information they have discovered and to find out what others have learned. The report may be oral or written and may be accompanied by audio-visual aids, such as charts, tables, maps, graphs, pictures, or tapes. It may be in one of a number of forms, including an oral report, a panel discussion, a skit, a more complete dramatization, a mural, or a multimedia computer presentation.

CULMINATION ACTIVITIES

At the end of the unit study, the different research groups present their reports to the whole class. The class critically examines the information that is presented, merges it with the core of information learned from the textbook and supplementary materials, and determines if the purposes of the unit have been met. If the class feels that not all of the original purposes have been met, the members may regroup to finish the task.

The teacher should help the students relate the findings to events in their own lives. An activity that immediately applies the findings to real situations would be beneficial because it would emphasize the relevance of the unit.

Table 9.1 presents the steps in unit development.

TABLE 9.1

Unit Development

Introduction	Development	Organization of Findings	Culmination
1. Build background and motivation 2. Connect unit to students' experiences	1. Core lessons presented through a directed reading approach, use of structured overviews, teaching of needed skills, study guides, language experience approach 2. Research groups 3. Needs groups	1. Discussion 2. Oral or written reports	1. Merging of information from diverse sources 2. Evaluation of effort 3. Application of information

SAMPLE UNIT IDEAS

**ENGLISH/
LANGUAGE
ARTS**

A unit in literature might be developed around a type of literature, such as "Tall Tales of the United States." The opening discussion could include an attempt to define "tall tales" and could provide opportunities for the students to name tall tales with which they are familiar. The teacher might use a video during the introductory stage to clarify the nature of tall tales. Different groups could be formed to read tall tales about different superhuman individuals, for example, Old Stormalong, Paul Bunyan, Mike Fink, and Pecos Bill. Other groups could concentrate on tall tales of other types, such as Washington Irving's "Rip Van Winkle" and "The Legend of Sleepy Hollow" or Mark Twain's "The Celebrated Jumping Frog of Calaveras County." As a culminating activity, each student could write a tall tale of the general type that he or she has read. The tales could be shared in oral or written form with the rest of the class.

**ENGLISH/
LANGUAGE
ARTS**

Meeks (1999) bases activities in a poetry unit for tenth-graders on Brian Cambourne's research about conditions for language learning. First, she immerses her students in poetry by having them read poems and choose favorites to copy for their portfolios and to share with the class on charts. She also shares her favorite poetry and her own poetry and has other teachers share their poetry also. She demonstrates the reading and writing of poetry to the students and then lets the students try. She makes clear her expectations for the students' poetry reading, writing, and collection, but she gives the students the responsibility for choosing group members, poets to study, topics for written assignments, and presentation formats. Students are given opportunities to use their new skills in risk-free ways before assessment— by doing several process-writing drafts, for example. Her students share their poems in real-world situations, such as reading them to senior citizens or posting them on the Internet. She responds to the students' poetry writing by using stickers or by highlighting interesting parts. Students also may respond to one another's work.

**SOCIAL
STUDIES**

Guzzetti, Kowalinski, and McGowan (1992) describe a literature-based unit on China that was used with sixth-graders to develop knowledge in social studies. It included brainstorming and formation of a semantic map of knowledge held about the subject, reading aloud to students from a literature selection, use of literature selections to answer questions about China, construction of question-and-answer books by the students, and activities to encourage reflective thinking. Many of the activities could easily be used in grades seven through twelve, and some of the same literature selections, such as *Dragonwings* by Laurence Yep, could be used, particularly for seventh- and eighth-graders. Other selections could be replaced by ones located through a selection aid such as *Selected Bibliography of Asian-American Literature: Redefining American Literary History* by Amy Ling (New York: MLA, 1990).

**SOCIAL
STUDIES**

The "Meeting the Challenge" vignette in this section includes excerpts from a unit on the Holocaust. The detailed planning that precedes the teaching of this unit makes it likely to be successful with students. Any unit on a content subject needs stated concepts to be learned, resources to be used, and instructional activities that are planned before the unit begins. Other resources and activities may be located and used as a result of student-teacher interactions as the unit progresses. Possible unit resources include textbooks, fiction and nonfiction trade books, electronic media (such as CDs and DVDs), and Internet sites.

SOCIAL STUDIES

All textbook presentations are by necessity brief and overly condensed. Good units provide much supplementary material that fills in gaps and fleshes out the information for students. The "Meeting the Challenge" vignette is part of a unit developed by a student in a graduate-level methods course who realized the limited viewpoint offered to students by a single textbook presentation. This unit originally had additional information for student use and teacher resources, but space does not allow their inclusion. The author of the unit found bountiful reading material that provided high levels of student interest and was pertinent to the topic.

Developing a unit similar to the one in this vignette would be possible in almost any content area. Both nonfiction and fiction trade books are available on a wide variety of subjects. These books can broaden the understanding of unit studies and add an element of student interest not always present when the textbook is the only reading material used. Librarians and media specialists are generally happy to work with classroom teachers in locating appropriate trade books to complement unit studies.

MEETING THE CHALLENGE

SOCIAL STUDIES

In an attempt to incorporate her knowledge of the values of student involvement in learning, multiple readings of various types, and integration of literature into content area study into a practical teaching plan, Jill Ramsey developed a unit plan for the study of the Holocaust.

Literature-Based Unit on the Holocaust

BEGINNING HOLOCAUST STUDIES

OVERALL OBJECTIVES OF THE UNIT

Through the reading of literature related to the Holocaust it is the hope that students:
- Gain an understanding of the concepts of diversity, culture, community, prejudice, and human rights, acting morally, and taking a stand.
- Share a vision of a world where people are embraced for their similarities and appreciated for their differences.
- Gain an understanding of the harm caused by prejudice and an ability to confront prejudice individually and as part of a community.
- Demonstrate an ability to think critically about human behavior.
- Demonstrate a desire to act morally.

PROCEDURES

I.   Literature Books to Be Used:
    A. Read Aloud: *Number the Stars*
    B. Historical fiction: *The Upstairs Room*

     C. Historical nonfiction: *Anne Frank: The Diary of a Young Girl*, *Anne Frank: Beyond the Diary*, *Tell Them We Remember*, *The Hidden Children*, *Surviving Hitler: A Boy in the Nazi Death Camp*

     D. Picture books: *The Butterfly*, *I Never Saw Another Butterfly*, *October '45: Childhood Memories of War*, *The Children of Topaz*, *Terrible Things*

II.   Oral testimony

III. Photographs

IV. PowerPoint presentation

V.   History

     A. Textbooks

     B. Research

     C. Internet sites

     D. Geography

     E. Timelines

VI. Narrow problem/question/issue/project unit

     A. How did children and adolescents make the best of the worst times in the history of mankind? In what ways were they resourceful, creative, and willing to make sacrifices that affected their entire lives?

     B. What happens when prejudice causes people to lose everything that they had, and then to start all over in a new place, where they are still not wanted?

     C. What are the lessons of this horrible time in history called the Holocaust? Why do we study them today?

VII. Connections to the Holocaust

     A. People, regardless of perceived or real differences, are fundamentally alike.

     B. Communities contain the potential for both acceptance and rejection of their members.

     C. Families in communities performed important functions that helped many.

     D. The Holocaust provides a context for exploring the dangers of remaining silent, apathetic, and indifferent in the face of others' oppression.

     E. Students must think about use and abuse of power and the roles and responsibilities of individuals, organizations, and nations when confronted with civil rights violations and/or policies of genocide.

     F. During the Holocaust, people had roles that were assumed or thrust upon them, such as victim, perpetrator, bystander, and rescuer.

     G. Students need to confront prejudice, deal with moral issues, and gain a deeper respect for human decency.

     H. Students can empathize with people who have survived hardship by listening to the stories of those who survived the Holocaust.

     I. Bystanders during the Holocaust closed their hearts and minds to the suffering of others; bystanders exist today; children need to learn values so that they are able to reason morally and take appropriate action; children can learn about the risks and rewards of taking action against injustice.

     J. Knowledge gives children the power to learn from the past and take action in the future.

VIII. Activities
    A. Student self-learning activities
        1. Literature circles
           a. Reading, discussion, journaling, researching
           b. Connecting other curricular areas with centers that incorporate the following: social studies, writing, science, geography, art, and music as appropriate to this subject matter.
    B. Research of a topic
    C. Peer learning activities
        1. Discussion
        2. Creation of timelines, tiles, bulletin boards
        3. Oral history interviews
        4. Use of research materials to locate answers to complex questions
        5. Study pair activities
        6. Small group shared reading/writing
    D. Teacher-directed or teacher-guided activities:
        1. Focus lessons
        2. Read aloud with overheads and text discussion
        3. KWL
        4. Semantic mapping, story mapping, concept maps
        5. Shared writing
        6. Lecture
        7. Shared reading
        8. Discussion

IX. Outcomes
    A. Children learn prejudice early in their lives. But, just as prejudice and hate can be taught, so can the opposite values of tolerance, acceptance, and love. Schools are one of the best hopes for instilling this in young students, reducing the possibility of future genocide.
    B. Children must understand that without knowledge and understanding history does repeat.
    C. Never Again!

X. Additional Ideas for Student Introduction
    A. Use a KWL about what is known about this time in history, and what students want to learn.
    B. Give historical time frame and background information. (Historical background not included for space considerations.)
    C. Begin a double timeline on adding machine tape with historical dates on the top, students to complete literature dates and activities on the bottom. This helps them put their books in accurate time frames of history.
    D. Show what resources may be used as references during readings in literature circles.
    E. Introduce vocabulary for literature of the Holocaust.

BUILDING A CONTEXT TO STUDY THE HOLOCAUST

TERRIBLE THINGS: AN ALLEGORY OF THE HOLOCAUST

OVERVIEW

Terrible Things is an award-winning picture book illustrated with black-and-white drawings. The Terrible Things of the title are never distinctly shown. They always appear as swirling dark clouds that sometimes suggest human shapes and at other times suggest huge, menacing animals.

An allegory is a picture or story that has a meaning beyond the one conveyed in the obvious story line. *Terrible Things* is a good starting point for trying to help students understand what happened during the Holocaust.

Together, read the book *Terrible Things* (try to have copies for at least every two students to share). Suggest that students take turns reading the roles of Little Rabbit, Big Rabbit, and the other animals.

After the class has had a chance to reflect on what they've just read, spend time on the discussion questions.

Then ask students to list on the chalkboard some of the questions Little Rabbit asks about the Terrible Things and the answers Big Rabbit gives.

LITTLE RABBIT'S QUESTIONS

- "Why did the Terrible Things want the birds?"
- "What's wrong with feathers?"
- "But why did the Terrible Things take them away?"
- "Do the Terrible Things want the clearing for themselves?"

BIG RABBIT'S RESPONSES

- "We mustn't ask."
- "The Terrible Things don't need a reason."
- "Be glad it wasn't us."
- "Just mind your own business."
- "We don't want them to get mad at us."

ASK STUDENTS

What is Big Rabbit trying to tell Little Rabbit? Do the answers satisfy Little Rabbit? How can you tell? What answers would you give to Little Rabbit's questions? What other questions would you ask? What does the story imply about non-Jews' reactions to the fate of the Jews and others during the Holocaust?

PROJECTS

Have students work individually or in groups to:
- Retell the story as a poem
- Adapt the story as a play or Readers' Theater.

- Write the next chapter and answer these questions:
- Where does Little Rabbit go?
- How does he "tell other forest creatures"? What happens then?

CLASS DISCUSSION

1. Why do you think the author told the story of the Holocaust in this symbolic way? Who is this story directed to?
2. Why do you think the Terrible Things take away the animals one group at a time?
3. In an allegory, people, places, and events are used as symbols. What can the clearing in the woods stand for? What about the different animals? The Terrible Things?
4. What kinds of excuses do the other animals offer to explain the fate of each group as it is taken away? How do these reactions help the Terrible Things?
5. How are the Terrible Things described? What verbs are used to describe their actions? How do the descriptions affect your feelings about the Terrible Things?
6. During the Holocaust, terrible things were done by real people, people with faces, names, and life histories. Why do you think the author shows the Terrible Things as anonymous?
7. What choices do the animals in the clearing have when the Terrible Things come?
8. What would you say to Big Rabbit's statement, "We are the White Rabbits. It couldn't happen to us"?
9. When the Terrible Things come for the rabbits, what do the rabbits do? What choice does Little Rabbit make? Why? What does this tell you about the Terrible Things?
10. Little Rabbit hopes someone will listen to him. Why might no one listen? Read Martin Niemoller's poem "First They Came for the Jews" and discuss its relationship with *Terrible Things*. (Activity details omitted for length considerations.)

BOOK TALK

GRADE LEVELS: MIDDLE AND HIGH SCHOOL

OBJECTIVES
- To create a journal reflecting upon a Holocaust-themed book.
- To discuss a Holocaust-themed book and a personal response to it with others using e-mail.

MATERIALS
1. sign-up sheet
2. directions worksheet
3. remote class (establish a relationship with a participating remote class prior to initiating the activity)
4. computer(s)
5. class collection of young adult books related to the Holocaust:
   Anne Frank: The Diary of a Young Girl
   Surviving Hitler: A Boy in the Nazi Death Camps

Tell Them We Remember
The Hidden Children
The Upstairs Room
6. paper
7. pens

PROCEDURES

Prior to initiating this activity with your class, establish a relationship with a remote classroom, preferably outside of your school. You may consider posting a message on an Internet message board for teachers interested in being involved in this project.

When you have a partner class established, explain to students that they will be engaged in a unit-long reading/writing project via e-mail, corresponding with a remote classroom. Every student will be paired with a student from the participating class, based on the book they choose to read.

To help students in deciding what books to read, you may wish to bring in the books for a class period and have a book swap. Students sit in a circle and have one minute to glance through the book, look at the cover, and read the back. When you say, "Switch," students pass their books along to the next students, clockwise, and repeat the process until all books have been passed around the circle.

Pass around a sign-up sheet, where students may write their names and the names of the Holocaust books they have chosen to read. E-mail the participating teacher with the list of students and books so that students may be paired.

As students read their selected books, have them keep response journals about what they are reading. Instead of summarizing the material, they are to reflect upon it and relate what they have read to their own lives: Responses might begin with a brief summary, or the statement, "The themes of this book are . . ." but the main portion of the responses states, "This reminded me of a time in my life when . . ." or "These themes are relevant today because . . ."

Students are to write in their journals and correspond with their remote reading partners once a week, sharing portions of their journals, questions they might have, new words, dilemmas, and issues brought up by the novel that left them puzzled. The mission is to create open book talks between the student pairs. E-mail correspondences are to be printed and kept within the journals. These will be collected at the end of the project.

After reading the book, each student is to complete one of the following projects:
- Write a letter through one character's perspective to another character in the book.
- Write a poem based on the book.
- Create a dictionary of terms that would help someone reading this book.
- Write a short story about the Holocaust.
- Write a one-act play based on the book; include appropriate stage directions.
- Any other ideas that are approved by the teacher.
- Students may share their final projects with their e-mail partners as well as with their class.

ASSESSMENT

Evaluation will be based on the students' journals and projects they have completed.

Anne Frank: Beyond the Diary
By Ruud van der Rol and Rian Verhoeven

SUMMARY

This book provides insight into the massive upheaval that tore apart Anne Frank's world. We are shown glimpses of her life before the family went into hiding and get some idea of the influences that formed her strong moral beliefs. We learn of her early childhood and the wretched conditions of the last years of her life, and we even hear testimony of the last persons to see her alive in the Bergen-Belsen concentration camp. The book does this through the use of photographs, maps, illustrations, interviews, historical essays, and most importantly, excerpts from the diary Anne Frank kept while in hiding in the Annex Building.

MATERIALS
Multiple copies of *Anne Frank: Beyond the Diary*

LESSON 1
Assign students to read pages 3–36. Discuss these elements in this section of the book:
• the birthday present
• the move from Frankfurt to Amsterdam
• the map showing where Anne lived during her brief life (pp. 12, 13)
• the segment on Hitler coming to power
• fleeing to another country
• German occupation of the Netherlands

LESSON 2
Assign students to read pages 37–86.
   Activity: The Nazis passed and implemented many anti-Jewish laws such as these— Jews may use only Jewish barbers; Jews must be indoors from 8:00 p.m. to 6:00 a.m., and so on. List at least six of these laws you have read about, pretend these laws were passed against your culture, and explain how the enforcement of such laws would change your life.
   Discuss these elements of the book:
• Dear Kitty
• actual pictures of Anne's diary and house
• deportation of Jews
• street map of Amsterdam
• sister Margot and cutaway view of the house
• going into hiding

LESSON 3
Assign students to read pages 87–107.
   Activity: Discuss with the students the following hypothetical situation: If Anne Frank were alive today and coming to speak to their school or community, what do they think her message would be? Ask the students to create a poster advertising her presentation.

Discuss these elements in this section of the book:
- the diary is left behind
- pictures from the concentration camps
- map of major concentration camps (pp. 91,95), containing information on estimated number of Jews killed in various countries during the war.

LESSON 4

Discuss the quotation from Anne Frank's diary that appears on page 106 of the book: "You've known for a long time that my greatest wish is to become . . . a famous writer" (May 11, 1944).
- How has her wish come true?
- Why is this considered ironic?
- Would her wish have come true if she had lived?
- Why?

LITERATURE-RELATED ACTIVITIES

The following are some suggestions that Jill included for possible literature-related activities. Others have been omitted for space considerations.

1. Read *Number the Stars* by Lois Lowry (Houghton Mifflin Co., 1989).

    In this story, a Christian family in Denmark risks their own lives to save the lives of a Jewish family. Discuss with the students that throughout history, there have been individuals or groups of people who have risked their lives in an effort to save others (e.g., the Underground Railroad to help free slaves in the United States). As a group, select one such effort, research it, and then create a full-page newspaper advertisement to let the world know about it. Finally, compare this effort with the efforts made to save the Jews during World War II.

    In addition to *Number the Stars*, the following books related to the Jewish resistance might be used:
    Rescue: The Story of How Gentiles Saved Jews in the Holocaust by Milton Meltzer (HarperCollins, 1991).
    Raoul Wallenberg by Michael Nicholson and David Winner (Morehouse, 1990).

2. Read some of the poems and share the drawings in *I Never Saw Another Butterfly* by Hana Volavkova (Schocken Books, 1978).

    After students have had the opportunity to peruse the book, ask them to create a poem with an illustration that will pay tribute to the children of Terezin and will demonstrate that they will always be remembered.

3. Read *Tell Them We Remember: The Story of the Holocaust* by Susan D. Bachrach (Little, Brown, and Co., 1994).

    Read the Afterword on page 86. The last paragraph states that the most pressing question on one of the tiles in the Holocaust Memorial Museum in Washington D.C., is "Why?" Discuss the "Why?" with your students—why and how could something as atrocious as the Holocaust happen?

Focus on Struggling Readers

Literature-Based and Thematic Approaches for Struggling Readers

Use of wordless picture books is beneficial in helping struggling readers develop oral and written language skills (Cassady, 1998). Students can discuss the pictures and then write about the content based upon the information that they have gained.

Read-alouds allow struggling readers to be exposed to content from books that are beyond their reading levels. Class discussion of these read-alouds builds background for the struggling readers to use as they read related material. Varied literature selections allow teachers to offer struggling readers trade books on the content topics that are within their reading capabilities. Heterogeneous group discussions let all students share the different content that they have learned from the trade books.

Thematic unit studies generally have hands-on activities, a wide variety of materials, and information sources in addition to print materials. This combination offers struggling readers a number of avenues for learning the content concepts. The activities that do not include reading and writing provide these students with needed background and scaffolding to approach the content reading.

Focus on English Language Learners

Literature-Based and Thematic Approaches for ELLs

When English language learners first begin learning a second language, they learn a great deal from listening to others speak and read aloud (Pinnell and Jaggar, 2003; Fisher, Flood, Lapp, and Frey, 2004).

ELLs learn best through meaningful talk, and literature discussions are good examples of meaningful talk. Listening to tapes of literature selections, viewing videos related to literature, such as *Hamlet* or *Shakespeare in Love;* viewing pictures of historical situations, such as conditions during the 1930s, when *The Grapes of Wrath* is being read; as well as lectures and discussions can help ELLs comprehend literature selections. It is preferable for all of the students to read the same book and discuss sections of the book as they read. Discussions only after an entire book has been read may not work well for these students (Wolfe, 2004).

Wordless picture books can be used as vehicles to develop oral language and writing skills with linguistically and culturally diverse students (Cassady, 1998). Picture books may make some content studies more comprehensible to ELLs (Ernst-Slavit, Moore, and Maloney, 2002). Narrative material is often good for introducing abstract concepts. Informational picture books have provided a good way to introduce content information and expository writing in a secondary English as a Second Language (ESL) classroom (Hadaway and Mundy, 1999).

Anticipation guides as prereading activities (see Chapter 4) let students think about their prior knowledge before reading a selection. Preteaching of vocabulary and use of graphic organizers are also beneficial for these students. Teaching of study skills (see Chapters 6 and 7) is also important.

SOCIAL STUDIES

Including a wide variety of literature from diverse cultures in the secondary school curriculum can help students better understand people from other countries and cultural groups. These books must be chosen carefully to avoid unacceptable use of stereotypes (Nilsson, 2005). Prereading instruction can help students acquire cultural, historical, and political background that affects the actions of characters from other cultures. This instruction may include such activities as participation in simulations and discussions, viewing videos, listening to lectures, and doing Internet research (Louie, 2005). Some cultural groups are represented in fewer books than are others. Hispanic characters, for example, are underrepresented, although books with Hispanic characters are increasing in number (Nilsson, 2005).

Thematic-unit activities offer hands-on activities and resources that do not require reading (videos, CDs, DVDs) to help ELLs develop concepts. These materials also provide preparation for reading content materials.

SUMMARY

Literature is valuable for study in itself and as a tool to enhance learning in other content areas. Teachers can use mini-lessons on reading strategies and literary elements, reading guides, electronic discussions, whole-class novel study, literature response groups, sustained silent reading, and directed reading lessons to help students learn more from and about the literature that they read. Teachers can encourage students to respond to literature through written responses, oral responses, and other responses based on multiple intelligences.

Literature is an extremely important resource in thematic units in the content areas. The topics that are covered briefly in text materials are enlarged upon, and the situations depicted allow the students to experience the material vicariously.

DISCUSSION QUESTIONS

1. How can trade books enhance content area instruction?
2. What are the values of literature response groups?
3. Which instructional techniques seem most useful for your teaching situation?
4. What types of literature could you use in your particular curricular area?

5.   What types of activities could you use in your content area to encourage student response to literature?

6.   How does unit teaching lend itself to differentiation of assignments?

7.   How can struggling readers and English language learners benefit from use of literature and thematic units in content area classes?

ENRICHMENT ACTIVITIES

*1.   Write out a plan for a directed reading lesson for a literature selection that you are currently using. Try it with your students, and report to the class concerning the results.

*2.   Develop a mini-lesson for a reading strategy or literary element. Use a think-aloud as a part of your lesson. Try it with your students, and report to the class concerning the results.

3.   Choose a topic, and locate trade books on a variety of difficulty levels that students could use when studying this topic.

*4.   Plan a unit from your chosen subject area. Try it with students in your class. Decide how you could improve the unit if you were to teach it again.

5.   Develop special literature activities to assist struggling readers and ELLs in learning content concepts.

6.   Choose a short story from a literature textbook. Choose prediction points for the selection that would allow you to use it for a DRTA. Discuss the stopping points that you have chosen with your college classmates.

*These activities are designed for in-service teachers, student teachers, and practicum students.

Chapter 10

Reading in the Content Areas: I

OVERVIEW

Developing the range of literacies that students need to negotiate the demands of content reading is a complex task. Content teachers need to understand the discourse and literacy demands, as well as curriculum goals and expectations of particular content areas, in order to teach strategies that students need to engage with both texts and multimedia materials. Understanding, interpreting, and using knowledge are basic learning processes in content subjects. In this chapter, we focus on techniques for guiding students in reading content and content-related materials in social studies, science, mathematics, English (language arts), and foreign languages.

PURPOSE-SETTING QUESTIONS

As you read this chapter, try to answer these questions:

1. What reading skills facilitate learning in each of these content areas: social studies, science, mathematics, English, and foreign languages?
2. What common writing patterns appear in each of the content areas discussed in this chapter?
3. How are multimedia materials, especially computer-based ones, changing content area studies and teaching in these areas?
4. Why is it important for students to interpret and use knowledge acquired in the content areas?

Introduction to Reading Content Material

"The texts and literate practices of everyday life are changing at an unprecedented and disorienting pace. This applies across a range of contexts" (Luke and Elkins, 1998, p. 4). As content teachers, we need a vision of the types of discourse and knowledge that our students will need in their lives. Instruction can help readers engage and interact with texts and media to comprehend, interpret, and assimilate knowledge into their frameworks of prior knowledge and experience (Unsworth, 1999).

The goals of content reading are different from those for reading literature and from those of elementary school reading instruction. Content textbooks in the secondary school differ from elementary school content textbooks that are written in narrative style rather than the expository style of secondary content textbooks.

In secondary content area reading, students are expected to retain important information. They are expected to understand topics deeply. They are also expected to apply the knowledge they gain (Graves, 1999). Content teachers can work with students as they comprehend nonfiction text. Students can learn to analyze information, synthesize information, and apply information. They can learn to recognize and apply knowledge of the major text structures (Bertelsen and Fischer, 2003/2004). Strategies for improving content learning, such as modeling active learning, using collaborative learning activities, and emphasizing thinking skills and application of knowledge in all types of learning materials, will help content students succeed (Grabe and Grabe, 2001). Research shows that the following are teaching methods and student strategies that teachers find helpful (Barry, 2002):

Teaching methods

Use of visual aids
Use of graphic organizers
Vocabulary activities
Anticipation guides

Student strategies

Note taking
Writing to learn
K-W-L
Summarizing
QAR

Broadening the way literacy is defined is important in content area instruction. New definitions of literacy include determining meaning from any type of representation of meaning presented (Kist, 2002). Video literacy, visual literacy, multimedia literacy, and hypertext literacy are important aspects of learning in all content subjects. The depth and breadth of information available on the Internet are virtually limitless. The comprehension strategies and interpretations that are appropriate for reading printed text (hard copy) are essentially the same for the Internet and many multimedia materials (Schmar-Dobler, 2003). Pailliotet (2001) identified parallel processes between print literacy and media literacy. Kymes (2005) found that use of think-alouds is an excellent teaching strategy for developing students' online comprehension. Students will find the skills of scanning, skimming, summarizing, locating information, brainstorming, and making inferences especially helpful in both content reading and Internet-based study (Tannock, 2002). Technology has a place in content learning in all subject areas.

The Internet provides teachers with a wealth of instructional materials, lesson plans, and teaching strategies. A useful professional site that includes lesson plans and links to other sites is http://eduref.org/cgi-bin/res.cgi/subjects. For example, a mathematics teacher visiting this site could find lesson plans for algebra, geometry, and statistics for various grade levels, while a foreign language teacher could find lesson plans for her students in Spanish, Chinese, French, German, Italian, Japanese, or Latin classes. In addition, this site has links to other sites that are of particular interest to content teachers. The Internet provides access to journals such as *Mathematics Teacher, Science Teacher, Journal of Adolescent & Adult Literacy,* as well as *English Teacher.* These teachers' sites include lesson plans and question-answering services, as well as many professional articles and materials.

ENGLISH/ LANGUAGE ARTS

FOREIGN LANGUAGES

MATHEMATICS

SCIENCE AND HEALTH

Content Area Discourse

Discourse in content textbooks and other sources is written to impart and explain information with patterns of organization that vary from subject to subject. The discourse in textbooks tends to be longer and more laden with facts than that found in magazines, newspapers, journals, and multimedia sources. These articles are usually short and direct, so that readers can read for specific bits of information or pick up a magazine and read an article as time permits, putting it aside when necessary and picking it up again at a later time. The information in these alternative sources tends to be written in short blocks or bulleted lists that many readers today prefer. These content-related materials can be timely and can help to spark students' interest in reading expository materials. Reading these materials in tandem with textbooks often helps prepare and motivate students to read content textbooks.

CRITICAL READING AND CRITICAL LITERACY

The array of content-related multimedia, print sources, and Internet sites requires both teachers and students to analyze the quality and veracity of the content. Readers must consider the sources of all material they read. Even textbooks should be read from a critical stance. For example, a study of secondary social studies textbooks revealed a surprising number of inaccuracies (Grady, 2002). Chapter 5 discusses critical reading and includes critical reading activities.

Critical literacy goes beyond critical reading because it invites readers to ask vital questions about content. These questions are appropriate to printed text literacy and media literacy. Luke (1999) asserted that teaching analytic skills through critical media literacy enabled both students and teachers to develop new strategies for thinking about meaning. Pailliotet (2001) suggests that guided analysis of print and visual information, whether from a content textbook or a television program, fosters student awareness of critical thinking about point of view, organization, fact versus opinion, bias, omission, argument, and rhetorical devices. Such analysis encourages students to think deeply about the subject at hand. Certainly, many secondary students are not ready to discuss all of these dimensions of an assignment at the same time, but they can gradually work through these thinking processes to achieve content goals.

Content Strategies and Assignments

What is the most effective content reading instruction?

SOCIAL STUDIES

The most effective content reading instruction occurs when teachers guide students in learning content concurrently with acquiring reading strategies (Rhoder, 2002). Content teachers have the expertise to identify the important ideas and concepts of the subject matter for the students. When planning lessons, teachers should ask themselves, "What do I want my students to know when they finish this chapter, unit, or lesson?" For example, in a unit or lesson in geography, the content learning objective might be for students to understand how geographic features are formed. A reading objective in this instance would be to recognize and understand sequence. After identifying content objectives, teachers select the learning strategies and materials their students need to achieve those objectives.

To plan content reading instruction, teachers also think through the learning task from the students' perspective, identifying the skills and strategies that will enable them to achieve the objectives, incorporating those strategies into the lesson, and giving students many opportunities to apply the strategies they learn to content materials (Rhoder, 2002). Strategy examples are included in Chapters 4, 5, 6, and 7 as well as this chapter.

Teaching strategies for the broad array of materials used in content reading include prereading strategies, during reading strategies, and after reading strategies that were introduced in Chapters 4 and 5. Writing has proven to be a very helpful process in developing content comprehension. The suggestions in Chapters 8 and 9 will help teachers integrate writing and literature with content learning.

AUTHENTIC READING ASSIGNMENTS

What are authentic reading assignments?

Authentic reading assignments involve activities concerned with actual problems and inquiries or simulations, which may include taking oral histories, solving community problems such as selecting toxic waste sites, or addressing other local political or school problems. These activities lead students into authentic experiences with reading, learning, and the application of ideas. Each section of this chapter introduces purposeful teaching strategies that can be adapted to various types of content, although the space constraints prohibit demonstrating every strategy with each type of content. Students who learn to use these strategies can apply them to printed materials and electronic media in their content studies.

Content Text Structures

Secondary teachers see their disciplines as organized bodies of knowledge with defined methods of inquiry. However, many students do not recognize the connections among the facts and ideas they study. Instead, they attempt to learn each detail or idea as a separate entity. They overlook main ideas and their relationships to details. These students recall content as a series of memorized fragments. The "Meeting the Challenge" vignette illustrates the fallacies in this approach to comprehension. Although this instance occurred in a biology class, it illustrates that students who understand the way knowledge is structured in any subject can better understand it.

MEETING THE CHALLENGE

SCIENCE AND HEALTH

Matthew Smith was a diligent student who read and reread his textbooks until he knew the material thoroughly. However, Matthew encountered a major challenge in tenth-grade biology. First, he found that no amount of rereading made the content sink into his memory. He did not have the time to read and reread his biology text and to read his other assignments as well. At the end of the first grading period, Matthew's grades were on a downward spiral, and he was deeply frustrated.

Matthew made an appointment with his guidance counselor, who set up a three-way conference with Matthew, the biology teacher, and himself. After some discussion, they asked the reading teacher to join them. She asked Matthew to demonstrate his reading and study strategies through a think-aloud and discovered that he was simply reading and rereading each sentence without grasping the overall concept of the unit and the chapter, which in this instance was "Genetics."

The reading teacher arranged four sessions with Matthew. During these sessions he learned how to use the table of contents as an overview and advance organizer. He learned to seek connections among the ideas he was reading and to connect them to his own experiences. Happily, Matthew began to grasp main ideas and supporting details, as well as the connections among ideas and concepts. He became a successful student whose grades improved throughout the school year. He finished the year with a B average in biology.

Professional educators meet to formulate plans for helping to alleviate their students' problems.
Copyright © Elena Rooraid/ Photo Edit

What is the
advantage of learning
to recognize
structures found in
content materials?

Five major patterns or organizational structures occur most frequently in content materials: chronological order, list structure, comparison/contrast, cause-and-effect, and problem-solution. The definition or explanation pattern is another common one. These structures are found in all subjects, sometimes alone, but often in combination. Among these patterns, chronological order and list structure are easiest to learn; therefore, students should examine these first. Identifying these patterns in different subjects helps students achieve broader understanding and gives them a feeling of greater control over complex subject matter. After examining the easier structures, students can move on to the more challenging ones. Instruction about structure should focus on the actual materials students will read in each subject area. A number of strategies have proved successful in developing students' awareness of text patterns including

Providing examples across topics and texts
Relating text patterns to real-life experiences
Having students identify signal words and make notes in the margins
Making visual representations of text patterns
Having students practice writing text patterns

Integrated Curriculum

Online Study Center

HM Video Case
Reading in the Content
Areas: An Interdisciplinary
Unit on the 1920s

TECHNICAL
EDUCATION

SOCIAL
STUDIES

Expanding our understanding of content literacy includes recognizing the literacy demands of an **integrated curriculum**, as well as individual literacy demands.

An integrated curriculum blends subjects together. For instance, math, science, social studies, fine arts, and language arts are sometimes integrated for effective learning. The integration is based on setting curricular priorities in each and finding the overlapping skills, concepts, attitudes, and content. An example of integrated curriculum in a content text is shown in the teachers' edition section in Example 10.1. In it, connections across the curriculum are identified for teachers. In addition, teachers are provided technology resources for the instructional unit. Teachers will also find that the majority of textbook publishers provide additional instructional resources and suggestions through Internet sites. Example 10.2 is a segment of an Internet site that classroom teachers can access. Appropriate sites are also available for students. These sites are updated to include current events and offer related teaching instructions. For example, many Internet sites were updated to provide teaching suggestions when the World Trade Center terrorist attacks occurred.

Teachers' editions for some content textbooks include suggestions for teaching students who are English language learners (ELLs), meeting the needs of gifted and talented students, and helping less proficient readers (Garcia et al., 2001). Teachers can find assistance in meeting the individual needs of content area students on Internet sites such as the *Content Literacy Information Consortium* (CLIC), which was developed by Thomas Estes and Kathie Burgess at the University of Virginia (http://curry.edschool.virginia.edu/curry/centers/clic).

EXAMPLE 10.1   An Integrated Curriculum

SOCIAL STUDIES

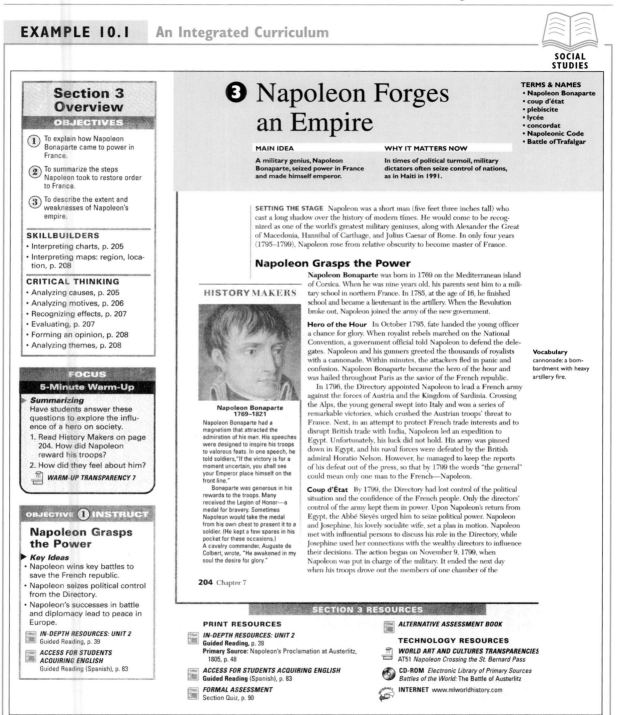

Section 3 Overview

OBJECTIVES

① To explain how Napoleon Bonaparte came to power in France.

② To summarize the steps Napoleon took to restore order to France.

③ To describe the extent and weaknesses of Napoleon's empire.

SKILLBUILDERS

- Interpreting charts, p. 205
- Interpreting maps: region, location, p. 208

CRITICAL THINKING

- Analyzing causes, p. 205
- Analyzing motives, p. 206
- Recognizing effects, p. 207
- Evaluating, p. 207
- Forming an opinion, p. 208
- Analyzing themes, p. 208

FOCUS
5-Minute Warm-Up

▶ **Summarizing**
Have students answer these questions to explore the influence of a hero on society.

1. Read History Makers on page 204. How did Napoleon reward his troops?
2. How did they feel about him?

🏛 *WARM-UP TRANSPARENCY 7*

OBJECTIVE ① INSTRUCT

Napoleon Grasps the Power

▶ **Key Ideas**
- Napoleon wins key battles to save the French republic.
- Napoleon seizes political control from the Directory.
- Napoleon's successes in battle and diplomacy lead to peace in Europe.

📖 *IN-DEPTH RESOURCES: UNIT 2*
Guided Reading, p. 39

📖 *ACCESS FOR STUDENTS ACQUIRING ENGLISH*
Guided Reading (Spanish), p. 83

---

❸ Napoleon Forges an Empire

TERMS & NAMES
- Napoleon Bonaparte
- coup d'état
- plebiscite
- lycée
- concordat
- Napoleonic Code
- Battle of Trafalgar

MAIN IDEA	WHY IT MATTERS NOW
A military genius, Napoleon Bonaparte, seized power in France and made himself emperor.	In times of political turmoil, military dictators often seize control of nations, as in Haiti in 1991.

SETTING THE STAGE Napoleon was a short man (five feet three inches tall) who cast a long shadow over the history of modern times. He would come to be recognized as one of the world's greatest military geniuses, along with Alexander the Great of Macedonia, Hannibal of Carthage, and Julius Caesar of Rome. In only four years (1795–1799), Napoleon rose from relative obscurity to become master of France.

Napoleon Grasps the Power

HISTORY MAKERS

Napoleon Bonaparte was born in 1769 on the Mediterranean island of Corsica. When he was nine years old, his parents sent him to a military school in northern France. In 1785, at the age of 16, he finished school and became a lieutenant in the artillery. When the Revolution broke out, Napoleon joined the army of the new government.

Hero of the Hour In October 1795, fate handed the young officer a chance for glory. When royalist rebels marched on the National Convention, a government official told Napoleon to defend the delegates. Napoleon and his gunners greeted the thousands of royalists with a cannonade. Within minutes, the attackers fled in panic and confusion. Napoleon Bonaparte became the hero of the hour and was hailed throughout Paris as the savior of the French republic.

In 1796, the Directory appointed Napoleon to lead a French army against the forces of Austria and the Kingdom of Sardinia. Crossing the Alps, the young general swept into Italy and won a series of remarkable victories, which crushed the Austrian troops' threat to France. Next, in an attempt to protect French trade interests and to disrupt British trade with India, Napoleon led an expedition to Egypt. Unfortunately, his luck did not hold. His army was pinned down in Egypt, and his naval forces were defeated by the British admiral Horatio Nelson. However, he managed to keep the reports of his defeat out of the press, so that by 1799 the words "the general" could mean only one man to the French—Napoleon.

Coup d'État By 1799, the Directory had lost control of the political situation and the confidence of the French people. Only the directors' control of the army kept them in power. Upon Napoleon's return from Egypt, the Abbé Sieyès urged him to seize political power. Napoleon and Josephine, his lovely socialite wife, set a plan in motion. Napoleon met with influential persons to discuss his role in the Directory, while Josephine used her connections with the wealthy directors to influence their decisions. The action began on November 9, 1799, when Napoleon was put in charge of the military. It ended the next day when his troops drove out the members of one chamber of the

Napoleon Bonaparte
1769–1821

Napoleon Bonaparte had a magnetism that attracted the admiration of his men. His speeches were designed to inspire his troops to valorous feats. In one speech, he told soldiers, "If the victory is for a moment uncertain, you shall see your Emperor place himself on the front line."

Bonaparte was generous in his rewards to the troops. Many received the Legion of Honor—a medal for bravery. Sometimes Napoleon would take the medal from his own chest to present it to a soldier. (He kept a few spares in his pocket for these occasions.) A cavalry commander, Auguste de Colbert, wrote, "He awakened in my soul the desire for glory."

Vocabulary
cannonade: a bombardment with heavy artillery fire.

204 Chapter 7

SECTION 3 RESOURCES

PRINT RESOURCES

📖 *IN-DEPTH RESOURCES: UNIT 2*
Guided Reading, p. 39
Primary Source: Napoleon's Proclamation at Austerlitz, 1805, p. 48

📖 *ACCESS FOR STUDENTS ACQUIRING ENGLISH*
Guided Reading (Spanish), p. 83

📖 *FORMAL ASSESSMENT*
Section Quiz, p. 90

📖 *ALTERNATIVE ASSESSMENT BOOK*

TECHNOLOGY RESOURCES

🏛 *WORLD ART AND CULTURES TRANSPARENCIES*
AT51 Napoleon Crossing the St. Bernard Pass

💿 **CD-ROM** *Electronic Library of Primary Sources*
Battles of the World: The Battle of Austerlitz

🌐 **INTERNET** www.mlworldhistory.com

THINK THROUGH HISTORY
A. Analyzing
Causes For what
reasons was
Napoleon able to
become a dictator?

national legislature. The legislature voted to dissolve the Directory. In its place, the legislature established a group of three consuls, one of whom was Napoleon. Napoleon quickly assumed dictatorial powers as the first consul of the French republic. A sudden seizure of power like Napoleon's is known as a coup—from the French phrase **coup d'état** (KOO day-TAH), or "blow of state."

At the time of Napoleon's coup, France was still at war. In 1799, British diplomats assembled the Second Coalition of anti-French powers—Britain, Austria, and Russia—with the goal of driving Napoleon from power. Once again, Napoleon rode from Paris at the head of his troops. Eventually, as a result of war and diplomacy, all three nations signed peace agreements with France. By 1802, Europe was at peace for the first time in ten years. Napoleon was free to focus his energies on restoring order in France.

Napoleon Rules France

At first, Napoleon pretended to be the constitutionally chosen leader of a free republic. In 1800, a **plebiscite** (PLEHB-ih-SYT), or vote of the people, was held to approve a new constitution, the fourth in eight years. Desperate for strong leadership, the people voted overwhelmingly in favor of the constitution, which gave all real power to Napoleon as first consul.

Restoring Order at Home Under Napoleon, France would have order and stability. He did not try to return the nation to the days of Louis XVI; instead, he kept many of the changes that had come with the Revolution. He supported laws that would both strengthen the central government and achieve some of the goals of the Revolution, such as a stable economy and more equality in taxation.

The first order of business was to get the economy on a solid footing. Napoleon set up an efficient tax-collection system and established a national bank. In addition to assuring the government a steady supply of tax money, these actions promoted sound financial management and better control of the economy.

Napoleon also needed to reduce government corruption and improve the delivery of government services. He dismissed corrupt officials and, in order to provide his government with trained officials, set up **lycées**, or government-run public schools. The students at the lycées included children of ordinary citizens as well as children of

Napoleon Brings Order After the Revolution

	The Economy	Government & Society	Religion
Goals of the Revolution	• Equal taxation • Lower inflation	• Less government corruption • Equal opportunity in government	• Less powerful Catholic Church • Religious tolerance
Napoleon's Actions	• Set up fairer tax code • Set up national bank • Stabilized currency • Gave state loans to businesses	• Appointed officials by merit • Fired corrupt officials • Created lycées • Created code of laws	• Recognized Catholicism as "faith of Frenchmen" • Signed concordat with pope • Retained seized church lands
Results	• Equal taxation • Stable economy	• Honest, competent officials • Equal opportunity in government • Public education	• Religious tolerance • Government control of church lands • Government recognition of church influence

SKILLBUILDER: Interpreting Charts
Napoleon's changes brought France closer to achieving the Revolution's goals.
1. Which goals of the Revolution did Napoleon achieve?
2. If you had been a member of the bourgeoisie in Napoleon's France, would you have been satisfied with the results of Napoleon's actions? Why or why not?

The French Revolution and Napoleon **205**

OBJECTIVE ② INSTRUCT

Napoleon Rules France

▶ **Key Ideas**
• Napoleon gains power; voters approve a fourth constitution.
• Napoleon gives France order and stability.
• The Napoleonic Code establishes a uniform set of laws for France.
• Napoleon crowns himself as emperor of France.

CRITICAL THINKING ACTIVITY
CLASS TIME: 15 MINUTES
Perceiving Cause and Effect Relationships
To help students understand Napoleon's accomplishments, have them make two-column charts in which they list his actions and the benefits of the actions.

Action	Benefit

History from Visuals

Napoleon Brings Order After the Revolution
Interpreting the Chart Show students how to read the chart in multiple ways: read each column to compare Napoleon's actions with the goals of the Revolution, and read each row to get a full overview.

Extension Activity Ask students to think of topics for additional columns they might add to the chart. *Possible Responses: education, land reform, aristocracy*
SKILLBUILDER

Economics Much of France's stability under Napoleon came from economic reforms. Discuss with students the practical meanings of these economic terms used in describing Napoleon's policies: *national bank*, *low inflation*, and *stable currency*.

A *national bank* system allows a central government to regulate banking activities. It eliminates problems that arise when private banks operate independently,

perhaps even issuing their own currencies. When a country has a national bank, people feel more secure about their bank deposits, so that their confidence in the government increases.

Inflation is a general rise in the level of prices. Increases in the prices of food, clothing, and housing are caused by decreases in the value of money. During extreme inflation, for example, a loaf of bread

might cost hundreds of dollars. Low inflation can lead to prosperity and political stability.

A *stabilized currency* results from a national banking system, low inflation, and other factors. Currency that does not change in value quickly and that is backed by a central government contributes to national stability and peace.

EXAMPLE 10.2   McDougal Littell Internet Site

SOCIAL
STUDIES

ART

ENGLISH/
LANGUAGE
ARTS

Creating America
Chapter 6 Links

Interdisciplinary Challenge: Fight for Representative Government!
Posters American Style
Gain inspiration to create your own poster or cartoon from this Smithsonian exhibition of poster art in America. Provides a wonderful selection of posters, as well as an examination of the motives, messages, and processes behind them.

USA Today Snapshot
For great ideas on the creative use of charts and graphs, browse this index of daily "snapshots" posted on the *USA Today* Web site.

Literature Connections: Revolution
Russian Revolution Resources
Collection of links to research materials including primary sources, biographies, and essays

Ireland's Troubled History
This washingtonpost.com special feature provides a thorough introduction to the history of the Irish struggle against British rule; it includes an overview, timeline, key points, Web links, and news

History Workshop: Raise the Liberty Pole
The Continental Colors
Account of the dedication or raising of liberty trees and poles, and images of the first flags flown on the Liberty Pole

"Liberty Tree" by Thomas Paine
The poem "Liberty Tree," written by Thomas Paine, celebrates the struggle against tyranny that the famous meeting spot underneath a large poplar tree came to symbolize

Section 1: Tighter British Control
George III (1760–1820)
Concise biography of George III followed by a guide to his ancestors and offspring

The Stamp Act Riots and Tar and Feathering
Examination of the outraged reaction of colonists to the Stamp Act of 1765

Sons of Liberty: Patriots or Terrorists?
Thoughtful essay that provides details about the formation, purpose, and actions of the Sons of Liberty and examines their legacy from both British and American perspectives

Section 2: Colonial Resistance Grows

Crispus Attucks

Account of the escape from slavery of Crispus Attucks, his subsequent years working as a sailor, and finally his role in the Boston Massacre

The Boston Tea Party

Overview of the Boston and the Edenton Ladies' Tea Parties, accompanied by an audio/video clip of scholar Pauline Majer describing the event

The Committee of Correspondence: Moving Towards Independence

Detailed essay on the formation, key figures, and impact of the Committee of Correspondence

Section 3: The Road to Lexington and Concord

The Intolerable Acts, 1774

Excerpts from the five acts, collectively known as the Intolerable Acts, designed to bring the colonies back into submission of the British King

MUSIC

Loyalist, British Songs & Poetry of the American Revolution

Complete text of twelve songs expressing Loyalist sentiments, followed by links to resources about Loyalist groups and to primary source documents such as protests against Thomas Paine's *Common Sense*

Paul Revere Biography

Information about Revere's life, times, work, and, of course, the Midnight Ride

Section 4: Declaring Independence

Abigail Adams

A look at the life of Abigail Adams—her girlhood, education, marriage, support of the Revolution, accomplished letter writing, and stance for the rights of women

The Second Continental Congress

Account of the conditions surrounding the formation of the Second Continental Congress, accompanied by an audio/video clip of scholar Richard Norton Smith speaking about George Washington and the Continental Congress

Declaring Independence: Drafting the Documents

Background information about the Declaration of Independence and a chronology of the events surrounding its writing, with links to the complete text of the document and to related sites

Social Studies Content

Social studies classes encompass many academic disciplines, including history, anthropology, geography, economics, political science, psychology, philosophy, and sociology. Recently, multicultural education has become an overarching theme in curriculum development. The primary objective of multicultural education is to help all students reach their potential through exploring cultural pluralism. Students learn that each culture has contributed to the culture of the United States. The Internet is an excellent source of materials for cultural studies. Internet sites such as Global Classroom and the Webquest Page will help you integrate the Web with content texts.

CRITICAL THINKING IN SOCIAL STUDIES

Why should students think critically in social studies?

Critical thinking has particular significance in the social sciences because understanding cause-and-effect relationships, distinguishing fact from opinion, separating relevant information from irrelevant information, and identifying and evaluating propaganda are essential skills for learning social studies. At the center of critical thinking is the understanding that we receive a limited amount of information about a particular event from one source (Cioffi, 1992); that is, content is presented from a particular point of view. For example, consider the terrorist attacks on the World Trade Center in New York and the Pentagon in Washington, D.C., on September 11, 2001, and think of the different perspectives of victims, victims' families, firefighters, police officers, Americans of the Muslim faith, and Arabs living in this country. These people no doubt shared feelings of horror, but each had different perspectives on the disaster. When learning about unfamiliar cultures, students need schemata that enable them to understand human behaviors outside of their experiences. Teachers find that anticipation guides, study guides, and advance organizers enhance critical thinking.

Comprehension of social studies content is enhanced when readers are prepared to

1. understand the ideas and viewpoints of others

2. acquire and retain a body of relevant concepts and information

3. think critically and creatively, thus developing new attitudes and values and the ability to make decisions

4. consult a variety of sources to develop more than one perspective regarding a topic

5. read critically about what has happened and why these events occurred

Social studies materials are written in a precise, factual, expository style that presents comprehension problems for a significant proportion of students. However, a student must comprehend 75 percent of the ideas and 90 percent of the vocabulary of

a selection in order to learn effectively from these materials. Through activities like those described in Chapter 3 and the activities that follow, word meanings are reinforced, and recall is enhanced. Beck and others (1991) found that revising social studies textbooks to reflect readers' cognitive processing increased their comprehensibility.

Study guides are maps to cognitive processing. A study guide may cover a chapter, a larger unit, a part of a chapter, or multiple materials on a topic. Students should have the study guide prior to reading an assignment, so they can reflect about the content while they read. Students should be encouraged to read critically in order to accomplish this. Example 10.3 illustrates a social studies study guide.

What is a concept guide?

A **concept guide** is a form of study guide that is concerned with developing students' understanding of an important content concept. Concept guides may be developed in a number of different ways. Example 10.4 is a concept guide based on a government text chapter on civil rights. A student would complete this guide after reading the chapter. Concept guides are also discussed in Chapter 3.

EXAMPLE 10.3   Social Studies Study Guide

SOCIAL STUDIES

Directions: Pay attention to the terms in Column A—they are important for understanding of this selection. After reading the selection, draw a line from the term in Column A to its meaning in Column B.

Column A	Column B
trade association	An organization designed to advance economic, social action, action, or other concerns of their members.
interest group	An organization of competing companies in one industry that sets industry standards and influences policies.
gross national product	The value of goods and services produced by a country for a given year.

Comprehension

Directions: Write short answers to the following questions:
1. What do economic interest groups try to influence?
2. What are four major categories of economic interest groups?
3. Why do economic interest groups focus on the government?
4. How do interest groups affect your life?
5. What are the positive qualities and the negative qualities of interest groups?

Directions: Write a short essay to answer this question:
6. What do interest groups for dentists and clothing manufacturers have in common?

EXAMPLE 10.4   Social Studies Concept Guide

SOCIAL STUDIES

Directions: Write a + before each term that is associated with civil rights, according to the information in your social studies textbook. Write a − before each word that is unrelated to the concept of civil rights. Be prepared to explain and support your answers by using your textbook.

_____	restrictive covenant	_____	affirmative action
_____	treason	_____	equality
_____	reverse discrimination	_____	private education
_____	segregation	_____	equal opportunity
_____	integration	_____	people's vote
_____	suspect classification	_____	open housing
_____	socialist government	_____	goods and services

WRITING PATTERNS

SOCIAL STUDIES

Social studies materials are dense with ideas and facts, but they are organized around writing patterns that help readers understand the cognitive relationships of key ideas, concepts, and information. When students recognize these patterns, they are better prepared to comprehend social studies content.

Cause-and-Effect Pattern

Why is the cause-and-effect writing pattern common in social studies?

Each area of social studies is concerned with chains of causes and effects: one cause results in certain effects that become causes of other effects. The passage in Example 10.5 is written in the **cause-and-effect writing pattern**.

Definition or Explanation Pattern

How is the definition or explanation writing pattern an example of main ideas and supporting details?

The **definition or explanation pattern** is used to define or explain important concepts. The concept is the main idea, and the supporting details constitute the elements of the definition or explanation. To comprehend this pattern of writing, the student must identify both the concept and the author's definition or explanation. This pattern is important to the reader because the knowledge included in the definition or explanation frequently serves as a basis for learning subsequent information on the topic. This pattern is illustrated in Example 10.6.

Chronological Order (Time Order) Pattern

In the **chronological order pattern**, events are arranged in order of occurrence. The teacher can help students develop a concept of time periods by having them

EXAMPLE 10.5   Cause-and-Effect Pattern (Social Studies)

SOCIAL
STUDIES

Technology Changes Life

World War I quickened the pace of invention. During the war, scientists developed new drugs and medical treatments that helped millions of people in the postwar years. The war's technological advances were put to use to improve transportation and communication after the war.

The Automobile Alters Society

The automobile benefited from a host of wartime innovations and improvements—electric starters, air-filled tires, and more powerful engines. Cars no longer looked like boxes on wheels. They were sleek and brightly polished, complete with headlights and chrome-plated bumpers. In prewar Britain, autos were owned exclusively by the rich. British factories produced 34,000 autos in 1913. After the war, prices dropped, and the middle class could afford cars. In 1923 the number of autos built in Britain had almost tripled. By 1937, the British were producing 511,000 autos a year.

Increased auto use by the average family led to lifestyle changes. More people traveled for pleasure. In Europe and the United States, new businesses, from motor hotels to vacation campgrounds, opened to serve the mobile tourist. The auto also affected where people lived and worked. People moved to suburbs and commuted to work.

Source: Roger B. Beck, Linda Black, Larry S. Krieger, Phillip Naylor, and Dahia Ibo Shabaka, *Modern World History*, page 418. Copyright © 1999 by McDougal Littell Inc., a division of Houghton Mifflin Company. All rights reserved. Reprinted by permission of McDougal Littell Inc., a division of Houghton Mifflin Company.

EXAMPLE 10.6   Definition or Explanation Pattern (Social Studies)

SOCIAL
STUDIES

Mining in the West

In 1859, gold and silver strikes drew fortune seekers to Colorado and Nevada. As many as 100,000 miners raced to the Rocky Mountains in Colorado after gold was discovered near Pikes Peak. Also in 1859, prospectors hit "pay dirt" at the Comstock Lode in western Nevada. (A lode is a deposit of a valuable mineral buried in layers of rock.) From 1859 to 1880, the Comstock mine produced some $300 million in silver and gold.

Nearby Virginia City, Nevada, became a **boomtown,** a town that has a sudden burst of economic or population growth. Population jumped from 3,000 in the 1860s to over 20,000 in the 1870s. The writer Samuel Clemens, better known as Mark Twain, captured the excitement of life there.

Source: Jesus Garcia, Donna M. Ogle, C. Frederick Risinger, Joyce Stevos, and Winthrop D. Jordan, *Creating America: A History of the United States.* Copyright © 2001 by McDougal Littell Inc., a division of Houghton Mifflin Company, p. 558. All rights reserved. Reprinted by permission of McDougal Littell Inc., a division of Houghton Mifflin Company.

What social studies writing pattern is developed through relating historical events to the reader's life?

consider time in relation to their own lives. Understanding time is necessary for comprehending social studies material, but reflecting on what one has read is more valuable than memorizing dates. Indefinite time references, such as "in the early days" or "in ancient times," may confuse readers; therefore, the teacher needs to clarify these terms. The chronological order pattern is presented in Example 10.7.

The teacher can relate a time sequence to a student's own experience with time and can help the student develop a concept of the past, present, and future. The student can relate historic occurrences to his or her own lifetime and the lifetimes of his or her parents and ancestors. For example, the Vietnam War probably occurred in the lifetime of the grandparents of present-day students.

EXAMPLE 10.7   Chronological Order or Time Order Pattern (Social Studies)

SOCIAL
STUDIES

Remaining Neutral

Britain made it hard for the United States to remain neutral. Late in 1792, the British began seizing the cargoes of American ships carrying goods from the French West Indies.

Washington sent Chief Justice John Jay to England for talks about the seizure of U.S. ships. Jay also hoped to persuade the British to give up their forts on the Northwest frontier. During the talks in 1794, news came of the U.S. victory at the Battle of Fallen Timbers. Fearing another entanglement, the British agreed to leave the Ohio Valley by 1796. In **Jay's Treaty,** the British also agreed to pay damages for U.S. vessels they had seized. Jay failed, however, to open up the profitable British West Indies trade to Americans. Because of this, Jay's Treaty was unpopular.

Like Jay, Thomas Pinckney helped the United States reduce tensions along the frontier. In 1795, **Pinckney's Treaty** with Spain gave Americans the right to travel freely on the Mississippi River. It also gave them the right to store goods at the port of New Orleans without paying customs duties. In addition, Spain accepted the 31st parallel as the northern boundary of Florida and the southern boundary of the United States.

Meanwhile, more American settlers moved west. As you will read in the next sections, change was coming back east as Washington stepped down.

Source: Jesus Garcia, Donna M. Ogle, C. Frederick Risinger, Joyce Stevos, and Winthrop D. Jordan, *Creating America: A History of the United States.* Copyright © 2001 by McDougal Littell Inc., a division of Houghton Mifflin Company, p. 302. All rights reserved. Reprinted by permission of McDougal Littell Inc., a division of Houghton Mifflin Company.

Comparison and/or Contrast Pattern

When using the **comparison and/or contrast pattern**, an author explains social studies ideas by using likenesses and differences to develop understanding. Example 10.8 shows this writing pattern.

EXAMPLE 10.8   Comparison and/or Contrast Pattern (Social Studies)

America's History Makers

John D. Rockefeller 1839–1937

John D. Rockefeller was born to a poor family in upstate New York. From his mother, he learned the habit of frugality—he avoided unnecessary spending. "Willful waste makes woeful want" was a saying that Rockefeller's mother passed down to him.

By 1897, he had made millions and millions of dollars. Instead of keeping all that vast fortune for himself and his family, he spent the rest of his life donating money to several worthy causes.

Andrew Carnegie 1835–1919

When Andrew Carnegie was 12, he and his family moved from Scotland to Pennsylvania. Carnegie's first job was in a cotton mill.

Later he worked in a telegraph office. There he was noticed by a railroad superintendent, who hired Carnegie as his assistant. Carnegie learned not only about running a big business but also about investing money. Eventually, he quit to start his own business.

Despite his fortune, Carnegie once wrote that none of his earnings gave him as much happiness as his first week's pay.

SOCIAL STUDIES

Compare the characters of Rockefeller and Carnegie. What do you think made each of them successful?

Source: Jesus Garcia, Donna M. Ogle, C. Frederick Risinger, Joyce Stevos, and Winthrop D. Jordan, *Creating America: A History of the United States.* Copyright © 2001 by McDougal Littell Inc., a division of Houghton Mifflin Company, p. 595. All rights reserved. Reprinted by permission of McDougal Littell Inc., a division of Houghton Mifflin Company.

The teacher and students may develop a chart to show comparisons and/or contrasts. The following chart is based on Example 10.8.

Comparison Chart for Social Studies

John D. Rockefeller	*Andrew Carnegie*
Poor parents	Poor in youth
Born in U.S.	Born in Scotland
Frugal	Hardworking
Made millions of dollars	Learned to run a business and to invest and made a fortune

Question-and-Answer Pattern

Authors sometimes use a **question-and-answer pattern** to organize social studies materials. In this pattern, the author asks a question and then answers it. Readers should be able to recall the author's questions and identify his or her answers. Example 10.9 illustrates this style of writing.

EXAMPLE 10.9   *Question-and-Answer Writing Pattern (Social Studies)*

SOCIAL
STUDIES

Slaves Ride the Underground Railroad

Antislavery forces did more than protect and rescue runaway slaves. In fact, they helped many slaves escape. A secret network known as the **Underground Railroad** guided some 100,000 fugitive slaves to freedom between 1780 and 1865.

What was the Underground Railroad? It was not a railroad, and it did not move underground. The Underground Railroad was a complex system of about 3,000 people—both blacks and whites—who helped transport escaped slaves. Under the cover of night, "conductors" led runaways to freedom, providing food and safe hiding places. They risked great danger in aiding slaves.

Source: Beverly J. Armento, Gary B. Nash, Christopher L. Salter, and Karen K. Wixson, *A More Perfect Union*, p. 333. Copyright © 1993 Houghton Mifflin Company. Reprinted by permission of Houghton Mifflin Company. All rights reserved.

Exercises

1. Give the students practice exercises such as the following one to enhance learning in social studies: from the list of words and phrases below, choose a word or phrase that is associated with each of the terms in the word list.

   Words and Phrases

   rules of conduct   control behavior
   power to interpret and apply law   self-government
   people's vote   rights of the people

   Word List

   1. jurisdiction   3. autonomy
   2. plebiscite   4. civil rights

2. An activity called "Possible Sentences" encourages students to learn word meanings and to predict ideas they will encounter when reading content (Tierney, Readence, and Dishner, 1990). For this activity, use the following steps:
   a. Identify important vocabulary in the reading selection and write the words on the chalkboard. Pronounce each word as you write it. The words below

are taken from a social studies text chapter that discusses democracy and socialism.

democracy   civil rights
socialism   laws

b. Ask each student to construct sentences using at least two of the words. Record these sentences on the chalkboard, underlining the important words. Continue eliciting sentences from the students as long as the sentences are creating new contexts.

In a <u>democracy</u>, <u>laws</u> are made by elected officials.

c. Have students read their textbooks to verify the accuracy of the sentences they constructed.
d. After they read the text, have the students evaluate each sentence using the text as a reference. Students may also use glossaries, dictionaries, and thesauruses. Have students modify the sentences if necessary.

3. The List-Group-Label lesson uses categorization to help students develop and refine concepts. This activity also encourages students to relate content to past experiences. It includes the following steps:
   a. Give students a topic drawn from the materials they are studying. An appropriate topic could be "The Geography of Georgia."
   b. Have students develop a list of words or expressions they associate with the topic. Record these words on the board until the list totals approximately twenty-five words.

Appalachian Mountains	Blue Ridge Mountains	Stone Mountain
Peanuts	Savannah River	
Altamaha River	Cotton	

   c. Have students group words from the large list, providing a label for each group.

Mountains	*Waterways*	*Products*
Blue Ridge Mountains	Savannah River	Peanuts
Stone Mountain	Altamaha River	Cotton
Appalachian Mountains		

4. Critical reading in social studies materials can be guided with questions like these:
   a. What was the author's purpose in writing this selection?
   b. Is the author knowledgeable and current about the subject?
   c. Is the author biased in his or her presentation? Why do you think so? An author's biases are likely to appear when causes of events are explained. The author's point of view may be affected by factors such as his or her age, nationality, religion, political views, race, family history, sex, and audience for the writing.
   d. Is the material well written and interesting?
   e. Does the author employ propaganda? If so, does the propaganda influence you?
   f. Does the author imply anything that is not directly stated? What is implied? What does the author say that leads you to this conclusion? (Hickey, 1990).

5. Technology, literature, newspapers, magazines, and field trips to museums and exhibits provide students with experiences to help build understandings of people, places, and events.

   a. A textbook chapter or unit on the western migration could be explored with a software program such as *Oregon Trail* (Riverdeep). This classic pioneer simulation software lets students experience history as they play the roles of emigrants traveling by covered wagon to Oregon and California on the Overland trails. Literature such as *Pioneer Women: The Lives of Women on the Frontier* (Peavy and Smith, 1996) and the *Western Historical Quarterly* would enrich this study. Copies of original documents and newspapers can be obtained from state historical societies.

   b. To study Vietnam, teachers could use software such as Passage to Vietnam (Against All Odds Prod.), a stunningly beautiful and very informative journey through Vietnam that could be used in conjunction with *Vietnam: Why We Fought—An Illustrated History* (Hoobler and Hoobler, 1990), *Portrait of a Tragedy: America and the Vietnam War* (Warren, 1990), and *Fallen Angels* (Myers, 1988). Newspapers from this period are available in most public libraries or in newspaper archives.

   c. The Internet enables students to visit national parks vicariously and see sites within the parks, which helps students develop geographic concepts.

Science and Health Content

SCIENCE AND HEALTH

The language of science is a unique hybrid (Lemke, 2004). There are at least four levels of science writing that require different reading approaches: (1) articles in the popular press (newspapers and magazines), (2) articles in popular scientific journals (for example, *Scientific American*), (3) science textbooks, and (4) articles in scientific research journals. Textbooks may include a wide spectrum of writing that ranges in style from popular articles to research papers. In a National Science Foundation study of textbooks, investigators found that textbooks often presented out-of-context facts. Moreover, popular texts failed to show the interrelationships and concepts students needed. These findings are cause for concern (Roseman, 1999).

The thesis that scientific language is a unique hybrid is supported by Lemke's examination of science texts (2004). He found diagrams included in footnotes and lengthy and complex research reports accompanied by complex diagrams. Experimental reports were presented in graphs and tables, but the written text referred to and commented on the information without explaining it. Mathematical material was not always explained in the language of the text.

Lemke (2004) videotaped one student during his chemistry lesson and found that the student had to interpret the following:

- A stream of rapid verbal English from his teacher
- Text and layout information presented on an overhead transparency
- Text, layout, diagrams, chemical symbols, and mathematical formulas in the open textbook in front of him

MATHEMATICS

- The display on his hand-held calculator
- Text, layout, diagrams, symbolic notations, and mathematics in his personal notebook
- The teacher's gestures, blackboard diagrams, and writing
- The actions and speech of other students, including their manipulation of demonstration apparatus
- The running commentary of his next-seat neighbor

The process for reading a science text is the same as that used by professional scientists for reading research articles. Readers of scientific texts must follow scientific thinking, the terse scientific writing style, and the dense content. They have to read slowly and more than once, with pencil and paper in hand, considering each new idea.

SCIENCE AND HEALTH

Written materials in health are similar to scientific materials and include a similar range of writing. Therefore, the same strategies will help students understand health materials. Health has become an important field of study as people take more responsibility for their own health and well-being. Health education seeks to help students understand both their physical bodies and their emotional growth and development.

In the past, 90 percent of science teachers relied on textbooks to convey scientific content (Lloyd and Mitchell, 1989); however, today's teachers create hands-on experiences and have students conduct experiments that illustrate the importance of science in daily life. The Internet provides access to up-to-date scientific content. The emphasis on authentic learning experiences increases students' need for interactive reading, which means they should relate questions, experiments, and problem solving to the text. Science students need study guides and strategies that will help them perceive connections and relationships. The following strategies and activities will help teachers develop students' understanding of scientific reading and writing.

Scientific terminology can be developed using the Frayer Model, which was introduced in Chapter 3. Example 10.10 illustrates this strategy.

WRITING PATTERNS

The main ideas and supporting details in scientific materials are frequently organized into classification patterns, definitions or explanations of technical processes, cause-and-effect patterns, and problem-solution patterns. Other patterns used to structure scientific content are the experimental pattern and the comparison pattern. These patterns and related strategies are illustrated in the following section.

Classification Pattern

How is information arranged in the classification pattern?

In the **classification pattern**, information is ordered under common headings and subheadings. The information sorted in this way may relate to living things, objects, or general ideas. This pattern is a type of outlining that shows a classification, the distinguishing characteristics of the members of the class, and examples (see Example 10.11). The classification represents a main idea, and the distinguishing characteristics and examples are treated as details.

EXAMPLE 10.10   Frayer Model Activity

SCIENCE AND
HEALTH

Concept: Adaptation

Essential Attributes
1. Improves chance of survival
2. Improves genetic selection

Nonessential Attributes
1. Seasonal changes
2. Changes that do not contribute to survival

Examples
1. Front legs of mole
2. Walrus tusks
3. Beak of black skimmer

Nonexamples
1. Albinism
2. Human beings with six fingers

EXAMPLE 10.11   Classification Pattern (Science)

SCIENCE AND
HEALTH

The Geologic Timetable

A geologist studying the rocks in a particular area can use the rules discussed in Topic 2 to determine the relative ages of the rocks in that area. If these rocks can be matched with the rocks in another area, their relative ages can also be determined. By matching rocks over large areas, geologists have determined the relative ages of most of the rocks on Earth's surface. Over many years, geologists have worked out a timetable that subdivides geologic time into units based on the formation of certain rocks.

The **geologic timetable,** shown in Figure 32.3 on pages 600–601, is a summary of the major events of Earth's history preserved in the rock record. Fossils are an important part of that history. In fact, many of the rock layers have been identified and matched based on the fossils in them.

The longest segments of geologic time are called **eras.** The oldest era is the **Archean** Era. The Archean Era began when Earth was formed between 4 and 5 billion years ago. The earliest known rocks formed during the Archean Era.

The **Proterozoic** Era began about 2.5 billion years ago. The difference between Archean and Proterozoic rocks is that Proterozoic rocks contain fossils of simple plants and worms that lived in the oceans. No evidence of life on land has been found in Proterozoic rocks.

The **Paleozoic** Era is marked by a more abundant fossil record. The rocks formed during the Paleozoic Era contain fossils of both land and ocean plants and animals. The Paleozoic Era began about 570 million years ago.

The **Mesozoic** Era began about 250 million years ago. Dinosaurs thrived during most of Mesozoic time.

Source: From *Earth Science* by Nancy Spaulding and Samuel Namowitz. Copyright © 2003 by McDougal Littell Inc., a division of Houghton Mifflin Company. All rights reserved. Reprinted by permission of McDougal Littell Inc., a division of Houghton Mifflin Company.

Outline of Example 10.11

I. The Geologic Timetable

    A. Major events of Earth's history

        1. As preserved in the rock record

        2. As preserved in fossils

    B. The longest segments of geologic time are eras.

        1. Archean Era

        2. Proterozoic Era

        3. Paleozoic Era

        4. Mesozoic Era

Definition or Explanation Pattern

SCIENCE AND HEALTH

The definition or explanation pattern occurs frequently in scientific content and health-related materials (see Example 10.12). This pattern may explain processes that are biological (the digestive process) or mechanical (the operation of an engine). It also may provide definitions for scientific terms, such as *atmosphere*. Diagrams often accompany this kind of pattern, so the reader must integrate written content information with the diagrams.

Exercises to help students comprehend the explanation of a process follow:

1. Have students attempt to restate an explanation in their own words.

2. Have students reread the explanation to check their comprehension.

3. Have students study the sequence of steps in a process and attempt to explain the process by recalling the steps in sequence.

4. Mask the labels in a diagram that accompanies a process explanation, and have students insert appropriate labels.

Cause-and-Effect Pattern

SCIENCE AND HEALTH

The cause-and-effect pattern often occurs in scientific or health-related materials. Example 10.13 shows the cause and effect pattern. Study guides can be developed to help students read this pattern. Example 10.14 presents a study guide in the form of a cause-and-effect map built on an earth science text passage.

EXAMPLE 10.12   Explanation Pattern (Science)

SCIENCE AND HEALTH

Magnetism

Some igneous rocks contain minerals that are magnetic. These minerals provide a record of the direction of Earth's magnetic poles at the time the rock formed. When this record was studied in igneous rocks on the continents, it was discovered that Earth's crust has apparently shifted or drifted since the rocks were formed. There is also evidence that Earth's magnetic poles had often been reversed. The present north magnetic pole became the south magnetic pole and the present south magnetic pole became the north magnetic pole. Scientists found that there have been four major periods of normal and reversed polarity within the past four million years (see Figure 13.5).

Magnetic polarity reversals also show in bands in the igneous rocks on the ocean floor. Where the lithospheric plates are moving apart, the polarity reversals occur in bands parallel to and on opposite sides of the plate boundaries. Scientists compared the magnetic bands found in the rock on both sides of the boundary with the actual age of the rock. They determined that the youngest rocks of the ocean floor are at the spreading plate boundaries, and that the ocean floor becomes increasingly older away from the boundaries.

Source: From *Earth Science* by Nancy Spaulding and Samuel Namowitz. Copyright © 2003 by McDougal Littell Inc., a division of Houghton Mifflin Company. All rights reserved. Reprinted by permission of McDougal Littell Inc., a division of Houghton Mifflin Company.

The following exercises can be used to provide practice with the cause-and-effect pattern and other writing patterns:

1. Writing (composition) can be used to reinforce reading comprehension in any content area or of any writing pattern. In the following paragraph, the student writer connected the earth science content he read to his own experiences.

   The climate is the average pattern of weather in a place. The climate affects the habitat, which includes the water, rocks, soil, and air that all living things need. Since the plants and animals need certain things to live, they exist in places where the habitat provides these things. The kinds of water, rocks, soil, and air that are available make a difference in the kinds of plants and animals that live in that place. Woodpeckers and sapsuckers live in North Carolina forests because they eat the insects that live in the pine trees growing in this state.

2. Ask students to write questions about the content they read. For example,
   a. Why do some animals become extinct?
   b. If Guilford County became a desert, what animals would become extinct?

For additional teaching suggestions, see the social studies section.

EXAMPLE 10.13   Science Cause and Effect Passage

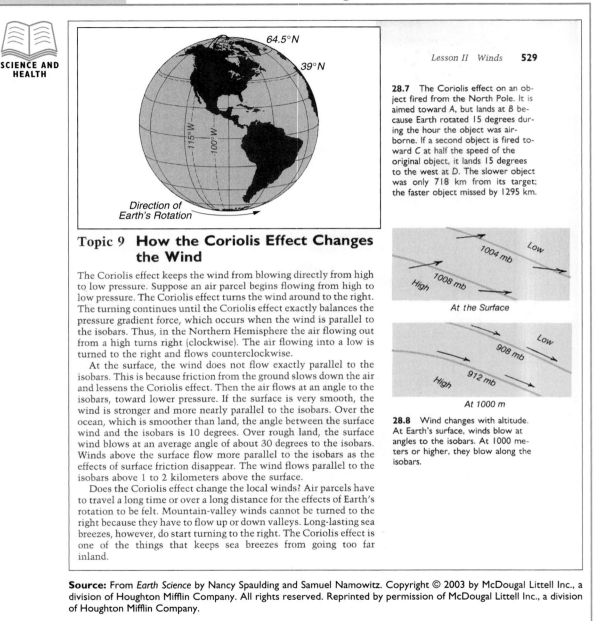

SCIENCE AND HEALTH

Lesson II   Winds   **529**

28.7   The Coriolis effect on an object fired from the North Pole. It is aimed toward *A*, but lands at *B* because Earth rotated 15 degrees during the hour the object was airborne. If a second object is fired toward *C* at half the speed of the original object, it lands 15 degrees to the west at *D*. The slower object was only 718 km from its target; the faster object missed by 1295 km.

Topic 9   How the Coriolis Effect Changes the Wind

The Coriolis effect keeps the wind from blowing directly from high to low pressure. Suppose an air parcel begins flowing from high to low pressure. The Coriolis effect turns the wind around to the right. The turning continues until the Coriolis effect exactly balances the pressure gradient force, which occurs when the wind is parallel to the isobars. Thus, in the Northern Hemisphere the air flowing out from a high turns right (clockwise). The air flowing into a low is turned to the right and flows counterclockwise.

At the surface, the wind does not flow exactly parallel to the isobars. This is because friction from the ground slows down the air and lessens the Coriolis effect. Then the air flows at an angle to the isobars, toward lower pressure. If the surface is very smooth, the wind is stronger and more nearly parallel to the isobars. Over the ocean, which is smoother than land, the angle between the surface wind and the isobars is 10 degrees. Over rough land, the surface wind blows at an average angle of about 30 degrees to the isobars. Winds above the surface flow more parallel to the isobars as the effects of surface friction disappear. The wind flows parallel to the isobars above 1 to 2 kilometers above the surface.

Does the Coriolis effect change the local winds? Air parcels have to travel a long time or over a long distance for the effects of Earth's rotation to be felt. Mountain-valley winds cannot be turned to the right because they have to flow up or down valleys. Long-lasting sea breezes, however, do start turning to the right. The Coriolis effect is one of the things that keeps sea breezes from going too far inland.

28.8   Wind changes with altitude. At Earth's surface, winds blow at angles to the isobars. At 1000 meters or higher, they blow along the isobars.

EXAMPLE 10.14   Cause-and-Effect Pattern and Map (Science)

SCIENCE AND
HEALTH

Earthquakes can occur for many reasons. The ground can shake from the eruption of a volcano, the collapse of a cavern, or even from the impact of a meteor. However, the major cause of earthquakes is the stress that builds up between two lithospheric plates.

Most of the time, friction between plates prevents movement along the plate boundary. Instead, the stresses cause the plates to deform, or change shape. Eventually, the stresses become great enough to overcome the frictional forces, and the plates suddenly move. This movement causes an earthquake. The plates then snap back to the shapes they had before they were deformed but at new locations relative to each other. This explanation for the cause of an earthquake is called the **elastic-rebound theory** and is fundamental to an understanding of earthquakes.

Source: From *Earth Science* by Nancy Spaulding and Samuel Namowitz. Copyright © 2003 by McDougal Littell Inc., a division of Houghton Mifflin Company. All rights reserved. Reprinted by permission of McDougal Littell Inc., a division of Houghton Mifflin Company.

Cause-and-Effect Map
Directions: Read the assigned selection and identify all of the causes in the selection. Label each of the boxes connected to the arrows that lead to "earthquakes," which is the effect in this reading. A completed map is shown.

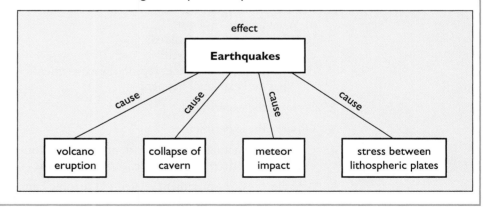

Problem-Solution Pattern

SCIENCE AND
HEALTH

The **problem-solution pattern** of writing is used in scientific and health-related materials to describe a real or hypothetical problem and its actual or suggested solution. For example, a writer might use this style of writing to explain how a vaccine was developed for polio.

To teach students to read and understand the problem-solution style of writing, the teacher may use the following techniques:

1. Ask students to identify the problem presented in a passage and to state it in their own words.

2. Ask students to locate the solution or solutions that the author suggests.

3. Ask students to prepare a problem and solution statement similar to the following:

   Problem: Why don't bacteria grow and divide in the region surrounding bread mold?
   Solution: Fleming found that mold gave off a chemical that killed the bacteria. He isolated the chemical and tested it against bacteria. He tested the chemical on animals with bacterial disease and on sick human volunteers.

Experimental Pattern

How is literal comprehension related to reading the experimental pattern?

SCIENCE AND HEALTH

The **experimental pattern** of writing is frequently used in scientific materials because experiments are the basis of much scientific knowledge and advancement. The reader must be able to read experiment directions and translate them into action. The reader must carry out the directions precisely and observe the outcomes carefully. The purpose of an experiment is comparable to a main idea, and experimental directions are comparable to details.

Following are the steps a reader should use when reading and conducting an experiment:

1. Ask the following questions:
   a. What am I to find out?
   b. What materials are needed?
   c. What processes are used?
   d. What is the order of the steps in the experiment?
   e. What do I expect to happen?

2. Perform the experiment.

3. Observe the experiment.

4. Compare the actual outcomes with predicted outcomes. (Success or failure of an experiment is determined by the learning that takes place.)

5. Ask: How is this experiment related to the topic I am studying?

Comparison Pattern

SCIENCE AND HEALTH

The comparison writing pattern also appears in science materials. In some content, writers use comparisons in the form of analogies to help readers understand scientific content.

Additional Skills

In addition to understanding technical terminology and the organizational patterns featured in scientific materials, the reader of science must have mathematical understandings and knowledge. He or she must know and be able to apply the abbreviations, equations, and symbols that appear in scientific content.

Mathematics Content

What are "real-world" mathematics problems?

MATHEMATICS

Mathematics requires a style of thinking involving modeling and abstraction. Mathematics has important applications in many areas of work and study, and students should explore these applications. Literacy is critical to mathematical reasoning and to exploring applications of mathematics. The standards developed by the National Council of Teachers of Mathematics (1998) point out that students need many opportunities to listen to, read about, write about, speak about, reflect on, and demonstrate mathematical ideas. They also indicate that teachers should continually encourage students to clarify, paraphrase, or elaborate. They must strive to engage a diverse student population in a variety of interesting and meaningful activities that are structured to develop critical thinking and problem solving.

Students need to develop extensive applications of mathematics concepts, as well as connections to everyday life. Today's mathematics instruction emphasizes the use of "real-world" mathematics problems and materials and of computer capabilities to develop conceptual understanding (National Council of Teachers of Mathematics, 1989). Current textbooks acquaint students with people who use math in their professions and businesses. Moreover, mathematics instruction builds connections with other subjects, and many teachers are striving to develop a broad, integrated mathematics curriculum in the middle school.

These current trends are illustrated in Example 10.15, taken from an Algebra I text.

WORDS AND SYMBOLS

MATHEMATICS

Mathematics is a highly compressed system of language in which a single **symbol** may represent several words; for example, the symbol > represents the words *greater than*. Writing in mathematics is generally denser and contains more ideas in each line and on each page than writing in the other disciplines.

In mathematics, as in some science material, words and symbols are mixed; comprehension depends not only on words and word relationships, but also on the relationships between words and symbols. Students have to read symbols, signs, abbreviations, formulas, equations, geometric figures, graphs, and tables as well as words.

Vocabulary knowledge is essential to understanding mathematics. Exactness in word knowledge is important because reading one word incorrectly can alter the meaning of an entire passage. Moreover, the reader has to integrate words and symbols into thought units. Some words, such as *odd* and *power*, have meanings in mathematics that are quite different from their meanings in everyday conversation. Students can keep mathematics journals in which they note key vocabulary terms and steps in solving various kinds of mathematics problems and patterns.

Many of the strategies introduced in Chapter 3 will help students acquire mathematics terminology. Another useful strategy involves defining concept characteristics. To use this approach, the teacher prepares an exercise for the students and asks them to identify the characteristics that describe each mathematical term in the exercise.

EXAMPLE 10.15   Critical Thinking in Math

MATHEMATICS

How Much Is Enough?

The number of calories that a particular athlete should consume depends on many factors including age, height, and activity level. The graph shown can help an athlete figure out how many calories from carbohydrates to include in a daily diet. Once the athlete's daily calorie needs are known, the number of calories from carbohydrates should be within the shaded region of the graph. As you will learn in this chapter, the graph represents a system of inequalities.

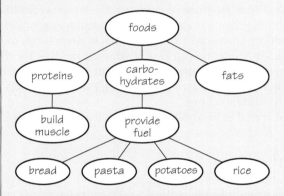

Nutrition for Athletes

(Calories from Carbohydrates vs. Daily Calorie Needs)

EXPLORE AND CONNECT

1. **Writing** According to the graph, if an athlete needs to consume 2200 Cal each day, about how many should come from carbohydrates? If another athlete needs to consume 1700 Cal from carbohydrates each day, about how many total calories does that athlete need?

2. **Research** In physics, a calorie is defined as a unit of heat. What is the relationship between calories used in physics and food calories? Find out how the numbers of calories in foods are determined.

3. **Project** The other 30–40% of an athlete's daily calorie intake should come from proteins and fats. What kinds of foods are high in proteins and fats? Create a poster showing how carbohydrates, fats, and proteins help the body to function.

Mathematics & Nancy Clark

In this chapter, you will learn more about how mathematics is related to sports nutrition.

Related Examples and Exercises

Section 7.1
- Example 1
- Exercises 34–36, 38

Section 7.5
- Exercises 29–31

Section 7.6
- Exercises 15–18

READING MATHEMATICS

MATHEMATICS

It is important for teachers to emphasize that mathematics content is different from other types of content. The reading involved in problem solving is particularly difficult because of the variety of cognitive processes that must be employed. Both linguistic and mathematics schemata are significant in understanding mathematics (Thomas, 1988). The following procedures are recommended for guiding mathematics comprehension.

Since the reading rate for mathematics is slower than that for other content areas, students should preread a section of the text at a moderate rate to get the general idea of the concept being introduced. On the second reading, they should go more slowly, taking notes and copying important information. As they read, students can paraphrase the content and devise questions relating to the assignment. Finally, they should reread any passages that are unclear and write questions regarding the information they need in order to clarify the material and focus attention on any illustrations (Henrichs and Sisson, 1980).

A directed reading lesson gives students a guide that can help them understand mathematics texts. The following set of steps can be used for directing the reading of a mathematics chapter:

1. *Introduce the new terms, using them in sentences.* Sentences from the text may be used. Give students an activity such as constructing a mathematics dictionary. Students may use their texts to help work out the meanings of the words.

2. *Ask students to preview the chapter and identify the topic.*

3. *Provide students with two or three silent reading purposes.* This step may be varied. If students have some background knowledge about the topic, they can help formulate silent reading purposes.

4. *Have students read the text silently.* Students should take notes on the content and formulate questions while reading.

5. *Work through examples and ask questions to clarify understanding.*

6. *Discuss the silent reading purposes and the questions students formulated in Step 4.*

Study guides such as the one in Example 10.16 can also be helpful.

EXAMPLE 10.16

Three-Level Study Guide for Mathematics (Developed by Stephanie Dykes, Jennifer Brown, and Keith Shakleford)

MATHEMATICS

Literal: What did the text say about adding and subtracting integers?

_____ 1. When adding integers with different signs, subtract the lesser absolute value from the greater absolute value. Give the result the same sign as the addend with the lesser absolute value.

_____ 2. When adding integers with different signs, subtract the lesser absolute value from the greater absolute value. Give the result the same sign as the addend with the greater absolute value.

_____ 3. For every number a, $a + (-a) = 0$.

_____ 4. To subtract a number, add its additive inverse. For any numbers a and b, $a - b = a + (-b)$.

_____ 5. To add integers with the same sign, add their absolute values. Give the result the opposite sign as the addends.

Interpretive: How exactly do the addition and subtraction laws apply to numbers?

_____ 1. $-5 + (-7) = -12$

_____ 2. $2 + (-3) = 1$

_____ 3. $-2 + 1 = -1$

_____ 4. The additive inverse of 5 is -5.

_____ 5. The additive inverse of -7 is $-1/7$.

_____ 6. $3 - (-1) = 3 + 1$

_____ 7. $-1 - (-7) = -1 + 7$

Applied: How can the use of adding and subtracting numbers (using positive and negative numbers) be applied to real life?

_____ 1. It might be useful in temperature scales.

_____ 2. It can be applied to telling time.

_____ 3. It could be applied to money situations, like balancing a checkbook.

Based on material from Foster, Gell, Gordon, et al. *Algebra 1: Applications and Connections.* Lake Forest, Illinois: Glencoe, 1992, pp. 55–57.

WRITING PATTERNS

MATHEMATICS

The writing patterns that occur most frequently in mathematics are the problem pattern and the demonstration pattern. In addition, graphs and charts are often used in math content reading.

Verbal Problems

MATHEMATICS

Solving **word problems** (**verbal problems**) is a very sophisticated task. Many readers have significant difficulties reading and understanding word problems, which are mathematical situations stated in words and symbols. Even when they can read the words and sentences with facility, they have difficulty choosing the correct process (operation) to solve the problem. Knifong and Holtran (1977) found that 95 percent of the students they studied could read all the words correctly in word problems; 98 percent knew the situation the problem was discussing; 92 percent knew what the problem was asking; yet only 36 percent knew how to work the problem.

MATHEMATICS

Kress (1989) recommends a technique similar to SQ3R for helping students solve word problems. This approach to solving verbal problems helps students identify the appropriate process or processes for solving a problem. The five steps in a mathematics reading technique similar to Kress's follow. Immediately after the description of the technique, the process is modeled.

1. *Survey.* Read the problem out loud. Try to visualize the situation.

2. *Question.* What is the problem asking you to find? This step gives students a purpose for reading the problem. It helps them know why they are reading.

3. *Question.* What is the correct process (e.g., addition, subtraction, division)?

4. *Read.* Read the problem out loud again.

5. *Work.* Work the problem.

MATHEMATICS

The process of reading and solving mathematics problems is applied to the text shown in Example 10.17 as follows:

Modeling the Process of Reading and Solving Mathematics Problems

1. *Survey.* The question sentence in this problem is: What are the length and width in meters that should be shown on the Canadian plans?

2. *Question.* What is this problem asking you to find? (Correct conversion of feet to meters.)

3. *Question.* What is the correct process? (Requires multiplication.)

4. *Read.* Read the written problem out loud. Refer to Example 10.17.

5. *Work.* Work the problem. To convert feet to meters, multiply by 0.3.

    57 ft. (0.3 m per ft.) = _____
    33 ft. (0.3 m per ft.) = _____

    Check your answer.

EXAMPLE 10.17   Verbal Problem (Mathematics)

Converting Customary Units to Metric Units

Objective: To convert customary units to metric units.

Because most other countries use the metric system, many United States companies convert the customary measurements of their products into metric units before exporting them. You can do this type of conversion using a chart like the one below.

When You Know	Multiply By	To Find
inches	2.54	centimeters
feet	0.3	meters
yards	0.91	meters
miles	1.61	kilometers
ounces	28.35	grams
pounds	0.454	kilograms
fluid ounces	29.573	milliliters
pints	0.473	liters
quarts	0.946	liters
gallons	3.785	liters

Example: Anderson Architects designs buildings worldwide. They recently designed a house that might be built in both the United States and Canada. The United States plans show that the length of the house is 57 ft and the width of the house is 33 ft. What are the length and width in meters that should be shown on the Canadian plans?

Source: Francis J. Gardella, Patricia R. Fraze, Joanne E. Meldon, et al., *Mathematical Connections*, p. 84. Copyright © 1992 by Houghton Mifflin Company. Reprinted by permission of Houghton Mifflin Company. All rights reserved.

MATHEMATICS

Another valuable approach to reading verbal problems was suggested by Earle (1976). In this technique, the teacher uses a series of steps to guide students through the written language of the problem. The following steps are based on those suggested by Earle:

1. Read the problem quickly to obtain a general understanding of it. Visualize the problem. Do not be concerned with the numbers.

2. Examine the problem again. Identify the question you are asked to answer. This question usually comes at the end of the problem, but it may occur anywhere in the problem.

3. Read the problem again to identify the information given.

4. Analyze the problem to see how the information is related. Identify any missing information and any unnecessary information.

5. Compute the answer.

6. Examine your answer. Label the parts of the solution to correspond with the question that the problem asks you to solve. Is your answer sensible?

See also the discussion of SQRQCQ in Chapter 7.

Demonstration Pattern

MATHEMATICS

The **demonstration pattern** is usually accompanied by an example that illustrates operations and concepts. This writing pattern is important in mathematics materials because it shows students how to work problems. Following are exercises to help students understand the strategies that they can use while reading the demonstration pattern.

1. The student should work through the example to determine whether he or she understands the process. If the student does not compute the same answer as shown in the example, he or she should work slowly through the example again, rereading each step carefully to determine the point in the process at which he or she erred.

2. The student should paraphrase the process in his or her own words.

3. The student should apply the process to other situations.

Example 10.18 shows the demonstration writing pattern.

Graphs and Charts

MATHEMATICS

Graphs and charts are often used to represent mathematical concepts in math materials as well as in other content textbooks, in newspapers, and in magazines. The graphs in Example 10.18 and Example 10.19 appear in mathematics textbooks.

Symbols, Signs, and Formulas

Students of mathematics must learn to read and use the special symbols, signs, and formulas found in mathematics textbooks. This is illustrated in Example 10.20. First, they need to realize the importance of knowing symbols, signs, and formulas. Then they must focus on the meaning of each and learn each in relationship to its meaning and application.

EXAMPLE 10.18   Demonstration Pattern (Mathematics)

MATHEMATICS

Integers on a Number Line

Objective: To recognize and compare integers and to find opposites and absolute values.

Terms to Know
- integers
- positive integers
- negative integers
- opposites
- absolute value

Data Analysis

The diagram at the right shows information about the highest and lowest points on Earth. The positive sign on $^+29,028$ tells you that the top of Mount Everest is 29,028 ft *above* sea level. The negative sign on $^-38,635$ tells you that the bottom of the Marianas Trench is 38,635 ft *below* sea level. Sea level is represented by 0. The numbers $^+29,028$, $^-38,635$, and 0 are examples of *integers*.

An integer is any number in the following set.

> **Earth's Greatest Ups and Downs**
>
> **Mount Everest**
> (Nepal-Tibet)
> +29,028 ft
>
> **Sea Level = 0 ft**
>
> **Marianas Trench**
> (Northern
> Pacific Ocean)
> –38,635 ft

$$\{\ldots, {}^-4, \quad {}^-3, \quad {}^-2, \quad {}^-1, \quad 0, \quad {}^+1, \quad {}^+2, \quad {}^+3, \quad {}^+4, \ldots\} \leftarrow$$ The braces { } mean *the set that contains.*

Integers greater than zero are called **positive integers.** Integers less than zero are called **negative integers.** Zero is neither positive nor negative. To make notation simpler, you generally write positive integers without the positive sign.

Another way to show the integers is to locate them as points on a number line. On a horizontal number line, *positive integers* are to the right of zero, and *negative integers* are to the left.

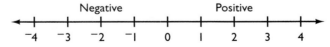

Numbers that are the same distance from zero, but on opposite sides of zero, are called **opposites.** To indicate the opposite of a number *n,* you write $-n$. You read $-n$ as "the opposite of *n.*"

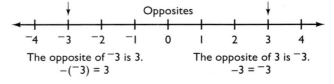

The opposite of $^-3$ is 3.   The opposite of 3 is $^-3$.
$-(^-3) = 3$ $-3 = {}^-3$

On the number line above, you see that the symbols −3 and ⁻3 represent the same number, negative three. To make notation simpler, this textbook will use the *lowered* sign to indicate a negative number. From this point on, you will see negative three written as −3.

The distance that a number is from zero on a number line is the absolute value of the number. You use the symbol | | to indicate absolute value. You read |n| as "the absolute value of n."

Example I

Find each absolute value.
a. |3| b. |−4|

Solution

3 is 3 units from 0, so |3| = 3.

−4 is 4 units from 0, so |−4| = 4.

Check Your Understanding

1. Name another integer that has an absolute value of 3.
2. What is the absolute value of 0?

When you compare numbers, you may want to picture them on a number line. On a horizontal number line, numbers increase in order from left to right.

Example 2

Replace each ___?___ with >, <, or =.
a. 1 ___?___ −3   b. −4 ___?___ −2

Solution

a. 1 is *to the right of* −3, so 1 > −3.

a. −4 is *to the left of* −2, so −4 < −2.

EXAMPLE 10.19   Graphing Equations (Mathematics)

MATHEMATICS

7.1

Learn how to...
• write and graph equations in standard form

So you can...
• solve problems with two variables, such as nutritional planning or telecommunications problems

Using Linear Equations in Standard Form

Nancy Clark recommends that runners replace their muscles' energy stores after a marathon. A runner should eat at least 0.5 g of foods containing carbohydrates for each pound of body weight within 2 h after the race. The athlete should eat at least this amount again 2 h later.

EXAMPLE 1   Interview: Nancy Clark

Leon should eat at least 70 g of carbohydrates after running a marathon. One cup of apple juice contains 30 g of carbohydrates, and 1 oz of pretzels contains 23 g. Write and graph an equation showing combinations of pretzels and juice that provide 70 g of carbohydrates.

SOLUTION

Step 1 Write an equation.

Let j = number of cups of juice.

Let p = number of ounces of pretzels.

$$\underset{\text{from juice}}{\text{Carbohydrates}} + \underset{\text{from pretzels}}{\text{Carbohydrates}} = 70$$

$$30j + 23p = 70$$

Step 2 Graph the equation.

j	p
0	3.0
1.0	1.7
2.3	0

First make a table of values.

Then graph each point and draw a line though the points.

Combinations of Pretzels and Juice Containing 70 g of Carbohydrates

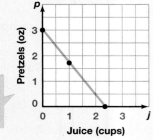

BY THE WAY

After the Boston Marathon, runners eat snacks such as pretzels and bread supplied by their sponsors. Ten small pretzels weigh about one ounce.

THINK AND COMMUNICATE

1. Why does the graph in Example 1 only make sense in the first quadrant?
2. How would the graph in Example 1 be different if you put cups of juice on the vertical axis?

Source: Miriam A. Leiva and Richard G. Brown, *Algebra I: Explorations and Applications* (Evanston, IL: McDougal Littell, 1997), p. 281. Reprinted by permission.

EXAMPLE 10.20   Symbols (Mathematics)

MATHEMATICS

Graphing Inequalities on a Number Line
Nearly ⅛ of the world's surface is desert and receives a yearly rainfall of less than 10 in.

The yearly amount of rainfall in deserts can be represented by an inequality.

Let *r* represent the number of inches of yearly rainfall.
The rainfall is less than 10 in.

$$r \quad < \quad 10 \quad \longleftarrow \boxed{\text{The < symbol indicates an inequality.}}$$

You can illustrate the inequality with a graph.

$r < 10$ The open circle indicates that 10 is not included.

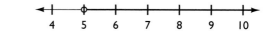

```
  5   6   7   8   9   10   11
```

The solid line represents the numbers that are
a solution to the given inequality.
(Assume numbers greater than zero in the solution.)

Some solutions are 6, 8, and 9.5.

The rainfall could have been 6 in., 8 in., or 9.5 in.

Think Aloud. Name three other possible solutions greater than zero. Include some decimal numbers.

Another example:
The amount of rainfall (*r*)
is greater than 5 in.

```
  4   5   6   7   8   9   10
```

$$r \quad > \quad 5$$

Some solutions are 7, 5.5, and 90.5.

Think Aloud. Name three other possible solutions.

Guided Practice
Name three possible solutions greater than zero for each inequality.

1. *x* > 5   2. *w* < 32

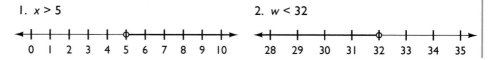

```
0  1  2  3  4  5  6  7  8  9  10          28  29  30  31  32  33  34  35
```

In Your Words. Explain the reason for your answer.

3. Is 5 included on the graph?

```
◄─┼─┼─┼─┼─┼─◇─┼─┼─┼─┼─┼─►
  0  1  2  3  4  5  6  7  8  9  10
```

4. Is 3.5 included on the graph?

```
◄─┼─┼─┼─◇─┼─┼─┼─┼─┼─┼─┼─►
  0  1  2  3  4  5  6  7  8  9  10
```

TEACHING MATHEMATICS CONTENT

MATHEMATICS

Teachers can use vocabulary strategies to introduce the important terms and concepts in meaningful contexts. Brainstorming will help students associate mathematics terms with previous experiences. Comprehension of mathematics content is facilitated with advance organizers, structured overviews, study guides, concept guides, and directed reading lessons to focus attention on understanding while reading. Example 10.21 illustrates a mathematics reading guide based on the textbook selection in Example 10.17.

EXAMPLE 10.21   **Mathematics Reading Guide (based on Example 10.17)**

MATHEMATICS

Part I: Facts of the Problem

Directions: Read the problem. Then in Column A, check the statements that contain the important facts of the problem. You may refer to the problem to verify your responses. In Column B, check the statements that will help you solve the problem.

A   B

____   ____   1. Anderson Architects designs buildings worldwide.
____   ____   2. These architects have been in business for five years.
____   ____   3. They recently designed a house for construction in the United States.
____   ____   4. This house can also be built in Canada.
____   ____   5. The United States plans show the length of the house is 57 feet.
____   ____   6. The United States plans show the width of the house is 33 feet.

Part II: Mathematical Ideas and Interpretations

Directions: Check the statements that contain mathematical concepts related to the problem. You may go back to Part I to review your responses.

_____ 1. Canadians measure in meters.

_____ 2. In the United States, measurement is generally stated in feet.

_____ 3. Canadians could convert meters to feet in order to interpret the house plans.

_____ 4. To convert feet to meters, multiply the measurements in feet by 0.3.

_____ 5. People in the United States are using metric measurement more frequently now than 25 years ago.

Part III: Computation

Directions: Below are possible mathematical calculations. Check those that apply to this problem. You may refer to Part I and Part II to verify your responses.

_____ 1. 57 ft + 33 ft = 90 ft

_____ 2. 57 ft − 33 ft = 24 ft

_____ 3. 57 ft (0.3 m per ft) = 17.1 m

_____ 4. 33 ft (0.3 m per ft) = 9.9 m

_____ 5. 57 ft ÷ 0.3 m per ft =

English (Language Arts) Content

**ENGLISH/
LANGUAGE
ARTS**

The language arts are listening, speaking, reading, writing, viewing, visually representing, and thinking. A command of English is essential to effective communication; therefore, study of the language arts focuses on effective use and appreciation of the English language. English has the most varied subject matter of all the content subjects. Study of English requires readers to work with grammar, composition, and many forms of literature—novels, short stories, poetry, biographies, and autobiographies.

VOCABULARY DEVELOPMENT

Vocabulary development is an important aspect of English instruction because students who have a large store of word meanings at their command are better communicators. Exploring changes in word meanings is one way to expand students' vocabularies.

Changes in Word Meanings

What examples can you suggest for the various types of changes in word meanings?

**ENGLISH/
LANGUAGE
ARTS**

Studying etymology shows students that meanings of certain words have changed over time. For example, the word marshal once meant "one who held horses," a meaning not quite as impressive as its present-day meaning. Daily use of words over the years leads to gradual change in their meanings, which can be systematically analyzed as illustrated in the following list:

1. *Amelioration.* The meaning of the word has changed so that the word means something better than it once did. For example, a person who was called *enthusiastic* was once considered a fanatic. Currently, enthusiasm is considered a desirable quality.

2. *Pejoration.* Pejoration indicates that the word has a more derogatory meaning than it did earlier in its history. For example, a *villain* once was a feudal serf or a servant from a villa. Currently, a villain is considered to be a scoundrel.

3. *Generalization.* Some words become more generalized in meaning. When generalization operates, the meaning of words is broadened. Earlier in history, *picture* meant painting, but now *picture* may mean a print, a photograph, or a drawing. In fact, a picture may not be representational at all, because in art a picture may not have a distinct form.

4. *Specialization.* The opposite of generalization is specialization. In this case, word meanings become more specific than they were in the past. At one time, *meat* meant any food, not just lamb, pork, or beef.

5. *Euphemism.* This term indicates the use of an affectation to convey elegance or the use of a more pleasant word for an unpleasant one. For example, a *janitor* is often called a "custodian" or a "maintenance engineer," and a person does not *die* but rather "passes away."

6. *Hyperbole.* This is an extreme exaggeration. For example, a man who is tired might say that he could "sleep for a year." Exaggeration is being used to make the point of extreme fatigue. Many people currently use the word *fantastic* to describe almost anything unusual, although *fantastic* means strange, wonderful, unreal, and illusory.

Activities such as the following can be used to develop word meanings through etymology:

1. Give students a list of words with instructions to determine the origin of each term and the types of changes that have occurred in its meaning. Words such as the following could be used in this activity: *city, ghetto, manuscript, lord, stench.*

2. Ask students to identify the origins of the names of the months or the days of the week. For example, *October* is from the Latin *Octo* (eight), because it was the eighth month of the Roman calendar. *Monday* means "day of the moon."

3. Encourage students to determine the origins and meanings of their first names and surnames. For example, *Susan* means "lily." Many surnames are related to

occupation or geographic origin. The surname *Butler* means a bottle maker; the surname *Hatfield* refers to a wooded field.

Types of Words

Word knowledge can be increased by exploring some of the unique characteristics of different types of words. Activities that involve acronyms, oxymorons, and homonyms, for example, will develop students' vocabularies. Following are definitions of some special types of words:

1. *Acronym.* A word composed of the first letters or syllables of longer terms, such as MADD, which means "*Mothers Against Drunk Driving.*"

2. *Oxymoron.* Two incongruous words used together, such as *cruel kindness.*

3. *Homonyms,* or *homophones.* Words that sound alike but are not spelled alike, such as *to, too, two; pare, pair; sum, some.*

4. *Heteronyms.* Words that have different pronunciations and meanings, although they are spelled exactly the same, such as:

   Don't *subject* me to that experience.
   What is the *subject* of your book?

5. *Coined word.* A word invented to meet specific needs. Words are often coined by using previously existing words and word parts. *Gerrymander, curfew, motel,* and *astronaut* are examples of coined words. Many product names are coined words, for example, *Jell-O* and *Bisquick.*

Denotative and Connotative Meanings of Words

Compare a denotative word meaning with the connotative meaning of the same word.

ENGLISH/
LANGUAGE
ARTS

The denotative and connotative meanings of words can be introduced through literature. **Denotation** is the literal definition of a word as defined by the dictionary. **Connotation** refers to the ideas and associations that are suggested by a term, including emotional reactions. For instance, the word *home* denotes the place where one lives, whereas it may connote warmth, love, and family. Readers must learn to recognize the connotations of words in order to comprehend a selection. By definition, *cunning* and *astute* are very similar, but when the word *cunning* is used to describe a person, it usually implies a negative quality, while describing a person as *astute* is complimentary.

Students can look for examples of both connotative and denotative uses of words in the literary selections they read. In addition, the following activities will increase their understanding of denotation and connotation:

1. In each pair, select the word that you would prefer to use for describing yourself. Tell why you chose the word.
   a. *creative* or *screwball*
   b. *stolid* or *easygoing*
   c. *conceited* or *proud*

2. Provide students with a list of words similar to the preceding list, and ask them to write a plus (+) beside each positive word, a minus (–) beside each negative word, and a zero (0) beside each neutral word.

Figurative language is connotative use of language. The author implies ideas through figurative language, and this expressive application of language makes written language more interesting to readers. Refer to Chapter 3 for suggestions to aid in instruction related to figurative language.

LITERATURE

**ENGLISH/
LANGUAGE
ARTS**

The goal of teaching literature is to develop in readers a lifelong interest in and appreciation for literature. Having students read and respond to interesting literary selections helps teachers achieve these goals. When students read material that is related to their interests and background experience, their schemata will enable them to read with greater comprehension. Many students need guides that will help them comprehend literature, such as anticipation guides, advance organizers, and three-level study guides.

Novels and Short Stories

**ENGLISH/
LANGUAGE
ARTS**

Reading novels and short stories is basic to the study of literature. A literature selection is an imaginative expression of a writer's ideas: the author shares an experience with the reader by relating incidents through a story. The longer form of the novel permits an author to develop literary elements, such as characterization, in greater depth than is possible within the form of the short story.

Response is concerned with the readers' reactions and feelings about reading content. Researchers have identified eight processes that are involved in a student's response to literature (Cooper and Purves, 1973). These processes are as follows:

1. *Description.* Students can restate in their own words what they have read.

2. *Discrimination.* Students can discriminate among different writings on the basis of type, author, theme, and so forth.

3. *Relation.* Students can relate to each other several aspects of a piece of literature. For example, students can discuss the relationship between a story's setting and plot or can compare the plots of two different stories.

4. *Interpretation.* Students can interpret the author's ideas and can support these interpretations.

5. *Generalization.* Students can use what they have learned in one piece of literature to understand another one.

6. *Evaluation.* Students can apply criteria to evaluate a piece of literature. For example, they might evaluate the quality of the element of characterization.

7. *Valuing.* Students can relate literature to their own lives.

8. *Creation.* Students can respond to literature by creating their own art, music, writing, drama, or dance.

When teaching novels or short stories, teachers activate students' schemata. Then they have students read through the story, although the reading may extend over several class sessions. Reading the entire selection enables students to understand the entire plot, character development, setting, and theme. If the reading of a selection is broken into chapters or smaller parts, the reader may not grasp the entire selection or the way the components of the selection fit together.

In addition to using the eight processes of responding to literature to guide instruction, the teacher asks students to support answers to questions with material from the selections they have read. Students may be asked to diagram story structure in the following manner:

Title

Setting	*Theme*	*Plot*	*Characters*
Place	Symbols	Episode #1	Main character
Time	Incidents	Episode #2	Supporting character
		Episode #3	

Poetry

ENGLISH/ LANGUAGE ARTS

Poetry is a condensed form of writing that expresses in a succinct fashion the writer's thoughts and emotions and stimulates the reader's imagination. Frequently, a poet can inspire a reader to perceive familiar things and ideas in a new way. Poets use rhythm, rhyme, imagery, and many other devices to make a reader see or feel what they are expressing.

Teachers may use the following techniques with poetry:

1. Poems should be read aloud.

2. Poems should be read in their entirety for full appreciation.

3. Poems should usually be read twice for full appreciation.

4. Prose and poetry on the same topic may be compared in order to understand the succinctness of poetry.

Drama

ENGLISH/ LANGUAGE ARTS

Drama is literature that is written to be acted. In drama, the characters tell the story. Drama includes stage directions needed to understand the plot. The reader should pay attention to all information in parentheses and italics. The name of the speaker is printed before his or her lines, and the reader must be alert to the names of the speakers in order to determine who is speaking and how the action unfolds.

The following teaching procedures help students understand drama:

1. Ask the students to visualize story action.

2. Have the students read the speeches aloud to aid comprehension.

3. Have the students act out described actions to arrive at a better understanding of the action.

4. Have the students write a play and act it out as described.

Essays and Editorials

What type of writing is found in essays, editorials, and position papers?

**ENGLISH/
LANGUAGE
ARTS**

Essays, editorials, and position papers are expository forms of writing. **Exposition** is used to explain information from a particular point of view. The author is usually trying to convince readers to accept his or her argument. Exposition contains a greater amount of information than fiction does. The strategies suggested in this chapter (and in Chapters 4, 5, and 11) for guiding the reading of content materials aid the teacher in teaching exposition. Following are activities that teachers can use to help students comprehend expository materials:

1. Identify the author's purpose.

2. Identify the author's argument.

3. Identify the details the author uses to support his or her argument and the sequence in which the author presents these details.

4. Identify the author's organizational pattern.

5. Identify the author's biases related to the topic and the audience.

The preceding activities can be used for discussions and study guides.

GENRE AND MULTIGENRE STUDIES

**ENGLISH/
LANGUAGE
ARTS**

Genre studies are those that include reading and/or writing a variety of materials reflecting a specific type of discourse (genre). These activities direct students' attention to the type of discourse they are reading, which is important for today's students, as diverse materials and multiple literacies become increasingly important to learning.

Multigenre reading and writing (reading and writing of many genres) are valuable instructional methods for projects, units, inquiry, and research papers. Moulton (1999) reports multigenre papers that included newspapers, lists, narrative stories, letters, journals, photos, documents, streams of consciousness, and maps. Students could conceivably use Internet materials, videos, photo essays, and magazines. See Chapter 8 for more on multigenre writing.

GRAMMAR AND COMPOSITION

**ENGLISH/
LANGUAGE
ARTS**

Textbooks are also used in many language arts classes to teach grammar and composition. Both electronic and print sources in today's classrooms that are designed to explain the grammar and punctuation of the English language use technical vocabulary words such as *complex sentences, interrogative,* and *adjective.* These textbooks and handbooks usually follow an expository pattern: a concept or idea is explained and illustrated, a definition or generalization is developed, and application exercises are provided. Many details are packed into a page, and students need to skim and scan when they need to find specific information. Frequently the material is almost in outline form, requiring readers to identify supporting details and main ideas. Some of the models and examples used in language arts textbooks are written in a narrative style, so that the reader must switch from expository to narrative style. Example 10.22 shows content from a grammar and composition text that is written in a definition or explanation pattern.

Many teachers use their text as a handbook or have students obtain handbooks to use as a reference. Students find handbooks such as *EasyWriter* (Lunsford and Connors, 1997) helpful.

Focusing on paraphrasing and finding applications for grammar, spelling, punctuation, and capitalization instruction helps students retain the information. Advance organizers, study guides, and concept guides are especially useful for teaching the conventions of language. The Internet offers websites for grammar, spelling, and punctuation.

EXAMPLE 10.22 Content from a Grammar and Composition Text

**ENGLISH/
LANGUAGE
ARTS**

*Lesson 6   **Placement of Phrases***

1   Here's the Idea

A common mistake that writers make is putting phrases in the wrong positions in sentences. This mistake usually involves phrases used as adjectives or adverbs.

Misplaced Phrases
A **misplaced phrase** is a phrase that is placed so far away from the word it modifies that the meaning of the sentence is unclear or incorrect. The types of phrases that are most often misplaced are prepositional phrases and participial phrases.

Draft
> Misplaced prepositional phrase
> The U.S. team in men's indoor volleyball won the most
> Olympic gold medals during the 1980s.

The sentence above says that the U.S. men's indoor volleyball team won more Olympic gold medals than any other team in any sport. This is not true.

Revision
> The U.S. team won the most Olympic gold medals
> in men's indoor volleyball during the 1980s.

Dangling Phrases

When the word or words that a phrase should modify are missing from a sentence, the phrase is called a **dangling phrase.** Most dangling phrases are participial phrases or infinitive phrases.

Draft

Dangling participial phrase

Failing to win a gold medal in the 1900s, the Olympic women's indoor volleyball competition has been disappointing.

The sentence above says that a competition won a gold medal.

Revision

Words modified

Failing to win a gold medal in the 1900s, the U.S. women's indoor volleyball team was disappointing at the Olympics.

Source: Mary Newton Bruder, Rebekah Caplan, Sharon Sicinski Skeans, and Richard Vinson, *Language Network, Grade 9*, p. 78. Copyright © 2001 by McDougal Littell Inc., a division of Houghton Mifflin Company. All rights reserved. Reprinted by permission of McDougal Littell Inc., a division of Houghton Mifflin Company.

Foreign Languages

The ability to read and speak foreign languages is a valuable skill in today's world because of increased travel and communication among the people of the world. Current approaches to foreign language study include meaning-centered activities with a cultural focus that emphasizes functional language use. See Example 10.23.

Learning to read a foreign language is very similar to learning to read one's native language. The teacher exposes students to oral language to develop their readiness for learning the new language. Listening comprehension of language precedes reading comprehension; and foreign language tapes, computer programs, and foreign language broadcasts on radio and television develop listening comprehension.

Prior to reading, students need to learn about the concepts and hear the vocabulary used in the assigned selections. Discussion and practice of common phrases and expressions are useful in developing readiness to read, as is using the context to understand words and expressions. In addition, the teacher should provide questions to guide the students' silent reading.

Reading for global meaning in a foreign language is more effective than translating a page or passage word by word. Stopping several times on each line to check English equivalents keeps students from effectively accessing the ideas from the written language. Students should have opportunities to listen to, speak, read, and write the language. These activities will help them learn both the semantics and the syntax of the language. Teachers can use the same methods in teaching students to read a foreign language that they use in teaching them to read English.

EXAMPLE 10.23   Teacher's Edition of a Spanish Text

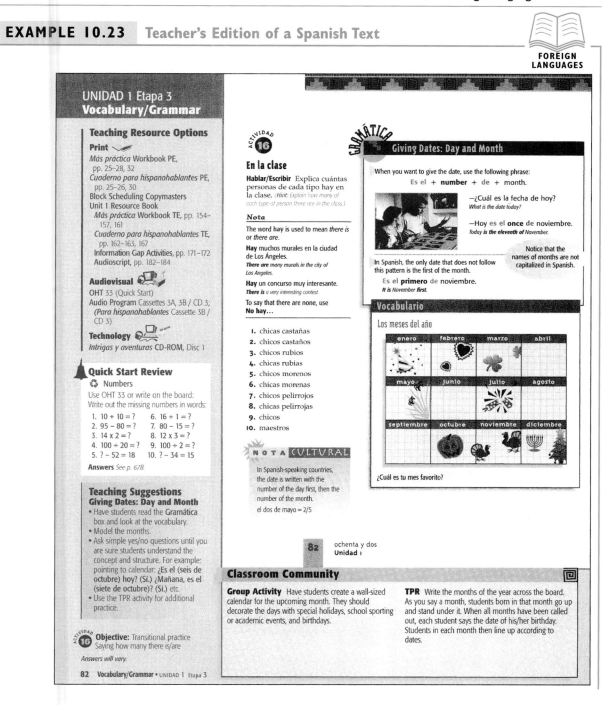

UNIDAD 1 Etapa 3
Vocabulary/Grammar

Teaching Resource Options

Print

Más práctica Workbook PE,
pp. 25–28, 32
Cuaderno para hispanohablantes PE,
pp. 25–26, 30
Block Scheduling Copymasters
Unit 1 Resource Book
  Más práctica Workbook TE, pp. 154–
  157, 161
  Cuaderno para hispanohablantes TE,
  pp. 162–163, 167
  Information Gap Activities, pp. 171–172
  Audioscript, pp. 182–184

Audiovisual

OHT 33 (Quick Start)
Audio Program Cassettes 3A, 3B / CD 3;
(*Para hispanohablantes* Cassette 3B /
CD 3)

Technology

Intrigas y aventuras CD-ROM, Disc 1

Quick Start Review

⚙ Numbers
Use OHT 33 or write on the board:
Write out the missing numbers in words:

1. 10 + 10 = ?	6. 16 + 1 = ?
2. 95 − 80 = ?	7. 80 − 15 = ?
3. 14 x 2 = ?	8. 12 x 3 = ?
4. 100 ÷ 20 = ?	9. 100 ÷ 2 = ?
5. ? − 52 = 18	10. ? − 34 = 15

Answers *See p. 67B.*

Teaching Suggestions
Giving Dates: Day and Month

• Have students read the **Gramática**
  box and look at the vocabulary.
• Model the months.
• Ask simple yes/no questions until you
  are sure students understand the
  concept and structure. For example:
  pointing to calendar: ¿Es el (seis de
  octubre) hoy? (Sí.) ¿Mañana, es el
  (siete de octubre)? (Sí.) etc.
• Use the TPR activity for additional
  practice.

🔶 **16 Objective:** Transitional practice
Saying how many there is/are
Answers will vary.

82 Vocabulary/Grammar • UNIDAD 1 Etapa 3

ACTIVIDAD 16
En la clase

Hablar/Escribir Explica cuántas
personas de cada tipo hay en
la clase. (*Hint: Explain how many of
each type of person there are in the class.*)

Nota

The word **hay** is used to mean *there is*
or *there are*.

Hay muchos murales en la ciudad
de Los Ángeles.
*There are many murals in the city of
Los Angeles.*

Hay un concurso muy interesante.
There is a very interesting contest.

To say that there are none, use
No hay...

1. chicas castañas
2. chicos castaños
3. chicos rubios
4. chicas rubias
5. chicos morenos
6. chicas morenas
7. chicos pelirrojos
8. chicas pelirrojas
9. chicos
10. maestros

NOTA CULTURAL

In Spanish-speaking countries,
the date is written with the
number of the day first, then the
number of the month.
el dos de mayo = 2/5

82 ochenta y dos
Unidad 1

GRAMÁTICA
Giving Dates: Day and Month

When you want to give the date, use the following phrase:

Es el + number + de + month.

—¿Cuál es la fecha de hoy?
What is the date today?

—Hoy es el **once** de noviembre.
Today is the eleventh of November.

In Spanish, the only date that does not follow
this pattern is the first of the month.

Notice that the
names of months are not
capitalized in Spanish.

Es el **primero** de noviembre.
It is November first.

Vocabulario

Los meses del año

enero	febrero	marzo	abril
mayo	junio	julio	agosto
septiembre	octubre	noviembre	diciembre

¿Cuál es tu mes favorito?

Classroom Community

Group Activity Have students create a wall-sized
calendar for the upcoming month. They should
decorate the days with special holidays, school sporting
or academic events, and birthdays.

TPR Write the months of the year across the board.
As you say a month, students born in that month go up
and stand under it. When all months have been called
out, each student says the date of his/her birthday.
Students in each month then line up according to
dates.

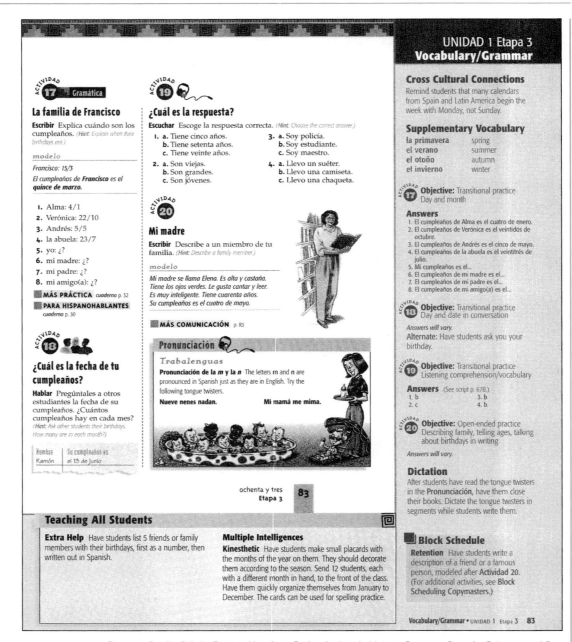

La familia de Francisco

Escribir Explica cuándo son los cumpleaños. *(Hint: Explain when their birthdays are.)*

modelo

Francisco: 15/3
El cumpleaños de **Francisco** es el quince de marzo.

1. Alma: 4/1
2. Verónica: 22/10
3. Andrés: 5/5
4. la abuela: 23/7
5. yo: ¿?
6. mi madre: ¿?
7. mi padre: ¿?
8. mi amigo(a): ¿?

■ **MÁS PRÁCTICA** cuaderno p. 32
■ **PARA HISPANOHABLANTES** cuaderno p. 30

¿Cuál es la fecha de tu cumpleaños?

Hablar Pregúntales a otros estudiantes la fecha de su cumpleaños. ¿Cuántos cumpleaños hay en cada mes? *(Hint: Ask other students their birthdays. How many are in each month?)*

Nombre	Su cumpleaños es
Ramón	el 13 de junio

¿Cuál es la respuesta?

Escuchar Escoge la respuesta correcta. *(Hint: Choose the correct answer.)*

1. a. Tiene cinco años.
   b. Tiene setenta años.
   c. Tiene veinte años.
2. a. Son viejas.
   b. Son grandes.
   c. Son jóvenes.
3. a. Soy policía.
   b. Soy estudiante.
   c. Soy maestro.
4. a. Llevo un suéter.
   b. Llevo una camiseta.
   c. Llevo una chaqueta.

Mi madre

Escribir Describe a un miembro de tu familia. *(Hint: Describe a family member.)*

modelo

Mi madre se llama Elena. Es alta y castaña. Tiene los ojos verdes. Le gusta cantar y leer. Es muy inteligente. Tiene cuarenta años. Su cumpleaños es el cuatro de mayo.

■ **MÁS COMUNICACIÓN** p. R3

Pronunciación

Trabalenguas

Pronunciación de la *m* y la *n* The letters m and n are pronounced in Spanish just as they are in English. Try the following tongue twisters.

Nueve nenes nadan.   Mi mamá me mima.

ochenta y tres
Etapa 3   83

Teaching All Students

Extra Help Have students list 5 friends or family members with their birthdays, first as a number, then written out in Spanish.

Multiple Intelligences
Kinesthetic Have students make small placards with the months of the year on them. They should decorate them according to the season. Send 12 students, each with a different month in hand, to the front of the class. Have them quickly organize themselves from January to December. The cards can be used for spelling practice.

UNIDAD 1 Etapa 3
Vocabulary/Grammar

Cross Cultural Connections
Remind students that many calendars from Spain and Latin America begin the week with Monday, not Sunday.

Supplementary Vocabulary

la primavera	spring
el verano	summer
el otoño	autumn
el invierno	winter

17 Objective: Transitional practice
Day and month

Answers
1. El cumpleaños de Alma es el cuatro de enero.
2. El cumpleaños de Verónica es el veintidós de octubre.
3. El cumpleaños de Andrés es el cinco de mayo.
4. El cumpleaños de la abuela es el veintitrés de julio.
5. Mi cumpleaños es el...
6. El cumpleaños de mi madre es el...
7. El cumpleaños de mi padre es el...
8. El cumpleaños de mi amigo(a) es el...

18 Objective: Transitional practice
Day and date in conversation

Answers will vary.
Alternate: Have students ask you your birthday.

19 Objective: Transitional practice
Listening comprehension/vocabulary

Answers (See script p. 67B.)
1. b   3. b
2. c   4. b

20 Objective: Open-ended practice
Describing family, telling ages, talking about birthdays in writing

Answers will vary.

Dictation
After students have read the tongue twisters in the **Pronunciación**, have them close their books. Dictate the tongue twisters in segments while students write them.

■ **Block Schedule**
Retention Have students write a description of a friend or a famous person, modeled after **Actividad 20**. (For additional activities, see Block Scheduling Copymasters.)

Vocabulary/Grammar • UNIDAD 1 Etapa 3   **83**

Following are some specific activities useful for helping students develop comprehension of a foreign language.

1. Teach students to use a foreign language dictionary.

2. Encourage students to write their own ideas in the language being studied.

3. List words in English that are derived from the language studied.

4. Ask students to describe a basketball, football, or soccer game in the language they are studying.

5. Provide students with direction cards written in English. Have them state the directions in the foreign language. For example, directions for finding the children's department in a department store could be provided.

6. The preceding activity can be reversed, with the directions printed in a foreign language and the students stating them in English.

7. Have students write, in a foreign language, an advertisement to sell an automobile.

8. Provide students with grocery advertisements, and ask them to write the foreign word for each item in the advertisement.

9. Provide students with objects to categorize by form, function, color, or texture in the foreign language.

10. Demonstrate a think-aloud for a foreign language reading selection, then have the students create their own think-alouds for content they are reading in the foreign language.

11. Access foreign language sites on the Internet.

Focus on Struggling Readers

Struggling Readers in Content Area Reading

One of the greatest content literacy problems facing struggling readers is their lack of concepts and vocabulary relating to the subject matter at hand (Grady, 2002). The extent to which readers are able to understand texts depends on prior knowledge and their ability to implement comprehension strategies. Struggling readers read infrequently, so they have not acquired the requisite background knowledge, skills, and vocabulary needed for comprehending content materials. Teachers need to build background for understanding and to illustrate the relationships between students' existing knowledge and the texts they are reading. Various kinds of reading support and scaffolding help these readers.

Reading coaches are a form of support that has been successful in helping struggling readers in the content areas. Bacon (2005) used a one-on-one peer coaching system wherein students acted as reading coaches for one another and learned to prompt, question, and probe their peers' thinking, in much the same way that a reading specialist does. A reading apprenticeship was developed as part of an academic literacy course in a San Francisco high school (Greenleaf et al., 2001). In this program, students were mentored as they read subject area texts. The mentors helped students understand how and why readers need vocabulary and concepts related to different texts. One of the questions addressed in this program was, "What do I need to know to be able to understand these different kinds of texts?" The author reports that the struggling readers in the program demonstrated significant gains on standardized reading comprehension measures. Moreover, the students indicated that they believed the mentoring approach affected them in positive ways.

Self-questioning is a highly effective strategy (Stoodt-Hill, 2005). Students require modeling prior to developing their own questions about the topic under study. Generating questions to find the answers through study encourages active reading. This helps students grasp the important ideas. After reading they remember more of the vital information and are better able to analyze and synthesize. Alverman (2004) analyzed the research on self-questioning and drew implications from these studies that indicate that self-questioning would serve science learning.

Explicitly teaching strategies for understanding text and monitoring comprehension help struggling readers understand content textbooks. The most valuable strategies for helping struggling readers are K-W-L, self-questioning, visual imagery, ReQuest (Reciprocal questioning), retelling, and question-answer relationships (Dole et al., 1996; Quatroche, 1999). All of these valuable strategies have been discussed previously in this text except ReQuest. Reciprocal questioning (ReQuest) improves comprehension and helps students develop questioning skills. This strategy is used most effectively in the classroom when the teacher models the process with a student and then pairs students to follow the procedure. The basic steps in ReQuest follow:

1. Both student and teacher silently read the first sentence of the selection. Then the student asks the teacher (or paired student) as many questions as possible about the sentence—with the book closed. The student attempts to ask the kinds of questions that the teacher would routinely pose for the class.

2. The teacher (or paired student) answers all the student's questions, asking the student to restate any question that was poorly stated. The teacher or partner restates any answers that the student does not fully understand.

3. After all the questions have been answered, the second sentence is read—and the teacher or second student now asks thought-provoking questions to ensure comprehension of the content. The teacher acts as a questioning model for the student and goes on to pose questions that require evaluation of prior student responses.

4. ReQuest continues until the student can confidently answer the questions, "What do you think is going to happen in the rest of this selection?" And "What have you read that causes you to make this prediction?" The student reads to the end of the selection to determine if the prediction was correct.

Focus on English Language Learners

English Language Learners and Content Area Reading

English language learners (ELLs) need cultural background to develop the fund of everyday knowledge needed to understand content textbooks (Moje et al., 2004). ELLs need resources to help them make sense of the United States. They also need a sense of both oral and written language as they exist in the United States. Effective instruction for ELLs requires teacher-planned scaffolding (Graves and Fitzgerald, 2003). Activating or building background knowledge is necessary, as is specific text knowledge. Graves and Fitzgerald (2003) suggest that ELLs write a list of what they know about a topic before reading. The goal is to prepare students to read the selection.

SUMMARY

This chapter focuses on content literacy for printed texts and media literacy because they require similar reading skills and strategies. Secondary students read content materials in social studies, science and health, mathematics, English (language arts), and foreign languages. Written materials and media in each of these content areas have characteristic patterns of language and organization that students can use to increase comprehension. Examples of content texts and strategies to increase understanding are presented throughout the chapter. Content literacy presents particular problems for struggling readers and for English language learners. These students tend to lack the background knowledge and concepts needed for successful content reading.

DISCUSSION QUESTIONS

1. How are social studies content and mathematics content alike in their demands? How are they different?
2. Why is critical reading important in all content areas?
3. How do multiple literacies relate to content reading?
4. How can teachers help students comprehend mathematics content?
5. What are the characteristics of science materials?
6. How can reading coaches help both struggling readers and English language learners?

ENRICHMENT ACTIVITIES

*1.   Prepare a study guide for a chapter in a social studies or science textbook. Use it with a secondary class.

*2.   Prepare a study guide for a verbal problem in a mathematics textbook. Use it with a secondary class.

3.   Develop a bibliography of trade books that could be used to enrich a textbook chapter. Let secondary students use books from this list as they read the chapter.

*4.   Prepare a multigenre assignment for your content area.

5.   Check professional journals such as *Social Education*, *Science Teacher*, *Mathematics Teacher*, and *English Journal* for articles dealing with reading of content material. Share your findings with the class.

6.   Check the readability level of a textbook and/or supplementary material used for one of the subjects treated in this chapter. See Chapter 12 for details.

7.   Review computer software that could be used to teach one of the content subjects in this chapter.

*8.   Identify Internet sites to use with your content area.

*These activities are designed for in-service teachers, student teachers, and practicum students.

Chapter 11

Reading in the Content Areas: II

OVERVIEW

The focus of this chapter is reading in vocational, workplace, and performance-based content areas. In recent years, the lines between academic and vocational education have become increasingly blurred as educators have recognized that all students need active involvement in constructing meaning and connecting learning to the world outside of school (Christ, 1995; Wonacott, 2002). Further major changes are taking place in workplace education as the curriculum becomes more demanding due to an upgraded core of academic courses. The content study and achievement required of **tech-prep students** are comparable to that required of college-prep students (Bottoms and Presson, 2000; Wonacott, 2002). Programs for these students are founded on the belief that blending the content of traditional college-preparatory studies in mathematics, science, and language arts with quality vocational and technical studies will provide a high-quality education for vocational and technical students (Plank, 2001; Roberson et al., 2001).

Evidence points to increasing reliance on technology in every occupational category (Smith, 2000; Sumner, 2001; Wonacott, 2001). Therefore, teachers need to prepare students to use technology communication skills for the workplace and to continuously update their knowledge in order to keep pace with technology.

PURPOSE-SETTING QUESTIONS

As you read this chapter, try to answer these questions:

1. Identify some ways that technology communication skills are necessary for students in career and vocational studies.
2. What reading skills increase comprehension of content information in physical education?
3. What reading skills are required in music and art?

continued

4. What strategies are useful for helping students comprehend the content and applications of vocational and technical materials?

5. Why are traditional college-preparatory studies important to preparing career-related education students?

Literacy for Career-Related Education

Work-based learning is a key factor in current models of career-related education (Hoyt, 2001). Today's students need basic skills and opportunities for practical applications of these skills as well as higher-order thinking skills in order to deal with the changes in work and the workplace (Hoyt and Wickwire, 2001). Career technical education contributes to our country's ability to compete in the global community. Its curriculum, standards, and organizing principles are drawn from the workplace (National Association of State Directors of Career Technical Education Consortium, 2001). An organized, comprehensive approach is needed to address changes in the work force and in national priorities and policies (Kerka, 1994). One strategy that addresses work force changes is the requirement of the Certificate of Initial Mastery, a document that students must earn in a growing number of states. This document shows that students have what it takes to graduate and succeed in the real world (Rothman, 1995). High school seniors in these programs are expected to work at least sixty hours on real-world projects.

However, the history of vocational education in this country shows that the programs also must keep the four-year college option open to students in a high school vocational curriculum; otherwise it will be difficult to attract ambitious students and to avoid acquiring a second-rate image. The 1990 Perkins Act and the 1994 School-to-Work Opportunities Act (Stern and Rahn, 1995) supported new educational options for vocational students.

Students who are preparing for careers in vocational and technical areas face more complex literacy demands than their predecessors did. Employees and those who seek employment must be prepared to find printed, oral, and graphic information. This task requires comprehension, analysis, synthesis, and evaluation necessary for gaining that information (Kibby, 2000; Mikulecky, 2000). Then they must transform information by writing and speaking about it and by visually representing it. Finally, they must transmit information through publishing or otherwise disseminating it (Kibby, 2000). Preparation for work now demands that students engage in the process of making meaning out of complex and layered combinations of messages that use video, audio, and print representations (Hobbs and Frost, 2003).

In **career-related education**, students reflect as they write about what they have seen and done in the workplace, and they discuss their writing in class. This process allows them to see how the problems they have confronted at work may relate to the subjects they have studied in school (Stern and Rahn, 1995). Students also need writing skills to report observations and data collected, to fill in job cards, and to complete projects.

Hobbs and Frost (2003) conducted media-literacy skill research with eleventh-grade students. One research group was instructed in media literacy skills for a year. This group achieved a higher level of comprehension skills than a second group which did not receive instruction in media literacy skills. This study illustrates that media-literacy skills can be taught. Computer literacy skills instruction is necessary because, although students may appear to be computer literate because they have computers at home and may be very adept at playing games on them, these students do not fare as well when they need to use the computer for work-related purposes.

TECHNICAL EDUCATION

Literacy is an integral part of technical and managerial jobs. People in these positions read to analyze problems, propose solutions, and carry out research. Managers and supervisors read to review, advise, assign, and develop organizational procedures and policies. They write materials such as letters, memos, policies, and training materials. Managers may have to create training programs when new equipment or material, such as a new type of cash register or a new version of accounting software, is installed. Business software must often be updated, and business files of customers, clients, and patients have to be systematically examined to ensure that they are current.

Aspects of Vocational Literacy

TECHNICAL EDUCATION

Since the amount of written material used in vocational subjects appears to be less than that required in other subjects, students and teachers may misjudge the difficulty of these materials. Many vocational materials are written in a concise expository style with technical vocabulary and are dense with information. Even brief vocational reading selections demand precise, careful reading. Students must be able to follow directions and to apply ideas and words to actual situations; misreading could be costly. See Figure 11.1 for a text illustrating the communication skills needed in the building trades.

TECHNICAL AND SPECIALIZED TERMINOLOGY

BUSINESS EDUCATION

HES/HUMAN ECOLOGY

Each career-related subject includes a great deal of specialized vocabulary that represents essential concepts. For example, the word *credit* has a special meaning in bookkeeping, where it refers to a bookkeeping entry that shows money paid on an account. ("You should place this entry on the *credit* side of the ledger.") In career-related subjects, technical terms usually represent concrete concepts. For example, in human environmental science (human ecology), *sauté* represents a particular way of cooking food that can be observed.

The precise meaning of a technical word usually cannot be derived from context clues or dictionary definition. Technical material often does not provide the necessary clues to help a reader define a term, and many dictionaries do not include the technical definitions of vocational terms. Therefore, vocabulary instruction is especially important in vocational subjects, and teachers need to develop word meanings as they teach these subjects. Teaching vocational and performance-based terminology means pointing out and defining new terms before assigning reading materials.

FIGURE 11.1

Text Illustration of the Communication Skills Needed in the Building Trades

Source: John L. Feirer, Gilbert R. Hutchings, and Mark D. Feirer, *Carpentry and Building Construction*, 5th ed. (New York: Glencoe McGraw-Hill, 1997), p. 939. Reprinted by permission of Glencoe McGraw-Hill.

Appendix E: Communication Skills

Good communication skills are needed in almost every job. Good communication skills are especially important in the building trades. Here, an error in communicating or understanding information can have serious consequences.

The Need to Communicate

It is the rare individual who works without the need to communicate with others. Almost everyone has to communicate with his or her fellow workers several times a day. Such communication can, of course, involve relatively unimportant information. It can also relate to serious matters. Communication with your coworkers is a necessary part of every job in the building trades. Because of this, it is important that you have good communication skills.

Verbal Skills

All who work in the building trades need the same general communication skills. They need to be able to communicate clearly. They need to be able to listen well. Some individuals, however, will need these skills in a greater degree than others. This is because they will have a greater need to rely on such skills in their jobs. The need for communication skills can depend on job responsibilities. For example, a worksite supervisor would generally have a need for a greater range of communication skills.

Regardless of your job, you must be able to tell your coworkers the information they need to do their jobs. If necessary, you must also be able to offer them clear instruction on work procedures.

Writing Skills

Depending on your job, you may need to prepare written instructions or reports for others. Work of this sort is usually done by those immediately supervising a worksite. For very large construction projects, the preparation of such reports may be done by those overseeing the general project. Small builders and contractors have to communicate with clients by means of written bids.

Ability to Read Plans

You may need to refer to plans, such as building plans. The number and type of plans you will need to refer to will depend on your job. In any case, you must be able to read and understand the plans that you work with. This will require that you have a knowledge of the symbols and conventions used in technical drawing.

Listening Skills

Having good communication skills also means that you must be a good listener. As well as being able to communicate clearly with others, you must be able to understand what they are telling you. This means that you must be able to listen well. It also means that you must be able to read and understand written instructions (such as those on plans and drawings). You must also be able to ask clearly worded questions when you do not understand something.

Instructors can demonstrate the concrete meanings of many technical terms by showing students the objects or activities the words represent. Students can develop dictionaries of technical terms by entering vocabulary in notebooks. This activity will help them learn word meanings and spellings. Pictures or drawings can be added to the terms to vary this activity. The teacher should give the students quizzes on these words every other week to check vocabulary development. Additional suggestions for developing word meanings are presented in Chapter 3.

FOLLOWING DIRECTIONS

TECHNICAL EDUCATION   **BUSINESS EDUCATION**

Every technical and vocational subject requires the student to read directions and to translate them into action. For example, students in technological education must read directions for operating and repairing various pieces of equipment. In business education, students read directions for operating computers and other business machines and for setting up bookkeeping systems. Reading directions is a slow, precise process. Students often need to reread and apply strategies such as SQ3R to achieve complete understanding. They will find the following questions useful for building comprehension:

1. What am I trying to do? (What is the task?)

2. What materials are required?

3. Do I understand all of the terms (words) used in these directions?

4. What is the sequence of steps?

5. Have I omitted anything?

6. Am I ready to perform the task?

7. Was I successful in accomplishing the task?

These questions can be incorporated into study guides. Additional suggestions for developing study guides are included later in this chapter and in Chapters 5 and 10. Suggestions for following directions are found in Chapter 7.

TECHNOLOGY

What computer applications can you add to those suggested here?

ART   **MUSIC**

TECHNICAL EDUCATION

There are many important computer applications in vocational and performance-based fields, including ones for securing up-to-date information and for solving problems. For example, in performance-based fields, students of dance can choreograph on computers; art students can explore art on the Internet and create art on a computer; and musicians can compose on computers.

Likewise, computers are used in vocational fields—for example, to diagnose automotive problems or to provide support in the business arena. The use of computers, fax machines, conference calls, and the Internet are nearly universal today. Therefore, students in all of these content areas will need to learn the computer applications and the Internet sites that are relevant to their work. Users need to apply critical reading skills to the materials they access.

Teachers and prospective teachers will find the Internet enormously helpful in their work. The Internet provides access to journals in agriculture, business, human environmental science (human ecology), career and technical education, nursing education, vocational education, art, and music. The Internet site http://www.eric.ed.gov includes lists of journals and lesson plans for specific subjects and grade levels. Lesson plans for architecture, computers in art, art history, Beethoven's Ninth Symphony, physical education, and vocational education were found in a recent visit to this site. There are links to electronic newsletters that help teachers stay up-to-date. (See Chapter 2 for more on computer use.)

GRAPHIC MATERIALS

What types of graphic materials do vocational and technical students have to read?

Vocational and technical students have to read a variety of **graphic materials**, such as blueprints, drawings, cutaways, patterns, pictures, and sketches. They must be able to visualize and interpret the scales and legends that accompany many graphic materials in order to understand both the illustrations and the textual materials.

Teachers should give students many opportunities to convert written directions, drawings, and blueprints into models and actual objects. Students must coordinate the text with any illustrations and perform such tasks as matching blueprints and diagrams with pictures of the finished products. These activities help students develop the ability to visualize written ideas. Having students prepare directions, diagrams, and blueprints for classmates to follow will help them to become more adept at understanding these written materials themselves.

Example 11.1 shows a diagram from a human environmental science (human ecology) text, and Example 11.2 shows graphic material from a physical education text.

READING RATE

Why do vocational students have to make many rate adjustments when reading?

Readers of vocational and technical materials must adjust their reading rates according to purpose, type of content, and familiarity with the subject, as is true of all readers. Vocational materials are often problem oriented and include many directions that require students to adjust their reading rates to accommodate variations in reading content. In vocational studies, students read a wide variety of materials that require frequent rate adjustments. Teachers can facilitate rate adjustment by having students identify appropriate rates for each type of content.

PROBLEM SOLVING

In vocational and performance-based subjects, the teachers' goals are to increase the students' ability to think on the job and to perform job-related tasks. Meeting these goals is facilitated when students bring real-life problems to class discussion and to reading. Students who have opportunities for work-based learning have an advantage because they can contribute actual experiences and problems to class discussions and problem solving.

Parts of the Sewing Machine (Human Environmental Science/Human Ecology)

EXAMPLE 11.1

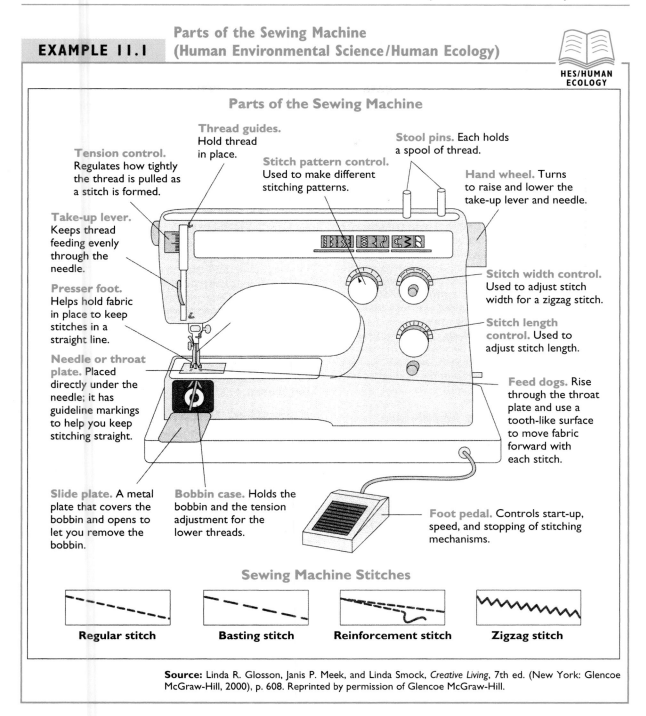

Parts of the Sewing Machine

Tension control. Regulates how tightly the thread is pulled as a stitch is formed.

Thread guides. Hold thread in place.

Stitch pattern control. Used to make different stitching patterns.

Stool pins. Each holds a spool of thread.

Hand wheel. Turns to raise and lower the take-up lever and needle.

Take-up lever. Keeps thread feeding evenly through the needle.

Presser foot. Helps hold fabric in place to keep stitches in a straight line.

Needle or throat plate. Placed directly under the needle; it has guideline markings to help you keep stitching straight.

Stitch width control. Used to adjust stitch width for a zigzag stitch.

Stitch length control. Used to adjust stitch length.

Feed dogs. Rise through the throat plate and use a tooth-like surface to move fabric forward with each stitch.

Slide plate. A metal plate that covers the bobbin and opens to let you remove the bobbin.

Bobbin case. Holds the bobbin and the tension adjustment for the lower threads.

Foot pedal. Controls start-up, speed, and stopping of stitching mechanisms.

Sewing Machine Stitches

Regular stitch   **Basting stitch**   **Reinforcement stitch**   **Zigzag stitch**

Source: Linda R. Glosson, Janis P. Meek, and Linda Smock, *Creative Living*, 7th ed. (New York: Glencoe McGraw-Hill, 2000), p. 608. Reprinted by permission of Glencoe McGraw-Hill.

EXAMPLE 11.2 Physical Education

PHYSICAL
EDUCATION

The Game of Volleyball

In 1895 William C. Morgan, a YMCA director in Holyoke, Massachusetts, invented a game called *mintonette* in an attempt to meet the needs of local businessmen who found the game of basketball to be too strenuous. The new game caught on quickly because it required only a few basic skills, easily mastered in limited practice time and by players of varying fitness levels. The original game was played with a rubber bladder from a basketball. Early rules allowed any number of players on a side. In 1896 the name was changed by Alfred T. Halstead, who, after viewing a game, felt that *volleyball* would be a more suitable name due to the volleying characteristic of play.

As the game has progressed, many changes in play have occurred. For example, the Filipinos are credited with adding the spike.

The game's status has changed from its being a recreational activity to being recognized as a strenuous sport as well. The Japanese added the sport to the Olympic Games program in 1964; this contributed to the fast growth of volleyball in the last 25 years.

The exciting aspect of volleyball is that it attracts all types of players—recreational to competitive, little skilled to highly skilled—and all ages. The game has great appeal because it requires few basic skills, few rules, few players (from two to six players on a side), and limited equipment, and it can be played on a variety of surfaces, from a hardwood floor to a sandy beach.

Playing a Game

The game of volleyball is played by two teams each having two to six players on a 30-foot square (9-meter square) court, the two courts separated by a net. The primary objective of each team is to try

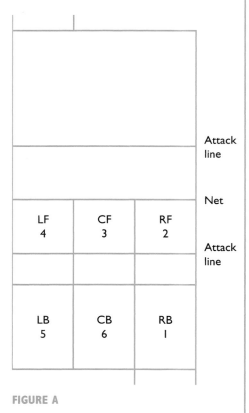

FIGURE A

Players arranged in proper rotational positions.

to hit the ball to the opponent's side in such a manner as to prevent the opponent from returning the ball. This is usually accomplished by using a three-hit combination of a forearm pass to a setter, followed by a set to an attacker, who spikes the ball into the opponent's court.

When there are six players on a side, three are called *forwards,* and three are called *backs.* The three players in the front row are called *left forward* (LF), *center forward* (CF), and *right forward* (RF). The three players in the back row are called *left back* (LB), *center back* (CB), and *right back* (RB). Players need to be in their correct *rotational positions* until the serve is executed. This means that players cannot overlap positions from front to back or from side to side (see Figure A). After the serve, players are allowed to play in any position on or off the court, with one restriction: back row players cannot leave the floor to hit the ball when in front of the attack line.

Source: Barbara L. Viera and Bonnie Jill Ferguson, *Volleyball Steps to Success* (Champaign, Ill.: Leisure Press, 1989), p. 1. Copyright © 1989 by Leisure Press. Reprinted by permission of Human Kinetics Publishers.

What is an example of problem-solving materials that could be used in vocational classes?

A problem-solving approach and student questions create a mental context for reading and thinking. The following problems were selected from problems posed by or for students in various content areas:

1. List the financial records and documents necessary for a businessperson who operates one of the following: a restaurant, a computer repair shop, an electronic sales company. The business could be designated as a small business with fewer than ten employees or a larger business with the number of employees specified.

2. Detail the materials and equipment needed to take a corn crop from planting to harvest.

3. List the tools you need to build a chair.

4. Identify the materials needed to build a specific item or machine.

5. Prepare menus for nutritionally balanced meals for a week for a family of three based on a specified budget.

6. Set up an office mailing system for a company.

The problem-solution writing pattern is common in career-related materials. These materials also include presentations of factual information and how-to-do-it directions. Reading instruction should focus on these types of content materials.

WRITING

Writing is an asset in retaining and understanding content materials. Through writing activities, students expand their understanding of technical and vocational language and their ability to express ideas effectively. Writing activities also develop students' knowledge of technical vocabulary, sentence structure, paragraph organization, and sequencing. Vocational and technical teachers need to model writing, provide guided practice, and give students feedback to guide their applications of writing in vocational subjects. In Chapter 8, suggestions for content area writing activities are given.

UTILIZING MOTIVATION

TECHNICAL EDUCATION

Many students are personally motivated to learn about vocational and technical subjects, so their interest can stimulate them to read. However, vocational and technical education teachers should stimulate their students to do further reading. The classroom library should include trade periodicals and Internet access, which provide information about new products, materials, and techniques. Periodicals also include general information about the various trades and careers. One issue of *Career World* discussed agribusiness, political careers, chefs, and physicians, as well as career guidance and interviewing strategies. Teachers can use trade- and career-related materials to develop their students' reading interests and understanding of the content area, thereby increasing students' ability to predict content and, consequently, to comprehend content materials. Following are some suggestions for using motivational strategies to increase comprehension of content materials:

Which would you choose as the most important motivational strategy suggested?

1. Display subject area books, magazines, and related materials appropriate to student interest and reading levels.

2. Suggest additional readings in magazines, newspapers, periodicals, books, and Internet sites.

3. Review and refer to relevant books.

4. Use learning activities such as field trips, movies, audio and video recordings, computer programs, and radio and television programs to build background and to stimulate a desire for further information.

5. Provide time in class for reading materials related to class topics.

6. Have students compare and contrast the way two or more authors have treated a topic.

7. Encourage students to discuss their readings with each other in pairs or in cooperative learning groups.

8. Permit students to work together so that good readers can help less able ones.

THE TEXTBOOK AS A REFERENCE

Teachers should make a particular effort to explain and demonstrate the use of textbooks and real-life printed materials as reference works, since vocational teachers use a wide variety of materials in a problem-solving format and students often are not acquainted with this approach. Instruction that familiarizes the students with the wealth of information provided in printed materials will help them to use these materials for acquiring knowledge and solving problems.

READING STRATEGIES

How does reading-to-learn contrast with reading-to-do?

Teachers need to prepare students to read vocational materials prior to reading, support them during reading, and follow up after reading. Reading-to-learn and reading-to-do are both kinds of reading that vocational and technical students are often required to do. **Reading-to-learn** is a task in which an individual reads with the intention of remembering and applying textual information. **Reading-to-do** is a task in which an individual uses the material as an aid to doing something else. In the latter situation, the materials often serve as "external memories" because the individual may refer to them to check information rather than to specifically learn the content. The most common on-the-job reading is reading-to-do, which may demand the following reading strategies:

1. **Read/rehearse**, which involves repeating the information or reading it again.

2. **Problem solve/question**, which involves answering questions posed by the text or searching for the information necessary to solve a specific problem.

3. **Relate/associate**, which is associating new information with the individual's existing store of information.

4. **Focus attention**, which involves reducing the amount of information to be remembered in some way, such as by underlining, outlining, or taking notes.

Why do you think directed reading lessons help vocational students comprehend?

Directed reading lessons are useful in helping vocational students learn to read textual materials. Example 11.3 is a directed reading lesson based on human environmental science (human ecology) content.

After students read a chapter and complete a study guide similar to the one in Example 11.5, which is based on vocational materials shown in Example 11.4, they should have an opportunity to discuss their answers and should be prepared to explain and support them by citing the text.

HES/HUMAN ECOLOGY

EXAMPLE 11.3

Directed Reading Lesson
(Human Environmental Science/Human Ecology)

Motivation and Building Background

1. Ask students the following questions: What kind of fabric is used in the clothing you are wearing today? What is your favorite kind of fabric? Here is a box of various types of fabric. Look at each piece, and try to determine the contents of each piece of fabric.

Skill-Development Activities

2. Discuss and pronounce each of the following vocabulary words. Be certain students have a concept for each type of fabric by giving them labeled samples of each to examine.

wool	brocade	satin	velvet
synthetic fabric	lamé	cotton	

Guided Reading

3. *Silent*—Provide students with *silent reading purposes* such as the following: How do you choose a suitable fabric to make a dress? How are synthetic fabrics different from natural fabrics? Have the students read the lesson silently.
4. *Discussion*—Discuss the silent reading purposes, and ask discussion questions such as the following: Do you prefer natural or synthetic fabrics? Why? What are the advantages of natural fabrics? What kind of dress pattern would you choose for a brocade fabric?

Follow-Up Activities

5. Have students reread as necessary to solve the problem of selecting an appropriate fabric for their next garment.

EXAMPLE 11.4   Sample Writing in Vocational Materials

Interior and Exterior Painting

TECHNICAL EDUCATION

Paints have been used for thousands of years to decorate and protect surfaces. Paint is now the most widely used finish on the exteriors and interiors of homes. Proper application of the material can prolong the life of a home and improve its appearance. Different effects and levels of protection can be obtained through the use of different kinds of paints. Outside surfaces require paints that will offer protection against weathering and moisture. Interior paints have various purposes:

- They make surfaces easy to clean.
- They impart wear resistance.
- They seal surfaces from moisture and vapor penetration.
- They complement or enhance a desired decorating effect.

This unit is divided into three sections. The first two (interior painting and exterior painting) cover tools and techniques. The third section discusses how to identify and solve paint problems.

Interior Painting

Many different kinds of interior paints are available. The most popular are the latex paints because they are easy to apply and dry quickly. For a high-gloss or semigloss finish, a good-quality enamel is better. Flat alkyd wall paints are also very popular because they are easy to apply, washable, and good for one-coat hiding. These paints are made from alkyds combined with special oils. They are excellent for covering almost any interior surface, including plaster, wood, wallboard, metal, or wallpaper.

Drywall and Plaster

Most plaster and drywall surfaces are finished with two coats of either flat, alkyd or latex paint. An initial treatment with size or sealer will improve holdout (reduce penetration of succeeding coats). Thus less paint will be needed for good coverage.

Kitchen and bathroom walls, which are exposed to high humidity and receive more wear, are best finished with one application of undercoater and two coats of semigloss enamel. This type of finish wears well, is easy to clean, and resists moisture.

Planning the Painting   On no other surface is skillful application of paint so important as it is for flat work on plaster walls and ceilings. Because paint must be distributed in a uniform film, extra care in brushing is necessary. Interior surfaces are normally under longer and closer observation than are exterior surfaces. Hence, the brushing on, smoothing out, and leveling off of the paint must be done with particular care.

Source: John L. Feirer, Gilbert R. Hutchings, and Mark D. Feirer, *Carpentry and Building Construction*, 5th ed. (New York: Glencoe McGraw-Hill, 1997), p. 838. Reprinted by permission of Glencoe McGraw-Hill.

EXAMPLE 11.5   Study Guide for Selection on Interior and Exterior Painting

**TECHNICAL
EDUCATION**

This selection introduces interior and exterior painting.

Vocabulary

Explain each of these terms in your own words and give examples where possible: *weathering, moisture, vapor penetration, latex, high-gloss, enamel, flat alkyd wall paint, drywall, uniform film, humidity*. Use a dictionary.

Directions: Use the selection to find the answers to these questions and write the answers in your own words.

Literal
  1. What is the most widely used finish for home interiors and exteriors?
  2. What are the purposes of interior paint?
  3. Why are latex paints popular?
  4. What are flat alkyd wall paints made from?
  5. How are most plaster and drywall surfaces finished?

Directions: Write a short answer to each of the following questions.

Interpretive
  6. Why is flat alkyd paint appropriate for interior rather than exterior surfaces?
  7. What will happen to an interior surface if you do not smooth out and level the paint?
  8. What will happen to kitchen or bathroom walls that are not finished with undercoater and two coats of semigloss enamel?

Applied
  9. Give an example of an item that you would not choose to finish with alkyd paint.
  10. Give an example of a room surface that you would not choose to finish with latex paint.
  11. How could you get a uniform film of paint without brushing?

Applications of Literacy Strategies

The sections that follow discuss how specific literacy skills and strategies can be applied to particular subject areas. However, the skills and strategies that are demonstrated can be used interchangeably in the various subject areas. In addition, the activities included in Chapter 10 can be used with the content areas discussed in this chapter.

TECHNICAL EDUCATION

**TECHNICAL
EDUCATION**

Technical content includes materials written about machine operation, woodworking, auto mechanics, drafting, electronics repair, and so forth. Obviously, these areas have large technical vocabularies that students must understand. Example 11.6 shows a selection from a carpentry text.

Readers must understand the following essential words in order to understand the selection in Example 11.6: *pulley, lever, triangulation, pivot, load, effort, movement, force, distance.*

Many of the terms that are used in technical education classes are related to tools and equipment. Demonstrating and labeling tools and equipment clearly in the classroom can help students learn to recognize these terms when they appear in textbooks.

Many reading tasks in technical education involve the students' ability to read and carry out directions. For example, students must know how to follow step-by-step directions for operating equipment, constructing furniture, or installing a carburetor. They must learn to follow the directions on "job sheets," which are used in technology education classes to assign daily work. Safety rules are very important reading content for technology education. Teachers should prepare study guides to help students comprehend and carry out complicated written instructions.

BUSINESS EDUCATION

**BUSINESS
EDUCATION**

Business education encompasses a wide variety of studies, including transcribing recorded material, typing, bookkeeping, computer applications, general business, business mathematics, business law, management, economics, and business communications. Each of the courses in business education has considerable written content. Courses in business rely heavily on reading as an important part of instruction. Many people in business face an increasing volume of transactions and the accompanying paperwork, due to the heavy use of computers and facsimile machines.

Many of the written materials used in business and industry are complex and have a high readability level. These materials are often filled with specialized concepts and loaded with information. However, business education textbooks probably do not reflect the diversity apparent in business reading materials. Generally, these textbooks fall into two categories: how-to-do-it manuals and informational books. Students must acquire the reading skills, not only to read the textbooks that

EXAMPLE 11.6   Technical Content

TECHNICAL
EDUCATION

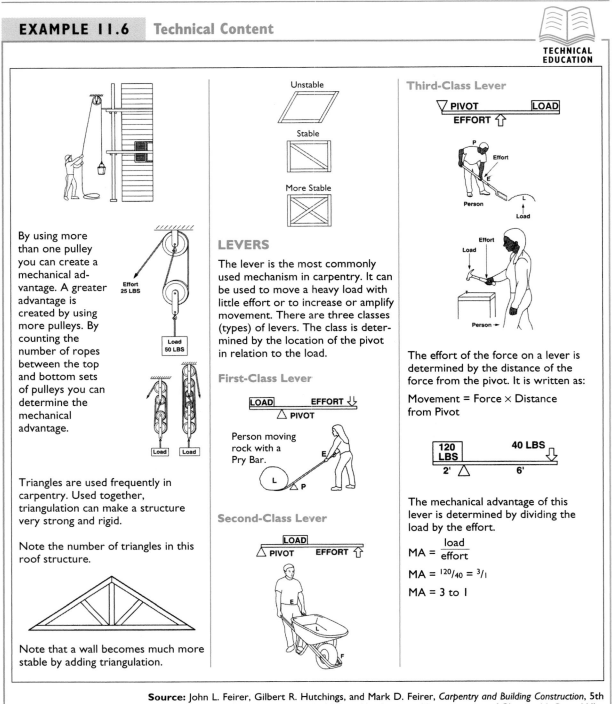

By using more than one pulley you can create a mechanical advantage. A greater advantage is created by using more pulleys. By counting the number of ropes between the top and bottom sets of pulleys you can determine the mechanical advantage.

Triangles are used frequently in carpentry. Used together, triangulation can make a structure very strong and rigid.

Note the number of triangles in this roof structure.

Note that a wall becomes much more stable by adding triangulation.

LEVERS

The lever is the most commonly used mechanism in carpentry. It can be used to move a heavy load with little effort or to increase or amplify movement. There are three classes (types) of levers. The class is determined by the location of the pivot in relation to the load.

First-Class Lever

Person moving rock with a Pry Bar.

Second-Class Lever

Third-Class Lever

The effort of the force on a lever is determined by the distance of the force from the pivot. It is written as:

Movement = Force × Distance from Pivot

The mechanical advantage of this lever is determined by dividing the load by the effort.

$$MA = \frac{load}{effort}$$

$$MA = {}^{120}/_{40} = {}^{3}/_{1}$$

$$MA = 3 \text{ to } 1$$

Source: John L. Feirer, Gilbert R. Hutchings, and Mark D. Feirer, *Carpentry and Building Construction*, 5th ed. (New York: Glencoe McGraw-Hill, 1997), p. 934. Reprinted by permission of Glencoe McGraw-Hill.

are often the basis of classroom instruction, but also to read the other business materials that will be important to their careers.

Business education students and people who work in business commonly apply literacy skills such as the following:

1. Reading directions or instructions and implementing them. Workers who have to stop others to ask for instructions or who complete tasks incorrectly slow down others and themselves.

2. Skimming and/or scanning to locate needed information. These skills may be used to locate materials needed in problem solving and report writing.

3. Reading and identifying main ideas and details in newspapers, magazines, and professional journals to learn about current trends in the business world.

4. Reading memos. Memos are organized differently from other types of written communication, and they often inform employees of changes in existing practices or policies in a business situation; therefore, the receiver must read these communications and remember the details.

5. Reading and responding to business letters. Business letters are organized differently, use more technical vocabulary, and use different semantics from social correspondence. Thus they require different reading skills.

6. Reading invoices to check their accuracy.

7. Reading computer printouts to locate needed information. These printouts may be used for problem solving or as a basis for planning programs to meet specific needs.

8. Reading reference materials such as interest tables, financial handbooks, and handbooks of business mathematics. Students must interpret and apply this information.

9. Reading and interpreting textbooks in order to complete class assignments that enable students to learn business skills.

10. Reading technical vocabulary. There are specific terms for each course.

Example 11.7 contains a selection from a business education textbook. Note the technical terminology, including *real estate, personal property tax, assessor, assessment, revenues,* and *tax base.* The preview guide, shown in Example 11.8, should be completed by students before they read the selection; it helps readers anticipate the selection content, thus increasing comprehension. After students have completed the preview guide and read the chapter, they should have an opportunity to discuss, ask questions, and support their answers.

EXAMPLE 11.7   Business Education Content

**BUSINESS
EDUCATION**

Property Tax

Local governments get a major share of their revenues from property taxes. This includes counties, cities, towns, townships, and school districts. About one-third of all revenues at this level comes from property tax. The state and federal governments have almost no revenue from this tax.

A **real estate property tax** is one on the value of land, and anything on the land such as houses, barns, garages, or other buildings. A second tax is the **personal property tax,** a tax applied to movable items such as automobiles, furniture, and machinery used by businesses. Because of the ease with which personal property can be hidden, the personal property tax is being used less and less. Real estate has thus become the most important property tax base and source of revenue for local communities.

The amount of real estate taxes is determined by first estimating the value of the property, and then multiplying the tax rate by the value. The amount at which the property is valued is called an **assessment,** and the government official who does the valuation is called an **assessor.**

Source: Betty Brown and John Clow, *General Business: Our Business and Economic World*, p. 231. Copyright © 1982 by Houghton Mifflin Company. Reprinted by permission of Houghton Mifflin Company.

EXAMPLE 11.8   Preview Guide

Directions: Place a check mark under the *Yes* column if you believe the selection will support the statement. Place a check under the *No* column if you believe the text will not support the statement. After you read the selection, review your responses.

Yes	No	
_____	_____	**1.** Property tax is levied on real estate and personal property.
_____	_____	**2.** Property tax is not levied on any personal property that can be bought and sold.
_____	_____	**3.** Personal property tax is applied to movable items.
_____	_____	**4.** Taxpayers may be exempted from paying tax on the full value of a property if there is a mortgage on it.
_____	_____	**5.** Taxpayers find it difficult to avoid paying personal property tax.
_____	_____	**6.** The assessed value of a property is the basis for calculating the amount of tax.

What is an example
of a way that business
students combine
skimming or scanning
with close reading?

Business students need to combine skimming and scanning with close reading after they locate the text they need to examine carefully. First, they should *skim* for the main idea or *scan* for specific information that they need to solve a problem, to compose a letter or memo, or to write a report. Then they should carefully and analytically read (*close reading*) the section or sections of content containing the information they need. Close reading for details and main ideas is important because in many situations even a small error can have serious consequences. For example, a bookkeeping error can make a company appear profitable when it is actually losing money; a secretary's error in typing and proofreading a business letter can change the entire meaning of an important communication or a contract; and a tiny error in a computer program may result in a program that will not run or gives incorrect results.

Chapters 3, 4, and 5 include suggestions for teaching students how to read for meaning. Teaching strategies such as preview guides, study guides, and directed reading lessons can help business education students refine vital comprehension skills. Each of these strategies can be applied to a specific area of business education.

Business education teachers need to link their classroom activities to real-world requirements. The "Meeting the Challenge" vignette on page 368 shows how one teacher did this. The guide that Ms. Carruthers developed was effective in helping the students link new information from the class to real-life needs.

A Reading Strategy for Business Education Materials

Explain the PRC
strategy in your own
words.

Students who must read the many kinds of materials identified earlier in this section can improve their reading comprehension by using a strategy like **PRC**. Its three phases are *prereading, reading,* and *consolidation.*

Prereading.   The prereading phase of the business reading process is the limbering up part. The readers survey the reading material to identify the type of content (e.g., memo, letter, report, text) and to set the stage for remembering it. During this phase, the readers identify topics around which they can cluster the ideas that are in the selection. They also identify the author's organization; knowing how the material is organized will help them pinpoint the main ideas when reading. During the prereading phase, the readers establish questions that will guide their reading, such as the sample questions that follow:

1. What new information does this selection tell me?

2. What is the main point?

3. What are the important details?

4. What questions will I be asked about this reading?

Reading.   The students read carefully if close reading is necessary or scan if that is adequate. If they are reading to gather data to write an important report, some close reading is in order. However, if the students are reading to locate specific pieces of information and those details are all that is needed from the content, then scanning is appropriate.

MEETING THE CHALLENGE

Lori Carruthers teaches business education courses in a large high school. Many of her students are employed in after-school and weekend jobs while enrolled in her classes. Although these students have opportunities to apply what they are learning in class, Lori has found that they do not relate their jobs to textbook assignments. When she asks questions in class discussion that should lead them to reflect on these relationships, the students look blank.

She decided to develop an application/reading guide that would lead them to apply the text to their experiences. The following guide is the first one she developed.

Teachers can help students apply text materials to experiences.
© John Henley/Corbis

Application Guide

1. How are the accounts receivable in your place of business similar to those described in this chapter? How are they different?
2. Does every business have to have financial records? Why or why not?
3. Does the business where you work have financial records? What kinds of records are kept?
4. Does the business where you are employed have computerized financial records? What are the advantages of computerized financial records? What are the disadvantages of computerized records?
5. What source documents are used for the financial records in your place of employment? How are the source documents similar to those discussed in this chapter?
6. How will understanding the process of recording charge sales, payments, and returns help you in other jobs that you might have in the future?

Consolidation.   During this phase, readers consolidate the information acquired from reading. Processing the information helps them organize it for long-term memory and for implementing the ideas presented when that is necessary. Readers may take notes to aid remembering and should ask themselves questions similar to the following:

1. What is it that I don't understand?

2. How does this information relate to what I already know?

3. What other examples can I think of?

4. How does this information change or alter what I already know?

5. How can I implement this information?

HUMAN ENVIRONMENTAL SCIENCE (HUMAN ECOLOGY)

Why is human environmental science (human ecology) considered a multidisciplinary field?

HES/HUMAN ECOLOGY

How are graphic aids related to literacy in human environmental science (human ecology)?

Human environmental science (human ecology) is a multidisciplinary field that emphasizes a synthesis of knowledge in the social and behavioral sciences. This content area focuses on child and family behavior, technological innovations, health, foods and nutrition, clothing and textiles, design, management, housing, home furnishings, and personal growth and development. Secondary students pursue these studies for both vocational and avocational purposes.

These students find that literacy plays an important role in studying the complex materials used in human environmental science (human ecology). Effective teaching strategies include guided reading lessons, study guides, and preview guides. Students have, in fact, requested that teachers provide them with such assistance. Students learn best from their reading when teachers guide them as they read a passage.

Human environmental science (human ecology) content includes many technical terms, for example, *developmental stages*, *teachable moment*, *top sirloin*, *kinship networks*, and *French seam*. Example 11.9 presents a selection from a textbook in this area. Notice that the reader must understand the following terms: *hue*, *primary colors*, *tint*, *value*, *shade*, and *intensity*. The study guide in Example 11.10, which follows the selection, will help students check their understanding of these terms and of the content.

Human environmental science (human ecology) students need to learn to read **graphic aids**, such as diagrams, patterns, drawings, graphs, and charts. Example 11.11 shows a diagram from a human environmental science textbook. Interpreting the pictures and the arrows is important to understanding this diagram. Example 11.12 shows a chart.

Human environmental science (human ecology) students should know how to interpret labels for specific information, such as the labels on foods, fabrics, and cleaning products that tell exactly how much of each item or ingredient is contained in the package. They also should know how to interpret directions for use of products. Teachers can prepare students for reading directions through directed reading lessons, study guides, and other instructional strategies suggested in Chapters 5 and 10.

EXAMPLE 11.9   Selection on Color (Human Environmental Science/Human Ecology)

Color

HES/HUMAN
ECOLOGY

ART

Color, the fifth element of clothing design, has many visual effects. Special terms—such as hue, value, shade, tint, and intensity—are used to describe the effects of color.

Hue is *a specific color name.* Green, red, and blue-violet are examples of hue. A color wheel is an arrangement of basic hues. It shows how the colors are related to each other. Although there are hundreds of hues, they are all blends of three primary colors: red, yellow, and blue, as shown in the color wheel on page 554.

When two primary colors are equally mixed, a secondary color results. The secondary colors are orange, green, and purple. Orange is a mixture of red and yellow and appears on the color wheel halfway between these hues. Green is a mixture of blue and yellow, and purple is a mixture of red and blue.

It is possible to create an infinite number of hues on the color wheel simply by mixing the primary colors in different amounts. For example, by adding more blue to a blue-yellow mixture you will obtain a bluish green commonly known as turquoise. By adding more yellow, you will get a bright yellow-green color often called chartreuse (shahr-TROOS).

White, black, and gray are considered neutrals. They are not included on the color wheel, but they are used to create different values of a hue. **Value** is *the lightness or darkness of a color.* Adding black to a color results in a *darker value,* or **shade,** of that color. Burgundy is a shade of red, for example. Adding white to a color results in a *lighter value,* or **tint,** of that color. Pink is an example of a tint of red.

Intensity is *the brightness or dullness of a color.* Hot pink and lemon yellow are bright. They are high in intensity. Navy blue and rust are examples of subdued colors that are low in intensity.

Color: A solid color outfit generally makes a person appear taller. Complementary colors—such as a yellow shirt and dark purple pants—break up the line of an outfit and make a person look shorter.

Space: The space within a garment can be defined in many ways. A jacket worn with a skirt divides the total space, making the wearer appear shorter than she would in a flowing garment. Pockets, belts, and trims further define space.

Source: Linda R. Glosson, Janis P. Meek, and Linda Smock, *Creative Living,* 7th ed. (New York: Glencoe McGraw-Hill, 2000), p. 553. Reprinted by permission of Glencoe McGraw-Hill.

EXAMPLE 11.10 Study Guide for Selection on Color

HES/HUMAN
ECOLOGY

ART

Introduction

This selection discusses color and terms to describe the effects of color, color classifications, and the relationships among colors. The terms include *primary colors, secondary colors, hues, value, shade, tint, and intensity*. Some of the relationships consist of shades and tints of colors, intensity, and complementary relationships.

Vocabulary

Find an example for each of the following terms:

primary colors   hue
secondary colors   intensity
shade   tint

Comprehension

Directions: Place a + beside each statement that is supported by the reading selection and a – beside each item that is not supported by the selection.

Literal
_____ 1. Intensity refers to brightness.
_____ 2. Colors are sorted into two basic groups.
_____ 3. All secondary colors are made by combining primary colors.

Interpretive
_____ 4. Special effects in dress can be created by individuals who understand the effect that colors have on people.
_____ 5. Short people would probably want to wear solid color outfits.
_____ 6. Green would appear on the color wheel between red and blue.

Applied
Directions: Write short answers for the following questions.
7. Identify three ways in which you can use the ideas in this article for planning your wardrobe.
8. Should you dress in solid colors or complementary colors? Why?
9. How can you form the color pink?

EXAMPLE 11.11   Human Environmental Science (Human Ecology) Diagram

HES/HUMAN ECOLOGY

BUSINESS EDUCATION

MATHEMATICS

How a Bank Uses Your Money as a Resource

When you deposit your money in a bank, the money is put to work in a number of ways. The bank lends deposited money to individuals who need it to buy goods or to pay for services. For example, if someone wants to buy a car or needs to pay for a college education and does not have enough money, the bank will make that person a loan. The bank also lends money to companies. For example, it may lend money to help build a new factory.

Each borrower pays interest to the bank for the use of the bank's money. In this way, the bank uses your deposit as a resource to make more money for itself.

You benefit, too.

The bank receives $100.00 from the depositor. It makes loans and receives $110.50 back. It pays the depositor $105.25. Thus, the bank's profit is $5.25 on the loan it made.

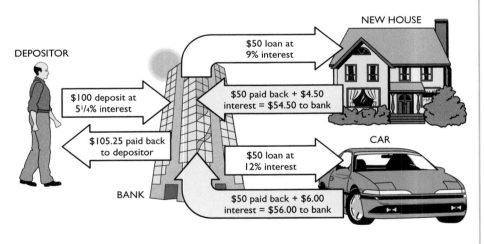

Source: *Teen Guide* by Valarie Chamberlain, with permission of Glencoe McGraw-Hill. A Macmillan/McGraw-Hill Company, Mission Hills, California, Copyright © 1990, p. 190.

EXAMPLE 11.12   Human Environmental Science (Human Ecology) Chart

HES/HUMAN
ECOLOGY

Strategies for Letting Off Steam

These strategies help control angry feelings.

Strategies That Work: Ten Ways to Let Off Steam

Everyone feels angry at times. You can't prevent it—but you can learn to deal with it effectively. Doing so can help prevent arguments from becoming violent.

Taking time to think before you react is a good idea. Take time to calm down and make a good decision about what approach to take. Think about how to communicate your feelings in acceptable ways.

Here are 10 ideas to help you calm down:

- Count to 10. Better yet, count to 20. You could even say the alphabet out loud.
- Breath deeply, concentrating on your breathing until you feel calmer.
- Call a time-out. Go into another room or outside until you cool off.
- Get a pencil and paper, and write down what caused the anger and why.
- Listen to music
- Phone a friend. If you can't reach a friend, phone for the weather.
- Be physically active. Do some sit-ups, go for a run, or ride a bike.
- Splash some cold water on your face, or take a warm bath.
- Hug a pillow.
- Lie down on the floor, and concentrate on a spot on the ceiling.

Making the Strategy Work

Think . . .

1. When people routinely blow up in anger, what effect does this have on those around them?
2. How does the saying "Think before you speak" apply to what you just read about anger?
3. On a scale of 1 to 10 (where 1 is poor and 10 is excellent), rate your own ability to manage anger. Explain your reasoning.

Try . . .

Which technique would be most effective for you when you are angry? Make a pledge to yourself to try using that technique when the need arises. Write your pledge, and place it where it can serve as a reminder to you.

Source: Linda R. Glosson, Janis P. Meek, and Linda Smock, *Creative Living*, 7th ed. (New York: Glencoe McGraw-Hill, 2000), p. 39. Reprinted by permission of Glencoe McGraw-Hill.

AGRICULTURE

AGRICULTURE

Agricultural education is focusing on adapting to agriculture's move from family farms to business conglomerates (Reese, 2001). Agriculture is a complex, multidisciplinary field, and agricultural literacy courses introduce students to the depth, breadth, and diversity of agriculture in our world today, including its impact on our daily lives. The recommended topics of study include the following (Matteson and Jensen, 1994):

- Agriculture science/production management
- Agriculture processing/food and fiber
- Agriculture supplies and services
- Agriculture mechanization/engineering and technical support services
- Agriculture resources management
- Professional employment in agriculture

This wide variety of subject matter creates a literacy challenge for students: each of these content areas involves a different technical vocabulary and has its own characteristic patterns of organizing content. These patterns include cause and effect, problem solving, comparison, experiment, directions, and chronological order. In addition, authors often use graphs, charts, diagrams, and pictures. Following is an example of agricultural content. Example 11.13 shows scientific content. Example 11.14 shows a mapping activity based on the content in Example 11.13.

EXAMPLE 11.13   Scientific Content

AGRICULTURE

SCIENCE AND HEALTH

What Are the Causes of Diseases Among Farm Animals?

A *disease* is considered in a broad sense to be any disorder of the body. (When the word is analyzed, it really means "lack of ease," which is probably its original meaning.)

Improper Feeding as a Cause of Diseases

Some diseases are caused entirely by improper feeding methods. The disease called *rickets,* in which the bones of an animal fail to develop properly, is due to improper amounts of certain minerals and vitamins. Young animals are sometimes born with enlargements in the throat region. This ailment, which is known as *goiter,* or "big neck," is caused by insufficient amounts of iodine in the ration of the mother animals during the period previous to the birth of the young. *Colic* in horses and *bloat* in cattle and sheep are usually caused by improper methods of feeding.

Animals may be poisoned by lead, which they can get through licking paint pails or freshly painted surfaces. They may also consume feeds that have a poisonous effect on their bodies. Poisonous weeds such as loco weed and white snakeroot are examples. The latter weed, if eaten by dairy cows, may injure not only the cows themselves but also the people who drink the cows' milk. Halogeton is a weed that has spread rapidly in semidesert areas; at times, it has caused the death of many sheep in some western states. Other plants that have a poisonous effect on livestock are alsike clover, when eaten wet; bouncing Bet, cocklebur, and corn cockle roadside plants; bracken fern, found in dry and abandoned fields; buttercup, when eaten green; larkspur; ergot; horse nettle; jimson weed; Johnson grass; nightshade; hemlock; milkweed; and wild cherry.

Ornamental plants toxic to goats include oleander, azalea, castorbean, buttercup, rhododendron, philodendron, yew, English ivy, chokeberry, laurel, daffodil, jonquil, and many members of the lily family. Even tomatoes, potatoes, rhubarb, and avocados contain toxic substances. Goats may also be harmed by toadstools, mushrooms, mistletoe, and milkweed.

Source: From Alfred H. Krebs, *Agriculture in Our Lives*, 5th ed. (Danville, Ill.: The Interstate Printers and Publishers, Inc., 1984), p. 405.

EXAMPLE 11.14   Mapping Activity for Cause and Effect in Agricultural Content

Improper feeding causes disease

Causes	Effects
Lack of iodine	Goiter
Improper feeding methods	Colic Bloat Rickets Goiter
Lead Weeds Ornamental plants	Poisoning

PHYSICAL EDUCATION

PHYSICAL EDUCATION

Physical education is a popular area of study today. The growing national interest in physical fitness has created a parallel surge of interest in physical education in the schools. The content of physical education studies can be used to motivate reluctant readers; students who may not be interested in reading other materials often willingly read physical education materials.

Reading serves five purposes in physical education:

1. Physical education topics can motivate students to read, and reading can motivate students to become involved in athletics.

2. Students can learn game rules and signals by reading.

3. Reading can be used to increase and refine students' skills.

4. Reading can increase understanding of a sport and thus can enhance the spectators' or participants' enjoyment.

5. Reading increases students' understanding that mind and body are not separate. Therefore, physical education contributes to mental function (Marlett and Gordon, 2004).

Sports and games present opportunities to develop thinking and reasoning skills (Landers et al., 2001). Physical education is taught in various ways; instructional material can be in the form of anything from a video to a piece of sculpture, to a magazine article or a computer game (Marlett and Gordon, 2004). Students also have reading tasks that include reading rules and directions for playing games and reading books and magazines to improve their techniques in various sports. For example, many books and magazine articles are available to help people improve their golf swings and tennis strokes.

Reading physical education material requires a number of reading skills. There is extensive specialized vocabulary in this reading content. Each sport has a separate set of terms to be learned (e.g., *love, touchdown, foul,* and *guard*). Notice that the word *love* from tennis and the terms *foul* and *guard*, which apply to several sports, are multiple-meaning terms for which students have other uses in their everyday vocabularies. Students must learn to translate physical education terms into action.

The team and individual sports taught in physical education classes require much special equipment. To learn the names and functions of the various pieces of equipment, students could illustrate each piece of equipment, label it, and describe its function. They could maintain a notebook for this purpose, in which the equipment for each sport is categorized and alphabetized. Teachers may wish to develop *inventories of terminology* related to each sport studied.

These inventories can be used both as preparation to introduce the sport and, after study, as a means to review students' understanding of this vocabulary. Students can supply synonyms or define terms in their own words and may develop an illustrated dictionary of sports terms. Examples of inventories of sports terms are shown in Example 11.15.

Critical (evaluative) reading is also important in physical education materials. Critical thinking is developed when students evaluate the strategies or equipment suggested by different authors. This is a good thinking activity, since various authorities suggest widely different approaches to a sport. Critical thinking also comes into play when students evaluate exercises and equipment for physical fitness. For example, recent television commercials recommend some equipment for exercising specific parts of the body, although many physical fitness authorities consider the equipment useless.

Example 11.16 shows an example of physical education text, and Example 11.17 shows a study guide based on this text.

EXAMPLE 11.15 Sports Term Inventories

PHYSICAL EDUCATION

Directions: Define the following terms in your own words.

Tennis	Basketball	Volleyball
racket	dribble	court
backhand	field goal	forearm pass
forehand	foul	setter
love	free throw	set
serve	pass	attacker
net	pivot	spike
game point	press	forwards
deuce	rebound	backs
match	shoot	rotational positions
fault	traveling	net
double fault	violation	attack line
volley	backboard	serve
lob	basket	dink
slice	drive	
chop	dunk	
overhead smash	charge	

EXAMPLE 11.16 Physical Education Text

PHYSICAL EDUCATION

STEP 8 Attack

There are three methods of attack in volleyball, each of which can be very effective. The first to learn of the three methods is the *dink*. It is often looked upon as a defensive maneuver to be performed when the conditions are not right for a more powerful attack. However, the dink is also an extremely effective offensive technique used to disrupt the timing patterns of the defensive team.

The *off-speed spike* is a second option for the attacker. As indicated by its name, less than maximum force is imparted at contact. Like the dink, it is an extremely effective offensive technique used to disrupt the timing patterns of the defensive team.

A third attack method is the *hard-driven spike,* the most exciting play in volleyball. It is also one of the most difficult of all sports skills to learn. In order to make a successful spike, you must jump into the air and sharply hit a moving object (the ball) over an obstacle (the net) so that it lands within the bounded area (the court). Due to the many variables associated with spiking, its timing is difficult and its success requires hours of practice.

Why Is the Attack Important?

When your opponents have mastered the timing of your attack, the dink can catch the opponents off-guard. It is much more difficult to cover the court defensively when a team effectively mixes the speed of their attack. A well-placed dink often "breaks the back" of the opposition and may help improve the momentum of the offense.

The attacking team attempts to have as many different options available to them as possible. The off-speed spike is similar in effect to the dink, but it is hit deeper into the opponent's court. When the off-speed spike is executed, placement is the emphasis, rather than power. The attacker hopes to force the defensive player to move from the starting defensive position and make an error in attempting to play the ball.

The hard-driven spike is the primary offensive weapon in volleyball. Most teams gain a majority of their points on successful spikes. The spike takes very little time to travel from the attacker's hand to the floor; therefore, there is little time for defensive players to move to the ball, and the defensive team must locate its players on the court in strategic positions before the ball is contacted on the spike. The hard-driven spike adds a great deal of excitement to the game and, thus, has tremendous spectator appeal.

How to Execute the Dink

The approach to all three types of attack is the same. It is important because it increases the height of your jump and increases the force you are able to impart on the ball. For a high set, you, the attacker, begin on the attack line, wait for the set to be half the distance to you from the setter, and then move toward the set. Approach the net attempting to cover the distance with as few steps as possible. The last two steps are the most important. Make a two-footed takeoff by planting your right foot heel first and closing with your left foot (bringing the left foot to a position even with the right foot) or taking a hop onto both feet. As you plant both feet heels first to change forward momentum into upward momentum, swing your arms to prepare for a jump. Swing forward both arms and reach high toward the set as you jump straight up into the air. Draw your hitting arm back, your elbow high and your hand close to your ear. As you swing at the ball, your nonhitting hand drops quickly to your waist. Gently contact the ball by using the upper two joints of the fingers of your hitting hand, slightly in front of your hitting shoulder at full arm extension. Contact the ball slightly below the center back. Direct the ball upward enough to barely clear the block but still drop quickly to the floor. Return to the floor with a two-footed landing (see Figure 8.1).

Preparation Phase
1. Wait on attack line
2. Watch setter
3. Eyes on ball after set
4. Weight forward
5. Anticipate approach to the net

FIGURE 8.1

Keys to Success: Dink

Execution Phase
1. Begin approach to net when ball is at peak of its trajectory
2. Cover distance with few steps
3. Last two steps right, close left or step to jump
4. Arms swing back to waist level
5. Both arms swing forward
6. Both arms swing high toward ball
7. Contact ball in front of hitting shoulder
8. Contact with upper two joints of fingers
9. Contact on lower back half of ball
10. Contact with full arm extension

Dink Keys to Success Checklist

When performing the dink, keep in mind that your attack needs to go over or by the opponent's block in order to be successful. Your body must be behind the ball so you

Error	Correction
1. The ball goes into the net.	1. Contact the ball just in front of your hitting shoulder; the greater the distance the ball is in front of you, the lower it drops before contact and the greater the chance of its being hit into the net.
2. The ball does not clear the block.	2. Make contact on the back lower half of the ball with your arm fully extended.
3. You stop your approach and wait for the ball.	3. You should not begin your approach until the ball is half the distance to you from the setter.
4. You contact the net.	4. The set must be at least 1 foot from the net; you must execute a heel plant to change horizontal momentum into vertical momentum.
5. You hit the ball too high, and it takes too long to hit the floor.	5. Contact the ball in front of your hitting shoulder.

can direct the ball to the most advantageous area of the opponent's court. Also, be aware that officials will usually call you for improper technique if you attempt to change the direction of the ball during dink performance. This causes your hand to be in contact with the ball too long, which is a held ball.

Follow-Through Phase
1. Hand follows ball to target
2. Land on both feet
3. Bend knees to cushion landing

Detecting Dink Errors

Most dink errors are associated with improper hand position in relation to the ball and poor timing during the approach. Dinking success is closely associated to your ability to disguise the fact that you are going to dink. Up until hand contact, your approach should be exactly the same as that for a spike.

Source: Barbara L. Viera and Bonnie Jill Ferguson, *Volleyball Steps to Success* (Champaign, Ill.: Leisure Press, 1989), pp. 81, 83. Copyright © 1989 by Leisure Press. Reprinted by permission of Human Kinetics Publishers.

EXAMPLE 11.17   **Study Guide for "Step 8: Attack"**

Objectives
1. Students should know:
   a. The three methods of attack
   b. The importance of attack
   c. The three phases of the methods of attack
   d. How to explain the execution of the dink in relation to footwork
   e. How to explain the execution of the off-speed spike in relation to hand and wrist
   f. How to demonstrate the execution of the hard-driven spike in relation to the hand, arm, and wrist.

Literal
1. Why is the dink an important tactic when attacking your opponent?
2. Why is the hard-driven spike the primary offensive weapon in volleyball?
3. What are the most important steps in the footwork relative to the dink?
4. When you snap your wrist and roll your fingers over the top of the ball in the off-speed spike, what type of spin develops?

Interpretive
1. What would happen if you contacted the underside of the ball with the heel of the open hand in the hard-driven spike?
2. What would happen if your footwork was incorrect in the dink?
3. Why is the footwork important in the dink?
4. What direction does the ball move when it is in a topspin?
5. Is the topspin useful in a volleyball game? Why or why not?

Applied
1. What steps could you take to improve your hard-driven spike?
2. What step would you take first to improve your hard-driven spike?
3. Practice the footwork for each of the three attacks described in this reading, and write a description of each in your own words.
4. Practice the hand and wrist movements described in the text so that you can show them to a classmate.

ART

ART

Art students use and study the media of artistic expression more frequently than they use and study textbooks. The study of art does not involve as much textbook reading as many other content areas, and fewer textbooks are available in this subject than in other areas. Nevertheless, art students need to have well-developed reading skills because they read many types of written content for a variety of purposes. For example, they read to acquire information about artistic techniques, art history, and the lives of important artists. Following is a summary of the reading strategies art students commonly use:

1. *Reading for information in materials such as reference books, art history books, biographies, and magazines.* Art students often read about exhibitions, artists, and techniques. They read to identify art styles or movements. They read such magazines as *Arts and Activities, School Arts, Popular Photography, Digital Camera, PC Photo, Art in America, The Artists Magazine, American Artists,* and *Craft Works* for information on current ideas, trends, and techniques. Reading for information involves identifying main ideas and supporting details.

2. *Reading to follow directions.* Art students must read and follow steps in sequential order. This kind of reading would occur when they read about topics such as new media and new techniques or how to make a woodcut.

3. *Reading to interpret charts and diagrams,* such as a color wheel. For example, art students need to learn about complementary colors.

4. *Reading critically.* The art student uses this skill when evaluating reviews of art shows or the impact of a medium or a style.

5. *Reading to implement information or directions.* After reading about a particular medium or style, an art student may experiment with it.

6. *Reading and organizing information for reports.* Art students may be required to write reports on the lives of artists, styles of art, or ways of interpreting moods and feelings in art. This reading task requires that the reader identify main ideas and details.

7. *Reading technical vocabulary related to art.* This vocabulary includes words like *linear, hue,* and *perspective.*

Study guides, preview guides, and vocabulary activities are particularly helpful to art students. In addition, many of the other strategies presented in Chapters 3, 4, 5, and 10 can be used to help art students develop appropriate literacy skills. Examples of art reading activities follow, including a vocabulary activity, a preview guide, and a study guide.

Example 11.18 includes material from a textbook used for teaching art. As you read this brief selection, note the many technical words and expressions used (e.g., *linear perspective, diminishing contrasts, hue, value, intensity of color, texture, two-dimensional surface, infinite concept, atmospheric perspective, pictorial composition, theme, picture plane, volume of deep space, softening edges of objects, scale,* and *middle ground*). Following the selection are two reading guides that are based on the passage (Examples 11.19 and 11.20).

EXAMPLE 11.18   Art Content

ART

Problem 1

In conjunction with linear perspective, artists of the past frequently used diminishing contrasts of hue, value, and intensity of color and texture to achieve deep penetration of space on a two-dimensional surface. This is known as the infinite concept of space or atmospheric perspective.

Create a pictorial composition based on the theme "Objects in Space." Conceive of the picture plane as the near side of a volume of deep space. Use the indications of space suggested in the opening paragraph, plus softening edges of objects as they are set back in depth. The human figure may be used to help suggest the scale of objects in space. Foreground, middle ground, and deep space may be indicated by the size of similar objects.

Source: Otto Ocvirk, Robert Bone, Robert Stinson, and Philip Wigg, *Art Fundamentals: Theory and Practice* (Dubuque, Iowa: William C. Brown Company, 1975), p. 114.

EXAMPLE 11.19   Preview Guide

Directions: Check *Yes* if you believe the reading selection will support the statement; check *No* if you believe the selection will not support the statement.

Yes	No	
_____	_____	1. The infinite concept of space and atmospheric perspective are the same thing.
_____	_____	2. Artists of the past used diminishing contrasts of hue, value, and intensity of color to achieve atmospheric perspective.
_____	_____	3. Students should conceive of the picture plane as the far side of a volume of deep space.
_____	_____	4. Trees are used to suggest scale.

EXAMPLE 11.20   Study Guide

Introduction

This selection poses a problem for art students to solve. If you have questions after you have read the problem, refer to books and articles in the bibliography on linear perspective.

Vocabulary

Provide an example for each of the following words: linear perspective, diminishing contrasts, hue, value, intensity, texture, two-dimensional surface, infinite concept of space, atmospheric perspective, pictorial composition, theme, picture plane.

Comprehension

Directions: Write a short answer to each question.

Literal
1. What does this selection ask you to do?
2. What concept is explained in the first paragraph?
3. What is the theme of the pictorial composition that you are to create?

Interpretive
4. Why does the author suggest that a human figure be used to suggest scale?
5. Will color play an important role in this composition?
6. What similar objects might be used to indicate foreground, middle ground, and deep space?

Applied
7. What materials will you need to complete this problem?
8. Can you create another composition that has the same title but uses a different object to show scale? If so, what could you use?

MUSIC

MUSIC

Written music is a form of language, and learning to read music is comparable to learning to read books. Both reading music and reading books rely on the student's ability to recognize likenesses and differences in sounds, shapes, and symbols (Badiali, 1984). Each piece of music can be considered a text (Morgan and Berg-O'Halloran, 1989). In studying music, students must be able to read the words, the music, and the technical language, as well as the accompanying expository and narrative text. Music instruction usually requires a high level of reading ability, including knowledge of notes, lyrics, and music theory. For example, music students read and interpret a large number of musical terms, such as *sonatina*, *spiritoso*, *andante*, and *allegretto*. In addition, special symbols are used in music books and scores. These symbols aid the student in interpreting the music. Students must be able to recognize symbols for elements such as treble clef, bass clef, notes (whole, half, quarter, etc.), rests (varying values corresponding to note values), sharps, flats, crescendo, and diminuendo. The teacher must frequently demonstrate musical terms, concepts, and technology using instruments and/or recorded music. Example 11.21 illustrates how a music teacher may demonstrate musical concepts.

Students must be able to understand material that is written about music in order to interpret the music. Instruction in music classes often is based on students' ability to read and understand the following types of content (Tanner, 1983):

> Expository and narrative materials about composers
> Critiques, reviews, and descriptions of performances
> Exposition—music history
> Reporting—current events related to music
> References—research, reviews
> Types of media—books, magazines, newspapers, scores

To help secondary students with the task of reading music and textbooks used in music classes, teachers may use the following strategies:

1. Anticipate students' problems before they read. Standardized reading tests and teacher-made inventories can provide data regarding students' reading skills. Observing students' performance in reading music is very helpful in isolating their strengths and weaknesses.

2. Teach the necessary vocabulary before students read a selection.

3. Develop and use illustrated dictionaries of musical terms.

4. Teach students how to study and prepare assignments (see Chapter 7). Demonstrating these techniques with music content can be helpful.

5. Use strategies such as study guides, directed reading lessons, structured overviews, preview guides, and vocabulary study to help students read and understand music content.

6. Consult Internet sites such as http://www.glencoe.com for teaching ideas.

EXAMPLE 11.21   Demonstrating Musical Concepts

MUSIC

TECHNICAL
EDUCATION

Electronic Timbres

Electronically generated sounds are all around us. The invention of new sound technology, particularly the extraordinary developments of the last quarter of the twentieth century, has enabled us to extend the range of musical timbres. The expressive potential of these sounds is infinite and only awaits the imagination of new composers to probe their possibilities. Already there are literally thousands of new musical compositions that owe their existence to this technology.

ACTIVITY   Realize the Potential
Listen to a demonstration of some samples of sounds and expressive effects that can be created on a synthesizer.

Listen to American composer Wendy Carlos (b. 1939) explain and demonstrate how she made the public conscious of the Moog synthesizer with her recording *Switched-On Bach,* the first classical album to go platinum.

What feats are required to make electronic music expressive and musical in a way similar to music made with acoustic instruments? Discuss such matters as vibrato, the need for overdubbing, touch sensitivity, and the need for taste.

Why is a perfect automated rhythm less exciting than a human's imperfectly performed rhythm?

Technology Option
Music with MIDI   Use a MIDI program to create a composition featuring unique and original sounds from your MIDI gear.

Most of us are so accustomed to electronic sounds in television commercials, on pop recordings, and in film scores that we may not be able to distinguish these sounds from the more traditional acoustic sources (musical instruments, voices). Although electronic technology has produced hundreds of new timbres, we do not yet have a common language or vocabulary to describe these new sounds. Quite often, however, sounds that are generated electronically deliberately mimic acoustic instruments or human voices and can be labeled accordingly. Often, instruments are electrified—the organ and guitar are common examples. The trick is to get our ears to distinguish sounds that are produced acoustically from those that are produced electronically.

Source: Charles Fowler, Timothy Gerber, and Vincent Lawrence, *Music! Its Role and Importance in Our Lives* (New York: Glencoe McGraw-Hill, 2000), p. 342. Reprinted by permission of Glencoe McGraw-Hill.

Example 11.22 is taken from a music text that provides students with guidance to help them read music-related text. The authors have identified the major objectives of the chapter, the vocabulary, and the specific names of artists that students are expected to learn. Such guidance gives students comprehension purposes and sets their expectations to learn the content that the teacher expects.

EXAMPLE 11.22   Music Text

MUSIC

Jazz

Jazz is America's musical gift to the world. This unique invention, born in New Orleans and bred largely in Memphis, St. Louis, Chicago, and New York, is still alive and kicking and going into its second century of high status. Without a doubt, it is the most original and influential music to emerge from the American continent—so far.

Objectives

By completing this chapter, you will:

- Learn about the beginnings of jazz.
- Become acquainted with the early contributions of Jelly Roll Morton, Fletcher Henderson, and Louis Armstrong.
- Be able to distinguish between the many styles of jazz, such as Dixieland, small band jazz, swing, bebop, and fusion.
- Learn some examples of classic jazz.
- Find out about the contributions of other jazz performers, such as Charlie Parker and Dizzy Gillespie, and learn what made them so great.

Vocabulary

bop	Dorian mode	scat singing
break	fusion	swing

Musicians to meet

Benny Goodman	Charlie Parker

Source: Charles Fowler, Timothy Gerber, and Vincent Lawrence, *Music! Its Role and Importance in Our Lives* (New York: Glencoe McGraw-Hill, 2000), p. 507. Reprinted by permission of Glencoe McGraw-Hill.

Hicks (1980) points out that in instrumental music, the reading process involves recognizing the notes, which represent pitch; the meter symbols, which indicate time; and various other interpretive and expressive markings. At the same time, an instrumentalist must physically manipulate valves, bows, slides, or keys. Hicks suggests that teachers present the early stages of music reading as a problem-solving activity involving simple duple and triple meters. He suggests presenting all songs in the same key, emphasizing continuity and repetition and using materials that have repeated patterns and a narrow range. He also recommends including familiar elements in each new activity. This activity could include such elements as the following:

1. Provide background information about the song.

2. Present the words of the song in poem form on a duplicated sheet (to avoid confusion that may result from all the accompanying signs and symbols on a music sheet).

3. Discuss any words that students may not recognize or comprehend, as well as the overall meaning of the lyrics.

4. The teacher and students should divide the words into syllables cooperatively. A duplicated sheet may again be prepared with words in this form.

After the musical aspects of the song are taught, the students can use the duplicated sheet (with divided words) to sing from. Later, they may use the music books that contain syllabicated words along with the notes and other symbols.

When preparing to perform a composition, music students must ask themselves a number of questions regarding the composition and their performance. Tanner (1983) asked a saxophone player in a high school band to identify the questions he had before playing a piece of music, and he produced a list similar to the following one:

1. What will playing this exercise show me?

2. What skills should I learn or develop?

3. What does this piece tell me about the composer?

4. What mood is conveyed?

5. What is the key signature?

6. What is the meter (time signature)?

7. What rhythms does the composer use?

8. What intervals are used?

9. What form does the piece have?

10. How long are the phrases?

11. How did the composer want the piece played?

12. What dynamic markings are shown, and why?

13. How many motives did the composer have?

14. Is this music challenging to play?

15. Can I play this successfully?

16. Do I want to play this piece?

17. Is this music too hard?

18. How can I play better?

19. Would it help me if I heard the song played by someone else?

20. Would it help me if I heard the lyrics?

The music text presented in Example 11.23 shows the type of text that music students are expected to read.

The study guide in Example 11.24 is based on the music text presented in Example 11.23. Teachers can use study guides similar to this one as one way of guiding students to comprehend music text.

EXAMPLE 11.23   Music Text

MUSIC

SOCIAL STUDIES

The 1940s and Bebop

Right after the Second World War, interest in jazz intensified. While big band jazz had become a formula, another style was emerging. Some of the younger jazz musicians wanted the freedom to create outside the confines of swing. This new style—called "bop" or "bebop"—was invented in Harlem jam sessions that took jazz back to a small combo. **Bop,** *a complex and sophisticated type of improvised jazz,* was an art for listening rather than dancing to. It was a reaction against the rigid conventions of swing. The jazz world was suddenly split into two camps: swing versus bop.

Trumpeter John Birks "Dizzy" Gillespie (1917–1996) and alto saxophonist Charlie "Yardbird" Parker (1920–1955) led this new movement and changed the face of jazz in the 1940s. They introduced melodic and harmonic innovations that established the style of contemporary jazz. These pioneers gave bop the sophistication of classical chamber music. Melodies became more chromatic. Harmonies and rhythms became far more complex. Beats were often doubled from four to eight, and constantly shifting accents created intricate polyrhythms. There were rapid tempos and dazzling technical displays but, at the same time, a seething soulfulness. Improvisations on the lips of these masterful musicians became more complex, dissonant, and daring. Parker's brilliance as an improviser was not measured just by the notes he could spin, but with the blues he could wrap them in. His bop could be melancholic. Through his improvisation a tune was transformed into a higher state—a reincarnation through invention.

Bebop or "modern jazz" was a more intimate art than the big band jazz. Jazz artists realized that what they were doing and saying went deeper than just easy entertainment or music for dancing. They could be profound and virtuosic, subtle and sophisticated, sensitive and expressive. With bebop, jazz declared itself an art, and the performers, artists. One of the goals of these beboppers was to see how far they could stretch a musical composition while still maintaining its basic formal structure. Fast and creatively complex improvisation became the highest form of art. Together Parker and Gillespie expanded the language of jazz, and other musicians studied their innovations and learned from them.

Source: Charles Fowler, Timothy Gerber, and Vincent Lawrence, *Music! Its Role and Importance in Our Lives* (New York: Glencoe McGraw-Hill, 2000), pp. 518–519. Reprinted by permission of Glencoe McGraw-Hill.

EXAMPLE 11.24   Study Guide

MUSIC

Introduction

The text shown in Example 11.23 discusses the development of bebop as a reaction to swing music.

Vocabulary

Explain the meaning of each of the following terms or phrases: *jazz, bop, bebop, modern jazz,* and *contemporary jazz.*

Comprehension

Directions: Write a short answer to the questions that follow.

Literal
  1. Why did bop or bebop develop?
  2. Where did bop develop?
  3. Who were the leaders of the bebop movement?

Interpretive
  4. Why was bop an art for listening rather than dancing to?
  5. Explain this statement from the text, "Parker's brilliance as an improviser was not measured just by the notes he could spin, but with the blues he could wrap them in."
  6. Why was improvisation so important in the development of bebop?

Applied
Directions: Write a short answer or follow the specific directions for each item below.
  7. Demonstrate how a musician can "stretch" a musical composition, either with recordings or with your own playing.
  8. Demonstrate the difference between swing and bebop, using recorded music or your own music.
  9. Why do you think that bebop raised jazz to the level of an art?
 10. Demonstrate how the rhythms and harmonies changed from jazz to bebop.

DANCE

MUSIC

PHYSICAL
EDUCATION

Dance textbooks focus on helping students to understand the language of movement and the elements of movement and to translate their understanding into action. Hanna (2001) illustrated how dance involves the same brain centers as sign language and uses the same coding to create meaning. Steps, gestures, and order are equivalent to words, sentences, and grammar. Meaning through the language of dance is created in many ways including metaphor; actualization; and who does what, when, where, how, and with whom (Marlett and Gordon, 2004). Dance is not a single language, but it comprises multiple languages such as ballet or classical East Indian. The dance text excerpt shown in Example 11.25 illustrates this characteristic, and the study guide in Example 11.26 demonstrates one approach to helping readers comprehend and apply written text in dance.

EXAMPLE 11.25 Dance Selection

PHYSICAL
EDUCATION

SCIENCE AND
HEALTH

2. An understanding of the body parts and their movement potential makes more intelligent movement possible.

You will experience your body as a whole and also in its separate parts. You know your nose from your toes, and have since earliest childhood, so a discussion of the parts of the body may seem superfluous. In dance, however, there are certain parts that need specific attention. These need to be clarified, so that you will speak not of the back, but of the lower, middle, or upper spine, and not of the hip bone when you really mean the hip joint.

The spine is basic to all human movement. It is a long series of bones extending from the base of the head, at about ear level, to the coccyx, or tailbone. It consists of 24 separate bones, or *vertebrae,* and two others, the sacrum and *coccyx.*

The spine has natural curves in it—a forward curve at the neck, a backward curve at the ribs, another forward curve at the waist, and a backward curve below the waist. These curves are meant to be there, but are not meant to be exaggerated. Fluidity of motion in the spine is a desirable asset to the dancer, and many of the things you will be asked to do are designed to give more mobility to the spine by working the curves opposite to their normal direction.

For convenience, you can speak of the spine in three sections. The *upper spine* extends from the base of the head to just below the shoulder blades. The *middle spine* continues from there to waist level, and the *lower spine* includes the remaining vertebrae, the sacrum, and the coccyx. Each of these areas can be trained to operate independently of the others, or together as a totality.

Learning Experience

Locate the 3 spinal areas on a friend or in yourself with your side to a mirror. Breathe into the upper spine while rounding it forward. Now deepen the curve by rounding the middle spine; now bend forward from the hip joint and breathe into the whole length of the spine and any place in the back or legs that feels tight.

Rounding in 3 areas of the spine.

The area of the hips is often a confusing one. The *hip bones,* first of all, are the prominent bones found on the front of the body, about three inches below the waist and about shoulder width apart. The *hip joint* is where the leg is attached to the torso.

Learning Experience

Put the heel of your hand on your hip bone and extend your fingers downward. Your palm will cross your hip joint. Lift your thigh forward and feel the break in your hip joint.

   Later, when you read "hips forward," this is the part of your hip that is directed forward—the whole area you just covered with your hand. The *side of your hip* is at the same level as your hip joint and can be felt as prominent bones on the sides of your body.

Source: Gay Cheney, *Basic Concepts of Modern Dance,* 3rd ed. (Princeton, N.J.: Princeton Book Company Publishers, 1989), pp. 22–23.

EXAMPLE 11.26   Study Guide for Dance Selection

Directions: Think about the following questions and exercises as you read this text. Try to visualize the various ideas the author introduces. Perform the learning experiences in the text and those in the application section of the study guide.

Literal
1. What part of the body is basic to all human movement?
2. Where are the hip bones?
3. Where is the hip joint?

Interpretive
1. Why do you think the author identified the hip area as a confusing one?
2. Why should dancers work spinal curves in different directions?
3. Visualize fluid movements. Describe fluid movements in your own words. You may have to do these movements to work out your descriptions.

Applied
1. Locate the three areas of your spine with the aid of a mirror.
2. Locate your hip bones, your hip joint, and the side of your hip.
3. Create a movement that will work the spine in a different direction, and be sure to breathe with the movement.

Focus on Struggling Readers

Helping Struggling Readers Read Vocational Content

Many times struggling readers are guided into vocational studies, but they lack the required skills to succeed. They have often spent much time outside of their classrooms for developmental instruction, which deprives them of the content exposure they need (Pisha and Coyne, 2001). Isolated skills instruction does not prepare them for content area learning (NCTE, 2004). Prior knowledge is necessary for building interest and desire to learn (NCTE, 2004; Tobias, 1994). Existing knowledge of the subject matter is the single most influential factor in determining what students will learn from reading a text about that subject matter (Grady, 2002). Struggling readers usually need to develop background for the materials they will read and review. Vocabulary related to the subject they are studying will help them read with understanding. Chapter 3 includes suggestions for vocabulary development. Teachers of vocational and performance subjects have special problems, because students must translate reading content to actual practice. However, computer programs and the Internet can help students understand (Grady, 2002).

Internet sites such as these are helpful for vocational subjects: Knowledge Network Explorer, which is found at http://www.kn.pacbell.com, provides educational sites in vocational, educational, technology, business, and many other areas. This site also connects to Blue Web'n, which is an online library of outstanding Internet sites categorized by subject, grade level, and format. The site http://teacher pathfinder.org/School/SchWork/schworkprogs.html links to resources for school-to-work programs.

Discussions with classmates will help students view topics from different perspectives; moreover, students can work together to construct meaning (Lloyd, 2004). Discussion of readings and classroom experiences encourage students to continue exploration of content subjects. After reading texts and exploring Internet sites, students should participate in discussion to clarify their understandings.

Focus on English Language Learners

Helping English Language Learners Read Vocational Content

Hernandez (2003) identified four key instructional dimensions for English language learners (ELLs).

1. Prior knowledge

2. Variety of instructional materials

3. Cognitive development

4. Study skills

Initially, ELLs may lack the prior knowledge necessary to comprehend content materials (Harper and de Jong, 2004). Teachers can relate the subject matter to students by asking questions regarding what they have learned about the content and eliciting what students know about the topic from their own life experiences. Vocational teachers can use communication-based instruction to develop students' readiness, as well as their vocabulary for studying the content subject. Reading and discussing texts with classmates in a cooperative learning experience helps students (Jacobs and Gallo, 2002). ELLs benefit from peer tutoring or coaching from students who are fluent users of English. These students and teachers model English for ELLs.

Vocational teachers may need to broaden their notions of text. They should present basic foundations of subject matter through visuals, hands-on experiences, guest speakers, field trips, and related readings (Hernandez (2003). ELLs benefit from experience with workplace materials that expose them to the level of English they will need in the future (Wade and Moje, 2000).Using simple syntax when discussing examples, differences, and similarities helps students develop oral fluency and comprehension. Lessons may need to be sequenced, so that students can be exposed to information needed as readiness for another subject.

ELLs need the cognitive development that will enable students to comprehend content materials (Hernandez, 2003). Texts can be used as references when students discuss points of view or main ideas and support them with examples. ELLs can summarize information, sequence events, infer conclusions, and compare and contrast. Text materials can be read to ELLs or recorded text can be played for them, so they can increase their comprehension and participation in reading and writing. In this manner, students can develop important comprehension skills (see Chapters 4 and 5).

ELLs also need study skills (Hernandez, 2003). They should learn the parts of a book and how to access information quickly. ELLs need to understand the difference between fiction and nonfiction. They also have to learn how to research information that will further their studies in content areas. Chapters 6 and 7 of this text will help teachers teach these skills.

SUMMARY

Efficient literacy is a prerequisite for successful learning. Our economy has changed, so that more and more people have changed their vocational goals and have sought retraining. These individuals need literacy skills to facilitate their life changes. Although many people believe that the literacy demands of vocational subjects are less rigorous than those of academic programs, literacy is equally important in these fields of study. Moreover, the current emphasis is on transferable skills and work-related learning that presents writing tasks as well as the need to implement technology.

Vocational and performance materials are written and organized to impart information, give directions, and provide solutions to problems. Teachers should use vocabulary strategies, advance organizers, study guides, preview guides, directed reading materials, mapping, and study methods to help students comprehend these materials. Systematic literacy instruction as a part of content instruction will improve students' learning in these courses. Struggling readers and English language learners need the same skills as other students, but they need to be taught in ways that will help them to succeed in vocational subjects.

DISCUSSION QUESTIONS

1. How is literacy for work-related education changing?
2. How and why is vocational education changing?
3. What kinds of literacy tasks do students encounter in vocational and technical studies?

4.   What strategies can teachers use to help students comprehend vocational materials?

5.   Discuss the increased integration of vocational education and academic education.

6.   How can teachers effectively teach the variety of content in human environmental science and agriculture?

7.   Why is literacy increasing in importance for contemporary students?

8.   What adjustments should vocational teachers make for struggling readers and English language learners?

9.   How does instruction for English language learners differ from instruction for struggling readers?

ENRICHMENT ACTIVITIES

*1.   Select a set of directions from a subject treated in this chapter, and rewrite the directions in simpler language for struggling readers.

2.   Develop an annotated bibliography of materials that could constitute a classroom library in one of the subjects treated in this chapter. Indicate readability levels whenever possible.

3.   Make a dictionary of terms for use in one of the areas treated in this chapter. You can use drawings and pictures from magazines, catalogs, and newspapers to illustrate the dictionary.

4.   Collect pamphlets, magazines, newspapers, and library books that could be used to develop understanding of vocabulary and concepts in a subject treated in this chapter. Use them with secondary school students.

5.   Select a section in a textbook on a subject treated in this chapter, and make a reading lesson plan for it.

6.   Prepare a presentation, describing how you would help teach a student to read one of the following: (a) an invoice or balance sheet; (b) a contract; (c) a tax form; (d) a physical education activity or game; (e) a critical review of art or music; (f) a specialized handbook; (g) a reference source.

7.   Examine materials from technology education, business education, and human environmental science (human ecology) textbooks. Locate examples of the common reading problems.

*8.   Prepare a vocabulary activity to teach new terms in a textbook chapter. Use it with a group of secondary school career-education students.

*9.   Prepare a study guide for a selection from one of the subjects discussed in this chapter. Use it with a group of secondary school career-education students.

10.   Use a readability formula to compute the readability level of a textbook for one of the content areas discussed in this chapter. (See Chapter 12 for a discussion of readability formulas.)

11.   Identify new applications of technology in your chosen field of study.

*These activities are designed for in-service teachers, student teachers, and practicum students.

Part 4

Instruction and Assessment of All Learners

Chapter 12

Content Literacy Assessment

A major purpose of this chapter is to assist the content area teacher in determining whether or not students possess the literacy and study skills necessary to deal successfully with course materials. To perform this evaluation, the content teacher must be aware of the literacy and study skills appropriate to the particular subject. Assessment involves collecting data from multiple sources in order to obtain a valid evaluation of students' capabilities (Brimijoin, Marquissee, and Tomlinson, 2003; Salvia and Ysseldyke, 2004). Teachers must recognize that students' performances on particular tasks are influenced by the tasks themselves, the background the students bring to the tasks, the students' ability related to task requirements, and the contexts in which the tasks take place. Such assessment is data collection designed to help teachers determine problem areas and make instructional decisions. Useful assessment is directly linked to instruction (Valencia, 2000; Serafini, 2000/2001; Brimijoin, Marquissee, and Tomlinson, 2003; Cobb, 2003/2004; Invernizzi, Landrum, Howell, and Warley, 2005).

Literacy assessment procedures have been changing. Some newer assessments are focusing more on processes (strategies used to understand text or revise written work) than on products (specific knowledge the student has acquired). Students are asked to produce or do something meaningful. The activity generally involves higher-level thinking and problem solving. Real-life problems and authentic techniques for solutions are featured (Herman, Aschbacher, and Winters, 1992). Because of the difficulties of developing norm-referenced measures that will reveal such processes, many of the new assessment procedures are classroom based and appear much like regular classroom instruction. There is also a recent focus on more self-assessment by students, making them active participants in the assessment process.

Many types of assessment are needed to obtain a complete picture of students' abilities and possibilities. Herman, Aschbacher, and Winters (1992) point out that performance assessments help teachers determine how well their students can apply information, but multiple-choice tests may be a more efficient way to determine how well the students have learned the basic facts and concepts. For this reason, teachers need to be familiar with a variety of assessment tools. In order to help students learn effectively, teachers must understand assessment data and their implications for instructional planning (Guskey, 2003).

Instructional material often is not written at its designated difficulty level. Teachers need to know whether their students can read at the level on which the textbook is written; to discover this, they need to know what this level actually is. Additionally, teachers need to understand the factors that influence readability and how to use readability formulas and other measures for determining the difficulty of materials.

In this chapter we discuss norm-referenced tests, criterion-referenced tests, classroom-based tests, assessment of the readability of printed materials, and computer applications to assessment. Criterion-referenced tests may be either commercially produced or teacher-constructed tests and may have objective written items or classroom-based performance tasks.

PURPOSE-SETTING QUESTIONS

As you read this chapter, try to answer these questions:

1. What are the functions of norm-referenced tests?
2. What changes are occurring in literacy assessment today?
3. What are criterion-referenced tests?
4. What are some classroom-based assessments of reading and writing achievement, and how can the results of each be used to help teachers plan instructional programs?
5. What is meant by portfolio assessment?
6. How are computers being applied in the area of assessment?
7. How is an understanding of the readability levels of textbook materials important to a teacher?
8. What assessment approaches are particularly appropriate for struggling readers and English language learners?

Norm-Referenced Tests

What types of information can norm-referenced tests give teachers?

Content teachers may administer and interpret certain types of **norm-referenced tests**, especially survey achievement tests, to check student performance in a wide range of literacy areas: reading, writing, language, reference skills, and others. Test results indicate the relative achievement of the groups tested in these areas. Teachers can compare a student's performance on a subtest in one subject with his or her performance on other subtests in a test battery. Therefore, the tests may reveal a pattern of strengths and weaknesses. Teachers also can learn how a student's performance on a test compares with his or her earlier or later performance on the same test, but scores from two different kinds of norm-referenced tests on the same topic (e.g., reading or writing) are not likely to be comparable.

Hoffman, Assaf, and Paris (2001) point out that standardized testing on a statewide basis has dramatically increased in recent years: "State-mandated standardized tests have become the centerpiece for standards-based reform" (p. 482). These researchers studied the high-stakes standardized testing (testing that results in severe penalties, such as denial of graduation, for failure) taking place in Texas and reported that such testing had numerous shortcomings and had a negative effect on both teachers and students. Similar concerns have been voiced about high-stakes testing throughout the United States, but because of the political pressure to have "objective" measures of literacy achievement, it is unlikely that such testing will disappear anytime soon.

CRITERIA FOR CHOOSING NORM-REFERENCED TESTS

Why are the validity and reliability of norm-referenced tests important?

A norm-referenced test should meet certain criteria. Its norms should be based on a population similar to the population being tested, and it should have high levels of **validity** and **reliability**. A valid norm-referenced reading test represents a balanced and adequate sampling of the instructional outcomes (e.g., knowledge and skills) that it is intended to cover. In addition to measuring the skills it claims to measure (validity) and having subtests that are long enough to yield reasonably accurate scores, a test should not result in a chance score with students obtaining high scores by luck or guessing (reliability). The reliability of a test refers to the degree to which the test gives consistent results.

A test is inappropriate if the sample population used to establish norms is significantly different from the class or group to be tested. A description of the norming population is usually contained in the test manual.

NORM-REFERENCED TESTS OF READING ACHIEVEMENT

Norm-referenced reading tests yield objective data about reading performance. They are designed so that each response to a test item is subject to only one interpretation. The types of norm-referenced reading tests that content teachers are most likely to hear about are **survey tests** and **diagnostic tests**.

What is the difference in the information obtained from a survey test and that obtained from a diagnostic test?

Reading survey tests measure general achievement in reading. The results can show how well students are performing in relation to others who have taken the test. Looking at scores of all students in a class gives an indication of the range of reading achievement in the class.

A single score on a survey test represents the student's overall reading achievement and does not reveal how the student will perform on specific reading tasks. However, some reading survey tests designed for secondary school students have separate sections that yield scores on vocabulary, comprehension, and reading rate. A wise teacher is not merely concerned with a student's total achievement score but wants to determine if the student is equally strong in all areas tested.

Diagnostic reading tests are used most frequently by special teachers of reading, but content teachers need some basic information about this type of test in order to discuss test results with special reading teachers. Diagnostic reading tests help to locate specific strengths and weaknesses of readers. Such tests often include subtests for comprehension, vocabulary, word identification skills, and rate of reading. Group diagnostic tests are usually given by reading specialists but sometimes are given by classroom teachers. Reading specialists usually administer individual diagnostic reading tests because they have the required experience and training. Additionally, time constraints generally make the use of diagnostic reading tests in the content area classroom impractical.

CONCERNS ABOUT TRADITIONAL STANDARDIZED READING TESTS

Tierney (1998, p. 376) states, "Changes in testing have not kept pace with shifts in our understanding of learning and literacy development." Traditional tests treat reading as if it were simply skill mastery of a variety of skills (a product) rather than a constructive, strategic process in which readers make use of their prior knowledge and techniques for unlocking meaning in the text in order to understand its message (a process). As long as the standardized tests available to educators fail to measure what happens in the classrooms and what teachers and students value—the constructive, strategic process involved in reading—and instead measure only skill mastery of a group of skills, it is inappropriate for these tests to control such important events as retention in grade and graduation. Well-constructed informal tests that teachers base on important curricular goals should be the ones that are given most credibility by the educational establishment. Popham (2001) says that teachers who want their students to score well on the traditional testing instruments may "teach to the test," resulting in inappropriate instruction in light of the current understanding of the reading process. Wittrock (1987, p. 736) explains to teachers that process-oriented comprehension measures "will not tell what your students have learned about a text passage. Nor will they tell you where your students' reading achievement lies in relation to that of other students. But process-oriented tests will tell you about the strategies your students use to make sense out of the text they read in your class. They will provide a way for you to understand the instruction in comprehension your students need."

Stiggins (2004) reports that one study showed small gains in test scores that could be attributed to high-stakes tests (Raymond and Hanushek, 2003). Other studies, however, have shown negative results of high-stakes tests, such as reduced achievement and graduation rates, as well as increased dropout rates (Amrein and Berliner, 2002). Participants in a survey of a random sample of the members of the Texas State Reading Association reported that the Texas Assessment of Academic Skills "does not measure what it purports, is unfair to minority students, is affecting instruction in negative ways, is leading both students and teachers to 'drop out,' and is being used in ways that are invalid" (Hoffman, Assaf, and Paris, 2001, p. 490).

Although use of high-stakes tests based on world-class standards is intended to cause students to work harder and learn more, the students will do so only if they *believe* that they will succeed with more effort. If they have a history of failure, the tests may instead be discouraging to them. With the current mandate to teachers to "leave no child behind" in meeting state standards, students who believe that they cannot attain these standards may give up. Teachers must build learning environments to convince students that they can succeed if they persevere (Stiggins, 2004).

Tierney (1998) thinks the goals for assessment should be tied to the teaching and learning that is going on within the classroom, should be set by the teachers and students involved, and should be flexible enough to be adjusted to changes that occur in the classroom. Obviously, traditional tests do not meet his criteria. He sees monitoring of students' reading and writing activities, keeping anecdotal records and holding conferences with students, and having students produce portfolios and keep journals as better ways to assess student performance. Invernizzi and others (2005, p. 612) believe that "test developers sometimes limit or avoid the use of more authentic, qualitative, or subjective measures, the reliability of which is difficult to establish, in favor of more contrived, quantitative, objective measures that can be more easily constructed to be reliable."

Sternberg (1991) points out that reading from traditional tests is different from reading in real life in these ways: recall on the tests is immediate and entirely intentional; the passages have tight reasoning; students are asked to evaluate, but not construct, arguments; the passages are emotionally neutral and often uninteresting; and distractions are minimized.

Still, Schmoker (2000) points out the usefulness of standardized tests in providing impetus for schools to improve instructional programs. He points out that they measure more than low-level skills: "Standardized tests are flush with items that assess students' ability to retain, interpret, and analyze text" (Schmoker, 2000, p. 65).

CHANGES IN SOME COMMERCIAL READING TESTS

There have been some attempts to develop commercial reading tests that reflect newer views of the reading process, but such attempts have encountered many difficulties. Prior knowledge of test takers is difficult to assess in a concise paper-and-pencil format; whole selections sometimes take unrealistically long periods of time to read; appropriate answers to questions involving different backgrounds of experience are hard to determine; reading strategy assessment is a more abstract concept than assessment of mastery of facts; reading fluency is difficult to assess; and construction of items that require higher-level thinking is more difficult than construction of test items at the literal level of thinking.

Criterion-Referenced Tests

What is the difference between norm-referenced tests and criterion-referenced tests?

Whereas norm-referenced tests compare the test taker's performance with that of others, **criterion-referenced tests** (CRTs) check the test taker against a performance criterion, which is a predetermined standard. Thus a criterion-referenced test might read, "Given ten paragraphs at the ninth-grade reading level, the student can identify the main idea in eight of them." In short, a CRT indicates whether or not the test taker has mastered a particular objective or skill rather than how well his or her performance compares with that of others. A norm-referenced test, on the other hand, may indicate that the student can identify the main idea of a paragraph better than 90 percent of the test takers in his or her age group.

The results of criterion-referenced tests can be used as instructional prescriptions; that is, if a student cannot perform the task of identifying the main idea in specified paragraphs, the need for instruction in that area is apparent. These tests are therefore useful in day-to-day decisions about instruction. Teachers often prefer criterion-referenced tests for this reason (Invernizzi et al., 2005).

However, there are a number of unresolved issues related to criterion-referenced tests. For example, the level of success demanded is one issue. Often the passing level is set arbitrarily at 80 or 90 percent, but there is no agreement as to the nature of mastery or how to measure it. Additionally, many criterion-referenced tests give the appearance that hundreds of discrete reading skills must be mastered separately, overlooking the fact that the skills are highly interactive and must be integrated with one another if effective reading is to occur. Some question exists about whether CRTs can measure complex domains such as critical/creative reading skills, reading appreciation, or attitude toward reading. CRTs may also be questioned in terms of reliability and validity. Any type of test *may* measure only knowledge of rules, rather than ability to use them, and a short set of items over a particular reading objective can be less than reliable, particularly in terms of individual assessment.

Both criterion-referenced tests and norm-referenced tests will likely continue to be important reading assessment tools, serving different purposes. In fact, both kinds of interpretation—individual and comparative—are offered by a number of tests. Content teachers may make frequent use of certain CRTs. They may construct these measures themselves, using banks of criterion-referenced test items that are available for all subject areas from some state educational departments or from places such as Educational Testing Services, which is located in Princeton, New Jersey. Teachers may choose appropriate items from such collections to construct tailor-made CRTs, or they may construct their own items.

Traditionally, content teachers have used their own criterion-referenced measures to assess the results of instruction. In such cases, definite instructional objectives are tested, and there is a definite standard of judgment or criterion for "passing." Example 12.1 shows an instructional objective that is measured by five items on a test prepared by a teacher. The criterion for demonstrating mastery of this objective is set at four out of five; that is, the student must answer four out of five items correctly to show mastery.

Note that each question in Example 12.1 is related to the objective. The criterion level for "passing" must be determined by the teacher. Results give the teacher precise information concerning what each student can and cannot do; therefore, the test results can be used to improve classroom instruction.

EXAMPLE 12.1 Criterion-Referenced Test

Objective: Utilize the information found on the content pages of the almanac.

Directions: Find answers to the following.
1. Who was the fifteenth president of the United States?
2. Who holds the world record for high diving?
3. What was the Academy Award winner for the Best Picture of 2004?
4. What are the names of the Kentucky Derby winner of 2003 and the jockey who rode the horse to victory?
5. Where is the deepest lake in the United States?

Classroom-Based Assessments

The term *classroom-based assessments* refers here to informal, primarily teacher-constructed assessments used daily in classrooms. Informal tests (tests not standardized against a specific norm or objective) are valuable aids to teachers in planning instruction. Most of them are constructed by teachers themselves. Other informal measures, such as observations, interviews/conferences, performance samples, and portfolio assessments provide much information. At present such measures are necessary in order for a teacher to assess outcomes of currently endorsed instructional procedures in reading because most current norm-referenced tests are not designed to do so. Teachers' feedback to students on class work, homework, and tests gives students strategies for improvement. Students must receive an opportunity to work on improvement and scaffolding to assist them in their endeavors.

INFORMAL TESTS OF ACHIEVEMENT

Teachers are expected to teach in a way that meets local, state, and even national standards related to their subject areas. Whenever possible, teachers should align both their teaching procedures and their informal evaluations with the standards that they are expected to follow.

Several informal tests of reading achievement can be useful to the teacher in revealing student reading achievement. Six of these measures are discussed in the sections that follow: (1) assessments of background knowledge, (2) group reading inventories, (3) written skill inventories, (4) informal reading inventories, (5) cloze tests, and (6) gamelike activities.

Assessments of Background Knowledge

Online Study Center

HM Video Case
Formative Assessment:
High School History Class

Since the background knowledge of the students plays a vital role in their comprehension of reading material (see Chapters 4 and 5), it is wise to assess background knowledge about a topic before asking students to read about that topic. When prior knowledge of the topics covered in the reading passages is lacking because students with diverse home backgrounds and mental capabilities have acquired different sets of background information, teachers should develop the missing concepts before assigning the reading. Students with varying backgrounds will often have difficulties with concepts in different content fields.

Background knowledge may be assessed in several ways. Oral methods of assessment may be better for less advanced students because they may actually know more than their writing skills allow them to express.

Some common ways to assess prior knowledge are brainstorming, word association, preliminary questioning by the teacher, and informal discussion. When students tell or write down all the facts they know about a topic before reading, they are *brainstorming*. This technique is more successful with older skilled readers than with younger students and less skilled older readers, who do not appear to be able to retrieve their knowledge as easily. *Word association* involves having the students tell everything they can think of about selected words that are subtopics of the main topic, one at a time. This technique may provide more information about prior knowledge than does brainstorming. The teacher may engage in *preliminary questioning* about

MEETING THE CHALLENGE

**ENGLISH/
LANGUAGE
ARTS**

Creative teachers have always found ways to adapt assessment techniques to their particular teaching situations. Katherine Dooley, an English teacher in a rural high school, worked out classroom-based assessment techniques to meet her students' needs. Here is her account of her experience:

In my first year of teaching, I quickly learned my expectations for a unit often could not be evaluated in one fifty-minute period; therefore, I divided tests into objective and subjective (essay-type) questions and gave the test over two days or allowed students to work on the essay part at home. I assumed (I should have known better than to assume) that they would HATE the idea of taking a longer test, and actually I think at first they did hate it.

Assessment methods may include performance measures.
© Richard Pasley/Stock, Boston, LLC

When I returned the tests, I noticed lots of smiles (something I thought was strange because the grades were average at best). Our discussion of the test turned into an evaluation of my evaluation of them. They loved the two-part test. Almost everyone had made a grade they were pleased with on at least one part of the test. Instead of receiving one mediocre grade, they had one great grade, and that made them feel good. In subsequent units, I continued the practice of at least two-part assessments.

The Shakespeare unit formed a new challenge. Shakespeare is my favorite, and more than anything I wanted to transfer my love of the Bard to them. In our pre-unit discussion, I discovered their negative feelings toward Shakespeare would make that difficult. In assessment, I was locked into several things by virtue of unwritten department policy. They would have to take an objective test, take a test about quotations, write an essay, and memorize the *Macbeth* dagger soliloquy; however, those things alone would only compound their dislike of Shakespeare. I wanted them to play with the play, and I knew a group of my students had been videotaping their parties and club meetings since elementary school. The solution was the fact that my students were video babies. I added a video assignment to their growing list and prepared for the groaning, complaining, and whining. But they were not upset about the workload as much as the instructions for the video project: "Videotape something related to *Macbeth* (act out scenes or do a newscast or ???). It should be at least seven minutes long." They begged for more directions; I refused. I wanted them to be creative, but I was secretly petrified that the project was going to bomb. A week before the due date, they became excited and secretive. One group refused to let me near them when they were discussing the video. Students guarded their groups' ideas for sports stories and funny commercials.

This project was the biggest success of the year. The videos, most of which were newscasts, were loaded with lines from the play and complex puns. My favorite was a live remote from the local Taco Bell where Fleance (one of my students in lovely purple tights) was "making a run for the border" after the murder of Banquo. Students told me this was the most fun they had had all year; parents, many of whom worked the camera or did makeup, called and sent gifts saying they "had a blast" helping with this assignment. After we watched all the videos, we voted, dressed up, and gave out the Doolies (huge pieces of minerals) for best actor, actress, cinematography, and picture. In their mandatory acceptance speeches, some thanked parents, some made political or social statements, but all said they would never forget *Macbeth*. I don't think they realized it, but that was the whole idea!

subtopics of the main topic to probe prior knowledge, but this approach requires expertise in question formulation and time for the preparation of questions. This technique offers the largest amount of information of the four types of assessments, and it provides the largest number of facts per minute of administration time. *Informal discussion* of the students' prior experiences with a topic often yields less information than the other three approaches, but is preferable to no assessment.

Langer (1981) developed the PreReading Plan (PReP) technique to help teachers to assess students' background knowledge about a content area topic and to activate their prior knowledge about the topic before they are asked to read the material. The PReP is a discussion activity for a group of approximately ten students, in which the teacher selects a key word, phrase, or picture about the topic to start the discussion. First, the teacher has the students brainstorm about the presented stimulus by saying something like, "What do you think of when you hear (the particular word or phrase) or see (the selected picture)?" The responses are recorded on the board. Then the students explain what made them think of the responses they gave, which develops an awareness of the networks of ideas they have in their experiential backgrounds and exposes them to the associations that their classmates have made. Finally, the teacher asks students if they have any new ideas about the word, phrase, or picture related to the topic of the content passage before they begin to read the text. The opportunity to elaborate on their prior knowledge often results in more refined responses, since students can use input from others to help in shaping responses.

After the PReP discussion ends, the teacher can analyze the responses to discover the students' probable ability to recall the content material after they have read it. Students who have much prior knowledge about the topic under discussion usually respond with superordinate concepts, definitions, analogies, and comparisons with other concepts. Those with some prior knowledge about the topic generally respond with examples or attributes of the concept. Those with little prior information about the topic usually make low-level associations, offering word parts (prefixes, suffixes, and/or root words) or sound-alike words or sharing not quite relevant personal experiences. Initial responses may fall into one category, and responses during the final elaboration may fall into a higher category of knowledge, showing that the process may activate knowledge as well as assess it. Langer states that responses that show much or some prior knowledge indicate that the students will be able to read the text with sufficient understanding. Responses that show little prior knowledge indicate that the students need direct instruction related to relevant concepts before they are asked to read the material.

Group Reading Inventories

What kind of information can a group reading inventory yield?

The content teacher may administer a **group reading inventory** (GRI) before asking students to use a particular text for study. A GRI of content material involves having students read a passage of 1,000 to 2,000 words from their textbooks and then asking them certain types of questions. This procedure can give some indication of how well students will be able to read a particular textbook. Content books to be studied should be written on a student's instructional or independent reading level (instructional for material to be worked on in class with the teacher's assistance; independent for material to be used by the students outside of class); trade and supplementary books should be on a student's independent level, since they are generally used for outside reading assignments. Therefore, by using a group reading inventory, the content teacher can decide whether or not to use material from a particular book for in-class or homework assignments and can decide which materials are inappropriate for use with particular students at any time.

The selection used in an inventory should be material that the students have not read previously. The teacher introduces the selection and directs the students to read it for the purpose of answering certain kinds of questions. As students read, the teacher may write the time on the board at 15-second intervals and have each student write down the last time recorded when he or she finishes reading the passage. Later, a words-per-minute score can be computed by dividing the time into the total number of words in the passage. When he or she is finished reading, the student closes the book and answers a series of questions of such types as the following:

1. Vocabulary (word meaning, word recognition, context, synonyms, antonyms, affixes)

2. Literal comprehension (main ideas, significant details, sequence)

3. Higher-order comprehension (inferential and evaluative)

A sample GRI from a secondary-level history textbook is provided in Example 12.2.

EXAMPLE 12.2   Sample Group Reading Inventory

SOCIAL
STUDIES

Name _____   Date _____

Motivation Statement: Read to find out why the Confederation Congress was unable to settle its foreign problems.

Selection: Dealing with Other Countries

The men who represent one country as it deals with other nations are called *diplomats.* Their work is called *diplomacy,* or the *foreign relations* of their country. The foreign relations of the Confederation were not very successful. Congress did not have the power to make the states or the people follow the agreements that it made with other countries. Under these conditions other nations had little respect for the United States.

The British had promised in the Treaty of Paris to leave the territory they had agreed was now part of the United States. Instead, they remained in their forts along the Great Lakes. They also used their Indian friends to keep settlers out of the Northwest Territory. There was much fighting between the frontiersmen and England's Indian allies.

Why did the English hold these forts? They hoped to keep their fur trade and the control it gave them over some Indian tribes. They even hoped to set up an Indian nation north of the Ohio River. Suppose the American government failed to last. Some British leaders thought that they could then move back into control of their former colonies. The reason they gave for keeping their grip on the Northwest was that the United States had not kept its treaty promise to help British creditors collect their debts in America.

In 1784 Congress tried to settle some of its problems with England. It sent John Adams to London. He tried to get the British to give up the forts on American soil and to increase trade with the United States. The British refused to give up the forts until American debtors had paid the money owed to British creditors since before the Revolutionary War. They refused to make any kind of trade treaty. Adams tried for three years, but could not get the British to change their minds.

Congress also tried to settle its troubles with Spain. In the Treaty of Paris, England had given Americans the use of the Mississippi River and the right to store their goods at New Orleans. This agreement was most important to the people who had moved into Kentucky and Tennessee. They had to use the Mississippi to get their goods to market. They also needed the right to deposit, or keep, their goods in New Orleans until a ship could load them for the trip across the ocean.

Spain held the lower Mississippi and New Orleans. Its rulers would not accept the agreement made by the British and Americans. They also hoped the new nation would not succeed so they could take part of it. Spanish officials urged the settlers south of the Ohio to secede, or take their territory out of the United States. They could then join the Spanish empire. Spain would give them the use of the Mississippi and New Orleans. Spain was still a strong nation. It proved this by getting Indians to attack the pioneers who settled near Spanish territory, and by holding onto Natchez, in American territory.

But Spain was willing to discuss such problems. In 1785 Don Diego de Gardoqui became the first Spanish minister to America. He and John Jay, the American Secretary of Foreign Affairs, soon began to bargain. By this time Spain had closed the lower Mississippi to American trade. Jay was told by Congress that he must get Spain to allow such trade. Don Diego was willing, but only if Spain would control the Mississippi, most of what is now Alabama and Mississippi, and parts of Tennessee, Kentucky, and Georgia. Spain claimed this land because it had held part of it while fighting the British as allies of the United States during the Revolutionary War. Don Diego also asked that Spain should hold all lands south of the thirty-fifth parallel.

John Jay refused to accept such claims. He insisted that the United States would accept only the terms of the Treaty of Paris, which made the thirty-first parallel the boundary between Florida and the United States. Businessmen in the North and East wanted to build up their trade with Spain. In August, 1786, Congress changed its position. It told Jay that he could give up American rights on the Mississippi River for 25 years, if Spain would in turn agree to allow more American trade in Spanish ports. This would have helped the businessmen of New England, but would have hurt the farmers and settlers in the South and West. There was a bitter debate in Congress, and the men who represented seven of the states voted for this plan. This was two states less than the nine that had to agree before Congress could make a treaty. The talks between Spain and the United States then ended. The problems between the two countries were not settled until the Pinckney Treaty of 1795.

Relations with France were also poor. Thomas Jefferson became our minister to France. He wrote that the French showed him little respect. The leaders of the French government were angry because the United States could not repay its wartime debts. However, Jefferson did get them to agree to allow more trade by American ships. The Confederation had no army, and could not do much about Indian attacks. It could not open up the Mississippi, build up trade with Europe, or make needed agreements with foreign governments. More people began to wonder why they had to have such a weak national government.

Source: Boyd Shafer et al., *A High School History of Modern America*, 3rd ed., pp. 104–105. Copyright 1977. By permission of LAIDLAW BROTHERS, a Division of Doubleday and Company, Inc.

Inventory Questions

Directions: Write a short answer to each question.

Vocabulary
1. What is meant by the term *diplomacy*?
2. Define *secede*.
3. Define *allies*.
4. What is a synonym for the word *treaty*?
5. Write the definition of the word *relations* as used in the passage.
6. What did the author mean by "keeping their grip on the Northwest"?

Literal Comprehension
1. What job did John Jay have in the Confederation government? (Detail)
2. Why did the English remain in forts along the Great Lakes? (Detail)
3. Why was the Treaty of Paris important to the people of Tennessee and Kentucky? (Detail)
4. List, in order, the sequence of steps in the discussion of problems with Spain. (Sequence)

Interpretive and Critical Comprehension
1. Do you agree with the directive of Congress to Jay in 1786? Why or why not? (Evaluation)
2. What do you think the people began to want from their national government? What makes you think this? (Inference)
3. Why did the U.S. have so much difficulty in dealing with other nations as described in this selection? (Conclusion)

Materials are suitable for instructional purposes if the student can comprehend 75 percent of what he or she reads, as indicated by performance on well-constructed comprehension questions. If students can comprehend 75 percent of what they read, their comprehension will probably increase if teachers introduce specialized vocabulary words, help with comprehension, teach a study method, and provide specific purposes for reading. Of course, students have many different reading levels, depending on their interests and the background information they possess on any specific topic. Thus, a GRI must be applied to the text in each specific content area. When the student comprehends 90 to 100 percent of what he or she reads, the material can be classified as being on his or her *independent* reading level. When the student comprehends 50 percent or less of what he or she reads, the material is on his or her *frustration* level. Students scoring 70 percent or below on a set of materials should be given an inventory on easier material; those who score 90 percent or above should be given an inventory on more difficult material.

Written Skill Inventories

Content teachers may want to know if students have developed the specific reading skills necessary to understand textbooks and other printed materials in their particular content areas. When teachers are preparing to teach particular chapters or units that involve reading content area materials, they should be aware of the nature of the assigned reading material. Teachers can prepare and administer skill inventories based on textbook chapters or units, modeling them after the skill inventories presented in this section. On the basis of the results, the teachers will become more aware of what activities are needed to prepare students to read and to understand the assigned materials.

Skill inventories may serve as a part of the total assessment program; that is, part of a test by a science teacher may require students to read a table or graph that appears in the text; questions about interpretation of a map that appears in the text might be used as part of a social science teacher's chapter or unit test; symbol knowledge and diagram-reading ability might be included in a mathematics teacher's test; questions on vocabulary words may be used to check understanding of the special terms in a content chapter or unit; assignments in outlining or note taking or adjusting reading rate to purpose and degree of difficulty may be included in tests by all content teachers. The ultimate purpose of skill inventories is that students master and comprehend the content found in their textbooks and in other printed materials used in the classroom. The following skills are common to all content areas:

1. Understanding and using parts of textbooks (table of contents, index, list of illustrations, appendixes, bibliography, glossary)

2. Interpreting maps, tables, charts, graphs, diagrams, cartoons

3. Comprehending specialized vocabulary

4. Using reference materials (encyclopedias, dictionaries, supplemental reference books)

5. Recognizing special symbols, formulas, and abbreviations

Other necessary general skills are using study methods, outlining, taking notes, and reading at a flexible rate. Of course, general comprehension skills are involved in all content areas, as suggested in the GRI.

The following items may be used to prepare skill assessments:

1. *Parts of textbooks.* Have students make use of different elements in their textbooks, such as preface, index, vocabulary lists, and appendixes.

2. *Maps, tables, charts, graphs, diagrams, cartoons.* Using examples from the students' textbooks, ask students to answer questions you have prepared.

3. *Specialized vocabulary, symbols, and abbreviations.* Use words from the glossaries of textbooks or supplemental materials and symbols and abbreviations that are frequently found in your content area.

4. *Reference materials.* Using the reference materials that are available for your content area, develop questions to see if students know the various reference sources and how to use them.

Examples 12.3 through 12.6 provide some sample reading skill tests.

EXAMPLE 12.3   **Finding Information in a Textbook—Skill Inventory**

Directions: Use your textbook to answer the following questions.
1. What is the title of your book?
2. When was it published? How did you find out? Where did you look?
3. Who wrote the book?
4. What are the titles of the first three chapters? Where did you look to find out?
5. How are the chapters arranged or grouped? How did you find out?
6. On what page does Chapter 4 begin? How did you find out?
7. Find the meaning of the term _____. Where did you look to find out?
8. What does the map on page _____ tell you?
9. On what page does the book explain the construction of a _____? Where did you find out?
10. What index entries are given for _____? Where did you look to find the index? How is it arranged?

EXAMPLE 12.4   Reading Graphs—Skills Inventory

Directions: Look at the graph and answer the questions about it.

SOCIAL
STUDIES

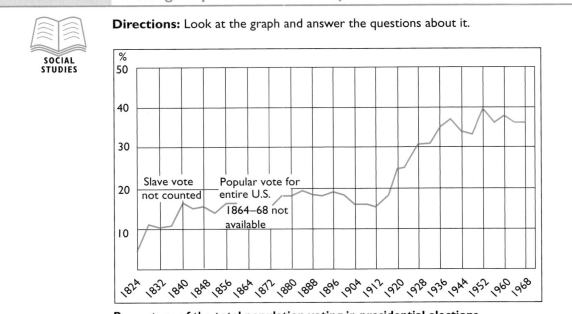

Percentage of the total population voting in presidential elections

Source: Historical Statistics and Statistical Abstract.

Questions

1. Was there a steady growth of voters from 1824 to 1860? Why do you think so?
2. Around what year was there a sudden increase in popular votes cast in presidential elections?
3. Does the graph show the percentage of voting-age citizens participating in presidential elections?
4. For what years are complete data not provided? What may have caused this?

EXAMPLE l2.5   Using Reference Sources—Skill Inventory

Directions: Find the following words in a dictionary, and list the guide words and page number on which each falls.

Word   *Guide Words*   *Page Number*

anachronism

epigram

foreshadowing

irony

soliloquy

Directions: Answer the following questions about reference materials.

1. How does the information in a dictionary differ from that in an encyclopedia?
2. How does information in a dictionary differ from that in a thesaurus?
3. What are guide words?
4. What is meant by cross-reference?
5. What is the purpose of the bibliographies at the ends of articles?
6. Where is the index located in a reference book?

EXAMPLE l2.6   Vocabulary—Skill Inventory

SOCIAL STUDIES

Directions: Study the terms listed below that were taken from a secondary history book. Use your knowledge of meanings of any of the word parts to help you understand the meanings of the whole words.

vaccination

pasteurization

radiation

evolution

genetics

sociology

psychology

Directions: Answer the following questions about the terms above.

1. What are the root words of the following words: *vaccination*, *pasteurization*, *radiation*, *evolution*, and *genetics*?
2. If you know the meanings of the root words, use these meanings to help you determine the meanings of the new words.

3. How is the word *pasteurization* different from the others? Does knowing the root word for this word help you? Why or why not?
4. Does being familiar with common suffixes help you figure out the meanings of these words?
5. What are the combining forms that make up the words *sociology* and *psychology*? If you know the meanings of these combining forms, use them to help you determine the meanings of the new words. Notice how knowing the meaning of one combining form can help you with two different words.

Directions: Define the italicized words.
1. When a person has been given a *vaccination*, an injection of a solution of weakened germs, he or she may be protected from contracting the disease.
2. The process of *pasteurization* of milk was invented by Louis Pasteur when he realized that bacteria could be killed by heat.
3. Uranium gives off *radiation* that is similar to X-rays.
4. The *evolution* of living things over time could result in one species slowly evolving into another, according to Darwin.
5. Genes carry the traits that are passed from parents to their children. Mendel did work that established the foundation of the science of *genetics*.
6. When searching for a set of laws under which human society operates, Comte invented the term *sociology* to describe his scientific study.
7. Those who wish to learn more about the mind and behavior may wish to major in *psychology*.

A skills chart can be developed for recording the instructional needs of students. A skills chart has a list of skills down the left side of a page and a list of students' names across the top of the page. The teacher places a check mark beside a skill under the name of a student who successfully achieves the skill. A glance at the chart shows which students need special help in developing a required skill. If most students need help with a particular skill, the teacher may plan a total-class instructional session around that skill. If only certain students lack a skill, the teacher may set up a small skill group to help students who need it. Skill groups are temporary groups in that they are dissolved when the members have mastered the skill. A skills file (collection of materials, equipment, and supplies) may provide the needed practice activities for some students.

Informal Reading Inventories

Commercial **informal reading inventories** (IRIs), which are compilations of graded reading selections with questions prepared to test the reader's comprehension, are

What information can informal reading inventories provide for teachers?

used to gauge students' reading levels. These types of inventories are often administered by the special or remedial reading teacher to students identified as problem readers, but they can also be used by regular classroom teachers for special situations. According to Bader and Wiesendanger (1989, p. 403), "If we examine the definitions of *informal* (not prescribed or fixed) and *inventory* (appraisal) we realize that the intention behind these devices is to provide a window on the reading process. The reader's confidence, willingness to risk error, ability to make semantically and syntactically sound substitutions, fluency, perception of organization, and a host of other understandings and abilities can be observed." They further point out that it may be inappropriate to expect reliability coefficients for alternative forms of informal reading inventories because of "the effect of content on attention, understanding, and recall." Professional judgment is needed to make decisions when greater prior knowledge about or interest in the content of a particular passage results in unusually high performance on that passage or when limited prior knowledge or interest in the content of a passage results in unusually low performance on that passage.

A chief purpose of these inventories is to identify the independent, instructional, frustration, and capacity reading levels of the student. Such inventories are valuable in that they not only provide an overall estimate of the student's reading ability, but they also make possible identification of the specific strengths and weaknesses of the reader. They are helpful in determining what books a student can read independently and how difficult assigned reading can be if it is to be used as instructional material. Although a reading specialist might give a student an entire series of inventory selections and locate all four of these levels, the content teacher may give a similar inventory based on textbooks used in a particular class to find out if students can benefit from using those books.

Although it is time-consuming, it is possible for a teacher to construct and administer an informal reading inventory for a specific content area. The steps below are suggested for this procedure:

1. Select a set of books (or other materials) used at various grade levels (such as sixth, seventh, eighth, ninth, tenth, eleventh, and twelfth), preferably a series used in the class.

2. From each book, select one passage to be used for oral reading and one passage to be used for silent reading (each of two hundred words or more).

3. Make a copy of each of the passages from each book. (Later, as the student reads from the book, the teacher marks the errors on the copy.)

4. Make up approximately ten questions for each passage. The questions should be of various types, including main idea, detail, vocabulary, sequence, inference, and cause and effect.

5. Direct the student to read the first passage orally. Mark and count his or her errors, using a system that allows you to identify types of errors, such as refusal to pronounce, mispronunciation, omission, insertion, reversal of word order

or word parts, and repetition. Mispronounced proper names and differences attributable to dialect should not be counted as errors. This, of course, requires the teacher to be familiar with the dialects spoken by the students in order to score the inventory properly. Some teachers have found it effective to tape a student's oral reading, replaying the tape to note the errors in performance.

6. Then ask questions prepared for the oral reading. Count the number of questions answered correctly.

7. Direct the student to read the second passage silently. Ask questions prepared for silent reading. Again, count the number of questions answered correctly.

8. Count the number of errors in oral reading. Subtract the number of errors from the number of words in the selection. Then figure the percentage correct by dividing by the number of words in the selection and multiplying the result by 100.

9. Total the number of correct answers to questions for both the oral and silent reading passages. Then figure the percentage correct by dividing by the number of questions and multiplying the result by 100.

10. Read higher levels of material aloud to the student until you reach the highest reading level for which he or she can correctly answer 75 percent of the comprehension questions. (The highest level achieved indicates the student's probable *capacity*, or potential, reading level.)

The following chart will help the teacher in estimating the reading levels of the reader:

Level	Word Recognition		Comprehension
Independent	99%	and	90%
Instructional	95%	and	75%
Frustration	<90%	or	<50%
Capacity			75%

Various writers in the field suggest slightly differing percentages relative to independent, instructional, frustration, and capacity levels. Originally, the criteria to establish the levels were developed by Betts (1946). The set of criteria given here for the reading levels is basically the one proposed by Johnson, Kress, and Pikulski (1987). An example of a published informal reading inventory selection is found in Example 12.7.

Some teachers may just want to choose passages for the texts being used in their classes, to decide if the students can read them independently or if they need teacher scaffolding.

EXAMPLE 12.7 Informal Reading Inventory Selection

SOCIAL STUDIES

TEACHER 11

◆ ◆

INTRODUCTORY STATEMENT: Read this story to find out some things Johnny Appleseed did.

There is some disagreement concerning the way in which Johnny went about planting apple trees in the wild frontier country. Some say that he scattered the seed as he went along the edges of marshes or natural clearings in the thick, almost tropical forests, others that he distributed the seeds among the settlers themselves to plant, and still others claim that in the damp land surrounding the marshes he established nurseries where he kept the seedlings until they were big enough to transplant. My Great-Aunt Mattie said that her father, who lived in a rather grand way for a frontier settler, had boxes of apples brought each year from Maryland until his own trees began to bear, and then he always saved the seeds, drying them on the shelf above the kitchen fireplace, to be put later into a box and kept for Johnny Appleseed when he came on one of his overnight visits.

Johnny scattered fennel seed all through our Ohio country, for when the trees were first cleared and the land plowed up, the mosquitoes increased and malaria spread from family to family. Johnny regarded a tea brewed of fennel leaves as a specific against what the settlers called "fever and ague," and he seeded the plant along trails and fence rows over all Ohio.

FORM A

Source: "Johnny Appleseed and Aunt Mattie," by Louis Bromfield, in *Pleasant Valley* (New York: Harper and Row, 1945).

SCORING AID
Word Recognition
%–Miscues
99–3
95–12
90–22
85–33
Comprehension
%–Errors
100–0
90–1
80–2
70–3
60–4
50–5
40–6
30–7
20–8
10–9
0–10
217 Words
(for Word Recognition)
217 Words
(for Rate)
WPM
13020

COMPREHENSION QUESTIONS

____ main idea	1.	What is the main idea of this story? (Johnny Appleseed planted apple trees and fennel seed.)
____ detail	2.	In what kind of country did Johnny plant trees? (wild frontier country; marshes; thick forests)
____ vocabulary	3.	What does the word "distributed" mean? (handed out to different people)
____ vocabulary	4.	What are the nurseries mentioned in the story? (places where trees, shrubs, and vines are grown until they are large enough to transplant)
____ inference	5.	Was Great-Aunt Mattie's father rich or poor? (rich) What in the story caused you to answer that way? (He lived in a grand way for a frontier settler and had boxes of apples brought from Maryland until his own trees began to bear.)
____ detail	6.	What did Great-Aunt Mattie's father save for Johnny? (seeds from his apples)
____ sequence	7.	Name, in order, the two things Great-Aunt Mattie's father did with the seeds. (He dried them on the shelf above the kitchen fireplace and then put them in a box.)
____ cause and effect/ inference	8.	What caused the spread of malaria through Ohio? (The increase in mosquitoes when the trees were first cleared and the land plowed up.)
____ inference	9.	What did the settlers call malaria? (fever and ague)
____ inference	10.	What did Johnny believe would help malaria sufferers? (a tea brewed of fennel leaves)

◆ 11 PASSAGE ◆

Source: Betty D. Roe, *Roe/Burns Informal Reading Inventory: Preprimer to Twelfth Grade*, 7th ed. Copyright © 2006 by Houghton Mifflin Company. Reprinted by permission of Houghton Mifflin Company.

Cloze Tests

An alternative method of assessment that can provide information similar to that provided by the informal reading inventory is the **cloze test** (Taylor, 1956; Bormuth, 1968a and b). This test is easy to construct, administer, and score, and it takes much less time to administer than the informal reading inventory. For these reasons, content area teachers are likely to find the cloze test procedure more attractive for classroom use than the informal reading inventory.

How is a cloze test administered?

For a cloze test, the student is asked to read selections of increasing levels of difficulty and to supply words that have been deleted from the passage. A sample cloze passage is given in Example 12.8.

Following are the steps used for constructing, administering, and scoring the cloze test:

1. Select a set of materials typical of those used in your classroom; from each level of these materials, select a passage of about 250 words. The chosen passages should be ones the students have not read previously.

2. Leave the first sentence intact, and then delete every fifth word until you have about fifty deletions. Replace the deleted words with blanks of uniform length.

3. Ask the student to fill in each blank with the exact word that has been deleted. Allow time to complete the test.

4. Count the number of correct responses. Do not count spelling mistakes as wrong answers; do not count synonyms as correct answers.

5. Convert the number of correct responses into a percentage.

The following criteria may be used in determining levels when cloze tests are used:

Accuracy	*Reading Level*
57% or greater	Independent reading level
44–57%	Instructional reading level
Below 44%	Frustration level

A student who achieves a percentage of accuracy at or above the instructional level is asked to complete the next higher-level cloze test until that student reaches his or her highest instructional level. The teacher can probably assign instructional reading of tested material to any student who achieves a score of between 44 and 57 percent on that material. A score of 57 percent or better on any passage means the teacher can use the material from which the passage was taken for independent reading. A score of less than 44 percent accuracy on a passage would indicate that the material from which the passage was taken is probably not suitable for that particular student.

Students should be given an explanation of the purpose of the procedure and a few practice passages to complete before a cloze test is used for assessment. Students need

EXAMPLE 12.8   Sample Cloze Passage

SCIENCE AND HEALTH

People rely on many different measures to control and prevent floods. Most of these measures _____ both advantages and disadvantages.
(1)

_____ way that people can _____ the impact of flooding _____ to
(2)   (3)   (4)
restore natural flood _____ that human activity has _____. In areas where
(5)   (6)
vegetation _____ been removed, replanting helps _____ control runoff. Re-
(7)   (8)
planting is _____ important at the headwater _____ of a river's drainage
(9)   (10)
_____. Such measures cannot prevent _____, however.
(11)   (12)

Dams are often _____ to control and prevent _____. When dams are built
(13)   (14)
_____ rivers, reservoirs can store _____ runoff. One example is _____
(15)   (16)   (17)
Tennessee River system where _____ 50 dams have been _____. Some of
(18)   (19)
the risks _____ with dams are that _____ can break, causing floods _____
(20)   (21)   (22)
may be more destructive _____ natural flooding. Dams also _____ sedi-
(23)   (24)
ment, which upsets the _____ between erosion and deposition _____. Less
(25)   (26)
deposition means more _____ of a floodplain, which _____ flooding. Dams
(27)   (28)
become less _____ at controlling floods once _____ fill up with sediment.
(29)   (30)
_____ can also damage river _____.
(31)   (32)

Artificial levees, such as _____ stacked on top of _____ river's natural
(33)   (34)
levees, are _____ method of flood control. _____ principle behind using arti-
(35)   (36)
ficial _____ is that a deeper _____ will hold more water. _____ problem
(37)   (38)   (39)
occurs, however, when _____ water level rises within _____ deeper channel.
(40)   (41)
As the _____ height increases, so does _____ velocity, creating a powerful
(42)   (43)
_____ force that can break _____ levees downstream, sometimes causing
(44)   (45)
_____ damage than might have _____ if the river had _____ allowed to
(46)   (47)   (48)
overflow the _____ levee onto the floodplain.
(49)

_____ the lower Mississippi, spillways control flooding.
(50)

Source: Text from Nancy E. Spaulding and Samuel N. Namowitz, *Earth Science*, page 292. Copyright ©
2005 by McDougal Littell Inc., a division of Houghton Mifflin Company. All rights reserved. Reprinted by
permission of McDougal Littell Inc., a division of Houghton Mifflin Company.

to be encouraged to use the information contained in the material surrounding each blank to make a decision about the correct word to place in the blank; otherwise they may simply guess without considering all of the available clues. Some students exhibit anxiety with this form of test, but practice may help alleviate this anxiety.

Although use of the traditional fifth-word deletion pattern is most common, some educators use a tenth-word deletion pattern, as suggested by Burron and Claybaugh (1974) for content area materials. This pattern is intended to compensate for the denseness of concepts and technical language in content materials.

Teachers who wish to discover the ability of their students to use semantic and syntactic context clues effectively may wish to administer the cloze test and accept as answers synonyms and reasonable responses that make sense in the passage. To obtain information about students' use of particular types of context clues, a teacher may wish to delete specific categories of words (for example, only nouns or only adjectives) in specific contexts, rather than every *n*th word. Of course, such modifications would make determination of reading levels according to the criteria indicated in this section inappropriate, but they would allow the teachers to see how the students process language as they read.

Cloze tests place heavy demands on short-term memory, because the reader must remember the words surrounding the blanks while searching for information in the selection to help in filling in the blanks. Therefore, because of the short-term memory demands, some students may not score as well on a cloze test as they would on another type of test.

Gamelike Activities

Some teachers use games to test students informally on the content just covered. Some base the games on the formats of popular television shows like *Jeopardy!* or competitions like *College Bowl*. Others use self-created game formats. Such activities take advantage of the students' attraction to fast-moving video games, and they offer students immediate knowledge of results to reinforce appropriate responses.

OBSERVATION

Systematic daily observation of students' reading performances can provide teachers with clues for planning effective instruction. Most decision making in the classroom is done by teachers as they observe classroom activities. Teachers, then, need to know how to look for patterns of behavior and to keep records related to the patterns observed. Without a written record of observations, teachers are likely to forget much of what they have seen or to remember it inaccurately. Various record-keeping devices that teachers use with observation, such as checklists, logs, class forms, and anecdotal records, can help them systematize observation and document findings.

Johnston and Costello (2005, p. 257) point out that "literacy assessment should reflect and encourage resilience—a disposition to focus on learning when the going gets tough, to quickly recover from setbacks, and to adapt." Teachers can best assess resilience through documented narratives of observed behaviors (Carr and Claxton, 2002; Johnston, 2004).

Teachers should try to observe students reading in a variety of settings in order to develop a complete picture of reading behaviors. Every reading activity the students engage in provides assessment data that teachers can record and analyze. Over a period of days or weeks, patterns of student development will become evident, providing a basis for instructional assistance. Teachers do need to be cautious about conclusions drawn from their observations because many biases can creep in. For example, people often base assessments on early evidence and ignore later evidence if they think that they are observing a stable characteristic, and they are more likely to think a poor paper is worse than it is if they see it just after a good one (MacGinitie, 1993).

The teacher should keep questions such as the following in mind during observation of each student:

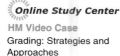

Online Study Center

HM Video Case
Grading: Strategies and
Approaches

1. Does the student approach the assignment with enthusiasm?

2. Does he or she apply an appropriate study method?

3. Can he or she find answers to questions of a literal type (i.e., detail questions)?

4. Does he or she understand ideas beneath the surface level (answering inferential- and critical-level questions)?

5. Can he or she ascertain the meanings of new or unfamiliar words? What word-recognition skills does the student use?

6. Can he or she use locational skills in books?

7. Can he or she use reference skills for various reference sources?

8. Is he or she reading at different rates for different materials and purposes?

In addition, when a student gives an oral report or reads orally, the teacher has the opportunity to observe the following:

Oral Report	*Oral Reading*
Pronunciation	Methods of word attack
General vocabulary	Word-recognition problems
Specialized vocabulary	Rate of reading
Sentence structure	Phrasing
Organization of ideas	Peer reactions
Interests	

Observations can be more valid assessment tools than standardized tests because they involve actual reading tasks, not artificial situations. Use of observation over an extended period allows patterns of performance in real reading situations to become evident. This makes the assessment more reliable than a single test can be.

INTERVIEWS/CONFERENCES

Interviews and teacher-student conferences can yield much information about literacy skill. Interviews are particularly good for collecting information about interests and attitudes. They are also useful for discovering why students have chosen particular strategies in their reading and writing activities. Teacher-student conferences about portfolios are discussed later in this chapter, and teacher-student conferences about students' writing pieces are discussed in Chapter 8.

PERFORMANCE SAMPLES

Performance samples can be either written or oral. Both can yield valuable data.

Retellings

What value does retelling have as an assessment technique?

Written work done for authentic purposes can be evaluated for effectiveness and sometimes can also be analyzed for ideas, organization, voice, style, and mechanics. Similarly, teachers may ask students to react in writing to narrative passages to discover whether they are attending to surface-level plot structures, underlying universal themes, or character development (Readence and Martin, 1989). This can be a form of written **retelling** of the story, which has the advantage over oral retelling of not requiring the individual attention of the teacher during the retelling. This written retelling can be a valuable piece to include in a student's portfolio. Later retellings can be added to demonstrate progress.

Assessing comprehension of material read by having students retell a selection in response to the reading can be effective (Glazer and Brown, 1993), but retelling is time-consuming, and it may be difficult for struggling readers. Readers construct a text in their minds as they read a particular selection. The texts constructed by better readers are more complete and accurate than those constructed by less skilled ones. The retelling technique shows what the students consider important in the text and how they organize that information, rather than showing if the students remember what the adults doing the testing consider important. A selection to be retold should be read silently and then retold to the teacher without interruption. When the retelling is completed, the teacher may request elaboration on some points, for the students may know more about the material than they can produce in a free recall situation. Teachers should listen for such things as identification of major characters, characteristics of the characters, the story's problem and solution, and an accurate sequence of events in retellings of narrative texts. They should listen for main ideas and important supporting details in expository texts (Richek, List, and Lerner, 1989). The retellings are a type of window to the reading comprehension process that goes on within a student and can be highly valuable in selected settings. Morrow (1989) cautions that retelling is difficult for students and suggests that teachers offer students guidance and practice with retelling before it is used for evaluation. She also stresses that students should be told before they read a story that they will be expected to retell it, and they should be given a purpose for the reading that is congruent with the information that the teacher is looking for in the evaluation.

Retellings can be evaluated by counting the number of idea units included (probably weighted for importance) and checking for appropriate sequence. Retellings can also be checked to determine such things as inclusion of literal and implied information, attempts to connect background knowledge to text information or to apply information to the real world, affective involvement with the text, appropriate language use, and control of the mechanics of spoken or written language (Morrow, 1989).

Rubrics

Rubrics can be developed to evaluate oral and written retellings as well as other oral and written responses to reading. Rubrics provide a set of criteria for each quality level of performance for a given assignment (Andrade, 2000). They clarify teacher expectations for students and help students see their strengths and weaknesses. A rubric for a written retelling might resemble the one in Example 12.9. A rubric is a scoring plan "that defines the level of accomplishment you desire for products (poems, essays, drawings, maps), complex cognitive processes (skills in acquiring, organizing, and using knowledge), use of procedures (physical movements, use of specialized equipment, oral presentations), and attitudes and social skills (habits of mind, cooperative group work)" (Tombari and Borich, 1999, p. 65).

Think-Alouds

How are think-alouds used to assess reading comprehension and strategy use?

Glazer and Brown (1993) suggest the use of oral think-alouds about reading that is in progress. Wade and Adams (1990) describe the use of a think-aloud procedure for comprehension assessment. With this procedure, students read short segments of passages in which they cannot be certain what the topic is until they have read the last segment. After reading each segment, they think aloud about the passage's meaning, generating hypotheses about the meaning from the clues in the segment just read. At the completion of the passage, the reader retells the complete passage. The activity can be recorded for later analysis as to how the reader generated hypotheses,

| **EXAMPLE 12.9** | **Rubric for Evaluating Written Retelling of Nonfiction** |

Score Level	Content
3	Includes all main ideas and at least one supporting detail for each one. Includes both literal and implied information (if appropriate). Includes no inaccurate content.
2	Includes at least one main idea with one or more supporting details. Includes only literal information even when implied information is appropriate. Includes no inaccurate content.
1	Includes only a main idea with no supporting details or only details without a main idea statement. Includes no inaccurate content.
0	Includes inaccurate content.

Score Level	Organization
3	Follows author's organization in retelling, with all parts included.
2	Generally follows author's organization, but omits or misplaces one part.
1	Attempts author's organization, but omits multiple parts.
0	Does not follow author's organization.

Score Level	Conventions Used
3	Uses standard English, correct spelling, and correct punctuation and capitalization consistently.
2	Generally uses standard English and mechanics, but has more than one deviation.
1	Has numerous deviations from some language aspects of standard English and mechanics, but shows control of other aspects.
0	Shows little evidence of standard English or correct mechanics of writing.

supported them with text information, related information to background experiences, integrated new information with existing knowledge, and so on. Such recordings can be included in students' portfolios.

Use of the think-aloud procedure can reveal students who are good comprehenders, those who overly rely on bottom-up (text-based) or top-down (knowledge-based) processing, and those who fail to integrate information in the different segments of the passage. Knowing these approaches to reading can help the teacher plan appropriate instruction, such as focusing on developing or activating prior knowledge to help students understand the text; helping them understand the function of background knowledge in comprehension; helping them link information from various sentences to form a unified, coherent idea; helping them develop flexibility in interpretations; and helping them learn to use metacognitive skills.

Videotape Analysis

Videotapes of a variety of learning events—oral reports, creative dramas, skits, debates, and group discussions, for example—can provide excellent performance samples. Videotapes made over a period of time filled with like activities can show growth in various areas, as well as continuing weaknesses.

Cloze Procedure

Baumann (1988) points out that the cloze procedure, described earlier in this chapter, is a type of process assessment because readers have to respond *while* they are working on figuring out the text. The readers use the semantic and syntactic clues in the supplied text to construct a meaningful whole text.

Problems

There are some special problems in the secondary school in using alternative assessments. These problems include very limited amount of time in classes, pressure to cover many specific concepts, and large numbers of students to be assessed by a single teacher.

PORTFOLIO ASSESSMENT

What types of items belong in a literacy portfolio?

Use of **portfolios** of students' work can be an effective way of accomplishing authentic classroom-based assessment of literacy skills. Portfolios allow teachers to examine real products of instruction, rather than a limited sample found on a test. In addition, portfolios can serve as an integral part of classroom instruction as the teacher and student confer about the contents and what the contents say about the student's literacy. Portfolios can be important, not only for teacher assessment, but also for self-assessment by the students, and they can aid the development of metacognition (Belanoff and Dickson, 1991; Sunstein, 1992; Serafini, 2000/2001). Such assessment is especially appropriate in the analysis of writing because, as Elbow and Belanoff (1991) indicate, an adequate picture of a student's writing proficiency cannot be obtained without examination of several pieces of writing produced on different days in a variety of genres. Belanoff and Dickson (1991, p. xx) point out, however, that portfolio assessment is "messy, bulky, nonprogrammable, not easily scored, and time-consuming (though . . . it's not as bad in these areas as its detractors paint it)."

Contents

Wolf and Siu-Runyan (1996, p. 31) say, "A portfolio is a selective collection of student work and records of progress gathered across diverse contexts over time, framed by reflection and enriched through collaboration, that has as its aim the advancement of student learning." Each student's portfolio should include materials showing that student's accomplishments as a reader and a writer. These materials can vary widely, depending on the function that the portfolio assessment is intended to serve. Possible purposes are "to promote student self-assessment, to document student learning, to guide teaching, to communicate with parents about their child's progress, or to provide administrators and policy makers with information about the impact of the school's or district's instructional program" (Wolf and Siu-Runyan, 1996, p. 32). Some examples of materials that might be included follow.

1. Writing samples judged to be the student's best efforts—either current samples or those chosen for the portfolio at regular intervals in order to show progress.

2. All prewriting materials and drafts for a piece that has been developed through to the publication stage, to show the process that was followed.

3. Recordings of a student's best oral reading (done with prior preparation), either current samples or those collected at regular intervals to show progress.

4. Written responses to literature that has been read and discussed in class (which can be analyzed for inclusion of information on theme, characters, setting, problem, events, solution, application, and personal response).

5. Journal entries that show analysis of literacy skills or that show interest or engagement in literary activities.

6. Functional writing samples (letters, lists, etc.).

7. Reading logs that show the number and variety of books read in various time periods.

8. Videotapes of group reading discussions, audience reading activities, reading/writing conferences, or literacy-based projects (creative dramatizations, readers' theater presentations, etc.).

9. Photographs of completed literacy-based projects, with attached captions or explanations.

10. Examples of writing-to-learn in content area activities. (See Chapter 8 for examples.)

11. Informal tests.

12. Checklists or anecdotal records made from observations by the teacher.

13. Questionnaires on attitudes toward reading and writing and on reading interests.

14. CDs of web pages or multimedia presentations developed.

15. The student's written explanation of portfolio contents and assessment of personal literacy achievements based on this evidence.

Purpose

Teachers or administrators must decide the purpose that the portfolios are to serve, the criteria for inclusion of materials, and who will place materials in the portfolios.

If the portfolios are to be used by the administration or outside agencies, this decision making may be entirely out of the hands of teachers and students. If the portfolios are for the teacher to use in making instructional decisions or in keeping parents informed of the student's progress or for the teacher and student to use in observing and documenting the student's progress and characteristics as a literate person, the student may make many or all of the decisions alone or in collaboration with the teacher. If the portfolios are primarily for evaluation or documentation for outside individuals, including parents and administrators, the teacher may take a more active role in the decision making than if the portfolios are only for classroom instructional purposes.

Teachers must be clear about the skills and strategies they want to assess and must require that the portfolios include a variety of products that demonstrate the use of these skills and strategies (Tombari and Borich, 1999). Portfolios "can measure growth and development of competence in cognitive areas such as knowledge construction (e.g., knowledge organization), cognitive strategies (analysis, interpretation, planning, organizing, revising), procedural skills (clear communication, editing, drawing, speaking, building), and metacognition (self-monitoring, self-reflection). They can also provide evidence of certain dispositions—or habits of mind—such as flexibility, adaptability, acceptance of criticism, persistence, collaboration, and desire for mastery" (Tombari and Borich, 1999, p. 170). Teachers must ensure that the instruction in their classes involves the skills and strategies needed for the construction of the portfolio.

Teachers may want students to keep separate portfolios for different purposes. The types of materials selected depend on the purpose of the portfolio (Wolf and Siu-Runyan, 1996). For example, one portfolio might focus on a student's best work in a variety of areas, whereas another portfolio might focus on the range of genres the student has experienced and experimented with in reading and writing. Still another portfolio might show the process used in developing written pieces or in evaluating reading selections. Some teachers may want evidence of all these varying literacy aspects in the same portfolio, which magnifies the importance of the organization of the material.

Selection and Evaluation

Why is it important to guide students in their selection of portfolio materials?

Ideally, the students will participate in the selection and evaluation of materials for their portfolios. They may need guidance, however, as to the criteria for inclusion because otherwise they may either put everything or very little into their portfolios. Including too much may obscure the information that is most helpful. Including too little may not offer sufficient input for decision making. They also need to know what scoring criteria will be used—what is being judged and the standards for acceptable materials. If the scoring criteria are vague, it will be difficult for the teacher to give a fair and consistent assessment. Students may participate in developing the criteria for evaluation (Gillespie et al., 1996). Collaborating with teachers to choose portfolio items that represent their progress over time and their current levels of achievement can help students to feel ownership of the learning process. Reflection about their learning activities not only leads them to choose assessment items but

What are some of the
possibilities for
organizing portfolios?

also helps them understand their strengths and weaknesses. It helps them understand what they need to do in the future as well (Wolf and Siu-Runyan, 1996).

Students should have the opportunity to organize their portfolios in ways that
help them best display their literacy products and processes. Labeling the materials
and indicating what criterion or criteria they meet can enhance clarity. Rief (1992,
p. 45) indicates that she sets the *external* criteria for her students' portfolios—"each
student's two best pieces chosen during a six-week period with all the rough drafts
that went into each piece, trimester self-evaluations of process and product, each
student's reading list, and, at year's end, a reading-writing project." However, her
"students determine the *internal* criteria—which pieces, for their own reasons."

Graves (1992a and b), on the other hand, asks students to decide which pieces
have particular value to them by asking them to label pieces that they like, that they
found hard to write, that surprised them as they were writing, that made them realize that they were learning something about the writing, that helped them learn
about the content they were writing about, that helped the reader picture the written ideas, that had good opening lines, that needed reworking, and so on. Then the
students can analyze the pieces for inclusion in the portfolio with a view as to what
they show about the writer and his or her ability to produce pieces that exhibit good
quality. Students' written explanations about materials in their portfolios can include the reason each item was included, what criterion it meets, when the work was
done, how long it took to complete and how they would evaluate its qualities (Simmons, 1992).

Students may be asked to rank their products from best to worst, arrange pieces
chronologically to show a picture of literacy activities for the period, choose pieces
to show a range of genres in their reading and writing experiences, or describe the
development of a long-term project. Portfolio assessment is flexible enough to fit individual class needs.

A portfolio can reflect the student's ability to understand and express ideas, recognize and use organization, understand and choose appropriate words, manage the
mechanics of writing, carry through to completion the reading, analysis, or writing
of a work, produce quality written products, revise, gain insight into material read,
and perform self-evaluation. It can also indicate the student's work habits, preferences, strengths and weaknesses, attitudes, and range of reading and writing activities (Simmons, 1992). Teachers can base portfolio grades on "effort, improvement,
commitment to the task, content of the work, mechanics, and volume" (Grace, 1993,
p. 27), among other criteria. Elbow (1991) feels that the use of portfolios encourages
analytic grading and the concept that humans have multiple types of intelligence
and skills.

Portfolio conferences can be opportunities to learn more about the process behind the development of the portfolio materials from the students. The students
should explain why they included what they did and what these items show about
them as literate people. The students can tell what they have learned, using the portfolio pieces as documentation, and then the teacher and students can plan future activities to work on any evident weaknesses or gaps in literacy achievement. The
teacher can listen to the students' self-assessments, point out areas of growth and

evidence of literacy skills, and ask questions to clarify points that the students made (Milliken, 1992; Rief, 1992).

Portfolios may contain both hard copies of written products and electronic works, such as videotapes, CDs, DVDs, or web pages. Electronic portfolios can include graphics, photographs, text, and audio and video segments. If the portfolios are in digital format, they can be transferred in part or in whole to videotapes or CDs for viewing, if desirable.

Category of Assessment

Portfolio assessment is a criterion-referenced, rather than a norm-referenced, approach. Instead of expecting students to end up distributed along a bell-shaped curve, users of this type of assessment would expect all students to pass eventually because they have had enough time and assistance to do what they have been asked to do (Elbow and Belanoff, 1991).

SELF-ASSESSMENT

Students need to be helped to monitor their own literacy learning, rather than depending exclusively on teacher monitoring. Teachers can facilitate this by asking students questions about how literacy tasks are going and how they can tell. This type of questioning lets them know that they are capable of evaluating their performance. Activities such as having students rank several examples of their own writing and asking them to tell the basis for the ranking encourages self-assessment (Johnston, 2005).

Self-assessment may also take place during whole-class or small-group discussion, as students discuss the strengths and weaknesses of their writing or the extent to which they understood the reading materials. Peer conferences about reading and writing can also be the basis for self-analysis. Involving students in self-assessment makes them partners in evaluation (Fryar, 2003; Van Kraayenoord, 2003).

Self-assessment techniques include the following:

1. *Discussion.* Self-assessment may focus on a single topic, such as word recognition, meaning of vocabulary, comprehension, study strategies, or problems in reading a particular textbook. With guiding questions from the teacher, the students can discuss, orally or in writing, their strengths and weaknesses in regard to the particular topic.

2. *Structured interview or conference.* The teacher may ask such questions as the following:
   a. How do you figure out the pronunciation or meaning of an unknown word?
   b. What steps are you taking to develop your vocabulary?
   c. What do you do to get the main ideas from your reading?
   d. Do you use the same rate of reading in most of your assignments?
   e. What method of study do you use most?
   f. How do you organize your material to remember it?

g. What special reference books have you used lately in the writing of a report?

h. How do you handle graphic aids that appear in the reading material?

i. How do you study for a test?

j. What could you do to become an even better reader?

3. *Self-rating checklist.* Checklists can focus on particular skills, such as reading to follow directions, or a broad range of skills. Students rate themselves.

4. *Learning logs.* Students keep learning logs to document daily progress and learning.

5. *Written reflections about work.* Portfolios should include students' written analyses of the materials included.

Self-evaluation can lead to the use of metacognitive strategies when students are reading. They ask themselves if they understand the material, and if not, what they can do to understand it better.

Tierney (1998, p. 375) believes that "readers and writers need to be both reflective and pragmatic . . . researching their own selves, considering the consequences of their efforts, and evaluating the implications, worth, and ongoing usefulness of what they are doing or have done." They need to be encouraged by teachers to keep samples of their accomplishments and to reflect on them. Journals, logs, and portfolios can serve this purpose. Conversations about their completed work and planned future work and what they have learned can result in effective assessment (Tierney, 1998).

ATTITUDE MEASURES

Students' affective responses to reading selections influence whether or not the students will become willing readers. Additionally, attitude is a factor in determining if students will read in specific content area textbooks or other content-related materials. Therefore, a measure of students' attitudes toward reading experiences in general and in specific content areas is an important aspect of the total assessment program. Reading takes many forms and means many different things to different students. One student might enjoy reading the sports page but be bored or even dislike reading a library book to complete an English assignment, whereas another student might prefer the library book.

Observation, interviewing, techniques in which reading is compared with another activity, sentence completion activities, questionnaires, summated rating scales (which involve having students respond to statements on a Likert-type scale), and semantic differentials (which involve having students choose descriptive adjectives to rate the items) have all commonly been used to assess attitudes in the United States. Multiple measures are recommended because single measures may give an incomplete picture (Alexander and Cobb, 1992).

Whether or not a student likes reading depends on what he or she is reading and for what purpose. Therefore, perhaps the most valid measure of a student's attitude toward reading is his or her oral or written responses to individual selections.

Students are not expected to respond positively to all their reading experiences, but if the majority of their responses indicate negative attitudes toward reading, something is amiss. A profile of individual scores may be kept as an ongoing assessment of each student's attitude toward reading. Content teachers should be concerned about the attitudes of students toward reading material; students who have negative attitudes may not comprehend well and will probably need additional motivation for reading. An assessment of this type carried out near the beginning of the school term should be valuable to content teachers.

INTEREST ASSESSMENTS

In reading, as in other areas, interest is often the key that unlocks effort. Consequently, study of students' reading and other interests is an important part of the teaching process. Teachers should plan ways to motivate students and show how a subject is related to their personal lives.

Content area teachers need to know the *specific* interests of each student in order to capitalize on them in recommending reading materials. One of the ways to learn a student's reading interests is through observation in daily classes. The teacher can note the books the student chooses to read, the degree of concentration and enjoyment with which he or she reads them, his or her eagerness to talk about them, and the desire expressed to read more books of similar nature or more books by the same author.

More detailed information about reading interests may be obtained from an interest inventory. A sample inventory is presented in Example 12.10.

COMPUTER APPLICATIONS TO ASSESSMENT

Some attempts have been made to apply computer technology to the area of assessment. The most appealing possibility to many educators may be on-computer testing, but most tests given on the computer are limited in form to objective questions that have definite single answers, limiting the scope of testing and the quality of items possible.

More commonly used are programs that enable teachers to construct multiple-choice, true-false, fill-in-the-blanks, and essay questions, store them, and allow various tests to be formed from different arrangements of the items. Additionally, when mark-sensitive answer sheets are used for responding to objective items, some tests can be computer scored when the answers are read by a special scanner or optical card reader. However, as Bitter, Camuse, and Durbin (1993, p. 91) point out, computers "may never be able to match the perception of a human teacher when evaluating essay answers."

EXAMPLE 12.10   Reading Interests Inventory

Name _____ Grade _____ Age _____

Reading Interests

1. How often do you go to the public library?
2. What are your favorite books that you own?
3. What things do you like to read about most?
4. Which comic books do you read?
5. Which magazines do you read?
6. What are some books you have enjoyed?
7. What parts of the newspaper do you read most frequently?
8. Do you like to read in your spare time?

Assessing the Readability of Printed Materials

What effect does readability of textbooks have on content area instruction?

Readability of printed materials is the reading difficulty of these materials. Selections that are very difficult to read are said to have high readability levels; those that are easy to read are said to have low readability levels.

Textbooks are sometimes written at higher levels of difficulty than the grade levels for which they are designed. Teachers need to know whether or not this is the case, because students will not learn content from textbooks that are too difficult for them to read with comprehension.

Since secondary school teachers frequently use textbooks for independent homework assignments and may expect students to read the complete textbooks, matching the textbooks assigned to students with the students' reading levels is particularly important. Just getting a book that fits the curriculum at a particular level will not necessarily result in an appropriate text. Kinder, Bursuck, and Epstein (1992) found that books designed for the same purpose may differ greatly in difficulty. They found the readability levels of ten American history textbooks published since 1985 to vary in difficulty from ninth- to fifteenth-grade level.

Textbook users often overlook the fact that different sections of the same textbook may have different readability levels, some topics may require more difficult language for their presentation, or different sections may be written by different authors with writing styles that vary in complexity or clarity. English teachers, in particular, should be aware of the wide differences in readability levels of selections in literature anthologies because different authors have written the materials. Stetson and Williams (1992) pointed out that the social studies textbooks they studied

SOCIAL STUDIES

ENGLISH/ LANGUAGE ARTS

SOCIAL
STUDIES

sometimes contained material that varied four or more years in difficulty from passage to passage.

Many factors influence the level of difficulty of printed materials. Some of these are vocabulary, sentence length, sentence complexity, abstract concepts, organization of ideas, inclusion of reading aids (such as underlining, boxing of information, and graphic aids), size and style of type, format, reader interest, and reader background. Concept load seems to be particularly important. If many new or technical concepts are introduced on each page or in each paragraph of text or if many of the concepts presented are abstract rather than concrete, the readability will be more difficult. Of the factors identified that influence the level of difficulty, two are directly related to the uniqueness of the reader: interest and background. A piece of literature may be of great interest to one student and yet have little appeal for another. A reader's areas of interest may be related to his or her background of experience. This background enables readers to understand easily material for which they have experienced vocabulary and concepts either directly or vicariously. (See Chapter 4 for a discussion of background experience as one area in which students exhibit individual differences.) Although all the other factors named here affect difficulty, vocabulary and sentence length have been found by researchers to be the most important in predicting readability.

READABILITY FORMULAS

Various formulas have been developed to measure the readability of printed materials. Most contain measures of vocabulary and sentence difficulty. Teachers should be aware that these formulas have been developed for use with connected prose; their use with other types of text, such as mathematics calculations, is inappropriate and will result in inaccurate scores.

The Fry Readability Graph is a relatively quick readability measure (Fry, 1972). To use the graph, the teacher selects three 100-word samples and determines the average number of sentences and the average number of syllables per 100 words. (The number of sentences in a 100-word sample is determined to the nearest tenth of a sentence.) With these figures, it is possible to use the graph to determine the approximate grade level of the selection. The Fry Graph and the instructions for using it are reprinted in Figure 12.1. The Fry Graph reflects an instructional reading level, the level at which a student should be able to read with teacher assistance. The authors of this text have found that, in many cases, secondary classroom teachers are more comfortable with this method than with more complex formulas, such as the Dale-Chall Readability Formula (Dale and Chall, 1948a and b) and the Flesch "Reading Ease" formula (Flesch, 1949). For that reason, the Fry Readability Graph is presented here in detail.

The readability measure just discussed and the others that were mentioned earlier are designed for use with long passages. Fry (1990) has also developed a formula for use with passages from 40 to 300 words long. The passage should contain at least three sentences. The user selects at least three key words needed to understand the passage, looks up the grade level of each key word in *The Living Word Vocabulary*

FIGURE 12.1

Fry Readability
Graph

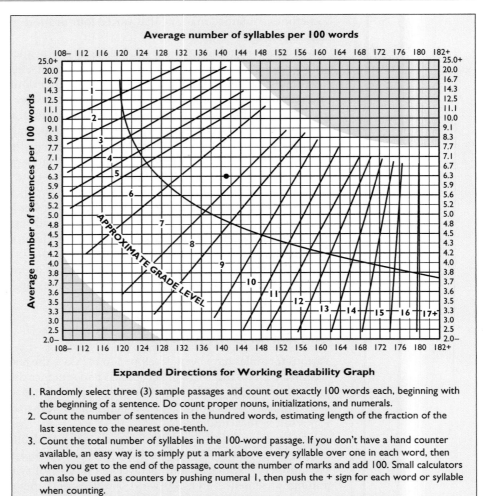

Expanded Directions for Working Readability Graph

1. Randomly select three (3) sample passages and count out exactly 100 words each, beginning with the beginning of a sentence. Do count proper nouns, initializations, and numerals.
2. Count the number of sentences in the hundred words, estimating length of the fraction of the last sentence to the nearest one-tenth.
3. Count the total number of syllables in the 100-word passage. If you don't have a hand counter available, an easy way is to simply put a mark above every syllable over one in each word, then when you get to the end of the passage, count the number of marks and add 100. Small calculators can also be used as counters by pushing numeral 1, then push the + sign for each word or syllable when counting.
4. Enter graph with *average* sentence length and *average* number of syllables; plot dot where the two lines intersect. Area where dot is plotted will give you the approximate grade level.
5. If a great deal of variability is found in syllable count or sentence count, putting more samples into the average is desirable.
6. A word is defined as a group of symbols with a space on either side; thus *Joe*, *IRA*, *1945*, and *&* are each one word.
7. A syllable is defined as a phonetic syllable. Generally, there are as many syllables as vowel sounds. For example, *stopped* is one syllable and *wanted* is two syllables. When counting syllables for numerals and initializations, count one syllable for each symbol. For example, *1945* is four syllables, *IRA* is three syllables, and *&* is one syllable.

Note: This "extended graph" does not outmode or render the earlier (1968) version inoperative or inaccurate; it is an extension. (REPRODUCTION PERMITTED — NO COPYRIGHT)

(Dale and O'Rourke, 1976), and averages the grade levels of the three hardest key words to find the Word Difficulty. Then he or she counts the number of words in each sentence and gives each sentence a grade according to a sentence length chart. An average of the grade levels of all sentences produces the score for Sentence Difficulty. The average of the Word Difficulty and Sentence Difficulty gives the readability estimate. This formula is designed for grades four through twelve.

Considering the number of factors that formulas fail to take into account, no formula can provide more than an approximation of level of difficulty. Determination of the relative difficulty levels of textbooks and other printed materials can be extremely valuable to a teacher, however. It has been demonstrated that estimating reading difficulty by using a formula produces much more consistent results than estimating without one.

If you are daunted by the prospect of counting syllables, words, sentences, and unfamiliar words and you have access to a computer and appropriate software, you can use one of these valuable aids to save you time and effort in making calculations. A number of programs can analyze the readability levels of texts according to a variety of readability formulas (Geisert and Futrell, 1995). Some grammar and style checker programs, including those built into word-processing programs, run the Flesch Reading Ease, the Gunning Fog Index, and the Flesch-Kincaid Grade Level formulas. These programs perform the calculations that teachers would ordinarily have to do manually. Teachers just have to enter the passages to be analyzed and read an on-screen menu that allows them to choose such things as which formulas to run.

Cautions and Controversies

Why should teachers use caution when interpreting readability scores?

All teachers should be familiar with at least one readability formula so that they can check the printed materials used in their classes. Then perhaps students will not be asked so frequently to read textbooks or supplementary materials that are too difficult for them. However, because of the limitations of the available formulas, teachers should always combine results obtained from the formulas with judgment based on personal experience with the materials and knowledge of the abstractness of the concepts presented, the organization and writing style of the author, the interests of the students in the class, the backgrounds of experience of the students, and other related factors such as size and style of type and format of the material. Because sampling procedures suggested by several formulas result in limited samples, teachers should be very cautious in accepting calculated grade levels as absolutes. They also should remember that textbooks vary in difficulty from section to section and should interpret samples with that in mind.

Readability formulas do not have any measure for abstractness or unfamiliarity of concepts covered. Familiar words, such as *run* and *bank*, do not always have their familiar meanings in school materials. A social studies text might discuss a "run on the banks," which would present a less familiar situation than reading about "fast movement by a person on the shore of a stream," which may be the meaning of these words that comes to mind immediately.

Authors may organize materials clearly, or they may have very poor organization, and the clarity of their writing styles may vary immensely, with some choosing to construct sentences in less common ways and others choosing familiar sentence structures. Readability formulas contain no measures for organization, style, or the cohesive structure of a text (the interrelationships of ideas in the text).

Factors within individual students help determine the readability of particular material for those students. Material that is interesting to students is easier for them to read because they are more motivated to read it. Other people with similar reading skills may find the material uninteresting and, thus, much more difficult to read. Likewise, readers who have had much experience related to the topic will find the material easier to read than those who have had little experience related to it. No formula has the power to foresee the interests and backgrounds of particular readers.

Formulas also do not contain measures for mechanical features such as size and style of type and format of the printed material. Type that is too small or too large may adversely affect readability, and some styles of type make reading the material more difficult than do other styles. Additionally, closely packed type, unrelieved by sufficient white space or illustrative material, can make reading more difficult.

OTHER METHODS OF READABILITY ASSESSMENT

There are means other than readability formulas of assessing the appropriateness of printed materials for specific students. Some of these are discussed next.

Checklists

A checklist approach has also been used to assess readability (Irwin and Davis, 1980). A checklist can include many considerations not covered by readability formulas. Items similar to the ones in Example 12.11 may be included in a checklist to help teachers estimate the readability of materials for their classes.

User Involvement Techniques

Some techniques involve trying out representative portions of the material on prospective users. These techniques take into account reader interest, reader background, author's writing style and organization, and abstractness of concepts, and, except for the cloze test, they also may consider format and type size and style. Three of these techniques are cloze tests, group reading inventory selections, and informal reading inventory selections, all discussed earlier in this chapter.

Chance (1985) found the cloze procedure to be a quick and reliable way to determine the readability of specific material for individual students. He also verified that subject matter teachers find it easy to construct cloze tests and to use them for determining readability.

EXAMPLE 12.11   Readability Checklist

1. _____ Is the vocabulary used appropriate for your students?

2. _____ Is the content presented appropriately for your students' prior knowledge and experiential backgrounds?

3. _____ Is there an effort to explicitly link new concepts to the students' prior knowledge or experiential backgrounds?

4. _____ Do concrete examples accompany the introduction of abstract concepts?

5. _____ Are new concepts introduced one at a time with sufficient examples?

6. _____ Are words defined clearly for the reading abilities of your students?

7. _____ Are the style and sentence structure appropriate for your class?

8. _____ Is the organization of the material clear, with main ideas clearly stated?

9. _____ Are important complex relationships (e.g., causality, conditionality, etc.) explicitly explained?

10. _____ Is the readability level indicated by a recognized readability formula appropriate for your students?

11. _____ Are aids to text organization (chapter introductions, summaries, headings, and subheadings; table of contents; glossary; and index) provided?

12. _____ Are there adequate graphic aids, such as maps, graphs, illustrations, to supplement prose descriptions of content area concepts?

13. _____ Are there both literal recall questions and higher order questions to check students' understanding?

14. _____ Are questions clear and unambiguous?

15. _____ Are interesting activities and applications included to increase student motivation?

16. _____ Does the book show how the information being learned is related to the students' real lives?

17. _____ Is the format (print size and style, use of illustrations, use of color, etc.) appealing to and appropriate for your students?

Focus on Struggling Readers

Assessment for Struggling Readers

Background knowledge can often be more accurately assessed for struggling readers through oral, rather than written, means. Limited writing ability may result in inaccurate results from written responses.

A modification of the cloze test that appears to be appropriate for struggling readers has been proposed by Baldauf and others (1980). This is a "matching" cloze: students select from the five words randomly ordered in the margin and copy the correct ones into the five blank spaces for one set of sentences of the passage, continuing this procedure for other sections of the passage.

Brozo (1990) makes a case for interactive assessment for struggling readers that resembles a directed reading lesson. First, there is a diagnostic interview to collect background information about the student's ideas about reading purposes and his or her reading strategies and ability, interests, and attitudes. Then the teacher determines passage placement in an informal reading inventory by letting the student work through the word lists, providing assistance with difficult words and offering strategies for unlocking them. To prepare the student to read, the teacher uses activities to activate and expand prior knowledge of the topic of the material, preteaches vocabulary, and sets purposes for the reading. The student reads silently first and then orally. As the student reads orally, the teacher observes use of strategies, asks questions about strategies, and models effective strategies as needed. After the reading takes place, the student retells the material. The teacher may probe for additional information through questions, allowing the student to look back through the passage to find answers. Comprehension is then extended through activities that connect the student's prior knowledge with the new content. A number of techniques found in this text—for example, semantic mapping and anticipation guides—may be used in both the preparation for reading step and this final step. This procedure is obviously time consuming, but it has the potential for uncovering a student's actual ability to perform in class work, rather than his or her ability to perform independently.

A dynamic form of assessment is also suggested for struggling readers by Kletzien and Bednar (1990). They suggest initial assessment and strategy analysis to establish the student's reading level and to determine his or her strategy knowledge and use. They also suggest an informal reading inventory for this purpose. The teacher observes the student's strategy application and questions the student about reading strategies used. Then the teacher plans a mediated learning mini-lesson to determine the reader's capacity for modifying his or her approach to reading. The teacher discusses the student's initial performance with him or her, stressing both strengths and limitations. Then the teacher chooses a strategy to teach, using independent-level materials. The student is taught how, when, and why the strategy can be used. The teacher models the strategy directly through a think-aloud procedure and then offers the student guided practice and independent practice. The teacher observes the student's attempts to learn the strategy. A postassessment and strategy analysis follows, using another form of the informal reading inventory that was used initially. Comparing the student's performance on the two assessment measures helps the teacher to determine his or her ability to integrate the targeted strategies into the reading process. This approach also takes quite a bit of time, although it yields useful information.

Focus on English Language Learners

Assessment for English Language Learners

Oral assessments of background knowledge are more helpful with ELLs than are written ones because the students' delayed instruction in writing may result in their being unable to adequately express themselves through writing. The "matching" cloze test and interactive and dynamic assessment that are explained in the "Focus on Struggling Readers" box are particularly appropriate for lower secondary school ELLs. ELLs have enough challenges when undergoing testing that giving them some scaffolding can make the task more manageable.

When teachers find it necessary to use standardized tests with ELLs, the tests can be adapted to help the student and the teacher. For example, the teacher can mark the work completed before the time limit by changing the color of the pencil and can then have the student complete the test. This technique will provide more satisfaction for the student and more information for the teacher. It will also help the teacher and the student understand what the student can accomplish as he or she acquires more fluency.

SUMMARY

Teachers at the secondary school level often need to interpret norm-referenced reading test results to learn about individual students' reading abilities and about the range of reading abilities within the classroom. Survey and diagnostic tests can both be useful.

Traditional achievement tests do not generally reflect current views of the reading process as a constructive strategic process in which readers make use of their prior knowledge and techniques for unlocking meaning in the text. Work is being done to develop standardized assessment procedures that reflect these views, however, and current tests do provide useful information.

Criterion-referenced tests, which check the test taker's performance against a performance criterion as a predetermined standard, can also be helpful to teachers. Results of criterion-referenced tests can be used as instructional prescriptions, making them useful in decisions about instruction.

Perhaps more useful to content teachers are informal tests, such as the group reading inventory (GRI), which gives an indication of how well students read a particular textbook; the informal reading inventory, which provides an overall estimate of a student's reading ability as well as a picture of some of his or her strengths and weaknesses; the cloze procedure, which provides the teacher with two types of information—an overall view of the student's reading ability and the appropriateness of text material for the student; and gamelike activities.

The type of assessment measure used most frequently by secondary school content teachers is the skill inventory, which provides information about whether or not students have developed the specific reading skills necessary to understand content material in the teacher's particular area.

Since teacher judgment enters into decisions about the level of each student's performance, the classroom teacher must carefully observe students as they perform daily tasks with printed materials. Retellings, written responses to writing, and portfolios for students are all informal procedures that, along with more common informal testing procedures, can facilitate assessment.

Student attitudes toward the reading experiences in the content classroom are an important aspect of the overall assessment program. Besides observation and discussion, there are teacher-made devices, self-evaluation devices, and other instruments available to show attitude. Similarly, since student interest often encourages effort, interest inventories can help content teachers plan ways to motivate the students and capitalize on student interests when selecting and using materials.

In order to adjust reading assignments to fit all students, teachers need to know the difficulty levels of classroom reading materials so they can match the materials to the students' reading levels. Difficulty levels can be determined by using readability formulas or other readability measures in conjunction with teacher judgment.

DISCUSSION QUESTIONS

1. What do you consider to be the major strengths and weaknesses of each of the major assessment procedures discussed in this chapter?
2. In what ways may a group reading inventory be useful to a content area teacher? An informal reading inventory?
3. Which reading skill inventory do you think would be most helpful to you as a content area teacher? Why?
4. Why might secondary teachers find the cloze test easy to use?

5. Do you think a self-assessment checklist would help you learn more about a student's reading of a content area textbook? If so, prepare a self-rating checklist that would be most appropriate for your classroom. If not, explain why not.

6. How would you revise the reading interests inventory to be most appropriate for your specific content area?

7. What are some effective uses of portfolios for evaluating different literacy concerns?

8. Why should teachers be concerned about the readability of content area reading materials?

9. What are some assessment approaches especially suited to struggling readers and English language learners, and why are these particularly appropriate?

ENRICHMENT ACTIVITIES

*1. Prepare a group reading inventory, using content area reading materials. Administer your inventory to a student, record your results, and share the findings with the class.

2. Using a textbook of your choice, develop at least two sample questions on each of the book parts listed. (If a particular book part is not included in your text, select examples from supplemental materials.)

   a. Preface, Introduction, or Foreword
   b. Table of Contents
   c. Index
   d. Appendix
   e. Glossary
   f. Unit or Chapter Introduction and/or Summary

*3. Prepare a reading skills inventory for a content area textbook. Administer it to a student, record your results, and share the findings with the class.

*4. Secure a published informal reading inventory, and administer it to a student. Report the results to the class.

*5. Prepare a cloze test for a passage of content area reading material. Administer it to a student. Report the results to the class.

*6. Prepare an interest checklist on one topic of study in your content area. If feasible, administer it to a student.

*7. Assemble a portfolio that represents your own literacy skills and features. Describe the criteria you used for including items in your portfolio.

*These activities are designed for in-service teachers, student teachers, and practicum students.

Glossary

aesthetic response: Readers' personal feelings about a story or text that may be expressed in relation to art, music, drama, or composition.

analogies: Comparisons of two similar relationships; using similarities of ideas for the sake of comparison.

assimilation: The process that occurs when a reader integrates new ideas with existing ideas stored in long-term memory.

attribute relations: A network of related characteristics.

audiobooks: Recordings of books that students can listen to as they read along in the text or listen to in order to understand better the dialect or style of the writing.

authentic purposes: The reasons for reading that relate to real life.

authentic reading tasks: Assignments and activities that are based on actual experiences that students may encounter.

blog: See Web log.

career-related education: A program that prepares students for employment.

cause-and-effect writing pattern: A common writing pattern in social studies and science that is concerned with the chains of causes and effects. This pattern recognizes that a cause results in effects that become causes of other effects.

CD: Compact disc; a digital data storage device from which information can be accessed in nonlinear fashion.

character journals: Diaries in which students assume the role of one of the main characters in a book.

chronological order pattern: This writing pattern is concerned with the time order of events.

classification pattern: A writing pattern that groups items into categories by types (objects, animals, ideas, rocks, soil, historical periods, etc.).

cloze test: An alternative method of determining students' reading levels in which the students are asked to read selections of increasing levels of difficulty and supply words that have been deleted from the passage; a method for matching students with reading materials.

cognitive flexibility: The ability to examine text from various perspectives or points of view.

cognitive processing: Thinking about content. It involves rehearsal (repeating information), review, comparing and contrasting, and drawing conclusions.

cognitive strategies: Approaches to understanding based on mental activities.

coherence (of text): Text that is organized in a cohesive manner to convey meaning.

college-prep students: Students who are enrolled in a high school curriculum that prepares them for a college education.

comparison and/or contrast pattern: A writing pattern that explains ideas through describing likenesses and differences.

computer-assisted instructional programs: Computer programs that present instructional material.

computer databases: Electronically searchable organized bodies of information.

concept: A mental construct derived from categories of experiences and related webs of ideas. For example, *cat* is a concept.

concept guide: A form of study guide that focuses on basic ideas in the content areas.

conceptual learning: Learning based on understanding relationships among ideas rather than lists of independent facts.

conceptual relationships: Connections among ideas; networks of words that are connected hierarchically or as examples or nonexamples.

connotation: The ideas and associations suggested by a term, including emotional reactions.

content area teachers: Teachers of classes in specific disciplines, for example, mathematics, science, or history.

445

content journals: Written records of content area learning activities that are personal and informal; learning logs.

content schemata: A reader's prior knowledge that permits him or her to comprehend content texts.

context: The words and phrases that surround a specific word.

context clues: The meaning clues in the text surrounding a word.

Cornell Note-Taking System: A type of split-page note taking that includes notes, questions answered in the notes, and a summary of each page of notes.

creative thinking: Cognitive activity that focuses on novel ways of viewing ideas, incidents, or characters.

criterion-referenced tests: Tests that check the test taker against a performance criterion, which is a predetermined standard.

critical readers: Individuals who question what they read, suspend final judgment until all facts are presented, evaluate, and decide.

critical thinking: Cognitive activity that requires evaluating information and ideas. The reader has to decide whether or not to believe content.

database programs: Computer programs that facilitate the development and searching of databases, organized bodies of information that can be sorted and searched electronically.

definition or explanation pattern: This writing pattern tells the meaning of a concept and/or explains a concept.

demonstration pattern: This writing pattern is usually accompanied by an example that illustrates operations and concepts.

denotation: The literal definition of a word as defined by the dictionary.

desktop-publishing programs: Computer programs that combine text and graphics for publishing newsletters, reports, brochures, and other documents.

diagnostic tests: Tests that help to locate specific strengths and weaknesses of readers.

dialogue journals: Journals in which a two-way written conversation is carried on between the teacher and each student.

digital literacy: The ability to understand, evaluate, and integrate information in multiple formats delivered by the computer.

direct instruction: Systematic, teacher-led instruction on targeted objectives.

directed reading lessons (DRL): A method for guiding students' comprehension of a reading selection.

directed reading-thinking activity (DRTA): A guided comprehension strategy involving predicting, reading, and confirming or rejecting predictions.

discourse: A major unit of language that is longer than a sentence.

DVD: A digital storage device that offers high-quality images and sound.

divergent thinking: Cognitive activity that follows different paths, that extends in different directions.

editing: Correcting spelling, grammar, and punctuation to polish the writing.

efferent response: Responses to content that focus on knowledge, information, and facts.

elaboration: Increasing complexity, adding detail to an idea or a word.

electronic mailing lists: Electronic distributors of messages on specific topics to groups of readers who have subscribed to the lists.

e-mail: Electronic mail; messages sent electronically from one computer user to another.

English language learners (ELLs): Students whose first language is not English.

experimental pattern: This pattern is often used in scientific materials. In this pattern, the steps for a hands-on exploration of a problem or discovery are described, so the reader can perform the steps involved.

exposition: Written or spoken language that explains.

expressive vocabulary: The words that an individual knows well enough to use in speaking and writing.

figurative language: Words that are used in a non-literal manner. Figurative language includes personification, similes, metaphors, hyperbole, euphemisms, and allusions.

flexibility of rate: The ability to vary rate according to purpose and difficulty of material.

fluency: Reading with speed, accuracy, automaticity, good phrasing, smoothness, and expression.

Frayer Model: A model of concept learning that includes examples and nonexamples.

freewriting: Writing that has no teacher restrictions on content.

full inclusion: This term refers to the practice of serving students with disabilities and other special needs entirely within the general classroom. In full inclusion settings, students spend the entire day in the general classroom.

graphic aids: Visual aids, such as maps, graphs, tables, charts, diagrams, and pictures.

graphic materials: Drawings such as blueprints, cutaways, patterns, pictures, and sketches.

graphic organizers: Visual representations or structured overviews that illustrate hierarchical and/or linear relationships among key concepts.

group reading inventory: A teacher-made test, based on the textbooks that the students are actually expected to use, designed to determine if the material is suitable for instructional purposes with the students.

homepage: The introductory page for a website.

hypermedia: Nonsequentially linked text, graphics, motions, and sounds that allow computer users to access information from different media in the order that they choose.

hypertext: Nonsequential text links that allow computers users to access text in the order that they choose.

I-Chart: A procedure for note taking for a research report, composed of a grid that has questions about the subject at the tops of columns and references consulted along the left-hand margin to form the row headings.

inclusion: This term describes the practice of including students with disabilities in general education classes.

in-depth word study: Exercises that increase vocabulary knowledge through association.

individualized education plan (IEP): An instructional plan to meet the needs of individual students who qualify for special education services.

Individuals with Disabilities Education Act (IDEA): This act provides that all children, including students with disabilities, are entitled to a free, appropriate public education.

inferential thinking: Cognitive activity that is concerned with deeper meanings that require reading between the lines rather than meanings that are directly stated.

informal reading inventory: A compilation of graded reading selections, accompanied by questions prepared to test the reader's comprehension, that is designed to determine students' reading levels and reading strengths and weaknesses.

integrated curriculum: A curriculum that blends subjects together based on overlapping skills, concepts, attitudes, and content identified for each subject. Subjects such as math, science, social studies, fine arts, and language arts are often integrated, although integration is not limited to these subjects.

integrated unit: A unit focused on a specific topic that is studied from the perspective of more than one content area.

Internet: An international "network of networks" that links a multitude of computers.

intertextuality: The links between the ideas gleaned from one text and those discovered in another text or texts.

K-W-L: A reading strategy that stands for Know–Want to Know–Learned.

language experience materials: Accounts that are written by individuals or groups of students of actual experiences that they have had.

literacy: The ability to read and write.

literal thinking: The cognitive activity of recognizing directly stated facts and ideas.

literature response groups: Also known as literature circles; several students who have chosen to read the same novel read a certain amount each week and meet in a group each week to discuss the reading.

media literacy: The ability to comprehend and produce material for media other than print.

metacognition: Thinking about one's own thinking and controlling one's own learning; comprehension monitoring.

metacognitive skills: Skills in comprehension monitoring.

mind mapping: Visual note taking that shows connections among ideas. Based on a central image, key words, colors, codes, and symbols.

morphological analysis: Word identification strategy based on identification of a root that carries the base meaning of the word and affixes that modify the base meaning.

multimedia: The use of a number of different media (graphics, text, moving images, sounds, etc.) in the same application.

multiple intelligences: Types of learning avenues, including verbal, logical, body, visual, musical, interpersonal, intrapersonal, naturalist, and existentialist.

multiple literacies: Reading and writing skills necessary for comprehension of content that vary according to the type of content.

newsgroups: Sometimes called electronic bulletin boards; network locations to which messages are posted so that interested computer users can read the messages electronically.

norm-referenced tests: Tests that compare students' performance with the performance of a norm group, a sampling of students in the same grade or of the same age.

organizational patterns: The structures used to organize texts. The common text patterns include sequential, comparison/contrast, cause/effect, definition or explanation, and enumeration.

outlining: Recording information from reading material in a way that makes clear the relationships between the main ideas and the supporting details.

paraphrasing: Putting material that one has read into one's own words.

PORPE: A technique to help students study for essay examinations: Predict, Organize, Rehearse, Practice, Evaluate.

portfolio: A collection of student-produced materials that teachers use to evaluate progress and achievement.

PRC: A study strategy that has three phases: prereading, reading, and consolidation.

preview guide: A guide completed prior to reading that helps the student relate prior knowledge to the topic.

prewriting: The initial stage in the writing process, used for selection and delimitation of topic, determination of audience, decisions about general writing approach, activation of prior knowledge of the topic, discussion of ideas with classmates, and organization of ideas.

print literacy: The ability to read printed language.

problem-solution pattern: A writing pattern that is often found in scientific and health-related content. In this pattern the writer identifies a difficulty and explains how to solve it.

problem-solving approach: This approach to comprehension encourages students to understand the question they need to answer, to state it in their own words, and then to brainstorm possible solutions. Finally, they need to evaluate the solutions.

PSRT: A teaching procedure that is helpful in enhancing students' study skills: Prepare, Structure, Read, Think.

publishing: Sharing writing with others in oral or written form.

question-and-answer pattern: This writing pattern is based on queries posed by the author and his or her response to these queries.

question/answer relationships (QARs): A strategy for increasing comprehension that focuses on the processes for generating answers to questions and on the relationships between questions and answers.

questions: Inquiries that call for replies. These inquiries are classified by various schemes such as literal, inferential, critical, and creative.

RAFT assignments: Writing assignments that include the Role of the writer, Audience for the writing, Format of the writing, and Topic to be written about.

read-alouds: Selections that the teacher reads aloud to the students because the students do not have the reading proficiency or motivation to read them for themselves.

readability: Reading difficulty level of texts that can be computed using statistical formulas.

reading: An active process in which the reader calls on experience, language, and schemata to anticipate and understand the author's written language.

reading comprehension: The process of understanding material that is read; a strategic process during which readers simultaneously extract and construct meaning. Reading comprehension is the product of vocabulary and language comprehension.

reading guide: A written guide that helps students comprehend and organize the material that they are reading.

reading response journals: A type of learning log for literature classes in which students comment on characters, setting, plot, author's writing style and devices, personal reactions, and other items related to a selection that has been read.

reader-response theory: This theory explains students' emotional and functional responses to written text.

reading-to-do: Tasks in which an individual uses the material read as an aid to doing something else.

reading-to-learn: Tasks in which an individual uses the material read with the intention of remembering and applying textual information.

receptive vocabulary: The words that readers recognize when they hear them and/or see them.

reciprocal teaching: A form of guided practice for comprehension. Readers apply simple, concrete strategies to achieve text comprehension.

rehearsal: A cognitive processing strategy that involves repeating information to oneself.

reliability: The degree to which a test gives consistent results.

response: See aesthetic response and efferent response.

retellings: Oral or written reconstructions of material that is read.

retention: The ability to remember what has been read.

revision: The stage in the writing process in which material is reexamined, reorganized, clarified, expanded, or in some other way changed to improve the presentation.

ROWAC: A general study method: Read, Organize, Write, Actively read, Correct predictions.

rubric: A set of criteria used to describe and evaluate a student's level of proficiency in a particular subject area.

scanning: Rapid reading to find a specific bit of information.

schema theory: Schemata (plural of schema) are abstract networks of knowledge, information, and experiences stored in long-term memory.

self-questioning: Inquiries that an individual poses to himself or herself.

semantic feature analysis: Comparing the attributes of related concepts.

semantic maps: Figures illustrating conceptual relationships.

semantics: Linguistic term referring to word meaning.

situational context: The setting in which one reads a text.

skimming: Reading to obtain a general idea or overview of material.

social constructivist perspective: A perspective in which the teacher provides a learning environment designed to engage students in a process of negotiating meaning through interaction of the reader, the text, the classroom community, the teacher, and the context.

social justice notebooks: Notebooks in which students write their stands on controversial human rights issues that they have read about in news articles or editorials.

socioeconomic status: Position in society based on such factors as social class, income, education level, and job held.

spreadsheets: Grids of rows and columns used to organize data into patterns, often used to store and manipulate numerical data.

SQ3R: A general study method: Survey, Question, Read, Recite, Review.

SQRC: A general study method: State, Question, Read, Conclude.

SQRQCQ: A study method for mathematics: Survey, Question, Read, Question, Compute, Question.

stance: The point of view or perspective that integrates the text and the situational context. The two major stances are aesthetic and efferent.

strategic reading: Actively reading the text by connecting text information with preexisting knowledge and using learned procedures to interact with the text.

study guides: A set of questions and/or suggestions designed to direct students' attention to the key ideas in a passage and sometimes to suggest the skills to apply for successful comprehension.

study skills: Techniques and strategies that aid readers in learning from written materials.

summarizing: Concisely restating what the author has said in a work or a section of a work.

summary: A concise restatement of what the author has said in a work or a section of a work.

survey tests: Tests that measure general achievement in reading.

sustained silent reading: A technique in which students are given a block of time to read self-selected materials for pleasure, without fear of testing or reporting being required.

symbols: Compressed language that may represent one or more words.

syntax: A linguistic term referring to word order in sentences and paragraphs.

tech-prep students: Students who are enrolled in a high school curriculum that prepares them for careers or employment in industry or applied science.

text coherence: A quality of text that moves from one idea to the next without confusing or losing the reader.

text organization: The way authors arrange text; the order of presentation in a text. Content authors organize text using these forms: comparison-contrast, sequential, cause-and-effect, definition or explanation, and question-answer.

textual context: The quality and difficulty of writing and organization found in texts.

textual schemata: Readers' organized knowledge of and experience with different forms of written discourse that prepare them to read a variety of content.

thematic teaching unit: A series of interrelated lessons or class activities organized around a theme, a literary form, or a skill.

themes: topics or major ideas.

validity: The extent to which a test measures what it is intended to measure.

vicarious experience: Experience acquired through using the imagination with a picture, film, model, etc., rather than firsthand experience.

videoconferencing: Holding conferences over the Internet with others who can be seen on the computer monitors and heard through speakers.

visualization: The process of forming mental images that depict reading content.

vocational literacy: The reading and writing skills that people need in order to perform the work in their careers or vocations.

wait time: The period of time a teacher waits between asking a question and expecting an answer.

web log (blog): A Web-based journal.

word identification skills and strategies: Skills and strategies used by students to decode unfamiliar words.

word problems (verbal problems): Mathematics problems that are presented in words and symbols.

word-processing programs: Computer programs designed to allow entry, manipulation, and storage of text.

work-based learning: Instruction that involves apprenticeship at a work site.

writing a draft: The second stage in the writing process, in which the writer puts ideas on paper without worrying about mechanics or neatness.

References

AAMR Ad Hoc Committee on Terminology and Classification. *Mental Retardation: Definition, Classification, and Systems of Support.* Washington, D.C.: American Association on Mental Retardation, 1992.

Aaron, Ira E., Jeanne S. Chall, Dolores Durkin, Kenneth Goodman, and Dorothy S. Strickland. "The Past, Present, and Future of Literacy Education: Comments from a Panel of Distinguished Educators, Part II." *The Reading Teacher* 43 (February 1990): 370–380.

Adams, Gerald, Thomas Gullotta, and Carol Markstrom-Adams. *Adolescent Life Experiences.* Pacific Grove, Calif.: Brooks/Cole, 1994.

Adams, Marilyn, and Ann Collins. "A Schema-Theoretic View of Reading." In H. Singer and R. Ruddell (eds.), *Theoretical Models and Processes of Reading.* Newark, Del.: International Reading Association, 1986, pp. 404–425.

Adams, Pamela E. "Teaching Romeo and Juliet in the Nontracked English Classroom." *Journal of Reading* 38 (March 1995): 424–432.

Albright, Lettie K., and Mary Ariail. "Tapping the Potential of Teacher Read-Alouds in Middle Schools." *Journal of Adolescent & Adult Literacy* 48 (April 2005): 582–591.

Alexander, J. Estill, and Jeanne Cobb. "Assessing Attitudes in Middle and Secondary Schools and Community Colleges." *Journal of Reading* 36 (October 1992): 146–149.

Alfassi, Miriam. "Reading for Meaning: The Efficacy of Reciprocal Teaching in Fostering Reading Comprehension in High School Students in Remedial Reading Classes." *American Educational Research Journal* 35 (Summer 1998): 309–332.

Alfred, Suellen. "Dialogue Journal." *Tennessee Reading Teacher* 19 (Fall 1991): 12–15.

Allen, Camille A. *The Multigenre Research Paper.* Portsmouth, N.H.: Heineman, 2001.

Allen, Virginia G. "Teaching Bilingual and ESL Children." In J. Flood, J. Jensen, D. Lapp, and J. Squire (eds.), *Handbook of Research in Teaching the English Language Arts.* New York: Macmillan, 1991, pp. 356–371.

Allington, Richard. *What Really Matters for Struggling Readers: Designing Research-Based Programs.* New York: Addison-Wesley, 2001.

Alverman, Donna E. "Multiliteracies and Self-Questioning in the Service of Science Learning." In E. Wendy Saul (ed.), *Crossing Borders in Literacy and Science Instruction: Perspectives on Theory and Practice.* Newark, Del.: International Reading Association, 2004, pp. 226–238.

Alvermann, Donna E., Kathleen A. Hinchman, David Moore, Stephen Phelps, and Diane R. Waff (eds.), *Reconceptualizing the Literacies in Adolescents' Lives.* Mahwah, N.J.: Erlbaum, 1998.

Alvermann, Donna E., Andrew Huddleston, and Margaret C. Hagood. "What Could Professional Wrestling and School Literacy Practices Possibly Have in Common?" *Journal of Adolescent & Adult Literacy* 47 (April 2004): 532–540.

Alvermann, Donna E., and David W. Moore. "Secondary School Reading." In R. Barr, M. L. Kamil, P. Mosenthal, and P. D. Pearson (eds.), *Handbook of Reading Research.* Vol. 2. New York: Longman, 1991, pp. 951–983.

Amrein, Audrey L., and David C. Berliner. "High Stakes Testing, Uncertainty, and Student Learning." *Education Policy Analysis Archives* 10, no. 18 (2002). Retrieved from http://epaa.asu.edu/epaa/v1On18/.

"Analyzing the NAEP Data: Some Key Points." *Reading Today* 11 (December 1993/January 1994): 1, 12.

Anderson, B. "The Missing Ingredient: Fluent Oral Reading." *Elementary School Journal* 18 (1981): 173–177.

Anderson, Richard C., Elfrieda H. Hiebert, Judith A. Scott, and Ian A. G. Wilkinson, *Becoming a Nation of Readers: The Report of the Commission on Reading.* Washington, D.C.: National Institute of Education, 1985.

Anderson-Inman, Lynne. "Electronic Journals in Technology and Literacy: Professional Development Online." *Journal of Adolescent & Adult Literacy* 41 (February 1998): 400–405.

Anderson-Inman, Lynne, and Mark Horney. "Computer-Based Concept Mapping: Enhancing Literacy with Tools for Visual Thinking." *Journal of Adolescent & Adult Literacy* 40 (December 1996/January 1997): 302–306.

Anderson-Inman, Lynne, and Mark Horney. "Electronic Books: Reading and Studying with Supportive Resources." *Reading Online* 2 (April 1999). Retrieved from http://www.readingonline.org.

Anderson-Inman, Lynne, and Carolyn Knox-Quinn. "Spell Checking Strategies for Successful Students." *Journal of Adolescent & Adult Literacy* 39 (March 1996): 500–501.

Anderson-Inman, Lynne, Carolyn Knox-Quinn, and Peter Tromba. "Synchronous Writing Environments: Real-Time Interaction in Cyberspace." *Journal of Adolescent & Adult Literacy* 40 (October 1996): 134–138.

Andrade, Heidi Goodrich. "Using Rubrics to Promote Thinking and Learning." *Educational Leadership* 57 (February 2000): 13–18.

Andrasick, Kathleen Dudden. *Opening Texts: Using Writing to Teach Literature.* Portsmouth, N.H.: Heinemann, 1990.

Andre, M., and T. Anderson. "The Development and Evaluation of a Self-Questioning Study Technique." *Reading Research Quarterly* 14, no. 4 (1978/1979): 605–622.

Andrews, Sharon E. "Using Inclusion Literature to Promote Positive Attitudes Toward Disabilities." *Journal of Adolescent & Adult Literacy* 41 (March 1998): 420– 426.

Applebee, Arthur, Judith Langer, M. Nystrand, and A. Gammoran. "Discussion-Based Approaches to Developing Understanding: Classroom Instruction and Student Performance in Middle and High School English." *American Educational Research Journal* 40 (2003): 685–730.

Armbruster, Bonnie B., and Thomas H. Anderson. *Content Area Textbooks.* Reading Education Report No. 23. Champaign: University of Illinois, July 1981.

Arreola, Daniel, Marci Deal, James Petersen, and Rickie Sanders. *World Geography.* Evanston, Ill.: McDougal Littell, 2003.

Ash, Gwynne. "Teaching Readers Who Struggle: A Pragmatic Middle School Framework." *Reading Online* 5, no. 7 (2002). Retrieved from http://www.readingonline.org/articles/art_index.asp?HREF=ash/index.html.

Au, Kathryn H. *Literacy Instruction in Multicultural Settings.* Fort Worth, Tex.: Holt, Rinehart and Winston, 1993.

Au, Kathryn H., Judith A. Scheu, Alice J. Kawakami, and Patricia A. Herman. "Assessment and Accountability in a Whole Literacy Curriculum." *The Reading Teacher* 43 (April 1990): 574–578.

Aubry, Valerie Sebern. "Audience Options for High School Students with Difficulties in Writing." *Journal of Reading* 38 (March 1995): 434–443.

Ausubel, D. *Educational Psychology: A Cognitive View.* 2nd ed. New York: Holt, Rinehart and Winston, 1978, pp. 523–525.

Ayers, Phyllis, and Jamelle Wilson. "Do It Write: IBM's Process Writing: Defining Ourselves in a Changing World." Paper presented at the National Council of Teachers of English Convention, Orlando, Florida, November 21, 1994.

Babbs, Patricia J., and Alden J. Moe. "Metacognition: A Key for Independent Learning from Text." *The Reading Teacher* 36 (January 1983): 422–426.

Bachman-Williams, Paula. "Promoting Literacy in Science Class." In Harriet Arzu Scarborough (ed.), *Writing Across the Curriculum in Secondary Classrooms.* Upper Saddle River, N.J.: Merrill/Prentice Hall, 2001, pp. 7–15.

Bacon, Stephanie. "Reading Coaches: Adapting an Intervention Model for Upper Elementary and Middle School Readers." *Journal of Adolescent & Adult Literacy* 48 (February 2005): 416–427.

Bader, Lois A., and Katherine D. Wiesendanger. "Realizing the Potential of Informal Reading Inventories." *Journal of Reading* 32 (February 1989): 402–408.

Badiali, B. "Reading in the Content Area of Music." In M. Dupuis (ed.), *Reading in the Content Areas: Research for Teachers.* Newark, Del.: International Reading Association, 1984, pp. 42–47.

Baines, Lawrence. "From Page to Screen: When a Novel Is Interpreted for Film, What Gets Lost in the Translation." *Journal of Adolescent & Adult Literacy* 39 (May 1996): 612–622.

Baker, Linda, Peter Afflerbach, and David Reinking. *Developing Engaged Readers in School and Home Communities.* Mahwah, N.J.: Erlbaum, 1996.

Baker, Scott K. "Vocabulary Acquisition: Curricular and Instructional Implications for Diverse Learners." Technical Report No. 14. Eugene, Ore.: National Center to Improve the Tools of Educators, 1995.

Balajthy, Ernest. "Text-to-Speech Software for Helping Struggling Readers." *Reading Online* 8 (January/February 2005). Retrieved from http://www.readingonline.org.

Baldauf, Richard B., Jr., Robert L. T. Dawson, John Prior, and Ivan K. Propst, Jr. "Can Matching Cloze Be Used with Secondary ESL Pupils?" *Journal of Reading* 23 (February 1980): 435–440.

Barron, Robert. "The Use of Vocabulary as an Advance Organizer." In H. Herber and P. Sanders (eds.), *Research in Reading in the Content Areas: First Year Report.* Syracuse, N.Y.: Syracuse University Press, 1969, pp. 29–39.

Barry, Arlene L. "The Staffing of High School Remedial Reading Programs in the United States Since 1920." *Journal of Reading* 38 (September 1994): 14–22.

Barry, Arlene. "Reading Strategies Teachers Say They Use." *Journal of Adolescent & Adult Literacy* 46 (October 2002): 132–141.

Barton, Keith C., and Lynne A. Smith. "Themes or Motifs? Aiming for Coherence Through Interdisciplinary Outlines." *The Reading Teacher* 55 (September 2000): 54–63.

Baskin, Barbara H., and Karen Harris. "Heard Any Good Books Lately? The Case for Audiobooks in the Secondary Classroom." *Journal of Reading* 38 (February 1995): 372–376.

Baumann, James F. *Reading Assessment: An Instructional Decision-Making Perspective.* Columbus, Ohio: Merrill, 1988.

Baumann, James, and Edward Kameenui. "Research on Vocabulary Instruction: Ode to Voltaire." In J. Flood, J. Jensen, D. Lapp, and J. Squire (eds.), *Handbook of Research on Teaching the English Language Arts.* New York: Macmillan, 1991, pp. 604–632.

Bean, Thomas W. "Teacher Literacy Histories and Adolescent Voices: Changing Content-Area Classrooms." In D. Alvermann, K. Hinchman, D. Moore, S. Phelps, and D. Waff (eds.), *Reconceptualizing the Literacies in Adolescents' Lives.* Mahwah, N.J.: Erlbaum, 1998, pp. 438–455.

Bean, Thomas W. "An Update on Reading in the Content Areas: Social Constructionist Dimensions." *Reading Online* 5, no. 5. Retrieved from http://www.readingonline.org (December/January 2001).

Bean, Thomas W., Shannon Bean, and Kristen Bean. "Intergenerational Conversations and Two Adolescents' Multiple Literacies: Implications for Redefining Content Area Literacy." *Journal of Adolescent & Adult Literacy* 42 (March 1999): 438–448.

Bean, Thomas, and B. Ericson. "Text Previews and Three Level Study Guides for Content Area Critical Reading." *Journal of Reading* 32 (January 1989): 337–341.

Beck, Ann. "A Place for Critical Literacy." *Journal of Adolescent & Adult Literacy* 48 (February 2005): 392–400.

Beck, I., M. McKeown, G. Sinatra, and J. Loxterman. "Revising Social Studies Text from a Text-Processing Perspective: Evidence of Improved Comprehensibility." *Reading Research Quarterly* 29 (1991): 230–281.

Beck, I., C. Perfetti, and M. McKeown. "Effects of Long-Term Vocabulary Comprehension." *Journal of Educational Psychology* 74 (1982): 506–521.

Belanoff, Pat, and Marcia Dickson, eds. *Portfolios: Process and Product.* Portsmouth, N.H.: Boynton/Cook, 1991.

Bell, Nancy, Debbie Cambron, Kathy Rey-Barreau, and Beverly Paeth. "Online Literature Groups." Handout for the National Council of Teachers of English Convention, San Diego, California, 1995.

Bempechat, Janine. "Learning from Poor and Minority Students Who Succeed in School." *Harvard Education Letter* (September–October 1999): 1–3.

Benson, Linda K. "How to Pluck an Albatross: The Research Paper Without Tears." *English Journal* 76 (November 1987): 54–56.

Berger, Linda R. "Reader Response Journals: You Make the Meaning . . . and How." *Journal of Adolescent & Adult Literacy* 39 (February 1996): 380–385.

Bertelsen, C. D., and J. M. Fischer. "Mediating Expository Text: Scaffolding and the Use of Multimedia Curricula." *Reading Online* 6 (December 2002/January 2003). Retrieved from http://www.readingonline.org/articles/Oakley.html.

"Best of the Blogs." *eSchool News* 8 (August 2005): 8.

Betts, Emmett A. *Foundations of Reading Instruction.* New York: American Book Company, 1946.

Beyer, B. "Developing a Scope and Sequence for Thinking Skills Instruction." *Educational Leadership* 45 (April 1988): 26–31.

Beyersdorfer, Janet M., and David K. Schauer. "Writing Personality Profiles: Conversations Across the Generation Gap." *Journal of Reading* 35 (May 1992): 612–616.

Biemiller, Andrew. "Vocabulary: Needed If More Children Are to Read Well." *Reading Psychology* 24 (October/December 2003): 323–335.

Biggers, Deborah. "The Argument Against Accelerated Reader." *Journal of Adolescent & Adult Literacy* 45 (September 2001): 72–75.

Binkley, Marilyn R. "New Ways of Assessing Text Difficulty." In Beverley L. Zakaluk and S. Jay Samuels (eds.), *Readability: Its Past, Present & Future.* Newark, Del.: International Reading Association, 1988, pp. 98–120.

Bintz, William P., and Karen S. Shelton. "Using Written Conversation in Middle School: Lessons from a Teacher Researcher Project." *Journal of Adolescent & Adult Literacy* 47 (March 2004): 492–507.

Bitter, Gary G., Ruth A. Camuse, and Vicki L. Durbin. *Using a Microcomputer in the Classroom.* 3rd ed. Boston: Allyn & Bacon, 1993.

Blachowicz, C., and B. Zabroske. "Context Instruction: A Metacognitive Approach for At-Risk Readers." *Journal of Reading* 33 (April 1990): 504–508.

Black, Paul, and Dylan Wiliam. "Inside the Black Box: Raising Standards Through Classroom Assessment." *Phi Delta Kappan* 89 (October 1998): 139–148.

Black, Rebecca W. "Access and Affiliation: The Literacy and Composition Practices of English-language Learners in an

Online Fanfiction Community." *Journal of Adolescent & Adult Literacy* 49 (October 2005): 118–128.

Blatt, G., and L. Rosen. "The Writing Response to Literature." *Journal of Reading* 28 (October 1984): 8–12.

Block, C. C., and M. Pressley, eds. *Comprehension Instruction: Research-Based Best Practices.* New York: Guilford, 2003.

Bloem, Patricia. "Correspondence Journals: Talk That Matters." *The Reading Teacher* 58 (September 2004): 54–62.

Bode, Barbara A. "Dialogue Journal Writing." *The Reading Teacher* 42 (April 1989): 568–571.

Borkowski, John G. "Metacognitive Theory: A Framework for Teaching Literacy, Writing, and Math Skills." *Journal of Learning Disabilities* 4 (April 1992): 253–257.

Bormuth, John. "Cloze Test Readability: Criterion Reference Scores." *Journal of Educational Measurement* 5 (Fall 1968a): 189–196.

Bormuth, John. "The Cloze Readability Procedure." *Elementary English* 45 (April 1968b): 429–436.

Bott, Christie "C.J." "Zines—The Ultimate Creative Writing Project." *English Journal* 92 (November 2002): 327–333.

Bottoms, Gene, and Alice Presson. *Using Lessons Learned: Improving the Academic Achievement of Vocational Students.* Educational Benchmarks 2000 Series. Atlanta, Ga.: Southern Regional Education Board, 2000.

Brazee, Ed. "Teaching Reading in Social Studies: Skill-Centered Versus Content-Centered." *Colorado Journal of Educational Research* 18 (August 1979): 23–25.

Brimijoin, Kay, Ede Marquissee, and Carol Ann Tomlinson, "Using Data to Differentiate Instruction." *Educational Leadership* 60 (February 2003): 70–73.

Britton, James, Tony Burgess, Nancy Martin, Alex McLeod, and Harold Rosen. *The Development of Writing Abilities* (11–18). London: Macmillan Education, 1975.

Broaddus, Karen, and Gay Ivey. "Surprising the Writer: Discovering Details Through Research and Reading." *Language Arts* 80 (September 2002): 23–30.

Bromley, Karen. *Journaling: Engagements in Reading, Writing, and Thinking.* New York: Scholastic, 1993.

Bromley, Karen. "Vocabulary Learning Online." *Reading Online* 6 (July/August 2002). Retrieved from http://www.readingonline.org.

Bromley, Karen D'Angelo, and Laurie McKeveny. "Précis Writing: Suggestions for Instruction in Summarizing." *Journal of Reading* 29 (February 1986): 392–395.

Brooks, Bruce. *Midnight Hour Encores.* New York: Harper & Row, Junior Books, 1986.

Brophy, Jere. "Probing the Subtleties of Subject-Matter Teaching." *Educational Leadership* 49 (April 1992): 4–9.

Brown, A. L., and J. D. Day. "Macrorules for Summarizing Texts: The Development of Expertise." *Journal of Verbal Learning and Verbal Behavior* 22, no. 1 (1983): 1–14.

Brown, A. L., J. D. Day, and R. Jones. "The Development of Plans for Summarizing Texts." *Child Development* 54 (1983): 968–979.

Brozo, William G. "Learning How At-Risk Readers Learn Best: A Case for Interactive Assessment." *Journal of Reading* 33 (April 1990): 522–527.

Brozo, William G., and Ronald V. Schmelzer. "Wildmen, Warriors, and Lovers." *Journal of Adolescent & Adult Literacy* 41 (September 1997): 4–11.

Bruce, Bertram. "New Literacies." *Journal of Adolescent & Adult Literacy* 42 (September 1998): 46–49.

Bruce, Bertram. "Searching the Web: New Domains for Inquiry." *Journal of Adolescent & Adult Literacy* 43 (December 1999/January 2000): 348–354.

Bruce, Bertram C. "Constructing a Once-and-Future History of Learning Technologies." *Journal of Adolescent & Adult Literacy* 44 (May 2001): 730–736.

Brumfield, Robert. "Computer Simulation for Students Is 'Making History.'" *eSchool News* 8 (October 2005): 28.

Brynildssen, Shawna. "Vocabulary's Influence on Successful Writing." ERIC Digest no. 157. Bloomington, Ind.: ERIC Clearinghouse on Reading, English, and Communication, December 2000.

Buehl, Doug. *Classroom Strategies for Interactive Learning.* 2nd ed. Newark, Del.: International Reading Association, 2001.

Burron, Arnold, and Amos L. Claybaugh. *Using Reading to Teach Subject Matter: Fundamentals for Content Teachers.* Columbus, Ohio: Merrill, 1974.

Busching, B., and R. Slesinger. "Authentic Questions: What Do They Look Like? Where Do They Lead?" *Language Arts* 72 (September 1995): 341–351.

Butcheri, Jan, and Jesse J. Hammond. "Authentic Writing Makes the Difference." *Journal of Reading* 38 (November 1994): 228–229.

Caine, Renate, and Geoffrey Caine. *Making Connections: Teaching and the Human Brain.* Reading, Mass.: Addison-Wesley, 1994.

Calfee, Robert C., and Pam Perfumo. "Student Portfolios: Opportunities for a Revolution in Assessment." *Journal of Reading* 36 (April 1993): 532–537.

Camp, Roberta, and Denise Levine. "Portfolios Evolving: Background and Variations in Sixth- Through Twelfth-Grade Classrooms." In Pat Belanoff and Marcia Dickson (eds.), *Portfolios: Process and Product.* Portsmouth, N.H.: Boynton/Cook, 1991, pp. 194–205.

Carlson, J. "Reading in the Content Area of Foreign Language." In M. Dupois (ed.), *Reading in the Content Areas: Research for Teachers*. Newark, Del.: International Reading Association, 1984, pp. 23–32.

Carnine, Douglas, Carlos Cortes, Kenneth Curtis, and Anita Robinson. *World History*. Evanston, Ill.: McDougal Littell, 2006.

Carr, E., and D. Ogle. "K-W-L Plus: A Strategy for Comprehension and Summarization." *Journal of Reading* 30 (1987): 626–631.

Carr, M., and G. Claxton. "Tracking the Development of Learning Dispositions." *Assessment in Education* 9 (1): 9–37.

Carrney, T. "Textuality: Infectious Echoes from the Past." *The Reading Teacher* 43 (March 1990): 478–484.

Carroll, David, and Patricia Carini. "Tapping Teachers' Knowledge." In Vito Perrone (ed.), *Expanding Student Assessment*. Alexandria, Va.: Association for Supervision and Curriculum Development, 1991, pp. 40–46.

Carroll, Pamela Sissi. "'i cant read i wont read': Will's Moment of Success." *English Journal* 81 (March 1992): 50–52.

Cassady, Judith K. "Wordless Books: No-Risk Tools for Inclusive Middle-Grade Classrooms." *Journal of Adolescent & Adult Literacy* 41 (March 1998): 428–432.

Chance, Larry. "Use Cloze Encounters of the Readability Kind for Secondary School Students." *Journal of Reading* 28 (May 1985): 690–693.

Chandler-Olcott, Kelly, and Donna Mahar. "Adolescents' *Anime*-Inspired 'Fanfictions': An Exploration of Multiliteracies." *Journal of Adolescent & Adult Literacy* 46 (April 2003): 556–566.

Chase, A., and F. Duffelmeyer. "VOCAB-LIT: Integrating Vocabulary Study and Literature Study." *Journal of Reading* 34 (November 1990): 188–193.

Chittenden, Edward. "Authentic Assessment, Evaluation, and Documentation of Student Performance." In Vito Perrone (ed.), *Expanding Student Assessment*. Alexandria, Va.: Association for Supervision and Curriculum Development, 1991, pp. 22–31.

Christ, G. "Curriculums with Real-World Connections." *Educational Leadership* 52 (May 1995): 32–35.

Christen, William L., and Thomas J. Murphy. "Increasing Comprehension by Activating Prior Knowledge." ERIC Digest no. 328-885. Bloomington, Ind.: ERIC Clearinghouse on Reading, English, and Communication, 1991.

Ciardiello, Angela V. "Did You Ask a Good Question Today? Alternative Cognitive and Metacognitive Strategies." *Journal of Adolescent & Adult Literacy* 42 (November 1998): 210–219.

Cioffi, G. "Perspective and Experience: Developing Critical Reading Abilities." *Journal of Reading* 36 (September 1992): 48–53.

Civello, Catherine A. "'Move Over Please': The Decentralization of the Teacher in the Computer-Based Classroom." *English Journal* 88 (March 1999): 89–94.

Clark, Charles H. "Assessing Free Recall." *The Reading Teacher* 35 (January 1982): 434–439.

Clark, Richard W., and Patricia Wasley. "Renewing Schools and Smarter Kids: Promises for Democracy." *Phi Delta Kappan* 90 (April 1999): 590–596.

Clarke, John. "Using Visual Organizers to Focus on Thinking." *Journal of Reading* (April 1991): 526–534.

Clarke, John H., James Raths, and Gary L. Gilbert. "Inductive Towers: Letting Students See How They Think." *Journal of Reading* 33 (November 1989): 86–95.

Cobb, Charlene. "Effective Instruction Begins with Purposeful Assessments." *The Reading Teacher* 57 (December 2003/January 2004): 386–388.

Cocking, Terry S., and Susan A. Schafer. "Scavenging for Better Library Instruction." *Journal of Reading* 38 (November 1994): 164–170.

Coley, J., and D. Hoffman. "Overcoming Learned Helplessness in At-Risk Readers." *Journal of Reading* 33 (April 1990): 497–502.

Collins, Cathy. "Reading Instruction That Increases Thinking Abilities." *Journal of Reading* 34 (April 1991): 510–516.

Collins, Norma Decker. "Freewriting, Personal Writing, and the At-Risk Reader." *Journal of Reading* 33 (May 1990): 654–655.

Collins, Vicki, Shirley Dickson, Deborah Simmons, and Edward Kameenui. *Metacognition and Its Relation to Reading Comprehension: A Synthesis of the Research*. National Center to Improve the Tools of Educators: University of Oregon, 1998.

Colvin, Carolyn, and S. Schlosser. "Developing Academic Confidence to Build Literacy: What Teachers Can Do." *Journal of Adolescent & Adult Literacy* 41 (December 1997/January 1998): 272–281.

Commander, Nannette Evans, and Brenda D. Smith. "Learning Logs: A Tool for Cognitive Monitoring." *Journal of Adolescent & Adult Literacy* 39 (March 1996): 446–453.

Condon, William, and Liz Hamp-Lyons. "Introducing a Portfolio-Based Writing Assessment: Progress Through Problems." In Pat Belanoff and Marcia Dickson (eds.), *Portfolios: Process and Product*. Portsmouth, N.H.: Boynton/Cook, 1991, pp. 231–247.

Conley, Mark W., and Kathleen A. Hinchman. "No Child Left Behind: What It Means for U.S. Adolescents and What We

Can Do About It." *Journal of Adolescent & Adult Literacy* 48 (September 2004): 42–50.

Conley, Maureen. "Teacher Decisionmaking." In Donna Alvermann and David Moore (eds.), *Research Within Reach: Secondary School Reading*. Newark, Del.: International Reading Association, 1987.

Cooper, Charles, and Ann Purves. *A Guide to Evaluation*. Lexington, Mass.: Ginn, 1973.

Cooper, John, S. Garrett, M. Leighton, P. Martorella, G. Morine-Dershimer, D. Sadker, M. Sadker, R. Shostak, T. TenBrink, and W. Weber. *Classroom Teaching Skills*. 5th ed. Lexington, Mass.: D. C. Heath, 1994.

Cooper, Winfield, and B. J. Brown. "Using Portfolios to Empower Student Writers." *English Journal* 81 (February 1992): 40–45.

Cooter, Robert B., Jr., and Robert Griffith. "Thematic Units for Middle School: An Honorable Seduction." *Journal of Reading* 32 (May 1989): 676–681.

Copeland, Matt, and Chris Goering. "Blues You Can Use: Teaching the Faust Theme Through Music, Literature, and Film." *Journal of Adolescent & Adult Literacy* 48 (February 2003): 436–441.

Coppola, Julie. "Meeting the Needs of English Learners in All English Classrooms: Sharing the Responsibility." In G. G. Garcia (ed.), *English Learners: Reading the Highest Level of English Literacy*. Newark, Del.: International Reading Association, 2003, 182–196.

Cote Parra, Gabriel Eduardo. "Learning English Through Online Discussion Groups." *Journal of Adolescent & Adult Literacy* 44 (September 2000): 36–38.

Cotton, Eileen Giuffré. *The Online Classroom: Teaching with the Internet*. Bloomington, Ind.: ERIC Clearinghouse on Reading, English, and Communication, 1996.

Cox, G. C., D. L. Smith, and T. A. Rakes. "Enhancing Comprehension Through the Use of Visual Elaboration Strategies." *Reading Research and Instruction* 33 (1994): 159–174.

Craven, Jerry. "A New Model for Teaching Literature Classes." *T.H.E. Journal* 22 (August 1994): 55–57.

Cruz, MaryCarmen E. "Writing to Learn as a Way of Making Sense of the World." In Harriet Arzu Scarborough (ed.), *Writing Across the Curriculum in Secondary Classrooms*. Upper Saddle River, N.J.: Merrill/Prentice Hall, 2001, pp. 71–89.

Cummins, James. "The Acquisition of English as a Second Language." In Karen Spangenberg-Urbschat and Robert Prichard (eds.), *Kids Come in All Languages: Reading Instruction for ESL Students*. Newark, Del.: International Reading Association, 1994, pp. 36–62.

Cunningham, James, and David Moore. "The Confused World of Main Idea." In James Baumann (ed.), *Teaching Main Idea Comprehension*. Newark, Del.: International Reading Association, 1986, pp. 1–17.

Cunningham, Patricia M., and James W. Cunningham. "Content Area Reading-Writing Lessons." *The Reading Teacher* 40 (February 1987): 506–512.

Curry, Adam, and Peter Ford. "What Are Schoolblogs?" Retrieved July 28, 2005 from http://www.schoolblogs.com/stories/storyReader$265.

Curtis, Mary, and Ann Longo. *When Adolescents Can't Read: Methods and Materials That Work*. Brookline, Mass.: Brookline Books, 1999.

Curtis, Mary, and Ann Longo. "Teaching Vocabulary to Adolescents to Improve Comprehension." *Reading Online* 5 (November 2001). Retrieved from http://www.reading online.org/vocabulary/curtis&longo/index.html.

Daedalus Group, Inc. DGI Home Page: Products & Services: What Is DIWE? (http://daedalus.com/info/diwe/diwe_info.html). Austin, Tex.: Daedalus Group, 1995.

Daisey, Peggy, and Cristina Jose-Kampfner. "The Power of Story to Expand Possible Selves for Latina Middle School Students." *Journal of Adolescent & Adult Literacy* 45 (April 2002): 578–587.

D'Angelo, Karen. "Précis Writing: Promoting Vocabulary Development and Comprehension." *Journal of Reading* 26 (March 1983): 534–539.

Dale, Edgar. *Audiovisual Methods in Teaching*. 3rd ed. New York: Holt, Rinehart and Winston, 1969.

Dale, Edgar, and Jeanne S. Chall. "A Formula for Predicting Readability." *Educational Research Bulletin* 27 (January 21, 1948a): 11–28.

Dale, Edgar, and Jeanne S. Chall. "A Formula for Predicting Readability: Instructions." *Educational Research Bulletin* 27 (February 18, 1948b): 37–54.

Dale, Edgar, and Joseph O'Rourke. *The Living Word Vocabulary*. Elgin, Ill.: Dome, 1976.

Dales, Brenda. "Trusting Relations Between Teachers and Librarians." *Language Arts* 67 (November 1990): 732–734.

Damico, Natalie W. "Portfolio Reflections—10 Activities to Promote Reflective Thinking." *Notes Plus* (March 1996): 3–4.

Danielson, Kathy Everts. "Picture Books to Use with Older Students." *Journal of Reading* 35 (May 1992): 652–654.

Davey, Beth. "Team for Success: Guided Practice in Study Skills Through Cooperative Research Reports." *Journal of Reading* 30 (May 1987): 701–705.

Davey, Beth. "How Do Classroom Teachers Use Their Textbooks?" *Journal of Reading* 31 (January 1988): 340–345.

Davis, Susan J., and Jean Hunter. "Historical Novels: A Context for Gifted Student Research." *Journal of Reading* 33 (May 1990): 602–606.

Dean, Deborah, and Sirpa Grierson. "Re-envisioning Reading and Writing Through Combined-Text Picture Books." *Journal of Adolescent & Adult Literacy* 48 (March 2005): 456–468.

Dede, Chris. "The Scaling-Up Process for Technology-Based Educational Innovations." In Chris Dede (ed.), *1998 Yearbook: Learning from Technology*. Alexandria, Va.: Association for Supervision and Curriculum Development, 1998, pp. 199–215.

Delett, Jennifer. "General Guidelines for Teaching Learning Strategies." *The NCLRC Language Resource* 1 (March 1997): 12–15.

Dettmer, Peggy, Linda P. Thurston, and Norma Dyck. *Consultation, Collaboration, and Teamwork for Students with Special Needs*. Boston: Allyn & Bacon, 1996.

Dever, Christine T. "Press Conference: A Strategy for Integrating Reading with Writing." *The Reading Teacher* 46 (September 1992): 72–73.

Dickson, Diane Skiffington, Dick Heyler, Linda G. Reilly, Stephanie Romano, and Bob DiLullo. "The Oral History Project." Handout at the 47th Annual Convention of the International Reading Association, San Francisco, Calif., April 29, 2002.

Dickson, Shirley V., Deborah C. Simmons, and Edward J. Kameenui. *Text Organization and Its Relation to Reading Comprehension: A Synthesis of the Research*. National Center to Improve the Tools of Educators: University of Oregon, 1995.

Doherty, Catherine, and Diane Mayer. "E-mail as a 'Contact Zone' for Teacher-Student Relationships." *Journal of Adolescent & Adult Literacy* 46 (April 2003): 592–600.

Dole, J. A., K. J. Brown, and W. Trathen. "The Effects of Strategy Instruction on the Comprehension Performance of At-Risk Students. *Reading Research Quarterly* 31 (1996): 62–88.

Dole, J., S. Valencia, E. Greer, and J. Wardrop. "Effects of Two Types of Prereading Instruction on the Comprehension of Narrative and Expository Text." *Reading Research Quarterly* 26, no. 2 (1991): 142–159.

Dolly, Martha R. "Integrating ESL Reading and Writing Through Authentic Discourse." *Journal of Reading* 33 (February 1990): 360–365.

Donahue, Patricia L., Kristin E. Voelkl, Jay R. Campbell, and John Mazzeo. *The NAEP 1998 Reading Report Card for the Nation and the States*. Washington, D.C.: U.S. Department of Education, Office of Educational Research and Improvement, National Center for Educational Statistics, 1999.

Donovan, Carol A., and Laura B. Smolkin. "Considering Genre, Content and Visual Features in the Selection of Trade Books for Science Instruction." *The Reading Teacher* 55 (March 2002): 502–520.

Dowhower, Sarah. "Supporting a Strategic Stance in the Classroom: A Comprehension Framework for Helping Teachers Help Students to Be Strategic." *The Reading Teacher* 52 (April 1999): 672–683.

Draper, Roni Jo. "School Mathematics Reform, Constructivism, and Literacy: A Case for Literacy Instruction in the Reform-Oriented Math Classroom." *Journal of Adolescent & Adult Literacy* 45 (March 2002): 520–529.

Dreher, Mariam Jean. "Searching for Information in Textbooks." *Journal of Reading* 35 (February 1992): 364–371.

Duke, Nell K., and P. David Pearson. "Effective Practices for Developing Reading Comprehension." In A. Farstrup and S. J. Samuels (eds.), *What Research Has to Say About Reading Instruction*. Newark, Del.: International Reading Association, 2002, pp. 205–242.

"A DVD Primer." *T.H.E. Journal* 26, no. 6 (1999): 23.

Earle, Richard. *Teaching Reading and Mathematics*. Newark, Del.: International Reading Association, 1976.

Elbow, Peter. "Why Teach Writing?" In Philip L. Brady (ed.), *The Why's of Teaching Composition*. Washington State Council of Teachers of English, 1978, pp. 57–69.

Elbow, Peter. "Foreword." In Pat Belanoff and Marcia Dickson (eds.), *Portfolios: Process and Product*. Portsmouth, N.H.: Boynton/Cook, 1991, pp. ix–xvi.

Elbow, Peter, and Pat Belanoff. "State University of New York at Stony Brook Portfolio-Based Evaluation Program." In Pat Belanoff and Marcia Dickson (eds.), *Portfolios: Process and Product*. Portsmouth, N.H.: Boynton/Cook, 1991, pp. 3–16.

El-Hindi, Amelia E. "Beyond Classroom Boundaries: Constructivist Teaching with the Internet." *The Reading Teacher* 51 (May 1998): 694–699.

Ellman, Neil. "The Impact of Competency Testing on Curriculum and Instruction." *NASSP Bulletin* 72 (February 1988): 49–52.

Ennis, Robert. "Critical Thinking and Subject Specificity: Clarification and Needed Research." *Educational Researcher* 18 (April 1989): 4–10.

Ernst-Slavit, Gisela, Monica Moore, and Carol Maloney. "Changing Lives: Teaching English and Literature to ESL Students." *Journal of Adolescent & Adult Literacy* 48 (October 2002): 118–128.

Ernst-Slavit, Gisela, and Margaret Mulhern. "Bilingual Books: Promoting Literacy and Biliteracy in the Second-Language and Mainstream Class." *Reading Online* 7 (September/October 2003). Retrieved from http://www.readingonline.org/articles/art_index.asp?HREF=/articles/ernst-slavit/index.html.

Farr, Roger, and Bruce Tone. *Portfolio and Performance Assessment.* Fort Worth, Tex.: Harcourt Brace, 1994.

Farstrup, Alan E. "Point/Counterpoint: State-by-State Comparisons on National Assessments." *Reading Today* 7 (December 1989/January 1990): 1, 11–15.

Faust, Mark A., and Ronald D. Kieffer. "Challenging Expectations: Why We Ought to Stand by the IRA/NCTE Standards for the English Language Arts." *Journal of Adolescent & Adult Literacy* 41 (April 1998): 540–547.

Fay, Leo. "Reading Study Skills: Math and Science." In J. Allen Figurel (ed.), *Reading and Inquiry.* Newark, Del.: International Reading Association, 1965, pp. 93–94.

Feathers, Karen M., and Frederick R. Smith. "Meeting the Reading Demands of the Real World: Literacy Based Content Instruction." *Journal of Reading* 30 (March 1987): 506–511.

Fennessey, Sharon. "Living History Through Drama and Literature." *The Reading Teacher* 49 (September 1995): 16–19.

Ferguson, Anne M., and Jo Fairburn. "Language Experience for Problem Solving in Math." *The Reading Teacher* 38 (February 1985): 504–507.

Ferris, Judith Ann, and Gerry Snyder. "Writing as an Influence on Reading." *Journal of Reading* 29 (May 1986): 751–756.

Finder, M. "Teaching to Comprehend." *Journal of Reading* 13 (May 1970): 611–636.

Fisher, Andrea L. "Implementing Graphic Organizer Notebooks: The Art and Science of Teaching Content." *The Reading Teacher* 55 (October 2001): 166–170.

Fisher, Douglas. "'We're Moving On Up': Creating a School-wide Literacy Effort in an Urban High School." *Journal of Adolescent & Adult Literacy* 45 (October 2001): 92–101.

Fisher, Douglas, James Flood, Diane Lapp, and Nancy Frey. "Interactive Read-Alouds: Is There a Common Set of Implementation Practices?" *The Reading Teacher* 58 (September 2004): 8–17.

Fisher, Douglas, and Nancy Frey. "Writing Instruction for Struggling Adolescent Readers: A Gradual Release Model." *Journal of Adolescent & Adult Literacy* 46 (February 2003): 396–405.

Fitzgerald, Jill. "Literacy and Students Who Are Learning English as a Second Language." *The Reading Teacher* 46 (May 1993): 638–647.

Fitzgerald, Jill. "Helping Young Writers to Revise: A Brief Review for Teachers." *The Reading Teacher* 42 (November 1988): 124–129.

Flesch, Rudolf. *The Art of Readable Writing.* New York: Harper & Row, 1949.

Forbes, Leighann S. "Using Web-Based Bookmarks in K–8 Settings: Linking the Internet to Instruction." *The Reading Teacher* 58 (October 2004): 148–153.

Franks, Leslie. "Charcoal Clouds and Weather Writing: Inviting Science to a Middle School Language Arts Classroom." *Language Arts* 78 (March 2001): 319–324.

Frayer, D. A., W. C. Frederick, and H. J. Klausmeier. *A Schema for Testing the Level of Concept Mastery.* Technical Report No. 16. Madison, Wis.: University of Wisconsin, R & D Center for Cognitive Learning, 1969.

Friend, Rosalie. "Teaching Summarization as a Content Area Reading Strategy." *Journal of Adolescent & Adult Literacy* 44 (December 2000/January 2001): 320–329.

Fry, Edward. "A Readability Formula That Saves Time." *Journal of Reading* 11 (April 1968): 513–516, 575–578.

Fry, Edward. *Reading Instruction for Classroom and Clinic.* New York: McGraw-Hill, 1972.

Fry, Edward. "Fry's Readability Graph: Clarifications, Validity and Extension to Level 17." *Journal of Reading* 21 (December 1977): 242–252.

Fry, Edward. *Fry Readability Scale (Extended).* Providence, R.I.: Jamestown Publishers, 1978.

Fry, Edward. "Graphical Literacy." *Journal of Reading* 24 (February 1981): 383–390.

Fry, Edward. "A Readability Formula for Short Passages." *Journal of Reading* 33 (May 1990): 594–597.

Fryar, R. "Students Assess Their Own Reporting and Presentation Skills." In H. Fehring (ed.), *Literacy Assessment.* Newark, Del.: International Reading Association, 2003, pp. 36–39.

Frymier, Jack. "Children Who Hurt, Children Who Fail." *Phi Delta Kappan* 74 (1992): 257–259.

Furr, Derek. "Struggling Readers Get Hooked on Writing." *The Reading Teacher* 56 (March 2003): 518–525.

Gahn, S. "A Practical Guide for Teaching Writing in the Content Areas." *Journal of Reading* 32 (March 1989): 525–531.

Gallagher, Janice Mori. "Pairing Adolescent Fiction with Books from the Canon." *Journal of Adolescent & Adult Literacy* 39 (September 1995): 8–14.

Garcia, Eugene. *Student Cultural Diversity: Understanding and Meeting the Challenge.* 3rd ed. Boston: Houghton Mifflin, 2000.

Garcia, Eugene. *Student Cultural Diversity.* Boston: Houghton Mifflin, 2002.

Garcia, Jesus, Donna Ogle, C. Frederick Risinger, Joyce Stevos, and Winthrop Jordan. *Creating America: A History of the United States.* Boston: McDougal Littell, 2001.

Garcia-Vazquez, Enedina, and Luis A. Vazquez. "In a Pen Pals Program: Latinos/as Supporting Latinos/as." *Journal of Reading* 38 (November 1994): 172–178.

Gardner, Howard. *Multiple Intelligences: The Theory in Practice.* New York: Basic Books, 1993, 1998.

Gardner, Howard. *Intelligence Reframed: Multiple Intelligence for the 21st Century.* New York: Basic Books, 1999.

Gee, J. P. *What Video Games Have to Teach Us About Learning and Literacy.* New York: Palgrave Macmillan, 2003.

Geisert, Paul G., and Mynga K. Futrell. *Teachers, Computers, and Curriculum: Microcomputers in the Classroom.* 3rd ed. Boston: Allyn & Bacon, 2000.

Gerber, Susan, and Jeremy D. Finn. "Learning Document Skills at School and at Work." *Journal of Adolescent & Adult Literacy* 42 (September 1998): 32–44.

Gergen, Kenneth J. *An Invitation to Social Construction.* Thousand Oaks, Calif.: Sage, 1999.

Gibbons, Pauline. *Scaffolding Language, Scaffolding Learning: Teaching Second Language Learners in the Mainstream Classroom.* Portsmouth, N.H.: Heinemann, 2002.

Gillespie, Cindy. "Questions About Student-Generated Questions." *Journal of Reading* 34 (December 1990): 250–257.

Gillespie, Cindy S. "Reading Graphic Displays: What Teachers Should Know." *Journal of Reading* 36 (February 1993): 350–354.

Gillespie, Cindy S., Karen L. Ford, Ralph D. Gillespie, and Alexandra G. Leavell. "Portfolio Assessment: Some Questions, Some Answers, Some Recommendations." *Journal of Adolescent & Adult Literacy* 39 (March 1996): 480–491.

Gilster, Paul. *Digital Literacy.* New York: Wiley, 1997.

Glasgow, Jacqueline N. "Motivating the Tech Prep Reader Through Learning Styles and Adolescent Literature." *Journal of Adolescent & Adult Literacy* 39 (February 1996): 358–367.

Glatthorn, Allen. "Thinking, Writing, and Reading: Making Connections." In Diane Lapp, James Flood, and Nancy Farnan (eds.), *Content Area Reading and Learning: Instructional Strategies.* Englewood Cliffs, N.J.: Prentice Hall, 1989.

Glazer, Susan Mandel, and Carol Smullen Brown. *Portfolios and Beyond: Collaborative Assessment in Reading and Writing.* Norwood, Mass.: Christopher-Gordon, 1993.

Glazer, Susan Mandel, and Lyndon W. Searfoss. "Reexamining Reading Diagnosis." In Susan Mandel Glazer, Lyndon W. Searfoss, and Lance M. Gentile (eds.), *Reexamining Reading Diagnosis: New Trends and Procedures.* Newark, Del.: International Reading Association, 1989, pp. 1–11.

Glencoe/McGraw Hill. *Glencoe Language Arts Guide to Using the Internet and Other Electronic Resources.* Westerville, Ohio: Glencoe/McGraw-Hill, 2000.

Godina, Heriberto. "The Canonical Debate—Implementing Multicultural Literature and Perspectives." *Journal of Adolescent & Adult Literacy* 39 (April 1996): 544–549.

Gollnick, Donna M., and Philip C. Chinn. *Multicultural Education in a Pluralistic Society.* Columbus, Ohio: Merrill, 2002.

"Good News, Bad News." *Reading Today* 21 (August/September 2003): 1, 4.

Gordon, Christine J., and Dorothy MacInnis. "Using Journals as a Window on Students' Thinking in Mathematics." *Language Arts* 70 (January 1993): 37–43.

Gordon, David T. "Curriculum Access in the Digital Age." *Harvard Education Letter* (January/February 2002): 3–7.

Gordon, K. *The Deluxe Transitive Vampire: The Ultimate Handbook of Grammar for the Innocent, the Eager, and the Doomed.* New York: Pantheon, 1993.

Grabe, Mark, and Cindy Grabe. *Integrating Technology for Meaningful Learning.* Boston: Houghton Mifflin, 2001.

Grabe, Mark, and Cindy Grabe. *Integrating the Internet for Meaningful Learning,* 4th ed. Boston: Houghton Mifflin, 2004.

Grace, Marsha. "Implementing a Portfolio System in Your Classroom." *Reading Today* 10 (June–July 1993): 27.

Grady, Karen. *Adolescent Literacy and Content Reading.* ERIC #176. Bloomington, Ind.: ERIC Clearinghouse on Adult, Career, and Vocational Education, December 2002.

Grant, Rachel. "Strategic Training for Using Text Headings to Improve Students' Processing of Content." *Journal of Reading* 36 (March 1993): 482–488.

Grant, Rachel, and Shelley Wong. "Barriers to Literacy for Language-Minority Learners: An Argument for Change in the Literacy Education Profession." *Journal of Adolescent & Adult Literacy* 46 (February 2003): 386–394.

Graser, Elsa R. *Teaching Writing: A Process Approach.* Dubuque, Iowa: Kendall/Hunt, 1983.

Graves, Donald H. "Help Students Learn to Read Their Portfolios." In Donald H. Graves and Bonnie S. Sunstein (eds.), *Portfolio Portraits.* Portsmouth, N.H.: Heinemann, 1992a, pp. 85–95.

Graves, Donald H. "Portfolios: Keep a Good Idea Growing." In Donald H. Graves and Bonnie S. Sunstein (eds.), *Portfolio Portraits.* Portsmouth, N.H.: Heinemann, 1992b, pp. 1–12.

Graves, Donald. "What I've Learned from Teachers of Writing." *Language Arts* 82 (November 2004): 88–94.

Graves, Michael F. "Fostering High Levels of Reading and Learning in Secondary Students." *Reading Online* (October 1999). Retrieved from http://www.readingonline.org.

Graves, Michael F., and Jill Fitzgerald. "Scaffolding Reading Experiences for Multilingual Classrooms." In Gilbert G.

Garcia (ed.), *English Language Learners: Reaching the Highest Level of English Literacy.* Newark, Del.: International Reading Association, 2003, pp. 96–124.

Greenleaf, Cynthia, Ruth Schoenbach, Christine Cziko, and Faye Mueller. "Apprenticing Adolescent Readers to Academic Literacy." *Harvard Educational Review* 71 (2001): 70–129.

Grierson, Sirpa T., Amy Anson, and Jacoy Baird. "Exploring the Past Through Multigenre Writing." *Language Arts* 80 (September 2002): 51–59.

Griffith, Lorraine, and Timothy Rasinski. "A Focus on Fluency: How One Teacher Incorporated Fluency with Her Reading Curriculum." *The Reading Teacher* 58 (October 2004): 126–137.

Guskey, Thomas R. "How Classroom Assessments Improve Learning." *Educational Leadership* 60 (February 2003): 7–11.

Guthrie, John T. "Children's Reasons for Success and Failure." *The Reading Teacher* 36 (January 1983): 478–480.

Guthrie, John. "The Director's Corner." *NRRC News: A Newsletter of the National Reading Research Center* (January 1997): 2.

Guthrie, John. "Contexts for Engagement and Motivation in Reading." In Michael Kamil, Peter Mosenthal, David Pearson, and Rebecca Barr (eds.), *Handbook of Reading Research.* Vol. III. New York: Erlbaum, 2000, pp. 403–422.

Guzzetti, Barbara J. T., and A. Wigfield. "Engagement and Motivation in Reading." In M. L. Kamil, P. B. Mosenthal, P. D. Pearson, and R. Barr (eds.), *Handbook of Reading Research* Volume III. New York: Erlbaum, 2000, 403–422.

Guzzetti, Barbara J., Barbara J. Kowalinski, and Tom McGowan. "Using a Literature-Based Approach to Teaching Social Studies." *Journal of Reading* 36 (October 1992): 114–122.

Hadaway, Nancy L., and JaNae Mundy. "Children's Informational Picture Books Visit a Secondary ESL Classroom." *Journal of Adolescent & Adult Literacy* 42 (March 1999): 464–475.

Haggard, Michael. "An Interactive Strategies Approach to Content Reading." *Journal of Reading* 29 (1986): 204–210.

Hall, Anne-Marie. "Math and Science in My English Class? Why Not?" In Harriet Arzu Scarborough (ed.), *Writing Across the Curriculum in Secondary Classrooms.* Upper Saddle River, N.J.: Merrill/Prentice Hall, 2001, pp. 17–31.

Hammond, Donald. "How Your Students Can Predict Their Way to Reading Comprehension." *Learning* 12 (1983): 62–64.

Hancock, Marjorie R. "Character Journals: Initiating Involvement and Identification Through Literature." *Journal of Reading* 37 (September 1993): 42–50.

Hanna, J. "The Language of Dance." *Journal of Physical Education, Recreation & Dance* 72 (2001): 40–45.

Harada, Violet H. "Breaking the Silence: Sharing the Japanese American Internment Experience with Adolescent Readers." *Journal of Adolescent & Adult Literacy* 39 (May 1996): 630–637.

Hare, V. C., and K. M. Borchardt. "Direct Instruction of Summarization Skills." *Reading Research Quarterly* 20, no. 1 (1984): 62–78.

Harmon, Janis M. "Vocabulary Teaching and Learning in a Seventh-Grade Literature-Based Classroom." *Journal of Adolescent & Adult Literacy* 41 (April 1998): 518–529.

Harmon, Janis M. "Teaching Independent Word Learning Strategies to Struggling Readers." *Journal of Adolescent & Adult Literacy* 45 (April 2002): 606–615.

Harp, Bill. "When the Principal Asks: 'Why Aren't You Using Peer Editing?'" *The Reading Teacher* 41 (April 1988): 828–829.

Harper, Candace, and Ester de Jong. "Misconceptions About Teaching English-Language Learners." *Journal of Adolescent & Adult Literacy* 48 (October 2004): 152–162.

Harris, Theodore, and Richard Hodges, eds. *A Dictionary of Reading and Related Terms.* Newark, Del.: International Reading Association, 1981.

Hartman, D. "Eight Readers Reading: The Intertextual Links of Able Readers Using Multiple Passages." *Reading Research Quarterly* 27, no. 2 (1992): 122–132.

Harvey, Stephanie. "Nonfiction Inquiry: Using Real Reading and Writing to Explore the World." *Language Arts* 80 (September 2002): 12–22.

Heckelman, R. G. "A Neurological Impress Method of Remedial Reading Instruction." *Academic Therapy* 4 (1969): 277–282.

Heide, Ann, and Dale Henderson. *The Technological Classroom: A Blueprint for Success.* Toronto: Trifolium Books, 1994.

Heinich, Robert, Michael Molenda, and James D. Russell. *Instructional Media and the New Technologies of Instruction.* New York: Macmillan, 1993.

Heinich, Robert, Michael Molenda, James D. Russell, and Sharon E. Smaldino. *Instructional Media and Technologies for Learning.* Columbus, Ohio: Merrill, 1999.

Heller, M. "How Do You Know What You Know? Metacognitive Modeling in the Content Areas." *Journal of Reading* 29 (February 1986): 415–422.

Henrichs, M., and T. Sisson, "Mathematics and the Reading Process: A Practical Application of Theory." *Mathematics Teacher* 1973 (April 1980): 253–256.

Henwood, Geraldine F. "A New Role for the Reading Specialist: Contributing Toward a High School's Collaborative

Educational Culture." *Journal of Adolescent & Adult Literacy* 43 (December 1999/January 2000): 316–325.

Herber, Harold. *Teaching Reading in Content Areas.* 2nd ed. Englewood Cliffs, N.J.: Prentice-Hall, 1978.

Herman, Joan L., Pamela R. Aschbacher, and Lynn Winters. *A Practical Guide to Alternative Assessment.* Alexandria, Va.: Association for Supervision and Curriculum Development, 1992.

Herman, William, Jr. "Reading and Other Language Arts in Social Studies Instruction: Persistent Problems." In R. Preston (ed.), *A New Look at Reading in Social Studies.* Newark, Del.: International Reading Association, 1969, pp. 5–9.

Hernandez, Ana. "Making Content Instruction Accessible for English Language Learners." In Gilbert G. Garcia (ed.), *English Learners: Reaching the Highest Level of English Literacy.* Newark, Del.: International Reading Association, 2003, pp. 125–149.

Hibbing, Anne Nielsen, and Joan L. Rankin-Erickson. "A Picture Is Worth a Thousand Words: Using Visual Images to Improve Comprehension for Middle School Struggling Readers." *The Reading Teacher* 56 (May 2003): 758–770.

Hickey, M. G. "Reading and Social Studies: The Critical Connection." *Social Education* (March 1990): 175–179.

Hicks, C. "Sound Before Sight: Strategies for Teaching Music Reading." *Music Education Journal* (April 1980): 53–67.

Hiebert, Elfrida H., P. David Pearson, Barbara M. Taylor, Virginia Richardson, and Scott G. Paris. *Every Child a Reader.* Ann Arbor, Mich.: Center for the Improvement of Early Reading Achievement (CIERA), 1998.

Hightshue, Deborah, Dott Ryann, Sally McKenna, Joe Tower, and Brenda Brumley. "Writing in Junior and Senior High Schools." *Phi Delta Kappan* 69 (June 1988): 725–728.

Hill, Margaret. "Writing Summaries Promotes Thinking and Learning Across the Curriculum—But Why Are They So Difficult to Write?" *Journal of Reading* 34 (April 1991): 536–539.

Hobbs, Renee and Richard Frost. "Measuring the Acquisition of Media-Literacy Skills." *Reading Research Quarterly* 38 (July/August/September 2003): 330–355.

Hodapp, Joan B., and Albert F. Hodapp. "Vocabulary Packs and Cued Spelling: Intervention Strategies." Paper presented at the National Association of School Psychologists Convention, Atlanta, Georgia, 1996.

Hoffman, James V. "Critical Reading/Thinking Across the Curriculum: Using I-Charts to Support Learning." *Language Arts* 69 (February 1992): 121–127.

Hoffman, James V., Lori Czop Assaf, and Scott G. Paris. "High-Stakes Testing in Reading: Today in Texas, Tomorrow?" *The Reading Teacher* 54 (February 2001): 482–492.

Holmes, Betty C., and Nancy L. Roser. "Five Ways to Assess Readers' Prior Knowledge." *The Reading Teacher* 40 (March 1987): 646–649.

Hoobler, D., and T. Hoobler. *Vietnam: Why We Fought—An Illustrated History.* New York: Knopf/Borzoi, 1990.

Horowitz, Robert. "Text Patterns: Part I." *Journal of Reading* 28 (February 1985a): 448–454.

Horowitz, Robert. "Text Patterns: Part II." *Journal of Reading* 28 (March 1985b): 534–541.

Hoyt, Kenneth. "Career Education and Education Reform: Time for a Rebirth." *Phi Delta Kappan* 83 (December 2001): 327–331.

Hoyt, Kenneth, and Pat Wickwire. "Knowledge-Information-Service Era Changes in Work and Education and the Changing Role of the School Counselor in Career Education." *Career Development Quarterly* 49 (March 2001): 238.

Hudley, C. A. "Using Role Models to Improve the Reading Attitudes of Ethnic Minority High School Girls." *Journal of Reading* 36 (November 1992): 182–189.

Hynd, Cinthia R. "Teaching Students to Think Critically Using Multiple Texts in History." *Journal of Adolescent & Adult Literacy* 42 (March 1999): 428–437.

Iannone, Patrick V. "Just Beyond the Horizon: Writing-Centered Literacy Activities for Traditional and Electronic Contexts." *The Reading Teacher* 51 (February 1998): 438–443.

"Ideas for Teaching with Interactive Whiteboards." *eSchool News* 8 (February 2005): 24.

Imel, S. *Vocational Education's Role in Dropout Prevention.* Columbus, Ohio: ERIC Clearinghouse on Adult, Career, and Vocational Education, 1993.

INC Sights: A Teacher's Guide to Writers INC. Burlington, Wis.: Write Source Educational Publishing House, 1989.

Invernizzi, Marcia A., Timothy J. Landrum, Jennifer L. Howell, and Heather P. Warley. "Toward the Peaceful Coexistence of Test Developers, Policymakers, and Teachers in an Era of Accountability." *The Reading Teacher* 58 (April 2005): 610–616.

Irwin, Judith. *Teaching Reading Comprehension Processes.* Englewood Cliffs, N.J.: Prentice-Hall, 1991.

Irwin, Judith Westphal, and Carol A. Davis. "Assessing Readability: The Checklist Approach." *Journal of Reading* 24 (November 1980): 124–130.

Ivey, Gay. "'The Teacher Makes It More Explainable': And Other Reasons to Read Aloud in the Intermediate Grades." *The Reading Teacher* 56 (May 2003): 812–814.

Jackson, J., and E. Evans. *Spaceship Earth: Earth Science.* Rev. ed. Boston: Houghton Mifflin, 1980, p. 19.

Jacobowitz, Tina. "Using Theory to Modify Practice: An Illustration with SQ3R." *Journal of Reading* 32 (November 1988): 126–131.

Jacobowitz, Tina. "AIM: A Metacognitive Strategy for Constructing the Main Idea of Text." *Journal of Reading* 33 (May 1990): 620–624.

Jacobs, George, and Patrick Gallo. "Reading Alone Together: Enhancing Extensive Reading via Student-Student Cooperation." *Reading Online* 5 (February 2002). Retrieved from http://www.readingonline.org/articles/art_index.asp?HREF=/articles/jacobs/index.html.

Jacobs, Vicki A. "What Secondary Teachers Can Do to Teach Reading." *Harvard Education Letter* (September/October 1999): 1–2.

Jacobs, Vicki. "What Secondary Teachers Can Do to Teach Reading." *Harvard Education Letter* (November/December, 2001): 1–4.

Jaeger, Elizabeth L. "The Reading Specialist as Collaborative Consultant." *The Reading Teacher* 49 (May 1996): 622–629.

Jenkins, J., B. Matlock, and T. Slocum. "Approaches to Vocabulary Instruction: The Teaching of Individual Word Meanings and Practice in Deriving Word Meaning from Context." *Reading Research Quarterly* 24 (1989): 215–235.

Jenkinson, Edward B. "'I Don't Know What to Write About Today': Some Ideas for Journal Writing." *Phi Delta Kappan* 69 (June 1988a): 739.

Jenkinson, Edward B. "Learning to Write/Writing to Learn." *Phi Delta Kappan* 69 (June 1988b): 712–717.

Jenkinson, Edward B. "Practice Helps with Essay Exams." *Phi Delta Kappan* 69 (June 1988c): 726.

Jetton, Tamara, and Patricia Alexander. "Learning from Text: A Multidimensional and Developmental Perspective." In Michael Kamil, Peter Mosenthal, David Pearson, and Rebecca Barr (eds.), *The Handbook of Reading Research*. Vol. III. New York: Erlbaum, 2000, chap. 7.

Jetton, Tamara L., and Patricia A. Alexander. "Learning from Text: A Multidimensional and Developmental Perspective." *Reading Online* 5, no. 1: http://www.readingonline.org (2001, July/August).

Jody, M., and M. Saccardi. *Computer Conversations: Readers and Books Online*. Urbana, Ill.: National Council of Teachers of English, 1996.

Johnson, Andrew, and Jay Rasmussen. "Classifying and Super Word Web: Two Strategies to Improve Productive Vocabulary." *Journal of Adolescent & Adult Literacy* 43 (November 1998): 204–207.

Johnson, D., and B. Johnson. "Highlighting Vocabulary in Inferential Comprehension Instruction." *Journal of Reading* 29 (April 1986): 622–625.

Johnson, Denise. "Web Watch: Internet Resources to Assist Teachers with Struggling Readers." *Reading Online* 4 (April 2001). Retrieved from http://www.readingonline.org/electronic/elec_index.asp?HREF=/electronic/webmatch/struggling/index.html.

Johnson, Eric. *How to Achieve Competence in English*. Pittsburgh, Pa.: Dorrance, 1994.

Johnson, M. S., R. A. Kress, and J. J. Pikulski. *Informal Reading Inventories*. 2nd ed. Newark, Del.: International Reading Association, 1987.

Johnson-Weber, Mary. "Picture Books for Junior High." *Journal of Reading* 33 (December 1989): 219–220.

Johnston, Peter. "Literacy Assessment and the Future." *The Reading Teacher* 58 (April 2005): 684–686.

Johnston, Peter, and Paula Costello. "Principles for Literacy Assessment." *Reading Research Quarterly* 40 (April/May/June 2005): 256–267.

Johnston, Peter H. *Reading Comprehension Assessment: A Cognitive Basis*. Newark, Del.: International Reading Association, 1983.

Johnston, Peter H. "Teachers as Evaluation Experts." *The Reading Teacher* 40 (April 1987): 744–748.

Johnston, Peter H. *Choice Words: How Our Language Affects Children's Learning*. York, Maine: Stenhouse, 2004.

Jones, Janet Craven. "Reading and Study Skills: Problems in the Content Areas." *Journal of Reading* 31 (May 1988): 756–759.

Jossart, Sarah A. "Character Journals Aid Comprehension." *The Reading Teacher* 42 (November 1988): 180.

Kaczynski, Michelle, and Jill White. "Integrating Language Arts, Social Studies, and Science Through Technology." Handout for the International Reading Association Convention, San Diego, May 1999.

Kameenui, Edward J., Donald Carnine, and R. Freschi. "Effects of Text Construction and Instructional Procedures for Teaching Word Meanings on Comprehension and Recall." *Reading Research Quarterly* 17 (1982): 367–388.

Kapitzke, Cushla. "Information Literacy: The Changing Library." *Journal of Adolescent & Adult Literacy* 44 (February 2001): 450–456.

Kapitzke, Cushla, Samuela Bogitini, Min Chen, Greg Mac Neill, Diane Mayer, Bruce Muirhead, and Peter Renshaw. "Weaving Words with the Dreamweaver: Literacy, Indigeneity, and Technology." *Journal of Adolescent & Adult Literacy* 44 (December 2000/January 2001): 336–345.

Kerka, S. *New Technologies and Emerging Careers: Trends and Issues Alert*. Columbus, Ohio: ERIC Clearinghouse on Adult, Career, and Vocational Education, 1994.

Kibby, Michael W. "What Will Be the Demands of Literacy in the Workplace in the Next Millennium?" *Reading Research Quarterly* 35 (July/August/September 2000): 380–381.

Kinder, Diane, Bill Bursuck, and Michael Epstein. "An Evaluation of History Textbooks." *The Journal of Special Education* 25 (1992): 472–491.

Kirby, Dan, and Tom Liner, with Ruth Vinz. *Inside Out: Developmental Strategies for Teaching Writing.* 2nd ed. Portsmouth, N.H.: Heinemann, 1988.

Kirk, Samuel A., James J. Gallagher, and Nicholas J. Anastasiow. *Educating Exceptional Children.* 10th ed. Boston: Houghton Mifflin, 2003.

Kist, William. "Finding 'New Literacy' in Action: An Interdisciplinary High School Western Civilization Class." *Journal of Adolescent & Adult Literacy* 45 (February 2002): 368–377.

Klauer, K. "Intentional and Incidental Learning with Instructional Texts: A Meta-analysis for 1970–1980." *American Educational Research Journal* 21 (1984): 323–340.

Kletzien, Sharon B. "Strategy Use by Good and Poor Comprehenders Reading Expository Text of Differing Reading Levels." *Reading Research Quarterly* 26 (1991): 67–86.

Kletzien, Sharon B., and Maryanne R. Bednar. "Dynamic Assessment for At-Risk Readers." *Journal of Reading* 33 (April 1990): 528–533.

Kletzien, Sharon, and B. Hushion. "Reading Workshop: Reading, Writing, Thinking." *Journal of Reading* 35 (March 1992): 444–450.

Knickerbocker, Joan L., and James Rycik. "Growing into Literature: Adolescents' Literary Interpretation and Appreciation." *Journal of Adolescent & Adult Literacy* 46 (November 2002): 196–208.

Knifong, J., and B. Holtran. "A Search for Reading Difficulties Among Erred Word Problems." *Journal for Research in Mathematics Education* 8 (May 1977): 230–247.

Knight, Janice Evans. "Coding Journal Entries." *Journal of Reading* 34 (September 1990): 42–47.

Konopak, Bonnie C., Michael A. Martin, and Sarah H. Martin. "Reading and Writing: Aids to Learning in the Content Areas." *Journal of Reading* 31 (November 1987): 109–115.

Kress, Roy A. "Trends in Remedial Instruction." *Journal of Reading* 32 (January 1989): 370–372.

Kucer, Stephen. "Authenticity as the Basis for Instruction." *Language Arts* 68 (November 1991): 532–540.

Kueker, Joan. "Prereading Activities: A Key to Comprehension." Paper presented at the International Conference on Learning Disabilities, Austin, Texas, 1990.

Kuhn, Melanie. "Helping Students Become Accurate, Expressive Readers: Fluency Instruction for Small Groups." *The Reading Teacher* 58 (December 2004/January 2005): 338–344.

Kuhn, M. E., and S. Stahl. *Fluency: A Review of Developmental and Remedial Practices* (CIERA Rep. No. 2-008). Ann Arbor: Center for the Study of Reading Achievement, 2000.

Kymes, Angel. "Teaching Online Comprehension Strategies Using Think-Alouds." *Journal of Adolescent & Adult Literacy* 48 (March 2005): 492–500.

Laflamme, John G. "The Effect of Multiple Exposure Vocabulary Method and the Target Reading/Writing Strategy on Test Scores." *Journal of Adolescent & Adult Literacy* 40 (1997): 372–384.

Lambeth, William. "Remaking Schools for the Information Age: What Media Centers Can and Must Do." *T.H.E. Journal* 25 (June 1998): 78–79.

Laminack, Lester. "Mr. T Leads the Class: The Language Experience Approach and Science." *Science and Children* 24 (1987): 41–42.

Landers, D. M., W. Maxwell, J. Butler, and L. Fagan. "Developing Thinking Skills in Physical Education. In A. L. Costa (ed.), *Developing Minds: Resource Book for Teaching Thinking.* Alexandria, Va.: Association for Supervision and Curriculum Development, 2001, pp. 343–351.

Landis, David. "Reading Engaged Readers: A Cross-Cultural Perspective." *Journal of Adolescent & Adult Literacy* 45 (March 2002): 472–480.

Landrum, Judith E. "Adolescent Novels That Feature Characters with Disabilities: An Annotated Bibliography." *Journal of Adolescent & Adult Literacy* 42 (December 1998/January 1999): 284–290.

Landrum, Judith. "Selecting Intermediate Novels That Feature Characters with Disabilities." *The Reading Teacher* 55 (November 2001): 252–258.

Langer, Judith A. "From Theory to Practice: A Prereading Plan." *Journal of Reading* 25 (November 1981): 152–156.

Langer, Judith A. "Learning Through Writing: Study Skills in the Content Areas." *Journal of Reading* 29 (February 1986): 400–406.

Langer, Judith A. *Envisioning Literature.* New York: Teachers College Press, 1995.

Langer, Judith, and Arthur Applebee. *How Writing Shapes Thinking: A Study of Teaching and Learning.* Urbana, Ill.: National Council of Teachers of English, 1987.

Lapp, Diane, James Flood, and Nancy Farnan. *Content Area Reading and Learning: Instructional Strategies.* Englewood Cliffs, N.J.: Prentice-Hall, 1989.

Lapp, Diane, James Flood, and Douglas Fisher. "Intermediality: How the Use of Multiple Media Enhances Learning." *The Reading Teacher* 52 (April 1999): 776–780.

Larson, R., L. Boswell, T. Kanold, and L. Stiff. *Course 2 Math.* Evanston, Ill.: McDougal Littell, 2005.

Laspina, James Andrew. "The Locus of Language in Digital Space." *Language Arts* 78 (January 2001): 245–254.

Latta, B. Dawn. "In-Process and Retrospective Journals: Putting Writers Back in Writing Processes." *English Journal* 80 (January 1991): 60–66.

Leal, Dorothy J., and Julia Chamberlain-Solecki. "A Newbery Medal–Winning Combination: High Student Interest Plus Appropriate Reading Levels." *The Reading Teacher* 51 (May 1998): 712–715.

Lederer, Robert. *Anguished English.* Charleston, S.C.: Wyrick, 1987.

Lehr, Susan, and Deborah L. Thompson. "The Dynamic Nature of Response: Children Reading and Responding to *Maniac Magee* and *The Friendship.*" *The Reading Teacher* 53 (March 2000): 480–493.

Lemke, Jay L. "The Literacies of Science." In E. Wendy Saul (ed.), *Crossing Borders in Literacy and Science Instruction: Perspectives on Theory and Practice.* Newark, Del.: International Reading Association, 2004, pp. 33–47.

Lerner, Janet. *Learning Disabilities: Theories, Diagnosis and Teaching Strategies.* 7th ed. Boston: Houghton Mifflin, 1997.

Leu, Donald J. "The New Literacies: Research on Reading Instruction with the Internet." In Alan E. Farstrup and S. Jay Samuels (eds.), *What Research Has to Say About Reading Instruction.* 3rd ed. Newark, Del.: International Reading Association, 2002, pp. 310–336.

Leu, Donald J., Jr., and Deborah Diadiun Leu. *Teaching with the Internet: Lessons from the Classroom.* Norwood, Mass.: Christopher-Gordon, 1999.

Levin-Epstein, Michael, Corey Murray, and Dennis Pierce. "Across-the-Board Instruction." *eSchool News* 8 (February 2005): 21–26.

Lewandowski, Lawrence J., and Brian K. Martens. "Test Review: Selecting and Evaluating Standardized Reading Tests." *Journal of Reading* 33 (February 1990): 384–388.

Lewis, J. "Redefining Critical Reading for College Critical Thinking Courses." *Journal of Reading* 34 (March 1991): 420–423.

Lipson, Marjorie, S. Valencia, K. Wixson, and C. Peters. "Integration and Thematic Teaching: Integration to Improve Teaching and Learning." *Language Arts* 70 (April 1993): 252–263.

Littrell, Annette B. *"My Space": Using Blogs as Literature Journals with Adolescents.* Dissertation. Cookeville: Tennessee Technological University, 2005.

Livo, Norma J., and Sandra A. Rietz. *Storytelling Activities.* Englewood, Colo.: Libraries Unlimited, 1987.

Lloyd, Carol V. "Engaging Students at the Top (Without Leaving the Rest Behind)." *Journal of Adolescent & Adult Literacy* 42 (November 1998): 184–191.

Lloyd, Carol, and J. Mitchell. "Coping with Too Many Concepts in Science Texts." *Journal of Reading* 32 (March 1989): 542–549.

Lloyd, Susan. "Using Comprehension Strategies as a Springboard for Student Talk." *Journal of Adolescent & Adult Literacy* 48 (October 2004): 114–124.

"Local Educators Gain Insight from Vanderbilt's 'Virtual Watershed' Science Program." *Crossville* (Tennessee) *Chronicle* (August 3, 1999): 3C.

Louie, Belinda. "Development of Empathetic Responses with Multicultural Literature." *Journal of Adolescent & Adult Literacy* 48 (April 2005): 566–578.

Love, Kristina. "Mapping Online Discussion in Senior English." *Journal of Adolescent & Adult Literacy* 45 (February 2002): 382–396.

Love, Mary Susan. "Multimodality of Learning Through Anchored Instruction." *Journal of Adolescent & Adult Literacy* 48 (December 2004/January 2005): 300–310.

Lowe, Ross E., Charles A. Malouf, and Annette R. Jacobson. *Consumer Education and Economics.* 4th ed. New York: Glencoe McGraw-Hill, 1997.

Lu, Mei-Yu. *Language Learning in Social and Cultural Contexts.* Bloomington, Ind.: ERIC Clearinghouse on Reading, English, and Communication Digest #131, September 1998.

Lubell, M., and R. Townsend. "A Strategy for Teaching Complex Prose Structures." *Journal of Reading* 33 (November 1989): 102–106.

Luke, Allan, and John Elkins. "Reinventing Literacy in 'New Times.'" *Journal of Adolescent & Adult Literacy* 41 (September 1998): 4–7.

Luke, C. "Media and Cultural Studies in Australia." *Journal of Adolescent & Adult Literacy* 42 (1999): 622–626.

Luna, Catherine. "Learning from Diverse Learners: (Re)writing Academic Literacies and Learning Disabilities in College." *Journal of Adolescent & Adult Literacy* 45 (April 2002): 596–605.

Lunsford, Andrea, and Robert Connors. *Easy Writer.* New York: St. Martin's Press, 1997.

Mace, Jane. *Talking About Literacy.* New York: Routledge, 1992.

MacGinitie, Walter H. "Some Limits of Assessment." *Journal of Reading* 36 (April 1993): 556–560.

Maimon, Elaine P. "Cultivating the Prose Garden." *Phi Delta Kappan* 69 (June 1988): 734–739.

Mallow, J. "Reading Science." *Journal of Reading* 34 (February 1991): 324–338.

Mandler, J., and N. Johnson. "Remembrance of Things Parsed: Story Structure and Recall." *Cognitive Psychology* 9 (1977): 111–151.

Manion, Betty Byrne. "Writing Workshop in Junior High School: It's Worth the Time." *Journal of Reading* 32 (November 1988): 154–157.

Manning, M. Lee, and Leroy G. Baruth. *Teaching Learners At-Risk*. Norwood, Mass.: Christopher-Gordon, 2000.

Manz, Suzanne Liff. "A Strategy for Previewing Textbooks: Teaching Readers to Become THIEVES." *The Reading Teacher* 55 (February 2002): 434–435.

Margulies, Nancy. *Mapping Inner Space*. Tucson, Ariz.: Zephyr Press, 1991.

Maring, Gerald. "Cyber Mentoring." http://depts.washington.edu/wctl/cybermentor.htm. 2001–2002. Accessed May 15, 2002.

Maring, Gerald H. "Video Conferencing." International Reading Association Convention, San Francisco, California, May 1, 2002.

Marlett, Paul, and Christine Gordon. "The Use of Alternative Texts in Physical Education." *Journal of Adolescent & Adult Literacy* 48 (November 2004): 228–237.

Marzano, R., E. Brandt, C. Hughes, B. Jones, B. Presseisen, S. Rankin, and C. Suhor. *Dimensions of Thinking: A Framework for Curriculum and Instruction*. Alexandria, Va.: Association for Supervision and Curriculum Development, 1988.

Mastropieri, Margo M., and Thomas E. Scruggs. *The Inclusive Classroom: Strategies for Effective Instruction*. Columbus, Ohio: Prentice Hall/Merrill, 2000.

Matteson, G., and R. Jensen. *Teaching Units from Agricultural Literacy*. Madison, Wis.: University of Wisconsin, 1994.

Matthews, Michael. "Electronic Literacy and the Limited English Proficient Student." *Reading Online* 3 (May 2000). Retrieved from http://www.readingonline.org/electronic/elec_index.asp?HREF=/electronic/matthews/index.html.

McDermott, J. Cynthia, and Sharon Setoguchi. "Collaborations That Create Real-World Literacy Experiences." *Journal of Adolescent & Adult Literacy* 42 (February 1999): 396–397.

McDougal Littell. *Language Network*. Boston: McDougal Littell, 2001.

McGee, Lea M., and Gail E. Tompkins. "Literature-Based Reading Instruction: What's Guiding the Instruction?" *Language Arts* 72 (October 1995): 405–414.

McGrath, Beth. "Partners in Learning: Twelve Ways Technology Changes the Teacher-Student Relationship." *T.H.E. Journal* 25 (April 1998): 58–61.

McKenna, M., R. Robinson, and J. Miller. "Whole Language: A Research Agenda for the Nineties." *Educational Researcher* 19 (November 1990): 3–6.

McLaughlin, Harry G. "SMOG Grading—A New Readability Formula." *Journal of Reading* 12 (May 1969): 639–646.

McLaughlin, Maureen, and Glenn DeVoogd. "Critical Literacy as Comprehension: Expanding Reader Response." *Journal of Adolescent & Adult Literacy* 48 (September 2004): 52–82.

McLaughlin, Maureen, and Mary Beth Allen. *Guided Comprehension: A Teaching Model for Grades 3–8*. Newark, Del.: International Reading Association, 2002.

McTighe, J., and F. Lyman, Jr. "Cueing Thinking in the Classroom: The Promise of Theory-Embedded Tools." *Educational Leadership* 45 (April 1988): 18–24.

Mealey, D. L., B. C. Konopak, M. A. Duchein, D. W. Frazier, T. R. Host, and C. Nobles. "Student, Teacher, and Expert Differences in Identifying Important Content Area Vocabulary." In N. D. Padak, T. V. Rasinski, and J. Logan (eds.), *Literary Research and Practice: Foundations for the Year 2000*. Fourteenth Yearbook of the College Reading Association. Pittsburg, Kans.: College Reading Association, 1992, pp. 117–123.

Medwin, Sherry, and Michael O'Donovan. "Computer-Mediated Discussion of Literature: An Opportunity for Collaboration, Inquiry, and Research." Paper presented at the National Council of Teachers of English Convention, San Diego, California, 1995.

Meeks, Lynn Langer. "Making English Classrooms Happier Places to Learn." *English Journal* 88 (March 1999): 73–80.

Memory, David M., and Carol Y. Yoder. "Improving Concentration in Content Classrooms." *Journal of Reading* 31 (February 1988): 426–435.

Merkley, Donna J., Denise Schmidt, and Gayle Allen. "Addressing the English Language Arts Technology Standard in a Secondary Reading Methodology Course." *Journal of Adolescent & Adult Literacy* 45 (November 2001): 220–231.

Meyers, Maria. "Using Cognitive Strategies to Enhance Second Language Learning." In Eileen Wood, Vera E. Woloshyn, and Teena Willoughby (eds.), *Cognitive Strategy Instruction for Middle and High Schools*. Brookline, Mass.: Brookline Books, 1995, pp. 226–244.

Mike, Dennis G. "Internet in the Schools: A Literacy Perspective." *Journal of Adolescent & Adult Literacy* 40 (September 1996): 4–13.

Mikulecky, Larry. "Real-World Literacy Demands: How They've Changed and What Teachers Can Do." In Diane Lapp, James Flood, and Nancy Farnan (eds.), *Content Area*

Reading and Learning: Instructional Strategies. Boston: Allyn & Bacon, 1996, pp. 153–163.

Mikulecky, Larry. "What Will Be the Demands of Literacy in the Workplace in the Next Millennium?" *Reading Research Quarterly* 35 (July/August/September 2000): 379–380.

Miller, G., and P. Gildea. "How Children Learn Words." *Scientific American* 257 (1987): 94–99.

Miller, Terry. "The Place of Picture Books in Middle-Level Classrooms." *Journal of Adolescent & Adult Literacy* 41 (February 1998): 376–381.

Milliken, Mark. "A Fifth-Grade Class Uses Portfolios." In Donald H. Graves and Bonnie S. Sunstein (eds.), *Portfolio Portraits.* Portsmouth, N.H.: Heinemann, 1992, pp. 34–44.

Mills-Courts, Karen, and Minda Rae Amiran. "Metacognition and the Use of Portfolios." In Pat Belanoff and Marcia Dickson (eds.), *Portfolios: Process and Product.* Portsmouth, N.H.: Boynton/Cook, 1991, pp. 101–112.

Mitchell, Judith P., Tammy V. Abernathy, and Linda P. Gowans. "Making Sense of Literacy Portfolios: A Four-Step Plan." *Journal of Adolescent & Adult Literacy* 41 (February 1998): 384–389.

Mohnsen, Bonnie. "Stretching Bodies and Minds Through Technology." *Educational Leadership* 55 (November 1997): 46–48.

Moje, Elizabeth, Kathryn Ciechanowski, Katherine Kramer, Lindsay Ellis, Rosario Carrillo, and Tehani Collazo. "Working Toward Third Space in Content Area Literacy: An Examination of Everyday Funds of Knowledge and Discourse." *Reading Research Quarterly* 39 (2004): 38–70.

Moje, Elizabeth B., and Dolores Handy. "Using Literacy to Modify Traditional Assessments: Alternatives for Teaching and Assessing Content Understanding." *Journal of Reading* 38 (May 1995): 612–625.

Moore, David, and A. Murphy. "Reading Programs." In D. Alvermann, D. Moore, and M. Conley (eds.), *Research Within Reach: Secondary School Reading.* Newark, Del.: International Reading Association, 1987.

Moore, David W., John E. Readence, and Robert J. Rickelman. *Prereading Activities for Content Area Reading and Learning.* 2nd ed. Newark, Del.: International Reading Association, 1989.

Moore, M. A. "Electronic Dialoguing: An Avenue to Literacy." *The Reading Teacher* 45 (December 1991): 280–286.

Morgan, H., and S. Berg-O'Halloran. "Using Music as a Text." *Journal of Reading* 32 (February 1989): 458–459.

Morrow, Lesley Mandel. "Retelling Stories as a Diagnostic Tool." In Susan Mandel Glazer, Lyndon W. Searfoss, and Lance H. Gentile (eds.), *Reexamining Reading Diagnosis:*

New Trends and Procedures. Newark, Del.: International Reading Association, 1989, pp. 128–149.

Mosenthal, Peter B., and Irwin S. Kirsch. "Document Strategies: Cycle Strategies in Document Search: From Here to There to Wherever." *Journal of Reading* 36 (November 1992): 238–242.

Mossberg, Walt. "Personal Technology: Search Engines Can Cut Time You Waste on the Web." Personal Technology from the *Wall Street Journal.* On-line at http://ptech.wsj.com/archive/ptech-19981112.html (12 November, 1998).

Moulton, Margaret R. "The Multigenre Paper: Increasing Interest, Motivation, and Functionality in Research." *Journal of Adolescent & Adult Literacy* 42 (April 1999): 528–539.

Mullis, Ina V. S., Jay R. Campbell, and Alan E. Farstrup. *Executive Summary of the NAEP 1992 Reading Report Card for the Nation and the States.* Washington, D.C.: Government Printing Office, 1993.

Murphy, Sandra, and Mary Ann Smith. *Writing Portfolios: A Bridge from Teaching to Assessment.* Markham, Ontario: Pippin, 1992.

Murray, Donald. *A Teacher Teaches Writing: A Practical Method of Teaching Composition.* New York: Houghton Mifflin, 1968.

Musthafa, Bachrudin. "Nurturing Children's Response to Literature in the Classroom Context." ERIC no: ED 398577, 1996.

Myers, W. D. *Fallen Angels.* New York: Scholastic, 1988.

"NAEP Achievement Standards Draw Criticism." *Reading Today* 11 (December 1993/January 1994): 12.

"NAEP Results Show Heartening Gains." *Reading Today* 16 (April–May 1999): 1, 4–5.

Nagy, William, P. A. Herman, and R. C. Anderson. "Learning Words from Context." *Reading Research Quarterly* 20 (1985): 233–253.

Nagy, William, and James Scott. "Vocabulary Processes." In Michael Kamil, Peter Mosenthal, P. David Pearson, and Rebecca Barr (eds.), *Handbook of Reading Research,* Vol. 3. Mahwah, N.J.: Erlbaum, 2000, pp. 269–284.

Naidoo, Beverly. "Crossing Boundaries Through Fiction: A Personal Account." *English in Education* 29 (1995): 4–13.

National Association of State Directors of Career Technical Education Consortium. *Career Technical Education: An Essential Component of the Total Educational System.* Washington D.C., 2001.

National Center for Education Statistics. "Reading Literacy in the United States: Findings from the IEA Reading Literacy Study." Washington, D.C.: U.S. Department of Education, 1996.

National Council of Teachers of Mathematics. *Curriculum and Evaluation Standards.* Reston, Va.: NCTM, 1989.

National Institute of Child Health and Human Development. *Teaching Children to Read: An Evidence-Based Assessment of the Scientific Research Literature on Reading and Its Implications for Reading Instruction.* Report of the National Reading Panel (NIH Publication No. 00-4769). Washington, D.C.: U.S. Government Printing Office, 2000.

Nelson, G. "Culture's Role in Reading Comprehension: A Schema Theoretical Approach." *Journal of Reading* 30 (February 1987): 424–429.

Nelson, G. "A Study of Middle School Science Textbooks—Project 2061." Washington, D.C.: American Association for the Advancement of Science, 1999.

Neubert, Gloria A., and Sally J. McNelis. "Peer Response: Teaching Specific Revision Suggestions." *English Journal* 79 (September 1990): 52–56.

Newly, Timothy J., Donald A. Stepich, James D. Lehman, and James D. Russell. *Instructional Technology for Teaching and Learning.* Columbus, Ohio: Merrill, 2000.

"New Study Supports Value of School Libraries." *Reading Online* 21 (April/May 2004). Retrieved from http://www.readingonline.org.

Ngeow, Karen. "Motivation and Transfer in Language Learning." *Education Digest* #138 (EDO-98-11). Bloomington, Ind.: ERIC Clearinghouse on Reading, English and Communication, November 1998.

Nilsen, Alleen Pace, and Don L. F. Nilsen. "The Straw Man Meets His Match: Six Arguments for Studying Humor in English Classes." *English Journal* 88 (March 1999): 34–42.

Nilsson, Nina. "How Does Hispanic Portrayal in Children's Books Measure Up After 40 Years? The Answer Is 'It Depends.'" *The Reading Teacher* 58 (March 2005): 534–548.

Noble, Susan. "Learning Standards Will Revitalize Schools." *Richmond Times-Dispatch* (May 16, 1999): G1.

Nolan, T. "Self-Questioning and Prediction: Combining Metacognitive Strategies." *Journal of Reading* 35 (October 1991): 132–138.

Noll, Elizabeth. "Social Issues and Literature Circles with Adolescents." *Journal of Reading* 38 (October 1994): 88–93.

Northwest Regional Educational Laboratory. *Scoring 6+1 Trait Writing.* Retrieved June 11, 2003, from http://www.nwrel.org/assessment/definitions.asp?d=1.

Norton-Meier, Lori. "Joining the Video-Game Literacy Club: A Reluctant Mother Tries to Join the 'Flow.'" *Journal of Adolescent & Adult Literacy* 48 (February 2005): 428–432.

Noskin, David Peter. "Teaching Writing in the High School: Fifteen Years in the Making." *English Journal* 90 (September 2000): 34–38.

Nua Internet Surveys. Computer Scope Ltd., Dublin, Ireland. http://www.nua.com, 2002.

Oberlin, Kelly J., and Sherrie L. Shugarman. "Purposeful Writing Activities for Students in Middle School." *Journal of Reading* 31 (May 1988): 720–723.

O'Donnell, Holly. "ERIC/RCS Report: Children Writing: Process and Development." *Language Arts* 56 (October 1979): 839–843.

Ogle, Donna. "A Teaching Model That Develops Active Reading of Expository Text." *The Reading Teacher* 39 (May 1986): 564–570.

Ogle, Donna. "Make It Visual: A Picture Is Worth a Thousand Words." In Maureen McLaughlin and Mary Ellen Vogt (eds.), *Creativity and Innovation in Content Area Teaching.* Norwood, Mass.: Christopher-Gordon, 2000, pp. 55–71.

Oley, Elizabeth. "Information Retrieval in the Classroom." *Journal of Reading* 32 (April 1989): 590–597.

Ollmann, Hilda E. "Creating High Level Thinking with Reading Response." *Journal of Adolescent & Adult Literacy* 39 (April 1996): 576–581.

Oral History Project Consortium. *Oral History Project Grades K–16.* CD. Pennsylvania: Oral History Project Consortium, BCD Interactive, 2000.

Owston, R. D., S. Murphy, and H. H. Wideman. "The Effects of Word Processing on Students' Writing Quality and Revision Strategies." *Research in the Teaching of English* 26 (1992): 249–276.

Paeth, Beverly, et al. "Kentucky Telecommunication Writing Program." Handout for the National Council of Teachers of English Convention, San Diego, California, 1995.

Pailliotet, Ann Watts. "Critical Media Literacy and Values: Connecting with the 5 Ws." In P. Schmidt and Ann Watts Pailliotet (eds.), *Exploring Values Through Literature, Multimedia and Literacy Events.* Newark, Del.: International Reading Association, 2001, pp. 20–46.

Palincsar, AnnMarie, and Ann Brown. *Reciprocal Teaching of Comprehension Monitoring Activities.* Technical Report No. 269. Champaign, Ill.: Center for the Study of Reading, 1984.

Palincsar, AnnMarie, and Ann Brown. "Interactive Teaching to Promote Independent Learning from Text." *The Reading Teacher* 39 (May 1986): 771–777.

Pallas, A., G. Natriello, and E. McDill. "The Changing Nature of the Disadvantaged Population: Current Dimensions and Future Trends." *Educational Researcher* 18 (June–July 1989): 16–22.

Pardo, Laura. "What Every Teacher Needs to Know About Comprehension." *The Reading Teacher* 58 (November 2004): 272–280.

Paterson, Katherine. *Bridge to Terabithia.* New York: Crowell, 1987.

Patthey-Chavez, G. Genevieve, Lindsay Clare Matsumura, and Rosa Valdes. "Investigating the Process Approach to Writing Instruction in Urban Middle Schools." *Journal of Adolescent & Adult Literacy* 47 (March 2004): 462–477.

Pauk, Walter. "On Scholarship: Advice to High School Students." *The Reading Teacher* 17 (November 1963): 73–78.

Pauk, Walter. *How to Study in College.* 7th ed. Boston: Houghton Mifflin, 2001.

Pavonetti, Linda M. "Joan Lowery Nixon: The Grand Dame of Young Adult Mystery." *Journal of Adolescent & Adult Literacy* 39 (March 1996): 454–461.

Pearson, Jenny Watson, and Carol M. Santa. "Students as Researchers of Their Own Learning." *Journal of Reading* 38 (March 1995): 462–469.

Peavy, L., and U. Smith. *Pioneer Women: The Lives of Women on the Frontier.* New York: Smithmark, 1996.

Pellicano, Richard. "At-Risk: A View of Social Advantage." *Educational Leadership* 44 (1987): 47–50.

Pellowski, Ann. *The Story Vine.* New York: Macmillan, 1984.

Perkins, David. *Outsmarting: The Emerging Science of Learnable Intelligence.* New York: Free Press, 1995.

Peters, Tim, Kathy Schubeck, and Karen Hopkins. "A Thematic Approach: Theory and Practice at the Aleknagik School." *Phi Delta Kappan* 76 (April 1995): 633–636.

Pflaum, Susanna, and Penny Bishop. "Student Perceptions of Reading Engagement: Learning from the Learners." *Journal of Adolescent & Adult Literacy* 48 (November 2004): 202–213.

Piazza, Carolyn L., and Carl M. Tomlinson. "A Concert of Writers." *Language Arts* 62 (February 1985): 150–158.

Pinnell, Gay S., and M. M. Jaggar. "Oral Language: Speaking and Listening in Elementary Classrooms." In James Flood, Diane Lapp, J. Squire, and J. Jensen (eds.), *Handbook of Research on Teaching the English Language Arts.* Mahwah, N.J.: Erlbaum, 2003, pp. 881–913.

Pisha, Bart, and Peggy Coyne. "Jumping Off the Page: Content Area Curriculum for the Internet Age." *Reading Online* 5 (November 2001): 1–18. Retrieved from http://www.readingonline.org.

Platt, Jennifer M., and Judith L. Olson. *Teaching Adolescents with Mild Disabilities.* Pacific Grove, Calif.: Brooks/Cole, 1997.

Plank, Stephen B. "A Question of Balance: CTE, Academic Courses: High School Perspective and Student Achievement." *Journal of Vocation Research* 26, no. 3, 2001.

Poindexter, Candace C. "Classroom Strategies That Convinced Content Area Teachers They Could Teach Reading, Too." *Journal of Reading* 38 (October 1994): 134.

Polloway, Edward A., and James R. Patton. *Strategies for Teaching Learners with Special Needs.* New York: Macmillan, 1993.

Polloway, Edward A., James R. Patton, and Loretta Serna. *Strategies for Teaching Learners with Special Needs.* Englewood Cliffs, N.J.: Prentice-Hall, 2001.

Pool, Carolyn R. "A New Digital Literacy: A Conversation with Paul Gilster." *Educational Leadership* 55 (November 1997): 6–11.

Popham, W. James. "Teaching to the Test?" *Educational Leadership* 58 (March 2001): 16–20.

Porter, Dwight. "Précis Writing in the ESL Classroom." *Journal of Reading* 33 (February 1990): 381.

Power, Brenda Miller. "Nutshells, Monkeys, and the Writer's Craft." *Voices from the Middle* 3 (April 1996): 10–15.

Powers, R. D., W. A. Sumner, and B. E. Kearl. "A Recalculation of Four Adult Readability Formulas." *Journal of Educational Psychology* 49 (April 1958): 99–105.

Prensky, M. "Digital Natives, Digital Immigrants." *On the Horizon* 9, no. 5 (2001): 1–6.

Pressley, Michael. "What Should Comprehension Instruction Be the Instruction Of?" In M. L. Kamil, P. Mosenthal, P. D. Pearson, and R. Barr (eds.), *Handbook of Reading Research.* Vol. 3. Mahwah, N.J.: Erlbaum, 2000.

Pressley, Michael. "Metacognition and Self-Regulated Comprehension." In Alan E. Farstrup and S. Jay Samuels (eds.), *What Research Has to Say About Reading Instruction.* 3rd ed. Newark, Del.: International Reading Association, 2002, pp. 291–309.

Pritchard, Ruie Jane. "Developing Writing Prompts for Reading Response and Analysis." *English Journal* 82 (March 1993): 24–32.

Proctor, Vikki, and Ken Kantor. "Social Justice Notebooks." *Voices from the Middle* 3 (April 1996): 31–35.

Professional Standards and Ethics Committee and the Advisory Group to the National Council of Accreditation of Teacher Education Joint Task Force. *Standards for Reading Professionals.* Newark, Del.: International Reading Association, 1998.

Purves, Alan C. *Elements of Writing About a Literary Work.* Champaign, Ill.: National Council of Teachers of English, 1968.

Quatroche, Diana. "Helping the Underachiever in Reading." ERIC Digest 141. Bloomington, Ind.: ERIC Clearinghouse on Reading, English and Communication, 1999.

Quatroche, Diana J., Rita M. Bean, and Rebecca L. Hamilton. "The Role of the Reading Specialist: A Review of Research." *The Reading Teacher* 55 (November 2001): 282–294.

Quinn, Kathleen Benson, Bernadette Barone, Janine Kearns, Susan A. Stackhouse, and Marie Ellen Zimmerman.

"Using a Novel Unit to Help Understand and Prevent Bullying in Schools." *Journal of Adolescent & Adult Literacy* 46 (April 2003): 582–591.

Rakes, Glenda C., Thomas A. Rakes, and Lana J. Smith. "Using Visuals to Enhance Secondary Students' Reading Comprehension of Expository Texts." *Journal of Adolescent & Adult Literacy* 39 (September 1995): 46–54.

Rakes, Sondra K., and Lana J. Smith. "Strengthening Comprehension and Recall Through the Principle of Recitation." *Journal of Reading* 31 (December 1987): 260–263.

Rand Corporation. *Reading for Understanding: Toward an R&D Program in Reading Comprehension.* Washington, D.C.: Rand Corporation, 2002.

Randall, Sally N. "Information Charts: A Strategy for Organizing Student Research." *Journal of Adolescent & Adult Literacy* 39 (April 1996): 536–542.

Raphael, Taffy. "Teaching Question Answer Relationships, Revisited." *The Reading Teacher* 39 (February 1986): 516–522.

Raphael, Taffy E., and Carol Sue Englert. "Writing and Reading: Partners in Constructing Meaning." *The Reading Teacher* 43 (February 1990): 388–400.

Raphael, Taffy, Carol Sue Englert, and Becky Kirschner. *The Impact of Text Structure Instruction and Social Context on Students' Comprehension and Production of Expository Text.* Research Series No. 177. East Lansing, Mich.: Institute for Research on Teaching, 1986.

Raphael, Taffy E., Becky W. Kirschner, and Carol Sue Englert. "Expository Writing Program: Making Connections Between Reading and Writing." *The Reading Teacher* 41 (April 1988): 790–795.

Rasinski, Timothy. "Speed Does Matter in Reading." *The Reading Teacher* 54 (October 2000): 146–151.

Rasinski, Timothy V., and James V. Hoffman. "Oral Reading in the School Literacy Curriculum." *Reading Research Quarterly* 38 (October/November 2003): 510–522.

Ratekin, N., M. Simpson, D. E. Alvermann, and E. K. Dishner. "Why Content Teachers Resist Reading Instruction." *Journal of Reading* 28 (February 1985): 432–437.

Raymond, Margaret E., and Eric A. Hanushek. "High Stakes Research." *Education Next* (Spring 2003). Retrieved from http://www.educationnext.org/20033/48.html.

Readence, John E., and Michael A. Martin. "Comprehension Assessment: Alternatives to Standardized Tests." In Susan Mandel Glazer, Lyndon W. Searfoss, and Lance M. Gentile (eds.), *Reexamining Reading Diagnosis: New Trends and Procedures.* Newark, Del.: International Reading Association, 1989, pp. 67–80.

"Reading." *The Nation's Report Card.* Retrieved from http://nces.ed.gov/nationsreport card/reading/results2002/.

Recht, Donna. "Teaching Summarizing Skills." *The Reading Teacher* 37 (March 1984): 675–677.

Reese, Susan. "Techniques: Connecting Education and Careers." *Agriculture Education* 76 (February 2001): 1–17.

Reid, J. M. "English as a Second Language Composition in Higher Education: The Expectations of the Academic Audience." In D. M. Johnson and D. H. Roen (eds.), *Richness in Writing.* New York: Longman, 1989, pp. 220–234.

Reinking, D., D. Mealey, and V. Ridgeway. "Developing Preservice Teachers' Conditional Knowledge of Content Area Strategies." *Journal of Reading* 36 (March 1993): 458–469.

Rekrut, Martha D. "Collaborative Research." *Journal of Adolescent & Adult Literacy* 41 (September 1997): 26–34.

Rekrut, Martha D. "Using the Internet in Classroom Instruction: A Primer for Teachers." *Journal of Adolescent & Adult Literacy* 42 (April 1999): 546–557.

Renner, S., and J. Carter. "Comprehending Text—Appreciating Diversity Through Folklore." *Journal of Reading* 34 (May 1992): 602–605.

Reynolds, Patricia. "Evaluating ESL and College Composition Texts for Teaching the Argumentative Rhetorical Form." *Journal of Reading* 36 (March 1993): 474–479.

Rhoder, Carol. "Mindful Reading: Strategy Training That Facilitates Transfer." *Journal of Adolescent & Adult Literacy* 45 (March 2002): 498–512.

Rhoder, Carol, and Patricia Huerster. "Use Dictionaries for Word Learning with Caution." *Journal of Adolescent & Adult Literacy* 45, no. 8 (May 2002): 730–735.

Richardson, Judy S. "Great Read-Alouds for Prospective Teachers and Secondary Students." *Journal of Reading* 38 (October 1994a): 98–103.

Richardson, Judy S. "A Read-Aloud for Science Classrooms." *Journal of Reading* 38 (September 1994b): 62–65.

Richardson, Judy S. "A Read-Aloud for Social Studies Classrooms." *Journal of Reading* 38 (February 1995): 402–404.

Richardson, Judy S., and Margaret Breen. "A Read-Aloud for Science." *Journal of Adolescent & Adult Literacy* 39 (March 1996): 504–506.

Richardson, Will. "Metablognition." *Weblogg-Ed* (2004). Retrieved July 28, 2005, from http://weblogg-ed.com/2004/04/27.

Richek, Margaret Ann, Lynne K. List, and Janet W. Lerner. *Reading Problems: Assessment and Teaching Strategies.* Englewood Cliffs, N.J.: Prentice-Hall, 1989.

Rief, Linda. "Eighth Grade: Finding the Value in Evaluation." In Donald H. Graves and Bonnie S. Sunstein (eds.), *Portfolio Portraits.* Portsmouth, N.H.: Heinemann, 1992, pp. 45–60.

Rigg, P. "Whole Language in Adult ESL Programs." *ERIC/CLL News Bulletin* 13 (1990): 1.4–5.8.

Robbins, Bruce, and Kris Fischer. "Vaporizing Classroom Walls: The Writing Workshop Goes Electric." *Voices from the Middle* 3 (April 1996): 25–30.

Roberson, Dana L., Jim Flowers, and Gary E. Moore. "The Status of Academic and Agricultural Education in North Carolina." *Journal of Career and Technical Education* 17 (Spring 2001): 51–59.

Robinson, Francis P. *Effective Study*. Rev. ed. New York: Harper and Row, 1961, chap. 2.

Roe, Betty D. "Using Technology for Content Area Literacy." In Shelley B. Wepner, William J. Valmont, and Richard Thurlow (eds), *Linking Literacy and Technology: A Guide for K–8 Classrooms*. Newark, Del.: International Reading Association, 2000, p. 155.

Roe, Betty D., and Elinor P. Ross. *Integrating Language Arts Through Literature & Thematic Units*. Boston: Pearson/Allyn and Bacon, 2006.

Roe, Betty D., and Sandy Smith. "TALK: Talking About Literature with Kids." Unpublished project description. Cookeville: Tennessee Technological University, 1996.

Roe, Betty D., and Sandy Smith. "University/Public Schools Keypals Project: A Collaborative Effort for Electronic Literature Conversations." In *Rethinking Technology and Learning Through Technology*. Proceedings of the Mid-South Instructional Technology Conference. Murfreesboro, Tenn.: Mid-South Technology Conference, 1997.

Roe, Betty D., Sandy H. Smith, and Paul C. Burns. *Teaching Reading in Today's Elementary Schools*. Boston: Houghton Mifflin, 2005.

Romano, Tom. *Writing with Passion: Life Stories, Multiple Genres*. Portsmouth, N.H.: Boynton/Cook, 1995.

Romano, Tom. "Crafting Authentic Voice." *Voices from the Middle* 3 (April 1996): 5–9.

Romano, Tom. *Blending Genre, Altering Style*. Portsmouth, N.H.: Boynton/Cook, 2000.

Roseman, Jo Ellen. *American Association for the Advancement of Science Project 2061*. Washington, D.C.: American Association for the Advancement of Science, 1999.

Rosenberg, E., H. Gurney, and V. Harlin. *Investigating Your Health*. Rev. ed. Boston: Houghton Mifflin, 1978, p. 313.

Rosenblatt, Louise. *The Reader, the Text, the Poem: The Transactional Theory of the Literary Work*. Carbondale: Southern Illinois University Press, 1978.

Rosenblatt, Louise. *Literature as Exploration*. New York: Noble and Noble, 1983.

Rosenblatt, Louise M. "Writing and Reading: The Transactional Theory." In Jana M. Mason (ed.), *Reading and Writing Connections*. Boston: Allyn & Bacon, 1989, pp. 153–176.

Rosenblatt, Louise M. "Literature—SOS!" *Language Arts* 68 (1991): 444–448.

Rosenblatt, Louise M. "The Transactional Theory of Reading and Writing." In Robert B. Ruddell, Martha R. Ruddell, and Harry Singer (eds.), *Theoretical Models and Processes of Reading*. 4th ed. Newark, Del.: International Reading Association, 1994, pp. 1057–1092.

Rosenholtz, Susan J. "Education Reform Strategies: Will They Increase Teacher Commitment?" *American Journal of Education* 95 (August 1987): 534–562.

Rosenshine, Barak. "Advances in Research on Instruction." In E. J. Kameenui and D. Chard (eds.), *Issues in Educating Students with Disabilities*. Mahwah, N.J.: Erlbaum, 1997, pp. 197–221.

Rosenshine, Barak, and Carol Meister. "Reciprocal Teaching: A Review of the Research." *Review of Educational Research* 64 (Winter 1994): 479–530.

Rosenshine, Barak, Carol Meister, and Susan Chapman. "Teaching Students to Generate Questions: A Review of the Intervention Studies." *Review of Educational Research* 66 (1996): 181–221.

Roser, Nancy, and James Hoffman. "Language Charts: A Record of Story Time Talk." *Language Arts* 69 (May 1992): 44–52.

Ross, Elinor P., and Betty D. Roe. *An Introduction to Teaching the Language Arts*. Fort Worth, Tex.: Holt, Rinehart and Winston, 1990.

Rothman, R. "The Certificate of Initial Mastery." *Educational Leadership* (May 1995): 41–45.

Ruddell, Martha R., and Brenda Shearer. "'Extraordinary,' 'tremendous,' 'exhilarating,' 'magnificent': Middle School At-Risk Students Become Avid Word Learners with the Vocabulary Self-Collection Strategy (VSS)." *Journal of Adolescent & Adult Literacy* 45 (February 2002): 353–363.

Ruddiman, James. "The Vocabulary Game: Empowering Students Through Word Awareness." *Journal of Reading* 36 (February 1993): 400–401.

Ryan, Mary E. *The Trouble with Perfect*. New York: Simon & Schuster, 1995.

Ryder, Randall J., and Michael F. Graves. "Using the Internet to Enhance Students' Reading, Writing, and Information Gathering Skills." *Journal of Adolescent & Adult Literacy* 40 (December 1996/January 1997): 244–254.

Sakta, Cathy Guerra. "SQRC: A Strategy for Guiding Reading and Higher Level Thinking." *Journal of Adolescent & Adult Literacy* 42 (December 1998/January 1999): 265–269.

Salvia, John, and James E. Ysseldyke. *Assessment*. 8th ed. Boston: Houghton Mifflin, 1995, 2001.

Salvia, John, and James E. Ysseldyke. *Assessment in Special and Inclusive Education*. Boston: Houghton Mifflin, 2004.

Samuels, S. Jay. "Toward a Theory of Automatic Information Processing in Reading, Revisited." In Robert Ruddell and

Norman Unrau (eds), *Theoretical Models and Processes of Reading*. 5th ed. Newark, Del.: International Reading Association, 2004, pp. 1127–1148.

Sanacore, Joseph. "Promoting the Lifelong Love of Writing." *Journal of Adolescent & Adult Literacy* 41 (February 1998): 392–396.

Sanacore, Joseph. "Genuine Caring and Literacy Learning for African American Children." *The Reading Teacher* 57 (May 2004): 744–753.

Santa, Carol, Lynn Havens, and Shirley Harrison. "Teaching Secondary Science Through Reading, Writing, Studying, and Problem Solving." In Diane Lapp, James Flood, and Nancy Farnan (eds.), *Content Area Reading and Learning: Instructional Strategies*. Englewood Cliffs, N.J.: Prentice-Hall, 1989.

Scharrer, Erica. "Making a Case for Media Literacy in the Curriculum: Outcomes and Assessment." *Journal of Adolescent & Adult Literacy* 48 (December 2002/January 2003): 354–358.

Schmar-Dobler, Elizabeth. "Reading on the Internet: The Link Between Literacy and Technology." *Journal of Adolescent & Adult Literacy* 47 (September 2003): 45–53.

Schmoker, Mike. "The Results We Want." *Educational Leadership* 57 (February 2000): 62–65.

Schmoker, Mike, and Robert J. Marzano. "Realizing the Promise of Standards-Based Education." *Educational Leadership* 56 (March 1999): 17–21.

Schon, Isabel. "Recent Noteworthy Young Adult Books About Latinos/as." *Journal of Adolescent & Adult Literacy* 42 (March 1999): 456–460.

School Renaissance Institute. *Supercharge Your Curriculum with Renaissance!* Wisconsin Rapids, Wis.: School Renaissance Institute, 2001.

Schumm, Jeanne Shay. "Identifying the Most Important Terms: It's Not That Easy." *Journal of Reading* 36 (May 1993): 679.

Schwartz, Jeffrey. "Let Them Assess Their Own Learning." *English Journal* 80 (February 1991): 67–73.

Schwartz, Robert M., and Taffy Raphael. "Concept of Definition: A Key to Improving Students' Vocabulary." *The Reading Teacher* 39 (1985): 198–205.

Schwarz, Gretchen E. "Graphic Novels for Multiple Literacies." *Journal of Adolescent & Adult Literacy* 46 (November 2002): 262–265.

Scruggs, T., and M. Mastropieri. "Reconstructive Elaborations: A Model for Content Area Learning." *American Educational Research Journal* 26 (Summer 1989): 311–327.

Seal, Kathy. "Transforming Teaching and Learning Through Technology." *Carnegie Reporter* 2 (Spring 2003): 1–4.

Seeley, C. "Increasing Access or Ensuring Failure? Policy Makers Throw a Hammer into the Wall." In National Council of Teachers of Mathematics (eds.), *Algebra for the Twenty-First Century: Proceedings of the August 1992 Conference*. Reston, Va.: NCTM, 1993.

Sefton-Green, Julian. "Computers, Creativity, and the Curriculum: The Challenge for Schools, Literacy, and Learning." *Journal of Adolescent & Adult Literacy* 44 (May 2001).

Seger, F. Dan. "Portfolio Definitions: Toward a Shared Notion." In Donald H. Graves and Bonnie S. Sunstein (eds.), *Portfolio Portraits*. Portsmouth, N.H.: Heinemann, 1992, pp. 114–124.

Sellars, G. "A Comparison of the Readability of Selected High School Social Studies, Science and Literature Textbooks." Ph.D. dissertation, Florida State University, 1988. *Dissertation Abstracts International* 48 (1988): 3085A.

Serafini, Frank. "Three Paradigms of Assessment: Measurement, Procedure, and Inquiry." *The Reading Teacher* 54 (December 2000/January 2001): 384–393.

Serim, Ferdi, and Melissa Koch. *Netlearning: Why Teachers Use the Internet*. Sebastopol, Calif.: Songline Studios, Inc., and O'Reilly & Associates, 1996.

Shanahan, Timothy. "Nature of the Reading-Writing Relationship: An Exploratory Multivariate Analysis." *Journal of Educational Psychology* 76 (1984): 466–477.

Shanahan, Timothy. "The Reading-Writing Relationship: Seven Instructional Principles." *The Reading Teacher* 41 (March 1988): 636–647.

Shannon, Albert J. "Using the Microcomputer Environment for Reading Diagnosis." In Susan Mandel Glazer, Lyndon W. Searfoss, and Lance M. Gentile (eds.), *Reexamining Reading Diagnosis: New Trends and Procedures*. Newark, Del.: International Reading Association, 1989, pp. 150–168.

Shannon, D. "Use of Top-Level Structure in Expository Text: An Open Letter to a High School Teacher." *Journal of Reading* 28 (February 1986): 426–431.

Sharer, Patricia L., Donna Peters, and Barbara A. Lehman. "Lessons from Grammar School: How Can Literature Use in Elementary Classrooms Inform Middle-School Instruction?" *Journal of Adolescent & Adult Literacy* 39 (September 1995): 28–34.

Sharp, Sidney J. "Using Content Subject Matter with LEA in Middle School." *Journal of Reading* 33 (November 1989): 108–112.

Shockley, B., B. Michalove, and J. Allen. *Engaging Families: Connecting Home and School Literacy Communities*. Portsmouth, N.H.: Heinemann, 1995.

Short, D. "Integrating Language and Culture in Middle School American History Classes." Educational Practice

Rep. No. 8. Santa Cruz, Calif., and Washington, D.C.: National Center for Research on Cultural Diversity and Second Language Learning, 1994.

Short, Kathy G., Gloria Kauffman, and Leslie Kahn. "'I Just *Need* to Draw': Responding to Literature Across Multiple Sign Systems." *The Reading Teacher* 54 (October 2000): 160–171.

Showers, Beverly, Bruce Joyce, Mary Scanlon, and Carol Schnaubelt. "A Second Chance to Learn to Read." *Educational Leadership* 55 (March 1998): 27–30.

Shugarman, Sherrie L., and Joe B. Hurst. "Purposeful Paraphrasing: Promoting a Nontrivial Pursuit for Meaning." *Journal of Reading* 29 (February 1986): 396–399.

Silver, E. "Rethinking 'Algebra for All,'" *Educational Leadership* 52 (March 1995): 30–33.

Simmons, Jay. "Portfolios for Large-Scale Assessment." In Donald H. Graves and Bonnie S. Sunstein (eds.), *Portfolio Portraits*. Portsmouth, N.H.: Heinemann, 1992, pp. 96–113.

Simons, Sandra McCandless. "PSRT—A Reading Comprehension Strategy." *Journal of Reading* 32 (February 1989): 419–427.

Simpson, Anne. "Not the Class Novel: A Different Reading Program." *Journal of Reading* 38 (December 1994/January 1995): 290–294.

Simpson, M. "Alternative Formats for Evaluating Content Area Vocabulary Understanding." *Journal of Reading* 30 (January 1987): 20–27.

Simpson, Michele L. "PORPE: A Writing Strategy for Studying and Learning in the Content Areas." *Journal of Reading* 29 (February 1986): 407–414.

Sinatra, Richard. "Integrating Whole Language with the Learning of Text Structure." *Journal of Reading* 34 (March 1991): 424–433.

Sinatra, Richard, and C. Dowd. "Using Syntactic and Semantic Clues to Learn Vocabulary." *Journal of Reading* 35 (November 1991): 224–229.

Sinatra, Richard, Jeffrey Beaudry, Josephine Stahl-Gemake, and E. Francine Guastello. "Combining Visual Literacy, Text Understanding, and Writing for Culturally Diverse Students." *Journal of Reading* 33 (May 1990): 612–614.

Singer, Jessie, and Ruth Shagoury Hubbard. "Teaching from the Heart: Guiding Adolescent Writers to Literate Lives." *Journal of Adolescent & Adult Literacy* 46 (December 2002/January 2003): 328–336.

Slavin, Robert. "A Cooperative Learning Approach to Content Areas: Jigsaw Teaching." In Diane Lapp, James Flood, and Nancy Farnan (eds.), *Content Area Reading and Learning: Instructional Strategies*. Englewood Cliffs, N.J.: Prentice-Hall, 1989, pp. 330–345.

Slavin, Robert E., Nancy L. Karweit, and Nancy A. Madden. *Effective Programs for Students at Risk*. Boston: Allyn & Bacon, 1989.

Slover, Josephine P., and Selene J. Payne. "Integrating Language Arts, Social Studies, and Science Through Technology." Paper presented at the International Reading Association Convention, San Diego, California, May 1999.

Smagorinsky, Peter. "Standards Revisited: The Importance of Being There." *English Journal* 88, no. 4 (March 1999): 82–88.

Smith, Carl. "Building a Better Vocabulary." *The Reading Teacher* 42 (December 1988): 238.

Smith, Carl. "Vocabulary Instruction and Reading Comprehension." ERIC Digest no. 126. Bloomington, Ind.: ERIC Clearinghouse on Reading, English, and Communication, 1998.

Smith, M. Cecil. "What Will Be the Demands of Literacy in the Workplace in the Next Millennium?" *Reading Research Quarterly* 35 (July/August/September 2000): 378–379.

Smith, Michael, and Jeffrey D. Wilhelm. "I Just Like Being Good at It: The Importance of Competence in the Literate Lives of Young Men." *Journal of Adolescent & Adult Literacy* 47 (March 2004): 454–461.

Smith, Patricia L., and Gail E. Tompkins. "Structured Notetaking: A New Strategy for Content Area Readers." *Journal of Reading* 32 (October 1988): 46–53.

Smith-D'Arezzo, Wendy M., and Brenda J. Kennedy. "Seeing Double: Piecing Writing Together with Cross-Age Partners." *Journal of Adolescent & Adult Literacy* 47 (February 2004): 390–401.

Smolin, Louanne Ione, and Kimberly A. Lawless. "Becoming Literate in the Technological Age: New Responsibilities and Tools for Teachers." *The Reading Teacher* 56 (March 2003): 570–577.

Snow, Catherine, M. Susan Burns, and Peg Griffin (eds.). *Preventing Reading Difficulties in Young Children*. Washington, D.C.: National Academy Press, 1998.

Soles, Derek. "The Prufrock Makeover." *English Journal* 88 (March 1999): 59–61.

Spaulding, Nancy, and Samuel Namowitz. *Earth Science*. Evanston, Ill.: McDougal Littell, 2005.

Spear-Swerling, Louise. "A Road Map for Understanding Reading Disability and Other Reading Problems: Origins, Prevention, and Intervention." In Robert B. Ruddell and Norman J. Unrau (eds.), *Theoretical Models and Processes of Reading*. 5th ed. Newark, Del.: International Reading Association, 2004, pp. 517–573.

Stabenau, J. "DVD: 'The Multimedium.'" *Syllabus* 12, no. 5 (1999): 40–43.

Stahl, Stephen. "To Teach a Word Well: A Framework for Vocabulary Instruction." *Reading World* 24 (1985): 16–27.

Stahl, Stephen. "Three Principles of Effective Vocabulary Instruction." *Journal of Reading* 29 (May 1986): 662–668.

Stahl, Steven A. *Vocabulary Development.* Brookline, Mass.: Brookline Books, 1999.

Stahl, Steven A., and B. Kapinus. "Possible Sentences: Predicting Word Meanings to Teach Content Area Vocabulary." *The Reading Teacher* 45 (September 1991): 65–70.

Standards for the English Language Arts. Urbana, Ill.: National Council of Teachers of English/International Reading Association, 1996.

Stauffer, Russell. *Teaching Reading as a Thinking Process.* New York: Harper & Row, 1969.

Stephens, Elaine, and Jean Brown. *A Handbook of Content Literacy Strategies.* Norwood, Mass.: Christopher-Gordon Publishers, 2005.

Stern, David, and M. Rahn. "Work-Based Learning." *Educational Leadership* 52 (May 1995): 35–40.

Sternberg, Robert J. "Are We Reading Too Much into Reading Comprehension Tests?" *Journal of Reading* 34 (April 1991): 540–545.

Stetson, Elton G., and Richard P. Williams. "Learning from Social Studies Textbooks: Why Some Students Succeed and Others Fail." *Journal of Reading* 36 (September 1992): 22–30.

Sticht, Thomas. *Literacy and Vocational Competence.* Columbus, Ohio: National Center for Research in Vocational Education, 1978.

Stiggins, Rick. "New Assessment Beliefs for a New School Mission." *Phi Delta Kappan* 86 (September 2004): 22–27.

Stivers, Jan. "The Writing Partners Project." *Phi Delta Kappan* 77 (June 1996): 694–695.

Stock, Patricia Lambert. "The Rhetoric of Writing Assessment." In Vito Perrone (ed.), *Expanding Student Assessment.* Alexandria, Va.: Association for Supervision and Curriculum Development, 1991, pp. 72–105.

Stoodt, Barbara. *Literacy in an Information Age.* Greensboro, N.C.: Center for Creative Leadership, 1985.

Stoodt, Barbara. "Literacy Instruction." In C. Baber (ed.), *Project Achieve.* Greensboro: University of North Carolina, 1990.

Stoodt, Barbara, and Linda Amspaugh. "Children's Response to Nonfiction." Paper presented at the International Reading Association Convention, Toronto, Canada, May 1994.

Stoodt-Hill, Barbara. "Classroom Observations of Successful Strategies for Struggling Readers." John Tyler Community College. A paper presented to the Virginia Association of Developmental Education (October 2005).

Stoodt-Hill, Barbara D. "Interviews with Teachers of At-Risk Students: Effective Content Reading Strategies." Unpublished paper, 2002.

Strackbein, Deanna, and Montague Tillman. "The Joy of Journals—With Reservations." *Journal of Reading* 31 (October 1987): 28–31.

Strichart, Stephen S., and Charles T. Mangrum II. *Teaching Study Strategies to Students with Learning Disabilities.* Needham Heights, Mass.: Allyn & Bacon, 1993.

Sullivan, Jane. "The Electronic Journal: Combining Literacy and Technology." *The Reading Teacher* 52 (September 1998): 90–92.

Sumner, Ann. "Implementing the Standards: A Classroom Teacher's Viewpoint." *Technology Teacher* 60 (February 2001): 38–40.

Sunstein, Bonnie S. "Introduction." In Donald H. Graves and Bonnie S. Sunstein (eds.), *Portfolio Portraits.* Portsmouth, N.H.: Heinemann, 1992, pp. xi–xvii.

"Survey Gauges Engagement Among High School Students." *Reading Today* 22 (October/November 2004): 4.

Sweet, Anne. *State of the Art: Transforming Ideas for Teaching and Learning to Read.* Washington, D.C.: U.S. Department of Education, Office of Educational Research and Improvement, 1993.

Swiderek, Bobbi. "Integrating Writing with Full Inclusion." *Journal of Adolescent & Adult Literacy* 41 (February 1998): 406–407.

Szymborski, Julie Ann. *Vocabulary Development: Context Clues versus Word Definitions.* M.A. project, Kean College of New Jersey, 1995.

Taba, H. *Teacher's Handbook for Elementary Social Studies.* Reading, Mass.: Addison-Wesley, 1967.

Tanner, M. "Reading in Music Class." *Music Education Journal* 60 (December 1983): 41–45.

Tannock, Susan. "Reading, Writing, and Technology: A Healthy Mix in the Social Studies Curriculum." *Reading Online* 5 (April 2002). Retrieved from http://www.readingonline.org.

Taylor, B., and S. Berkowitz. "Facilitating Children's Comprehension of Content Material." In M. Kamil and A. Moe (eds.), *Perspectives on Reading Research and Instruction.* Twenty-ninth Yearbook of the National Reading Conference. Washington, D.C.: National Reading Conference, 1980, pp. 64–68.

Taylor, Wilson L. "Recent Developments in the Use of Cloze Procedure." *Journalism Quarterly* 33 (Winter 1956): 42–48, 99.

Tchudi, Stephen N., and Joanne Yates. *Teaching Writing in the Content Areas: Senior High School.* Washington, D.C.: National Education Association, 1983.

Terban, M. *Checking Your Grammar*. New York: Scholastic, 1993.

Thayer, Yvonne. "Virginia's Standards Make All Students Stars." *Educational Leadership* 57 (February 2000): 70–72.

Thomas, D. "Reading and Reasoning Skills for Math Problem Solvers." *Journal of Reading* 32 (December 1988): 244–249.

Thousand, J. S., and R. A. Villa. "Strategies for Educating Learners with Severe Disabilities Within Their Local Home Schools and Communities." *Focus on Exceptional Children* 23 (1990): 1–24.

Tierney, Robert. "Redefining Reading Comprehension." *Educational Leadership* 47 (March 1990): 37–42.

Tierney, Robert J. "Literacy Assessment Reform: Shifting Beliefs, Principled Possibilities, and Emerging Practices." *The Reading Teacher* 51 (February 1998): 374–390.

Tierney, Robert, and J. Cunningham. "Research on Teaching Reading Comprehension." In P. D. Pearson (ed.), *Handbook of Reading Research*. New York: Longman, 1984, pp. 609–656.

Tierney, Robert J., John E. Readence, and Ernest K. Dishner. *Reading Strategies and Practices*. Boston: Allyn & Bacon, 1990.

Tipton, J. "Extending Context Clues to Composition and Cooperative Learning." *Journal of Reading* 35 (September 1991): 50.

Tobias, Sigmund. "Interest, Prior Knowledge, and Learning." *Review of Educational Research* 64 (Spring 1994): 37–54.

Tombari, Martin, and Gary Borich. *Authentic Assessment in the Classroom*. Columbus, Ohio: Merrill, 1999.

Tone, Bruce. "Guiding Students Through Research Papers." *Journal of Reading* 32 (October 1988): 76–79.

Toppo, Greg. "Teachers Are Getting Graphic." *USA Today* (May 4, 2005): 1D–2D.

Tornow, J. *Link/Age: Composing in the On-Line Classroom*. Logan: Utah State University Press, 1997.

Tucker, Chris. "The Search Goes On." *Spirit* (May 1999): 38–42.

Tuman, Myron C., and Ann Arbor Software. *Instructor's Guide for Use with Norton Textra Connect: A Networked Writing Environment*. New York: W. W. Norton, 1994.

Unrau, Norman J., and Robert B. Ruddell. "Interpreting Texts in Classroom Contexts." *Journal of Adolescent & Adult Literacy* 39 (September 1995): 16–27.

Unsworth, Len. "Develop Critical Understanding of the Specialized Language of School Science and History Texts: A Functional Grammatical Perspective." *Journal of Adolescent & Adult Literacy* 42 (April 1999): 508–521.

U.S. Census Bureau, Population Division, Journey-To-Work & Migration Statistics Branch. "The Foreign-Born Population." Online at www.census.gov/population/www/socdemo/foreign.html (21 May, 1999).

U.S. Department of Education. *To Assure the Free Appropriate Public Education of All Children with Disabilities*. Seventeenth Annual Report to Congress on the Implementation of the Individuals with Disabilities Education Act. Washington, D.C.: Government Printing Office, 1995.

U.S. Department of Education. *Eighteenth Annual Report to Congress on the Implementation of the Individuals with Disabilities Education Act*. Washington, D.C.: U.S. Department of Education, 1996.

U.S. Department of Education. *Twentieth Annual Report to Congress on the Implementation of the Individuals with Disabilities Education Act*. Washington, D.C.: U.S. Department of Education, 1998.

Valencia, Sheila. In R. Tierney, D. Moore, S. Valencia, and P. Johnson, "How Will Literacy Be Assessed in the Next Millennium?" *Reading Research Quarterly* 35 (2000): 244–250.

Valmont, William J. *Technology for Literacy Teaching and Learning*. Boston: Houghton Mifflin, 2003.

Van Horn, Leigh. "Reading and Writing Essays About Objects of Personal Significance." *Language Arts* 78 (January 2001): 273–278.

Van Kraayenoord, C. "Toward Self-Assessment of Literacy Learning." In H. Fehring (ed.), *Literacy Assessment*. Newark, Del.: International Reading Association, 2003, pp. 44–54.

Venezky, Richard L. "Literacy." In Theodore L. Harris and Richard E. Hodges (eds.), *The Literacy Dictionary: The Vocabulary of Reading and Writing*. Newark, Del.: International Reading Association, 1995, p. 142.

Vigil, A. *The Corn Woman: Stories and Legends of the Hispanic Southwest*. Englewood, Colo.: Libraries Unlimited, 1994.

Vygotsky, L. *Thought and Language*. Cambridge, Mass.: MIT Press, 1962.

Wade, S., and B. Adams. "Effects of Importance and Interest on Recall of Biographical Text." *Journal of Literacy* 22 (1990): 331–353.

Wade, S., G. Schraw, W. Buxton, and M. Hayes. "Seduction of the Strategic Reader: Effects of Interest on Strategies and Recall." *Reading Research Quarterly* 28 (Spring 1993): 93–114.

Wade, Suzanne, and Elizabeth Moje. "The Role of Text in Classroom Learning: Beginning an Online Dialogue." *Reading Online* 5 (November 2001). Retrieved from http://www.readingonline.org.

Wagner, M. *The Benefits of Secondary Vocational Education for Young People with Disabilities*. Menlo Park, Calif.: SRI International, 1991.

Wait, S. S. "Textbook Readability and the Predictive Value of the Dale-Chall, Comprehensive Assessment Program and Cloze." Ph.D. dissertation, Florida State University. *Dissertation Abstracts International* 48 (1987): 357A.

Warren, J. *Portrait of a Tragedy: America and the Vietnam War.* New York: Lothrop, Lee and Shepard, 1990.

Watts Pailliotet, Ann, Ladislaus Semali, Rita K. Rodenberg, Jackie K. Giles, and Sherry L. Macaul. "Intermediality: Bridge to Critical Media Literacy." *The Reading Teacher* 54 (October 2000): 208–219.

Wheatley, E., D. Muller, and R. Miller. "Computer-Assisted Vocabulary Instruction." *Journal of Reading* 37 (October 1993): 92–102.

Whimbey, Arthur. "A 15th-Grade Reading Level for High School Seniors?" *Phi Delta Kappan* 69 (November 1987): 207.

White, Theodore G., Michael Graves, and William Slater. "Growth of Reading Vocabulary in Diverse Elementary Schools." *Journal of Educational Psychology* 42 (1989): 343–354.

Wildstrom, Stephen H. "Search Engines with Smarts." *Business Week* (February 8, 1999): 22.

Williams, Bronwyn T. "What They See Is What We Get: Television and Middle School Writers." *Journal of Adolescent & Adult Literacy* 48 (April 2003): 546–554.

Willis, Jerry W., Elizabeth C. Stephens, and Kathryn I. Matthew. *Technology, Reading, and Language Arts.* Boston: Allyn & Bacon, 1996.

Willis, William. "Software: Focus on Videotapes." *T.H.E. Journal* 25, no. 6 (1998): 24–26.

Winer, Dave. "The History of Weblogs." *Weblogs.Com News* (2002). Retrieved July 28, 2005, from http://newhome.weblogs.com/historyofweblogs.

Winograd, Peter, Scott Paris, and Connie Bridge. "Improving the Assessment of Literacy." *The Reading Teacher* 45 (October 1991): 108–116.

"Wired Education: The Internet: A Valuable, Integral Part of the Teaching Process." *Curriculum Administrator* 30 (April 1996): 8.

Wittrock, Merlin C. "Process Oriented Measures of Comprehension." *The Reading Teacher* 40 (April 1987): 734–737.

Wolf, D. P. "Portfolio Assessment: Sampling Student Work." *Educational Leadership* 46, no. 7 (1989): 35–39.

Wolf, Kenneth P. "From Informal to Informed Assessment: Recognizing the Role of the Classroom Teacher." *Journal of Reading* 36 (April 1993): 518–523.

Wolf, Kenneth, and Yvonne Siu-Runyan. "Portfolio Purposes and Possibilities." *Journal of Adolescent & Adult Literacy* 40 (September 1996): 30–37.

Wolfe, Paula. "'The Owl Cried': Reading Abstract Literary Concepts with Adolescent ESL Students." *Journal of Adolescent & Adult Literacy* 47 (February 2004): 402–413.

Wolfe, R., and A. Lopez. "Structured Overviews for Teaching Science Concepts and Terms." *Journal of Reading* 36 (December 1992/January 1993): 315–317.

Wollman-Bonilla, J. "Why Don't They 'Just Speak'? Attempting Literature Discussion with More and Less Able Readers." *Research in the Teaching of English* 28 (October 1994): 231–258.

Wonacott, Michael E. "Technological Literacy." ERIC Digest no. 233 (2001).

Wonacott, Michael E. *High Schools That Work: Best Practices for CTE.* Research Triangle Park, N.C.: Research Triangle Institute, 2002.

Wood, Karen D. "Fostering Collaborative Reading and Writing Experiences in Mathematics." *Journal of Reading* 36 (October 1992): 96–103.

Worthy, Jo, and Karen Broaddus. "Fluency Beyond the Primary Grades: From Group Performance to Silent, Independent Reading." *The Reading Teacher* 55 (December 2001/January 2002): 334–343.

Wren, Sebastion, Brian Litke, Deborah Jenkins, Susan Paynter, Jennifer Watts, and Iliana Alanis. *The Cognitive Foundations of Learning to Read: A Framework.* Austin, Tex.: Southwestern Educational Development Laboratory, 2000.

"Writing." *The Nation's Report Card.* Retrieved from http://nces.ed.gov/nationsreport card/writing/results2002/.

Young, Petey, and Cynthia Bastianelli. "Retelling Comes to Chiloquin High." *Journal of Reading* 34 (November 1990): 194–196.

Zessoules, Rieneke, and Howard Gardner. "Authentic Assessment: Beyond the Buzzword and into the Classroom." In Vito Perrone (ed.), *Expanding Student Assessment.* Alexandria, Va.: Association for Supervision and Curriculum Development, 1991, pp. 47–71.

Zhao, Yong, Sophia Hueyshan Tan, and Punya Mishra. "Teaching and Learning: Whose Computer Is It?" *Journal of Adolescent & Adult Literacy* 44 (December 2000/January 2001): 348–353.

Zucca, Gary. "Online Writing Clinics on the World Wide Web." *Syllabus* 10, no. 3 (October 1996): 48–49.

Name Index

Subject Index